THE
WHITEWATER
SOURCEBOOK

SECOND EDITION

THE WHITEWATER SOURCEBOK

SECOND EDITION

A Directory of
Information on
American
Whitewater
Rivers

Richard Penny

INCLUDING

RIVER DESCRIPTIONS

GAUGE READINGS BY TELEPHONE

PERMITS

MAPS

GUIDEBOOKS

LITERATURE

ORGANIZATIONS

GOVERNMENT OFFICES

MENASHA RIDGE PRESS
BIRMINGHAM, ALABAMA

Library of Congress Cataloging-in-Publication Data

Penny, Richard, 1956–
    The whitewater sourcebook : a directory of information on
American whitewater rivers/Richard Penny. —2nd ed.
        p.   cm.
    Includes bibliographical references (p.) and indexes.
    ISBN 0-89732-078-6
    1. White-water canoeing—United States—
Directories.   2. Rafting (Sports)—United States—
Directories.   3. Rivers—United States—Recreational
use—Directories.   I. Title.
GV776.A2P46 1990
797.1'22'02573—dc20   90-19492
                                                            CIP

Text design by Hollie Taylor.
Cover design by Alexa Dilworth.

Menasha Ridge Press
3169 Cahaba Heights Road
Birmingham, Alabama 35243

Dedicated to John Muir

CONTENTS

PART I. INFORMATION SOURCES FOR POPULAR WHITEWATER RIVERS, BY STATE

*Rivers for which permits, reservations, or registration is required (but not including those requiring camping or fire permits) are indicated by the letter **P** following the page number. Most sections are followed by "General Information Sources" for that state.*

*Not to be confused with the Salmon River (Idaho).

PART II. THE WILD AND SCENIC RIVER SYSTEM

PART III. SOURCES OF MAPS AND INFORMATION

PART IV. ORGANIZATIONS, SCHOOLS, AND FESTIVALS

ORGANIZATIONS

WHITEWATER SCHOOLS

PART V. BOOKS AND PERIODICALS

SOURCES OF BOOKS

GUIDEBOOKS

INSTRUCTION

PART VI. TOOLS

APPENDICES

INDEXES

ACKNOWLEDGMENTS
First Edition

Many people deserve my gratitude for their contributions to The Whitewater Sourcebook. My spouse, Anne Penny, provided needed encouragement, criticism, good company, much help, and good Alf imitations on river trips. My publisher, Bob Sehlinger; and editors, Carol Offen, Barbara Williams, and Jessica Letteney, were fantastic. My good friend Mike Sawyer, the consummate outdoorsman, made many contributions; he deserves special thanks for his radical ideas and comments and for his voluminous knowledge of places and maps.

Numerous National Weather Service hydrologists and staff members generously provided their time and help, and deserve my thanks, including Sam Baker, Ernest Cathey, Jim Gross, Bud Hild, Scott Kiser, Charles Matthews, Gary McDivett, Leo Harrison, Todd Mendell, John Monro, Lee Morgan, John Patton, Russell Post, Burt Reeves, Alan Ringo, Fred Ronco, Tim Scram, Clint Stiger, Robert Thompson, Bob Tivi, Ed Vanblargen, and many others. Staff members of the United States Geological Survey (USGS) also gave me their help and deserve thanks; these include Steve Addington, Tim Hale, Bob Helm, Glen Hess, E. F. Hubbard, Myron Lys, Lloyd Wagner, and others. Great help also came from Tom Hughes of the Bureau of Reclamation and from Gary Marsh, Carol McDonald, and David Meier of the Bureau of Land Management, from Judith Ladd of the Soil Conservation Service, and from Barbara Payne of the National Park Service.

The help of several United States Department of Agriculture (USDA) Forest Service officials should also be especially acknowledged, including Robert Addison, Jim Braggs, Greg Reynolds, Fred Schaub, Ken Vines, Jay Whittek, and many others. Officials of state and city agencies who went out of their way to provide assistance include Jim Barnes of the Idaho Department of Parks and Recreation, Jack Easton of the Virginia Water Control Board, Jack Fulton, director of Public Safety for the City of Richmond, Andy Goldbloom and Joel Seffel of Texas Parks and Wildlife, Tom Greenwood of Montana Fish, Parks and Wildlife, Bill Hansell of the California Department of Water Resources, Steve Mueller of the Minnesota Department of Natural Resources, Allen White of the California Department of Boating and Waterways, and many others.

Outfitters and guides who were generous with their time and knowledge include Charles Albright of Sierra Nevada Whitewater. Frank Barton of the Trail Shop in Little Rock, Susan Bechdel of Canyons Inc., George Collins of Upper Yough Whitewater Expeditions, Bill Dallam of Eastern River, John Dolbeare and John Reynolds of the Nantahala Outdoor Center, Steve Miller of New Wave Rafting, Matt Gaynes of Sierra South, Guy Newhall of Wilderness House, Craig Niller of Saco Bound, Judo Patterson of Sundance, Doug Proctor of Class VI River Runners, George Stesanyshyn of Superior Whitewater, Jim Walker of Batten Kill Canoes, Michael Zaber of Wild Water Outfitters, and others. Thanks are also due to Beth Rundquist of Rivers and Mountains.

Staff members of a number of organizations were enormously generous with their help; these include Eric Leaper and Mary McCurdy of the National Organization for River Sports, Cathy Schmising of the American Canoe Association and Jim Caveney of the World Footbag Association.

Several whitewater authors were extremely helpful, including John Connelly, Ed Grove, Tom Kennon, Rena Margulis, Don McClaran, William Nealy, John Porterfield, and Bob Sehlinger. Other authors of the numerous excellent guidebooks to whitewater rivers in the United States (listed elsewhere in this volume) deserve thanks; their works served as sources of invaluable information. The late Randy Carter is appreciated for two revolutionary ideas: for painting paddlers' gauges at rivers and for recruiting people to read those gauges and report the readings over the phone.

Finally, my many friends in the Bluff City Canoe Club and the Volunteer Group of the Sierra Club deserve thanks for their help and encouragement, with special thanks to John Spence, Jim Surprise, Sonny Saloman, Roxann Hanning, Julie Wood, Karen Hopkins, and Bill Hopkins. Other knowledgeable and experienced paddlers who gave me the benefit of their time and assistance include Beck Bryant, Walter Cushwa, Michael Skalvos. and Bryan Tooley.

Last but not least, I should mention my paddling buddy Dennis Rhodes, without whom this book could not have been written; he deserves special thanks for rescuing me from the Dam Breach Rapid on the St. Francis (where I certainly otherwise would have drowned). There are many other good stories to tell about Dennis, but I'll restrain myself.

Second Edition

I would particularly like to thank Joe Greiner of the Carolina Canoe Club for generously helping with gathering updated material on Southeastern rivers. His contribution was enormous!

Some government folks that helped out and deserve my sincere gratitude include LuVerne Grussing, Gail Marsh, Terry Humphrey, Chuck Otto, Brad Palmer, and Barry Thelps of the Bureau of Land Management; Jim Braggs, Martha Crusius, Edward Gastellum, David Stimson, and Harvey Wickware of the National Park Service; Al Peterson of the National Weather Service; MaryJane Brooks of New York State Parks; Mark Reed of the Ohio Department of Watercraft; Tina Barnes, Marge Cline, Tom Contrares, Kevin Craig, Julie Gardner, John Kramer, Bill Lea, and Lee Redding of the USDA Forest Service; and Gary Woodring of the Department of Parks and Recreation in El Dorado County, California. Members of the boating community that contributed to the Second Edition include Terry Schering of Adventure Calls Rafting; Pope Barrow of the American Whitewater Affiliation; Bob Taylor of Appomattox River Company; Les Bechdel of Canyons Inc.; David Cooper of El Vado Ranch; Bill Guheen of Grand Teton Lodge; Mary McCurdy of the National Organization for River Sports; Roger Scott of the Outdoor Sports Center; Beth and Dale Rundquist of Rivers and Mountains; Charles Albright of Sierra Nevada Whitewater; Tom Moore and Mark Ritchie of Sierra South; Harold Theiss of the U.S. Canoe Association; Loie Evans of Westwater Books; Bill Kallner of Whitewater Specialties; Jennie Goldberg (the Girl from Riffles Magazine); Sonny Salomon; James Snyder; and Jim Reed.

Two fine persons and splendid paddlers who made contributions when I first wrote *The Sourcebook* were no longer there for me to turn to for help with the Second Edition. John Dolbeare of the Nantahala Outdoor Center was drowned in Coming Home Sweet Jesus Rapid on the Lower Meadow in 1989. Matt Gaynes of Sierra South was tragically killed that same year in a taxicab accident near Jaipur, India, while on an expedition to make a first descent of the Chenab River. Both of these explorers will be greatly missed by the rest of the paddling community.

THE WHITEWATER SOURCEBOOK

SECOND EDITION

INTRODUCTION
Second Edition

Purpose of *The Whitewater Sourcebook*

My goal in writing *The Whitewater Sourcebook* is to assist you, the reader, to get in touch with the many resources that are available for use in expanding your paddling horizons. Using The Sourcebook as a starting point, you can learn new boating skills, meet other addicts of the sport, join conservation organizations, explore new rivers, find peak water, and get permits for the Western cruising rivers! The more you take advantage of these various resources and opportunities provided by contacts in the paddling community, government, and elsewhere, the more you will advance in the sport and enjoy your boating! It's also my hope that folks with other reasons for interest in rivers, such as conservationists and river managers, will also find The Sourcebook a useful reference tool.

What's Inside

The section titled "Information Sources for Popular Whitewater Rivers, by State" makes up about two-thirds of this book; it consists of a series of concise entries of information on hundreds of the most popular or noteworthy American whitewater rivers, arranged alphabetically by state. The purpose of this section is to provide a handy reference that you may use while you are on the phone or while planning a trip; each river entry should give you all the information you need to put it together, including sources of river levels, maps, guidebooks, and permits. At the end of every state's section, you'll also find a summary page that lists the phone numbers for the most significant sources of river levels for that state and surrounding areas; after each number will be a complete list of the river gauge readings you can obtain from that source.

Further back in the volume, you'll find a long section titled "Sources of Maps and Information." Use the contacts you'll discover there to track down maps, get forecasts of river levels, or to talk, for example, to the rangers that manage the Kern River in California.

Keep flipping the pages, and you'll discover more useful lists of all kinds of federal offices, of clubs and organizations,

1

and of books and periodicals. The list of whitewater guide-books in *The Whitewater Sourcebook* is probably the most thorough ever published; it should include sources for obtaining just about every guidebook now in print. In the Appendices, you'll find material created by other folks that I have reproduced for your benefit, including every permit application form I could get hold of. I hope it serves you well.

I gathered the information here by reading guidebooks, by talking to other outfitters, authors, and paddlers, by writing nice letters to the Forest Service, the Weather Service, and everyone else, by writing threatening letters when the nice ones didn't work, and by making hundreds of phone calls. I visited a lot of the rivers in this book, but I haven't been to most of them (maybe someday). After the book was almost finished, we mailed out sections of it to experienced paddlers around the country and asked them to look for errors. Any errors that these kind folks found, we fixed. There may still be a few left. Worrying about them keeps my publisher and me awake at night. If in your use of *The Whitewater Sourcebook,* you find someplace I have slipped up, or if you discover a valuable source of information we missed, let me know through Menasha Ridge Press. We'll try to get the fix in the next edition.

Permits and Reservations

I started out blissfully writing about phones, books, maps, forests, parks, and rivers. It wasn't long before I was re-minded of two unfortunate facts of life: permits and reserva-tions. Well, barring a peoples' revolt and a repeal of Malthu-sian principles, we'll be stuck with permits and reservations. So I write about them too, and I try where I can to take away the pain. Detailed descriptions of permit systems are de-scribed in each river entry in the section named "Information Sources for Popular Whitewater Rivers, by State." Flip through the Table of Contents, and you will discover that every river requiring a permit, reservation, or registration is indicated by a bold letter **P**. Turn to the back and you'll find an index titled "Index of Rivers Requiring Permission"; this index lists every river in the lower 48 states that, to my knowledge, requires permission from a governmental regulatory body for you to run it.

Look in Appendix One and you'll see copies of all the permit or reservation application forms I could find. (A few agencies wouldn't let me have a form. Sorry.) Many of them you may photocopy and pop in the mail. But, in other cases the managing agencies will not accept photocopies of permit application forms. These are reproduced anyway so that you'll know what's involved. You'll have to call and get originals of these. Good luck in the lottery.

Two other warnings: First, agencies may change their policies on accepting photocopies of application forms. If you're worried, call and check. Second, many managing agencies accept permit applications only at particular times of the year. Check the river entry.

What's Not Inside

Please remember that the river entries in *The Whitewater Sourcebook* are not as fully descriptive as those in a good regional guidebook. A guidebook will tell you stuff like "At mile 4.2, portage on the left around Talking Heads Falls, which drops 200 feet in one-fifth mile." While I tried to mention obvious dangers, I couldn't get all that detail in and still have a book that would fit in your VW van. Look at the guidebook too (a list of guidebooks for areas covered by *The Whitewater Sourcebook* is in the section titled, "Books and Periodicals").

The same goes for choosing safe levels. For each river listed I have tried to include a little information on interpret-ing the gauge reading. In most cases I have suggested low, medium, and high (i.e., maximum) levels. This information is intentionally brief, intended for quick reference while you are on the phone, and is not intended to be definitive. Before you drive eight hours for a run that may be near minimum, or decide to put onto a river that has water in the trees, I recommend that you (1) consult a boater experienced with the river, (2) consult the more detailed description that will be present in a regional guidebook, and (3) honestly assess your skills.

On Gauge Readings

Paddlers are interested in water levels because in order to boat a river, there has to be enough water in it, but not too much. The federal government is also interested in how much water is in the nation's rivers—not because members of Congress do a lot of paddling—but because the government is interested in flood control, resource allocation, and the like. Paddlers can use this shared interest with the feds to their advantage by scoring the information the various government agencies have on hand. In this book, I'm going to tell you how to do it.

The United States Geological Survey and, to a lesser extent, the Army Corps of Engineers, the USDA Forest Service, the Tennessee Valley Authority, the Salt River Project, the Bureau of Reclamation, the Bureau of Land Management, the National Park Service, various public and private utilities, and probably some other folks too, maintain systems of automated river gauges on rivers and streams around the country. These hydrologic gauges (recognizable as cylindrical concrete or metal structures on the riverbank, about 3 feet in diameter and about 15 feet high) measure the height of the water surface as gauge height (feet and tenths of feet). Usually gauges will have a graduated staff on the outside that a paddler can look at and read.

Some hydrologic gauges store their readings on site and a civil servant has to drive out once a month or so to collect the data. These aren't too useful to us. Others are telemetering *gauges.* A telemetering gauge has a phone it can answer; it provides its reading to the civil servant calling it as a coded set of beeps. The telemetering gauges on whitewater rivers are enormously useful provided someone calls them daily; a paddler can usually find out this reading from the National Weather Service. Finally, many gauges are linked to a National Weather Service satellite system that obtains continuous updates of their status. It is easy to find a source to report gauges that interface to the satellite system. (See the section titled "Sources of Maps and Information" for more on hydrologic gauges.)

Often we have to depend on other, less sophisticated gauges. Graduated sticks may be mounted on bridge abutments by various agencies. I refer to these as "staff gauges" in the text. Paddlers will often paint gauges on bridge abutments, with 0 feet indicating minimum, and additional marks placed at 1 foot, 2 feet, and so on. I refer to these as "paddlers' gauges" in the text.

Those of you who are out for primo runs at high water levels will be well advised to supplement the gauge readings that we help you find with forecasts and a little voodoo. You should be aware that the National Weather Service, the main source to the public of river levels in the U.S., can also provide a two-to-three-day forecast of most gauging stations that they monitor. Ask for it. Get the weather forecast too, and study it.

To take a case in point, during August 1985, Hurricane Danny left the Gulf and headed across Mississippi to the Cumberland Plateau of Tennessee. Friday's TVA reading for the Big South Fork was 310 cfs, but we put our faith in the Weather Channel and headed for the river. Despite rain for the entire drive, the river was only running about 600 cfs when we arrived. The next morning, after an allnight downpour, we were still disappointed to find that the river was running only about 1000 cfs at the take-out. However, when we got to the put-in, we found that Clear Fork (a tributary) was in flood. We dropped down the Clear Fork onto the Big South Fork, which had risen to 10,000 cfs. Within two and a half hours we were at the take-out 11 miles below. The river was still rising, and in the afternoon we ran it again at 14,000 cfs. This second run took only an hour and a half. The purpose of this story is to remind you that the gauge reading on Thursday or Friday should be taken as only one indicator of the future behavior of the river over the weekend; other factors come into play as well.

On Using This Book as a Whitewater Phonebook

In the pages that follow are more phone sources for river levels than I ever dreamed existed before I really started searching. I hope that you can use them to find good water and do some good paddling.

But before you cut loose on your mom's phone, let me encourage a little restraint. Except in the case of recordings, someone is going to have to answer at the other end. That person may have other responsibilities too, so don't call frivolously. Try to be especially parsimonious with calls to numbers that ring directly at National Weather Service offices (the so-called "administrative lines"). The busy civil servants at that organization don't like answering the phone much, and are apt to change their numbers once they decide the constant ringing is getting to be a drag.

Many of the telephone numbers provided in this book are for private businesses including outfitters and operators of campgrounds and restaurants. These people are extremely generous to provide us with water level information; pay them back by eating in their restaurants or staying at their campgrounds. Call at reasonable times, don't call unnecessarily, and above all, do remember that these people are doing you a tremendous favor.

One of my favorite such persons is Ms. Jean Houston, the proprietor of the Canyon Mouth Campground, located at the bottom of one of the greatest Southeastern whitewater rivers, Little River Canyon in Alabama. Ms. Houston has always been extremely kind about providing river levels, and she and her husband have always been killer additions to the impromptu parties after the runs.

I can remember only one occasion when she may have been a little put out with us. The Great Flood of 1985 brought the Little River to previously unheard-of levels. Canyon Mouth Campground lay in the path of the flood, which rolled in so quickly that Ms. Houston was forced to take refuge on the roof of her house, from which she was subsequently rescued by helicopter. As the floodwaters traveled further downstream they caused tremendous damage to the town of Fort Payne, Alabama. Dennis Rhodes and I saw the report of the Great Flood on the news that evening, and it seemed logical that we should go take a ride on the ebbing floodwaters.

Picture the following: a forlorn woman squishes back through her yard after returning from a helicopter rescue and a night in an emergency shelter. She looks out over the devastated campground (two years of work destroyed) and then enters her house. The phone is ringing. She wades through the mud and mess and finds the phone. It's Dennis, and he wants to know if the river is still up.

She forgave us later, and we did get in our run the next day at 11,700 cfs. I hope the rest of you can manage a little more tact.

HOW TO USE
THE RIVER INFORMATION
SECTION

This section consists of a series of concise entries of information on popular or noteworthy American rivers, arranged alphabetically by state. Only the lower 48 states with especially significant whitewater were included. If I left out your state, I'm sorry. Have you ever thought of moving to a state that has *mountains?*

The purpose of this section is to provide a handy reference for use while you are on the phone or planning a trip. A typical entry might include the following headings and information; some headings may be deleted if irrelevant.

Sections: Provides the beginning and end points of the section or sections, and any informal name of the section. The overall difficulty of the section is indicated as a range (e.g., Class II-IV) using the International Scale of River Difficulty (see the Tools chapter for an explanation of this scale). If only a few rapids exceed this difficulty, or if the degree of difficulty associated with high water is well known, then this is indicated. If more than one river section is described they are numbered (1), (2), (3), and so on. Descriptions further down the page and specific to a given section will use these numbers as reference, as in "For Section (3) the minimum is about 3 feet on the gauge."

Length of Run: Provided in both miles and days. Trips requiring a day or less are always described as "Day trip," even if the run requires only a few hours.

Location: The county and state is indicated so that you can go find your county map. Other significant features of the location may be listed, such as a national park.

Maps: The relevant USGS topographic quads are listed, always in the 7.5-minute (1:24,000) series unless otherwise indicated. In some parts of the country, only the 15-minute series are available; such maps will be listed as: "Havasupai Point (15')." Other useful maps may be listed, too. See the Maps and Literature (USGS Topographic Maps) section for more information.

Times Runnable: An approximate season is indicated, based on flow records. Remember, it also may be possible to paddle out of the usual season. In the Southeast, for example, after a hurricane we can often make late summer runs of creeks normally runnable only in late winter or early spring.

Permit: If permits for private boaters are required, an address, phone, and protocol for obtaining such is provided. If the permit is easily obtainable on site, the method is explained. If a permit application form exists, and I was able to purloin a copy, it is reproduced in Appendix One.

Reservations: If prior reservations are required, typically only in the case of federally managed touring rivers in the West, the mechanism for obtaining such is explained, and an address, phone number, and mechanism for applying is provided. If a reservation application form exists, and the managing agency was kind enough to let me have one, then it is reproduced in Appendix One. If no reservations are required then this section will not appear. In a few cases the managing agencies will not accept photocopies of permit or reservation application forms. You'll have to call and get originals of these. One other warning. Many managing agencies accept applications only at particular times of the year. Check the river entry.

Restrictions: If a managing agency has issued specific restrictions of use, these are indicated. This information is subject to change; for example, fire regulations may change according to weather, so check with the managing folks for the current scoop. If there are no specific restrictions of use, then this section will not appear.

Gauge: Listed here is the name and approximate location of the principal gauge from which river level readings can be obtained. If no gauge exists then the fact is so noted. Read the entry titled "The W.D.S. Method" in the Tools section to learn volume estimation on rivers with no gauge. Those of you who regularly paddle rivers with no gauge are hereby encouraged to put aside your sloth and paint a Randy Carter-style paddlers' gauge for your river in time to get it into the next edition. It's easy. Put zero at about minimum and slap on some lines for one foot, two feet, and so on.

Source of Levels: One or more telephone sources for readings from the principal gauge are listed by name and number. If there is no choice but to drive there and to get out of the van and glissade down the muddy bank to look at the gauge, then the entry will read "Visual inspection only."

How Reported: In feet or in cubic feet per second (cfs).

Additional Gauge: If a second gauge is in use, then its name and approximate position is provided here.

Source of Levels: One or more telephone sources for readings from the second gauge are listed by name and number. If there is no choice but to drive there and to get out of the van and belly-slide down the muddy bank to look at the gauge, then the entry will read "Visual inspection only."

How Reported: Whether the second gauge reports (reads) in feet or in cfs.

Interpretation of Levels: Low, optimum, and high levels are listed, in terms of the principal gauge. If there are complexities to the gauge interpretation, these are explained. The specified low, medium, and high levels are aimed primarily at boaters who should be independently competent on the river in question and who are paddling in a group that includes folks familiar with the river and skilled at rescue. On many rivers, folks of intermediate or lesser skill and those paddling with weaker parties may prefer lower levels than the one that I suggest is optimum. Generally, the "low" or "minimum" level should be sufficient to have fun, rather than merely to scrape down. The "high" level will often be very similar to that listed in the guidebooks as "maximum." "Extremely high" means levels at which only a relatively few experts have made runs. Generally, non-experts should *not* paddle when rivers are high or extremely high. I have avoided the use of the term "maximum" because it is my belief that maximum levels are (1) personal things, dependent on a paddler's skill, preferences, and goals, and (2) very dependent on the advance of the sport. Try asking a group of advanced paddlers to recommend the primo level on their local river. It will often be well above the maximum in any guidebook published more than a few years prior. Having said this, it probably won't hurt to remind the reader once more that most rivers are more difficult and dangerous at high water.

Source of More Information: Usually this will be an organization familiar with the river or its surrounds, such as a prominent outfitter, a Forest Service office, or a local club. Sometimes you can get level information from these sources if others fail, if only in the form of "It's been raining two days" or "There's folks up here with boats on their cars."

Best Guidebooks: A few of the most current and authoritative guidebooks describing the river are listed by the name of the author (books with more than two authors use "et al." after the first author's name) and an abbreviated title. Complete references and sources for guidebooks are listed in the "Books and Periodicals" section. In a few cases, short maps/guides will also be listed here. These shorter works will not be referenced in the Books and Periodicals section, so an explanation of how to obtain the maps or guides will be included immediately after the entry.

Further Comments: Anything else I had to say. I may mention dams, waterfalls, or portages here if I know about them. If I don't mention them, that doesn't mean they are not there. There's no need to kid you—I haven't run all these rivers.

Gauge Conversions: I prefer to measure water flow in cubic feet per second (cfs) rather than by means of gauge height (feet). The cfs scale is a much better system of measurement and conveys a great deal more information. For those of you who understand this stuff, the cfs scale is a linear, ratio scale. The scale of feet is a much more primitive ordinal scale. Using the cfs system, it is immediately obvious that 4000 cfs is twice the flow of 2000 cfs. With the scale of feet, the relationship of 4 feet to 2 feet is not at all clear (especially in the case of a USGS gauge, where 2 feet might represent no water at all; less so in the case of a paddlers' gauge where a 0 is usually around minimum). Anyway, where I have been able to get the information, I have included a conversion table from feet to cfs. If the river has more than one gauge in common use, an approximate conversion from one to the other is often included.

One other thing. Without fail, when I talk to a USGS hydrologist and order a gauge rating table (that's what they call the table that converts gauge feet to cfs), he or she issues the following caveat: the rating table is subject to change over time and has to be recalibrated from year to year, especially for lower flows. That should be obvious to whitewater paddlers, who are all aware that rivers move rocks, trees, and dirt around. At any rate, all values in this book were the current ratings from the USGS at the time of this writing.

Following the river descriptions for each state appears a section titled "General Information Sources." On this page will be listed a summary of the most important telephone sources of river information for the state, such as National Weather Service River Forecast Centers, state boating and recreation offices, or recreational river recordings.

To help you with the recordings (which often sound like Alvin the Chipmunk), I list in order all the river gauges reported, including rivers that may be in another state. However, for sources where you have to ask for the information, I list only the river gauges that fall within the state's boundaries. Please note that this list is very inclusive, and may therefore include many gauges and rivers not described in the preceding river descriptions section. Some of the gauges may not be of interest, but you may also discover some gems of which you were not aware.

PART 1

INFORMATION
SOURCES FOR
POPULAR
WHITEWATER
RIVERS,
BY STATE

ALABAMA

LITTLE RIVER CANYON

Sections: (1) Suicide Section, Hwy. 35 bridge through Cable Falls, Class V-VI.
    (2) Upper-Three-Mile, Cable Falls to the Chairlift, Class IV-V.
    (3) Chairlift to Canyon Mouth Campground, Class III-IV.

Length of Run: (1) Day trip, 2.5 miles
    (2) Day trip, 3 miles
    (3) Day trip, 6 miles

All three sections can be run in one day, but it is a very long day.

Location: Dekalb and Cherokee Counties, Alabama

Maps: USGS quads: Fort Payne, Jamestown, Little River

Times Runnable: In the dry 1985-86 record year, there were 38 days of good water; in the relatively wet 1984-85 season, 130 days. Best times are from late November into May. There is usually very little water from June through October except after periods of heavy thunderstorms or after a hurricane.

Permit: None required

Gauge: USGS at Canyon Mouth (referred to by the USGS as Little River near Blue Pond).

Source of Levels: Canyon Mouth Campground, 205-779-6814.

How Reported: Levels are reported in feet.

Interpretation of Levels: For the Upper-Three-Mile Section and the Chairlift Section, consider 4 feet to be minimum (360 cfs) and 6 feet (2750) to be high. Dennis Rhodes, Sonny Salomon, and I ran these sections at 9.5 feet (11,740 cfs; extremely high), but we carried Humpty Dumpty (Class V+) and Deep Throat (Class V+). The uppermost section (which has the slightly hysterical name of "Suicide Section") descends from the base of Desoto Falls at the Hwy. 35 bridge to the start of the

Upper-Three-Mile. Use your own judgment about water levels if you run this totally aggro section (Class V and VI with portages likely). My only run of this section was at 4.5 feet (606 cfs) on the Canyon Mouth gauge.

Additional Gauge: A second gauge is located on a bridge abutment on the east side of the Hwy. 35 bridge. The levels on this gauge are normally discussed in inches, with 0 inches being minimum and 1.5 feet being very high.

Source of Levels: None

Source of More Information: Desoto State Park, Rt. 1, Box 210, Fort Payne, AL 35967; 205-845-0052.

Birmingham Canoe Club, Box 951, Birmingham, AL 35201.

Best Guidebooks: Suicide Section: none
Upper-Three-Mile: none
Chairlift: Sehlinger et al., *Appalachian Whitewater, Vol. 1*; Sehlinger and Otey, *Northern Georgia Canoeing.*

Further Comments: Because the Suicide Section and the Upper-Three-Mile are not yet in a guidebook, it is worth mentioning the locations of the put-ins. For the Suicide Section, carry your boat down a trail on river-left from the Hwy. 35 bridge at Desoto Falls; within a quarter mile or so the trail will descend to the river. To find the put-in for the Upper-Three-Mile, from Hwy. 35, drive south along river-right on Canyon Rim Road. Drive until you reach a huge boulder that bisects the road. Now turn around and go back north about one hundred yards until you reach a dirt pull-out on the canyon side. Lower your boat about one-half mile straight down into the canyon along the goat trail here. Put in immediately below Cable Falls (Class VI) and above Roadblock (Class IV). The take-out for all sections is the same: Canyon Mouth Campground. (Taking out at Chairlift would be crazy— it's straight up.)

Gauge Conversions: USGS Gauge Conversion Feet to cfs

Feet	Cfs	Feet	Cfs	Feet	Cfs
2.0	1.5	5.4	1669	7.2	5680
3.0	46	5.6	2030	7.4	6190
4.0	360	5.8	2369	8.0	7481
4.2	450	6.0	2750	8.5	8770
4.4	548	6.2	3200	9.0	10,190
4.6	670	6.4	3700	9.5	11,740
4.8	820	6.6	4200	10.0	14,430
5.0	1025	6.8	4700	11.0	17,240
5.2	1314	7.0	5200	12.0	21,660

LOCUST FORK OF THE WARRIOR RIVER

Sections: US 231 to Nectar Bridge, Class II-III (Class III-IV at high water)

Length of Run: 8 miles

Location: Blount County, Alabama

Maps: USGS quads: Blountsville, Cleveland, Nectar

Times Runnable: Late winter and spring after rain

Gauge: Paddlers' gauge, US 231 bridge

Permit: None required

Source of Levels: Pardue Grocery, 205-274-2586.

How Reported: Feet

Interpretation of Levels: A minimum level is about 2.0 feet. Many folks consider 3.0 feet to be ideal. High is around 4-6 feet. I caught the Locust Fork once at about 9.5 feet and had fun, but saw several open canoes lost that day to trees and to the whirlpool-eddy at Skirum Bluff.

Source of More Information: Birmingham Canoe Club, Box 951, Birmingham, AL 35201.

Best Guidebooks: Nealy, *Whitewater Home Companion,* Vol. 1; Sehlinger et al., *Appalachian Whitewater, Vol. 1.*

MULBERRY FORK OF THE BLACK WARRIOR RIVER

Sections: Hwy. 31 to Birmingham Canoe Club take-out at Hawaii 5-0 Rapid (1 mile off Hwy. 31, reached via a dirt road), Class II

Length of Run: Day trip, 4 miles

Location: Blount and Cullman Counties, Alabama

Maps: USGS quads: Garden City, Nectar, Blount Springs

Times Runnable: Late winter and spring after rain

Permit: None required

Gauge: Paddlers' gauge on US 31 bridge

Source of Levels: Visual inspection only

How Reported: Feet

Additional Gauge: Extrapolate from the paddlers' gauge on the Locust Fork nearby.

Source of Levels: Pardue Grocery, 205-274-2586.

How Reported: Feet

Additional Gauge: USGS Mulberry Fork of the Black Warrior River at Cordova

Source of Levels: National Weather Service, Birmingham; 205-942-1811.

How Reported: Feet

Interpretation of Levels: In terms of the Hwy. 31 bridge gauge, minimum is about 1.0 feet. Optimum levels range from about 1.5 to 2.5 feet. Above about 3.0 feet the best stuff washes out, but because of trees and so forth, the overall difficulty between 3 and 4 feet is about Class III. If you call Pardue Grocery for a Locust Fork Level, it is a good rule of thumb that the Mulberry Fork Highway 31 gauge will be about 1 foot lower. I don't know of any paddlers who are using the Cordova USGS gauge reading from the National Weather Service, but I would recommend that boaters start checking it so that an interpretation can be worked out.

Source of More Information: Birmingham Canoe Club, Box 951, Birmingham, AL 35201.

Best Guidebooks: Foshee, *Alabama Canoe Rides and Float Trips.*

TOWN CREEK

Sections: High Falls to Guntersville Lake, Class III+ (and one Class VI usually portaged)

Length of Run: Day trip, 11 river miles plus 1.5 miles of flatwater on Lake Guntersville

Location: Dekalb County, Alabama

Maps: USGS quad: Grove Oak

Times Runnable: Late winter and spring after rain

Permit: None required

Gauge: Geraldine gauge

Source of Levels: Tennessee Valley Authority, 615-632-8000.

How Reported: Cfs

Interpretation of Levels: About 500 cfs is low, and 2000 cfs is high.

Source of More Information: Birmingham Canoe Club, Box 951, Birmingham, AL 35201.

Best Guidebooks: None

Further Comments: Since Town Creek is not yet in a guidebook, it is worth giving some more direction here. To find the put-in, drive south on Highway 227 from Guntersville, Alabama. Cross a reservoir and reach a stop sign at an intersection. A sign at this intersection will point left to "Bucks Pocket." Turn right (away from Bucks Pocket), staying on Highway 227 as it becomes a four-lane highway. At 2.2 miles from the turn, you'll reach a gravel jeep road entering on the left from Lake Guntersville, just prior to the beginning of a guardrail. This is the take-out trail from the lake. To reach the put-in, continue south on 227 another 5.4 miles. Highway 227 will turn right; stay with it. Pass two churches on the right, and then turn right on a paved road immediately after the second (Mt. Pleasant Church). Continue across a creek and go up a hill, passing the Flat Rock Church on the left after 0.9 mile from the turn, and the Welcome Hill Baptist Church on the right after 1.2 miles. Take the next left onto a gravel road at 1.4 miles. Bear to the left and drive to Mr. Oliver's house and farm. Ask for permission to park vehicles and to carry boats 0.25 mile down his private road to the river. Put in immediately below High Falls. Town Creek has 22 distinct Class III rapids, all of which are great fun. About three-quarters of the way down the river, however, is an obvious Class VI boulder-jumble and falls, "the Blockage." This rapid is almost always carried, although it has been run on occasion by notable paddlers including John Kennedy and Nolan Whitsell.

After reaching Lake Guntersville, paddle for 1.5 miles down the cove created by the flooding of Town Creek. Watch for a road-cut above a marshy area on the right side of the lake. The take-out will be around the next point, marked by a small fishing shack. Take out here and carry your boat up the steep trail about 0.5 mile to Highway 227.

OTHER WHITEWATER RIVERS IN ALABAMA

In addition to Town Creek (described earlier in this section), there are several more whitewater creeks that drain the Sand Mountain plateau of northeastern Alabama. These gnarly creeks cut steep gorges in the sedimentary rock that forms the plateau, and all have the difficulties and dangers (undercuts, cracks, pinning spots, and so forth) associated with steep gorges cut through soft rock. Check with local boating clubs and outfitters for more information, but make sure that you understand the difficulty of these streams, and that you boat with someone that knows the way! Some that are boated include:

Short Creek

South Sauty Creek (since even Dennis Rhodes thinks this one is tough, it must be!)

Shoal Creek

Whippoorwill Creek

GENERAL INFORMATION SOURCES FOR ALABAMA

The National Weather Service Forecast Office in Birmingham monitors river levels for many Alabama rivers: 205-942-1811.

They receive readings updated daily for the following gauges:

Tallapoosa River
  Release from Harris Dam
  At Wadley
  Release from Martin Dam
  Release from Yates Dam
  Release from Thurlow Dam
  At Milstead
  At Tallapoosa Water Plant
Coosa River
  Release from Weiss Dam
  At Gadsden
  Release from Neely Henry Dam
  Release from Logan Martin Dam
  At Childersburg
  Release from Lay Dam
  Release from Mitchell Dam
  Release from Jordan Dam
  At Wetumpka
Cahaba River
  At Centreville
  At Marion Junction
Alabama River
  At Montgomery
  Inflow to Jones Bluff Reservoir
  Outflow from Jones Bluff Reservoir
  At Selma
  Inflow to Millers Ferry Reservoir
  Outflow from Millers Ferry Reservoir
  Inflow to Claiborne Dam
  Outflow from Claiborne Dam
Catoma Creek, at Montgomery
Sipsey Fork of the Black Warrior River, at Smith Dam
Mulberry Fork of the Black Warrior River, at Cordova
Black Warrior River
  Inflow to Bankhead Dam
  Outflow from Bankhead Dam
  Inflow to Holt Dam
  Outflow from Holt Dam
  Inflow to Oliver Dam
  Outflow from Oliver Dam
  Inflow to Warrior Dam
  Outflow from Warrior Dam
Tombigbee River
  Inflow to Aliceville Dam
  Outflow from Aliceville Dam
  Inflow to Gainesville Dam
  Outflow from Gainesville Dam
  Inflow to Demopolis Dam
  Outflow from Demopolis Dam
  Inflow to Coffeeville Dam
  Outflow from Coffeeville Dam
Sucarnoochee River, at Livingston
Mobile River, Release from the Barry Steam Plant
Choctawatchee River
  At Newton
  At Geneva
  At Caryville FL
Conecuh River
  At River Falls
  At Brewton
Pea River, at Elba

COLORADO RIVER IN THE GRAND CANYON

(See Colorado and Utah for additional sections of the Colorado River.)

Sections: Lees Ferry to Pearce Ferry; opinion varies on difficulty, maybe Class IV

Length of Run: 10 to 30 days, 230 river miles, 47 lake miles, depending on choice of section

Location: Coconino and Mohave Counties, Arizona; Grand Canyon National Park

Maps: USGS quads: Lees Ferry (15'), Tanner Wash (15'), Emmett Wash (15'), Nankoweap (15'), Vishnu Temple (15'), Bright Angel (15'), Havaupai Point (15'), Supai (15'), Kanab Point (15'), Powell Plateau (15'), Tuckup Canyon (15'), National Canyon (15'), Vulcans Throne, Whitmore Rapids, Vulcans Throne SW, Whitmore Point SE, Granite Peak, Travertine Rapids, Separation Canyon, Spencer Canyon, Devils Slide Rapids, Quartermaster Canyon, Bat Cave, Columbine Falls, Snap Canyon West.

Times Runnable: Year-Round

Permit: Required. Permits are issued only to trips with reservations. Grand Canyon National Park currently issues 223 noncommercial permits for trips between April 16 and April 15 of the following year. One trip per day is allowed during the summer season (April 16 through October 15) and no more than 40 trips during the winter season (October 16 through April 15).

Reservations: Required. Send in an application during February of any year to be placed on the waiting list for trip leaders of prospective trips; there is a form in Appendix One. Provide your name and address, daytime phone number and social security number, and include a money order or cashier's check for $25. Every subsequent year you will have to inform the Park Service as to whether you want to stay on the list.

The trip leader must be in charge of the trip and must accompany the trip for its entire duration. There are thousands of names on the waiting list. Rip van Winkle might be a good candidate as a trip leader.

River trips are scheduled from the waiting list in numerical order. Each October the top 300 people are notified of their waiting list number and are asked to submit requested launch dates. On January 1, permit applications are distributed with the scheduled launch date indicated. Once you get a launch date, you'll have to submit another fee—$30 this time.

There is another strategy that you can take that will enormously improve your chances of getting on the river before senility. Once you're on the waiting list, call the Park Service frequently, and ask about cancellations. Starting in early January of each year, it is often possible to reserve launch dates that others have had to give up.

Restrictions: The trip size limit is 16 persons. The maximum trip length is restricted to 18 days from April 16 to October 15; to 21 days from October 16 to November 30 and from March 1 to April 15. No-show penalty. There is a limit of one trip per person per year. The trip leader and boatmen must have experience in the Grand Canyon or one or more comparable whitewater rivers; at least one of these persons must be familiar with the Grand Canyon. There are numerous other restrictions and rules; the National Park will send you a list.

Gauge: Release from Glen Canyon Dam

Source of Levels: Bureau of Reclamation, Salt Lake City UT Recording, 801-539-1311. National Park Service, Grand Canyon National Park, 602-638-7843.

How Reported: Cfs

Interpretation of Levels: The amount of water released from Glen Canyon Dam fluctuates each day according to power demands, ranging from as little as 500 cfs to as much as 20,000. The rapids are considered most difficult around 25,000 cfs. Lower down, they lose much of their kick and higher up, they wash out a little. Peak releases in June generally approach 45,000 cfs.

Source of More Information: National Park Service, address and phone above.

Grand Canyon Natural History Assoc., PO Box 399, Grand Canyon, AZ 86023, 602-638-2771.

Best Guidebooks: Belknap and Evans, *Belknap's Water-*

Surfing Diamond Rapid on The Salt River. Photo by Curt Smith.

proof Grand Canyon River Guide; Stevens, *The Colorado River in Grand Canyon.*

Further Comments: Bring a geology guide, too. Take time for trips up the side canyons. If you get a permit, call and invite me.

SALT RIVER

Sections:
(1) The Flying V Gorge, Arizona Rt. 9 to U.S. 60, very continuous Class III-IV (to Class IV-V high), plus two at Class V and a 2 mile portage around an unrunnable gorge.

(2) The Upper Salt, U.S. 60 to diversion dam above the HW 288 bridge at Roosevelt Reservoir, Class II-IV (plus one Class VI, Quarzite Falls, that you will want to line or portage).

Length of Run:
(1) 1-2 days, 25 miles
(2) 2-3 days, 52 miles

Location: Gila County, Arizona; Tonto National Forest; Fort Apache Indian Reservation

Maps: USGS quads: Forks Butte, Cone Butte, Popcorn Canyon, Carrizo SE, Becker's Butte, Blue Horse Mtn. (15'), Haystack Butte, Rockinstraw Mtn. (15')

Times Runnable: February through June. Peaks in March.

Permit: Section (1) and the put-in for Section (2) are within the Fort Apache Reservation; you'll need to pay a fee and get a permit for about $10. Permits are available from the small store located near the put-in for Section (2). For further information, contact the White Mountain Fish and Game Department, Attn: Mr. John Caid, White River, AZ 85941; 602-338-4385.

Gauge: For Section (1), Salt River Project gauge, Salt River at Salt River Canyon, 0.2 mile above US 60.

Source of Levels: Salt River Project recording, 602-236-5929.

How Reported: Cfs

Additional Gauge: For Section (2), Salt River Project gauge near Highway 288 (inflow to Roosevelt Lake)

Source of Levels: Salt River Project, 602-236-8888

How Reported: Cfs

Interpretation of Levels: Low for either Section is about 900 cfs. Medium water is considered 2400 cfs; at this level on Section (1) you'll probably want to portage Little Lava Falls. During high water (2500 to 6000 cfs) you'll probably want to avoid Section (1).

Source of More Information: USDA Forest Service, Globe Ranger District, Tonto National Forest, Rt. 1, Box 33, Globe, AZ 85502; 602-425-7180

Shuttles: Jack's Journeys; 602-425-3307.

Salt River Guide, c/o Dana Hollister, PO Box 56784, Phoenix, AZ 85079.

Best Guidebooks: The best guide to the Flying V Gorge (sometimes also called the Upper, Upper Salt) is not in a guidebook at all. Get hold of the February 1990 issue of River Runner and read *Arizona's Salt River* by Robert Miller. For Section (2), use Hollister, *The Salt River*.

Further Comments: Section (1), the Flying V Gorge, is considered by most river folks as a thundering, extremely continuous Class III and IV wilderness run with long portages, appropriate for experts only. The Forest Service, unfazed by the facts, continues to list it as unrunnable Class VI in their publications. Decide for yourself who to believe. Don't bring rafts on this section—there is at least one mandatory portage of at least 2 miles, plus possible portages around two Class V rapids.

Section (2) is a popular rafting run. The Forest Service rates Quartzite Falls, 32 miles into Section (2) as Class VI. You'll want to line or portage this one. At the trip's end, make sure to take out above the dangerous diversion dam, located about a mile above the US 280 bridge.

Portaging Quartzite Falls, Salt River. Photo by Curt Smith.

VERDE RIVER
Wild and Scenic River

Sections: (1) Childs, Arizona to Horseshoe Reservoir, Class I-III
(2) Bartlett Reservoir to confluence with the Salt River, Class I-II

Length of Run: (1) 1-2 days, 25 miles, 2 on reservoir
(2) Day trip, 19 miles

Location: Yavapai and Gila Counties; Tonto National Forest

Maps: USGS quads: Verde Hot Springs, Wet Bottom Mesa, Chalk Mtn., Horseshoe Dam, Bartlett, McDowell, Granite Reef Dam

Times Runnable: Section (1) is runnable only in spring; Section (2) is runnable year-round

Permit: None required

Gauge: For Section (1), inflow to Horseshoe Reservoir

Source of Levels: Salt River Project, 602-236-5929.

How Reported: Cfs

Additional Gauge: For Section (2), release from Bartlett Reservoir

Source of Levels: Salt River Project, 602-236-5929.

How Reported: Cfs

Interpretation of Levels: For both sections, 100 cfs is minimum for canoe or kayak, and about 600-700 cfs is minimum for a raft. About 1100 cfs is optimum, and 15,000 is high (not recommended by the Forest Service). Peak flow has been as high as 40,000 cfs.

Source of More Information: USDA Forest Service, Verde Ranger District, Tonto National Forest, Star Route, Box 1100, Camp Verde, AZ 86322; 602-567-4121.

Best Guidebooks: Anderson and Hopkinson, *Rivers of the Southwest*; Tonto National Forest, "Verde River Runner Map" (available from Forest Service, address above).

Further Comments: Section (2) is a nice afternoon run for Phoenix boaters. In the summer it is extremely popular with tubers; summer is also a good time for the voyeur kayaker to head for the Verde—nudity is plentiful.

GENERAL INFORMATION SOURCES FOR ARIZONA

Levels for rivers in Arizona and Utah can be obtained by calling Salt Lake City for the recorded Bureau of Reclamation River Observations: 801-539-1311.

Gauge readings updated daily at 4 am are reported for the following rivers:

Colorado River Basin
Colorado River, at Westwater
Gunnison, at Gun Summit
Dolores River, at Bedrock
Dolores River, near Cisco
Colorado River, near Cisco
Colorado River, Cataract Canyon
Colorado River, at Lees Ferry
Virgin River, near Littlefield
Muddy, near Emory

Green River Basin
Yampa River, at Maybell
Little Snake River, near Lily
Yampa River, at the Mouth
Green River, near Jensen
White River, near Watson
Green River, near Green River, Utah
San Rafael, near Green River, Utah
Dirty Devil, at Hanksville

Great Basin
Weaver, near Oakley
Weaver, below Echo
Sevier, above Clear Creek

San Juan Basin
Animas, near Durango
San Juan River, near Bluff

Dam Releases
Flaming Gorge Dam, Green River
Glen Canyon Dam, Colorado River
Navaho Dam, San Juan River
McPhee Dam, Dolores River

The Salt River Project Lake and River Recording reports lake inflows and outflows for dams and reservoirs under its jurisdiction: 602-236-5929. For further information, call: 602-236-8888.

The recording includes the following:

Salt River
At Salt River Canyon
Below Roosevelt Lake
Inflow from Tunnel Creek
Below Stewart Mountain Dam

Verde River
At Camp Verde River
Inflow to Horseshoe Reservoir
Below Horseshoe Reservoir
Below Bartlett Dam

ARKANSAS

BAKER CREEK

Sections: Ed Banks Road to low-water bridge on Weyerhauser Logging Road 52200 (on the way to the Cossatot put-in), Class IV

Length of Run: Day trip, 3 miles

Location: Howard County, Arkansas

Maps: USGS quad: Umpire (15')

Times Runnable: When the Cossatot is over 2000 cfs.

Permit: None required

Gauge: None. If water is over the low-water bridge at the take-out, then there should be enough water. Generally this happens only when the Cossatot River is over 2000 or 3000 cfs.

Source of Levels: For Cossatot: Army Corps of Engineers' Lake and Stream Report; 501-378-5150.

How Reported: Cfs

Source of More Information: Take a Hike Shop, 615 N. Beechwood, Little Rock, AR 72205; 501-664-2423.

Best Guidebooks: Kennon, *Ozark Whitewater*

Further Comments: A tough, technical run on a small tributary of the Cossatot. It makes a good early-morning trip before paddling the Cossatot in the afternoon.

BIG PINEY CREEK

Sections:
(1) Highway 123 bridge to Treat (Helton's Farm), Class I-II
(2) Treat (Helton's Farm) to Longpool Camp, Class II
(3) Longpool Camp to Twin Bridge, Class I-II

Length (1) Day trip, 9 miles
of Run: (2) Day trip, 9 miles
(3) Day trip, 5 miles

Location: Johnson and Pope Counties, Arkansas; Ozark National Forest

Maps: USGS quads: Treat, Fort Douglas

Times Runnable: From late September through mid-June in a normal rainfall year. Best from late February through May.

Permit: None required

Gauge: Big Piney at Long Pool near Dover

Source of Levels: US Army Corps of Engineers recording, 501-378-5150.

How Reported: Feet

Interpretation of Levels: Low is about 2.5 feet, medium is 3 to 4 feet, and high is 5 to 8 feet.

Source of More Information: Moore Outdoors, Big Piney Creek Outpost, Hwy. 164W at Twin Bridge, Rt. 2, Dover, AR 72837; 501-331-3606.

USDA Forest Service, Bayou Ranger District, Ozark National Forest, Rt. 1, Box 36 Hector, AR 72843; 501-284-3150.

Best Guidebooks: Kennon, *Ozark Whitewater*.

COSSATOT RIVER

Sections: (1) Highway 246 to Ed Banks Road bridge, Class II-III
(2) Ed Banks Road bridge to Falls low-water bridge, Class III-IV
(3) Falls low-water bridge to Highway 4 bridge, Class III, IV (to Class IV-V at high water)

Length (1) Day trip, 3 miles
of Run: (2) Day trip, 2 miles
(3) Day trip, 4.5 miles

Location: Howard County, Arkansas

Maps: USGS quads: Umpire (15'), Gillam Dam (15'). Also: Ozark National Forest Visitor Map.

Times Runnable: Late winter and spring after heavy rain and very occasionally from September through December.

Permit: None required

Gauge: Cossatot, inflow to Gillam Reservoir (located at Highway 246 bridge)

Source of Levels: US Army Corps of Engineers, 501-378-5150.
Gillam Reservoir, 501-378-6238.

How Reported: Cfs

Interpretation of Levels: About 700 cfs is low, 1500 cfs is medium, and 3000 and over is high.

Source of More Information: Take a Hike Shop, 615 N. Beechwood, Little Rock, AR 72205; 501-664-2423.

Best Guidebooks: Kennon, *Ozark Whitewater*.

Further Comments: The Cossatot is a super river, but its watershed has suffered from clearcutting. The runoff is so fast that I've known the Cossatot to go from 10,000 cfs Wednesday (too high), to 2000 on Thursday (just right), and to 300 on Friday (too low). The Cossatot Five-falls area provides superb Class IV whitewater; at high water this section becomes a single Class IV-V rapid (some folks say Class V). Be careful of Devil's Hollow Falls, Class III-IV, downstream. It's possible to pin here if you don't run the drop right.

LITTLE MISSOURI RIVER

Sections: (1) Albert Pike Campground to Arizona Highway 84 bridge, Class II-III
(2) Arizona Highway 84 bridge to US Highway 70 bridge, Class I-II

Length (1) Day trip, 8.5 miles
of Run: (2) Day trip, 11.5 miles

Location: Polk, Montgomery and Pike Counties, Arkansas; Albert Pike Recreation Area, Ouachita National Forest

Maps: USGS quads: Athens (15') and Center Point NE (15'). Also: Ouachita National Forest Visitor Map.

Times Runnable: Late winter and spring after rain

Permit: None required

Gauge: None, exactly. Levels are reported in terms of air space under the low-water bridge at Albert Pike. Or, check the Cossatot level with the US Army Corps. If it's up, then the Little Missouri is probably up, too.

Source of Levels: Mr. and Mrs. Langley, Langley Campground, Albert Pike Recreation Area; 501-356-3964.

How Reported: Inches of air space

Additional Gauge: Paddlers' gauge at Hwy. 84 bridge

Source of Levels: None. Visual inspection only.

How Reported: Feet

Interpretation of Levels: Minimum is 8 inches at Hwy. 84 or about 27 inches of air space at the low bridge. Optimum ranges from 8 inches to 2.5 feet at the Hwy. 84 bridge or about 12 to 20 inches of air space at the low bridge. High is above 3 feet at the Hwy. 84 bridge or 8 inches or less of air space at the low bridge.

Source of More Information: USDA Forest Service, Caddo Ranger District, Ouachita National Forest, Glenwood, AR 71943; 501-356-3523.
Take a Hike Shop, 615 N. Beechwood, Little Rock, AR 72205; 501-664-2423.

Best Guidebooks: Kennon, *Ozark Whitewater.*

RICHLAND CREEK

Sections: (1) Forest Service Road 1203 to Richland Creek Campground, Class IV
(2) Richland Creek Campground to Forest Service Road 1201, Class III-III+

Length of Run: (1) Day trip, 6 miles
(2) Day trip, 10 miles

Location: Newton County, Arkansas; Ozark National Forest

Maps: USGS quads: Moore

Times Runnable: Late winter and spring after rain

Permit: None required

Gauge: None. Correlate to the Scottsdale gauge on the Illinois Bayou or the Big Piney at Long Pool reported by the US Army Corps of Engineers.

Source of Levels: US Army Corps of Engineers recording, 501-378-5150.

How Reported: Feet

Interpretation of Levels: Richland Creek will probably be runnable if the Illinois Bayou is 9 feet or over, or if the Big Piney is over 4 feet; 7.5 to 9.0 feet on the Big Piney at Long Pool is a good level.

Source of More Information: Take a Hike Shop, 615 N. Beechwood, Little Rock, AR 72205; 501-664-2423.

USDA Forest Service, Buffalo Ranger District, Ozark National Forest, Jasper, AR 72641; 501-446-5122.

Best Guidebooks: Kennon, *Ozark Whitewater*

Further Comments: The upper section is a tough, technical run for advanced to expert paddlers only. There have been several near-misses, lost boats, and so on. If you are not sure, consider running the lower section. The first two miles of the lower section are the hardest, so if you have trouble you can carry back to the campground.

GENERAL INFORMATION SOURCES
FOR ARKANSAS

Levels for rivers in Arkansas can be obtained by calling the US Army Corps of Engineers' lake and stream recording at 501-378-5150.

Some levels are reported in feet and others in cfs. The recording is updated daily at 10 a.m. Gauge readings reported include:

Buffalo River
   At Silver Hill
   At Buffalo Point
   At Steel Creek
   At Pruett

Big Piney Creek at Long Pool, near Dover
Frog Bayou near Rudy
Illinois Bayou, at Scottsdale
Lee Creek, at Van Buren
Mulberry River, at Mulberry
Cossatot River
   Inflow to Gillam Reservoir
   Release from Gillam Reservoir

The Take A Hike Shop in Little Rock acts as a clearinghouse of information on Arkansas whitewater:

Take A Hike Shop, 615 N. Beechwood, Little Rock, AR 72205; 501-664-2423.

CALIFORNIA/NEVADA

AMERICAN RIVER, MIDDLE FORK

Sections: Tunnel Chute Run, Oxbow Bend to Hwy. 49 bridge, Class IV (one at V-VI)

Length of Run: 1-2 days, 25 miles

Location: El Dorado and Placer Counties, California; El Dorado National Forest

Maps: USGS quads: Michigan Bluff, Foresthill, Georgetown, Auburn, Greenwood

Times Runnable: May to September

Permit: None required

Gauge: Flow below Oxbow Dam

Source of Levels: Department of Water Resources, Flood Operations Whitewater Recording, (The Flow Phone); 916-653-9647.

How Reported: Cfs

Interpretation of Levels: Minimum is about 500 cfs. Optimum is 1200 cfs. Low-moderate levels range from 800 to 1500 cfs. Over 2000 cfs, it becomes difficult to reenter the river after portaging the Tunnel Chute entrance rapid.

Source of More Information: Department of Boating and Waterways, 1629 "S" St., Sacramento, CA 95814-7291; 916-445-2616.

California Department of Parks and Recreation, Folsom Lake Area Headquarters, 7806 Folsom-Auburn Rd., Folsom, CA 95630; 916-988-0205.

El Dorado National Forest, 100 Forni Rd., Placerville, CA 95667; 916-622-5061.

Best Guidebooks: Cassady and Calhoun, *California Whitewater;* Holbeck and Stanley, *A Guide to the Best Whitewater in the State of California;* Mandel et al.,

Bye-bye at Tunnel Chute, Middle Fork of the American River. Photo by Curt Smith.

Airbracing on the American River. Photo by Curt Smith.

American River; Friends of the River, "American River Recreation Area" Map/guide.

Further Comments: You may want to portage the Tunnel Chute Entrance rapid, Class IV at regular levels to VI at high levels.

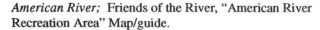

AMERICAN RIVER, NORTH FORK
Wild and Scenic River

Sections:
(1) Generation Gap, Tadpole Creek to Euchre Bar Rd., Class V
(2) Giant Gap, Euchre Bar to Colfax-Iowa Hill Rd., Class IV, V
(3) Chamberlain Falls, Colfax-Iowa Hill Rd., to Colfax-Foresthill Rd., Class IV, V
(4) Ponderosa Way Run, Colfax-Foresthill Bridge to Ponderosa Way Bridge, Class II-III.

Length of Run:
(1) Day trip, 12 miles
(2) Day trip, 14.5 miles
(3) Day trip, 5 miles
(4) Day trip, 5 miles

Location: Placer County, California; Tahoe National Forest

Maps: USGS quads: (1) Duncan Peak, Westville, Dutch Flat; (2) Dutch Flat, Forest Hill, Colfax; (3) Colfax; (4) Colfax

Times Runnable: Spring

Permit: None required

Gauge: Inflow to Lake Clementine

Source of Levels: Department of Water Resources, Flood Operations Whitewater Recording (the Flow Phone); 916-653-9647.

How Reported: Cfs

Interpretation of Levels: For Section (1), minimum is about 600 cfs. Optimum is 1500 cfs. Low to moderate levels range from 600 to 1200 cfs (about Class III-IV), and moderate to high levels range from 1200 to 2000 cfs (about Class IV-V). Above 2000 is very high.

For Section (2), minimum is about 600 cfs. Optimum is 1000 cfs. Low to moderate levels range from 600 to 1200 cfs (about Class III-IV+), and moderate to high levels range from 1200 to 3000 cfs (about Class IV-V+). Above 3000 is very high.

For Section (3), minimum is about 800 cfs. Optimum is 1500 cfs. Low to moderate levels range from 800 to 1500 cfs (about Class III-IV), and moderate to high levels range from 1500 to 4000 cfs (about Class IV-V). Above 4000 is very high.

For Section (4), minimum is about 500 cfs. Optimum is 1200 cfs. Low to moderate levels range from 500 to 1500 cfs (about Class II+), and moderate to high levels are over 1500 cfs (about Class III+).

Source of More Information: California Department of Parks and Recreation, Folsom Lake Area Headquarters, 7806 Folsom-Auburn Rd., Folsom, CA 95630; 916-988-0205.

Department of Boating and Waterways, 1629 "S" St., Sacramento, CA 95814-7291; 916-445-2616.

Tahoe National Forest, Highway 49 and Coyote St., Nevada City, CA 95959; 916-265-4531.

Best Guidebooks: Cassady and Calhoun, *California Whitewater;* Holbeck and Stanley, *A Guide to the Best Whitewater in the State of California;* Mandel et al., *American River;* Friends of the River, "American River Recreation Area" Map/guide.

AMERICAN RIVER, SOUTH FORK

Sections:
- (1) Kyburz Run, Kyburz to Riverton, Class III-IV+ (Class IV-V high, plus two portages: one Class V with logs and one Class VI)
- (2) Riverton to Peavine, Class III-IV
- (3) Chili Bar Run, Chili Bar to Marshall Gold Discovery State Park in Coloma, Class III (one at III-IV, Troublemaker)
- (4) South Fork Gorge, Marshall Gold Discovery State Park, continuing past Camp Lotus to Salmon Falls Bridge, Class III+

Length of Run:
- (1) Day trip, 9.6 miles
- (2) Day trip, 3.5 miles
- (3) Day trip, 6 miles
- (4) Day trip, 14.5 miles

Other put-in and take-out options exist.

Location: El Dorado County, California; El Dorado National Forest

Maps: USGS quads: Kyburz, Riverton, Garden Valley, Coloma, Pilot Hill

Times Runnable: Sections (1) and (2) are runnable in the spring; Section (3) is runnable year-round.

Permit: The Department of Parks and Recreation of El Dorado County requires every boat on the South Fork of the American to bear a permit tag. These permits are available free at kiosks located at Camp Lotus, Chili Bar, Marshall Gold Discovery State Park in Coloma, and in Lotus. Once you have a tag, it's good forever. For more information, contact the El Dorado County Department of Parks and Recreation at 916-621-5353.

The Parks and Recreation Department of the State of California charges $3.00 for take-out and launch fees at Marshall Gold Discovery State Park in Coloma and at the Salmon Falls launch facility. Chili Bar and Camp Lotus are both privately owned, and both charge parking and launch fees.

Gauge: For Sections (1) and (2), flow at Kyburz

Source of Levels: Department of Water Resources, Flood Operations Whitewater Recording (the Flow Phone); 916-653-9647.

How Reported: Cfs

Additional Gauge: For Section (3), flow at Chili Bar

Source of Levels: Department of Water Resources, Flood Operations Whitewater Recording (the Flow Phone); 916-653-9647.

How Reported: Cfs

Interpretation of Levels: For Section (1), minimum is about 700 cfs, optimum is 1200 cfs and high is 3000 cfs. For Section (2), minimum is about 700 cfs, optimum is 1500 cfs and high is 4000 cfs. For Sections (3) and (4), minimum is about 700 cfs; optimum is 2000 cfs, and high is 6000 to 7000 cfs.

Source of More Information: Bureau of Land Management, Folsom Resource Area, 63 Natoma St., Folsom, CA 95630; 916-985-4474.

El Dorado County Department of Parks and Recreation; 916-621-5353.

Department of Boating and Waterways, 1629 "S" St., Sacramento, CA 95814-7291; 916-445-2616.

USDA Forest Service, El Dorado National Forest, 100 Forni Rd., Placerville, CA 95667; 916-622-5061.

The River Store, 1032 Lotus Road, Lotus, CA 95651; 916-626-3425.

American River Coalition, 909 12th St., Suite 207A, Sacramento, CA 95814; 916-448-1045.

Save the American River Association, PO Box 19496, Sacramento, CA 95819.

Best Guidebooks: Cassady and Calhoun, *California Whitewater;* Holbeck and Stanley, *A Guide to the Best Whitewater in the State of California;* Department of Boating and Waterways. "Rafting on the South Fork of the American River" Map/guide; Mandel et al., *American River.*

Further Comments: The South Fork of the American is an extremely popular intermediate run, located in the scenic Gold Country of California. Sadly, the American is a continual object of the nefarious schemes of the evil dam-mavens, who are constantly promoting the construction of the Auburn Dam, and the resultant destruction of the South Fork. Do your part to protect this stellar river!

Portage one Class VI and probably a Class V on Section (1). Watch for logjams on this section, too.

CARSON RIVER, EAST FORK

Sections: (1) Upper, Cane Rock to Hangman's Bridge, Class III

(2) Wilderness Run, Markleeville to BLM Boat Ramp at Route 395, Class II

Length of Run: (1) Day trip, 7 miles

(2) Day trip, 20 miles

Location: Alpine County, California; Toiyabe National Forest

Maps: USGS quads: Markleeville (15'), Topaz Lake (15'), and Mt. Siegel (15')

Times Runnable: Spring

Permit: None required

Gauge: Flow at Gardnerville

Source of Levels: Department of Water Resources, Flood Operations Whitewater Recording (the Flow Phone); 916-653-9647.

How Reported: Cfs

Interpretation of Levels: Minimum is about 500 cfs. Optimum is 1500 cfs. Medium-high levels range from 1000 to 5000 cfs (from about Class III to Class III+).

Source of More Information: USDA Forest Service, Carson Ranger District, Toiyabe National Forest, 1536 S. Carson St., Carson City, NV 89701; 702-882-2766.

Bureau of Land Management, Carson City District, 1535 Hot Springs Rd., Suite 300, Carson City, NV 89701; 702-882-1631.

Department of Boating and Waterways, 1629 "S" St., Sacramento, CA 95814-7291; 916-445-2616.

Best Guidebooks: Cassady and Calhoun, *California Whitewater;* Holbeck and Stanley, *A Guide to the Best Whitewater in the State of California.*

Further Comments: Take out above the dam at Highway 395.

EEL RIVER, MAIN
Wild and Scenic River

Sections: (1) Pillsbury Run, Scott Dam to Bucknell Creek, Class III+

(2) Dos Rios to Alderpoint, Class II-III

Length of Run: (1) Day trip, 6 miles

(2) 4-6 days, 45 miles

Location: Mendocino and Lake Counties, California; Mendocino National Forest

Maps: USGS quads: (1) Lake Pillsbury; (2) Dos Rios, Iron Peak, Updegraff Ridge, Lake Monta, Jewett Rock, Alderpoint

Times Runnable: December to May

Permit: None required

Gauge: For Section (1), release from Lake Pillsbury

Source of Levels: Department of Water Resources, Flood Operations Whitewater Recording (the Flow Phone); 916-653-9647.

How Reported: Cfs

Additional Gauge: For Section (2), flow at Fort Steward

Source of Levels: Department of Water Resources, Flood Operations Whitewater Recording (the Flow Phone); 916-653-9647.

How Reported: Cfs

Interpretation of Levels: For Section (1), minimum is about 200-700 cfs. High is 5000 to 6000 cfs. For Section (2), minimum is about 500 to 800 cfs. High is 20,000 cfs.

Source of More Information: USDA Forest Service, Upper Lake Ranger District, Mendocino National Forest, PO Box 96, Upper Lake, CA 95485; 707-275-2361.

Department of Boating and Waterways, 1629 "S" St., Sacramento, CA 95814-7291; 916-445-2616.

Best Guidebooks: Cassady and Calhoun, *California Whitewater;* Holbeck and Stanley, *A Guide to the Best Whitewater in the State of California.*

EEL RIVER, MIDDLE FORK

Sections: Black Butte River to Dos Rios, Class II-IV (one at V)

Length of Run: 2-3 days, 30 miles

Location: North Bay County, California; Mendocino National Forest

Maps: USGS quads: Covelo East, Newhouse Ridge

Times Runnable: March to May

Permit: None required

Gauge: None. Extrapolate from the Main Eel at Fort Steward.

Source of Levels: Department of Water Resources, Flood Operations Whitewater Recording (the Flow Phone); 916-653-9647.

How Reported: Cfs

Interpretation of Levels: Minimum is about 700 cfs. High is 10,000. Before April, the Middle Fork provides about half of the water in the Main Eel, so multiply the Fort Steward reading by 0.5 to get the flow on the Middle Fork. Later in the season, dams cut off the bulk of the Main Eel's flow, so multiply the Fort Steward reading by about 0.8 to get the flow on the Middle Fork. If you're puzzled, contact the BLM; they should have a good idea of conditions.

Source of More Information: Bureau of Land Management, Ukiah District, 555 Leslie St. (PO Box 940), Ukiah, CA 95842; 707-462-3873.

USDA Forest Service, Covelo Ranger District, Mendocino National Forest, Covelo, CA 95428; 707-983-6118.

Department of Boating and Waterways, 1629 "S" St., Sacramento, CA 95814-7291; 916-445-2616.

Best Guidebooks: Cassady and Calhoun, *California Whitewater;* Holbeck and Stanley, *A Guide to the Best Whitewater in the State of California.*

Further Comments: You'll probably want to portage Coal Mine Falls, Class V-VI. Watch out for flash flood conditions after heavy rain.

EEL RIVER, SOUTH FORK

Sections: Ten-mile Creek to the confluence with the South Fork and continuing to Big Bend, Class IV-V (one at V-VI)

Length of Run: Day trip, 16 miles

Location: Mendocino and Lake Counties, California; Mendocino National Forest

Maps: USGS quads: Leggett, Lincoln Ridge and Tanoak Point

Times Runnable: December to early April after rain

Permit: None required

Gauge: Flow at Leggett

Source of Levels: Department of Water Resources, Flood Operations Whitewater Recording (the Flow Phone); 916-653-9647.

How Reported: Cfs

Interpretation of Levels: Minimum is about 1500 to 2000 cfs. High is 8000.

Source of More Information: Big Bend Lodge, PO Box 111, Leggett, CA 95455; 707-984-6321.

Department of Boating and Waterways, 1629 "S" St., Sacramento, CA 95814-7291; 916-445-2616.

USDA Forest Service, Upper Lake Ranger District, Mendocino National Forest, PO Box 96, Upper Lake, CA 95485; 707-275-2361.

Best Guidebooks: Cassady and Calhoun, *California Whitewater;* Holbeck and Stanley, *A Guide to the Best Whitewater in the State of California.*

FEATHER RIVER, EAST BRANCH OF THE NORTH FORK

Sections: Virgilia to Belden, Class IV (IV-V high)

Length of Run: Day trip, 10 miles

Location: Plumas County, California; Plumas National Forest

Maps: USGS quads: Twain, Caribou

Times Runnable: Spring

Permit: None required

Gauge: None. Runnable during peak runoff of a highwater year.

Interpretation of Levels: Apply the W.D.S. method when you get there. Low is about 600 to 1500 cfs. Medium is about 1500 to 3000 (Class IV). High is over 3000 (Class IV- V). At much higher flows, stay in camp and play Hacky.

Source of More Information: USDA Forest Service, Quincy Ranger District, Plumas National Forest, PO Box 69, Quincy, CA 95971; 916-283-0555.

Department of Boating and Waterways, 1629 "S" St., Sacramento, CA 95814-7291; 916-445-2616.

Best Guidebooks: Holbeck and Stanley, *A Guide to the Best Whitewater in the State of California.*

FEATHER RIVER, MIDDLE FORK
Wild and Scenic River

Sections: Gorge, Nelson Point to Milsap Bar, Class V-V+

Length of Run: 3 days, 32 miles

Location: Plumas and Butte Counties, California, Plumas National Forest

Maps: USGS quads: Blue Nose Mtn., Onion Valley, Cascade, Brush Crk.

Times Runnable: Spring

Permit: Campfire permit required. Apply to: USDA Forest Service, Quincy Ranger District, Plumas National Forest, PO Box 69, Quincy, CA 95971; 916-283-0555

Restrictions: Shovel required as a condition of the campfire permit.

Gauge: None, but check the inflow to the new Bullards Bar Reservoir on the North Fork of the Yuba. Flow on the Middle Fork of the Feather should be about half this.

Source of Levels: Department of Water Resources, Flood Operations Whitewater Recording (the Flow Phone); 916-653-9647.

How Reported: Cfs

Interpretation of Levels: Minimum is about 200-300 cfs. Optimum is 500 cfs. Moderate flows range from 600 to 1000 cfs. 1200 is very high.

Source of More Information: USDA Forest Service, Quincy Ranger District, Plumas National Forest, PO Box 69, Quincy, CA 95971; 916-283-0555.

USDA Forest Service, Beckworth Ranger District, Plumas National Forest, PO Box 7, Blairsden, CA 96103; 916-445-2616.

Best Guidebooks: Cassady and Calhoun, *California Whitewater*; Holbeck and Stanley, *A Guide to the Best Whitewater in the State of California*.

Further Comments: Spectacular and difficult Class V. There is a portage at Granite Dome Falls and possibly elsewhere.

KERN RIVER
Wild and Scenic River

Sections: Forks of the Kern
(1) Forks of the Kern, from the Forks of the Kern to the Johnsondale Bridge, Class IV and V (Class V high)

Upper Kern
(2) Limestone Run, from Johnsondale Bridge to Fairview Dam, Class III-IV (IV high)
(3) Fairview Run (Calkins Run), from Fairview Dam to Calkins Flat Camping Area, Class III (plus Bombs Away, Class V, just below Fairview Dam, usually skipped).
(4) Chamise Gorge, from Calkins Flat to just above Salmon Falls, Class IV-V
(5) Gold Ledge Run, from Ant Canyon to Camp 3 Campground, Class V
(6) Camp 3 Run, from Camp 3 Campground to Powerhouse No. 3, Class I

The Kern near Kernville
(7) Powerhouse Run, from Southern California Edison Powerhouse KR3 to Riverside Park in Kernville, Class II-III
(8) Riverside Park Rapid, Class II
Lower Kern
(9) Isabella Dam to Sandy Flat, Class III+
(10) Sandy Flat launch area to the Highway 178 Bridge, Class IV (one portage at Royal Flush, Class V-VI)
(11) Highway 178 to Democrat Hot Springs Campground, Class IV.

Length of Run:
(1) 1-2 day trip, 14 miles, plus a 2 mile carry to the put-in
(2) Day trip, 2.4 miles
(3) Day trip, 2.8 miles
(4) Day trip, 2.2 miles
(5) Day trip, 7.2 miles
(6) Day trip, 2.4 miles
(7) Day trip, 2 miles
(8) Play spot, 0.2 mile
(9) Day trip, 6.3 miles
(10) Day trip, 7.6 miles
(11) Day trip, 4 miles

Location: Kern County, California; Sequoia National Forest

Maps: USGS quads: Hocket Peak (15'), Kernville (15'). Also: Sequoia National Forest Map.

Tom Moore cruising Carsons Falls. Photo by Anne Penny.

Times runnable: In Kernville, from about December through August, there is usually enough water to practice at the slalom gates below Riverside Park. Just above, the fine play rapid at Riverside Park generally has enough water from February through August. The Powerhouse Section can generally be run from February through May or June.

On the Upper Kern, the Limestone Section generally also becomes runnable in February or March, and it can be run through the spring runoff period, extending into May or June (or longer in wet years). Sadly, just below Limestone five hundred cfs of water is stolen from the river by the hydropower boondoggle at Fairview, diverted through a flume, and returned far downstream at the Southern California Edison Powerhouse KR3, two miles above Kernville. The sad result is that the rest of the Upper Kern below Fairview has a much shortened season during the spring runoff period.

The Forks of the Kern become runnable in late March or early April; like the Limestone Section, the Forks can be run only the spring runoff period, extending into May or June (or longer in wet years).

The water for the Lower Kern originates from Lake Isabella, but can arrive on the Lower Kern by either of two routes. During the summer, the U.S. Army Corps releases 1000 to 3000 cfs directly from the Isabella Dam at Lake Isabella to provide water for irrigation in San Joaquin Valley near Bakersfield. It's these releases that provide the prime boating season on the Lower Kern, allowing paddlers to run Sections (9), (10) and (11) at optimal levels. The length and volume of the irrigation releases vary from year to year, depending on water supply. Check with the Army Corps for the release schedule: 619-379-2742.

A flume also originates at the dam and leads about six miles downstream to the Southern California Edison Borel Powerhouse. During most of the year, 400 to 600 cfs is diverted through this flume and into the Borel Powerhouse where it turns some turbines and lights some lights, before being returned to the river. This low volume flow is enough to allow kayaks and canoes to run Sections (10) and (11) of the Lower almost year-round, but rafters will want to wait for the higher volume summer releases.

During drought years, when the pool elevation at Lake Isabella is extremely low, the mouth of the diversion flume is left high and dry, and the Army Corps is unable to divert any water to Cal Edison's Borel Powerhouse. The year-round releases of 400 to 600 cfs continue, but now the water is allowed to flow directly out of the Isabella Dam, opening up Section (9) for low-water runs as well.

Permit: Forks of the Kern: permits are required from May 15 to September 15. There is a maximum of 15 users per day; permits must be picked up in person before 9 am at the Kernville Office on the launch day. Permits are currently issued to the trip leader, and he can specify how many persons will accompany him. Once again, this system may change, and each individual boater may be required to have a permit. Check with the Forest Service!

For the Kernville section, including the Powerhouse Run and the Riverside Park Rapid, no permit is required.

On the Upper and Lower Kern, permits are required from May 15 to September 15. There is no maximum number of users per day. Permits are currently issued to the trip leader, and he can specify how many persons will accompany him. This system may change and each individual boater may be required to have a permit. Check with the Forest Service! Permits for either Section must be picked up in person at the Groveland or Kernville Office prior to 9 am on the launch day.

USDA Forest Service, Cannell Meadow Ranger District, Sequoia National Forest, PO Box 6, Kernville, CA 93238; 619-376-3781.

USDA Forest Service, Greenhorn Ranger District, Sequoia National Forest, 15701 Highway 178, Bakersfield, CA 93306; 805-871-2223 (located at the mouth of the Kern River Canyon).

A California Campfire Permit is required for fires or stoves; check with the Forest Service office.

Reservations: Reservations are required during the controlled season (May 15 to September 15) for the Forks, the Upper Kern, and the Lower Kern, but not for the Powerhouse Run and Riverside Park sections in Kernville. You may either mail in an application form or phone the Kernville Office. An application form is reproduced in the Appendix One. Applications are accepted beginning April 15. An individual may hold only one weekday or three weekend permits at one time. Apply to the Kernville Office :

USDA Forest Service, Cannell Meadow Ranger District, Sequoia National Forest, PO Box 6, Kernville, CA 93238; 619-376-3781.

Restrictions: PFDs are required. Group size is limited to 15 people. Each raft must have an extra oar or paddle, a throw line, and a 20' mooring line. Overnight trips must carry portable toilets. On the Forks, firepans are required. There is a no-show penalty. See also Further Comments, below.

Gauge: Kern River, flow at Kernville. Applies to Sections (1) to (8) above.

Source of Levels: Department of Water Resources, Flood Operations Whitewater Recording (the Flow Phone); 916-653-9647.

How Reported: Cfs

Additional Gauge: Release from U.S. Army Corps of Engineers Isabella Dam, applies to Sections (9), (10) and (11)

Source of Levels: U.S. Army Corps of Engineers, Lake Isabella; 619-379-2742.

How Reported: Release schedule and flow in cfs.

Additional Gauge: Release from Southern California Edison Borel Powerplant

Source of Levels: U.S. Army Corps of Engineers, Lake Isabella; 619-379-2742.

How Reported: Release schedule and flow in cfs.

Interpretation Of Levels: Optimum flow on all sections is about 1200 cfs. The minimum for kayaks is about 400 cfs, and 800 is about minimum for rafts. Above 2000 cfs, difficulty ratings on the Upper Kern go up to about Class V; Lower Kern ratings go up about half a grade at this level. The Forks is most difficult when very low (under 600 cfs) and when very high (over 2000), and is easiest at intermediate flows.

Remember that 500 cfs is removed from the river between Fairview Dam and Powerhouse KR3, so you'll need a gauge reading of least 1000 cfs at Kernville to boat most of the Upper Sections. If in doubt, check with the Forest Service or Sierra South.

Source of More Information: USDA Forest Service Offices listed above.

Department of Boating and Waterways, 1629 "S" St., Sacramento, CA 95814-7281; 916-445-2616.

Sierra South, PO Box Y, Kernville, CA 93238; 619-376-3745.

Best Guidebooks: Cassady and Calhoun, *California Whitewater;* Holbeck and Stanley, *A Guide to the Best Whitewater in the State of California;* Interagency Whitewater Committee, *River Information Digest;* Cassady and Calhoun, set of four "Kern River Maps" (see the Maps and Literature section, California).

Further Comments: The Kern River is the longest whitewater river in California, and is graced by more miles carrying the Wild and Scenic designations than any other river system in the continental U.S.! Because of its tremendous variety of sections and rapids, it is extremely popular with boaters from Southern California and the Central Valley.

KINGS RIVER
Wild and Scenic River

Sections: (1) Kings Canyon Run, Yucca Point Trail to Mill Flat Campground, Class V+
(2) The Garnet Dike or Banzai Run, Garnet Dike Campground to Kirch Flat Campground, Class III+

Length of Run: (1) Day trip, 14.5 miles
(2) Day trip, 10 miles

Location: Fresno County, California; Sierra and Sequoia National Forests

Maps: USGS quads: Tehipite Dome (15'), Patterson Mtn. (15')

Times Runnable: Summer

Permit: None required

Gauge: Flow at Rodgers Crossing

Source of Levels: Department of Water Resources, Flood Operations Whitewater Recording (the Flow Phone); 916-653-9647.

How Reported: Cfs

Interpretation of Levels: For Section (1), minimum is about 800 cfs. Optimum is about 1500. High is 2500 cfs. For Section (2), minimum is about 800 cfs. Optimum is 1500 cfs. Low levels range from 1000 to 3000 cfs, and moderate levels range from 3000 to 5000 cfs. High is over 5000 (Class IV).

Source of More Information: USDA Forest Service, Kings River Ranger District, Sierra National Forest, Trimmer Route, Sanger, CA 93657; 209-855-8321.

Department of Boating and Waterways, 1629 "S" St., Sacramento, CA 95814-7291; 916-445-2616.

County of Fresno, Parks Division, 2220 Tulare St., Fresno, CA 93721; 209-488-1650.

Best Guidebooks: Cassady and Calhoun, *California Whitewater;* Holbeck and Stanley, *A Guide to the Best Whitewater in the State of California.*

Further Comments: You will probably want to portage several rapids in the tough Class V Garlic Falls section on Section (1) at mile 5.

KLAMATH RIVER
Wild and Scenic River

Sections:
(1) Hell's Corner run, John Boyle Power house to Copco Lake, Class IV+
(2) Sarah Totem Campground to Green Riffle, Class II-III
(3) Ike Falls run, Ishi Pishi Bridge to Orleans, Class III-IV (IV-V high)

Length of Run:
(1) 1-2 days, 17 miles
(2) 4 days, 72 miles, shorter sections possible
(3) Day trip, 7 miles

Location: Siskiyou and Humboldt Counties, California; Klamath County, Oregon; Klamath National Forest

Maps: USGS quads: Section (1), Surveyor Mtn. (15'), Macdoel (15'); Section (2), Seiad Valley (15'), Happy Camp (15'), Ukonom Lake (15'), Dillon Mtn. (15'), Orleans (15'); Section (3), Orleans (15'), Forks of Salmon (15').

Times Runnable: Section (1) is runnable from April to October except in June, when flows are around 600 cfs, and a few weeks in July, when the power plant is closed for maintenance. Sections (2) and (3) are runnable year-round.

Permit: None required

Gauge: For Section (1), flow at J.C. Boyle Plant

Source of Levels: Department of Water Resources, Flood Operations Whitewater Recording (the Flow Phone); 916-653-9647.

Pacific Power and Light; 800-547-1501.

How Reported: Cfs

Additional Gauge: For Sections (2) and (3), flow at Orleans

Source of Levels: Department of Water Resources, Flood Operations Whitewater Recording (the Flow Phone); 916-653-9647.

How Reported: Cfs

Interpretation of Levels: For Section (1), minimum is about 500 to 800 cfs. Peak releases rarely exceed 2000 cfs. For Sections (2) and (3), the minimum is about 500 cfs. Optimum is 4000 cfs. Low to moderate levels range from 1000 to 4000 cfs, and moderate to high levels range from 4000 to 10,000 cfs.

Source of More Information: USDA Forest Service, Happy Camp Ranger District, Klamath National Forest, Happy Camp, CA 96039; 916-493-2243.

USDA Forest Service, Ukonom Ranger District, Klamath National Forest, 99300 Highway 96, Somes Bar, CA 95568; 916-469-3331.

USDA Forest Service, Klamath National Forest, 1312 Fairlane Rd., Yreka, CA 96097; 916-842-6131.

USDA Forest Service, Six Rivers National Forest, 507 "E" St., Eureka, CA 95501; 707-442-1721.

Department of Boating and Waterways, 1629 "S" St., Sacramento, CA 95814-7291; 916-445-2616.

Bureau of Land Management, Redding District, 355 Hemstead, Redding, CA 96002; 916-246-5325.

Best Guidebooks: Cassady and Calhoun, *California Whitewater;* Holbeck and Stanley, *A Guide to the Best Whitewater in the State of California;* US Forest Service, "Klamath River Map/guide."

Further Comments: Don't forget to take out at Green River for Section (2), avoiding Ishi Pishi Falls, Class VI, downstream.

MERCED RIVER
Wild and Scenic River

Sections:
(1) The Hotels Section, from Riverside Lodge in El Portal to the Chevron Station, Class IV-V (V-V+ high)
(2) The Lower El Portal Section, from the Chevron Station to the Highway 140 Bridge, Class IV+ (V high)

(3) Highway 140 Bridge to Redbud Picnic Area, Class IV- (V- high)

(4) Redbud Picnic Area to the Suspension Bridge, Class III-IV (IV high)

(5) Suspension Bridge to the BLM Launch Site at Briceburg, Class II (III high)

(6) The Lower Merced Canyon, from the Briceburg BLM Launch Site to Merced Irrigation District Landing on Lake McClure at Bagby, Class IV (IV-V high), plus one portage around North Fork Falls, Class VI

Length of Run:
(1) Day trip, 1.5 miles
(2) Day trip, 1 mile
(3) Day trip, 1 mile
(4) Day trip, 9 miles
(5) Day trip, 6 miles
(6) Day trip, 13 miles

Location: Mariposa County, California; Sierra National Forest

Maps: USGS quads: El Portal, Kinsley, Feliciana Mtn., Yosemite, Bear Valley, Hornitos

Times Runnable: March to June

Permit: The landing at Bagby on Highway 49 at the end of Section (6) is in the evil clutches of the Merced Irrigation District. They will charge you a fee to bring a car down to the landing, and another fee for allowing you the privilege of removing your boat from the river. Resist these abhorrent dam-mavens if you can. Their phone number is 800-468-8889.

Gauge: Inflow to Lake McClure

Source of Levels: Department of Water Resources, Flood Operations Whitewater Recording (the Flow Phone); 916-653-9647.

How Reported: Cfs

Interpretation of Levels: For the sections of the river along Highway140, Sections (1) through (5), minimum is about 800 cfs, and optimum is 1500 cfs. Low to moderate levels here range from about 1000 to 2000 cfs, and moderate to high levels from about 2000 to 4000 cfs. Above 4000 is high. For Section (6), the Lower Canyon between Highway 140 and Highway 49, minimum is about 600 cfs. Optimum is 1500 cfs. Low to moderate levels range from 800 to 2000 cfs. Above 2000 is high. If Lake McClure is full, then you'll have to paddle two miles of flatwater at the end of the Canyon before reaching Bagby. Check with the Merced Irrigation District by calling 800-468-8889.

Rafting on the Merced River. Photo by Curt Smith.

Source of More Information: Bureau of Land Management, Folsom Resource Area, 63 Natoma St., Folsom, CA 95630; 916-985-4474.

USDA Forest Service, Mariposa Ranger District, Sierra National Forest, PO Box 747, Mariposa, CA 95338; 209-966-3638.

California Department of Parks and Recreation, Four Rivers Area, 31426 West Highway 152, Santa Nella, CA 95322; 209-826-1196.

Department of Boating and Waterways, 1629 "S" St., Sacramento, CA 95814-7291; 916-445-2616.

Best Guidebooks: Cassady and Calhoun, *California Whitewater;* Holbeck and Stanley, *A Guide to the Best Whitewater in the State of California.*

Further Comments: The Merced River drains the famous Yosemite Valley of Yosemite National Park. Soon after it leaves the Park, descending along the side of Highway 140, the splashy and continuous Merced provides section after section of glorious whitewater. In season, the floral display by the numerous redbuds, *Cercis occidentalis,* can't be matched. In the Lower Canyon, below Briceburg, the character of the river changes to that of a pool-drop river. The river's bed is more constricted; the rapids have more of a big-water feel, and funny-water effects abound. If you've paddled in the East, you'll be reminded of the Nolichucky River.

MOKELUMNE RIVER

Sections: Electra run, Electra picnic area to Highway 49, Class II (Class III above 3000 cfs)

Length of Run: Day trip, 3 miles

Location: Amador County, California

Maps: USGS quads: Mokelumne Hill

Times Runnable: Year-round

Permit: None required

Gauge: Inflow to Pardee Reservoir

Source of Levels: Department of Water Resources, Flood Operations Whitewater Recording (the Flow Phone); 916-653-9647.

How Reported: Cfs

Interpretation of Levels: Minimum is about 300 to 500 cfs. Optimum is 1200 cfs. Low levels range from 500 to 1500 cfs, and moderate levels range from 1500 to 3000 cfs (Class II+). High levels range from 3000 to 6000 cfs (about Class III).

Source of More Information: Bureau of Land Management, Folsom Resource Area, 63 Natoma St., Folsom, CA 95630, 916-985-4474.

Department of Boating and Waterways, 1629 "S" St., Sacramento, CA 95814-7291; 916-445-2616.

Best Guidebooks: Cassady and Calhoun, *California Whitewater;* Holbeck and Stanley, *A Guide to the Best Whitewater in the State of California.*

SACRAMENTO RIVER

Sections: (1) Box Canyon, Box Canyon Dam to Dunsmuir, Class IV (IV+ high)

(2) Dunsmuir to Castle Crag, Class III-IV (IV high)
(3) Castle Crag to Sims Road, Class III-IV (IV high, with one at V)
(4) Sims Flat to Lake Shasta, Class IV

Length of Run: (1) Day trip, 7.5 miles
(2) Day trip, 5 miles
(3) Day trip, 9 miles
(4) Day trip, 13 miles

Location: Siskiyou and Shasta Counties, California; Shasta-Trinity National Forest

Maps: USGS quads: Dunsmuir (15'), Weed (15'), Lamoine (15')

Times Runnable: December to mid-June

Permit: None required

Gauge: Release from Lake Siskiyou

Source of Levels: Department of Water Resources, Flood Operations Whitewater Recording (the Flow Phone); 916-653-9647.

How Reported: Cfs

Interpretation of Levels: Minimum is about 500 cfs. Optimum levels range from 800 to 1000 cfs for Sections (1)-(3). Optimum is about 1500 cfs for Section (4). High levels range from 1500 to 2500 cfs, and are about one grade in difficulty harder than at moderate levels.

Source of More Information: USDA Forest Service, Mt. Shasta Ranger District, Shasta-Trinity National Forest, 204 Alma St., Mt. Shasta, CA 96067; 916-926-4511.

Department of Boating and Waterways, 1629 "S" St., Sacramento, CA 95814-7291; 916-445-2616.

Best Guidebooks: Cassady and Calhoun, *California Whitewater;* Holbeck and Stanley, *A Guide to the Best Whitewater in the State of California.*

Further Comments: This constricted gorge becomes much more difficult at higher levels.

SALMON RIVER, MAIN
(Not to be confused with the Salmon River, Idaho)

Sections: Forks of Salmon to Somes Bar, Class IV-V

Length of Run: 2-3 days, 19 miles

Location: Siskiyou County, California; Klamath National Forest

Maps: USGS quads: Forks of Salmon (15')

Times Runnable: April to June

Permit: None required

Gauge: Salmon River at Somes Bar

Source of Levels: Department of Water Resources, Eureka Office, North Coast Whitewater Recording (the North Flow); 707-443-9305.

How Reported: Cfs

Interpretation of Levels: Minimum is about 300 to 500 cfs. Moderate flows from about 500 to 2000 cfs have an overall difficulty of about Class IV+; high flows from 2000 to 5000 cfs have an overall difficulty of about Class V. Very high is over 5000 cfs.

Source of More Information: Otter Bar Lodge, Forks of Salmon, CA 96031; 707-442-3712.

Department of Boating and Waterways, 1629 "S" St., Sacramento, CA 95814-7291; 916-445-2616.

USDA Forest Service, Klamath National Forest, 1312 Fairland Rd., Yreka, CA 96097; 916-842-6131.

USDA Forest Service, Happy Camp Ranger District, Klamath National Forest, Happy Camp, CA 96039; 916-493-2243.

USDA Forest Service, Ukonom Ranger District, Klamath National Forest, 99300 Highway 96, Somes Bar, CA 95568; 916-469-3331.

Best Guidebooks: Cassady and Calhoun, *California Whitewater;* Holbeck and Stanley, *A Guide to the Best Whitewater in the State of California.*

Further Comments: At mile 10.5 there is a probable portage at Butter Creek Ledge, Class V-VI. At high water, most boaters put in below this rapid in order to miss the toughest upper section.

SALMON RIVER, SOUTH FORK

(Not to be confused with the Salmon River, Idaho)

Sections: Limestone Bluffs to Matthews Creek Campground, Class IV-V

Length of Run: Day trip, 6 miles

Location: Siskiyou County, California; Klamath National Forest

Maps: USGS quads: Cecilville

Times Runnable: Winter and spring

Permit: None required

Gauge: Flow at Somes Bar

Source of Levels: Department of Water Resources, Flood Operations Whitewater Recording (the Flow Phone); 916-653-9647.

How Reported: Cfs

Interpretation of Levels: The South Fork will have about half of the flow at Somes Bar, so divide the Somes Bar readings by 2. Minimum is about 300 cfs. Optimum is 800 cfs. High is 1000 cfs.

Source of More Information: USDA Forest Service, Klamath National Forest, 1312 Fairland Rd., Yreka, CA 96097; 916-842-6131.

USDA Forest Service, Happy Camp Ranger District, Klamath National Forest, Happy Camp, CA 96039; 916-493-2243.

USDA Forest Service, Ukonom Ranger District, Klamath National Forest, 99300 Highway 96, Somes Bar, CA 95568; 916-469-3331.

Department of Boating and Waterways, 1629 "S" St., Sacramento, CA 95814-7291; 916-445-2616.

Best Guidebooks: Cassady and Calhoun, *California Whitewater;* Holbeck and Stanley, *A Guide to the Best Whitewater in the State of California.*

Further Comments: You are likely to portage several of the more difficult drops.

SCOTT RIVER

Sections: Indian Scotty Campground to Scott Bar, Class IV-V

Length of Run: Day trip, 14 miles

Location: Siskiyou County, California; Klamath National Forest

Maps: USGS quads: Scott Bar (15')

Times Runnable: April to late June

Permit: Campfire permit is required from May 15 to October 31. Check with the Forest Service.

Gauge: None. Extrapolate from the Klamath at Orleans.

When the Klamath is between 5000 and 10,000, then the Scott should be running.

Source of Levels: Department of Water Resources, Flood Operations Whitewater Recording (the Flow Phone); 916-653-9647.

How Reported: Cfs

Interpretation of Levels: Minimum is about 400 or 500 cfs. Optimum levels range from 600 to 2000 cfs, and high levels range from 2000 to 4000 cfs.

Source of More Information: USDA Forest Service, Scott River Ranger District, Klamath National Forest, 11263 South Highway 3, Ft. Jones, CA 96032; 916-468-5351.

Department of Boating and Waterways, 1629 "S" St., Sacramento, CA 95814-7291; 916-445-2616.

Best Guidebooks: Cassady and Calhoun, *California Whitewater;* Holbeck and Stanley, *A Guide to the Best Whitewater in the State of California.*

SMITH RIVER, MAIN
Wild and Scenic River

Sections: The Oregon Hole Gorge, from the Route 199 Bridge to the South Fork Road, Class IV+

Length of Run: Day trip, 5 miles

Location: Del Norte County, Six Rivers National Forest

Maps: USGS quads: Hiouchi

Times Runnable: November to May

Permit: A campfire permit is required. Check with the Forest Service.

Gauge: USGS Smith River at Jedediah Smith State Park

Source of Levels: Department of Water Resources, Flood Operations Whitewater Recording, (The Flow Phone); 916-653-9647.

How Reported: Cfs

Interpretation Of Levels: Minimum is about 800 cfs. Optimum is 2500 cfs. Low to moderate levels range from 800 to 2500 cfs, and moderate to high levels range from 2000 to 8000 cfs (Class IV-V).

Source of More Information: USDA Forest Service, Gasquet Ranger District, Six Rivers National Forest, PO Box 228, Gasquet, CA 95543; 707-457-3131.

Department of Boating and Waterways, 1629 "S" Street, Sacramento, CA 95814-7291; 916-445-2616.

Best Guidebooks: Cassady, *California White Water;* Holbeck and Stanley, *A Guide to the Best Whitewater in California.*

Further Comments: The various sections of the Smith River near Jedediah Smith State Park (including this section of the Main Smith, and the two upper forks described below) offer unmatched boating! The water is crystal clear, and the river is surrounded by dense forests of the giant rain trees: the coastal redwoods (*Sequoia sempervirens).* The best rapids occur in constricted, miniature rock gorges, reminiscent of the shut-ins found on whitewater rivers in the Ozarks.

SMITH RIVER, NORTH FORK
Wild and Scenic River

Sections: The North Fork Gorge, Low Divide Road to the confluence with the Middle Fork, Class III and IV (IV-V high)

Length of Run: Day trip, 13 miles

Location: Del Norte County, California; Six Rivers National Forest

Maps: USGS quads: Gasquet (15'), Crescent City (15')

Times Runnable: November to May

Permit: A campfire permit is required. Check with the Forest Service.

Gauge: Extrapolate from the flow on the Main Smith at Jedediah Smith State Park. The North Fork should have about 1/4 to 3/8 of this volume.

Source of Levels: Department of Water Resources, Flood Operations Whitewater Recording (the Flow Phone); 916-653-9647.

How Reported: Cfs

Interpretation of Levels: Minimum is about 200 to 400 cfs. Optimum is 2000 cfs. Low to moderate levels range from 800 to 2000 cfs, and moderate to high levels range from 2000 to 4000 cfs (Class IV-V-).

Source of More Information: USDA Forest Service, Gasquet Ranger District, Six Rivers National Forest, PO Box 228, Gasquet, CA 95543; 707-457-3131.

Department of Boating and Waterways, 1629 "S" St., Sacramento, CA 95814-7291; 916-445-2616.

Best Guidebooks: Cassady and Calhoun, *California Whitewater;* Holbeck and Stanley, *A Guide to the Best Whitewater in the State of California.*

SMITH RIVER, SOUTH FORK
Wild and Scenic River

Sections: Smith Fork Road Bridge to Smith River confluence, Class III, IV+

Length of Run: Day trip, 13 miles

Location: Del Norte County, California; Six Rivers National Forest

Maps: USGS quad: Hiouchi

Times Runnable: October to mid-June

Permit: A campfire permit is required. Check with the Forest Service.

Gauge: Extrapolate from the Main Smith at Jedediah Smith State Park. Roughly 1/3 to 1/2 of this water should be available on the South Fork.

Source of Levels: Department of Water Resources, Flood Operations Whitewater Recording (the Flow Phone); 916-653-9647.

How Reported: Cfs

Interpretation of Levels: Minimum is about 700 to 800 cfs. Optimum is 1000 cfs. Moderate to high levels range from 1200 to 5000 cfs.

Source of More Information: USDA Forest Service, Gasquet Ranger District, Six Rivers National Forest, PO Box 228, Gasquet, CA 95543; 707-457-3131.

Department of Boating and Waterways, 1629 "S" St., Sacramento, CA 95814-7291; 916-445-2616.

Best Guidebooks: Cassady and Calhoun, *California Whitewater;* Holbeck and Stanley, *A Guide to the Best Whitewater in the State of California.*

Further Comments: Below mile 11.6 is a continuous Class IV gorge. Take out above here if you're not up for an expert run.

STANISLAUS RIVER, MAIN

Sections: Goodwin Dam Section, Goodwin Dam to Knight's Ferry, Class V

Length of Run: Day trip, 4 miles

Location: Tuolumne and Stanislaus counties, California

Maps: USGS quads: Knight's Ferry

Times Runnable: Once or twice a year when the Army Corp releases water

Permit: None required

Gauge: The flow at Orange Blossom

Source of Levels: Department of Water Resources, Flood Operations Whitewater Recording (the Flow Phone); 916-653-9647.

How Reported: Cfs

Interpretation of Levels: Minimum is about 500 cfs. Low levels range from 500 to 1000 cfs. Optimum is 1000 to 2000 cfs. High levels range from 2000 to 4000 cfs.

Source of More Information: Park Manager, Stanislaus River Parks, US Army Corps of Engineers, Sacramento Ranger District, PO Box 1229, Oakdale, CA 95261; 209-847-0225.

Department of Boating and Waterways, 1629 "S" St., Sacramento, CA 95814-7291; 916-445-2616.

Best Guidebooks: Cassady and Calhoun, *California Whitewater;* Holbeck and Stanley, *A Guide to the Best Whitewater in the State of California.*

STANISLAUS RIVER, MIDDLE FORK

Sections: (1) Dardanelles Run, Baker Campground to Clark Fork Bridge, Class IV-V (plus two unrunnable gorges)
(2) Donells Run, Clark Fork Road to Donells Lake, Class IV-V (three portages)
(3) Sand Bar Flats Run, Sand Bar Flat Dam to Mount Knight, Class IV-V (four portages)
(4) Mt. Knight Run, Mt. Knight Trail to Camp 9 powerhouse, Class V (three portages).

Length of Run: (1) Day trip, 9 miles
(2) Day trip, 6 miles
(3) Day trip, 6 miles
(4) Day trip, 8 miles

Location: Tuolumne, Stanislaus, Alpine Counties, California; Stanislaus, Toiyabe National Forests

Maps: USGS quads: (1) The Dardanelles;
(2) Dardanelles Cone (15'); (3) Crandell Peak,
Stanislaus;
(4) Crandell Peak, Strawberry, Liberty Hill

Times Runnable: Spring

Permit: None required

Gauge: For Sections (1) and (2), inflow to Donnell's
Lake

Source of Levels: Call the Department of Water Resources
ahead of time and ask them to get this information from
Pacific Gas and Electric: Department of Water Resources, 916-445-3553.

How Reported: Cfs

Additional Gauge: For Sections (3) and (4), release from
Sand Bar Dam

Source of Levels: Call the Department of Water Resources
ahead of time and ask them to get this information from
Pacific Gas and Electric: Department of Water Resources, 916-445-3553.

How Reported: Cfs

Interpretation of Levels: For Section (1), minimum is
about 300 cfs. Optimum is 500 cfs, and high is 600 cfs.
For Section (2), minimum is about 400 cfs. Optimum is
700 cfs, and high is 800 cfs. For Section (3), minimum is
about 800 cfs. Optimum is 1200 cfs, and high is 1500
cfs. For Section (4), minimum is about 1200 cfs,
moderate is 1200 to 2000 cfs (about Class IV), and high
is 2000 to 3000 cfs (about Class V).

Source of More Information: Park Manager, Stanislaus
River Parks, US Army Corps of Engineers, Sacramento
Ranger District, PO Box 1229, Oakdale, CA 95261; 209-
847-0225.

Department of Boating and Waterways, 1629 "S" St.,
Sacramento, CA 95814-7291; 916-445-2616.

Best Guidebooks: Cassady and Calhoun, *California
Whitewater;* Holbeck and Stanley, *A Guide to the Best
Whitewater in the State of California.*

TRINITY RIVER, UPPER
Wild and Scenic River

Sections: Pigeon Point Campground at the confluence
of the North Fork to China Slide, Class III+
(for the first 5 miles, Class II+ and lower)

**Length
of Run:** Day trip, 25 miles

Location: Trinity County, California; Shasta-Trinity
National Forest

Maps: USGS quads: Helena (15'), Hayfork (15'),
Hyampom (15'), Ironside Mtn. (15')

Times Runnable: Year-round, but best from late spring to
summer

Permit: None required

Gauge: 6/10 of the flow at Hoopa

Source of Levels: Department of Water Resources, North
Coast Whitewater Recording; 704-443-9305.

How Reported: Cfs

Interpretation of Levels: Minimum is about 300-500 cfs.
Peak flow will be around 8000.

Source of More Information: Bureau of Land Management, Redding Resource Area, 355 Hemsted Dr.,
Redding, CA 96001; 916-246-5325.

World of Whitewater Kayak School, Big Flat, PO Box
708, Big Bar, CA 96010; 916-623-6588.

Department of Boating and Waterways, 1629 "S" St.,
Sacramento, CA 95814-7291; 916-445-2616.

Best Guidebooks: Cassady and Calhoun, *California
Whitewater;* Holbeck and Stanley, *A Guide to the Best
Whitewater in the State of California.*

TRINITY RIVER, BURNT RANCH GORGE
Wild and Scenic River

Sections: Burnt Ranch Gorge, China Slide to
Hawkins Bar, Class V

**Length
of Run:** Day trip, 8.5 miles

Location: Trinity County, California; Shasta-Trinity
National Forest

Maps: USGS quads: Iron Side Mtn. (15'), Willow Creek
(15')

Times Runnable: Summer after peak runoff is over

Permit: None required

Gauge: Extrapolate from the flow at Hoopa. About 2/3 of
the flow there should be about right.

Source of Levels: Department of Water Resources, Flood
Operations Whitewater Recording (the Flow Phone);
916-653-9647.

How Reported: Cfs

Interpretation of Levels: Minimum is about 300 to 500 cfs. Optimum is 1500 cfs. Low to moderate levels range from 500 to 2500 cfs (about Class V), and moderate to high levels range from 2500 to 3000 cfs.

Source of More Information: USDA Forest Service, Big Bar Ranger District, Shasta-Trinity National Forest, Star Rt. 1, PO Box 10, Big Bar, CA 96010; 916-623-6106.

Bureau of Land Management, Redding Resource Area, 355 Hemsted Dr., Redding, CA 96001; 916-246-5325.

Department of Boating and Waterways, 1629 "S" St., Sacramento, CA 95814-7291; 916-445-2616.

Best Guidebooks: Cassady and Calhoun, *California Whitewater;* Holbeck and Stanley, *A Guide to the Best Whitewater in the State of California.*

Further Comments: The three tough Class V rapids in the Burnt Ranch Falls area can be readily portaged.

TRINITY RIVER, SOUTH FORK
Wild and Scenic River

Sections: Highway 36 to Low Bridge Site, Class V (plus one portage)

Length of Run: 3-4 days, 48 miles

Location: Trinity County, California; Shasta-Trinity National Forest; Six Rivers National Forest

Maps: USGS quads: Pickett Peak (15'), Hyampon (15'), Willow Creek (15'), Pilot Creek (15')

Times Runnable: April to May

Permit: None required

Gauge: None. Extrapolate from the Trinity at Hoopa. About 1/4 of the flow at Hoopa should be about right for the South Fork.

Source of Levels: Department of Water Resources, Flood Operations Whitewater Recording (the Flow Phone); 916-653-9647.

How Reported: Cfs

Interpretation of Levels: Minimum is about 500 cfs. High is 4000 cfs.

Source of More Information: Shasta-Trinity National Forest, Hay Fork Rd., PO Box 159, Hay Fork, CA 96401; 916-628-5227.

Department of Boating and Waterways, 1629 "S" St., Sacramento, CA 95814-7291; 916-445-2616.

Best Guidebooks: Cassady and Calhoun, *California Whitewater;* Holbeck and Stanley, *A Guide to the Best Whitewater in the State of California.*

Further Comments: You'll probably want to carry around the toughest Class V rapids in addition to Winton Flat, Class VI; and Big Slide Falls, Class VI.

TRUCKEE RIVER

Sections: (1) Fanny Bridge at the outflow from Lake Tahoe to Alpine Meadows Road, Class I
(2) Alpine Meadows Road to Floriston, Class II, III (to IV high)
(3) Farad Powerhouse to Verdi, Class III (to IV high)

Length of Run: (1) Day trip, 4 miles
(2) 2-3 days, 27 miles, many possibilities for shorter runs
(3) Day trip, 8 miles

Location: Placer and Nevada Counties, California; and Washoe County, Nevada; Tahoe and Toiyabe National Forests

Maps: USGS quads: Tahoe City, Truckee, Martis Park, Boca, Mt. Rose NW, Verdi

Times Runnable: (1) Spring to fall; (2) and (3) Year-round; highest in late winter through June

Permit: None required

Gauge: For Section (1), Truckee River, release from Lake Tahoe at Fanny Bridge.

Source of Levels: Department of Water Resources, Flood Operations Whitewater Recording (the Flow Phone); 916-653-9647.

How Reported: Cfs

Additional Gauge: For Section (2), in midsummer or fall, it is probably fairly accurate to take the release from Boca Reservoir to Truckee River and add it to the reading for Truckee River release from Lake Tahoe at Fanny Bridge.

Source of Levels: Department of Water Resources, Flood Operations Whitewater Recording (the Flow Phone); 916-653-9647.

How Reported: Cfs

Additional Gauge: For Sections (2) or (3), the USGS gauge at Farad (near the California-Nevada border) provides the best readings.

Source of Levels: National Weather Service, Reno; 702-784-5402.

If you're desperate, you could try the Nevada State Watermaster. He'll know the reading, but I'm warning you that he doesn't want to talk to you very much. Call 702-784-5241.

How Reported: Cfs

Interpretation of Levels: For Section (1), 450 cfs is the standard summer release from Lake Tahoe for family float-rafting. On Sections (2) and (3), 450 to 1000 cfs is low; 1000 to 2000 is medium; 2000 to 5000 is high; and 5000 to 10,000 is very high.

Source of More Information: Charles Albright, Sierra Nevada Whitewater; 916-677-0164.

Best Guidebooks: Cassady and Calhoun, *California Whitewater;* Holbeck and Stanley, *A Guide to the Best Whitewater in the State of California.*

Further Comments: Section (1) is extremely popular for float-rafting in small rental rafts; decked boaters other than beginners will prefer lower sections. Section (2) is Class II-III at lower flows, with the exception of Bronco Rapid, immediately above the bridge off Highway 80 at Floriston, which is hard Class III+ low, Class IV at medium levels (1000-4000), and Class IV-V higher. Immediately downstream of the rapid and bridge is a dangerous diversion dam; don't fail to take out. Section (3) is popular with Tahoe and Reno-area paddlers at high water. It's a good idea to run Section (3) the first time with someone who knows the way; it has several dams and diversions, and during high water a riverwide hole develops at one spot, due to natural causes.

TUOLUMNE RIVER
Wild and Scenic River

Sections: (1) Cherry Creek Section, Cherry Creek to Lumsden Falls, Class V (V+ high)
(2) The Lower T, Lumsden Campground to Ferry Bridge, Class IV

Length of Run: (1) Day trip, 6 miles
(2) 1-2 days, 18 miles

Location: Tuolumne County, California; Stanislaus National Forest

Maps: Jawbone Ridge, Duckwall Mtn, Groveland, Moccasin, Standard

Times Runnable: Best from May through October. Water is often diverted on weekends, so weekdays generally have better flows.

Permit: Required from May 1 through September 30. Each year 3500 commercial and 3500 private permits are issued (a remarkably fair system, don't you think?).

Reservations: Recommended. Application forms for advance reservations are available after January 1 from: USDA Forest Service, Groveland Ranger District, Stanislaus National Forest, PO Box 709, Groveland, CA 95321; 209-962-7825.

A permit application form is included in Appendix One. You must include a $10 fee with the application. Applications are not accepted before January 1. Confirmations are sent promptly. Apply in time to receive confirmation at least 7 days before launch; if confirmation is not received, call. Permits must be picked up at the Groveland District Office on your launch day before 10 a.m.

Restrictions: Reservations are limited to 6 weekend launches per person per year. There is a no-show penalty. The maximum group size is 26 persons and 6 rafts. The maximum length of stay is 3 days. A group first-aid kit and repair kit is required. PFDs and helmets are required. Each boat must carry an extra oar or paddle, a throw line, and would you believe a 20-foot mooring line and a coil of at least 100 feet of extra line for emergencies? Inflatable boats must carry a pump. Portable toilets must be carried on multiple-day trips, except for kayak trips without support craft. Build fires in firepans only; carry out your ashes and your garbage. Any party of more than two persons must carry at least 2 extra PFDs. Please also note that during the summer the road to Lumsden Campground may be closed due to fire danger. Call ahead and check with the Groveland Ranger Station!

Gauge: Release from Holm Powerhouse

Source of Levels: Department of Water Resources, Flood Operations Whitewater Recording (the Flow Phone); 916-653-9647

How Reported: Cfs

Additional Gauge: Tuolumne River, flow at Meral's Pool

Additional Gauge: Tuolumne River, inflow to Don Pedro Reservoir

Source of Levels: Groveland Ranger Station, 209-962-7825.

Department of Water Resources, Flood Operations Whitewater Recording (the Flow Phone); 916-653-9647.

How Reported: Cfs

Interpretation of Levels: For the Cherry Creek Section, at the put-in your flow will equal the Release from Holm Powerhouse. About a mile downstream, at the confluence with the main Tuolumne, you will generally receive an additional 200 cfs coming downstream from Hetch Hetchy; but sometimes at peak runoff, quite a bit more will be released by Hetch Hetchy and will be coming in here. Optimal releases for Cherry Creek are between 600 and 1500 cfs (about Class V overall), and high is over 1500 cfs (Class V+). You can expect good releases on Cherry Creek almost year-round, especially during the week!

For the Lower T, the reading for the Meral's Pool gauge is preferred; the Don Pedro gauge is downstream and may read 10 to 25 percent high for this section. Low is from about 600 to 1500 cfs (difficulty IV-) medium is 1500 to 4000 (difficulty IV), optimum is 2500 cfs, high is 4000-8000 cfs (difficulty IV+), and very high is above 8000 (difficulty V).

Source of More Information: USDA Forest Service, Groveland Ranger District; 209-962-7825.

For search and rescue: Tuolumne County Sheriff's Dept., 209-533-5911.

Best Guidebooks: Cassady and Calhoun, *California Whitewater;* Interagency Whitewater Committee, *River Information Digest;* Holbeck and Stanley, *A Guide to the Best Whitewater in the State of California.*

Further Comments: I can think of perhaps three rivers in the country that have established themselves as proving grounds for expert boaters of the first rank. In Idaho, it's the North Fork of the Payette. In Kentucky, it's the Russell Fork. And in California, the Cherry Creek Section of the Tuolumne!

Although the Lower T is of more moderate difficulty, it remains significant in its own right. It's on the Tuolumne, more than any other river, where California commercial and private rafters developed the ability to run rivers that combined high technical difficulty with high volume. Besides, the T is fun! Super rapids, great camping, and stunning surroundings!

WALKER RIVER, WEST FORK

Sections: Highway 395 bridge to Walker, Class IV (V above 1000 cfs)

Length of Run: Day trip, 11 miles

Location: Mono County, California; Toiyabe National Forest

Maps: USGS quads: Chris Flat

Times Runnable: Spring

Permit: None required

Gauge: USGS West Fork of the Walker River, at Coleville

Source of Levels: National Weather Service, Reno; 702-784-5402.

How Reported: Cfs

Interpretation of Levels: Low to medium-high is 600 to 1000 cfs; high is over 1000.

Source of More Information: None.

Best Guidebooks: Cassady and Calhoun, *California Whitewater;* Holbeck and Stanley, *A Guide to the Best Whitewater in the State of California.*

Further Comments: The Walker is the gnarliest expert run on the eastern slope. Think of this section as a single, extremely continuous 11-mile-long rapid. Don't swim here.

YUBA RIVER, NORTH FORK

Sections:
(1) Wild Plum Campground above Sierra City to just above Ladies Canyon, very continuous Class IV+ (Class V overall when high)
(2) Ladies Canyon to Union Flat Campground, Class III-IV (1 at V and 1 at IV if you run Ladies Canyon Rapid and its runout)
(3) Union Flat Campground to Shangri-La Bridge, Class IV+ (2 at V; V overall when high)
(4) Shangri-La Bridge to Downieville, Class III-IV
(5) Rossasco Canyon, Downieville to Goodyears Bar Bridge, Class IV+ (1 at V; Class V overall when high)
(6) Goodyears Bar, Goodyears Bar to Highway 49 Bridge, Class III-IV (1 at V; Class IV+ overall when high)

Length of Run:
(1) Day trip, 6 miles
(2) Day trip, 1 miles

(3) Day trip, 3 miles
(4) Day trip, 3 miles
(5) Day trip, 4 miles
(6) Day trip, 8.5 miles

Location: Sierra County, California; Tahoe National Forest

Maps: USGS quads: Downieville, Goodyears Bar, Challenge, French Corral

Times Runnable: Spring

Permit: None required

Gauge: Inflow to Bullards Bar, for Sections (1) to (3)

Source of Levels: Department of Water Resources, Flood Operations Whitewater Recording (the Flow Phone); 916-653-9647.

How Reported: Cfs

Additional Gauge: Release from Bullards Bar Dam, for Section (4)

Source of Levels: Department of Water Resources, Flood Operations; 916-445-3555.

How Reported: Cfs

Interpretation Of Levels: For Sections (1) through (4), minimum is about 500 cfs. Optimum is 1200 cfs. Low to moderate levels range from 500 to 1200 cfs (about Class IV), and moderate to high levels range from 1200 to 2500 cfs (about Class IV-V). Very high is over 2500 cfs (Class V with portages). For Section (5), minimum is about 700 cfs. Optimum is 1200 cfs. Low to moderate levels range from 700 to 1500 cfs (Class IV+). High is over 1500 cfs (Class V with portages). For Section (6), minimum is about 700 cfs. Optimum is 1500 cfs. Low to moderate levels range from 700 to 2500 cfs (Class III-IV with 1 at V), and high levels to very high levels are between 2500 and 8000 (Class IV+).

Source of More Information: Tahoe National Forest, Hwy. 49 and Coyote St., Nevada City, CA 95959; 916-265-4531.

Department of Boating and Waterways, 1629 "S" St., Sacramento, CA 95814-7291; 916-445-2616.

Best Guidebooks: Cassady and Calhoun, *California Whitewater;* Holbeck and Stanley, *A Guide to the Best Whitewater in the State of California.*

Further Comments: The North Fork of the Yuba is one of my favorite rivers in California. Particularly on the upper sections, the rapids are nonstop, and the river is overhung by trees and surrounded by lush foliage. The views of the Sierra Buttes are incredible! Expect to portage or sneak a dam at mile 3 on Section (1). Expect to scout several times on every section. Rapids that are often portaged include Gillespie Dam on Section (1), Ladies Canyon Rapid at the start of Section (2), a big Class V rapid on Section (5) about a mile below Downieville, and Maytag, a Class V located six miles below Goodyears Bar on Section (6). You may also choose to portage other drops on any of these sections.

The upper sections of this river are extremely continuous. If the water is high, I strongly suggest that you drive home, rent a video, and chill.

YUBA RIVER, SOUTH FORK

Sections:
(1) Kingvale to Indian Springs Campground, Class IV+
(2) Indian Springs to Lake Spaulding, Class IV-V
(3) Washington to Edwards, Class III-IV
(4) Edwards to Purdons Crossing, Class III-IV (IV+ high)
(5) Purdons Crossing to Route 49, Class IV-V (V high)
(6) Route 49 to Bridgeport, Class IV-V

Length of Run:
(1) Day trip, 9 miles
(2) Day trip, 5.5 miles
(3) Day trip, 14 miles
(4) Day trip, 4 miles
(5) Day trip, 4 miles
(6) Day trip, 7 miles

Location: Nevada County, California; Tahoe National Forest

Maps: USGS quads: Soda Springs, Cisco Grove, Blue Canyon, Washington, North Bloomfield, Nevada City

Times Runnable: Spring

Permit: None required

Gauge: For Sections (1) and (2), inflow to Spaulding Reservoir

Source of Levels: Department of Water Resources Flood Operations, 916-445-3555.

How Reported: Cfs

Additional Gauge: For Sections (3)-(6), release from Spaulding Reservoir

Source of Levels: Department of Water Resources Flood Operations, 916-445-3555.

How Reported: Cfs

Interpretation of Levels: For both Sections (1) and (2), minimum is about 400 cfs. Optimum is 800 cfs, and high is 1000 cfs. For Section (3), minimum is about 700 cfs. Optimum is 1500, and high is 2000. For Section (4), minimum is about 800 cfs. Low to moderate levels range from about 800 to 2000 cfs (about Class III-IV). Optimum is 1500 cfs. Moderate to high levels range from 2000 to 3000 cfs (Class IV+). For section (5), minimum is about 800 cfs. Optimum is 1500 cfs. Moderate to high levels range from 1500 to 3000 cfs. For Section (6), minimum is about 1000 cfs. Optimum is 1500 cfs, and high is 2000 cfs.

Source of More Information: USDA Forest Service, Tahoe National Forest, Highway 49 and Coyote, Nevada City, CA 95959; 916-639-2342.

South Yuba River Citizens' League, PO Box 841, Nevada City, CA 95959; 916-265-5962.

Department of Boating and Waterways, 1629 "S" St., Sacramento, CA 95814-7291; 916-445-2616

Best Guidebooks: Cassady and Calhoun, *California Whitewater;* Holbeck and Stanley, *A Guide to the Best Whitewater in the State of California.*

GENERAL INFORMATION SOURCES FOR CALIFORNIA AND NEVADA

Levels for rivers in California can be obtained from the Flood Operations whitewater recording produced by the Department of Water Resources in cooperation with the Department of Boating and Waterways (the Flow Phone): 916-653-9647.

They report the following gauge readings in cfs:

Smith River, at Jedediah State Park
Trinity River
    Release from Lewiston Dam
    Flow at Hoopa
Salmon River, flow at Somes Bar
Klamath River
    Flow at J.C. Boyle Plant
    Release from Iron Gate
    Flow at Orleans
    Flow at Klamath & Glen
Eel River
    Release from Lake Pilsbury to Van Arsdale
    Release from Van Arsdale to Russian River
    Release from Van Arsdale to Eel River
    Flow at Fort Steward
South Fork of the Eel River, flow at Leggett
Russian River
    Flow at Hopland
    Flow at Healdsburg
    Flow at Hacienda Bridge
McCloud River, near Shasta
Sacramento River
    Release from Lake Siskiyou
    Release below Lake Shasta from Keswick Dam
Feather River, release from the Oroville Complex
Yuba River
    Release from Englebright Dam
    Inflow to New Bullards Bar Reservoir (North Fork)
    Flow at Spaulding
South Fork of the American River
    Flow at Kyburz
    Stream inflow to Slab Creek
    Release from Chili Bar Powerhouse
Middle Fork of the American River, release from
    Oxbow Powerhouse
North Fork of the American River
    Inflow to Lake Clementine
    Inflow to Folsom Lake
    Below Folsom Lake, release from Nimbus Dam
Cache Creek, flow at Rumsey Bridge
Cosumnes River, flow at Michigan Bar
Mokelumne River
    Inflow to Pardee Reservoir

Stanislaus River, flow at Orange Blossom
Tuolumne River
    Release from Helm Powerhouse
    Flow at Meral's Pool
    Inflow to Don Pedro Reservoir
    Below La Grange Diversion Dam
Merced River
    Inflow to Lake McClure
    Release from Merced Falls Dam
Kings River
    Flow at Rodgers Crossing
    Inflow to Pine Flat Reservoir
    Release from Pine Flat Reservoir
Kaweah River, inflow to Terminus Reservoir (Lake
    Kaweah)
Kern River
    Flow at Kernville
    Inflow to Lake Isabella
    Release from Lake Isabella
East Fork of the Carson River, flow at Gardnersville
Truckee River
    Release from Lake Tahoe Pass at Fanny Bridge
    Release from Boca Reservoir to Truckee River

The Department of Water Resources also maintains a recording at its Eureka office, reporting levels of rivers in northern California: Eureka Flood Center Recording; 707-443-9305.

They report the following gauge readings in cfs:

Smith River
    At Jed Smith State Park
    At Dr. Fine Bridge
Trinity River
    Release from Lewiston Dam
    At Hoopa
Klamath River, Upper Klamath River Gauge
Salmon River
    At Somes Bar
    At Orleans
    At Turwar Creek (Klamath Glen)
Redwood Creek
    At O'Kane
    At Orick
Mad River
    Release from Ruth Dam
    At Arcata (Highway 299 Bridge)
Van Duzen River
    At Grizzly Creek State Park
Eel River South Fork
    At Leggett
    At Miranda
Eel River Middle Fork, at Fort Seward
Eel River
    At Scotia
    At Fernbridge

For additional information on streamflow in California, call the Department of Water Resources at: 916-445-3553. The Eureka office can be contacted at 707-433-8467.

The Department of Boating and Waterways of the State of California serves as a clearinghouse for whitewater information:

Department of Boating and Waterways, 1629 "S" St.,

Sacramento, CA 95814-7291; 916-445-2616.

So does the Department of Parks and Recreation: California Department of Parks and Recreation, 915

Capitol Mall, Sacramento, CA 95814; 916-445-8828.

The National Weather Service Forecast Office in Reno, Nevada receives daily readings for river gauges in Nevada: 702-784-5402.

Readings are received for the following gauges:

Truckee River
    At Farad
    At Reno (Kietzke)
    At Sparks
    At Vista
    At Tracy
    At Nixon
Carson River
    At Carson City
    At Fort Churchill
West Fork of the Carson River, at Woodfords
East Fork of the Carson River, at Gardnerville
West Fork of the Walker River, at Coleville
    Humboldt River, at Palisade

Charles Albright of Sierra Nevada Whitewater maintains a recording of upcoming river trip information for California and Nevada boaters: 916-677-0164.

The Pacific Power and Light Company in Portland maintains a recording that reports reservoir levels and dam releases. Call 800-547-1501. They report the following releases:

Lewis River, North Fork, Release from Merwin Dam
Klamath River
    Release from Keno Dam
    Release from J.C. Boyle Powerhouse
    Release from Irongate Dam

International Whitewater Explorer maintains a hotline and answering machine to help Northern California Boaters locate and join river trips: 707-887-1149.

Two organizations maintain hotlines for booking rafting trips in California:

River Travel Center, 707-882-2255.

Friends of the River, 415-771-0400.

Other useful resources in California include:

California Representative, Interagency Whitewater Committee, USDA Forest Service, 900 W. Grand Ave., Porterville, CA 93257; 209-784-1500.

National Park Service Regional Information, 415-556-0122.

Bureau of Land Management, California Information, 415-484-4724.

California Department of Forestry Information, 916-445-9920.

Sierra South, 619-376-3745.

Sonoma County Water Agency, 707-544-2736

Northern California Rainfall Report, 707-462-5256

COLORADO

ANIMAS RIVER

Sections: The Animas River Gorge, from Silverton to the High Truss Bridge near Silverton, Class V

Length of Run: 1-2 Days, 26 miles (or 28 if you continue to the Rockwood Cut)

Location: San Juan and La Plata Counties, Colorado; San Juan National Forest

Maps: USGS quads: Silverton, Snowden Peak, Mountain View Crest, Electra Lake, Hermosa

Times Runnable: May to July, except when too high

Permit: None required

Gauge: USGS gauge, Animas River at Durango

Source of Levels: Department of Water Resources, Watertalk Station; 303-831-7135.

How Reported: Cfs

Interpretation of Levels: The water level should be low at the put-in, because many tributaries contribute water along the section. Use the W.D.S. method to estimate— 400 to 600 cfs should be about right. If you use the Durango USGS gauge below the take-out, about 1800 to 4500 cfs is optimum.

Source of More Information: USDA Forest Service, Animas Ranger District, San Juan National Forest, 701 Camino Del Rio, Durango, CO 81301; 303-247-4874.

Mountain Waters, 108 W. Sixth St., PO Box 2681, Durango, CO 81302-2681; 303-259-4191.

Best Guidebooks: Stohlquist, *Colorado Whitewater;* Wheat, *Floater's Guide to Colorado;* Interagency Whitewater Committee, *River Information Digest.*

Further Comments: The Animas River Gorge is a remote, dangerous run for expert kayakers only. There are numerous tough rapids; be on the particular watch for No-name Falls; it's a Class V or VI drop at about mile 12. There is another unnamed, difficult rapid downstream of an abandoned steel truss footbridge at mile 15. If you're not sure you're up for the run, take a ride first on the famous Durango and Silverton narrow gauge railway on its scenic trip up and down the Gorge!

It's safest to take out at the High Truss Bridge at mile 26.0, and then drag your boats downstream along the railway to Rockwood Cut. While you can boat all the way to Rockwood, the eddy at the take-out is small and a big gnarly hole lies just upstream. If you somehow miss this last chance to get out of the canyon, you're in deep trouble. Downstream lies the dreaded Animas Box Canyon, filled with numerous thundering Class VI drops that descend to a grand finale at a giant log jam that totally blocks the river. Any and all boaters or swimmers that tried this stretch would certainly be chopped and radiated.

Dennis Rhodes tells the amusing tale of the time he led the British Kayak Racing Team down the Animas. As he probed the final drop approaching the takeout at Rockwood, he was gulped by the hole I told you about above. Every now and again, as he was fighting with the hole, he would glance upstream at the dudes from England. Each and every one was smeared on a wall, with every finger and tongue in their possession jammed in cracks and crevices, as they watched, heart in mouth, to see whether Dennis would make the critical eddy. He made it, of course, and the Brits were able to detach and crank for the take-out.

Richard Penny squirting Pine Creek Canyon. Photo by Anne Penny.

ARKANSAS RIVER

Sections:
(1) Granite to Pine Creek, Granite Canyon, Class III-IV
(2) Pine Creek to Campground, Pine Creek Canyon, Class V-VI
(3) Campground to above Mt. Harvard Estates Bridge, The Numbers, Class IV+ (V high)
(4) Below Mt. Harvard Estates Bridge to Buena Vista Baseball Field, Frog Rock Run, Class II-III
(5) Baseball Field to Ruby Mountain Campground, Milk Run, Class II-III
(6) Ruby Mountain Campground to Highway 291 Bridge, Brown's Canyon, Class III-IV
(7) Highway 291 Bridge to Parkdale, lower river, Class III
(8) Parkdale to Canon City, Royal Gorge, Class IV (IV-V high)

Length of Run:
(1) Day trip, 3.5 miles
(2) Day trip, 3.1 miles
(3) Day trip, 4.6 miles
(4) Day trip, 6.4 miles
(5) Day trip, 4.2 miles
(6) Day trip, 9.2 miles
(7) 3 days, 54 miles, many possibilities for shorter runs
(8) Day trip, 6 miles

Location: Chaffee, Fremont Counties, Colorado

Maps: USGS quads: Granite, South Peak, Harvard Lakes, Buena Vista West, Buena Vista East, Nathrop, Salida West, Salida East, Wellsville, Howard, Coaldale, Cotopaxi, Arkansas Mtn., Echo, McIntyre Hills, Royal Gorge

BLM map: The Arkansas River: Granite to Parkdale, from address below

Times Runnable: Late March or early April to September; optimum from May through June

Permit: None required for noncommercial use

Gauge: Paddlers' gauge on the small bridge near the put-in for Section (3), the Numbers.

Source of Levels: Colorado Kayak Supply monitors this gauge during the paddling season; 719-395-2421.

How Reported: Feet

Additional gauge: USGS gauge near Buena Vista

Julia Wood flashing through the Numbers.

radical at higher levels (I caught it at 4500 and had a blast). Don't miss the eddy at the incline railway; stop for ice cream and to impress the tourists.

You might want to skip Pine Creek Rapid (it's hard), but tell everyone you did it. The last time I ran Pine Creek, one of my buddies was trashed in a hole and came out of his boat. I was the only guy close enough to try to help him, and, unfortunately, I was paddling a cut-down race boat. With him clinging to my ridiculous excuse for a watercraft, we must have hit five or six boulders as we tried to make for the bank. I would squirt up and over, but he always gave them a good body-slam. As you might imagine, this did my friend no good. And so, the rest of the day was occupied with rigging ropes, doing vertical raises, and loading the ambulance. Don't take this run lightly.

Source Of Levels: Department of Water Resources, Watertalk Station; 303-831-7135.

How Reported: Cfs

Additional gauge: USGS gauge near Buena Vista

Source Of Levels: Department of Water Resources, Watertalk Station; 303-831-7135.

How Reported: Cfs

Interpretation Of Levels: For most sections, 1500 to 3000 cfs is optimum (about 2.5 to 4.5 feet on the paddlers' gauge), with the exception of Pine Creek, where the optimum for sane boaters is pretty damn low (between 1.8 and 2.7 on the paddlers' gauge). The minimum for most sections is around 600 cfs (about 1.6 feet).

Source of More Information: Colorado Kayak Supply, PO Box 3059, Buena Vista, CO 81211; 719-395-2421.

Rocky Mountain Outdoor Center, 10281 US Highway 50R, Howard, CO 81233; 719-942-3214.

Bureau of Land Management, Royal Gorge Resource Area, 831 Royal Gorge Blvd., PO Box 1470, Canon City, CO; 719-275-7578 (Ask for the BLM's "Arkansas River Map" and the "User's Guide to Outdoor Recreation on Public Lands in Colorado.")

Best Guidebooks: Staub, *The Upper Arkansas River*; Stohlquist, *Colorado Whitewater;* Wheat, *Floater's Guide to Colorado*.

Further Comments: The Arkansas is whitewater heaven. If you're in the area, and a good boater, try to run the Numbers and the Royal Gorge. If you're expert, skip Brown's Canyon (it's boring). The Royal Gorge is

BLUE RIVER

Sections:	Green Mountain Canyon, Green Mountain Reservoir to Spring Creek Road, Class II (III high)
Length of Run:	Day trip, 4.5 miles

Location: Summit and Grand Counties, Colorado

Maps: USGS quad: Mt. Powell

Times Runnable: June to August

Permit: None required

Gauge: Release from Green Mountain Dam

Source of Levels: Department of Water Resources, Watertalk Station; 303-831-7135.

How Reported: Cfs

Interpretation of Levels: Low is from 400 to 600 cfs; medium is from 600 to 1000, and high from 1000 to 2000 cfs. Flows rarely exceed 2000 cfs.

Source of More Information: USDA Forest Service, Arapaho National Forest, 240 W. Prospect Rd., Fort Collins, CO 80526-2098; 303-498-1100.

Bill Dvorak Kayak and Rafting Expeditions, 17921 US Highway 285, Nathrop, CO 81236; 719-539-6851.

Boulder Outdoor Center, 2510 N. 47th, Boulder, CO 80301; 303-444-8420.

Colorado Kayak Supply, PO Box 3059, Buena Vista, CO 81211; 719-395-2421.

Colorado Outward Bound School, 945 Pennsylvania St., Denver, CO 80203; 303-837-0880.

Rocky Mountain Outdoor Center, 10281 US Highway 50, Howard, CO 81233; 719-942-3214.

Best Guidebooks: Stohlquist, *Colorado Whitewater;* Wheat, *Floater's Guide to Colorado.*

CACHE LA POUDRE RIVER
Wild and Scenic River

Sections:	(1) First Meadow to Rustic, Class IV
	(2) Dadd Gulch to Kelly Flats, Class III-IV
	(3) Kelly Flats to the Narrows, Class IV
	(4) Upper Narrows, Class VI+, don't run
	(5) Middle Narrows, Class IV-V
	(6) Lower Narrows, Class V-VI, not recommended
	(7) Narrows to Mishawaka Bar, Class IV
	(8) Mishawaka Bar to Diversion Dam, Class IV
Length of Run:	(1) Day trip, 10 miles
	(2) Day trip, 4 miles
	(3) Day trip, 5 miles
	(4) No trip, 0.5 mile
	(5) One rapid, 1 mile
	(6) One rapid, 0.2 mile
	(7) Day trip, 7 miles
	(8) Day trip, 4 miles

Location: Larimer County, Colorado; Roosevelt National Forest

Maps: USGS quads: Kinnikinnik, Rustic, Big Narrows, Poudre Park, Laporte

Times Runnable: May to August

Permit: A permit used to be required from the Larimer County Sheriff's Department in Fort Collins, but no longer.

Restrictions: An approved PFD is required, and your address and phone number must be permanently affixed to your boat.

Gauge: USGS gauge on the Cache La Poudre near Fort Collins

Source of Levels: Department of Water Resources, Watertalk Station; 303-831-7135.

How Reported: Cfs

Interpretation of Levels: Low is around 500 cfs. Optimum for all sections is around 1000 to 2000 cfs. Above

Gary Stacks on the Cache la Poudre. Photo by Julia Wood.

2000 is high; most sections increase in difficulty one full class at this level.

Source of More Information: USDA Forest Service, Estes-Poudre District, Arapaho and Roosevelt National Forests, 148 Remington St., Ft. Collins, CO 80524; 303-482-3822.

Bill Dvorak Kayak and Rafting Expeditions, 17921 US Highway 285, Nathrop, CO 81236; 719-539-6851.

Boulder Outdoor Center, 2510 N. 47th, Boulder, CO 80301; 303-444-8420.

Colorado Kayak Supply, PO Box 3059, Buena Vista, CO 81211; 719-395-2421.

Colorado Outward Bound School, 945 Pennsylvania St., Denver, CO 80203; 303-837-0880.

Rocky Mountain Outdoor Center, 10281 US Highway 50, Howard, CO 81233; 719-942-3214.

Best Guidebooks: Stohlquist, *Colorado Whitewater;* Wheat, *Floater's Guide to Colorado;* Interagency Whitewater Committee, *River Information Digest.*

Further Comments: A true story. After a few days of hanging around the Poudre, running various sections, and driving by the Lower Narrows, it occurred to me that it would be completely aggro to try a run through the Lower Narrows at about 1000 cfs. My buddies and I scouted it for about half an hour. A crowd of tourists and local boaters stopped to watch in anticipation of my eventual glorious demise. To postpone the inevitable, I decided to run the Middle Narrows as a warm-up. This went well enough, until I neared a drop above a rock arch that extended from the canyon wall on river-right. The rock arch was an obvious and classic undercut, with large volumes of water piling up in front, going under, and bubbling out into the eddy below. I didn't want any part of this thing, so I moved left. Tourists following along slowly were able to watch from their car windows as my boat ski-jumped over the drop far to the left, pitoned a rock, flipped, and surfed upside-down to river-right above the arch. As I rolled up, I discovered that I was about to execute a smear with my face. A quick flip back down, and I began a subterranean journey. Under water, upside-down, bumping along under Rick's Rock, I decided for no particularly rational reason to put off swimming until the boat began to hang up under the rock. It did for a minute, and I had a hand on my grab loop (I use Kevlar climbing cord for this application), and then the boat was moving again. No need to swim yet. After a bit, I emerged from the downstream side and rolled up. I suppose you won't be surprised to hear that the descent of the Lower Narrows was put off for a more propitious day.

Best Guidebooks: Stohlquist, *Colorado Whitewater;* Wheat, *Floater's Guide to Colorado;* Interagency Whitewater Committee, *River Information Digest.*

COLORADO RIVER, GORE CANYON
(See Utah and Arizona for additional sections.)

Sections: Grand County Road 12 near Kremmling to Grand County Road 1, Class V-VI

Length of Run: Day trip, 11 miles

Location: Grand County, Colorado

Maps: USGS quads: Kremmling, Mt. Powell, Radium

Times Runnable: May to August, except when too high

Permit: None required

Gauge: USGS gauge on the Colorado River near Kremmling

Source of Levels: Department of Water Resources, Watertalk Station; 303-831-7135.

How Reported: Cfs

Interpretation of Levels: Minimum is about 1000 cfs; optimum is about 2000. Above 2500, stay in camp and practice Hacky.

Source of More Information: Bureau of Land Management, Kremmling Resource Area, PO Box 68,

Kremmling, CO 80459; 303-724-3437.

Bill Dvorak Kayak and Rafting Expeditions, 17921 US Highway 285, Nathrop, CO 81236; 719-539-6851.

Boulder Outdoor Center, 2510 N. 47th, Boulder, CO 80301, 303-444-8420.

Colorado Kayak Supply, PO Box 3059, Buena Vista, CO 81211; 719-395-2421.

Colorado Outward Bound School, 945 Pennsylvania St., Denver, CO 80203; 303-837-0880.

Rocky Mountain Outdoor Center, 10281 US Highway 50, Howard, CO 81233; 719-942-3214.

Best Guidebooks: Stohlquist, *Colorado Whitewater;* Wheat, *Floater's Guide to Colorado.*

COLORADO RIVER, UPPER
(See Utah and Arizona for additional sections.)

Sections: (1) Pumphouse to State Bridge, Class I-II
   (2) State Bridge to the confluence of the Eagle River at Dotsero, Class I-II

Length of Run: (1) Day trip, 14 miles
   (2) 2-3 days, 44 miles

Location: Grand and Eagle Counties, Colorado

Maps: USGS quads: Radium, McCoy State Bridge, Blue Hill, Burns South, Sugarloaf Mtn., Dotsero

Times Runnable: May to June

Permit: None required

Gauge: USGS gauge on the Colorado River near Dotsero

Source of Levels: Department of Water Resources, Watertalk Station; 303-831-7135.

How Reported: Cfs

Interpretation of Levels: Minimum is around 1000 cfs; peak flows are around 3000 to 4000.

Source of More Information: For Section (1), Ask for the BLM river map/guide: Bureau of Land Management, Kremmling Resource Area, PO Box 68, Kremmling, CO 80459; 303-724-3437.

For Section (2), Ask for the BLM river map/guide: Bureau of Land Management, Glenwood Springs Resource Area, PO Box 1009, Glenwood Springs, CO 81602; 303-945-2341.

Bill Dvorak Kayak and Rafting Expeditions, 17921 US Highway 285, Nathrop, CO 81236; 719-539-6851.

Boulder Outdoor Center, 2510 N. 47th, Boulder, CO 80301; 303-444-8420.

Colorado Kayak Supply, PO Box 3059, Buena Vista, CO 81211; 719-395-2421.

Colorado Outward Bound School, 945 Pennsylvania St., Denver, CO 80203; 303-837-0880.

Rocky Mountain Outdoor Center, 10281 US Highway 50, Howard, CO 81233, 719-942-3214.

Best Guidebooks: Wheat, *Floater's Guide to Colorado;* Interagency Whitewater Committee, *River Information Digest*

Further Comments: Section (1) is Colorado's most popular rafting trip.

COLORADO RIVER, GLENWOOD CANYON
(See Utah and Arizona for additional section.)

Sections: (1) Shoshone Section, Shoshone Powerhouse to Grizzly Creek, Class IV
(2) Grizzly Creek to New Castle, Class II-III (if you stay out of the holes)

Length of Run: (1) Day trip, 1 mile
(2) Day trip, 19 miles

Location: Garfield County, Colorado; White River National Forest

Maps: USGS quads: Glenwood Springs, Storm King Mtn., New Castle

Times Runnable: April to July

Permit: None required

Gauge: USGS gauge, Colorado River at Glenwood Springs

Source of Levels: Department of Water Resources, Watertalk Station; 303-831-7135.

How Reported: Cfs

Interpretation of Levels: Low is about 2000 cfs; optimum is about 4000 to 6000, and high is over 10,000 (Class V)

Source of More Information: USDA Forest Service, Eagle Ranger District, White River National Forest, PO Box 720, Eagle, CO 81631; 303-328-6388.

Bill Dvorak Kayak and Rafting Expeditions, 17921 US Highway 285, Nathrop, CO 81236; 719-539-6851.

Boulder Outdoor Center, 2510 N. 47th, Boulder, CO 80301; 303-444-8420.

Gary Stacks and Richard Penny doing a cheap stunt. Photo by Julia Wood.

Colorado Kayak Supply, PO Box 3059, Buena Vista, CO 81211; 719-395-2421.

Colorado Outward Bound School, 945 Pennsylvania St., Denver, CO 80203; 303-837-0880.

Rocky Mountain Outdoor Center, 10281 US Highway 50, Howard, CO 81233; 719-942-3214.

Best Guidebooks: Stohlquist, *Colorado Whitewater;* Wheat, *Floater's Guide to Colorado;* Interagency Whitewater Committee, *River Information Digest.*

Further Comments: Section 1 is a big water run. Radically fun. Put in below the two obvious Class VI drops.

CONEJOS RIVER

Sections: Pinnacle Gorge, Forest Rd. 105 to Spectacle Lakes Campground, Class III (one at IV)

Length of Run: Day trip, 11 miles

Location: Conejos County, Colorado; Rio Grande National Forest

Maps: USGS quads: Cumbres, Spectacle Lake

Times Runnable: April to July

Permit: None required

Gauge: USGS gauge on the Conejos below Platoro Reservoir

Source of Levels: Department of Water Resources, Watertalk Station; 303-831-7135.

How Reported: Cfs

Interpretation of Levels: Minimum is about 300 cfs, optimum is about 1000; above 1500 is high.

Source of More Information: USDA Forest Service, Rio Grande National Forest, 1803 W. Highway 60, Monte Vista, CO 80225; 303-236-7386.

Bill Dvorak Kayak and Rafting Expeditions, 17921 US Highway 285, Nathrop, CO 81236; 719-539-6851.

Boulder Outdoor Center, 2510 N. 47th, Boulder, CO 80301; 303-444-8420.

Colorado Kayak Supply, PO Box 3059, Buena Vista, CO 81211; 719-395-2421.

Colorado Outward Bound School, 945 Pennsylvania St., Denver, CO 80203; 303-837-0880.

Rocky Mountain Outdoor Center, 10281 US Highway 50, Howard, CO 81233; 719-942-3214.

Best Guidebooks: Stohlquist, *Colorado Whitewater;* Wheat, *Floater's Guide to Colorado;* Interagency Whitewater Committee, *River Information Digest.*

CRYSTAL RIVER

Sections:
(1) Marble Bridge to Bogan Flats, Class IV
(2) Bogan Flats to Redstone, Class IV
(3) Redstone to USGS gauging section. Don't run this section; most of the rapids are small with the exception of Meat Grinder, a deadly, logjammed Class VI+ rapid.
(4) USGS gauging station to BRB Ranch, Class IV.
(5) Lower river, Class II.

Unnamed runs exist above Marble; difficult and continuous.

Length of Run:
(1) Day trip, 2 miles
(2) Day trip, 8 miles
(3) Forget it
(4) Day trip, 6 miles
(5) Day trip, as far as you want to go.

Location: Gunnison and Pitkin Counties, Colorado

Maps: USGS quads: Marble, Chair Mountain, Placita, Redstone, Mount Sopris, Carbondale

Times Runnable: May to July.

Permit: None required

Gauge: USGS gauge above Avalanche Creek near Redstone, CO

Source of Levels: Department of Water Resources, Watertalk Station; 303-831-7135.

Interpretation of Levels: About 500 cfs is minimum and 1500 is optimum

Source of More Information: Bill Dvorak Kayak and Rafting Expeditions, 17921 US Highway 285, Nathrop, CO 81236; 719-539-6851.

Boulder Outdoor Center, 2510 N. 47th, Boulder, CO 80301; 303-444-8420.

Colorado Kayak Supply, PO Box 3059, Buena Vista, CO 81211; 719-395-2421.

Colorado Outward Bound School, 945 Pennsylvania St., Denver, CO 80203; 303-837-0880.

Rocky Mountain Outdoor Center, 10281 US Highway 50, Howard, CO 81233; 719-942-3214.

Best Guidebooks: Stohlquist, *Colorado Whitewater;* Wheat, *Floater's Guide to Colorado.*

Further Comments: The Crystal is a beautiful river; its headwaters are in the Snowmass Wilderness. Watch out for downed trees on the upper sections. Before running the Bogen Flats to Redstone Section, scout the culverts under the Highway 133 bridge so that you can recognize them from upstream. These are often logjammed, so carry around them.

DOLORES RIVER

Sections:
(1) Rico to Dolores, Class I-III
(2) Dolores Canyon, Dolores Canyon Ranch to Slick Rock, Class III (one at IV-V, often portaged)
(3) Little Glen and Slick Rock Canyons, Slick Rock to Bedrock, Class II-III
(4) Bedrock to Gateway, CO, Class II-IV
(5) Gateway, CO into Utah and continuing to the Colorado River, Class II-IV

Length of Run:
(1) 2 days, 37 miles
(2) 2-3 days, 50 miles
(3) 2-3 days, 45 miles
(4) 2-3 days, 44 miles
(5) 2 days, 32 miles

Location: Montezuma and Dolores Counties, Colorado; Grand County, Utah

Maps: USGS quads: (1) Rico, Orphan Butte, Wallace Ranch, Stoner, Boggy Draw, Dolores East; (2) Doe Canyon, The Glade, Secret Canyon, Joe Davis Hill, Slick Rock; (3) Slick Rock, Anderson Mesa, Paradox; (4) Paradox and Gateway; (5) Gateway, Coates Creek, Polar Mesa, Cisco

Times Runnable: April to June or mid-July

Permit: None required for Sections (1)-(4). For section (5) in Utah, a permit is required. A sample application form is included in Appendix One, but don't use it. Write away for a fresh one. Apply to: Bureau of Land Management, Grand Resource Area, PO Box M, Moab, UT 84532; 801-259-8193.

Reservations: Required, but it is no real problem. The Dolores is not really crowded, and there is no lottery. On your application form, specify when you want to launch. The BLM will approve your application if it is in order and send you back notice. There is no fee.

Restrictions: For Section (5), only one launch is permitted per day. Maximum group size is 25. Firepans and portable toilets are required on overnight trips (except unsupported kayak and canoe trips). PFDs are required. Each boat must carry an extra PFD and an extra oar, paddle or spare motor (do you know a good source for spare kayak motors?). Rafts must carry a bail bucket or bilge pump. Each group must carry a first-aid kit, a patch kit, and an air pump. Carry out waste.

Gauge: For Section (1), Dolores River near Rico

Source of Levels: Department of Water Resources, Watertalk Station; 303-831-7135.

How Reported: Cfs

Additional Gauge: For Section (2), Dolores River below McPhee Reservoir

Source of Levels: Department of Water Resources, Watertalk Station; 303-831-7135.

Bureau of Reclamation, Salt Lake City Recording; 801-539-1311.

How Reported: Cfs

Additional Gauge: For Section (3) or (4), Dolores River below Bedrock

Source of Levels: Department of Water Resources, Watertalk Station; 303-831-7135.

Bureau of Reclamation, Salt Lake City; 801-539-1311.

How Reported: Cfs

Additional Gauge: For Section (5), Dolores River near Cisco

Source of Levels: Department of Water Resources, Watertalk Station; 303-831-7135.

Bureau of Reclamation, Salt Lake City; 801-539-1311.

How Reported: Cfs

Interpretation of Levels: Minimum is about 1000 cfs. The average peak at Bedrock is about 8000 cfs.

Source of More Information: Colorado Sections: Bureau of Land Management, San Juan District, 701 Camino Del Rio, Durango, CO 81301; 303-247-4082.

Bureau of Land Management, Grand Junction Resource Area, 764 Horizon Dr., Grand Junction, CO 81501; 303-243-6552.

Utah Section: Bureau of Land Management, Grand Resource Area, PO Box M, Moab, UT 84532; 801-259-8193.

Bill Dvorak Kayak and Rafting Expeditions, 17921 US Highway 285, Nathrop, CO 81236; 719-539-6851.

Boulder Outdoor Center, 2510 N. 47th, Boulder, CO 80301; 303-444-8420.

Colorado Kayak Supply, PO Box 3059, Buena Vista, CO 81211; 719-395-2421.

Colorado Outward Bound School, 945 Pennsylvania St. Denver, CO 80203; 303-837-0800.

Rocky Mountain Outdoor Center, 10281 US Highway 50, Howard, CO 81233; 719-942-3214.

Best Guidebooks: Stohlquist, *Colorado Whitewater;* Wheat, *Floater's Guide to Colorado;* Nichols, *River Runner's Guide to Utah;* Interagency Whitewater Committee, *River Information Digest.*

EAGLE RIVER

Sections:
(1) Minturn Canyon, Cross Creek confluence to bridge off Highway 24, Class III
(2) Dowds Chutes, Bridge off Highway 24 to Rock Dam, Class IV (one at V)

Richard Penny in Dowds Chutes on the Eagle River. Photo by Anne Penny.

Length of Run: (1) Day trip, 4 miles
(2) Day trip, 3 miles

Location: Eagle County, Colorado

Maps: USGS quads: Minturn, Edwards, Wolcott and Eagle

Times Runnable: May to July except when too high

Permit: None required

Gauge: Eagle River near Gypsum

Source of Levels: Department of Water Resources, Watertalk Station; 303-831-7135.

How Reported: Cfs

Interpretation of Levels: Minimum is around 500 to 800 cfs; optimum for Section (1) is about 1000 and for Section (2) 1500 cfs; high for both is about 2000 (causing the overall difficulty of Section (2) to move to Class V).

Source of More Information: Bill Dvorak Kayak and Rafting Expeditions, 17921 US Highway 285, Nathrop, CO 81236; 719-539-6851.

Boulder Outdoor Center, 2510 N 47th, Boulder, CO 80301; 303-444-8420.

Colorado Kayak Supply, PO Box 3059, Buena Vista, CO 81211; 719-395-2421.

Colorado Outward Bound School, 945 Pennsylvania St., Denver, CO 80203; 303-837-0880.

Rocky Mountain Outdoor Center, 10281 US Highway 50, Howard, CO 81233; 719-942-3214.

Best Guidebooks: Stohlquist, *Colorado Whitewater;* Wheat, *Floater's Guide to Colorado.*

GREEN RIVER

See Utah.

GUNNISON RIVER

Sections: Lower Gunnison Canyon, Chucker Trail to the confluence with the North Fork of the Gunnison, Class III-IV

Length of Run: Day trip, 14 miles

Location: Montrose and Delta Counties, Colorado

Maps: USGS quads: Red Rock Canyon, Smith Fork

Times Runnable: December to June

Permit: None required

Gauge: Gunnison River at Delta

Source of Levels: Department of Water Resources, Watertalk Station; 303-831-7135.

How Reported: Cfs

Interpretation of Levels: 1000 cfs is minimum, and 1500 is optimum.

Source of More Information: Bill Dvorak Kayak and Rafting Expeditions, 17921 US Highway 285, Nathrop, CO 81236; 719-539-6851.

Boulder Outdoor Center, 2510 N. 47th, Boulder, CO 80301; 303-444-8420.

Colorado Kayak Supply, PO Box 3059, Buena Vista, CO 81211; 719-395-2421.

Colorado Outward Bound School, 945 Pennsylvania St., Denver, CO 80203; 303-837-0880.

Rocky Mountain Outdoor Center, 10281 US Highway 50, Howard, CO 81233; 719-942-3214.

Best Guidebooks: Stohlquist, *Colorado Whitewater;* Wheat, *Floater's Guide to Colorado.*

Further Comments: You may need a 4WD on the shuttle.

NORTH PLATTE RIVER

See Wyoming.

RIO GRANDE RIVER

See New Mexico.

ROARING FORK

Sections: (1) Slaughterhouse Canyon, Fisherman's Parking Lot to Cemetary Road Bridge, Class IV+ (plus one possible portage at John Denver Falls)

(2) Woody Creek Canyon, Cemetary Road Bridge to second Cemetary Road bridge, Class III-IV

(3) Toothache, second Cemetary Road Bridge to Old Snowmass Bridge, Class III-IV

Length of Run: (1) Day trip, 5 miles
(2) Day trip, 4 miles
(3) Day trip, 4.5 miles

Location: Pitkin County, Colorado; White River National Forest

Maps: USGS quads: Aspen, Highland Peak, Woody Creek, Basalt

Times Runnable: May to July

Permit: None required

Gauge: Roaring River near Aspen

Source of Levels: Department of Water Resources, Watertalk Station; 303-831-7135.

How Reported: Cfs

Interpretation of Levels: Around 500 cfs is minimum. Optimum is between 1000 and 1200, and high is 1500.

Source of More Information: White River National Forest, PO Box 948, Glenwood Springs, CO 81602; 303-945-2521.

Bill Dvorak Kayak and Rafting Expeditions, 17921 US Highway 285, Nathrop, CO 81236; 719-539-6851.

Boulder Outdoor Center, 2510 N. 47th, Boulder, CO 80301; 303-444-8420.

On the Slaughterhouse Section of the Roaring Fork. Photo by Anne Penny.

Colorado Kayak Supply, PO Box 3059, Buena Vista, CO 81211; 719-395-2421.

Colorado Outward Bound School, 945 Pennsylvania St., Denver, CO 80203; 303-837-0880.

Rocky Mountain Outdoor Center, 10281 US Highway 50, Howard, CO 81233; 719-942-3214.

Best Guidebooks: Stohlquist, *Colorado Whitewater;* Wheat, *Floater's Guide to Colorado.*

Further Comments: The Slaughterhouse section is a run for advanced and expert paddlers only. Especially at high water, boaters tend to lose boats and have hair swims here.

YAMPA RIVER, CROSS MOUNTAIN GORGE

Sections: Cross Mountain Gorge, west of Maybell to Deerlodge Park, Class IV-IV+ (IV-V with one VI when high)

Length of Run: Day trip, 3.8 miles

Location: Moffat County, Colorado

Maps: USGS quads: Elk Springs

Times Runnable: April to July, but may be too high in May or June

Permit: None required

Gauge: Yampa near Maybell, CO

Source of Levels: Department of Water Resources, Watertalk Station; 303-831-7135.

Bureau of Reclamation, Salt Lake City; 801-539-1311.

How Reported: Cfs

Interpretation of Levels: Minimum is about 300 cfs; optimum is around 3,000 to 5,000, high (Class IV to V+) is about 5000 to 10,000.

Source of More Information: Bill Dvorak Kayak and Rafting Expeditions, 17921 US Highway 285, Nathrop, CO 81236; 719-539-6851.

Boulder Outdoor Center, 2510 N. 47th, Boulder, CO 80301; 303-444-8420.

Colorado Kayak Supply, PO Box 3059, Buena Vista, CO 81211; 719-395-2421.

Colorado Outward Bound School, 945 Pennsylvania St., Denver, CO 80203; 303-837-0880.

Rocky Mountain Outdoor Center, 10281 US Highway 50E, Howard, CO 81233; 719-942-3214.

Best Guidebooks: Stohlquist, *Colorado Whitewater;* Wheat, *Floater's Guide to Colorado.*

Further Comments: This section is extremely big and continuous at high water, but is more reasonable when it's lower.

YAMPA RIVER, DINOSAUR NATIONAL MONUMENT

Sections: Yampa through Dinosaur, Deerlodge Park to confluence with the Green River and continuing to the Split Mountain Boat Ramp, Class II-III (one at IV)

Length of Run: 4-7 days, 72 miles (46 on the Yampa and 26 on the Green)

Location: Moffat County, Colorado and Uintah County, Utah; Dinosaur National Monument

Maps: USGS quads: Elk Springs, Indian Water Canyon, Haystack Rock, Tanks Peak, Hells Canyon, Canyon of Lodore South, Jones Hole, Island Pk., Split Mtn., Dinosaur Quarry

Times Runnable: Year-round, but best from April through June or July

Permit: Required, and so are reservations!

Reservations: Required. A sample reservation application form is in Appendix One, but don't use it. Photocopies of applications are not accepted. Write or call: River Office, National Park Service, P.O. Box 210, Dinosaur, CO 81610; 303-347-2468.

For multi-day trips, the high-use season begins the second Monday in May and continues to the second Friday in September. During this period, a total of 300 noncommercial trips are allowed to launch. Applications to the lottery are accepted from December 1 through January 15. You must specify the launch date you desire on your form, and chances are improved by choosing a less popular date. Selected permittees are notified by March 15. If you don't hear anything, you lose. After the lottery, folks may telephone and request unfilled slots whether or not they participated in the lottery. If you are a lucky winner, then you must submit a confirmation list with names, addresses and phone numbers for everyone no later than four weeks before the launch date.

The low-use season begins the second Friday in September and continues to the second Monday in May. One launch per day is available. Requests for permits to launch during this period are accepted after March 1, either by mail (postcards only), by phone, or in person. Permits are issued on a first-come, first-served basis.

Restrictions: Groups must have at least 2 members and no more than 25. No permittees or trip leaders may be under the age of 18, although passengers or boatman under 18 are okay.

PFDs are required, and must be worn. Rafts, canoes and dories must have an extra PFD and at least one spare oar or paddle. Decked canoes must be equipped with floatation. One major first aid kit is required for each group and minor first aid kits must be in every boat. Hard boaters must wear helmets. Maps are required.

A dishwater strainer, portable toilets, and a firepan are required.

There are no-show and late cancellation penalties.

Gauge: Yampa at the Mouth

Source of Levels: Bureau of Reclamation, Salt Lake City; 801-539-1311.

How Reported: Cfs.

Interpretation of Levels: Optimum is about 10,000 cfs.

Source of More Information: Adventure Bound, Inc. 2932 H Road, Grand Junction, CO 81505; 303-241-5633.

Best Guidebooks: Anderson and Hopkinson, *Rivers of the Southwest;* Belknap, *Dinosaur River Guide;* McGinnis, *Whitewater Rafting;* Wheat, *Floater's Guide to Colorado.*

Further Comments: A tour through fantastically beautiful Canyonlands. Indian pictographs are numerous on the lower cliffs and in the side-canyons. Hiking and bird-watching opportunities are plentiful. Unfortunately, it's tough to get a permit; the best approach is to be aggressive in trying to occupy cancelled and unfilled slots.

COLORADO

GENERAL INFORMATION SOURCES
FOR COLORADO

The Department of Water Resources maintains the Watertalk Network, a convenient and sophisticated system for gaining access to river gauge readings and reservoir levels in the state of Colorado. Call 303-831-7135, and use your touchtone phone to navigate the system, responding to queries and prompts as instructed. You'll be able to obtain readings for the following gauges:

Division One

1 Adams Tunnel
2 Bear Creek, at Morrison
3 Bear Creek, Reservoir
4 Bear Creek, at Sheridan
5 Big Thompson, at mouth near LaSalle
6 South Boulder Creek, below Gross Reservoir
7 South Boulder Creek, near Eldorado Springs
8 Boulder Creek, at Boulder
9 Boulder Creek, near Orodell
10 Big Thompson River, above Lake Estes
11 Big Thompson River, below Lake Estes
12 North Fork, Big Thompson River, near Drake
13 Big Thompson River, at mouth of Canyon
14 Burlington Canal
15 Chatfield Reservoir
16 Cheesman Reservoir
17 Cherry Creek Reservoir
18 Cache La Poudre River, at Fort Collins
19 Cache La Poudre, at Canyon Mouth, near Fort Collins
20 Cache La Poudre, near Greeley
21 Clear Creek, at Derby
22 Clear Creek, near Golden
23 Clear Creek, near Lawson
24 Four Mile Creek, near Hartsel
25 Four Mile Creek, near Lawson
26 Grand River Ditch
27 Hansen Feeder Canal Waste-way
28 Hoosier Pass Tunnel
29 Jefferson Creek, near Jefferson
30 Laramie-Poudre Tunnel
31 Lower Latham Canal
32 Michigan Creek, above Jefferson
33 Metro Sewer effluent, at Denver
34 Middle Fork, at Prince
35 Middle Fork, at Santa Maria
36 Moffat Tunnel
37 Ohler Gulch, near Jefferson
38 Olympus Tunnel
39 South Platte River, near Balzac
40 South Platte River, below Cheesman Reservoir

41 South Platte River, at Denver
42 North Fork of the South Platte River, at Grant
43 Platte River, above Elevenmile Reservoir
44 South Platte River, at Henderson
45 South Platte River, at Julsburg, Left Channel
46 South Platte River, at Julsburg, Right Channel
47 South Platte River, near Kersy
48 South Platte River, at Fort Lupton
49 South Platte River, above Spinney Reservoir
50 South Platte River, at South Platte
51 South Platte River, below Strontia Springs
52 South Platte River, at Waterton
53 South Platte River, near Weldona
54 Riverside Canal
55 Roberts Tunnel
56 South Fork Platte River, above Antero Reservoir
57 North Sterling Canal
58 Saint Vrain Creek, at Lyons
59 Saint Vrain Creek, at Mouth
60 Tarryall Creek, at US 285, near Como
61 Union Ditch, near Gilcrest

Division Two

1 Amity Canal
2 Arkansas River, near Avondale
3 Arkansas River, at Catlin Dam, near Fowler
4 Arkansas River, near Coolidge, Kansas
5 Arkansas River, at Granada
6 Arkansas River, below John Martin Reservoir
7 Arkansas River, at La Junta
8 Arkansas River, at Las Animas
9 Arkansas River, near Nepesta
10 Arkansas River, at Portland
11 Arkansas River, above Pueblo
12 Arkansas River, near Wellsville
13 Bob Creek, at Canal
14 Charles H. Boustead Tunnel
15 Busk-Ivanhoe Tunnel
16 Crooked Arroyo, near Swink
17 Catlin Canal, at Catlin Dam, near Fowler
18 Cheyenne Creek, near Kansas stateline
19 Colorado Canal, at Mile 3.8 near Boone
20 Columbine Ditch
21 Ewing Ditch
22 Fort Lyon Storage Canal
23 Fort Lyon Canal
24 Fountain Creek, near Pinion
25 Frontier Ditch, Kansas
26 Lake Henry Reservoir, content and outflow
27 Holbrook Canal at Mile 3.4, near Rocky Fork
28 Homestake Tunnel
29 Horse Creek, at Highway 194
30 John Martin Reservoir, at Caddoa
31 Kicking Bird Canal

32   Lake Creek below Twin Lakes
33   Lamar Canal
34   Larkspur Ditch, at Marshall Pass
35   Lake Fork Creek, below Sugarloaf
36   Lake Fork Creek, above Turquoise Reservoir
37   Merredith Reservoir inflow, near Ordway
38   Merridith Reservoir content and outflow
39   Oxford Farmers Ditch Company
40   Pueblo Reservoir, near Pueblo
41   Pueblo Waterworks Diversion
42   Purgatorie River, below Trinidad Reservoir
43   Purgatorie River, near Las Animas
44   Purgatorie River, at Madrid
45   Purgatorie River, at Nine-Mile Dam, near Higbee
46   Purgatorie River, near Thatcher
47   Rocky Ford Highline Canal, at Mile 4.9 near Boone
48   Timpas Creek, near Rocky Ford
49   Twin Lakes Tunnel
50   Wurtz Ditch, near Tennessee Pass
51   Cucharas River, above Cucharas Reservoir
52   Cucharas River, below Cucharas Reservoir
53   Cucharas Reservoir
54   Cucharas Reservoir Seepage Flume
55   Fountain Creek, at Colorado
56   Fountain Creek, near Security
57   Fountain Creek, near Fountain
58   Fountain Creek, at Pueblo
59   Arkansas River, near Nathrop
60   Arkansas River, near Park Dale

Division Three

1   Alamosa Creek, above Terrace Reservoir
2   Closed Basin Project Canal, near Alamosa
3   Conejos River, near Magote
4   Conejos River, below Platoro Reservoir
5   Continental Reservoir, near Creede
6   La Jara Creek, at Gallegos Ranch
7   Los Pinos River, near Ortiz
8   North Channel Conejos River, near Lasauses
9   Platoro Reservoir
10   Rio Grande River, at Alamosa
11   Rio Grande Canal, near Del Norte
12   Rio Grande, near Del Norte
13   Rio Grande, near Lobatos
14   Rio Grande, at Thirty Mile Bridge
15   Rio Grande, at Monte Vista
16   Rio Grande Reservoir
17   South Fork, Rio Grande River, South Fork
18   Rio Grande River, above Trinchera Creek
19   Sagauche Creek, near Sagauche
20   San Antonio River, at Ortiz
21   South Channel, Conejos River, near Lasauses
22   Tabor Ditch at Spring Creek Pass
23   Terrace Reservoir

Division Four

1   Blue Mesa Reservoir, Gunnison County
2   Cimarron River, near Cimarron, Gunnison
3   Dallas Creek, near Ridgeway, Ouray County
4   Dolores River, near Bedrock, Montrose County
5   East River, at Almont
6   Gunnison River, below East Portal
7   Gunnison River, at Delta, Delta County
8   Gunnison River, near Grand Junction
9   Gunnison River, near Gunnison County
10   Muddy Creek, above Paonia Reservoir, Gunnison
11   Muddy Creek, below Paonia Reservoir, Gunnison
12   North Fork of the Gunnison River, Somerset
13   Paonia Reservoir, near Bardine
14   Redlands Canal, near Grand Junction
15   Ridgeway Reservoir, near Ridgeway, Ouray
16   San Miguel River, at Naturita, Montrose County
17   San Miguel River, near Placerville
18   Silver Jack Reservoir, near Cimarron
19   South Canal, near Montrose, Montrose County
20   Surface Creek, at Cedaredge, Delta County
21   Surface Creek, near Cedaredge, Delta County
22   Taylor River, at Almont
23   Taylor Park Reservoir, Gunnison County
24   Trout Lake Reservoir, San Miguel County
25   Trout Lake Reservoir, out-flow
26   Uncompahgre River, at Colona, Montrose
27   Uncompahgre River, below Ridgeway Reservoir
28   Uncompahgre River, near Ridgeway, Ouray County

Division Five

1   Blue River, below Dillon, Summit County
2   Blue River, below Green Mountain Reservoir, Summit
3   Colorado River, near Cameo
4   Colorado River, near Dotero, Eagle County
5   Colorado River, below Granby Reservoir, Grand County
6   Colorado River, below Glenwood Springs
7   Colorado River, near Kremmling
8   Colorado River, near Granby, Grand County
9   Colorado River, Hot Sulphur Springs, Grand County
10   Colorado River, near Colorado-Utah state line
11   Crooked Creek, at Tabernash
12   Crystal River, above Avalanche Creek, Redstone
13   Dillon Reservoir, Summit County
14   Eagle River, below Gypsum, Eagle County
15   Eagle River, at Red Cliff
16   Fraser River, near Windy Gap
17   Fryingpan River, near Reudi, Eagle County
18   Fryingpan River, near Thomasville, Pitkin County
19   Government Highline Canal

COLORADO

20 Granby Reservoir
21 Grand Valley Canal
22 Green Mountain Reservoir, Summit County
23 Grass Valley Canal
24 Lower Fraser River, near Winter Park
25 Lincoln Creek, below Grizzly Reservoir
26 Piney River, near State Bridge
27 Plateau Creek, near Cameo
28 Ranch Creek, above Tabernash
29 Rifle Gap, below Gap Reservoir
30 Roaring Fork River, near Aspen
31 Roaring Fork River, below Maroon Creek
32 Roaring Fork River, at Glenwood Springs
33 Roaring Fork River, above Lost Man Creek
34 Ruedi Reservoir, near Basalt
35 Shadow Mountain Reservoir, Grand County
36 Saint Louis Creek, above Fraser
37 Strawberry Creek, near Granby
38 Upper Fraser River, above Winter Park
39 Vasquez Creek, at Winter Park
40 Willow Creek Pump Canal, Grand County
41 Williams Fork, below Williams Fork Reservoir, Grand County
42 Willow Creek Reservoir, Grand County
43 Willow Creek, below Willow Creek Reservoir, Grand County
44 Williams Fork Reservoir

Division Six

1 Bear River, near Toponas, Garfield County
2 Coal Creek, at Mouth, near Yampa
3 Elk River, at Clark, Routt County
4 Illinois River
5 Little Snake River, near Dixon, Wyoming
6 Little Snake River, near Lilly
7 Little Snake River, near Slater, Routt County
8 Michigan Creek, near Gould
9 North Platte River, near Gateway
10 Pot Creek, near Vernal, Utah, Daggett County
11 White River, near Meeker
12 Yampa River, at Maybell
13 Yampa River, near Oak Creek
14 Yampa River, above Stage Coach Reservoir
15 Coalo Reservoir
16 Yampa River at Deer Lodge Park

Division Seven

1 Animas River, near Cedar Hill, New Mexico
2 Animas River, at Durango
3 Azotea Outlet Tunnel, Chama, New Mexico
4 Cherry Creek, at Mouth, near Red Mesa
5 Dolores River, below McPhee Reservoir
6 Dolores River, at Dolores, Montezuma County
7 Dolores River, near Rico

8 Dolores Tunnel Outlet, near Dolores
9 Florida River, above Lemon Reservoir, near Durango
10 Florida River, below Lemon Reservoir
11 La Plata River, at Hesperus, La Plata County
12 La Plata River, at Colorado-New Mexico state line
13 Long Hollow, at the Mouth, near Red Mesa
14 Lost Canyon Creek, at Dolores, Montezuma County
15 La Plata and Cherry Creek Ditch, near Hesperus
16 Mancos River, near Mancos
17 Lone Pine Canal, at Great Cut Dike, near Dolores
18 Navajo River, below Oso Diversion Dam, near Chromo
19 Pine River, below Vallecito Reservoir, near Bayfield
20 Rio Blanco, below Blanco Diversion Dam, at Pagosa
21 San Juan River, at Farmington, New Mexico
22 San Juan River, at Pagosa Springs
23 Vallecito Reservoir

You can contact the Department of Water Resources for further information at 1313 Sherman Street, Room 818, Denver, CO 80203; 303-866-3581.

The Colorado TravelBank maintains a computer bulletin board of Colorado travel information, accessible by modem. The bulletin board includes a list of gauge readings for popular Colorado rivers, updated on Monday, Wednesday and Friday. Set the communications program on your computer as follows: 300 to 2400 baud, 8 bits, no parity, and 1 stop bit. Then dial up 303-671-7669, to get online. There is no access fee. For more information, contact the sysop, Jay Melnick, at Colorado TravelBank, PO Box 20594, Denver, CO 80220; 303-320-8550.

The TravelBank provides readings for the following gauges:

The North Platte River at North Gate
The Cache la Poudre River, 9 mi NW of Fort Collins
The North Fork of the Big Thompson at Drake
Big Thompson Creek at Mouth of Canyon
The St. Vrain River at Lyons
Clear Creek at Golden
Bear Creek at Morrison
Boulder Creek at Orodell
The North Fork of the South Platte River near Grant
The South Platte River at South Platte
The South Platte River at Deckers
The South Platte River at Denver near 19th St.
Lake Creek below Twin Lakes
The Arkansas River at Wellsville
The Arkansas River at Parkdale
The Little Snake River at Lily

The Elk River, at Clark
The Yampa River, at Steamboat Springs
The Yampa River, at Maybell
The Yampa River, at DeerLodge Park
The Colorado River, at Hot Sulphur Springs
The Colorado River, at Kremmling
The Colorado River, at Glenwood Springs
The Colorado River, at Utah State Line
The Blue River, below Dillon
The Blue River, below Green Mountain Reservoir
The Eagle River, at Redcliff
The Eagle River, at Gypsum
The Roaring Fork, one mile upstream of Aspen
The Roaring Fork, at Glenwood Springs
The Crystal River, at Redstone
The Frying Pan River, at Thomasville
The Frying Pan River, at Ruedi Reservoir
The Taylor River, at Almont
The Gunnison River, at Gunnison Tunnel
The Gunnison River, at Delta
The San Juan River, at Pagosa Springs
The Animas River, at Durango
The Dolores River, below McPhee Reservoir
The Dolores River, at Bedrock
The San Miguel River, at Naturita
The Uncompahgre River, at Ridgeway
The Rio Grande River, at Del Norte
The Rio Grande River, at New Mexico State Line
The Conejos River, below Platoro
The Conejos River, at Mogote

A few readings relevant to Colorado are included in the Salt Lake City Bureau of Reclamation River Observations Recording: 801-539-1311.

Gauge readings, updated daily at 4 a.m., are reported for the following rivers:

Colorado River Basin
Colorado River, at Westwater
Gunnison River, at Gun Summit
Dolores River
    At Bedrock
    Near Cisco
Colorado River
    Near Cisco
    Cataract Canyon
    At Lee's Ferry
Virgin River, near Littlefield
Muddy River, near Emory

Green River Basin
Yampa River, at Maybell
Little Snake River, near Lily
Yampa River, at the mouth
Green River, near Jensen

White River, near Watson
Green River, near Green River, Utah
    San Rafael, near Green River, Utah
    Dirty Devil, at Hanksville
Great Basin
Weaver, near Oakley
Weaver, below Echo
Sevier, below Clear Creek
San Juan Basin
Animas, near Durango
San Juan River, near Bluff
Dam Releases
Flaming Gorge Dam, Green River
Glen Canyon Dam, Colorado River
Navajo Dam, San Juan River
McPhee Dam, Dolores River

A few readings relevant to Colorado are available from the National Weather Service in Albuquerque, New Mexico; 505-243-1453.

Colorado rivers reported by this office include:

Rio Grande River
    At Del Norte, CO
    At Monte Vista, CO
    At Alamosa, CO
    At Mogote, CO
    At State Line, CO-NM

CONNECTICUT

BANTAM RIVER

Sections: (1) Litchfield to Bantam, Class III
                    (2) Bantam to the confluence with the
                        Shepaug and continuing to the Rt. 47
                        Bridge, Class I-II

Length   (1) Day trip, 9 miles
of Run: (2) Day trip, 5 miles

Location: Litchfield County, Connecticut

Maps: USGS quads: Litchfield, New Preston

Times Runnable: A brief season during March and April

Permit: None Required

Gauge: Painted gauge at the Hwy. 47 bridge on the Shepaug

Source of Levels: Visual inspection only, but you might try: Appalachian Mountain Club, Hartford Chapter, Whitewater Hotline; 203-582-6978.

How Reported: Feet

Interpretation of Levels: Minimum is 0.5 feet; medium is about 1.0 to 1.5, and high is 2.0 to 3.0.

Source of More Information: River Running Expeditions, Inc., Main St., Falls Village, CT 06031; 203-824-5579 and 203-824-5286.

Mt. Tom State Park, Rt. 202, Bantam, CT 06750; 203-567-8870.

Best Guidebooks: AMC, *AMC River Guide: Massachusetts, Rhode Island and Connecticut.*

BLACKLEDGE AND SALMON RIVERS

Sections: Connecticut Hwy. 66 to confluence with the

Salmon and continuing to covered bridge at Connecticut Hwy. 16, Class II-III

Length of Run: Day trip, 8 miles

Location: Tolland county, Connecticut

Maps: USGS quads: Marlboro, Moodus

Times Runnable: For about 4 weeks in February and March

Permit: None required

Gauge: Painted gauge at covered bridge at the take-out

Source of Levels: Visual inspection only, but you might try: Appalachian Mountain Club, Hartford Chapter, Whitewater Hotline; 203-582-6978.

How Reported: Feet

Interpretation of Levels: Minimum is about 1.4. Medium levels range from 2 to 3 feet.

Source of More Information: River Running Expeditions, Inc., Main St., Falls Village, CT 06031; 203-824-5579 and 203-824-5286.

Best Guidebooks: Weber, *Canoeing Massachusetts, Rhode Island and Connecticut;* AMC, *AMC River Guide: Massachusetts, Rhode Island and Connecticut.*

Tariffville Gorge, Farmington River. Photo by John Porterfield.

FARMINGTON RIVER, TARIFFVILLE GORGE

(See the following entry and Massachusetts for additional sections.)

Sections: Tariffville Gorge, from Tariffville to Hwy. 187, Class II-IV

Length of Run: Play spot, 1 mile

Location: Hartford County, Connecticut

Maps: USGS quads: Tariffville

Times Runnable: Year-round, dam released

Permit: None required

Gauge: USGS gauge: Farmington River at Tariffville

Source of Levels: National Weather Service River Forecast Center, Bloomfield, CT; 203-240-3514.

Perhaps also: Appalachian Mountain Club, Hartford Chapter, Whitewater Hotline; 203-582-6978.

How Reported: Feet

Interpretation of Levels: Minimum is about 1.2 feet (250 cfs); ideal is 2 to 4.5 feet (800-3200); can be run by sufficiently competent boaters to floodstage.

Source of More Information: River Running Expeditions, Main St., Falls Village, CT 06031; 203-824-5579 and 203-824-5286.

Best Guidebooks: Connelly and Porterfield, *Appalachian Whitewater, Vol. III;* Gabler, *New England Whitewater River Guide;* AMC, *AMC River Guide: Massachusetts, Rhode Island and Connecticut.*

Gauge Conversions: USGS gauge: Farmville at Tariffville

Feet	Cfs	Feet	Cfs	Feet	Cfs
1.0	250	2.4	1117	4.5	2650
1.2	350	2.6	1287	5.0	3760
1.4	459	3.0	1650	5.5	4453
1.6	569	3.2	1827	6.0	5250
1.8	680	3.4	2008	6.5	6100
2.0	809	3.6	2207	7.0	7000
2.2	957	3.8	2425		

FARMINGTON RIVER, LOWER

(See the preceding entry and Massachusetts for additional sections.)

Sections:
(1) Hogback Road to Riverton, Class I-II
(2) Riverton to Satan's Kingdom parking area, Class I-III
(3) Collinsville to Unionville, Class III

Length of Run:
(1) Day trip, 2 miles
(2) Day trip, 11 miles
(3) Day trip, 6 miles

Location: Litchfield County, Connecticut

Maps: USGS quads: Winsted, New Hartford, Collinsville, Avon, New Britain

Times Runnable: February to mid-April and after scheduled fall releases

Permit: None required

Gauge: For Section (1), releases from dams on the East and West Branches at Hogback

Source of Levels: Farmington River Watershed Association, 203-658-4442.

How Reported: Cfs, release schedule

Additional Gauge: For Section (2), release from the Colebrook Basin, supplemented above Satan's Kingdom by releases from the Barkhamsted Reservoir

Source of Levels: Farmington River Watershed Association, 203-658-4442.

How Reported: Cfs, release schedule

Additional Gauge: For Section (3), release from the Collinsville power dam

Source of Levels: Farmington River Watershed Association, 203-658-4442.

How Reported: Cfs, release schedule

Additional Gauge: For Section (3), paddlers' gauge at the Connecticut Hwy. 7 bridge in Unionville

Source of Levels: Visual inspection only

How Reported: Feet

Interpretation of Levels: I suggest that you follow the recommendations of the folks at the Farmington River Watershed Association for interpreting the levels they report. For section (3), 2.0 feet on the paddlers' gauge in Unionville is a good level, and 3.0 is high.

Source of More Information: Farmington River Watershed Association, 749 Hopmeadow St., Simsbury, CT 06070; 203-658-4442.

River Running Expeditions, Inc., Main St., Falls Village, CT 06031; 203-824-5519.

People's State Forest, East River Rd., Pleasant Valley, CT 06063; 203-379-2464.

American Legion State Forest, PO Box 161, Pleasant Valley, CT 06063; 203-379-2469.

Best Guidebooks: Farmington River Watershed Association, *The Farmington River and Watershed Guide;* Gabler, *New England Whitewater Guide;* AMC, *AMC River Guide: Massachusetts, Rhode Island and Connecticut.*

Carved Kettleholes frame Bill Adamson's descent of Stairway Rapid on the Bulls Bridge section of the Housatonic River. Photo by Jim Michaud.

HOUSATONIC RIVER

Sections:
(1) Bulls Bridge Section, Bulls Bridge to Route 7 take-out, Class IV (V high)
(2) Falls Village hydro plant to Swifts Bridge, Class II (with one at IV when high)

Length of Run:
(1) Day trip, 2.25 miles
(2) Day trip, 13.5 miles

Location: Litchfield County, Connecticut

Maps: USGS quads: Kent, Dover Plains, South Canaan, Sharon, Cornwall, Ellsworth

Times Runnable: February to April and in the summer during evening releases

Permit: None required

Gauge: USGS at Gaylordsville

Source of Levels: National Weather Service River Forecast Center, Bloomfield, CT; 203-240-3514.

Clarke Outdoors, 203-672-6365.

Appalachian Mountain Club, Hartford Chapter, Whitewater Hotline; 203-582-6978.

How Reported: Feet

Interpretation of Levels: Minimum is about 2.0 feet (385 cfs) and extremely high is 8.0 feet (8400 cfs).

Source of More Information: Clarke Outdoors, Box 302, Rt. 7, West Cornwall, CT 06796; 203-672-6365.

Housatonic Meadows State Park, Highway 7, Cornwall, CT 06754; 203-672-6139.

Macedonia Brook State Park, Kent, CT 06757; 203-927-3238.

Best Guidebooks: Connelly and Porterfield, *Appalachian Whitewater, Vol. III.*

Further Comments: The reading at Gaylordsville may be misleading during dry weather, because flows are often diverted through a canal. Check with Clarke Outdoors, they'll know the scoop. Section (1) is similar in difficulty to the Upper Gauley in West Virginia; use caution if the river is high.

Gauge Conversions: USGS Housatonic at Gaylordsville

Feet	Cfs	Feet	Cfs	Feet	Cfs
2.0	385	3.8	1600	5.6	3888
2.2	470	4.0	1806	5.8	4214
2.4	567	4.2	2030	6.0	4554
2.6	677	4.4	2259	6.5	5437
2.8	800	4.6	2503	7.0	6375
3.0	936	4.8	2760	7.5	7374
3.2	1084	5.0	3017	8.0	8442
3.4	1241	5.2	3290	8.5	9582
3.6	1410	5.4	3580	9.0	10800

JEREMY AND SALMON RIVERS

Sections: Jeremy River at Rt. 2 bridge to confluence with the Salmon river and continuing to covered bridge above Rt. 16, Class I-II

Length of Run: Day trip, 5 miles

Location: Tolland County, Connecticut

Maps: USGS quads: Moodus

Times Runnable: February to March for about four weeks

Permit: None required

Gauge: Staff gauge at Comstock Covered Bridge at Hwy. 16

Source of Levels: Visual inspection only, but you might try: Appalachian Mountain Club, Hartford Chapter, Whitewater Hotline; 203-582-6978.

How Reported: Feet

Interpretation of Levels: Minimum is 1.4 feet and medium is 3.0.

Source of More Information: River Running Expeditions, Inc., Main St., Falls Village, CT 06031; 203-824-5579 and 203-824-5286.

Best Guidebooks: AMC, *AMC River Guide: Massachusetts, Rhode Island and Connecticut.*

Further Comments: Portage one dam.

NATCHAUG RIVER

Sections: (1) England Rd. to Rt. 198 bridge at Diana's Pool, Class IV
(2) Diana's Pool to Bassett's Bridge, Class II

Length of Run: (1) Day trip, 1 mile
(2) Day trip, 3 miles

Location: Tolland County, Connecticut

Maps: USGS quads: Spring Hill and Hampton

Times Runnable: Short season during peak runoff in March or April, or after heavy rain

Permit: None required

Gauge: There is a paddlers' gauge on river-right at Diana's Pool, upstream of Rt. 198 bridge.

Source of Levels: Visual inspection only, but you might try: Appalachian Mountain Club, Hartford Chapter, Whitewater Hotline; 203-582-6978.

How Reported: Feet

Interpretation of Levels: Minimum is about 1.75 feet; ideal is between 2.5 and 3.5. The gauge runs out at 4 feet.

Source of More Information: River Running Expeditions, Inc., Main St., Falls Village, CT 06031; 203-824-5579 and 203-824-5286.

An open boater cuts the slot in low water above the third bridge on Sandy Brook. Photo by Robert Hall

Pounding turbulence surrounds Risa Shimoda during a high water descent of the Stairway Rapid at Bulls Bridge. Photo by Sharon O'Brien.

Mansfield Hollow State Park, Rural Rt. 2, Box 82, North Windham, CT 06256; 203-455-9057.

Natchaug State Forest, Eastford, CT 06242; 203-974-1562.

Best Guidebooks: Connelly and Porterfield, *Appalachian Whitewater, Vol. III;* Gabler, *New England Whitewater River Guide;* AMC, *AMC River Guide: Massachusetts, Rhode Island and Connecticut.*

SANDY BROOK

Sections:	Rt. 183 bridge to Rt. 8 bridge, following along Sandy Brook Rd., Class IV (to V high)
Length of Run:	Day trip, 4 miles

Location: Litchfield County, Connecticut

Maps: USGS quads: South Sandisfield, Tolland, Winsted

Times Runnable: February to March after heavy rains; comes up and down very quickly

Permit: none required

Gauge: Paddlers' gauge on river-right, on a pillar of the first Rt. 8 bridge, above the take-out

Source of Levels: Visual inspection only, but you might try: Appalachian Mountain Club, Hartford Chapter, Whitewater Hotline; 203-582-6978.

How Reported: Feet

Interpretation of Levels: Low is about 3.5 feet. Ideal is between 4 and 5 feet. High is 5 feet, and extremely high is 6 feet.

Source of More Information: Clarke Outdoors, Box 302, Rt. 7, West Cornwall, CT 06796; 203-672-6365.

River Running Expeditions, Inc., Main St., Falls Village, CT 06031; 203-824-5579 and 203-824-5286.

Best Guidebooks: Connelly and Porterfield, *Appalachian Whitewater, Vol. III;* Gabler, *New England Whitewater River Guide;* AMC, *AMC River Guide: Massachusetts, Rhode Island and Connecticut.*

SHEPAUG RIVER

Sections:	(1)	Woodville to Bee Brook (at CT Rt. 47), Class I-II
	(2)	Bee Brook Rest Area on CT Rt. 47 to Steep Rock Reservation, Class II
	(3)	Steep Rock Reservation to Roxbury Station and Hwy. 317, Class II
Length of Run:	(1)	Day trip, 6 miles
	(2)	Day trip, 5 miles
	(3)	Day trip, 4.5 miles

Location: Litchfield County, Connecticut

Maps: USGS quads: New Preston (15'); and Roxbury

Times Runnable: March and some of April

Permit: None required

Gauge: Painted gauge at the Bee Brook Rest Area on the Hwy. 47 bridge

Source of Levels: Visual inspection, but try: Appalachian Mountain Club, Hartford Chapter, Whitewater Hotline; 203-582-6978.

How Reported: Feet

Interpretation of Levels: Low is about 0.5 feet, medium is 1.0, and high is 2.0.

Source of More Information: Mount Tom State Park, Rt. 202, Bantam, CT 06750; 203-567-8870.

River Running Expeditions, Inc., Main St., Falls Village, CT 06031; 203-824-5579 and 203-824-5286.

Best Guidebooks: Connelly and Porterfield, *Appalachian Whitewater, Vol. III;* Gabler, *New England Whitewater River Guide;* AMC, *AMC River Guide: Massachusetts, Rhode Island and Connecticut.*

Further Comments: Don't fail to take out at Roxbury; downstream is an unrunnable falls. It is difficult to stop above the falls or to portage it.

GENERAL INFORMATION SOURCES
FOR CONNECTICUT

The New England River Forecast Center of the National Weather Service in Bloomfield, Connecticut, is also the headquarters. for the Southern New England Hydrological Service Area: 203-240-3514.

The US Army Corps of Engineers and other managers of water projects coordinate many of the scheduled releases through the Appalachian Mountain Club.

Appalachian Mountain Club, New England Rivers Center, Boston, 5 Joy St., Boston, MA; 617-523-0636.

The Connecticut chapter of the Appalachian Mountain Club also maintains a river hotline which reports levels and events for Connecticut and surrounding areas: AMC Connecticut Chapter Whitewater Hotline, Hartford Recording; 203-582-6978.

The New England River Forecast Center of the National Weather Service in Bloomfield, Connecticut, is also the headquarters for the Southern New England Hydrological Service Area: 203-240-3514.

They can provide gauge readings, updated twice daily, for rivers in Connecticut and Massachusetts. Don't call before 11:30 a.m., as they are busy putting out the forecast. Reports are available for the following Connecticut gauges:

Housatonic River
    At Great Barrington, MA
    At Gaylordsville
    Below Stedson Dam
Connecticut River
    At Montague City
    At Holyoke, MA
    At Enfield
    At Hartford
    At Middletown
Shetucket River, at Willomantic
Farmington River, at Tariffville
West Branch of the Farmington River, at New Boston

AMICALOLA CREEK

Sections: (1) Goshen Rd. to Highway 53, Class II-III
(2) Highway 53 to Etowah river, Class III-IV

Length of Run: (1) Day trip, 10 miles
(2) Day trip, 10 miles

Location: Dawson County, Georgia

Maps: USGS quads: Amicalola, Nelson, Juno, Matt

Times Runnable: March to July

Permit: None required

Gauge: Paddlers' gauge on river-right above Highway 53 bridge

Source of Levels: None

How Reported: Feet

Interpretation of Levels: Minimum is about 1.0 feet; medium-high is 2.5 feet, and high is 3.5 feet.

Source of More Information: High Country, Inc., 6300 Powers Ferry Rd., Atlanta, GA 30339; 404-892-0828.

Best Guidebooks: Sehlinger et al., *Appalachian Whitewater, Vol. I;* Sehlinger and Otey, *Northern Georgia Canoeing.*

CARTECAY RIVER

Sections: Georgia Highway 52 to East Ellijay, Class I-III

Length of Run: Day trip, 10.5 miles

Off the Wall, Amicalola Creek. Photo by Don Ellis.

Edge of the World Rapid, Amicalola Creek. Photo by Don Ellis.

Location: Gilmer County, Georgia

Maps: USGS quads: Tickanetly, Ellijay

Times Runnable: Almost year-round

Permit: None required

Gauge: USGS gauge at East Elijay

Source of Levels: Mountain Tour Outdoor Expeditions, 404-635-2524.

How Reported: Feet

Interpretation of Levels: About 1.4 feet (83 cfs) is minimum; medium is 2.0 to 2.6 feet (210-470 cfs); high is 3.0 feet (720 cfs), and very high is 4.0 feet (1570 cfs). Runnable to floodstage by expert decked boaters.

Source of More Information: Mountain Tour Outdoor Expeditions, PO Box 86, Elijay, GA 30540; 404-635-2524.

Best Guidebooks: Sehlinger et al., *Appalachian Whitewater, Vol. I;* Sehlinger and Otey, *Northern Georgia Canoeing.*

Gauge Conversions:

Feet	Cfs	Feet	Cfs	Feet	Cfs
1.4	83	3.2	880	6.0	3750
2.0	210	3.4	1020	7.0	5140
2.4	360	3.6	1210	8.0	6780
2.6	470	3.8	1390	9.0	8700
2.8	590	4.0	1570	10.0	11000
3.0	720	5.0	2550	-	-

CHATTAHOOCHEE RIVER, UPPER

Sections:	(1) Forest Service Rd. 44 to Robertson, Class II-IV
	(2) Robertson to GA 115, Class I-II
	(3) GA 115 to Duncan Rd., Class II-III

Length of Run:	(1) Day trip, 7 miles
	(2) Day trip, 16 miles
	(3) Day trip, 4 miles

Location: White, Habersham and Hall Counties, Georgia

Maps: USGS quads: Jacks Gap, Cowrock, Helen, Leaf, Clarkesville, Lula

Times Runnable: Almost all year

Permit: None required

Gauge: Paddlers' gauge at GA 115 bridge

Source of Levels: Wildewood Shop, Chattahoochee Outpost; 404-865-4451 or 404-878-2541.

How Reported: Feet

Additional Gauge: USGS at Helen, GA (at Hwy. 17-75 bridge)

Source of Levels: National Weather Service, Atlanta; 404-762-1186.

How Reported: Feet

Interpretation of Levels: In terms of the Paddlers' gauge, minimum is about 1.0 feet. Very high is about 6 feet. In terms of the Helen USGS gauge, minimum is around 100 cfs.

Source of More Information: Wildewood Shop,

Chattahoochee Outpost, PO Box 119, River St., Helen, GA 30545; 404-878-2541 or 404-865-4451.

USDA Forest Service, Chattahoochee National Forest, 601 Broad St., NE, Gainesville, GA 30501; 404-536-0541.

Unicoi State Park, PO Box 256, Helen, GA 30545; 404-878-2824.

Best Guidebooks: Nealy, *Whitewater Home Companion, Vol. I;* Sehlinger et al., *Appalachian Whitewater, Vol. I;* Sehlinger and Otey, *Northern Georgia Canoeing.*

Gauge Conversions:

Feet	Cfs
0.4	45
0.6	70
0.8	100
1.0	140
1.2	189
1.4	247
1.6	315
1.8	392
2.0	480
2.2	579
2.4	690
2.6	798

CHATTOOGA RIVER
Wild and Scenic River

Sections:	(1) Section 1: West Fork of the Chattooga to its confluence with the Chattooga River, and continuing to Highway 28, Class I and II.
	(2) Section 2: Georgia Hwy. 28 to Earls Ford, Class I-II
	(3) Section 3: Earls Ford to US 76 bridge, Class III-IV
	(4) Section 4: US 76 bridge to Lake Tugaloo, Class IV (one class VI usually carried or snuck)
Length of Run:	(1) Day trip, 4 miles.
	(2) Day trip, 7.5 miles
	(3) Day trip, 10.5 miles
	(4) Day trip, 6 miles plus 2 1/4 of flatwater on Lake Tugaloo

Location: Rabun County, Georgia and Oconee County, South Carolina

Maps: USGS quads: Satolah, Whetstone and Rainy Mountain Forest. Service map: Chattooga National Wild and Scenic River

A brave splat onto Pillow Rock. Photo by Richard Penny.

Times Runnable: Winter, spring, early summer and after rain. The Chattooga is famous for its excellent watershed.

Permit: Self-issuing permits are required for each party boating on the Chattooga. A sample is reproduced in Appendix One, but do not use it. Permit forms are available at a self-issuing station near the dressing area and parking lot at the Section 3 take-out/Section 4 put-in area.

Organized groups planning to boat the Chattooga must apply for special permits and reservations. Apply by letter to: USDA Forest Service, Stumphouse Ranger Station, Andrew Pickens Ranger District, Sumter National Forest, Star Route, Walhalla, SC 29691. In your letter, mention the name of your group, the date and time you would like to launch, the section(s) you will run, and the number of members in the party.

Reservations: For organized groups (see above.)

Restrictions: Minimum party size: two persons, one craft above Earls Ford, two persons, two craft below. Inner tubes or other unsuitable craft are prohibited. PFDs must be worn. All persons in decked boats and all persons on Section 4 must wear a helmet. Camping is restricted to areas more than 1/4 mile from a road and more than 50 feet from a trail, stream or the river.

Gauge: Two USGS staff gauges are located at the Highway 76 bridge at the put-in for Section 4. The first of these is attached to a bridge abutment on the South Carolina side, and the second is about 100 feet downstream, also on the South Carolina side. Most folks go by this bridge gauge, which reads about one inch higher than the lower gauge.

Seven Foot Falls, Section IV, Chattooga River. Photo by Slim Ray.

Source of Levels: Chattooga Whitewater Shop; 803-647-9083.

Wildwater Ltd.; 803-647-9587.

Southeastern Expeditions; 404-329-0433.

How Reported: Feet

Interpretation of Levels: For Section 3, about 1.2 feet (240 cfs) is minimum, 2 feet (840 cfs) is high, and 3-4 feet (2000-3400 cfs) is very high. For Section 4, 1 foot is about minimum and 2 feet is high. Optimum on section 4 is often thought to be around 1.7 to 1.8 feet (568 to 652 cfs).

Source of More Information: USDA Forest Service, Stumphouse Ranger Station, Andrew Pickens Ranger District, Sumter National Forest, Star Route, Walhalla, SC 29691; 803-638-9568.

Chattooga Whitewater Shop, Highway 76, Box 147, Long Creek, SC 29658; 803-647-9083.

Nantahala Outdoor Center, Star Route, Box 68, Bryson City, NC 28713; 704-488-2175.

Southeastern Expeditions, 1955 Cliff Valley Way, NE, Suite 220, Atlanta, GA 30029; 404-329-0433.

Wildwater, Ltd., Long Creek, SC 29658; 803-647-9587.

Best Guidebooks: Nealy, *Whitewater Home Companion, Vol. I;* Sehlinger et al., *Appalachian Whitewater, Vol. I;* Sehlinger and Otey, *Northern Georgia Canoeing.*

Gauge Conversions:

Feet	Cfs	Feet	Cfs	Feet	Cfs
1.0	155	1.7	568	2.8	1750
1.1	195	1.8	652	3.0	2000
1.2	240	1.9	742	3.4	2550
1.3	293	2.0	840	3.6	2840
1.4	353	2.2	1040	4.0	3450
1.5	420	2.4	1280	5.0	5200
1.6	491	2.6	1510	-	-

Further Comments: The famous Chattooga River is one of the last undammed rivers in the Southeast, and one of the first to be included in the Wild and Scenic River system. Its watershed is in fine condition, and so the Chattooga offers a surprisingly long season of scenic and challenging whitewater paddling.

If you boat Sections (3) or (4), please be careful of the dangerous potholes and undercut rocks. And, although Woodall Shoals on Section (4) may not look too nasty, it is! I watched, horrified, as famous hair-boater Roger Beaman was thoroughly chundered in this terminal hydraulic. Happily for Roger, Dennis Rhodes paddled in and pulled him out.

CHAUGA RIVER

Sections: (1) Upper, Blackwell Bridge to Cassidy Bridge, Class II-IV, (plus one portage of a multiple Class VI falls section).
(2) Lower (Chauga River Gorge), Cassidy Bridge to Cobbs Bridge, Class IV-V

Length of Run: (1) Blackwell to Cassidy, 4.2 miles
(2) Cassidy to Cobbs, 8.0 miles

Location: Oconee County, South Carolina

Maps: USGS quads: Whetstone, Holly Springs

Times Runnable: Late winter and spring

Permit: Not required

Gauge: Levels can be extrapolated from the USGS gauge at the Highway 76 bridge on the Chattooga River nearby.

Source of Levels: Chattooga Whitewater Shop; 803-647-9083.

Black Hole, Chauga Gorge, South Carolina. Photo by Don Ellis.

Wildwater Ltd.; 803-647-9587.

Southeastern Expeditions; 404-329-0433.

How Reported: Feet

Additional Gauge: Paddlers' gauge painted on Cassidy Bridge on the Chauga.

Source of Levels: There is no source of readings for this gauge by phone.

Interpretation of Levels: 1.7-2.0 feet on the Chattooga gauge is about minimum for the Chauga, and 3 feet is very high. In terms of the paddlers' gauge at the Cassidy Bridge, 3" is about minimum and 1 foot is high. I ran the upper section on one occasion at -1". You can get down at this level, but I don't recommend it.

Source of More Information: USDA Forest Service, Stumphouse Ranger Station, Andrew Pickens Ranger District, Sumter National Forest, Star Route, Walhalla, SC 29691; 803-638-9568.

Chattooga Whitewater Shop, Highway 76, Box 147, Long Creek, SC 29658; 803-647-9083.

Nantahala Outdoor Center, Star Route, Box 68, Bryson City, NC 28713; 704-488-2175.

Southeastern Expeditions, 1955 Cliff Valley Way, NE, Suite 220, Atlanta, GA 30029; 404-329-0433.

Wildwater, Ltd., Long Creek, SC 29658; 803-647-9587.

Best Guidebooks: Sehlinger et al., *Appalachian Whitewater, Vol. I;* Sehlinger and Otey, *Northern Georgia Canoeing.*

Further Comments: Both sections are beautiful in the extreme, surrounded by lush vegetation resembling a tropical rain forest. The Chauga Gorge from Cassidy Bridge to Cobbs Bridge is a difficult expert run. The upper section is less difficult, but has its drawbacks. Numerous downed trees are in the riverbed; many of these would become hazardous at higher water. One-half mile into the section, after a right-hand bend, the paddler reaches a series of three falls, which drop a total of 45 feet in one-fifth mile. The first of these is a razorback falls on river-right, about 15 feet in height, Class VI. After a short pool, the river then descends a nozzlelike trough on river-left, dropping about 25 feet in 50 feet, Class VI. This second drop is rumored to have been run by resin-fried crazies. Make a single portage around both drops on river-right along a steep trail; it will take about 20 minutes. You can put back in after the second drop and then paddle about 200 feet to the last falls, a slanting 10-foot slide, partly obstructed by an overhanging undercut rock to the left. With enough water, a sneak might develop here that would not risk this undercut, at which point the drop would be Class IV. If you don't like it, carry on the left. Don't forget to watch out for downed trees all along this section—it's like paddling through a giant game of pick-up sticks.

CONASAUGA RIVER

Sections: (1) Chicken Coop Gap to Georgia Hwy. 2, Class II-IV

(2) Georgia Hwy. 2 to US 411 in Tennessee, Class I-II (one at III)

Length of Run: (1) Day trip, 5.5 miles
(2) Day trip, 12 miles

Location: Murray County, Georgia, Polk and Bradley Counties, Tennessee; Chattahoochee National Forest, Georgia; Cherokee National Forest, Tennessee

Maps: USGS quads: Tennga, Parksville

Times Runnable: (1) January to June after rain
(2) December to March after rain

Permit: None required

Gauge: None

Interpretation of Levels: If it looks high enough, then it is.

Source of More Information: USDA Forest Service, Ocoee Ranger District, Cherokee National Forest, Rt., 1, Parksville, Highway 64, Benton, TN 37307; 615-338-5201.

USDA Forest Service, Chattahoochee National Forest, 601 Broad St., NE, Gainesville, GA 30501; 404-536-0541.

High Country, Inc., 6300 Powers Ferry Rd., Atlanta, GA 30339; 404-892-0828.

Best Guidebooks: Sehlinger et al., *Appalachian Whitewater, Vol. I;* Sehlinger and Otey, *Northern Georgia Canoeing.*

TALKING ROCK CREEK

Sections: (1) Georgia Hwy. 5 in Plaine to Georgia Hwy. 136, Class I-III
(2) Georgia Hwy. 136 to Carters Lake Reservoir, Class I-III

Length of Run: (1) Day trip, 6.5 miles
(2) Day trip, 18 miles

Location: Pickens, Gilmer, Gordon, and Murray Counties, Georgia

Maps: USGS quads: Talking Rock, Oakma

Times Runnable: January to June

Permit: None required

Gauge: Paddlers' gauge at Hwy. 136 Bridge

Source of Levels: None.

How Reported: Feet

Interpretation of Levels: Minimum is 1.5 feet, 4 feet is high, and 5 feet is very high.

Source of More Information: High Country, Inc., 6300 Powers Ferry Rd., Atlanta, GA 30339; 404-892-0828.

Best Guidebooks: Sehlinger et al., *Appalachian Whitewater, Vol. I;* Sehlinger and Otey, *Northern Georgia Canoeing.*

Dick Creek Falls, Section III, Chattooga River, Georgia. A. Photo by Slim Ray.

GENERAL INFORMATION SOURCES FOR GEORGIA AND SOUTH CAROLINA

The National Weather Service Forecast Office in Atlanta can provide levels for rivers in Georgia: 404-762-1186.

They get daily readings for the following:

Coosa River Basin
Etowah River, at Canton
Oostanaula River
  At Resaca
  At Rome
Big Cedar Creek, at Cedartown

Chattahoochee River Basin
Chattahoochee River
  At Helen
  At Norcross
Peachtree Creek, at Atlanta
Chattahoochee River, at Vinings
Sweetwater River, at Austell
Chattahoochee River
  At Whiteburg
  At Columbus
  Release from Walter F. George Lock and Dam
  Release from George W. Andrews Lock and Dam

Flint and Appalachicola River Basins
Flint River
  Near Culloden
  At Montezuma
Kinchafoonee Creek
  At Preston
  At Dawson
Flint River
  At Albany
  At Newton
Seminole River, release from Woodruff Dam
Appalachicola River, at Blountstown, FL

Ocmulgee River Basin
Ocmulgee River
  At Macon
  At Hawkinsville
  At Lumber City

Oconee River Basin
Apalachee River, near Bostwick
Oconee River, at Penfield
Little River, near Eatonton
Murder Creek, at Monticello
Oconee River
  At Milledgeville
  At Dublin

Altamaha River Basin
Altamaha River
  At Baxley
  At Jesup
  At Doctortown

Ogeechee River Basin
Ogeechee River
  At Midville
  At Scarboro
  At Eden

Saltilla and Alapaha River Basins
Saltilla River, at Waycross
Alapaha River, at Stateville

Savannah River and Tributaries
Broad River, at Carlton
Savannah River
  At Augusta
  At Burton's Ferry
  At Clyo

The National Weather Service Forecast Office in Columbia, SC, can provide levels for rivers in South Carolina: 803-822-8135.

They get daily readings for the following gauges:

Congaree River, at Columbia
Great Pee Dee, at Cheraw
Reedy River, at Greenville
Saluda River, at Chappels
Little Pee Dee River, at Galivants Ferry
Broad River, at Gaffney
Great Pee Dee, at Pee Dee
Lynches River, at Effingham
Santee River, at Buckingham Lodge
Edista River, at Givhans Ferry
Black Creek, at Quinby
Broad River, at Blair
Saluda River, at Pelzer
Waccamaw River, at Conway
Black River, at Kingstree
Congaree River, at St. Mathews
Santee River, at Jamestown
North Edista River, at Orangeburg
Wateree River, at Camden
Enoree River, at Whitmire
Broad River, at Carlisle
Tyger River, at Delta
Broad River, at Alston

IDAHO

BOISE RIVER

Sections:
    (1) Troutdale to Willowdale Campground, Class II (III high)
    (2) Barber Park to Ann Harrison Park, Class I when high)
    (3) Glenwood St. Bridge in Boise to Caldwell, Class I

Length of Run:
    (1) Day trip, 10 miles
    (2) Day trip, 6 miles
    (3) 2 days, 34 miles

Location: Boise, Ada Counties, Idaho

Maps: USGS quads: (1) Twin Springs, Arrowrock Res., NE; (2) Lucky Peak, Boise S; (3) Eagle, Star, Middleton, Caldwell

Times Runnable: (1) June to mid-July; (2) All summer; (3) April to mid-June

Permit: None required

Gauge: Boise River, near Glenwood

Source of Levels: National Weather Service, Boise, 208-334-9867.

Idaho Department of Water Resources, 208-327-7900.

How Reported: Cfs

Interpretation of Levels: Optimum is around 600 and 1500 cfs.

Source of More Information: USDA Forest Service, Boise National Forest, 1750 Front St., Boise, ID 83702; 208-334-1516.

Idaho Department of Parks and Recreation, Statehouse, 2200 Warm Springs, Boise, ID 83720; 208-334-2284.

Best Guidebooks: Moore and McClaran, *Idaho Whitewater.*

Further Comments: A remote and pristine run through

Boise River, a tributary of Snake River. Photo by Curt Smith.

giant moss-covered boulders. Watch out for the Irish Railroad Rapid at high levels; it's tough!

BOISE RIVER, MIDDLE FORK

Sections: Troutdale to Willow Creek Campground, Class III

Length of Run: Day trip, 10 miles

Location: Boise and Elmore Counties, Boise National Forest

Maps: USGS Quads: Barber Flat, Sheep Creek, Twin Spring

Times Runnable: Spring

Permit: None required

Gauge: None

Source of Levels: None

Interpretation of Levels: You'll have to estimate the flow. About 1000 cfs is about right.

Source of More Information: USDA Forest Service, Boise National Forest, 1750 Front St., Boise, ID 83702; 208-364-4100.

Idaho Department of Parks and Recreation, Statehouse, 2200 Warm Springs, Boise, ID 83720; 208-334-2284.

Best Guidebooks: Moore and McClaran, *Idaho Whitewater.*

Further Comments: A very fine Class III run through a dense forest of ponderosa pine (*Pinus ponderosa*).

CLEARWATER RIVER, NORTH FORK

Sections: Orogrande Creek to Aquarius Campground, Class IV (One at V when high)

Length of Run: 2 days, 30 miles

Location: Clearwater County, Idaho; Clearwater National Forest

Maps: USGS quads: Sheep Mtn., Clark Mtn., The Nub

Times Runnable: June to July

Permit: None required

Gauge: Clearwater, near Canyon

Source of Levels: National Weather Service, Boise; 208-334-9867.

How Reported: Cfs

Interpretation of Levels: Minimum is around 1000 or 2000 cfs. High is around 10,000 cfs, and the peak flow will be about 30,000 cfs.

Source of More Information: USDA Forest Service, Clearwater National Forest, 12730 Highway 12, Orofino, ID 83544; 208-476-4541.

Idaho Department of Parks and Recreation, Statehouse, 2200 Warm Springs, Boise, ID 83720; 208-334-2284.

Barker River Trips, 2124 Grelle, Lewiston, ID 83501; 208-743-7459.

Best Guidebooks: Graeff, *River Runner's Guide to Idaho;* Moore and McClaren, *Idaho's Whitewater.*

Further Comments: The Irish Railroad rapid is very difficult at high levels (Class V).

HENRYS FORK

Sections: The Lower, from below Lower Mesa Falls to Ashton, Class III

Length of Run: Day trip, 13 miles

Location: Fremont County, Targhee National Forest

Maps: USGS quads: Snake River Butte, Warm River, Ashton

Times Runnable: June to August

Permit: None required

Gauge: Release from Island Park Dam

Source of Levels: Island Park Ranger District, Targhee National Forest, 208-558-7301.

How Reported: Cfs

Interpretation of Levels: Between 1000 and 3000 cfs is optimum.

Source of More Information: USDA Forest Service, Island Park Ranger District, Targhee National Forest, PO Box 220, Island Park, ID 83429; 208-558-7301.

Jacklin's Fly Shop, 105 Yellowstone Ave., West Yellowstone, MT 59758; 406-646-7336.

Idaho Department of Parks and Recreation, Statehouse, 2200 Warm Springs, Boise, ID 83720; 208-334-2284.

Best Guidebooks: Moore and McClaran, *Idaho Whitewater.*

Further Comments: The Lower Henrys Fork is a fantastically beautiful Class III run through a deep and awesome gorge!

JARBRIDGE AND BRUNEAU RIVERS

Sections:
(1) Murphy Hot Springs on the Jarbridge to Indian Hot Springs at the confluence with the Bruneau River, Class II-III (plus two Class IV-V rapids and one at Class VI, all three generally portaged)
(2) Indian Hot Springs to the take-out, Class II-IV

Length of Run:
(1) 2 days, 30 miles
(2) 3 days, 40 miles

Location: Owyhee County, Idaho

Maps: USGS quads: Poison Butte, The Arch, Inside Lake, Indian Hot Springs, Cave Draw, Stiff Tree Draw, Winter Camp, Austin Butte, Crowbar Gulch, Hot Spring, Sugar Valley

Times Runnable: Late April to June

Permit: Mandatory registration is required. Register with the Boise District Office of the Bureau of Land Management. An application form is reproduced in Appendix One. Bureau of Land Management, Boise District, 3948 Development Dr., Boise, ID 83705; 208-334-1582.

Reservations: Not required.

Restrictions: Party size is limited to 12 persons. Pack out your trash. Firepans are suggested.

Gauge: Bruneau near Hot Springs

Source of Levels: National Weather Service, Boise; 208-334-9867

Idaho Department of Water Resources; 208-327-7900.

Bureau of Land Management; 208-334-1582.

How Reported: Cfs

Interpretation of Levels: Minimum is around 1000 or 2000 cfs. Optimum is between 2000 and 8000 cfs. High is around 10,000 cfs, and the peak flow will be about 30,000 cfs.

Source of More Information: BLM; address and phone above.

Hughes River Expeditions, PO Box 217, Cambridge, ID 83610; 208-257-3477.

Idaho Department of Parks and Recreation, Statehouse, 2200 Warm Springs, Boise, ID 83720; 208-334-2284.

Best Guidebooks: Moore and McClaran, *Idaho Whitewater;* BLM, "Bruneau-Jarbridge River Guide."

Further Comments: The Jarbridge and Bruneau flow through absolutely fantastic canyons cut through igneous rock. On Section (2), plan to portage two dangerous wiers. Be on the lookout for low fences spanning the river.

LOCHSA RIVER

Sections:
(1) Papoose Creek to Grave Creek, Class III (III+ high)
(2) Grave Creek to Wilderness Gateway Bridge, Class IV (IV+ high)

(3) Wilderness Gateway Bridge to Split Mountain Pack Bridge, Class IV

(4) Split Mountain Pack Bridge to Lowell, Class III (IV-V high)

Length of Run:
(1) Day trip, 20 miles
(2) Day trip, 13 miles
(3) Day trip, 9 miles
(4) Day trip, 15 miles

Location: Idaho County, Idaho; Nez Perce National Forest

Maps: USGS quads: Cool Water Mtn., Lowell

Times Runnable: Late April to July or August

Permit: None required

Gauge: Lochsa River near Lowell

Source of Levels: National Weather Service, Boise, 208-334-9867.

Idaho Department of Water Resources, 208-327-7900.

How Reported: Cfs

Additional Gauge: A Forest Service staff gauge has been installed on a bridge at Lowell (at Milepost 97).

Source of Levels: USDA Forest Service, Lochsa Ranger District, Clearwater National Forest; 208-926-4275.

Interpretation of Levels: Minimum is around 1000 or 2000 cfs. Optimum is between 2000 and 8000 cfs. High is around 10,000 cfs, and the peak flow will be about 30,000 cfs.

Source of More Information: USDA Forest Service, Lochsa Ranger District, Clearwater National Forest, Rt. 1, Box 398, Kooskia, ID 83539; 208-926-4275.

Holiday River Expeditions of Idaho, Rt. 2, Box 755, Grangeville, ID 83550; 208-983-1518.

Gravity Sports, McCall, ID 83638; 208-634-8530.

Idaho Department of Parks and Recreation, Statehouse, 2200 Warm Springs, Boise, ID 83720; 208-334-2284.

Best Guidebooks: Moore and McClaran, *Idaho Whitewater.*

Further Comments: The Lochsa offers some of the best roadside boating around! Expect to find very continuous rapids with big holes.

OWYHEE RIVER, EAST FORK
(See Oregon for lower sections of the main Owyhee.)

Sections:
(1) Duck Valley Indian Reservation, Class III (with several portages; Class IV high)
(2) Crutchers Crossing to Three Forks, Oregon, Class III (with several portages; IV high)

Length of Run:
(1) 3 days, 50 miles
(2) 3 days, 35 miles

Location: Owyhee County, Idaho; Malheur County, Oregon

Maps: USGS quads: Jarvis Pasture, Red Basin, Piute Basin East, Piute Basin West, Brace Flat, Pickshooter Ridge, Bull Basin Camp

Times Runnable: April to June

Permit: Registration is mandatory. Register with: Bureau of Land Management, PO Box 700, Vale, OR 97918; 503-473-3144.

Gauge: Owyhee near Rome

Source of Levels: National Weather Service, Boise, 208-334-9867.

Idaho Department of Water Resources, 208-327-7900.

National Weather Service, River Forecast Center, Portland; 503-249-0666.

Bureau of Land Management, Rome Launch Site, 503-586-2612.

How Reported: Cfs

Interpretation of Levels: Minimum is around 1000 cfs. Optimum is between 3000 cfs. High is around 4000 to 5000 cfs. A river-wide hole in Garet Gorge becomes unportageable over 8000 cfs. Stay home and watch the Ninja Turtles.

Source of More Information: Idaho Department of Parks and Recreation, Statehouse, 2200 Warm Springs, Boise, ID 83720; 208-334-2284.

Bureau of Land Management, Boise District Office, 3948 Development Ave., Boise, ID 83705; 208-334-1582.

Best Guidebooks: Moore and McClaran, *Idaho Whitewater;* BLM, "Owyhee River Boating Guide".

Further Comments: The East Fork of the Owyhee may provide some of the most remote wilderness boating in the lower 48 states! The river descends through steep-walled canyons, studded with pinnacles and spires. Expect to make numerous difficult portages; leave your portable refrigerator and VCR at home.

PAYETTE RIVER, MAIN

Sections: Banks to a culvert 3 miles above Gardena, Class III

Length of Run: Day trip, 9 miles

Location: Boise County, Boise National Forest

Maps: USGS Quads: Banks, Horseshoe Bend

Times Runnable: Spring and Summer

Permit: None required

Gauge: USGS Payette River near Horseshoe Bend

Source of Levels: National Weather Service, Boise, 208-334-9867.

Idaho Department of Water Resources, 208-327-7900.

How Reported: Cfs

Interpretation of Levels: Optimum flow is between 1500 and 5000 cfs.

Source of More Information: USDA Forest Service, Boise National Forest, 1750 Front St., Boise, ID 83702; 208-364-4100.

Payette River Co., Box 1889, Boise, ID 83701; 208-343-3226.

Idaho Department of Parks and Recreation, Statehouse, 2200 Warm Springs, Boise, ID 83720; 208-334-2284.

Best Guidebooks: Moore and McClaran, *Idaho Whitewater.*

Further Comments: Fun, easy rapids, nice beaches and warm water make the Main Payette an extremely popular beginner and intermediate run!

PAYETTE RIVER, NORTH FORK

Sections:
(1) The Upper-upper Section, Pearl Creek Bridge to Fisher Creek, Class IV (IV+ to V high)
(2) McCall Section, Rotary Peak to Sheep Bridge, Class III
(3) Sheep Bridge to Hartsell Bridge, Class II

(4) Cascade to Cabarton, Class I
(5) Cabarton Run, Cabarton Bridge to Smiths Ferry, Class III
(6) Smiths Ferry to Banks, Class V (V+ high)

Length of Run:
(1) Day trip, 4 miles
(2) Day trip, 2.5 miles
(3) Day trip, 18 miles
(4) Day trip, 10 miles
(5) Day trip, 10 miles
(6) Day trip, 15 miles

Location: Valley and Boise Counties, Idaho; Payette and Boise National Forests

Maps: Granite Lake, McCall, No Business Mtn, Cascade, Smiths Ferry, Banks

Times Runnable: June to August

Permit: None required

Gauge: For Sections (1)-(3), USGS Gauge at McCall Fish Hatchery

Source of Levels: National Weather Service, Boise, 208-334-9867

Idaho Department of Water Resources, 208-327-7900

How Reported: Cfs.

Gauge: For Sections (4)-(6), Cascade Dam Outflow

Source of Levels: National Weather Service, Boise, 208-334-9867.

Idaho Department of Water Resources, 208-327-7900.

Cascade Dam, 208-382-4258.

How Reported: Cfs.

Interpretation of Levels: For Sections (1)–(3), minimum is around 800 cfs, 1000 cfs, 1000 to 1200 is low, and 2000 is optimum. For Sections (4) to (6), minimum is around 1000 cfs. First time boaters will want between 1200 and 1500 cfs. Optimum is between 1000 and 2000 cfs, and high is 2000 to 3000 cfs.

Source of More Information: Idaho Department of Parks and Recreation, Statehouse, 2200 Warm Springs, Boise, ID 83720; 208-334-2284

USDA Forest Service, Emmett Ranger District, Boise National Forest, 1648 N. Washington, Emmett, ID 83617; 208-336-9140.

Gravity Sports, McCall, ID 83638; 208-634-8530.

Best Guidebooks: Moore and McClaran, *Idaho Whitewater.*

Further Comments: The North Fork of the Payette! The Smiths Ferry to Banks section deserves its reputation as the premier expert run in the United States! What other river has rapids that are continuous Class IV and V without let-up for 15 miles?

PAYETTE RIVER, SOUTH FORK

Sections:
(1) Grandjean to Lowman, Class III (IV high)
(2) Canyon Run, Deadwood to Danskin Station, Class IV (IV+ high)
(3) Old Swirley Canyon, Danskin Station to Hot Springs Campground, Class III
(4) Alder Creek Section, Alder Creek Bridge to the confluence of the Middle Fork and the South Fork, Class II
(5) Staircase Section, Deer Creek Bridge to Banks, Class III+ (one at IV, overall Class IV when high)

Length of Run:
(1) 2-3 days, 33 miles
(2) Day trip, 9 miles
(3) Day trip, 5 miles
(4) Day trip, 7 miles
(5) Day trip, 4.5 miles

Location: Boise County, Idaho; Boise National Forest

Maps: USGS Quads: Grandjean, Eight Mile Mtn, Tyee Mtn, Jackson Pk, Lowman, Pine Flat, Garden Valley, Banks

Times Runnable: End of May through July

Permit: None required

Gauge: South Fork of the Payette River near Lowman

Source of Levels: National Weather Service, Boise; 208-334-9867.

Idaho Department of Water Resources; 208-327-7900

How Reported: Cfs

Interpretation of Levels: 500 cfs is minimum and 1000 to 2000 cfs is optimum.

Source of More Information: Idaho Department of Parks and Recreation, Statehouse, 2200 Warm Springs, Boise, ID 83720; 208-334-2284.

USDA Forest Service, Emmett Ranger District, Boise National Forest, 1648 N. Washington, Emmett, ID 83617; 208-336-9140.

Payette River Co., Box 1889, Boise, ID 83701; 208-343-3226.

Best Guidebooks: Moore and McClaran, *Idaho Whitewater.*

Further Comments: The South Fork of the Payette offers the greatest variety of whitewater in the state! Every section is a different experience.

SALMON RIVER, MAIN FORK
Wild and Scenic River

Sections: Main Salmon River of No Return, Corn Creek to Vinegar Creek, Class III (IV high)

Length of Run: 5 days, 85 miles

Location: Idaho County, Idaho; Frank Church-River of No Return Wilderness

Maps: USGS quads: Hot Springs, Kelly Mtn., Burgdorf, Warren, Square Top, Butts Creek, Long Tom Mtn., Waugh Mtn., Sheep Mtn., Hidapoint.

Also: Forest Service River Guide Map: "Middle Fork of the Salmon"; Challis National Forest visitor map; Frank Church-River of No Return Wilderness, North Half; Frank Church-River of No Return Wilderness, South Half.

Times Runnable: Year-round unless it's too cold.

Permit: Permits are required year-round. During the control period, these can be obtained only by reservation (see below). At other times, permits are available at a self-issue station at the launch site, or can be obtained from the North Fork District Office. Apply to:

USDA Forest Service, North Fork Ranger District, Salmon National Forest, River Contact: James F. Wiley, North Fork, ID 83446; 208-865-2383.

Reservations: Advance reservations are required from June 20 through Sept. 7. Before and after this period, reservations are not needed. Application forms are available from the Forest Service beginning October 1 (however, note that a form is also reproduced in Appendix One.) Boaters may apply for launch reservations for the Salmon, Middle Fork of the Salmon, Selway and Snake Rivers on one application form. Applications are accepted by the Forest Service at the address above from December 1 through January 31. Applications received earlier or later are rejected. Only one application per person. There is a $5 non-refundable application fee. Reservations are issued in late February or early March. Unassigned or cancelled launches will be allocated by telephone on a first-come, first-served basis beginning at

8 a.m. on the second Monday after April 15 and continuing through the control period. Call from 8 a.m. to 4:30 p.m. Monday to Friday: 208-865-2383.

Restrictions: The maximum party size is 30 persons. Campsites are assigned. The maximum trip duration is 10 days. Only one trip per person is allowed during the control period. Portable toilets, firepans and ash containers are required.

Gauge: North Fork Lodge gauge

Source of Levels: National Weather Service, Boise, 208-334-9867.

Idaho Department of Water Resources, 208-327-7900.

North Fork Ranger District, 208-865-2383.

How Reported: Cfs

Additional Gauge: Whitebird, Idaho gauge (near end of trip)

How Reported: Cfs

Source of Levels: National Weather Service, Boise, 208-334-9867.

Idaho Department of Water Resources, 208-327-7900.

North Fork Ranger District, 208-865-2383.

Interpretation of Levels: Low is 5000 cfs; medium is 5000 to 10,000, and high is over 20,000 cfs. Average flow in June can approach 50,000 to 60,000 cfs, in July 10,000 to 40,000, and August 5,000 to 10,000. Flow levels in June are considered hazardous by the Forest Service.

Source of More Information: USDA Forest Service, North Fork (address and phone above). These folks will send you three publications: "A User's Guide: Frank Church-River of No Return Wilderness," a "Float Trip Information Sheet," and the flyer entitled, "Centralized Private Float Reservation System for the Salmon, Snake, Middle Fork Salmon and Selway Rivers."

Idaho Department of Parks and Recreation, Statehouse, 2200 Warm Springs, Boise, ID 83720; 208-334-2284.

Canyons, Inc., Box 823. McCall, ID 83638; 208-634-4303.

Echo: The Wilderness Company, 6529 Telegraph Ave., Oakland, CA 94609; 415-652-1600.

Best Guidebooks: Garren, *Idaho River Tours;* Moore and McClaran, *Idaho Whitewater.*

Further Comments: One of the best wilderness runs for beginning and intermediate boaters.

SALMON RIVER, LOWER
Section (1)-(4)

Sections:
    (1) Vinegar Creek to French Creek, Class III
    (2) French Creek to Allison Creek, Class III
    (3) Allison Creek Campground to Riggins, Class III
    (4) Riggins to Whitebird, Class III (IV and V high)

Length of Run:
    (1) Day trip, 7 miles
    (2) Day trip, 8 miles
    (3) Day trip, 7 miles
    (4) 2 days, 30 miles

Location: Idaho and Nez Perce Counties, ID; Nez Perce National Forest

Maps: USGS quads: (1) Kelly Mtn., Burgdorf; (2) Riggins Hot Springs, Kelly Mtn; (3) Riggins, Riggins Hot Springs; (4) Whitebird, Slate Creek, Lucille, Riggins

Times Runnable: From spring to fall, unless the river is too high for your skill and experience

Permit: Voluntary registration at put-in sites (no form in Appendix)

Gauge: Salmon River at Whitebird

Source of Levels: National Weather Service, Boise, 208-334-9867.

Idaho Department of Water Resources, 208-327-7900.

North Fork Ranger District, 208-865-2383.

How Reported: Cfs

Interpretation of Levels: Minimum about 1000 cfs, 4000 to 12,000 is about optimum; with 10,000 to 20,000 being considered high, and over 20,000 extra high.

Source of More Information: Idaho Department of Parks and Recreation, Statehouse, 2200 Warm Springs, Boise, ID 83720; 208-334-2284.

Bureau of Land Management, Route 3, Box 181, Cottonwood, ID 83522; 208-962-3245.

USDA Forest Service, Salmon River Ranger District, Nez Perce National Forest, Whitebird, ID 83554; 208-839-2211.

Canyons, Inc., Box 823, McCall, ID 83638; 208-634-4303.

Best Guidebooks: Moore and McClaran, *Idaho Whitewater.*

SALMON RIVER, LOWER
Section (5)

Sections: (5) Whitebird, Idaho to confluence with Snake and on to the Mouth of the Grande Ronde River, Class II-IV

Length of Run: (5) 3-5 days, 72 miles

Location: Idaho, Lewis and Nez Perce Counties, Idaho

Maps: USGS quads: Whitebird, Fenn, Moughner Pt., Bolles, West Lake, Hoover Pt., Cactus Mtn., Rattlesnake Ridge, Deadhorse Ridge

Times Runnable: April to August

Permit: Required and is self-issuing. Complete at the Lower Salmon put-in point (no form in the Appendix).

Reservations: None required

Restrictions: The maximum party size is 30. Fire pans are required. June flows are considered hazardous to unrunnable by the BLM. Open canoes are not encouraged.

Gauge: Whitebird gauge

Source of Levels: National Weather Service, Boise; 208334-9867.

How Reported: Cfs

Interpretation of Levels: Under 5000 cfs is low; 5000 to 10,000 is considered moderate, and above 10,000 is considered hazardous. Optimum is thought to be around 4000 to 8000 cfs. The BLM discourages boating during June high water when flows can exceed 50,000 cfs.

Source of More Information: Bureau of Land Management, Route 3, Box 181, Cottonwood, ID 83522; 208-962-3245.

Idaho Department of Parks and Recreation, Statehouse, 2200 Warm Springs, Boise, ID 83720; 208-334-2284.

Idaho Guide Service, PO Box 1230; Sun Valley, ID 83353; 208-734-8872.

Canyons, Inc., Box 823, McCall, ID 83638; 208-634-4303.

Best Guidebooks: Garren, *Idaho River Tours;* Interagency Whitewater Committee, *River Information Digest;* Forest Service, "Lower Salmon River Guide;" Graeff, *River Runner's Guide To Idaho;* Moore and McClaren, *Idaho Whitewater.*

Further Comments: Watch out for jet boats!

SALMON RIVER, MIDDLE FORK
Wild and Scenic River

Sections: Boundary Creek to the Main Salmon, Class III+ (IV high)

Length of Run: 5-6 days, 100 miles

Location: Valley County, Idaho; Frank Church-River of No Return Wilderness

Maps: USGS quads: Greyhound Ridge, Chinnook Mtn., Pungo Mtn., Sliderook Ridge, Morton Ridge, Ramey Hill, Apparejo Pt., Pudding Mtn., Longtom Mtn.,

Buttes Creek Pt. Also: Forest Service River Guide Map: "Middle Fork of the Salmon." Challis National Forest Visitor Map. Frank Church-River of No Return Wilderness, North Half; Frank Church-River of No Return Wilderness, South Half.

Times Runnable: May through September

Permit: Required year-round. Obtain from: USDA Forest Service, Middle Fork Ranger District, Challis National Forest, Challis, ID 83226; 208-879-5204.

Reservations: Advance reservations are required June 1 through September 3. Before and after this period launches are given out on a first-come, first-served basis. Application forms are available from the Forest Service beginning October 1 (however, I've reproduced one in Appendix One). Boaters may apply for launch reservations for the Salmon, Middle Fork of the Salmon, Selway and Snake Rivers on one application form. Applications are accepted by the Forest Service at the address above from December 1 through January 31. Applications received earlier or later are rejected. Only one application per person. There is a $5 nonrefundable application fee. Reservations are issued in late February or early March. Unassigned or cancelled launches will be allocated by telephone on a first-come, first-served basis after the initial lottery and continuing through the control period. Call from 8 a.m. to 4:30 p.m. Monday to Friday 208-879-5204.

Restrictions: The maximum party size is 24 persons. Campsites are assigned. There is an 8-day visit limit. Self-contained toilets are required. Only one trip per person is allowed during the control period. Fire pans and ash containers are required. There is a no-show penalty.

Gauge: Painted staff gauge at the Boundary Creek Put-in

Source of Levels: Middle Fork Ranger District, Challis National Forest; 208-879-5204.

How Reported: Feet

Additional Gauge: USGS Salmon River at Middle Fork Lodge

How Reported: Cfs

Interpretation of Levels: In terms of the gauge at the Boundary Creek put-in, optimum is between 4 and 6 feet. Above 6 feet the river is high and dangerous! In terms of the USGS gauge, minimum is 800 cfs; low is 1000 to 2500; medium is 2500 to 4500, and high is over 4500 cfs. During May and June, runoff ranges between 3000 and 10,000 cfs, averaging from 4000 to 6000. The river is more difficult at these times; it is considered very difficult above 6000 cfs. From mid-June through July the river ranges from 1500 to 3000 cfs and is considered ideal.

Source of More Information: USDA Forest Service, Challis (address and phone above). These folks will send you "A User's Guide: Frank Church-River of No Return Wilderness," a descriptive flyer, "Middle Fork of the Salmon River," a "Float Trip Information Sheet," and the flyer entitled "Centralized Private Float Reservation System for the Salmon, Snake, Middle Fork Salmon and Selway Rivers."

Idaho Department of Parks and Recreation, Statehouse, 2200 Warm Springs, Boise, ID 83720; 208-334-2284.

Idaho Guide Service, PO Box 1230, Sun Valley, ID 83353; 208-734-8872.

Canyons Inc., Box 823, McCall, ID 83638; 208-634-4303.

Gravity Sports, McCall, ID 83638; 208-634-8530.

Best Guidebooks: Moore and McClaren, *Idaho Whitewater*; Garren, *Idaho River Tours*.

Further Comments: The Middle Fork of the Salmon is the primo wilderness run in the US of A! Through most of its run through the Frank Church River of No Return Wilderness, the Middle Fork is fast, rough and turbulent. Expect to encounter over 100 individual rapids during your descent!

SALMON RIVER, SOUTH FORK

Sections: The Overnighter, South Fork Salmon Road to Vinegar Creek on the Main Salmon, Class IV (two at V, Class V overall when high—over 6 feet)

Length of Run: 2 Days, 31 miles on the South Fork plus 20 on the Main Salmon

Location: Valley and Idaho Counties; Payette and Nez Pierce National Forests; Frank Church River of No Return Wilderness and Gospel Hump Wilderness

Maps: USGS quads: Williams Peak, Parks Peak, Pilot Peak, Chicken Peak, Wolf Fang Peak, Warren, Burgdorf

Times Runnable: Spring and Summer

Permit: None required

Gauge: Staff gauge on the South Fork of the Salmon River below Krassel Work Center

Source of Levels: Payette National Forest, 208-634-8151.

How Reported: Feet

Interpretation of Levels: Optimum is around 4 to 5 gauge feet. Above 5 feet, this river is huge, and should be run by experts only!

Source of More Information: USDA Forest Service, Payette National Forest, 106 West Park St., PO Box 1026, McCall, ID 83530; 208-634-8151.

Idaho Department of Parks and Recreation, Statehouse, 2200 Warm Springs, Boise, ID 83720; 208-334-2284.

Best Guidebooks: Moore and McClaran, *Idaho Whitewater*.

Further Comments: An excellent two to three day wilderness trip, offering fine water and superb scenery. There are two major Class V rapids that you may choose to portage: Devil Creek and Fall Creek.

Rafting on the Selway River. Photo by Curt Smith.

SELWAY RIVER

Sections: Paradise Launch Point to Race Creek take-out near Selway Falls, Class IV

Length of Run: Day trip, 48 miles

Location: Lemhi County, Idaho; Selway-Bitteroot Wilderness, Salmon National Forest

Maps: USGS quads: Selway Falls, Fog Mountain, Mink Peak, Moose Ridge, Dog Creek, Gardiner Peak

Times Runnable: April to July

Permit: Required year-round. Obtain from: USDA Forest Service, Middle Fork Ranger District, Challis National Forest, Challis, ID 83226; 208-879-5204. Or USDA Forest Service, West Fork Ranger District, Bitteroot National Forest; Darby, MT 59829; 406-821-3269.

Reservations: Advance reservations are required May 15 through July 31. Before and after this period launches are given out on a first-come, first-served basis. Application forms are available from the Forest Service beginning October 1 (however, I've reproduced one in Appendix One). Boaters may apply for launch reservations for the Salmon, Middle Fork of the Salmon, Selway and Snake Rivers on one application form. Applications are accepted by the Forest Service at the address above from December 1 through January 31. Applications received earlier or later are rejected. Only one application per person. There is a $5 nonrefundable application fee. Reservations are issued in late February or early March. Unassigned or cancelled launches will be allocated by telephone on a first-come, first-served basis after the initial lottery and continuing through the control period. Call from 8 a.m. to 4:30 p.m. Monday to Friday 208-879-5204.

Restrictions: The maximum party size is 16 persons. Only one trip per year per person is permitted. Campsites are not assigned. Only one launch is allowed per day. Motors are prohibited. Pack out your trash. Firepans are recommended. Open canoes are considered unsuitable.

Gauge: Staff gauge at the put-in at Paradise

Source of Levels: USDA Forest Service, West Fork Ranger District, Bitteroot National Forest; 406-821-3269.

How reported: Feet

Additional gauge: USGS Selway River near Lowell

Source of Levels: National Weather Service, Boise; 208-334-9867.

Idaho Department of Water Resources, 208-327-7900.

Interpretation of Levels: In terms of the USGS gauge at Lowell, minimum is around 2500 cfs. Low is anywhere on up to 5000; medium is 5000 to 8000, and peak high flow is around 15,000 cfs. n terms of the staff gauge at Paradise, about 2 feet is minimum; 3.5 to 6 feet is optimum, and 6 or over is very high (experts only!).

Source of More Information: USDA Forest Service, addresses and phones above.

Don Hatch River Expeditions, Inc., PO Box 1150, Vernal, UT 84078; 801-789-4316.

Northwest River Company, PO Box 403, Boise, ID 83701; 208-344-7119.

Best Guidebooks: Moore and McClaran, *Idaho Whitewater.*

SNAKE RIVER, BIRDS OF PREY

Sections: Birds of Prey Section, Swan Falls Dam to Walters Ferry, Class II

Length of Run: Day trip, 18 miles

Location: Ada County; Birds of Prey Natural Area

Maps: USGS quads: Walters Butte, Sinker Butte, Initial Pt

Times Runnable: Spring and summer

Permit: None required

Gauge: Release from Swan Falls Dam

Source of Levels: National Weather Service, Boise; 208-327-9867.

Idaho Department of Water Resources; 208-327-7900.

How Reported: Cfs

Interpretation of Levels: Ideal flow is between 10,000 and 20,000 cfs.

Source of More Information: Birds of Prey Natural Area, Bureau of Land Management, Boise District Office, Boise, ID 83705; 208-334-9225.

Idaho Department of Parks and Recreation, Statehouse, 2200 Warm Springs, Boise, ID 83720; 208-334-2284.

MacKay Bar, 3190 Airway, Boise, ID 83705; 208-344-1881.

Best Guidebooks: Moore and McClaran, *Idaho Whitewater.*

Further Comments: This easy and pleasant cruising trip takes you through one of the most dense populations of raptors (eagles, hawks and falcons) in the United States. Bring your camera and binoculars.

SNAKE RIVER, HELLS CANYON
Wild and Scenic River
(See Wyoming for upper sections of the Snake River.)

Sections:
    (1) Hells Canyon Dam to Pittsburgh Landing, Class III-IV
    (2) Pittsburgh Landing to Heller Bar, Class IV

Length of Run:
    (1) 2-3 days, 35 miles
    (2) 2-3 days, 46 miles

Location: Adams County, Idaho and Wallowa County, Oregon; Hells Canyon National Recreation Area and Nez Perce National Forest

Maps: USGS quads: He Devil, Kerman Pt. (15'), Kirkwood Creek, Grave Pt., Wolf Creek, Cactus Mtn., Deadhorse Ridge, Wapshilla Creek, Jim Creek Butte, Limekiln Rapids. Also: Forest Service "Snake River Guide Map"

Times Runnable: April to October

Permit: Required during the regulated period beginning the Friday before Memorial Day and continuing through September 15. Permits are issued to boaters with reservations at the Hells Canyon launch site from 7:45 a.m. to 4:30 p.m., 7 days a week during the regulated season. Permits are not required at other times.

Reservations: Advance reservations and permits are required during the regulated period beginning the Friday before Memorial Day and continuing through September 15. Application forms are available beginning October 1 (however, one is also reproduced in Appendix One of this book). Applications are accepted from December through January. Applications received at other times will rejected. Boaters may apply for launch reservations for the Salmon, Middle Fork of the Salmon, Selway, and Snake Rivers on one application form. Three launches are reserved each day during the control period. A computerized lottery is held in February and the lucky winners have reservations issued beginning the first weekend in

February. Beginning the third Monday in March and continuing through the control period, you may call the Forest Service at the number below to request an unfilled or cancelled slot. If no slot in which you are interested is

Above the take-out on the Snake River, Hell's Canyon. Photo by Curt Smith.

available, you may be placed on a waiting list.

Submit applications to: USDA Forest Service, Hells Canyon National Recreation Area, Wallowa Whitman National Forest, 3620-B Snake River Ave., Lewiston, ID 83501; 208-743-2297.

Restrictions: Confirmation is required. There are penalties for no-shows. The maximum party size is 30 persons. No fires are permitted from July 1 through September 15. Firepans are recommended at other times. Portable toilets are required at the upper or lower Granite sites. Canoes are considered unsuitable craft.

Gauge: Release from Hells Canyon Dam

Source of Levels: Idaho Power Company, 208-383-2864; 800-422-3143 (within Idaho); 800-521-9102 (surrounding states). These friendly and helpful folks answer their area code 208 phone line 24 hours a day and will provide the current release, the projected minimum and the projected maximum for the day, as well as the projection for the next few days. The 800 numbers access a recording that provides the same information. National Weather Service, Boise; 208-334-9867. Idaho Department of Water Resources, 208-327-7900.

How Reported: Cfs

Interpretation of Levels: Volume can range from 3000 to 35,000 cfs. Dam discharges can vary widely during the day. Optimum levels range from 10,000 to 12,000 cfs. Above 15,000 is considered very high. I called the day I wrote this (June 24), and was told that the current release (11 a.m.) was 10,010 cfs, the projected maximum 15,000 and the minimum 8,000.

Source of More Information: USDA Forest Service, above. Write or call for a package of information that includes a bunch of things, the most especially useful of which is the pamphlet, "Some Things Every Hells Canyon Floater Should Know." Pay a dollar and get the Forest Service "Snake River Guide Map."

River Odysseys West, PO Box 579, Coeur D'Alene, ID 83814; 208-765-0841.

Best Guidebooks: Garren, *Idaho River Tours;* Moore and McClaran, *Idaho Whitewater.*

Further Comments: The most famous of Idaho's whitewater rivers, the Snake through Hells Canyon offers fine intermediate to advanced boating. Some folks claim that Hells Canyon is the deepest in the U.S., but I've seen that assertion made for the canyons of the Kings River in California and the Columbia River in Oregon and Washington too. Choose for yourself.

SNAKE RIVER, MILNER AND MURTAUGH

(See Wyoming for sections of the Snake River further upstream.)

| Sections: | (1) Milner Section, Milner Dam to Take-out, Class V (with one Class VI below 12,000 cfs) |
| | (2) Murtaugh Section, Murtaugh to Twin Falls Reservation, Class IV |

| Length of Run: | (1) Day trip, 1.3 miles |
| | (2) Day trip, 22 miles |

Location: Twin Falls and Jerome Counties, Idaho

Maps: USGS quads: Milner Butte, Milner, Murtaugh, Eden, Kimberly, and Twin Falls

Times Runnable: A new diversion project prevents the Milner Section from being runnable except in extreme high-water years. The Murtaugh section is runnable from April to May and September to October.

Permit: None required

Gauge: Snake River at Milner

Source of Levels: National Weather Service, Boise; 208-327-9867.

Idaho Department of Water Resources; 208-327-7900.

Milner Dam, 208-436-4187.

Interpretation of Levels: The Milner run is at its screaming best at high water, 12,000 to 15,000 cfs. Below

12,000 cfs, a river-wide hole forms. Scout before the run and be prepared to portage. At any level, the Milner run is for experts that can shrolp!! For the Murtaugh run, consider minimum to be about 2000 cfs, and ideal between 6000 and 10,000. High is 12,000. Normal peak is around 17,000.

Source of More Information: Bureau of Land Management, PO Box 2B, Shoshone, ID 83352; 208-886-2206.

Best Guidebooks: Moore and McClaran, *Idaho Whitewater.*

Further Comments: The Murtaugh Run offers big-water boating at times of the year when other rivers are getting boney. The Murtaugh is a fine run for advanced boaters, but the Milner is definitely experts only!

ST. JOE RIVER

Sections:	(1) Heller Creek Run, Heller Creek Campground to Spruce Tree Camp ground, Class III-IV.
	(2) Spruce Tree Campground to Gold Creek Campground, Class III
	(3) Gold Creek Run, Gold Creek Camp ground to Bluff, Class III+ (IV high)

Length of Run:	(1) Day trip, 17 miles
	(2) Day trip, 7 miles
	(3) Day trip, 7 miles

Location: Shoshone County, Idaho; Idaho Panhandle (St. Joe) National Forest

Maps: USGS quads: Illinois Peak, Bacon Peak, Simmons Peak, Three Sisters, Thor Mtn., Fishhook Crk., Wallace, Hoyt Mtn, Calder, St Joe

Gauge: Painted gauge at Avery Ranger Station, Idaho Panhandle National Forest

Times Runnable: April-August

Permit: None required

Source of Levels: National Weather Service, Boise; 208-327-9867.

Idaho Department of Water Resources; 208-327-7900.

How Reported: Feet and cfs

Interpretation of Levels: Unrunnably low is around 7 feet (200 cfs). Minimum is 9 feet (1000 cfs). Very high is about 11 feet (5000 cfs). Peak flow can sometimes reach 12 feet (7000 cfs).

Source of More Information: Idaho Panhandle National
Forest (St. Joe), 1201 Ironwood Dr., Coeur D'Alene, ID
83814; 208-765-7223.

Heyburn State Park, Rt. 1, Box 139, Plummer, ID 83851;
208-686-1308.

Best Guidebooks: Moore and McClaran, *Idaho
Whitewater.*

Further Comments: Watch for a logjam on section (1).

Gauge Conversions:

Feet	Cfs
7.0	200
9.0	1000
9.5	1500
10.0	2200
11.0	5000
12.0	7000

GENERAL INFORMATION SOURCES
FOR IDAHO

The Idaho Department of Water Resources can provide current readings for all telemetered or satellite-polled gauges in Idaho. Call 208-327-7900.

Levels for rivers in Idaho can also be obtained by calling the National Weather Service River Forecast Center in Boise, at 208-334-9867. This ring-through recording reports the river stages listed below. Stay on the line for further information.

    South Fork of the Payette River, Deadwood Dam
        outflow
    Fall River, near Squirrel
    Snake River, at Milner (Murtaugh section)
    Bruneau River, near Hot Springs
    Owyhee River, near Rome, Oregon
    Middle Fork and South Forks of the Boise River, near
        their confluence

    South Fork of the Boise River
    Boise River (main), near Glenwood
    South Fork of the Payette River, near Lowman
    North Fork of the Payette River, Cascade Dam outflow
    Payette River (main), at Horseshoe Bend
    Snake River, Hells Canyon Dam outflow
    Salmon River, at Salmon
    Middle Fork of the Salmon River, at Middle Fork
        Lodge
    Little Salmon River, at Riggins
    Salmon River, at Whitebird
    Grande Ronde, at Tracy
    Selway River, near Lowell
    Lochsa River, near Lowell
    South Fork of the Clearwater River, at Stites
    North Fork of the Clearwater River, near Canyon

The Idaho Department of Parks and Recreation serves as a clearinghouse for river information in Idaho:

Idaho Department of Parks and Recreation, Statehouse Mail, Boise, ID 83720; 208-334-2284.

KENTUCKY

CUMBERLAND RIVER, BIG SOUTH FORK

See Tennessee.

CUMBERLAND RIVER, NORTH FORK

Sections: Below the Falls, Cumberland Falls to the mouth of the Laurel River, Class III

Length of Run: Day trip, 11.3 miles

Location: McCreary and Whitley Counties, Kentucky

Maps: USGS quads: Cumberland Falls, Sawyer

Times Runnable: Water levels are best in spring and early summer. This section terminates on Lake Cumberland; when the pool elevation is high, many of the best rapids are covered by the lake, and the flatwater paddle to the take-out can become as long as 7 miles. In the fall and winter the lake is drawn down; more rapids are exposed, and the flatwater paddle is shortened to 3 miles. Check the pool elevation before you go.

Permit: None required

Gauge: Williamsburg Gauge

Source of Levels: Streamflow and the pool elevation of Lake Cumberland are available from: Army Corps of Engineers, Nashville District Recording; 615-736-5455.

How Reported: Cfs

Interpretation of Levels: Minimum streamflow is about 400 or 500 cfs, medium is 800 to 1500, and high is about 2000 to 3000. During the summer, pool elevation at Lake Cumberland is allowed to reach levels as high as 726 feet and in the winter can fall as low as 686 feet. Pool elevations of 718 or lower expose the mid-run rapids, and below 710 expose all the good rapids. Stay home if Lake Cumberland is higher than 718 feet.

Source of More Information: Sheltowee Trace Outfitters, 117 Hawkins Ave., Somerset, KY 42501; 606-679-5026. You can arrange with these folks for a tow across the lake ($5), lunch on the pontoon boat ($5 more), and for shuttle (another $5).

Cumberland Falls State Resort Park, KY-90, Carbin, KY 40701; 606-528-4121.

Best Guidebooks: Sehlinger et al., *Appalachian Whitewater, Vol. I*; Nealy, *Whitewater Home Companion, Vol II*

ELKHORN CREEK

Sections: US 460 bridge to Hwy. 1900 bridge, Class II

Length of Run: Day trip, 7.5 miles

Location: Franklin County, Kentucky, northeast of Frankfort

Maps: USGS quads: Switzer and Polsgrove

Times Runnable: January to mid-June

Permit: None required

Gauge: Hand-painted gauge at US 460 bridge

Source of Levels: Kentuckiana Wilderness Outfitters, 812-923-9546.

How Reported: Feet

Interpretation of Levels: Minimum runnable is 1/2 foot; optimal is 2–3 feet, and high is over 3 feet.

Source of More Information: Kentuckiana Wilderness Outfitters, 812-923-9546.

Best Guidebooks: Sehlinger, *A Canoeing and Kayaking Guide to the Streams of Kentucky.*

ROCKCASTLE RIVER

Sections: The Narrows, Kentucky Highway 80 to Bee Rock Boat Ramp at Cumberland River Lake, Class II–IV

Length of Run: Day trip, 16 miles

Location: Laurel and Pulaski Counties, Kentucky

Maps: USGS quads: Bernstadt, Billows, Ano, Sawyer

Times Runnable: January to late July

Permit: None required

Gauge: Rockcastle River at Bellows, Kentucky

Source of Levels: Army Corps of Engineers, Nashville District, Stream and Lake Recording; 615-736-5455.

Tennessee Valley Authority, 615-632-8000.

How Reported: Cfs

Interpretation of Levels: Minimum is about 300 cfs, and high is about 700.

Source of More Information: Sheltowee Trace Outfitters, 117 Hawkins Ave., Somerset, KY 42501; 606-679-5026.

Best Guidebooks: Sehlinger, *A Canoeing and Kayaking Guide to the Streams of Kentucky.*

THE RUSSELL FORK OF THE LEVISA FORK OF THE BIG SANDY RIVER

Sections: The Breaks, Flanagan Dam on the Pound River to its confluence with the Russell Fork and continuing to Elkhorn City, Class V+

Length of Run: Day trip, 10.3 miles (including 3 miles on the Pound River)

Location: Dickenson County, Virginia; and Pike County, Kentucky; Breaks Interstate Park, Kentucky

Maps: USGS quad: Elkhorn City

El Horrendo Rapid, Russell Fork of the Levisa Fork of the Big Sandy River. Photo by Bill Millard.

Times Runnable: The Army Corps, working with the Pike County Office, schedules two optimal releases of 1300 cfs on two successive October weekends.

Permit: None required

Gauge: Release from John W. Flanagan Dam on the Pound Reservoir

Source of Levels: Pike County Judges' Offices; 606-432-6247.

How Reported: Release schedule

Interpretation of Levels: 1300 cfs is optimum.

Source of More Information: U. S. Army Corps of Engineers, John W. Flanagan Dam; 309-529-5604.

Pike County Offices, 324 Main St., Rm 101, Pikeville, KY 41501; 606-432-6247.

Precision Rafting, PO Box 185, Friendsville, MD 21531; 301-746-5290.

Best Guidebooks: Sehlinger et al., *Appalachian Whitewater Vol. I.*

Further Comments: The Russell Fork is the greatest and most popular of the Eastern hair runs, and since 1987, the most difficult commercially rafted river in the East. If it's your goal to prove yourself as a demented expert, head for the Russell Fork. Bring a videocam for El Horrendo. See if you can arrange for helicopter support.

Source of More Information: USDA Forest Service, Stanton Ranger District, Daniel Boone National Forest, 705 W. College Avenue, Stanton, KY 40380; 606-663-2852.

Best Guidebooks: Sehlinger, *A Canoeing & Kayaking Guide to the Streams of Kentucky.*

UPPER RED RIVER

Sections: Hwy. 746 to Hwy. 715 (Wolfe County), Class II (III)

Length of Run: Day trip, 11.1 miles

Location: Wolfe and Menifee Counties, Kentucky

Maps: USGS quads: Lee City, Cannel City, Hazel Green, Pomeroyton

Times Runnable: January to early May (with luck)

Permit: None required

Gauge: None, visual inspection required.

Source of Levels: Stanton Ranger District, Daniel Boone National Forest; 606-663-2852.

How Reported: Runnable or unrunnable

Interpretation of Levels: Rangers check the Upper Red daily and provide nontechnical (high, low, flood) representations of water conditions.

GENERAL INFORMATION SOURCES
FOR KENTUCKY

The U.S. Army Corps of Engineers Nashville District Office maintains a recorded report of Cumberland River Basin reservoir levels and streamflows at 617-736-5455. At the end of the long message, you'll hear readings for the following gauges:

Cumberland River, near Williamsburg
Rockcastle River, near Bellows
Big South Fork of the Cumberland River near Stearns

MAINE

DEAD RIVER

Sections: Grand Falls to West Forks at the confluence with the Kennebec, Class II-III (IV when high)

Length of Run: Day trip, 15 miles

Location: Somerset County, Maine

Maps: USGS quads: Pierce Pond, The Forks

Times Runnable: There are generally two high-volume releases of about 7000 cfs during May that produce Class IV water. At other times during the late spring and early summer, Kennebec Water Power Company schedules low to medium releases that yield Class II and III difficulty. Call the Kennebec Water Power Company to find out the schedule.

Permit: Camping and fire permit required: Bureau of Forestry, Department of Conservation, State of Maine, State House Station 22, Augusta, ME 04333; 207-289-2791.

Gauge: Release from Kennebec Water Power Company's Long Falls Dam on Flagstaff Lake

Source of Levels: Kennebec Water Power Company; 207-872-6624

National Weather Service, Portland; 207-773-0352

How Reported: Feet

Interpretation of Levels: Low to medium releases are usually around 900 to 1200 cfs, and give this section a difficulty in the range of Class II to III. High volume releases are around 7000 cfs, and these up the difficulty to Class IV.

Source of More Information: Eastern River Expeditions, Inc., Box 113, Greenville, ME 04441; 207-695-2411.

Northern Outdoors, PO Box 100, The Forks, ME, 04985; 207-663-4466.

Rafting in Ripogenus Gorge, West Branch of the Penobscot. Photo by Eastern River Expeditions.

Unicorn Rafting Adventures, PO Box T, Brunswick, ME; 207-725-2255.

Best Guidebooks: Connelly and Porterfield, *Appalachian Whitewater, Vol. III;* Appalachian Mountain Club, *AMC Whitewater Guide: Maine;* Gabler, *New England Whitewater.*

KENDUSKEAG STREAM

Sections: Kenduskeag to Bangor, Class II-III+

Length of Run: Day trip, 6 miles

Location: Penobscot County, Maine

Maps: USGS quads: Bangor

Times Runnable: March to June

Permit: Camping and fire permit is required: Bureau of Forestry, Department of Conservation, State of Maine, State House Station 22, Augusta, ME 04333; 207-289-2791.

Gauge: None. Impression only.

Bill Zollinger heads straight into the teeth of Magic Falls during one of the early descents of the Kennebec Gorge. Photo by Eric Bader.

Source of Levels: Hanson Sports, Bangor; 207-989-7250.

How Reported: Impression

Interpretation of Levels: Minimum is about 300 cfs (use the W.D.S. method). Too high is floodstage.

Source of More Information: Eastern River Expeditions, Inc., Box 113, Greenville, ME 04441; 207-695-2411.

Unicorn Rafting Adventures, PO Box 50, The Forks, ME 04985; 207-663-2258.

Best Guidebooks: Connelly and Porterfield, *Appalachian Whitewater, Vol. III;* Appalachian Mountain Club, *AMC Whitewater Guide: Maine.*

KENNEBEC RIVER

Sections: (1) Kennebec River Gorge, George Harris Station Dam to Carry Brook, Class III-IV+
              (2) Carry Brook to Crusher Pool, Class II-III

Length of Run: (1) Day trip, 4 miles
              (2) Day trip, 9 miles

Location: Somerset County, Maine

Maps: USGS quads: Moosehead Lake (15'), Brassua Lake (15')

Times Runnable: May to October after dam releases

Permit: Check in at the gate with the Central Maine Power

Co. personnel. In addition, a camping and fire permit are required: Bureau of Forestry, Department of Conservation, State of Maine, State House Station 22, Augusta, ME 04333; 207-289-2791.

Gauge: Release from George Harris Station Dam

Source of Levels: Central Maine Power Co., 207-672-4848.

Eastern River Expeditions, 207-695-2248.

Northern Outdoors, 207-663-4466.

How Reported: Cfs

Interpretation of Levels: Levels may vary widely according to power demands. Minimum is about 2000 cfs. The Kennebec can be run much higher, according to your skill and experience.

Source of More Information: Eastern River Expeditions, Inc., Box 113, Greenville, ME 04441; 207-695-2411.

Unicorn Rafting Adventures, PO Box T, Brunswick, ME; 207-725-2255.

Best Guidebooks: Connelly and Porterfield, *Appalachian Whitewater, Vol. III;* Appalachian Mountain Club, *AMC Whitewater Guide: Maine.*

Further Comments: Pioneered just over a decade ago, the Kennebec has now become one of the classic whitewater touring rivers in the United States. Over 30,000 people go down the Kennebec in commercial rafts every year.

KENNEBEC RIVER, EAST OUTLET OF MOOSEHEAD LAKE

Sections: Moosehead Lake Route 15 Bridge to Indian Pond, Class II-III

Length of Run: Day trip, 3 miles

Location: Somerset County, Maine

Maps: USGS quads: Moosehead Lake, Brassau Lake

Times Runnable: May to October

Permit: A camping and fire permit is required: Bureau of Forestry, Department of Conservation, State of Maine, State House Station 22, Augusta, ME 04333; 207-289-2791.

Gauge: Release from dam at Moosehead Lake

Source of Levels: Kennebec Water Power Co., 207-872-6624.

How Reported: Cfs

Interpretation of Levels: 1200 cfs is the standard release.

Source of More Information: Eastern River Expeditions, Inc., Box 113, Greenville, ME 04441; 207-695-2411.

Unicorn Rafting Adventures, PO Box T, Brunswick, ME; 207-725-2255.

Best Guidebooks: Connelly and Porterfield, *Appalachian Whitewater, Vol. III;* Appalachian Mountain Club, *AMC Whitewater Guide: Maine.*

MATTAWAMKEAG RIVER

Sections: Mattawamkeag Wilderness Park (Scatterrack Rapid) to Mattawamkeag, Class II-IV+

Length of Run: Day trip, 7 miles

Location: Penobscot County, Maine

Maps: USGS quads: Mattawamkeag, Wytopitlock

Times Runnable: May to July

Permit: Camping and fire permit required: Bureau of Forestry, Department of Conservation, State of Maine, State House Station 22, Augusta, ME 04333; 207-289-2791.

Gauge: None. Impression only.

Source of Levels: Mattawamkeag Wilderness Park, 207-736-4881.

How Reported: Feet

Interpretation of Levels: There is no gauge, but Mr. Davis at the Mattawamkeag Wilderness Park drives by the river daily and can report his impression. In general, if it looks high enough, it is.

Source of More Information: Mattawamkeag Wilderness Park, Box 104, Mattawamkeag, ME 04459; 207-736-4881.

Eastern River Expeditions, Inc., Box 113, Greenville, ME 04441; 207-695-2411.

Unicorn Rafting Adventures, PO Box T, Brunswick, ME; 207-725-2255.

Best Guidebooks: Connelly and Porterfield, *Appalachian*

Whitewater, Vol. III; Appalachian Mountain Club, *AMC Whitewater Guide: Maine.*

Dusk silhouettes a canoeist at Class V+ Hulling Machine on the East Branch of the Penobscot. Photo by Zip Kellogg.

PENOBSCOT RIVER, EAST BRANCH

Sections: Mattagamon Dam on Grand Lake to logging road on right side of river, Class III-V

Length of Run: Day trip, 12 miles

Location: Penobscot County, Maine

Maps: USGS quads: Traveler Mtn., Shir Pond, Stacyville

Times Runnable: May to June after dam releases

Permit: A camping and fire permit is required: Bureau of Forestry, Department of Conservation, State of Maine, State House Station 22, Augusta, ME 04333; 207-289-2791.

The fee for camping in the Penobscot River Corridor is $3 per night for Maine residents and $6 for nonresidents.

Gauge: Release from Mattawamkeag Dam on Grand Lake

Source of Levels: Bangor Hydroelectric Company, PO Box 932, Bangor, ME 04401; 207-945-5621.

How Reported: Cfs

Interpretation of Levels: 1000 cfs is about minimum.

Source of More Information: Baxter State Park, 64 Balsam Dr., Millinocket, ME 04462; 207-695-2248.

Eastern River Expeditions, Inc., Box 113, Greenville, ME 04441; 207-695-2411.

Northern Outdoors, PO Box 100, The Forks, ME 04985; 207-663-4466.

Unicorn Rafting Adventures, PO Box T, Brunswick, ME; 207-725-2255.

Best Guidebooks: Connelly and Porterfield, *Appalachian Whitewater, Vol. III;* Appalachian Mountain Club, *AMC Whitewater Guide: Maine.*

PENOBSCOT RIVER, SOUTH BRANCH

Sections: Canada Falls Dam to Pittston Farm, Class III-V+ (many of the harder drops can be portaged)

Length of Run: Day trip, 3.5 miles

Location: Somerset County, Maine

Maps: USGS quads: Seboomook Lake

Times Runnable: May to September, and when the dam releases water

Permit: A camping and fire permit is required: Bureau of Forestry, Department of Conservation, State of Maine, State House Station 22, Augusta, ME 04333; 207-289-2791.

The fee for camping in the Penobscot River Corridor is $3 per night for Maine residents and $6 for nonresidents, plus entry fee at Golden Road ($4 for residents, $8 for nonresidents).

Gauge: Release from Canada Falls Dam

Source of Levels: Great Northern Paper Co., 207-723-6743.

How Reported: Cfs

Interpretation of Levels: Minimum is about 300 cfs.

Source of More Information: Eastern River Expeditions, Inc., Box 113, Greenville, ME 04441; 207-695-2411.

Northern Outdoors, PO Box 100, The Forks, ME 04985; 207-663-4466.

Unicorn Rafting Adventures, PO Box T, Brunswick, ME; 207-725-2255.

Best Guidebooks: Connelly and Porterfield, *Appalachian Whitewater, Vol. III;* Appalachian Mountain Club, *AMC Whitewater Guide: Maine.*

Further Comments: Numerous steep ledges and falls.

PENOBSCOT RIVER, WEST BRANCH

Sections: (1) Ripogenus Gorge, Ripogenus Dam to Big Eddy, Class V
(2) Lower West Branch, Big Eddy to Pockwockamus, Class III-IV

Length of Run: (1) Day trip, 1.5 miles
(2) Day trip, 17 miles

Location: Piscataquis County, Maine

Maps: USGS quads: Harrington Lake, Katahdin

Times Runnable: April through October

Permit: A camping and fire permit is required: Bureau of Forestry, Department of Conservation, State of Maine, State House Station 22, Augusta, ME 04333; 207-289-2791.

The fee for camping in the Penobscot River corridor is $3 per night for Maine residents and $6 for nonresidents, plus entry fee at Golden Road ($4 for residents, $8 for nonresidents).

Gauge: Release from Great Northern Power Company's McKay Power Station

Neil Erickson makes this descent of Nesowadnehunk Falls look easy. Photo by Jim Michaud.

Source of Levels: Great Northern Paper Company; 207-723-6743

How Reported: Cfs

Interpretation of Levels: Flows are constant, usually around 1500 to 3500 cfs.

Source of More Information: Eastern River Expeditions, Inc., Box 113, Greenville, ME 04441; 207-695-2411.

Northern Outdoors, PO Box 100, The Forks, ME 04985; 207-663-4466.

Unicorn Rafting Adventures, PO Box T, Brunswick, ME; 207-725-2255.

Best Guidebooks: Connelly and Porterfield *Appalachian Whitewater, Vol. III;* Appalachian Mountain Club, *AMC Whitewater Guide: Maine.*

Further Comments: An article that appeared in Canoe Magazine in 1977 called the Ripogenus Gorge unrunnable. So much for their crystal ball—it's now an extremely popular run both for commercial rafters and decked boaters!

PENOBSCOT RIVER, WEST BRANCH, SEBOOMOOK SECTION

Sections: Seboomook Section, McKay Power Station at Seboomook Lake to Roll Dam Camping Area, Class III-IV

Length of Run: Day trip, 2.5 miles

Location: Somerset County, Maine

Maps: USGS quads: North East Carry

Times Runnable: From May to September after releases from McKay Power Station

Permit: You must register with the Great Northern Paper Company as you enter their land.

Gauge: Release from the McKay Power Station at Seboomook Lake

Source of Levels: Great Northern Paper Company recording; 207-723-6743

How Reported: Cfs

Interpretation of Levels: Minimum is about 300 cfs.

Source of More Information: Eastern River Expeditions, Box 113, Greenville, ME 04441; 207-695-2411.

Best Guidebooks: Connelly and Porterfield, *Appalachian Whitewater III.*

Further Comments: Fantastic glacial terrain and plenty of ledge-pool rapids make the Seboomook run a breathtaking trip! Don't expect to find a dam at Roll Dam; there isn't one!

PISCATAQUIS RIVER

Sections: Blanchard to Route 15 bridge, Class II-III+

Length of Run: Day trip, 10 miles

Location: Piscataquis County, Maine

Maps: USGS quads: Greenville, Kingsbury

Times Runnable: April to June

Permit: A camping and fire permit is required: Bureau of Forestry, Department of Conservation, State of Maine, State House Station 22, Augusta, ME 04333; 207-289-2791.

Gauge: Piscataquis near Dover-Foxcroft

Source of Levels: National Weather Service, Portland; 207-773-0352.

How Reported: Feet

Interpretation of Levels: This is a natural flow river. Minimum is about 200 cfs.

Source of More Information: Eastern River Expeditions, Inc., Box 113, Greenville, ME 04441; 207-695-2411.

Unicorn Rafting Adventures, PO Box T, Brunswick, ME; 207-725-2255.

Best Guidebooks: Connelly and Porterfield, *Appalachian Whitewater, Vol. III;* Appalachian Mountain Club, *AMC Whitewater Guide: Maine.*

Gauge Conversions: Piscataquis near Dover-Foxcroft

Feet	Cfs	Feet	Cfs	Feet	Cfs
2.0	82	4.0	1050	6.5	3668
2.4	194	4.2	1219	7.0	4280
2.6	259	4.4	1402	7.5	4923
2.8	337	4.6	1590	8.0	5560
3.0	427	4.8	1778	8.5	6216
3.2	530	5.0	1978	9.0	6900
3.4	646	5.5	2516	9.5	7616
3.6	772	6.0	3100	10.0	8360
3.8	905	—	—	—	—

RAPID RIVER

Sections: Richardson Lake to Umbagog Lake, Class III-IV

Length of Run: Day trip, 7 miles

Location: Oxford County, Maine

Maps: USGS quads: Oquossoc (15')

Times Runnable: July to August

Permit: None required

Gauge: Release from Richardson Lake

Source of Levels: Union Water Power Company; 207-784-4501.

How Reported: Cfs

Interpretation of Levels: Union Water Power Company releases water into the Rapid River only during the summer, in order to augment flows in the Androscoggin River downstream. Releases of 1000 cfs are usually enough for good boating.

Source of More Information: Downeast Whitewater, PO Box 119, Center Conway, NH 03813; 603-447-3002.

Best Guidebooks: Armstead, *Whitewater Rafting in Eastern North America, 2nd Ed.*

Further Comments: One of the steeper commercially rafted rivers in the East, the Rapid River drops 360 feet through heavily glaciated terrain during the course of this run!

SHEEPSCOT RIVER

Sections: North Whitefield to Head Tide, Class I-II

Length of Run: Day trip, 13 miles

Location: Lincoln County, Maine

Maps: USGS quads: Vassalboro, Wiscasset

Times Runnable: March to May

Permit: A camping and fire permit is required: Bureau of Forestry, Department of Conservation, State of Maine, State House Station 22, Augusta, ME 04333; 207-289-2791.

Gauge: None

Source of Levels: Probably none, but you could always try the Merrimack Valley Paddlers' recording at 603-432-6870.

Interpretation of Levels: The Sheepscot is a natural flow river. Check at the put-in. If it looks like there is enough water, then there is.

Source of More Information: Eastern River Expeditions, Inc., Box 113, Greenville, ME 04441; 207-695-2411.

Unicorn Rafting Adventures, PO Box T, Brunswick, ME; 207-725-2255.

Best Guidebooks: Connelly and Porterfield, *Appalachian Whitewater, Vol. III;* Appalachian Mountain Club, *AMC Whitewater Guide: Maine.*

SOUADABSCOOK STREAM

Sections: Manning Mill Bridge to Rt. 1A in Hampden, Class II-V+

Length of Run: Day trip, 4 miles

Location: Penobscot County, Maine

Maps: USGS quad: Bangor

Times Runnable: March to June

Permit: A camping and fire permit is required: Bureau of Forestry, Department of Conservation, State of Maine, State House Station 22, Augusta, ME 04333; 207-289-2791.

Gauge: None

Source of Levels: Probably none, but you could always try the Merrimack Valley Paddlers' recording at 603-432-6870.

Interpretation of Levels: The Souadabscook is a natural flow stream. If water is flowing through the trees upstream of the put-in, then there is plenty of water. The minimum is around 500 cfs.

Source of More Information: Eastern River Expeditions, Inc., Box 113, Greenville, ME 04441; 207-695-2411.

Unicorn Rafting Adventures, PO Box T, Brunswick, ME; 207-725-2255.

Best Guidebooks: Connelly and Porterfield, *Appalachian Whitewater, Vol. III;* Appalachian Mountain Club, *AMC Whitewater Guide: Maine.*

ST. CROIX RIVER

(Not to be confused with the St. Croix River on the Minnesota/Wisconsin Border)

Sections: Vanceboro to Loon Bay, Class II (one rapid, Little Falls, at IV)

Length of Run: 1-2 days, 21 miles

Location: Washington County, Maine, along the Maine-New Brunswick border

Maps: USGS quads: Vanceboro (15'), Kellyland (15') and Forest (15'), plus Canadian topographic maps: 21 g/11 West McAdam, 21 g/6 West Rolling Run. Canadian topographic maps are available from: Map Distribution Office, Dept. of Energy, Mines and Resources, 615 Booth St., Ottawa, Ontario, Canada.

Times Runnable: May to mid-June

Permit: A camping and fire permit is required: Bureau of Forestry, Department of Conservation, State of Maine State House Station 22, Augusta, ME 04333; 207-289-2791.

Gauge: St. Croix near Baring, ME

Source of Levels: National Weather Service, Portland; 207-773-0352.

How reported: Feet

Interpretation of Levels: 700 cfs is about minimum. Average flow in March is about 1000 cfs, an optimum level.

Source of More Information: Eastern River Expeditions, Inc., Box 113, Greenville, ME 04441; 207-695-2411.

Northern Outdoors, PO Box 100, The Forks, ME 04985; 207-663-4466.

Best Guidebooks: Appalachian Mountain Club, *AMC Whitewater Guide: Maine.*

Gauge Conversions:

Feet	Cfs	Feet	Cfs	Feet	Cfs
4.0	553	5.4	1581	7.5	4510
4.4	774	5.6	1770	8.0	5509
4.6	913	5.8	1977	8.5	6636
4.8	1068	6.0	2204	9.0	7906
5.0	1227	6.5	2838	9.5	9304
5.2	1403	7.0	3620	10.0	10860

GENERAL INFORMATION SOURCES FOR MAINE

The Great Northern Power Company maintains a recording that reports releases from the dams that they control; 207-723-6743.

Penobscot River, South Branch, release from Canada Falls Dam
Penobscot River, West Branch, release from Seboomook Dam
Penobscot River, West Branch, release from McKay Power Station

The US Army Corps of Engineers and other managers of water projects coordinate many of the scheduled releases through the Appalachian Mountain Club. Call the office of the Appalachian Mountain Club in Boston; they should have a printed list they can mail out (I don't recommend that you call the New England Division of the Army Corps—they don't want to hear from you). Appalachian Mountain Club, New England Rivers Center, Boston, 5 Joy St., Boston, MA; 617-523-0636.

The Northern New England Hydrological Service Area of the National Weather Service in Portland, Maine can provide gauge readings for Maine and New Hampshire, call: 207-773-0352.

Reports are available for the following Maine gauges; levels are reported in feet except where indicated otherwise:

St. John River
    At Fort Kent
    At Dickey
    At Nine-Mile Bridge

Aroostook River
    At Washburn
    At Masaidis
Penobscot Riverz
    At West Enfield
    At Eddington
Kennebec River
    At Sidney
    Release from Wyman Dam near Bingham (cfs)
    Weston Station near Skachegan (cfs)
Androscoggin River
    At Auburn
    At Rumford
    At Gulf Island (cfs)
Little Androscoggin River, at West Paris
Moose River, at Brassua
Dead River, release from Long Falls Dam on Flagstaff Lake
Dennys River, at Dennysville
Royal River, at Yarmouth
Presumpscot River, at Westbrook
Fish River, at Fort Kent
St. Croix River, at Baring
Nezinscot River, at Turner
Piscataquis River, near Dover-Foxcroft
Wild River, at Guiliad
Swift River, at Roxbury
Carrabasset River, at North Anson
Saco River
    At Hiram Falls (cfs)
    At West Boxton (cfs)

MARYLAND

ANTIETAM CREEK

Sections: Poffenburger Rd. to Harper's Ferry Road, Class I-II

Length of Run: 1-2 days, 21.5 miles, shorter sections possible

Location: Washington County, Maryland

Maps: USGS quads: Funkstown and Keedysville

Times Runnable: Winter and spring

Permit: None required

Gauge: Staff gauge on Burnside Bridge, 1 mile south of Hwy. 34

Source of Levels: National Weather Service River Forecast Center, Harrisburg; 717-234-6812

How Reported: Feet

Additional Gauge: Extrapolate from the USGS gauge on the Monocacy River at Frederick, MD.

Source of Levels: National Weather Service River Forecast Center, Harrisburg; 717-234-2251.

How Reported: Feet

Interpretation of Levels: In terms of the Burnside gauge, low is about 3 feet. In terms of the Frederick gauge, low is about 4 feet for upper sections and 3 feet for lower sections; high is about 6.5 or 7 feet at Frederick.

Source of More Information: Antietam National Battlefield, PO Box 158, Sharpsburg, MD 21782; 301-432-5124.

C&O Canal National Historic Park, PO Box 4, Sharpsburg, MD 21782; 301-739-4200.

Best Guidebooks: Grove et al., *Appalachian Whitewater, Vol. II.*

Further Comments: Portage the dam at Devil's Backbone Park. Watch for downed trees.

GUNPOWDER FALLS

Sections: Route 1 to Route 40, Class II-III (III-IV high)

Length of Run: Day trip, 3.3 miles

Location: Baltimore County, Maryland

Maps: USGS quads: White Marsh

Times Runnable: Winter and spring after heavy rain

Permit: None required

Gauge: Paddlers' gauge on Rt. 1 at the put-in

Source of Levels: Visual inspection only

How Reported: Feet

Interpretation of Levels: Minimum is 0 feet at the Route 1 gauge. Optimum is 1 to 2 feet. High is 4 feet, still a good level for competent paddlers (Class III-IV).

Source of More Information: Gunpowder Falls State Park, 10815 Harford Rd., Glen Arm, MD 21057; 301-592-2897.

Best Guidebooks: Grove et al., *Appalachian Whitewater, Vol II;* Gertler, *Maryland and Delaware Canoe Trails.*

POTOMAC RIVER (MAIN)

See Virginia/District of Columbia.

POTOMAC RIVER, NORTH BRANCH

Sections:
(1) Gormania, West Virginia to Kitzmiller Maryland, Class III-IV at moderate levels
(2) Barnum, West Virginia to Bloomington, Maryland, Class II-III

Length of Run:
(1) Day trip, 11 miles
(2) Day trip, 6 miles

Location: (1) Mineral and Grant Counties, West Virginia and Garrett County, Maryland; (2) Garrett County, Maryland

Maps: (1) USGS quads: Gorrnan, Kitzmiller, Mount Storm; (2) USGS quads: Kitzmiller, Westernport

First big ledge below the railroad bridge on the North Branch of the Potomac, above Kitzmiller. Photo by Hoyt Reel.

Times Runnable: (1) Winter and spring after snowmelt or heavy rain; (2) Late summer and early fall dam releases from Bloomington Lake; water is released only several days a year, mainly from August to October.

Permit: None required

Gauge: For Section (1), USGS gauge at Kitzmiller

Source of Levels: National Weather Service River Forecast Center, Harrisburg; 717-234-6812.

National Weather Service, Washington; 703-260-0305.

How Reported: Feet

Additional Gauge: For Section (1), Steyer gauge, 2 miles downstream from put-in on river left

Source of Levels: Visual inspection only

How Reported: Feet

Interpretation of Levels: On Section (1) in terms of the Kitzmiller gauge, the minimum is 4.5 feet and high is 6.5 feet. In terms of the Steyer gauge, the minimum is 2.9, 4.2 is high.

Additional Gauge: For Section (2), release from Randolph Jennings Dam on Bloomington Lake

Source of Levels: US Army Corps of Engineers, Baltimore; 301-962-4616.

How Reported: Release schedule, flow in cfs

Interpretation of Levels: On Section (2), minimum is about 600 cfs, and the maximum release is around 1250 cfs.

Corkscrew Ledge, North Branch of the Potomac above Kitzmiller. Photo by Hoyt Reel.

Source of More Information: Potomac State Forest, Rt. 3, Box 256, Deer Park, MD 21550; 301-334-2038.

Cheat River Outfitters, PO Box 134; Albright, WV 25619; 304-329-2029.

Blue Ridge Outfitters, PO Box 750; Harpers Ferry, WV 25425; 304-725-3444.

Best Guidebooks: Grove et al., *Appalachian Whitewater, Vol. II;* Davidson et al., *Wildwater West Virginia;* Gertler, *Maryland and Delaware Canoe Trails.*

Gauge Conversions: USGS North Branch of the Potomac at Kitzmiller

Feet	Cfs	Feet	Cfs	Feet	Cfs
4.5	706	5.5	1528	6.4	2767
4.6	768	5.6	1641	6.5	2937
4.7	834	5.7	1760	7.0	3900
4.8	903	5.8	1885	7.5	5003
4.9	977	5.9	2016	8.0	6300
5.0	1054	6.0	2153	8.5	7874
5.1	1135	6.1	2297	9.0	9700
5.2	1220	6.2	2447	9.5	11670
5.3	1317	6.3	2603	10.0	13890
5.4	1420	—	—	—	—

SAVAGE RIVER

Sections: Below the Savage River Dam to confluence with the North Branch of the Potomac, Class III-IV at lower levels (Class IV-V at high)

Length of Run: Day trip, 4 miles

Location: Garrett County, Maryland

Maps: USGS quads: Westernport, Barton, Bittinger

Times Runnable: Paddling on the Savage River is dependent on releases from the Savage River Dam on the Westernport Reservoir. These are scheduled about four times a year, generally in March, May, September, and November. Two releases will be for races; some parts of the river are restricted at that time.

Permit: None required

Gauge: Release from the Savage River Dam on Westernport Reservoir

How Reported: Release schedules and anticipated flows in cfs

Source of Levels: National Weather Service River Forecast Center, Harrisburg; 717-234-6812.

National Weather Service, Washington; 703-260-0305.

Additional Gauge: USGS Savage River at Savage, MD

Source of Levels: National Weather Service, Washington, DC; 202-899-7378.

National Weather Service, Washington; 703-899-7378.

National Weather Service River Forecast Center, Harrisburg; 717-234-2251.

How Reported: Feet

Interpretation of Levels: Below 800 cfs is considered low (about Class III-IV); from 800 to 1200 cfs is medium (Class IV); above 1200 cfs is high, Class IV-V.

Source of More Information: Savage River State Forest, Rt. 2, Box A-63, Grantsville, MD 21536; 301-895-5759.

Canoe Cruisers of Greater Washington, DC, Inc., PO Box 572, Arlington, VA 22216.

Savage River at 3,000 cfs. Photo by Bill Kirby.

Best Guidebooks: Gertler, *Maryland and Delaware Canoe Trails;* Grove et al., *Appalachian Whitewater, Vol. II.*

Further Comments: About a mile or so downstream of the put-in is the 5-foot-high Piedmont Dam. A metal flume on the left provides a safe route.

Gauge Conversions: USGS Savage River at Savage, MD, gauge feet to cfs

Feet	Cfs	Feet	Cfs
0.6	2	3.8	1214
0.8	6.8	4.0	1401
1.0	15.3	4.2	1605
1.2	28.0	4.4	1827
1.4	61.0	4.6	2066
1.6	93.9	4.8	2323
1.8	135.9	5.0	2600
2.0	187.8	5.2	2895
2.2	250.4	5.4	3211
2.4	324.3	5.6	3546
2.6	410.2	5.8	3902
2.8	508.8	6.0	4279
3.0	620.8	6.2	4678
3.2	746.6	6.4	5099
3.4	887.0	6.6	5542
3.6	1043.0	6.8	6008

YOUGHIOGHENY RIVER, TOP SECTION
(See Pennsylvania for a lower section.)

Sections: Top, Swallow Falls State Park to Sang Run, Class IV-V

Length of Run: Day trip, 6 miles

Location: Garrett County, Maryland

Maps: USGS quads: Sang Run, Oakland

Times Runnable: The upper half of this section is dependent on natural flow, and is runnable during winter or spring after snowmelt. Halfway down, Hoyes Run joins the Top Yough, and, by putting in there, you can paddle after releases by the Pennsylvania Electric Project at Deep Creek Lake into Hoyes Run.

Check with the Pennsylvania Electric Project for the release schedule; usually the best times to expect releases are weekdays. Releases, typically 600 cfs in volume, often last as little as three hours, but by starting out with the first crest of the release, it is possible to spend five hours on the river without running out of water.

Permit: None required

Gauge: USGS gauge at Friendsville, MD

Source of Levels: National Weather Service River Forecast Center, Harrisburg; 717-234-6812.

National Weather Service, Maryland; 301-260-0305.

National Weather Service, Pittsburgh; 301-644-2890.

Precision Rafting; 301-746-5290.

How Reported: Release schedules and levels in feet

Additional Gauge: Release from the Pennsylvania Electric Power Project at Deep Creek Lake onto Hoyes Run.

Source of Levels: Pennsylvania Electric Power Company recording; 814-533-8911.

How Reported: Schedule of releases

Additional Gauge: Staff gauge at Sang Run Road Bridge

Source of Levels: Visual inspection only

How Reported: Feet

Interpretation of Levels: Most paddlers discuss levels on the Top Yough in terms of the Sang Run gauge. Low is 1.7 feet at Sang Run, and high is 3.6 feet at Sang Run. Low is 3 feet on the Friendsville gauge, and high is 4 feet at Friendsville.

Source of More Information: Precision Rafting, PO Box 185, Friendsville, MD 21531; 301-746-5290.

Upper Yough Whitewater Expeditions, Inc., River Rd., PO Box 158, Friendsville, MD 21531; 301-746-5808.

Garrett State Forest, Rt. 3, Box 256, Deer Park, MD 21550; 301-334-2038.

Swallow Falls State Park, RFD 5, Box 122, Oakland, MD 21550; 301-334-9180.

Best Guidebooks: Grove et al., *Appalachian Whitewater, Vol. II;* Gertler, *Maryland and Delaware Canoe Trails.*

Gauge Conversions: Friendsville readings can be approximately converted to Sang Run Readings by subtracting 1.3 from Friendsville. See the Upper Yough section for the conversion from feet to cfs for the Friendsville gauge.

YOUGHIOGHENY RIVER, UPPER SECTION
(See Pennsylvania for a lower section.)

Sections: Natural Land Trust Fund put-in at Sang Run

Jon Lugbill and Dutch Downey at National Falls on the Top Youghiogheny. Photo by Colleen Laffey.

Bridge to Friendsville, Maryland,
Class IV-V

Length of Run: Day trip, 9.5 miles

Location: Garrett County, Maryland

Maps: USGS quads: Sang Run, Friendsville

Times Runnable: During the winter and spring, it is often possible to run the Upper Yough after snowmelt or rain. Most of the time, however, boating is dependent on releases by the Pennsylvania Electric Project at Deep Creek Lake into Hoyes Run. Hoyes Run is a tributary that joins the Top Yough.

Check with the Pennsylvania Electric Project for the release schedule; usually the best times to expect releases are weekdays. Releases, typically 600 cfs in volume, often last as little as three hours, but by starting out with the first crest of the release, it is possible to spend five hours on the river without running out of water. Add about 1.5 hours to the time that Pennsylvania Electric schedules the start of a release in order to estimate the time at which the water will arrive at the put-in at Sang Run.

Permit: None required

Gauge: Friendsville gauge

Source of Levels: National Weather Service River Forecast Center, Harrisburg; 717-234-6812.

National Weather Service, Maryland; 301-260-0305.

National Weather Service, Pittsburgh; 301-644-2890.

Precision Rafting; 301-746-5290.

How Reported: Release schedules and levels in feet

Additional Gauge: Release from the Pennsylvania Electric Power Project at Deep Creek Lake onto Hoyes Run.

Source of Levels: Pennsylvania Electric Company recording; 814-533-8911.

How Reported: Schedule of releases.

Additional Gauge: Staff gauge on Sang Run Road Bridge

Source of Levels: Visual inspection only

How Reported: Feet

Interpretation of Levels: In terms of Friendsville gauge, 2.9 feet is the minimum, and 3.8 is high. In terms of the Sang Run gauge, 1.6 feet is the minimum and 2.5 is high.

Source of More Information: Precision Rafting, PO Box 185, Friendsville, MD 21531; 301-746-5290.

Upper Yough Whitewater Expeditions, Inc., PO Box 158, Friendsville, MD 21531; 301-746-5808.

Best Guidebooks: Grove et al., *Appalachian Whitewater, Vol. II;* Gertler, *Maryland and Delaware Canoe Trails.*

Further Comments: A classic, technical, expert run. Expect several pins and other trouble if you paddle with a group of good boaters who don't know the river.

Gauge Conversions: Friendsville readings can be approximately converted to Sang Run readings by subtracting 1.3 from Friendsville.

USGS gauge at Friendsville conversion:

Feet	Cfs	Feet	Cfs	Feet	Cfs
2.5	168	3.2	610	3.8	1355
2.6	211	3.3	712	4.0	1673
2.7	261	3.4	826	4.5	2588
2.8	317	3.5	952	5.0	3533
2.9	380	3.6	1077	5.5	4558
3.0	449	3.7	1211	6.0	5620
3.1	526	-	-	-	-

GENERAL INFORMATION SOURCES FOR MARYLAND

The National Weather Service in Pittsburgh reports gauge readings for the Monongahela River basin in Pennsylvania, and for parts of Maryland and West Virginia: National Weather Service, Pittsburgh; 412-644-2890.

They get readings for the following Maryland gauge:
Upper Yough, Deep Creek Gauge (at Friendsville)

The National Weather Service Washington, DC District Office is responsible for the Potomac and Rappahannock River basins. They prepare a recording, updated daily at 10 a.m. and 8 p.m. The 10 a.m. edition is more inclusive, with data for the Monongahela and James River Basins.

National Weather Service, Washington, DC; 703-260-0305.

They report the following readings:

Rappahannock River Basin
    Rapidan, at Culpeper, VA
    Rappahannock, at Remington, VA

Potomac River Basin
    North Branch of the Potomac River, at Kitzmiller, MD
    Savage River, at Savage, MD
    North Branch of the Potomac River, at Cumberland, MD
    South Branch of the Potomac River
        At Petersburg, WV
        At Springfield, WV
    Potomac River
        At Paw Paw, WV
        At Hancock, WV
        At Williamsport, MD
        At Shepardstown, WV
    North Fork of the Shenandoah River
        At Cootes Store, VA
        At Strasburg, VA
    South Fork of the Shenandoah River
        At Lynnwood, VA
        At Front Royal, VA
    Shenandoah River
        At Millville, WV
    Potomac River
        At Point of Rocks, MD
        At Little Falls, DC

James River and Tributaries
    Maury River, at Buena Vista, VA
    James River
        At Bent Creek, VA
        At Cartersville, VA
        Westham gauge at Richmond, VA

Bill Warren running Meat Cleaver, Upper Youghiogheny. Photo by Bill Millard.

Monongahela River and Tributaries
    Tygart River, at Belington, WV
    Cheat River, at Parsons, WV
    Youghiogheny River, at Confluence, PA
    Casselman River, at Markleton, PA
    Upper Yough, Deep Creek Gauge (at Friendsville)
    Big Sandy Creek, at Rockville, WV

The National Weather Service Forecast Center in Harrisburg, PA, acts as the hydrologic service office for the Delaware and Susquehanna River Basins. They also receive information on the Potomac and James River Basins relayed from the Washington, DC, and Richmond, VA, forecast offices.

National Weather Service River Forecast Center, Harrisburg; 717-234-6812

Dialing this line accesses a ring-through recording. If you don't hear what you need on the recording, stay on the line and ask for it. Here's what you'll hear:

Susquehanna River Basin
    Susquehanna River at Harrisburg
    Susquehanna River at Wilkes Barre
    Susquehanna River at Sunberry
    West Branch of the Susquehanna River at Carson
    West Branch of the Susquehanna River at Renovo
    Pine Creek at Cedar Run
    Judiana River at Newport
    Condoquinet Creek at Hoyestown
    Yellow Breeches Creek near Camp Hill
    Swatara Creek at Hershey

Other Stages:
    Swatara Creek at Harpers Tavern

Codorus Creek near York
Little Judiana River at Spruce Creek
Loyalsock Creek at Loyalsockville
Penns Creek near Penns Creek
Tioga River at Mansfield

Schylkill River at Fern
Bushgill River at Showmaker
Lehigh River at Whitehaven
Flow from Walter Dam at Whitehaven

MASSACHUSETTS

DEERFIELD RIVER

Sections: (1) The Upper Deerfield Drys, Monroe Bridge to Bear Swamp Reservoir, Class III and IV.
(2) Bear Swamp Reservoir to Route 2, Class II+ (1 at III, Zoar Gap Rapid)

Length of Run: (1) Day trip, 4 miles
(2) Day trip, 9.5 miles

Location: Franklin County, Massachusetts

Maps: USGS quad: Rowe

Times Runnable: Section (1) is runnable only during periods of peak runoff during early spring. Water is usually diverted by evil dam-mavens through a canal to the power plant at the Bear Swamp Project downstream. I suppose you can guess then why this section is called the Drys. Section (2) is dam-controlled and can be run after releases, which are best during dry months and rare on Sundays or holidays.

Permit: None required

Gauge: For Section (1), none

Source of Levels: None

How Reported: Not known

Additional Gauge: For Section (2), release from dam at New England Power Bear Swamp Pumped Storage Project

Source of Levels: Wild Water Outfitters; 413-586-2323.

How Reported: Cfs

Additional Gauge: Also for Section (2), USGS gauge on river-left, downstream of Charlemont

Source of Levels: National Weather Service, Bloomfield, CT; 203-240-3514.

How Reported: Feet

Interpretation of Levels: Minimum is about 3.9 feet at Charlemont.

Source of More Information: Mohawk Trail State Forest, Rt. 2, Charlemont, MA 01339; 413-339-5504.

Wild Water Outfitters, 93 Boltwood Walk, Amherst, MA 01002; 413-586-2323.

Best Guidebooks: AMC, *AMC River Guide: Massachusetts, Connecticut, and Rhode Island.*

Further Comments: Section (1) of the Deerfield is a terrific whitewater river; sadly, as it stands now, you'll rarely get to boat it, since the Bear Swamp boys have stolen all the water. The American Whitewater Affiliation is leading a fight to challenge the relicensing of the Bear Swamp Project. If you would like to help, contact J. Valera, 91 High St., Fitchburg, MA 01420.

On Section (2), be on the watch for Zoar Gap Rapid, Class III, which is considerably harder than the rest of the run. During the racing season, you'll see slalom racers training in the gates at this rapid; try not to get in their way.

Gauge Conversions: USGS at Charlemont

Feet	Cfs	Feet	Cfs
3.0	911	6.0	4860
3.5	1360	6.5	5850
4.0	1870	7.0	6930
4.5	2460	7.5	8070
5.0	3150	8.0	9290
5.5	3960	8.5	10600

FARMINGTON RIVER
(See Connecticut for a lower section.)

Sections: Upper Farmington Section (A.K.A. New Boston section), Tolland Forest Bridge off Rt. 8 to New Boston, Class III-IV (IV+ high). This section is paralleled by Massachusetts Rt. 8.

Length of Run: Day trip, 3 miles

Location: Berkshire and Hampden Counties, Massachusetts

Maps: USGS quads: Otis, Tolland Center

Times Runnable: During March of high-water years. Also after dam releases from Otis Reservoir in the fall.

Permit: None required

Gauge: None (the gauge at Rainbow has been discontinued)

Source of Levels: None.

Additional Gauge: Scheduled fall releases from Otis Reservoir, usually the third weekend in October.

Source of Levels: A schedule can be obtained from: Appalachian Mountain Club, New England Rivers Center, Boston; 617-523-0636.

How Reported: Cfs

Interpretation of Levels: In terms of the USGS gauge, minimum is about 4.0 feet; can be run to floodstage by sufficiently competent boaters. In the case of releases from Otis Reservoir, 250-300 cfs is considered low to medium (Class III-IV) and appropriate for open boats.

Source of More Information: Tolland State Forest, Rt. 8, Otis, MA 02542; 413-269-7268.

Wild Water Outfitters, 93 Boltwood Walk, Amherst, MA 01002; 413-586-2323.

Best Guidebooks: Connelly and Porterfield, *Appalachian Whitewater, Vol. III;* AMC, *AMC River Guide: Massachusetts, Connecticut, and Rhode Island.*

GREEN RIVER

Sections: (1) Green River, Vermont to West Leyden, Massachusetts, Class II
(2) Leyden to Greenfield Pump Station, Class I

Length of Run: (1) Day trip, 7 miles
(2) Day trip, 6 miles

Location: Windham County, Vermont and Franklin County, Massachusetts

Maps: USGS quads: Brattleboro, Colrain, Bernardston

Times Runnable: During peak runoff in early April

Permit: None required

Gauge: Flow is usually measured in terms of the amount of water spilling over the Low Head Dam at Stewartsville on Section (1).

Source of Levels: Sawmill at Stewartsville (Colrain township), C.A. Dennison Lumber Co., Inc.; 413-624-3225.

How Reported: Impression

Additional Gauge: USGS East Colrain gauge, on river-right, 0.5 mile upstream from the take-out for section (1) and put-in for section (2).

Source of Levels: Visual inspection only

How Reported: Feet

Interpretation of Levels: If the folks at the sawmill think there is enough water, then there is. In terms of the East Colrain gauge, minimum is about 3.9 feet.

Source of More Information: Leyden State Forest, c/o Mohawk Trail State Forest, Box 7, Charlemont, MA 01339; 413-339-7779.

Wild Water Outfitters, 93 Boltwood Walk, Amherst, MA 01002; 413-586-2323.

Best Guidebooks: AMC, *AMC River Guide: Massachusetts, Connecticut, and Rhode Island;* Gabler, *New England Whitewater River Guide.*

Further Comments: The shuttle for Section (1) is bad in spring if you want to put in at Green River; however, you can drive on paved roads from the take-out to the Stewartsville Dam and put in there. Portage the dam at Stewartsville.

Gauge Conversions: USGS gauge at East Colrain

Feet	Cfs	Feet	Cfs	Feet	Cfs
3.0	125	3.7	333	4.4	694
3.1	147	3.8	376	4.5	757
3.2	171	3.9	424	4.6	818
3 3	197	4.0	475	4.7	882
3.4	225	4.1	525	4.8	948
3.5	255	4.2	578	4.9	1020
3.6	292	4.3	635	5.0	1090

MILLERS RIVER

Sections: (1) Upper Millers, South Royalston to Athol, Class III
(2) Lower Millers, Erving to Millers Falls, Class II

Length of Run: (1) Day trip, 7 miles
(2) Day trip, 6 miles

Location: Franklin County, Massachusetts

Maps: USGS quads: Royalston, Athol

Times Runnable: March and April

Permit: None required

Gauge: For Section (1), USGS gauge at South Royalston

Source of Levels: Outdoor Center of New England; 413-659-3926.

How Reported: Feet

Additional Gauge: For Section (2), USGS gauge at Farley Flats

Source of Levels: Same as above

How Reported: Feet

Interpretation of Levels: For Section (1), minimum at South Royalston is 5 feet; medium is 6.5, and 7.5 is high. For Section (2), minimum at Farley Flats is 3.5, medium is 4 to 5 feet, 6.5 feet is high, and 8.5 feet is extremely high.

Source of More Information: Otter River State Forest, New Winchendon Rd., Baldwinville, MA 01436; 508-939-8962.

Erving State Forest, Rt. 2A, Erving, MA 01364; 508-544-3939.

Outdoor Center of New England; 413-659-3926.

Best Guidebooks: AMC, *AMC River Guide: Massachusetts, Connecticut, and Rhode Island;* Gabler, *New England Whitewater River Guide.*

Further Comments: The Millers is a popular and fun Class II and III river with plenty of nice surfing waves.

Gauge Conversions: USGS gauge at South Royalston

Feet	Cfs	Feet	Cfs	Feet	Cfs
4.6	200.0	5.8	765.0	7.0	1770
4.8	269.0	6.0	899.0	7.2	1990
5.0	347.0	6.2	1050.0	7.4	2220
5.2	436.0	6.4	1210.0	7.6	2480
5.4	540.0	6.6	1380.0	7.8	2750
5.6	646.0	6.8	1570.0	8.0	3050

USGS gauge at Earley Flats

Feet	Cfs	Feet	Cfs	Feet	Cfs
3.0	480.0	4.2	1420	5.4	2820
3.2	601.0	4.4	1620	5.6	3110
3.4	740.0	4.6	1830	5.8	3430
3.6	887.0	4.8	2040	6.0	3750
3.8	1050.0	5.0	2280	6.5	4610
4.0	1230.0	5.2	2540	—	—

QUABOAG RIVER

Sections: Lucy Stone Park in Warren to Rt. 67, Class II-IV (IV overall when high)

Length of Run: Day trip, 5.5 miles

Location: Hampden, Worchester Counties, Massachusetts

Maps: USGS quad: Warren

Times Runnable: Mid-March to April

Permit: None required

Gauge: West Brimfield gauge, off Highway 67, 0.8 mile north of the Mass. Turnpike Bridge

Source of Levels: Visual inspection only

How Reported: Feet

Interpretation of Levels: Minimum is 3.9 feet; high is 5 feet, and extremely high is 6 feet.

Source of More Information: Wild Water Outfitters, 93 Boltwood Walk, Amherst, MA 01002; 413-586-2323.

Best Guidebooks: Connelly and Porterfield, *Appalachian Whitewater, Vol. III;* AMC, *AMC River Guide: Massachusetts, Connecticut, and Rhode Island.*

WALKER BROOK

Sections: Rt. 20 to Chester, Class IV (V high)

Length of Run: Day trip, 3.5 miles

Sue Talbot takes on the Broken Dam Rapid on the Quaboag River at 4.5 feet. Photo by Dave Rego.

Location: Berkshire and Hampden Counties, Massachusetts

Maps: USGS quads: Becket, Chester

Times Runnable: March and April after heavy rain

Permit: None required

Gauge: None. Correlate to the Huntington gauge on the West Branch of the Westfield.

Source of Levels: Visual inspection only.

How Reported: Feet

Interpretation of Levels: Extrapolating from the Westfield, minimum should be around 3.5 feet, and very high around 5.5

Source of More Information: Becket State Forest, 413-442-8992. Mail to: c/o Pittsfield State Forest, Cascade St., Pittsfield, MA 01201.

Best Guidebooks: Connelly and Porterfield, *Appalachian Whitewater, Vol. III.*

WESTFIELD RIVER, WEST BRANCH

Sections: Becket to Chester, Class III-IV (V to V+ high)

Length of Run: Day trip, 9.5 miles

Location: Berkshire and Hampden Counties, Massachusetts

Maps: USGS quads: Chester, Becket

Times Runnable: March and April after heavy rain

Permit: None required

Gauge: Huntington gauge at Huntington, MA near confluence with North Branch

Source of Levels: Visual inspection only

How Reported: Feet

Additional Gauge: You might check the USGS gauge on the Westfield, far downstream at the city of Westfield. If it's up, then there may be water on the West Branch.

Source of Levels: National Weather Service, Bloomfield, CT; 203-240-3514.

How Reported: Feet

Interpretation of Levels: Minimum is 3.0 feet at Huntington. Can be run by extremely good boaters to floodstage. Not for dweebs.

Source of More Information: Wild Water Outfitters, 93 Boltwood Walk, Amherst, MA 01002; 413-586-2323.

Best Guidebooks: Connelly and Porterfield, *Appalachian Whitewater, Vol. III.*

WESTFIELD RIVER, NORTH BRANCH

Sections: Knightville Dam to Huntington, Class II-III (III+ high)

Length of Run: Day trip, 5.2 miles

Location: Hampshire and Hampden Counties, Massachusetts

Maps: USGS quads: Westhampton, Woronoco

Times Runnable: March to May after releases from Knightville Dam

Permit: None required

Gauge: Release from Army Corps Knightville Dam on Knightville Reservoir

Source of Levels: National Weather Service, Bloomfield, CT; 213-240-6870.

How Reported: Cfs

Interpretation of Levels: Low is about 400 cfs, medium is 1000, and high is 2000 cfs.

Source of More Information: C.M. Gardner State Park, 413-532-3995. Mail c/o: Hampden Pond State Park, Box 537, Apremont Rd., Westfield, MA 01085.

Wild Water Outfitters, 93 Boltwood Walk, Amherst, MA 01002; 413-586-2323.

Best Guidebooks: Connelly and Porterfield, *Appalachian Whitewater, Vol. III.*

GENERAL INFORMATION SOURCES FOR MASSACHUSETTS

The US Army Corps of Engineers and other managers of water projects coordinate all scheduled releases through the Appalachian Mountain Club. Call the office of the Appalachian Mountain Club in Boston; they should have a printed list they can mail out (I don't recommend that you call the New England Division of the Army Corps—they don't want to hear from you). Appalachian Mountain Club, New England Rivers Center, Boston, 5 Joy St., Boston, MA; 617-523-0636.

The New England River Forecast Center of the National Weather Service in Bloomfield, Connecticut, is also the headquarters for the Southern New England Hydrological Service Area: 203-240-3514.

They can provide daily updated gauge readings for rivers in Massachusetts. Don't call before 11:30 a.m., as they are busy putting out the forecast. Reports are available for the following Massachusetts gauges:

Merrimack River, at Lowell
Charles River, at Dover
Neponset River, at Norwood
Nashua River, at East Pepperell
Concord River, at Lowell
Westfield River
    Release from Littleville Dam
    At Westfield

BLACK RIVER

Sections: (1) County Rd. 513 Bridge to US 2 Bridge, Class I (one at II)
(2) Covered Bridge at Blackjack Ski Area to Narrows Roadside Park, Class I
(3) Narrows to Potawatomi Falls, Class II-IV, one portage
(4) Gorge Falls to Lake Superior, Class IV, two portages

Length of Run: (1) Day trip, 8 miles
(2) Day trip, 9.5 miles
(3) Day trip, 3.5 miles
(4) Day trip, 4 miles

Location: Gogebic County, Michigan; Ottawa National Forest

Maps: USGS quads: North Ironwood (15')

Times Runnable: During high-water periods in spring and fall

Permit: None required

Gauge: None, but the Forest Service plans to install one in the future. In the meantime, they make visual inspections.

Source of Levels: USDA Forest Service, Bessemer Ranger District, Ottawa National Forest; 906-667-0261.

How Reported: Impression only

Interpretation of Levels: If the Forest Service says there is enough water, then there is.

Source of More Information: Department of Natural Resources, Wakefield Field Office, US Highway 2, Wakefield, MI 49945; 906-224-2771.

Trek and Trail, US Highway 2, Bessemer, MI 49911; 906-663-4791.

USDA Forest Service, Bessemer Ranger District, Ottawa National Forest, Bessemer, MI 49911; 906-667-0261.

Best Guidebooks: Dennis and Date, *Canoeing Michigan Rivers.*

Further Comments: There is one probable portage on Section (1) and numerous portages on Section (2). Sections (3) and (4) continue to Lake Superior and contain numerous waterfalls in a deep gorge. There is one mandatory portage on Section (3), Conglomerate Falls, 35 feet. This falls has been run, but some folks have broken their ankles in the attempt. Section (4) is runnable at moderate levels by teams of experts. It includes two unrunnable drops, Sandstone and Rainbow Falls.

MENOMINEE RIVER

See Wisconsin.

MONTREAL RIVER

See Wisconsin.

ONTONAGON RIVER, EAST BRANCH

Sections: East Branch Road (Forest Service 208) to bridge at Highway 45, Class I-III

Length of Run: Day trip, 7.5 miles

Location: Ontonagon County, Michigan; Ottawa National Forest

Maps: USGS quads: Rockland (15')

Times Runnable: Spring, summer and fall

Permit: None required

Gauge: USFS staff gauge on river-right below the put-in

Source of Levels: Visual inspection, but you might try: USDA Forest Service, Ontonagon Ranger District, Ottawa National Forest, Ontonagon, MI 49953; 906-884-2411.

How Reported: Feet

Interpretation of Levels: About 250 to 500 cfs is low, 500 to 2000 is medium, and above 2000 is high.

Source of More Information: Department of Natural Resources, Wakefield Field Office, US Highway 2,

Wakefield, MI 49945; 906-224-2771.

Trek and Trail, US Highway 2, Bessemer, MI 49911; 906-663-4791.

USDA Forest Service, Bessemer Ranger District, Ottawa National Forest, Bessemer, MI 49911; 906-667-0261.

Best Guidebooks: Dennis and Date, *Canoeing Michigan Rivers.*

PRESQUE ISLE RIVER

Sections: (1) Michigan Highway 28 Bridge to Steiger's Bridge, Class III-IV.
(2) Steiger's Bridge to South Boundary Bridge, Class III-IV

Length of Run: (1) Day trip, 8.5 miles
(2) Day trip, 9 miles
Sections (1) and (2) are usually run together as a *very long* day trip. (Steiger's Road is often closed.)

Location: Gogebic and Ontonagon Counties, Michigan; Ottawa National Forest

Maps: USGS quads: Thomaston (15')

Times Runnable: April to May, with peak high water in April

Permit: None required

Gauge: Staff gauge below the South Boundary Road Bridge at the take-out, on the right bank

Source of Levels: Visual inspection, but you might try: USDA Forest Service, Bessemer Ranger District, Ottawa National Forest; 906-667-0261.

How Reported: Feet

Interpretation of Levels: Optimum is around 7.5 feet; high is 8 feet. Peak flow was measured by the USGS once as being around 1500 cfs. Low flow in August is around 40 cfs.

Source of More Information: Department of Natural Resources, Wakefield Field Office, US Highway 2, Wakefield, MI 49945; 906-224-2771.

Trek and Trail, US Highway 2, Bessemer, MI 49911; 906-663-4791.

USDA Forest Service, Bessemer Ranger District, Ottawa National Forest, Bessemer, MI 49911; 906-667-0261.

Porcupine Mountains Wilderness State Park, Mailstop 107, Rt. 2, Ontonagon, MI 49953; 906-885-5798

Best Guidebooks: Dennis and Date, *Canoeing Michigan Rivers.*

Further Comments: Some of the best whitewater in Michigan. Section (1) includes long pools with Class II-III drops, followed by two short, Class IV gorges. Section (2) is quite different. It has *continuous* Class II-III rapids with many Class IV drops at low to medium levels. At higher flows (7.7 to 8.0 feet), Class III to IV conditions are found. At 8.0 feet or higher, the sheer-walled gorge below Steiger's Bridge is very dangerous to enter.

TWO HEARTED RIVER

Sections:
(1) High Bridge on County Road 407 to Reed and Green Bridge on County Road 410, Class I
(2) Reed and Green Bridge to Rivermouth, Class I

Length of Run:
(1) Day trip, 9.5 miles
(2) Day trip, 11 miles

Location: Luce County, Michigan

Maps: USGS quads: Muskallonge Lake SE, Muskalonge Lake East, Betsy·Lake NW

Times Runnable: Spring and early summer

Permit: None required

Gauge: None

Source of Levels: Mark's Rod and Reel, Canoe Livery; 906-293-5855.

How Reported: Impression only

Interpretation of Levels: If Mark thinks it's O.K., then it is.

Source of More Information: Department of Natural Resources, Wakefield Field Office, 309 W. McMillen Ave., PO Box 445, Newberry, MI 49868; 906-293-5131.

Mark's Rod and Reel, Canoe Livery, Rt. 1, Box 428, Newberry, MI 49868; 906-293-5855.

Lake Superior State Forest, Box 445, Newberry, MI 49868; no phone.

Best Guidebooks: Dennis and Date, *Canoeing Michigan Rivers.*

Further Comments: Beautiful and popular canoeing river.

GENERAL INFORMATION SOURCES FOR MICHIGAN

The National Weather Service Forecast Office in Ann Arbor can report river stages for Michigan rivers: 313-668-2220.

They receive updates daily for the following gauges:

The Clinton River, at Fraser
The North Branch of the Clinton River, at Mt. Clemens
The Clinton River, at Mt. Clemens
The Upper Rouge River, at Detroit
The Middle Rouge River, at Garden City
The Raisin River
    At Adrian
    At Monroe
The Huron River, at Ann Arbor
The Red Cedar River
    At Williamston
    At East Lansing
The Grand River
    At Lansing
    At Portland

The Flat River, at Smyrna
The Grand River, at Ionia
The Thornapple River
    At Hastings
    At Caledonia
The Grand River, at Grand Rapids
The Kalamazoo River, at Comstock
The Muskegon River, at Newaygo
The Cass River, at Wahjamega
The Chippewa River, at Mt. Pleasant
The Tittabawassee River, at Midland
The Shiawassee River, at Owosso
The South Branch of the Flint River, at Columbiaville
Kearsley Creek, at Davison
Thread Creek, at Flint
Swartz Creek, at Flint
The Flint River
    At Otisville
    At Flint
The Saginaw River, at Saginaw
The Sturgeon River, at Sidnaw

BAPTISM RIVER

Sections:

(1) Finland to Superior National Forest Campground, Class III-IV (with one difficult portage)

(2) Superior National Forest Campground to Lake Superior, Class III-IV (and several portages)

Length of Run:

(1) Day trip, 6.5 miles

(2) Day trip, 4.5 miles

Location: Lake County, Minnesota; Superior National Forest

Maps: USGS quads: Finland, Illgen and Silver Bay (15'); Also Superior National Forest Visitor Map

Times Runnable: Early spring during peak runoff or in late spring after heavy rain

Permit: None required

Gauge: None

Source of Levels: None

Source of More Information: Information Center, Department of Natural Resources, 500 Lafayette Rd., St. Paul, MN 55155-4040; 612-296-6699, 800-652-9747 (inside Minnesota).

Superior Whitewater, PO Box 17223, St. Paul, MN 55117; 218-384-4637.

Superior National Forest, PO Box 338, Duluth, MN 55801; 218-720-5324.

Best Guidebooks: Palzer and Palzer, *Whitewater/ Quietwater.*

Further Comments: A remote expert run with several waterfalls to portage. Run this one with someone who has been there.

BIG FORK RIVER

Sections: Dora Lake to confluence with the Rainy River in Ontario

Length of Run: 7-10 days, 165 miles, shorter sections possible

Location: Itasca and Koochichung Counties, Minnesota

Maps: USGS quads: Dora Lake, Coddington Lake, Wirt, Pomroy, Wildwood SE, Spring Lake, Big Fork, Effie, Effie SE, Craigville, Effie NW, Wildwood NE, Big Falls SE, Johnson Landing, Johnson Landing NW, Big Falls, Big Falls NW, Lindford SW, Lindford SE, Lindford, Little Fork NW, Devlin

Times Runnable: Generally, most sections are canoeable all season.

Permit: None required

Gauge: DNR gauge #1 on the downstream side of State Highway 38 Bridge

Source of Levels: Information Center, 612-296-6699; 800-652-9747 (inside Minnesota).

How Reported: Feet

Additional Gauge: DNR gauge #2 on the middle piling, downstream side, of the railroad trestle at Big Falls

Source of Levels: DNR, as above

How Reported: Feet

Interpretation of Levels: Not available at this time.

Source of More Information: Information Center, Department of Natural Resources, 500 Lafayette Rd., St. Paul, MN 55155-4040; 612-296-6699, 800-652-9747 (inside Minnesota).

USDA Forest Service, Chippewa National Forest, Cass Lake, MN 56633; 218-335-2226.

Big Fork State Forest Area Forester, Box 157, Deer River, MN 56636; 218-246-8343.

Pine Island State Forest, Area Forester, Little Fork, MN 56653; 218-278-6651.

Superior Whitewater, PO Box 17223, St. Paul, MN 55117; 218-384-4637.

Best Guidebooks: Breining and Watson, *A Gathering of Waters;* DNR Map/guide, "Big Fork: Canoe Route," (available from the DNR, address above.)

Further Comments: Portage the two waterfalls and the dam.

BRULE RIVER

(Not to be confused with the Brule River at the Michigan-Wisconsin border or the Bois Brule River in Wisconsin)

Sections: (1) Northern Light Lake to Sauna Bath Rapids, Class II-IV (one at V-VI)
(2) Sauna Bath Rapids to Lake Superior, Class IV-V (one at VI and two falls)

Length of Run: (1) Day trip, 16 miles
(2) Day trip, 6 miles

Location: Cook County, Minnesota; Grand Portage State Forest

Maps: USGS quads: Tom Lake, Marr Island; also Superior National Forest Visitor Map

Times Runnable: Spring during peak runoff

Permit: None required

Gauge: None

Source of Levels: Probably none.

Interpretation of Levels: Previous runs have been at about 600 to 900 cfs (estimated).

Source of More Information: Information Center, Department of Natural Resources, 500 Lafayette Rd., St. Paul, MN 55155-4040; 612-296-6699, 800-652-9747 (inside Minnesota).

Superior Whitewater, PO Box 17223, St. Paul, MN 55117; 218-384-4637.

Judge C. R. Magney State Park, Grand Marais, MN 55604; 218-387-2929.

Grand Portage State Forest, Area Forestry Ranger, 613 Rice Lake Rd., Duluth, MN 55803; 218-723-4669.

Best Guidebooks: Palzer and Palzer, *Whitewater/ Quietwater.*

Further Comments: This North Shore expert run includes portages of waterfalls and numerous difficult rapids. Go with someone who has been there.

KETTLE RIVER

Sections: Highway 23 Bridge to Sandstone, MN, Class III-IV at Spring Flow

Length of Run: Day trip, 5 miles

Location: Pine County, Minnesota; Banning State Park

Maps: USGS quads: Sandstone (15')

Times Runnable: Mid-March to early July

Permit: None required

Gauge: DNR #13 at Banning State Park on the upstream side of the east pier of State Highway 23 Bridge

Source of Levels: Information Center, 612-296-6699; 800-652-9747 (inside Minnesota).

How Reported: Feet

Interpretation of Levels: Minimum is 1 foot; low is from 1 to 1.5 feet; medium/good is from 1.5 to 2.5 feet, and high is over 2.5 feet. The upper limit for an open canoe is 3 feet.

Source of More Information: Information Center, Department of Natural Resources, 500 Lafayette Rd., St. Paul, MN 55155-4040; 612-296-6699, 800-652-9747 (inside Minnesota).

Banning State Park, PO Box V, Sandstone, MN 55012; 612-245-2668.

Wilderness Campgrounds on Long Lake, Canoe Livery, Willow River, MN 55795; 612-333-5747.

Superior Whitewater, PO Box 17223, St. Paul, MN 55117; 218-384-4637.

Best Guidebooks: Breining and Watson, *A Gathering of Waters;* DNR Map: "Kettle River: Canoe Route" (available from the DNR, address above).

Gauge Conversions:

Feet	Cfs
1.0	275
2.0	700
3.0	1500
4.0	2400
5.0	3600

SNAKE RIVER
(Not to be confused with the Snake River in Idaho)

Sections: Silver Star Road access to County Road 3, Class I-IV

Length of Run: 2 days, 22 miles (shorter runs possible)

Location: Aitkin and Kanabec Counties, Minnesota

Maps: USGS quads: McGrath, Kroschell, Pomroy Lake, Kanabec

Times Runnable: April to June

Permit: None required

Gauge: DNR #37, upstream of the put-in at State Highway 65 retainer wall, on the downstream side and facing east. DNR #38 at Kanabec Ford Township Bridge, on the south wall and facing north. DNR #39, on County Road 3 Bridge at the take-out, on the west wall and facing east.

Source of Levels: Information Center; 612-296-6699, 800-652-9747 (inside Minnesota).

How Reported: Feet

Interpretation of Levels: In terms of the Highway 65 gauge (DNR #37), 2 feet is minimum; 2.3 to 2.8 feet is low; 4.0 feet is optimum; and 4.3 or over is high water.

Source of More Information: Information Center, Department of Natural Resources, 500 Lafayette Rd., St. Paul, MN 55155-4040; 612-296-6699, 800-652-9747 (inside Minnesota).

Superior Whitewater, PO Box 17223, St. Paul, MN 55117; 218-384-4637.

Best Guidebooks: Breining and Watson, *A Gathering of Waters;* DNR Map/guide, "Snake River: Canoe Route" (available from the DNR, address above.)

ST. CROIX RIVER
Wild and Scenic River
(Not to be confused with the St. Croix River, Maine)

Sections: Norway Point at St. Croix River State Park to Soderbeck Landing at the Snake River confluence, Class I-II

Length of Run: Day trip, 10 miles

Location: Pine County, Minnesota and Burnett County, Wisconsin

Maps: USGS quads: Grantsburg (15') and Pine County (15')

Times Runnable: Mid-March to early July

Permit: None required

Gauge: DNR 32, St. Croix State Park Boat Ramp. DNR #33, Highway 70 Bridge, west pier on upstream end. DNR #34, Highway 243, center pier on upstream end.

Source of Levels: Information Center; 612-296-6699, 800-652-9747 (inside Minnesota).

How Reported: Feet

Additional Gauge: USGS gauge near Stillwater, MN (roughly 40 miles downstream)

How Reported: Feet

Source of Levels: National Weather Service, Minneapolis; 612-725-6090.

Interpretation of Levels: In terms of the DNR #33 gauge at the Highway 70 Bridge, a medium to good level is around 6.3 to 7.5.

Source of More Information: National Park Service, St. Croix National Scenic Riverway, PO Box 708, St. Croix Falls, WI 54024; 715-483-3284.

Information Center, Department of Natural Resources, 500 Lafayette Rd., St. Paul, MN 55155-4040; 612-296-6699, 800-652-9747 (inside Minnesota).

St. Croix River State Park, Rt. 3, Box 174, Hinckley, MN 55037; 612-384-6591.

St. Croix Wild River State Forest, Chengwatana State Forest, Rt. 2, 701 S. Kenwood, Mooselake, MN 55767; 218-485-4474.

Taylors Falls Canoe Rental, Highway 8, Box 225, Taylors Falls, MN 55004; 612-465-6315 or 612-462-7550.

Best Guidebooks: Breining, *A Gathering of Waters*.

Further Comments: Portage the dam near St. Croix Falls.

ST. LOUIS RIVER, BELOW SCANLON DAM

Sections: Highway 61 bridge (south of Duluth near Jay Cooke State Park) to Thomson, Class II-IV

Length of Run: Day trip, 3 miles

Location: Carlton County, Minnesota

Maps: USGS quads: Cloquet, Esko

Times Runnable: May to September

Permit: None required

Gauge: Release from Minnesota Power Co. Scanlon Dam

Source of Levels: Superior Whitewater, 612-728-4217.

How Reported: Cfs

Interpretation of Levels: Bare-bones minimum is about

500 cfs, with minimum for fun being around 1500. Medium-low is from 1500 to 6000 cfs (about Class II-III). Medium-high is from 6000 to 15,000 cfs (about Class III-IV). Very high is 15,000 to 18,000 cfs (Class IV).

Source of More Information: Superior Whitewater, PO Box 17223, St. Paul, MN 55117; 218-384-4637.

Jay Cooke State Park, 500 East Highway 210, Carlton, MN 55718; 218-384-4610.

Best Guidebooks: None

Further Comments: This big-water section is popular for both kayaking and commercial rafting. Access is a problem. The put-ins and take-outs are on posted land; however, this proscription apparently is not enforced. Be careful and considerate.

VERMILION RIVER

Sections: (1) Vermilion Dam to Highway 24, Class III-IV (one at V)
(2) Highway 24 to Crane Lake, Class III-IV (one at VI)

Length of Run: (1) Day trip, 15 miles
(2) 1-2 days, 24 miles

Location: St. Louis County, Minnesota Superior National Forest

Maps: USGS quads: Vermilion Dam, Picket Lake, Buyck, Kabastasa Lake, Elephant Lake, Johnson Lake, Crane Lake

Times Runnable: Spring to fall

Permit: None required

Gauge: USGS below Vermilion Dam

Source of Levels: DNR Outdoor Information Center, 612-296-6699, 800-652-9747 (inside Minnesota).

How Reported: Feet

Interpretation of Levels: Minimum is about 4 feet.

Source of More Information: Information Center, Department of Natural Resources, 500 Lafayette Rd., St. Paul, MN 55155-4040; 612-296-6699, 800-652-9747 (inside Minnesota).

Superior Whitewater, PO Box 17223, St. Paul, MN 55117; 218-384-4637.

Superior National Forest, PO Box 338, Duluth, MN 55801; 218-720-5324.

Best Guidebooks: DNR Map/guide, *Vermilion River Canoe Route.*

Further Comments: Portage High Falls, Class VI, on Section (2). Possible portages of other difficult rapids on both sections.

ADDITIONAL NORTH SHORE RIVERS

In addition to the Baptism and the Brule, several other difficult whitewater rivers are found on the North Shore of Lake Superior in Minnesota. Many are Class IV to V in difficulty and are made more difficult by their extreme remoteness and by numerous waterfalls requiring portages. Some North Shore rivers include: the Manitou River, the Cascade River, and the Devil's Track.

None are described in guidebooks. For more information, contact: Superior Whitewater, PO Box 17223, St. Paul, MN 55117; 218-384-4637. Or Information Center, Department of Natural Resources, 500 Lafayette Rd., St. Paul, MN 55155-4040; 612-296-6699, 800-652-9747 (inside Minnesota).

GENERAL INFORMATION SOURCES FOR MINNESOTA

The National Weather Service Forecast Office in Minneapolis can report river stages for rivers in Minnesota: 612-725-6090.

They receive the following Minnesota readings daily:

Mississippi River
    At Aitkin
    At Ft. Ripley
    At Minneapolis
    At St. Paul
    At Hastings
    At Red Wing
    At Lake City
    At Wabasha
Minnesota River
    At Montevido
    At Mankato
    At Jordan
    At Savage
St. Croix River, at Sillwater
Zumbro River, at Zumbro Falls
Root River, at Houston
Crow River, at Rockford

The Minnesota Department of Natural Resources Information Center serves as a clearinghouse of river information in Minnesota. The staff at the Center would like you to call before you paddle in Minnesota; they will be able to recommend the best rivers according to conditions and your level of ability. They should be able to answer most other questions as well.

Information Center, Department of Natural Resources, 500 Lafayette Rd., St. Paul, MN 55155-4040; 612-296-6699, 800-652-9747 (inside Minnesota).

The DNR Information Center also continually monitors river levels based on information provided to them by paddlers and other observers. Included in Appendix Three is a Department of Natural Resources River Level Inventory Form. After you paddle, send in a copy of this form with your observations and help them out. They keep track of the following gauges:

Gauge No.	River	Location
1.	Big Fork River	Hwy. 38 bridge crossing
2.	Big Fork River	Railroad trestle at Big Falls
3.	—	—
4.	Cannon River	CSAH 1 bridge in Dundas
5.	Cannon River	5th Street bridge above dam in Northfield
6.	Cannon River	Hwy. 20 bridge in Cannon Falls
7.	Cannon River	CSAH 7 bridge in Welch
8.	Cloquet River	County Rd. 44 bridge
9.	Cloquet River	US 53 bridge
10.	Crow Wing River	County Rd. 12 bridge
11.	Crow Wing River	MN 210 bridge near Motley
12.	Des Moines River	MN 60/US 71 bridge in Windom
13.	Kettle River	Banning State Park SH. 23 bridge
14.	Kettle River	MN 48 bridge, near Hinckley
15.	Little Fork River	Railroad trestle in Cook
16.	Little Fork River	US 217 bridge
17.	Minnesota River	CSAH bridge 10 near Upper Sioux State Park
18.	Minnesota River	MN 4 bridge near Fort Ridgely State Park
19.	Mississippi River	Bridge at Coffee Pot access
20.	Mississippi River	CSAH bridge 5, west of Bemidji
21.	Mississippi River	Grant Valley Township Road wooden bridge
22.	Mississippi River	US 2 bridge
23.	Mississippi River	CSAH bridge 441 at Blackberry
24.	Mississippi River	MN 6 bridge, north of Crosby
25.	Mississippi River	MN 24, east of Clearwater
26.	North Fork of the Crow River	CSAH 2 bridge at Forest City
27.	North Fork of the Crow River	Rockford Hwy. 55
28.	Pine River	County Rd. 11 retainer wall, 6 miles north of Crosby
29.	Rum River	County Rd. 25 bridge near Onamia
30.	Rum River	MN 95 bridge in Mille Lacs County
31.	Rum River	MN 95 bridge in Cambridge, Isanti County
32.	St. Croix River	St. Croix State Park boat ramp
33.	St. Croix River	MN 70 bridge, 10 miles east of Pine City
34.	St. Croix River	Hwy. 243 bridge, south of Franconia
35.	St. Louis River	CSAH bridge 8, at Floodwood
36.	St. Louis River	US 2 bridge, southeast of Brookston
37.	Snake River	MN 65 bridge, northeast of McGrath
38.	Snake River	Ford Township bridge, east of Woodland
39.	Snake River	County Rd. 3 bridge, northeast of Mora

40.	Snake River	County Rd. 6 bridge, west of Mora
41.	Snake River	County Rd. 9 bridge, northeast of Pine City
42.	Straight River	Rose Street bridge in Owatonna
43.	Straight River	RR trestle in Morehouse Park, Owatonna
44.	Straight River	CSAH 24 bridge in Medford
45.	Vermilion River	CSAH 24 bridge in Buyck
46.	Zumbro River	US 63 bridge in Zumbro

MISSOURI

ST. FRANCIS RIVER

Sections: The Shutins, Highway 72 Bridge to D Low Bridge, Class III+

Length of Run: Day trip, 5.25 miles

Location: Madison County, Missouri; Mark Twain National Forest

Maps: USGS quads: Lake Killarney, Ironton

Times Runnable: Fall, winter, and spring after rain

Gauge: USGS gauge at Roselle

Permit: None required

Source of Levels: US Army Corps of Engineers Recording, 314-928-1194.

How Reported: Feet on the Roselle gauge. Convert this to the D Bridge paddlers' gauge (see below).

Additional Gauge: The D Bridge paddlers' gauge

Source of Levels: Mark Twain National Forest, 314-783-7225.

How Reported: Most paddlers go by the D Bridge gauge at the take-out, and this is the gauge that will be reported by the National Forest Rangers. The nomenclature on this gauge is a little confusing, so follow closely: when water is below the top of the D low-water bridge, the level is reported in terms of inches on the gauge immediately downstream. The top of the bridge is equivalent to about 40 inches on this gauge. Once the water reaches the top of D Bridge, then the level is reported in terms of the number of feet above the bridge.

Interpretation of Levels: Low water is 0 inches to 15 inches. Medium is 15 inches on up to the bridge. High is from the top of the bridge to 2 1/2 feet over its top. Floodstage is anything above that. Be warned that at levels from the top of the bridge to 1 foot over the bridge, the Dam Breach Rapid at Silvermine develops a monster hole and becomes serious Class V+. At levels beyond that the Breach is Class VI.

Source of More Information: USDA Forest Service, Fredericktown Ranger District, Mark Twain National Forest, Rt. 2, Box 175, Fredericktown, MO 63645; 314-783-7225.

Best Guidebooks: Kennon, *Ozark Whitewater.*

Further Comments: A true story. A bunch of the fine Memphis paddlers and I ran the St. Francis once at floodstage, seven feet over the D Bridge at the take-out. Lots of fun and big water! When we arrived at the dam at Silvermine, as you might imagine, the Breach on river-left was awesome. A tremendous green tongue arched smoothly down for 20 feet into the most awesome hole you'll ever see. Enough water was backed up behind the broken dam that the pool was filled and four inches or so were flowing over the intact top of the dam to river-right. Even I wasn't stupid enough to go boating through the Breach, but I did get the insane idea of paddling over the top of the dam, and plunging over 20 feet down to the eddy below. Smart! I was immediately sucked back against the face and hammered. No way to roll—the force of water falling on my head was too much, so it was time to swim.

Once I was out of my boat, I had another problem. The whirlpool-eddy in which I was floundering fed directly into the maw of the monster Dam Breach hole! Luckily for me, Dennis Rhodes was standing in the flow on top of the dam, and was able, after three attempts, to hit me with a rope just before I flushed into the hole and my certain doom. Then he ran toward the bank, while I made rappel-hops along the dam face, allowing me to breath from time to time. Now this was excellent fun!

Gauge Conversion: The conversion from the Roselle (Army Corps) gauge to the D Bridge (paddlers') gauge and to cfs is as follows:

Roselle	D Bridge	Cfs
2.7 feet	-6 inches	
3.6 feet	+8 inches	292
3.9 feet	+13 inches	407
4.43 feet	+20 inches	661
5.1 feet	+27 inches	1005
7.95 feet	2.5 feet over	1772
9.41 feet	3.5 feet over	3740
10.5 feet	4.0 feet over	7750
14.9 feet	12.3 feet over	19,140

MONTANA

BLACKFOOT RIVER

Sections: Whitaker Bridge to McNamara Bridge at Johnsrud State Park, Class II-III

Length of Run: Day trip, 6 miles

Location: Missoula County, Montana; Lolo National Forest

Maps: USGS quads: Sunflower, Potomac

Times Runnable: Best during high water in May and June; runnable from April to August.

Permit: None required

Gauge: Blackfoot River near Bonner

Source of Levels: National Weather Service, Great Falls; 406-453-2081.

Trail Head, 406-543-6966.

How Reported: Cfs

Interpretation of Levels: High water extends from about the 1st to the 15th of June, with peak around 7000 cfs. Minimum is about 1000 cfs, and optimum is around 2000 to 5000.

Source of More Information: Montana Department of Fish, Wildlife and Parks, Region 2 Headquarters, 3201 Spurgin Rd., Missoula, MT 59801; 406-542-5500.

USDA Forest Service, Lolo National Forest, Building 24, Missoula, MT 59801; 406-329-3750.

Trail Head, 501 S. Higgins Ave., Missoula, MT 59801; 406-543-6966.

Western Waters, 333 Knowles St., Missoula, MT 59801; 406-728-6161.

Best Guidebooks: Fischer, *Floaters' Guide to Montana.*

CLARK FORK

Sections: Alberton Gorge, St. John's access to Forest Grove access, Class II-III (with two at IV at optimum levels)

Length of Run: Day trip, 21 to 23 miles

Location: Mineral County, Montana; Lolo National Forest

Maps: USGS quads: Alberton (15'), Petty Mountain (15')

Times Runnable: Year-round, except when frozen in winter.

Permit: None required

Gauge: Clark Fork above Missoula

Source of Levels: National Weather Service, Great Falls, 406-453-2081.

How Reported: Cfs

Additional Gauge: Clark Fork below Missoula

Source of Levels: National Weather Service, Great Falls; 406-453-2081.

Trail Head, Missoula; 406-543-6966.

How Reported: Cfs

Interpretation of Levels: Minimum is 2000 cfs. Medium ranges from 4000 to 10,000. From 10,000 to 20,000 cfs is high. Peak flows range from 15,000 to 40,000 in June (experts only, approaching Class V overall).

Source of More Information: Montana Department of Fish, Wildlife and Parks, Region 2 Headquarters, 3201 Spurgin Rd., Missoula, MT 59801; 406-542-5500.

USDA Forest Service, Lolo National Forest, Building 24, Missoula, MT 59801; 406-329-3750.

Trail Head, 501 S. Higgins Ave., Missoula, MT 59801; 406-543-6966.

Western Waters, 333 Knowles St., Missoula, MT 59801; 406-728-6161.

Best Guidebooks: Fischer, *Floater's Guide to Montana.*

Further Comments: The Clark Fork is tough and dangerous at spring levels, but is a safe and fun play river in July and August. Be careful; there have been a number of drownings of insufficiently experienced boaters here lately.

FLATHEAD RIVER, MAIN STEM

Sections: Buffalo Rapids, from Kerr Dam below Polson to first bridge, Class III

Length of Run: Day trip, 6 miles

Location: Lake and Sands Counties, Montana

Maps: USGS quads: Polson, Buffalo Bridge

Times Runnable: Year-round; best in spring and summer

Permit: A tribal recreation permit is required from the Flathead Indian Reservation. These are available for $5 at most sporting goods stores in Montana, and are good for a year. A stamp to allow fishing is an extra $10. For further information, contact the Tribal Information Center at 406-675-2700.

Reservations: None required

Gauge: Release from Kerr Dam on Flathead Lake

Source of Levels: Montana Power Office at Kerr Dam, 406-883-4450.

How Reported: Cfs

Interpretation of Levels: Releases of water fluctuate widely on this section of the Flathead, due to variations in power demands. Levels vary from 2000 to 25,000 cfs, averaging in the summer around 10,000 to 13,000. Optimum is between 10,000 to 18,000 cfs. Many rapids are more difficult lower; higher water causes many rapids to wash out, but funny water effects do increase.

Source of More Information: Glacier Raft Co., Box 264, West Glacier, MT 59936; 406-888-5541, 800-332-9995 (inside Montana), 406-883-5838 (Polson Outpost).

Best Guidebooks: Fischer, *Floaters' Guide to Montana.*

FLATHEAD RIVER, MIDDLE FORK
Wild and Scenic River

Sections:
(1) Schaeffer Meadows air access to Bear Creek, Class III, IV (Class V in the opinion of the Forest Service)
(2) Bear Creek to West Glacier, Class III-IV

Length of Run:
(1) 1-2 days, 25 miles
(2) 2-3 days, 35 miles (shorter sections possible)

Location: Flathead County, Montana; Glacier National

Park and Flathead National Forest

Maps: USGS quads: Pinnacle, Stanton Lake, Nyack, West Glacier, Lake McDonald West

Times Runnable: On Section (1), flows are fickle; generally the brief season extends from June into July. Section (2) is usually runnable, except when it's too cold.

Permit: Backcountry permits are required for camping on the Glacier National Park side of the river: Glacier National Park, West Glacier, MT 59936; 406-888-5441.

Gauge: Middle Fork of the Flathead, near West Glacier

Source of Levels: National Weather Service, Great Falls; 406-453-2081.

USDA Forest Service, Hungry Horse Ranger District; 406-387-5243.

How Reported: Cfs

Interpretation of Levels: The average low flow in winter at the USGS gauging station is about 1000 cfs (still runnable); the peak flows in May approach 11,000 cfs (probably in the Class IV range).

Source of More Information: Glacier National Park, West Glacier, MT 59936; 406-888-5441.

USDA Forest Service, Hungry Horse Ranger District, Flathead National Forest, Hungry Horse, MT 59919; 406-387-5243.

Glacier Raft Co., Box 264, West Glacier, MT 59936; 406-888-5541, 800-332-9995 (inside Montana).

Best Guidebooks: Fischer, *Floaters' Guide to Montana;* Interagency Whitewater Committee, *River Information Digest.*

Further Comments: The upper section may be too difficult for many boaters at peak flows.

GALLATIN RIVER

Sections: (1) Red Cliff access to Big Sky, Class II
(2) Big Sky to Greek Creek, Class III
(3) Greek Creek to Squaw Creek Bridge, Class III-IV
(4) Squaw Creek to Williams Bridge, Class III

Length of Run: (1) Day trip, 6 miles
(2) Day trip, 6 miles
(3) Day trip, 4 miles
(4) Day trip, 8 miles

Location: Gallatin County, Montana; Gallatin National Forest

Maps: USGS quads: Garnet Mtn. (15'), Spanish Peaks (15'), Anceney (15'), Bozeman (15')

Times Runnable: May to June during high water

Permit: None required

Gauge: USGS near Gallatin Gateway (near Squaw Creek)

Source of Levels: National Weather Service, Great Falls; 406-453-2081.

USDA Forest Service, Bozeman Ranger District, Gallatin National Forest; 406-587-6920.

Yellowstone Raft Co., Big Sky Outpost; 406-995-4613.

How Reported: Cfs

Interpretation of Levels: Minimum is about 500 cfs. Moderate flows range from about 1000 to 1800 cfs. Above 2000 is usually considered too high.

Source of More Information: USDA Forest Service, Bozeman Ranger District, Gallatin National Forest, 601 Nickles, Bozeman, MT 59715; 406-587-6920.

Northern Lights Trading Co., 1627 W. Main St., Bozeman, MT 59715; 406-586-2225.

Yellowstone Raft Co., Box 46AG, Gardiner, MT 59030; 406-848-7777, 406-995-4613 (Big Sky outpost).

Montana Department of Fish, Wildlife and Parks, RIII, 1400 S. 19th, Bozeman, MT 59715; 406-994-4042.

Best Guidebooks: Fischer, *Floaters' Guide to Montana.*

MADISON RIVER

Sections: Bear Trap Canyon, Ennis Lake to Hwy. 84 near Red Bluff, Class II-III (one at IV, increasing to IV-V at high water)

Length of Run: Day trip, 10 miles

Location: Madison County, Montana; Bear Trap Canyon Wilderness

Maps: USGS quads: Ennis (S) (15'), Norris (15')

Times Runnable: Spring and summer

Permit: None required

Gauge: Release from Montana Power Madison Dam on Ennis Lake

Source of Levels: Bureau of Land Management, Bear Trap Canyon Wilderness; 406-683-2337. Or use the sign posted at the put-in, updated daily by the BLM.

How Reported: Cfs

Interpretation of Levels: Flows range from 900 to 10,000 cfs (but are rarely over 6000). Optimum is about 1500 to 2200 cfs. High is 2500 cfs. Very high is 4000 to 10,000.

Source of More Information: Bureau of Land Management, Bear Trap Canyon Wilderness, Ibey Building, PO Box 1048, Dillon, MT 59725; 406-683-2337.

Butte District Office, Bureau of Land Management, PO Box 3388, Butte, MT 59702; 406-494-5059.

Northern Lights Trading Co., 1627 W. Main St., Bozeman, MT 59715; 406-586-2225.

Yellowstone Raft Co., Box 46AG, Gardiner, MT 59030; 406-848-7777 or 406-995-4613 (Big Sky outpost).

Best Guidebooks: Fischer, *Floaters' Guide to Montana;* BLM, "Floaters' Guide to Bear Trap Canyon" (available from the BLM address above).

MISSOURI RIVER
Wild and Scenic River

Sections: Fort Benton to Fred Robinson Bridge, Class I

Length of Run: 5-7 days, 149 miles, shorter sections possible

Location: Chocteau, Blaine, and Fregos Counties, Montana; Missouri Breaks National Wild and Scenic River

Maps: USGS quads: Fort Benton, O'Hanlon Coulee, Loma West, Rocky Lake, Loma East, Stranahan, Boggs Island, Verona, Lonetree, Coulee, Pilot Rock, Eagle Buttes, Dark Butte, Last Chance, Starve-Out Flat, P N Ranch, Council Island, Gallatin Rapids, Taffy Ridge, Leroy, Bird Rapids, Sturgeon Island, Low Island. Also: BLM "Upper Missouri National Wild and Scenic River Maps 1 & 2," and BLM "Upper Missouri National Wild and Scenic River Maps 3 & 4."

Times Runnable: Year-round, unless it's too cold.

Permit: All boaters must check in with a ranger or self-register at the put-in. In addition, groups of boaters associated with organizations or universities must have a special use permit. An application form is included in Appendix One.

Gauge: Missouri at Fort Benton

Source of Levels: National Weather Service, Great Falls, 406-453-2081.

Bureau of Land Management, 406-538-7461.

How Reported: Cfs

Additional Gauge: Missouri River near Virgelle

Source of Levels: National Weather Service, Great Falls; 406-453-2081.

Bureau of Land Management, 406-538-7461.

How Reported: Cfs

Additional Gauge: Missouri River near Landusky

Source of Levels: National Weather Service, Great Falls; 406-453-2081.

Bureau of Land Management, 406-538-7461.

How Reported: Cfs

Interpretation of Levels: Follow the recommendation of the BLM.

Source of More Information: River Manager, Bureau of Land Management, 80 Airport Rd., Lewiston, MT 59457; 406-538-7461.

Best Guidebooks: Fischer, *Floaters' Guide to Montana;* Interagency Whitewater Committee, *River Information Digest;* BLM, Maps (above); BLM, "Some Hazards on the Upper Missouri National Wild and Scenic River" (from BLM, address above); BLM, "Highlights of the Upper Missouri National Wild and Scenic River and the Lewis and Clark National Historic Trail" (from BLM, address above).

Further Comments: A trip down the Missouri provides an unmatched experience of the Northern Great Plains!

STILLWATER RIVER

Sections: (1) Woodbine Campground to Mouat Mine, Class IV, V
(2) Mouat Mine (below Chrome Mine Rapids) to Moraine, Class I, II
(3) Moraine to Cliffswallow, Class III, IV
(4) Cliffswallow to Absarokee, Class II

Length of Run: (1) Day trip, 3 miles
(2) Day trip, 9 miles
(3) Day trip, 8 miles
(4) Day trip, 8 miles

Location: Stillwater County, Montana

Maps: USGS quads: Mt. Wood (15'), Beehive, Cow Face Hill, Sandborn Creek, Absarokee

Times Runnable: Mid-May to early July

Permit: None required

Gauge: Stillwater near Absarokee

Source of Levels: National Weather Service, Great Falls; 406-453-2081.

How Reported: Cfs

Interpretation of Levels: About 1000 to 2000 cfs should be O.K.

Source of More Information: Montana Department of Fish, Wildlife and Parks, 1420 East 6th Ave., Helena, MT 59624; 406-444-2535.

Best Guidebooks: Fischer, *Floaters' Guide to Montana.*

Further Comments: Watch out for low bridges between Moraine and Cliffswallow.

YELLOWSTONE RIVER

Sections: Yankee Jim Canyon, Joe Brown Trail to public access at Corbella, along Highway 89, Class III (to IV high)

Length of Run: Day trip, 4.5 miles

Location: Park County, Montana

Maps: USGS quads: Miner (15')

Times Runnable: Year-round, unless it's too cold

Permit: None required

Gauge: Yellowstone at Corwin Springs

Source of Levels: National Weather Service, Great Falls; 406-453-2081.

Yellowstone Raft Co., 406-848-7777.

How Reported: Cfs

Interpretation of Levels: The river is lowest in January— around 1000 to 2000 cfs, but is still runnable. The crest is in June, usually around 19,000 to 20,000 cfs, but it has been as high as 36,000. Low levels range from 1000 to 5000; medium from 5000 to 10,000, and high is from 10,000 to 20,000. For kayaks, 5000 to 6000 is optimum.

Source of More Information: Montana Department of Fish, Wildlife and Parks, 1420 East 6th Ave., Helena, MT 59624; 406-444-2535.

Yellowstone Raft Co., Box 46AG, Gardiner, MT 59030; 406-848-7777.

Best Guidebooks: Fischer, *Floaters' Guide to Montana.*

GENERAL INFORMATION SOURCES FOR MONTANA

The National Weather Service Forecast Office in Great Falls, Montana serves as the hydrologic service office for Montana: 406-453-2081.

They can report readings for the following gauges:

Columbia River Basin:
   Kootenai River, below Libby Dam
   Fisher River, near Libby
   Kootenai River, at Libby
   Yaak River, near Troy
   Rock Creek, near Clinton
   Blackfoot River, near Bonner
   Clark Fork, above Missoula
   Bitterroot River, near Darby
   Clark Fork, below Missoula
   St. Regis River, at St. Regis
   Clark Fork, at St. Regis
   North Fork of the Flathead River, near Columbia Falls
   Middle Fork of the Flathead River, near West Glacier
   South Fork of the Flathead River
      Above Twin Creek
      Below Hungry Horse
   Flathead River, at Columbia Falls
   Swan River, near Big Fork
   Clark Fork, near Plains

Missouri River Basin:
   St. Mary River, at Babb
   Red Rock River, below Lima Reservoir
   Beaverhead River, at Twin Bridges
   Jefferson River, at Three Forks
   Madison River
      Below Hebgen Dam
      Below Ennis
   Gallatin River
      Near Gallatin Gateway
      At Logan
   Missouri River, at Toston
   Smith River, at Fort Logan

Missouri River, near Ulm
Sun River, near Vaughn
Missouri River, at Fort Benton
Marias River
   At Shelby
   Near Chester below Tiber Dam
Missouri River
   At Virgelle
   Near Landusky
Musselshell River
   At Harlowton
   At Roundup
Big Dry Creek, at Van Norman
Milk River, at Western Crossing
North Fork of the Milk River
   Above Canal
   Near Boundary
Milk River, at Eastern Crossing
Big Sandy Creek, at Havre
Clear Creek, near Chinook
Battle Creek, near Chinook
Milk River
   Near Harlem
   At Saco
   At Nashua
Missouri River
   Near Wolf Point
   Near Culberson

Yellowstone River Basin:
   Yellowstone River
      At Corwin Springs
      At Livingston
   Boulder River, at Big Timber
   Stillwater River, near Absarokee
   Clarks Fork of the Yellowstone River, near Belfry
   Yellowstone River, at Billings
   Big Horn River
      Near St. Xavier
      At Big Horn
   Tongue River, at Miles City
   Yellowstone River, at Miles City
   Powder River, at Locate
   Yellowstone River, at Sidney

NEW HAMPSHIRE

AMMONOOSUC RIVER

Sections: (1) River Road to Pierce Bridge, Class II+
(2) Pierce Bridge to Rt. 116, Class II-IV

Length of Run: (1) Day trip, 3 miles
(2) Day trip, 7 miles

Location: Grafton County, New Hampshire

Maps: USGS quads: Littleton (15'), Whitefield (15')

Times Runnable: Short season during peak runoff in March and April

Permit: None required

Gauge: Bethlehem USGS gauge, 0.2 mi. upstream from the Hwy. 302 Bridge at the take-out for Section (1)

Source of Levels: National Weather Service, Portland, ME; 207-773-0352.

Perhaps one of the following, too:

Merrimack Valley Paddlers' Recording, 603-432-6870.

Saco Bound, Center Conway, NH, 603-447-2177/3801.

How Reported: Feet

Additional Gauge: USGS gauge at Bath (downstream from Bath, NH)

Source of Levels: National Weather Service, Portland, ME, 207-773-0352.

How Reported: Feet

Interpretation of Levels: Both gauges read similarly. Minimum is about 4 feet; medium is 5, and high is 6.

Source of More Information: Saco Bound, Box 119, Center Conway, NH 03913; 603-447-2177, 603-447-3801.

Best Guidebooks: Gabler, *New England Whitewater River Guide*.

Gauge Conversions:

Bethlehem Gauge

Feet	Cfs	Feet	Cfs	Feet	Cfs
3.0	400	5.0	1290	7.0	3220
3.2	470	5.2	1430	7.2	3460
3.4	540	5.4	1570	7.4	3720
3.6	610	5.6	1730	7.6	3980
3.8	680	5.8	1890	7.8	4240
4.0	755	6.0	2070	8.0	4500
4.2	845	6.2	2270	8.5	5150
4.4	945	6.4	2380	9.0	5830
4.6	1050	6.6	2740	9.5	6550
4.8	1170	6.8	2980	10.0	7310

Bath Gauge

Feet	Cfs	Feet	Cfs	Feet	Cfs
3.0	600	5.2	2050	7.4	4560
3.2	695	5.4	2230	7.6	4840
3.4	795	5.6	2410	7.8	5120
3.6	900	5.8	2600	8.0	5400
3.8	1010	6.0	2800	8.2	5720
4.0	1130	6.2	3040	8.4	6040
4.2	1260	6.4	3280	8.6	6360
4.4	1400	6.6	3520	8.8	6680
4.6	1550	6.8	3760	9.0	7000
4.8	1710	7.0	4000	9.5	7900
5.0	1870	7.2	4280	10.0	8800

ANDROSCOGGIN RIVER

Sections: Errol to Pontook School, along Highway 16, Class I (II high)

Length of Run: Day trip, 20 miles

Location: Coos County, New Hampshire

Maps: USGS quads: Berlin, Errol (15'), Milan (15')

Times Runnable: After scheduled releases from Pontook Dam during the summer

Permit: None required

Gauge: Dam release at Errol

Source of Levels: A schedule of releases is available from: Saco Bound, Box 119, Center Conway, NH 03913; 603-447-2177.

How Reported: Feet

Interpretation of Levels: Low but runnable is 1500 cfs. Anything above that is good.

Source of More Information: Saco Bound, Box 119, Center Conway, NH 03913; 603-447-2177, 603-447-3801.

Best Guidebooks: Gabler, *New England Whitewater River Guide.*

Further Comments: A good place to play when nothing else is running in the summer.

ASHUELOT RIVER

Sections:
(1) Marlow to Gilsum Gorge, Class III-IV (IV high)
(2) Below Gilsum Gorge to Shaws Corner, Class II
(3) Ashuelot to Hinsdale, Class III-IV

Length of Run:
(1) Day trip, 3.5 miles
(2) Day trip, 4 miles
(3) Day trip, 3.5 miles

Location: Cheshire County, New Hampshire

Maps: USGS quads: Lovewell Mtn., Bellows Falls

Times Runnable: April

Permit: None required

Gauge: For Sections (1) and (2), a stage marker on a concrete wall upstream river left of a stone arch bridge above Gilsum Gorge, between Sections (1) and (2)

Source of Levels: Probably only by visual inspection, but you might try:

Merrimack Valley Paddlers' Recording; 603-432-6870.

How Reported: Feet

Additional Gauge: For Section (3) it was once the practice to use the US Army Corps telemetering gauge at Hinsdale. However, since the Army Corps will no longer give readings to the public, you might try to use the release from Surry Mountain Dam way upstream, which you can get from the NWS.

Source of Levels: National Weather Service, Portland, ME; 207-773-0352.

How Reported: Cfs

Interpretation of Levels: For Sections (1) and (2), low is about 5 feet; medium is 6 feet, and very high is 7.5 feet (Gilsum gauge). The interpretation of the Surry Mountain release for Section (3) is unknown, but since it reads in cfs, you ought to be able to figure it out pretty quickly. Section (1) has been run as high as 12 feet by experts (they described it as being "very, very exciting").

Best Guidebooks: Gabler, *New England Whitewater River Guide.*

Further Comments: Gilsum Gorge (Class IV+ to V) is located between Sections (1) and (2). It is usually carried. There are three dams on Section (3).

COLD RIVER

Sections: (1) South Acworth to Vilas Pool, Class II
(2) Alsted to Drewsville, Class II

Length (1) Day trip, 5.5 miles
of Run: (2) Day trip, 2 miles

Location: Sullivan County, New Hampshire

Maps: USGS quads: North Conway (15'), Fryeburg (15')

Times Runnable: Late spring or after heavy rain

Permit: None required

Gauge: Drewsville gauge on river-left, just upstream of the Highway 123A Bridge below the take-out.

Source of Levels: Probably only by visual inspection, but you might try:

Merrimack Valley Paddlers' Recording; 603-432-6870.

How Reported: Feet

Interpretation of Levels: Minimum is 4 feet, and optimum is about 5 feet.

Source of More Information: Saco Bound, Box 119, Center Conway, NH 03913; 603-447-2177, 603-447-3801.

Best Guidebooks: Gabler, *New England Whitewater River Guide.*

Further Comments: There are two dams in the stretch that separates Section (1) from Section (2). There is a falls to portage near the take-out for Section (2).

CONTOOCOOK RIVER

Sections: Freight Train Section, Western Avenue to take-out above West Henniker Dam, Class III-IV

Length Day trip, 2 miles
of Run:

Location: Hillsborough County, New Hampshire

Maps: USGS quads: Hillsborough (15')

Times Runnable: Spring, summer, and fall

Permit: None required

Gauge: Western Avenue Gauge near Henniker

Source of Levels: Probably only by visual inspection, but you might try:

Merrimack Valley Paddlers' Recording; 603-432-6870.

How Reported: Cfs

Interpretation of Levels: About 1000 cfs is minimum, 4000 is high.

Source of More Information: Saco Bound, Box 119, Center Conway, NH 03913; 603-447-2177, 603-447-3801.

Best Guidebooks: Connelly and Porterfield, *Appalachian Whitewater, Vol. III.*

MAD RIVER

Sections: Highway 49 Bridge at Waterville Valley to Highway 49 Bridge at Goose Hollow, Class III-IV

Length (1) Day trip, 8.5 miles
of Run:

Location: Grafton County, New Hampshire

Maps: USGS quads: Plymouth (15')

Times Runnable: Brief runoff for a few weeks in April; very difficult to catch.

Permit: None required

Gauge: Paddlers' gauge on rock on left at 6-mile bridge

Source of Levels: Probably only by visual inspection, but you might try:

Merrimack Valley Paddlers' Recording; 603-432-6870.

How Reported: Feet

Additional Gauge: Mad River at Compton Pond

Source of Levels: National Weather Service, Portland, ME; 207-773-0352.

How Reported: Feet

Interpretation of Levels: On the paddlers' gauge, 1.5 feet is minimum; 2.5 is medium, and 3 is high. If the Compton Pond gauge is at 11 feet, then there is usually enough water.

Source of More Information: Saco Bound, Box 119, Center Conway, NH 03913; 603-447-2177, 603-447-3801.

Best Guidebooks: Gabler, *New England Whitewater River Guide.*

MASCOMA RIVER

Sections: Mascoma Lake to Rt. 4, Lebanon, Class II-III (IV high)

Length of Run: Day trip, 4 miles

Location: Grafton County, New Hampshire

Maps: USGS quads: Mascoma (15'), Hanover

Times Runnable: After heavy rains from March to May or in the fall after releases by the New Hampshire Water Resources Board

Permit: None required

Gauge: Release from Mascoma Lake

Source of Levels: Schedules for the fall drawdown are available from the New Hampshire Water Resources Board, 603-271-1110.

How Reported: Dates and predicted levels in feet

Additional Gauge: Staff gauge on river-left just downstream of the put-in below Mascoma Lake

Source of Levels: Visual inspection, but maybe Merrimack Valley Paddlers' Recording, 603-432-6870.

How Reported: Feet

Interpretation of Levels: 2.5 feet is a moderate level and is the standard release.

Source of More Information: Ledyard Canoe Club, Dartmouth College, Hanover, NH 03756; 603-646-2753.

Best Guidebooks: Connelly and Porterfield, *Appalachian Whitewater, Vol. III.*

Further Comments: Just downstream of the take-out is an unrunnable dam; in Lebanon there is a Class VI-VI+ section.

MERRIMACK RIVER

Sections: Arms Park in the city of Manchester below Amoskeag Dam, Class II-III (a runnable Class V Section is upstream)

Length of Run: Playspot, 0.25 mile

Location: Hillsborough County, New Hampshire

Maps: USGS quads: Manchester North

Times Runnable: All year, dam released

Permit: None required

Gauge: Amoskeag Falls Dam at Manchester

Source of Levels: National Weather Service, Portland, ME, 207-773-0352.

Interpretation of Levels: Runnable and fun year-round.

Source of More Information: Don's Sport Center, Manchester, NH; 603-668-4440.

Best Guidebooks: Connelly and Porterfield, *Appalachian Whitewater, Vol. III*

Further Comments: Water quality is poor.

PEMIGEWASSET RIVER

Sections: Bristol Gorge, Bristol to Coolidge Woods Road, Class II-III (IV high)

Length of Run: Day trip, 2.5 miles

Location: Grafton and Belknap Counties, New Hampshire

Maps: USGS quads: Holderness

Times Runnable: Year-round (dam released)

Permit: None required

Gauge: Release from power dam at Ayres Island, Bristol

Source of Levels: Perhaps from: Merrimack Valley Paddlers' Recording, 603-432-6870.

How Reported: In numbers of tubes (or turbines)

Interpretation of Levels: Minimum is release from one tube, about 500 cfs. Ideal is 2 (1000 cfs) or 3 (1500 cfs). Can be run by sufficiently competent paddlers to floodstage (release through the spillway).

Source of More Information: Saco Bound, Box 119, Center Conway, NH 03913; 603-447-2177, 603-447-3801.

Best Guidebooks: Connelly and Porterfield, *Appalachian Whitewater, Vol. III.*

Further Comments: The Pemigewasset is favorite summertime play river for New England boaters.

PEMIGEWASSET RIVER, EAST BRANCH

Sections: Confluence of Franconia Brook at Pemigewasset Wilderness Area to North Woodstock, Class III-IV when low (IV medium; IV+ high; V extremely high)

Length of Run: Day trip, 3 miles

Location: Grafton County, New Hampshire; White Mountains National Forest

Maps: USGS quads: Mt. Osceola, Lincoln

Times Runnable: March to May after heavy rain

Permit: None required

Gauge: Paddlers' gauge on Kancamagus Bridge at the put-in.

Source of Levels: Saco Bound, 603-447-2177.

Pemigewasset Ranger Station, 603-536-1310.

How Reported: Feet

Interpretation of Levels: From .5 feet is low, 1.0 to 2.0 is medium, and 3.0 is high. Extremely high is 3.5 feet or over.

Source of More Information: Saco Bound, Box 119, Center Conway, NH 03913; 603-447-2177, 603-447-3801.

USDA Forest Service, Pemigewasset Ranger District, White Mountain National Forest, NH; 603-536-1310.

Best Guidebooks: Connelly and Porterfield, *Appalachian Whitewater, Vol. III.*

Squirts on a dynamic eddy line at the take-out of Bristol Gorge on New Hampshire's Pemigewasset River. Photo by John Porterfield.

SACO RIVER

Sections: Crawford Notch to Bartlet along Highway 302, Class III+ to III-IV

Length of Run: Day trip, 6.5 miles

Location: Carroll and Grafton Counties, New Hampshire; White Mountains National Forest

Maps: USGS quads: Crawford Notch (S) (15')

Times Runnable: Almost all summer

Permit: None required

Gauge: Paddlers' gauge on rock on river-right at take-out (recently damaged by extreme high water)

Source of Levels: Saco Bound, 603-447-2177, 603-447-3801.

How Reported: Feet

Additional Gauge: USGS Saco River at Conway

Source of Levels: National Weather Service, Portland, ME, 207-773-0352.

How Reported: Feet

Interpretation of Levels: Before the paddlers' gauge was damaged, 1.0 feet was low; 3-4 feet ideal and 4.0 feet was high. Nowadays, check with Saco Bound.

Source of More Information: Saco Bound, Box 119, Center Conway, NH 03913; 603-447-2177, 603-447-3801.

Bob Potter in Ray's Rapid on the Smith River at a level of over three feet. Photo by Jim Jackson.

The formidable Lower Falls at the put-in for the Swift River. Photo by Roger Belson.

Best Guidebooks: Gabler, *New England Whitewater River Guide;* Saco Bound, "Map of the Saco."

Best Guidebooks: Connelly and Porterfield, *Appalachian Whitewater, Vol. III.*

SMITH RIVER

Sections: Hill Center Road to Old Route 104 in Bristol, Class IV

Length of Run: Day trip, 5 miles

Location: Grafton and Merrimack Counties, New Hampshire; White Mountain National Forest

Maps: USGS quads: Cardigan and Holderness

Times Runnable: March to April; water levels dependent on recent rain or consistent runoff

Permit: None required

Gauge: Paddlers' gauge on Cass Mill Bridge, left abutment

Source of Levels: Probably only by visual inspection, but you might try:

Merrimack Valley Paddlers' Recording; 603-432-6870.

How Reported: Feet

Interpretation of Levels: Minimum is about 0.5 feet; optimum is 1 to 2 feet; high is 2.5 feet or more.

Source of More Information: Saco Bound, Box 119, Center Conway, NH 03913; 603-447-2177, 603-447-3801.

Bristol, NH Chamber of Commerce, 603-744-2150.

SWIFT RIVER

Sections:
(1) Kancamagus Highway to Lower Falls access. Class III-IV
(2) Lower Falls access area along Rt. 112 to Darby Field sign, Class III-IV

Length of Run:
(1) Day trip, 1.2 miles
(2) Day trip, 4.0 miles

Location: Carroll County, New Hampshire

Maps: USGS quads: Crawford Notch (15'), Mt. Chocura (15')

Times Runnable: March to May after heavy rains

Permit: None required

Gauge: Gauge rock in Swift Gorge on right

Source of Levels: USDA Forest Service, Saco District Ranger Station, White Mountain National Forest, (24-hr. ring-through recording during the season); 603-447-5448.

How Reported: Feet

Interpretation of Levels: 1.0 feet is very low; optimum ranges from 1.5 to 3.0 feet; high is 3.5 feet or over.

Source of More Information: USDA Forest Service, Saco District Ranger Station, White Mountain National Forest,

RFD. 1, Box 94, Kancamagus Highway, Conway, NH 03818; 603-447-5448.

Saco Bound, Box 119, Center Conway, NH 03913; 603-447-2177, 603-447-3801.

Downeast Whitewater Rafting, PO Box 119, Center Conway, NH 03813; 603-447-3002.

Best Guidebooks: Connelly and Porterfield, *Appalachian Whitewater, Vol. III;* Gabler, *New England Whitewater River Guide.*

Further Comments: Great place to show off for the tourists.

GENERAL INFORMATION SOURCES
FOR NEW HAMPSHIRE

The US Army Corps of Engineers and other managers of water projects coordinate many of the scheduled releases through the Appalachian Mountain Club. Call the office of the Appalachian Mountain Club in Boston; they should have a printed list they can mail out (I don't recommend that you call the New England division of the Army Corps—they don't want to hear from you). Appalachian Mountain Club, New England Rivers Center, Boston, 5 Joy St., Boston, MA 02108; 617-523-0636.

The Merrimack Valley Paddlers have established a river phone line that reports upcoming trips and that may include levels on various rivers. Call 603-432-6870.

The Northern New England Hydrological Service Area of the National Weather Service in Portland, Maine, can provide updated gauge listings for Maine and New Hampshire. Call: 207-773-0352.

Reports are available for the following New Hampshire gauges, levels in feet except where indicated otherwise:

Saco River, at Conway
Ammonoosuc River
    At Bethlehem
    At Bath
    At Dalton
Ashuelot River, release from Surry Mountain Dam
Pemigewasset River
    At Plymouth
    At Woodstock
Piscataquog River, at Goffstown
Mad River, at Compton Pond
Baker River, at Rumney
Soucook River, at Soucook
Merrimack River
    At Amoskeag Falls in Manchester
    At Concord
    At Goffs Falls
    At Hopkinton Dam
    At Franklin Falls
Connecticut River
    At West Lebanon
    At Walpole
    At North Stratford

NEW MEXICO

CHAMA RIVER
Wild and Scenic River

Sections:
    (1) Upper Chama Run, Plaza Blanca to El Vado Lake, Class III
    (2) Wilderness Run, El Vado Ranch to Chavez Canyon Take-out, Class II
    (3) Chavez Canyon to Adobe Ruins, Class III

Length of Run:
    (1) Day trip, 15 miles
    (2) Day trip, 22 miles
    (3) Day trip, 9 miles

Runs (2) and (3) are often combined to make a two-day wilderness trip.

Location: Rio Arriba and Santa Fe Counties, New Mexico; Chama River Wilderness of Santa Fe National Forest; Carson National Forest; Taos Resource Area of the Bureau of Land Management.

Maps: USGS quads: Tierra Amarilla (15'), Navajo Peak, Laguna Peak, Echo Amphitheatre, Ghost Ranch, Canones, Abiquiu

Times Runnable: Section (1) is runnable from April into early June. Sections (2) and (3) are runnable from May until early August, with occasional weekend recreational releases extending the season into early September.

Permit: For the Wilderness Run, Section (2), register with the BLM ranger stationed at the private resort at El Vado Ranch. El Vado Ranch also charges fees of $1 per person as a launch fee, $2 per night per auto for parking, and $2 per auto for camping. For more information, contact: El Vado Ranch, PO Box 129, Tierra Amarilla, NM 87575; 505-588-7354, or Taos Resource Area, Bureau of Land Management, PO Box 1045, Taos, NM 87571; 505-758-8851 or 505-758-8148 (recording).

Restrictions: No more than two nights may be spent on Section (2).

Gauge: For Section (1), inflow to El Vado Lake

Source of levels: Bureau of Reclamation; 505-766-3719.

Bureau of Land Management recording; 505-758-8148.

How Reported: Cfs

Additional gauge: Release from El Vado Lake

Source of levels: National Weather Service, Albuquerque; 505-243-1453.

Bureau of Reclamation; 505-766-3719.

How Reported: Cfs

Interpretation of Levels: For Section (1), minimum is about 600 cfs. It stays good to peak releases. For Sections (2) and (3), minimum is about 800 cfs. Peak release is about 4000 cfs, which is still fun and safe.

Source of More Information: New Wave Rafting; Rt. 5, Box 302; Santa Fe, NM 87501; 505-984-1444.

New Mexico State Parks, Natural Resources Division; 141 East de Varen; PO Box 1147; Santa Fe, NM 87503; 505-827-7465.

El Vado Ranch, PO Box 129, Tierra Amarilla, NM 87575; 505-588-7354.

Chama River Park, PO Box 306, Chama, NM 87520; 505-756-2306.

USDA Forest Service, Coyote Ranger District, Santa Fe National Forest Coyote, NM 87504; 505-638-5526.

Taos Resource Area, Bureau of Land Management, PO Box 1045, Taos, NM 87571; 505-758-8851, 505-758-8148 (recording).

Best Guidebooks: New Mexico State Parks. *New Mexico Whitewater.* BLM map/guide, "Rio Chama: A Wild and Scenic River"

Further Comments: Part of Section (3) of the Chama is in danger of being inundated by proposed additional storage by Abiquiu Lake. Legislation to protect the Chama by inclusion in the National Wild and Scenic River System is before Congress. Write to your representatives in Washington.

GILA RIVER

Sections:

   (1) State Highway 15 Bridge at East Fork to Forest Road 155 at Turkey Creek, Class II-III

   (2) Mogollon Creek to FS 809, Class I

   (3) Middle Box, FS 809 to Red Rock, Class II-III

   (4) Lower Box, Red Rock to Virden, Class I

Length of Run:

   (1) 3-4 days, 32 miles
   (2) 1-2 days, 20 miles
   (3) 1-2 days, 18 miles
   (4) 1-2 days, 20 miles

Location: Catron and Hidalgo Counties, New Mexico; Gila National Forest

Maps: USGS quads: (1) Gila Hot Springs, Little Turkey Park, Granny Mountain, Canyon Hill, Canteen Canyon; (2) Canteen Canyon, Cliff (15'); (3) Cliff (15'), Red Rock (15'); (4) Red Rock (15'), Canador Peak (15')

Times Runnable: Short season of several weeks in late March or April

Permit: None required

Gauge: USGS Gila River near Gila, New Mexico

Source of Levels: National Weather Service, Albuquerque Recording (April through June); 505-588-7354.

How Reported: Cfs

Interpretation of Levels: Minimum is around 200 cfs. Optimum ranges from 450 to 1000 cfs. Very high is 1500.

Source of More Information: For Sections (1) and (2): USDA Forest Service, Silver City Ranger District, Gila National Forest, Rt. 8, Box 1244, Silver City, NM 88061; 505-538-2771.

For Sections (3) and (4): Bureau of Land Management, Los Cruces Resource Area, PO Box 1420, Los Cruces, NM 88004; 505-525-8228.

New Wave Rafting, Rt. 5, Box 302, Santa Fe, NM 87501; 505-984-1444.

New Mexico State Parks, Natural Resources Division, 141 East de Varen, PO Box 1147, Santa Fe, NM 87503; 505-827-7465.

Best Guidebooks: New Mexico State Parks, *New Mexico Whitewater;* Interagency Whitewater Committee, *River Information Digest.*

Further Comments: Section (1) is an excellent wilderness trip. On all sections, watch out for fences, logjams, and diversion dams. The Middle Box is threatened by a proposed dam.

PECOS RIVER

Sections: Antonchico Canyon, Villanueva State Park to Tecolotito, Class III

Length of Run: Day trip, 19 miles

Location: San Miguel and Guadalupe Counties, New Mexico

Maps: USGS quads: Villanueva (15'), San Juan (15'), Antonchico (15')

Times Runnable: May and possibly June in a good year

Permit: None required

Gauge: USGS Pecos River near Santa Rosa

Source of Levels: National Weather Service, Albuquerque Recording (April through June); 505-243-1453.

How Reported: Cfs

Interpretation of Levels: About 600 cfs is minimum, and 1200 to 1500 is ideal. The Pecos is fun at even higher levels.

Source of More Information: New Wave Rafting, Rt. 5, Box 302, Santa Fe, NM 87501; 505-984-1444.

New Mexico State Parks, Natural Resources Division, 141 East de Varen, PO Box 1147, Santa Fe, NM 87503; 505-827-7465.

USDA Forest Service, Santa Fe National Forest, 120 St. Francis Dr., PO Box 1689, Santa Fe, NM 97504; 505-988-6940.

Villanueva State Park, General Delivery, Villanueva NM 87583; 505-421-2957.

Best Guidebooks: New Mexico State Parks, *New Mexico Whitewater.*

Further Comments: This is a *very long* one-day trip. Expect at least two portages of dams and many around fences.

RIO GRANDE RIVER
(See Texas for sections of Big Bend.)

Sections:
(1) The Ute Mountain Run, Lobatos Bridge, Colorado, to Lee Trail, Class I and II
(2) Razorblade Section, Lee Trail to Chiflo Campground, Class IV (to V high)
(3) Class V-VI Section, Chiflo Camp ground to Red River confluence; boating prohibited
(4) Red River confluence to Dunn Bridge, Class II (one at III). [Sections (1) through (4) are often referred to collectively as the Upper Box.]
(5) The Taos Box (or the Lower Box), Dunn Bridge to Taos Junction Bridge, Class IV+ (to V at high water)
(6) State Park Section, Taos Junction Bridge to Pilar, Class I-II
(7) Pilar Race Course Section, Pilar to County Line, Class III (IV high)

Length of Run:
(1) 2 days, 24 miles, plus hike out
(2) Day trip, 8 miles, plus hike in and out
(3) Portage or shuttle around
(4) Day trip, 8 miles, plus hike in and out
(5) Day trip, 16 miles
(6) Day trip, 7 miles
(7) Day trip, 6 miles

Location: Conejos and Costilla Counties, Colorado; Taos and Rio Arriba Counties, New Mexico

Maps: USGS quads: Kiowa Hill, Sky Valley Ranch, Ute Mtn., Sunshine, Arroyo Hondo, Los Cordovas, Taos SW, Carson, Trampas, Velarde, Lyden, San Juan Pueblo, Espanola, White Rock, Cochiti Dam

Times Runnable: Section (2) can be run only from April to July; the others, year-round.

Permit: Required by the BLM for Sections (1), (2), (4) and (5). Permits are not required for Sections (6) and (7); permission is denied for Section (3). Permits for Section (5), the Taos Box, are issued by the ranger at the launch point. Permits for other sections can be obtained from the BLM office, but it seems that you should apply well ahead of time; see below.

Reservations: Required for Sections (1), (2) and (4). Apply as early as 30 days prior to launch. For the Taos Box, Section (5), reservations are required only if you plan to camp along the river. Apply to the BLM in time to obtain your permits by mail at least two weeks prior to launch: Bureau of Land Management, Taos Resource Area, PO Box 1045, Taos, NM 87571; 505-758-8851. There is no application form.

Restrictions: These are numerous, and are well-described in the BLM literature. Here are the high points. The following equipment is required: first-aid kit, PFD, throw ropes in each boat, patch and repair kit, spare oars and paddles, gear and food in waterproof bags, firepans, and an ash receptacle. On the Taos Box, Section (5),

Kayaker below Government Rapid, San Juan River. Photo by Curt Smith.

rafts shorter than 11 feet must be with larger craft capable of carrying the smaller rafts' passengers in case the little ones get chewed. No open canoes are allowed on sections rated higher than III unless they are specially approved by the BLM. The maximum party size on the Upper Box, Section (4), is 15 persons, and 30 is the maximum on the Main Taos Box, Section (5). Bury feces away from the river. Carry out your garbage. Motors are prohibited (great!). When the flow is over 4000 cfs or the air temperature is below 60 degrees, single-boat launches are prohibited, rafts are required to have flip lines, and folks are required to wear drysuits, wetsuits, or polypro.

Gauge: BLM Rio Grande at the Taos Box

Source of Levels: Bureau of Land Management, Taos Resource Area; 505-758-8851.

How Reported: Cfs

Additional Gauge: USGS Rio Grande River at state line

Source of Levels: National Weather Service, Albuquerque Recording (April through June); 505-243-1453.

How Reported: Cfs

Interpretation of Levels: For most sections, about 600 to 800 cfs is considered minimum, and about 1500 to 3000 is considered optimum. Above 4000 cfs or below 60 degrees air temperature, the BLM considers the river hazardous and applies special restrictions (see above). New Wave Rafting and other outfitters rafted the Box at levels near 7000 cfs during the 1987 season; big waves and souse holes put the river in the Class V range at 4000 cfs or higher.

Source of More Information: For Sections (1) through (5)

contact the BLM, address and phone above. These folks will send you a packet of information. Include 25 cents and you can get the BLM's "Rio Grande Wild and Scenic River Map and Guide."

New Wave Rafting, Rt. 5, Box 302, Santa Fe, NM 87501; 505-984-1444.

New Mexico State Parks, Natural Resources Division, 141 East de Varen, PO Box 1147, Santa Fe, NM 87503; 505-827-7465.

Best Guidebooks: Anderson and Hopkinson, *Rivers of the Southwest;* New Mexico State Parks, *New Mexico Whitewater;* BLM, "Rio Grande Wild and Scenic River Map and Guide" (available from the BLM, address above).

Further Comments: Although commercial outfitters regularly run the Taos Box at all levels with few problems, many private boaters come to grief, especially at high water, when scouting becomes very difficult. Make sure you know what you're doing before you put in. Section (2) is an experts-only wilderness run with carries in and out.

A True Story. Tom Moore of Sierra South told me this one. He and a group of brave and hearty professional boatmen from Texas were making one of the earliest attempts at a high water descent of the Box. Tom hit a breaking wave at just the wrong instant with his oar rig, and the wave exploded, flipping the raft, and tossing him in the drink. What followed was Tom's ultimate swim, as he plunged through waves, holes, surge, vortices and whirlpools between the narrow canyon walls before he eventually found a place to crawl out, now over a mile downstream. Apparently, the entire experience had addled him a bit, because when he began to catch his breath, he discovered that he was still clutching a ten foot-long oar!

Far below the rest of the group found a safe eddy, and then looked upstream to discover Tom's boat upside-down, following them from the canyon. It was quite some time before they were to discover his fate.

SAN JUAN RIVER
(See Utah for additional sections.)

Sections: (1) Navajo Dam to Blanco, Class I, II
              (2) Blanco to Shiprock, Class II (plus two apparently runnable dams, Class II to IV)
              (3) Shiprock to Four Corners, Class I

Length	(1) 1-2 days, 17 miles
of Run:	(2) 2-3 days, 50 miles
	(3) 2-3 days, 31 miles

Location: San Juan and Rio Arriba Counties, New Mexico

Maps: USGS quads: (1) Navajo Dam (15'), Aztec (15'), Bloomfield (15'); (2) Bloomfield (15'), Horn Canyon, Farmington, South Kirtland, Fruitland, Waterflow, Hogback North (15'); (3) Chimney Rock (15'), Rattlesnake (15')

Times Runnable: Year-round

Permit: None required

Gauge: For Section (1), Release from Navajo Dam

Source of Levels: National Weather Service, Albuquerque; 505-243-1453.

Bureau of Reclamation, Salt Lake City; 801-539-1311.

How Reported: Cfs

Additional Gauge: For Sections (2) and (3), San Juan River at Farmington

Source of Levels: Colorado Department of Water Resources; 303-831-7135.

How Reported: Cfs

Interpretation of Levels: Minimum is about 500 cfs, and 2000 is very high.

Source of More Information: New Wave Rafting, Rt. 5, Box 302, Santa Fe, NM 87501; 505-984-1444.

The Mexican Hat, visible from the San Juan River. Photo by Curt Smith.

New Mexico State Parks, Natural Resources Division, 141 East de Varen, PO Box 1147, Santa Fe, NM 87503; 505-827-7465.

Navajo Lake State Park, 1448 NM Highway 511, #1 Navajo Dam, NM 87419; 505-632-2278.

Best Guidebooks: New Mexico State Parks, *New Mexico Whitewater.*

GENERAL INFORMATION SOURCES FOR NEW MEXICO

The National Weather Service Forecast Office in Albuquerque, New Mexico, serves the New Mexico Hydrological Service Area. Call 505-243-1453, 505-243-0702.

They can report readings for the following river gauges:

Reservoirs
Rio Grande River, release from Rio Grande Reservoir
San Juan River, release from Navajo Reservoir
Chama River
    Release from El Vado Reservoir
    Release from Abiquiu Reservoir
Canadian River, release from Conchas Reservoir
Jemez River, release from Jemez Reservoir
Willow Creek (tributary of the Chama), release from Heron Reservoir
Rio Grande River, release from Cochiti Reservoir

Rio Grande Basin
Rio Grande River
    Release from Rio Grande Reservoir
    At Del Norte, CO
    At Monte Vista, CO
    At Alamosa, CO
    At Mogote, CO
    At State Line CO-NM
    At Embudo, NM
    At Chamita, NM
    At Espanola, NM
    At Otowi, NM
    At Albuquerque, NM
Animas River, at Cedar Hill, NM
San Juan River
    At Pagosa Springs, NM
    At Farmington, NM
La Plata River, at La Plata, NM

Pecos Basin
Pecos River
    At Pecos, NM
    At Santa Rosa, NM
    At Damsite No. 3, near Carlsbad, NM

Canadian Basin
Coyote Creek, at Golendrinas, NM
Gila Basin
San Francisco River, at Glenwood, NM
Gila River, at Gila, NM
Red Rock River, at Red Rock, NM

The U.S. Army Corps of Engineers can report both inflows and outflows for the dams they manage in New Mexico: U.S. Army Corps of Engineers, Albuquerque; 505-766-2636.

They can report inflow and outflow for the following dams and reservoirs:

Pecos River, Santa Rosa Dam and Reservoir
Canadian River, Conchas Dam and Reservoir
Rio Grande River, Cochiti Dam and Reservoir
Jemez River, Jemez Canyon Dam and Reservoir
Chama River, Abiquiu Dam and Reservoir

The Bureau of Reclamation can report both inflows and outflows for the dams they manage in New Mexico: Bureau of Reclamation, Albuquerque; 505-766-3719.

They can report inflow and outflow for the following dams and reservoirs:

Rio Nambe, Nambe Falls Dam and Reservoir
Willow Creek, Heron Dam and Reservoir
Chama River, El Vado Dam and Reservoir

NEW YORK

BLACK RIVER

Sections: Adirondack River Outfitters in Watertown to Fish Island boat access in Dexter, Class IV (V high)

Length of Run: Day trip, 8 miles

Location: Jefferson County, New York

Maps: USGS quads: Watertown, Dexter

Times Runnable: The Black is too high to be run during the regular spring season. But from May to October a system of flood control dams upstream usually maintain its flow at perfect levels!

Permit: None required

Gauge: USGS Black River at Watertown, NY (Van Deuzee Street)

Source of Levels: Adirondack River Outfitters, 315-369-3536.

Merrimack Valley Paddlers Recording, 603-432-6870.

How Reported: Feet and cfs

Interpretation of Levels: Minimum is about 2.6 feet (944 cfs). Maximum is 5.3 feet (5313 cfs). Water levels may fluctuate several times during a trip. There is a mandatory portage of 30 foot-high "The Falls" partway down the run; at high water (above about 5.3 feet or 5313 cfs), the portage for "The Falls" is underwater. Stay home and watch the Ninja Turtles on video.

Source of More Information: Adirondack River Outfitters, PO Box 563, 143 Newell St., Watertown, NY 13601; 315-369-3536.

Adirondack Wildwaters, PO Box 801, Corinth, NY 12811; 518-696-2953.

Best Guidebooks: Connelly and Porterfield, *Appalachian Whitewater, Vol. III.*

Further Comments: The Black River is a popular high-volume, pool-drop river. The scenery, as the river flows through the city of Watertown is turn-of-the-century industrial, similar to the James River in Richmond. My suggestion to the commercial rafters and private boaters that run the Black: why not pool your resources and build a safe, all-season portage ramp at "The Falls"?

Gauge Conversion:

Feet	Cfs	Feet	Cfs
2.0	467	3.8	2429
2.2	607	4.0	2746
2.4	766	4.2	3084
2.6	944	4.4	3443
2.8	1143	4.6	3822
3.0	1360	4.8	4222
3.2	1597	5.0	4643
3.4	1854	5.3	5313
3.6	2131	—	—

BOREAS RIVER

Sections: Rt. 28N to confluence with the Hudson River and continuing to the Minerva Bridge on Highway 28, Class IV (V high)

Length of Run: Day trip, 12.5 miles

Location: Essex and Warren Counties, New York; Adirondack Park

Maps: USGS quads: Thirteenth Lake, Newcomb

Times Runnable: March and April

Permit: None required

Gauge: Extrapolate from the Hudson River at North Creek

Source of Levels: National Weather Service, Albany, 518-869-6347.

How Reported: Feet

Additional Gauge: Painted gauge at Minerva Bridge at take-out

Source of Levels: Telemark beep gauge, 518-251-2777.

How Reported: Feet

Interpretation of Levels: The Boreas should be runnable when the Hudson is over 7 feet. In terms of the paddlers' gauge at the Minerva Bridge, about 1 foot is minimum.

Source of More Information: Adirondack River Outfitters, PO Box 563, 143 Newell St, Watertown, NY 13601; 315-369-3536.

Adirondack Wildwaters, PO Box 801, Corinth, NY 12811; 518-696-2953.

Eastern River Expeditions, Box 1173, Greenville, ME 04441; 207-695-2248, 207-695-2411.

Best Guidebooks: Connelly and Porterfield, *Appalachian Whitewater, Vol. III;* Proskine, *Adirondack Canoe Waters, South and West.*

Further Comments: This mostly continuous Class IV river is among the most difficult rivers commonly run in the Adirondacks.

CATTARAUGUS CREEK

Sections: (1) Scoobie Hill Road and Dam near Highway 219 to Burts Landing, Class I-II
(2) Zoar Valley, Burts Landing to Gowanda, Class III (Class III+ to IV high)

Length of Run: (1) Day trip, 8 miles
(2) Day trip, 10 miles

Location: Cattaraugus and Erie Counties

Maps: USGS quads: Ashford Hollow, Collins Center and Gowanda

Times Runnable: Late March to the end of May

Permit: None required

Gauge: USGS Cattaraugus Creek at Gowanda

Source of Levels: National Weather Service, Buffalo; 716-632-2223

Adventure Calls Rafting; 716-343-4710.

How Reported: Feet

Additional Gauge: Painted paddlers' gauge at Burts Landing

Source of Levels: Adventure Calls Rafting; 716-343-4710.

How Reported: Feet

Interpretation of Levels: In terms of the USGS gauge, about 1.5 to 2 feet is minimum for canoes, and 2 feet for rafts. Between 2 and 2.6 feet is optimum; 2.6 and 3.6 feet is high, and over 3.6 feet is very high and dangerous. In terms of the Burts Landing gauge, about 1 foot is minimum for canoes and 1.5 feet for rafts; 2 to 3 feet is optimum, and 4 feet and above is very high and dangerous.

Source of More Information: Adventure Calls Rafting, 20 Ellicott Avenue, Batavia, NY 14020; 716-343-4710.

Best Guidebooks: Armstead, *Whitewater Rafting in Eastern North America. 2nd Ed.*

Further Comments: As it descends to Lake Erie, the Cattaraugus Creek provides kayakers and rafters a thrilling ride through a deep glacial chasm. Expect chilly, snow-melt water!

CEDAR RIVER

Sections: New York 28 Bridge to junction with the Hudson River, Class IV+

Length of Run: Day trip, 13 miles

Location: Hamilton and Essex Counties, New York; Adirondack Park

Maps: USGS quads: Newcomb, Blue Mtn., Indian Lake, West Canada Lakes

Times Runnable: April to mid-May

Permit: None required

Gauge: None

Source of Levels: Impression only

Interpretation of Levels: If it looks runnable, then it is.

Source of More Information: Adirondack Park, Department of Environmental Conservation, Rt. 86, Ray Brook, NY 12977; 518-891-1370.

Mountain Sports, 1135 Commercial Dr., New Hartford, NY 13413; 315-736-5336.

Adirondack River Outfitters, PO Box 563, 143 Newell St., Watertown, NY 13601; 315-369-3536.

Adirondack Wildwaters, PO Box 801, Corinth, NY 12811; 518-696-2953.

Best Guidebooks: Proskine, *Adirondack Canoe Waters, South and West.*

FISH CREEK

Sections: Point Rock Bridge to Blossvale Road off Highway 69, Class III

Length of Run: Day trip, 8 miles

Location: Oneida County, New York; Adirondack Park

Maps: USGS quads: Point Rock, Lee Center

Times Runnable: Spring after heavy rain

Permit: None required

Gauge: Painted gauge at Talking Bridge

Source of Levels: Mountain Sports, 315-736-5336.

How Reported: Feet

Interpretation of Levels: Minimum is 1.5 to 2.5 feet, and maximum is around 4.5 to 5 feet.

Source of More Information: Adirondack Park, Department of Environmental Conservation, Rt. 86, Ray Brook, NY 12977; 518-891-1370.

Adirondack River Outfitters, PO Box 563, 143 Newell St., Watertown, NY 13601; 315-369-3536.

Adirondack Wildwaters, PO Box 801, Corinth, NY 12811; 518-696-2953.

Best Guidebooks: Connelly and Porterfield, *Appalachian Whitewater, Vol. III;* Proskine, *Adirondack Canoe Waters, South and West.*

Further Comments: Portage Boyd Dam.

GENESEE RIVER

Sections: Letchworth State Park, Lees Landing to St. Helenas, Class II (Class III high)

Length of Run: Day trip, 6 miles

Location: Wyoming and Livingston Counties; Letchworth State Park

Maps: USGS quads: Portageville, Nunda and Mount Morris

Times Runnable: The third weekend in April to the end of October

Permit: Required. An application form is reproduced in Appendix One. Have everyone in your party sign it, and send it in along with your $5 fee (warning: this may go up soon!) Apply to: Genesee State Parks Region, Letchworth State Park, Castille NY 14427; 716-493-2611. If you plan to take out at the Army Corps of Engineers Dam at Mt. Morris (downstream of St.

Helena), you'll have to get permission from the Corps. Call 716-493-2611.

Reservations: Required, but easy to get. Just mail your permit application early enough that it is received by the folks at Letchworth State Park at least 2 working days before you plan to boat. When you get to the river, check in at the Park Office.

Restrictions: Boaters must be at least 18 and have whitewater experience, with the exception that young folks between the ages of 12 and 18 may also boat if a release signed by their parent accompanies the permit application. Every person under 18 must be accompanied by an adult, with one adult for every youngster, and the release form must state this adult's name. There must be at least 2 boats in every party, and the group must stay together. Just hard boats (kayaks and canoes) are permitted; only commercial outfitters are allowed to run rafts. All boaters must wear PFDs, and helmets are recommended.

Boating is only allowed between the third weekend in April and the end of October. The park manager may cancel boating permits if he decides the river is dangerously high (over 5000 cfs).

Boating groups may not stop, go ashore, picnic, take extended lunch breaks, go on side trips or hikes, or engage in any other activity! *Isn't this the craziest thing you have ever read? Aren't we in America, Land of the Free?*

Entry to the river must be at Lees Landing and at no other spot. You must take out at St. Helena or at the Army Corps of Engineers Mt. Morris Dam, and nowhere else. You must notify the Letchworth Park administration at 716-658-4220 when your trip is over and you're off the river. If you don't get an answer at the Park number, then call the Genesee Sheriff's Office at 716-243-1212 and ask them to use their radio to let the Letchworth Park Police know you're off the river.

Gauge: USGS Genesee River at Portageville

Source of Levels: Letchworth State Park; 716-493-2611.

How Reported: Cfs

Interpretation of Levels: About 900 cfs is minimum; 3000 is optimum, and 5000 is very high. In terms of gauge feet, about 8.6 is minimum, 9 to 12 is optimum, and above 12 feet is very high.

Source of More Information: Letchworth State Park, Castille NY 14427; 716-493-2611.

Adventure Calls Rafting, 20 Ellicott Avenue, Batavia, NY 14020; 716-343-4710.

Buried up to his gunwales, Jim Michaud successfully runs Otter Slide on the Indian Creek section of the Hudson. Photo by John Barry.

Best Guidebooks: Armstead, *Whitewater Rafting in Eastern North America. 2nd Ed.*

Further Comments: The Genesee is a fun and splashy run through a sensational sandstone canyon, popular for commercial rafting! Unfortunately, this excellent section suffers from arbitrary and excessive regulation, the worst I've seen in the U.S. of A. In the words of the Park Manager, "we do not encourage canoe trips down the Genesee River within the Park." I think he needs to relax a little bit, don't you?

If you visit the Genesee, you might encourage the Park personnel there to develop a more enlightened and positive outlook.

HUDSON RIVER

Sections: The Hudson River Gorge, Indian River to its confluence with the Hudson River and continuing to Barton Mines Road, Class III-IV (IV+ high)

Length of Run: Day trip, 12.5 miles (including 3.5 miles on Indian River)

Location: Hamilton, Essex and Warren Counties, New York

Maps: USGS quads: Utica, Thirteenth Lake and Newcomb

Times Runnable: Boating in the Hudson River Gorge is dependent on releases from Abanahee Dam on the Indian River below Indian Lake. It releases from April into early June and again in the fall from Labor Day to the first weekend of October.

Permit: None required

Gauge: USGS Hudson River at North Creek

Source of Levels: National Weather Service; Albany, 518-869-6437.

Whitewater Challengers, 717-443-8345.

Telemark beep gauge, 518-251-2777.

How Reported: Feet

Interpretation of Levels: Minimum is about 3 feet (600 cfs); high is 8 feet, and extremely high is 10 feet (17,000 cfs). Commercial rafters rarely run over 8 feet.

Source of More Information: Whitewater Challengers, Star Route, Box 6A1, White Haven, PA 18661; 717-443-8345, 800-443-RAFT.

Adirondack River Outfitters, PO Box 563, 143 Newell St., Watertown, NY 13601; 315-369-3536.

Adirondack Wildwaters, PO Box 801, Corinth, NY 12811; 518-696-2953.

Eastern River Expeditions, Box 1173, Greenville, ME 04441; 207-695-2411.

Best Guidebooks: Connelly and Porterfield, *Appalachian Whitewater, Vol. III;* Proskine, *Adirondack Canoe Waters, South and West.*

Further Comments: The Hudson offers some of the best and most reliable whitewater in the Northeast. During a single season, over 20,000 commercial raft patrons descend the river!

MOOSE RIVER

Sections: (1) Lower section, Old Iron Bridge to Fowlerville Road Bridge, Class III-V+
(2) Bottom section, Fowlerville Bridge to Lyons Falls, Class V+

Length of Run: (1) Day trip, 10 miles
(2) Day trip, 4 miles

Location: Lewis County, New York

Maps: USGS quads: Utica, Port Leyden, Brantingham

Times Runnable: Section (1) is runnable in April, and section (2) from May to July after rain.

Permit: None required

Salmon fight their way upstream, or: one way *not* to run 12-Foot Falls on the Bottom Moose! Photo by Jim Michaud.

Gauge: About a quarter mile upstream of the Old Iron Bridge in Fowlerville

Source of Levels: Hudson River-Black River Regulating District, 315-788-5440.

Whitewater Challengers, 717-443-8345, 800-443-RAFT.

How Reported: Feet

Interpretation of Levels: Around 3 feet 8 inches is minimum for Section (1). For Section (2), about 3 feet is minimum, and 5 feet is extremely high.

Source of More Information: Adirondack River Outfitters, PO Box 563, 143 Newell St., Watertown, NY 13601; 315-369-3536.

Adirondack Wildwaters, PO Box 801, Corinth, NY 12811; 518-696-2953.

Eastern River Expeditions, Box 1173, Greenville, ME 04441; 207-695-2411.

Best Guidebooks: Connelly and Porterfield, *Appalachian Whitewater, Vol. III;* Proskine, *Adirondack Canoe Waters, South and West.*

Further Comments: I can think of three rivers that best typify the difficult, big-water, Eastern pool-drop river. The Gauley in West Virginia is one. The Ripogenous Gorge of the West Branch of the Penobscot in Maine is another. And the Moose River in New York is the third.

The Moose is a fantastic river, with super Class V rapids, terrific scenery, and a geology lesson at every turn. Don't take it lightly though, it's a toughy. Section (1) is about as difficult as the Upper Gauley of West Virginia, and Section (2) is even harder. Expect to portage one dam on Section (2), plus any Class V rapids you don't like!

RAQUETTE RIVER

Sections: (1) Piercefield to logging road below Sevey, Class II-III
(2) Sevey to Carry Falls Dam, Class II-III

Length of Run: (1) Day trip, 13.5 miles
(2) Day trip, 10 miles

Location: St. Lawrence County, New York; Adirondack Park

Maps: USGS quads: Tupper Lake (15'), Mount Matumba, Childwood, Carry Falls, Reservoir

Times Runnable: Year-round except when it's too cold

Permit: None required

Gauge: Release from Piercefield Dam

Source of Levels: Apparently none

Interpretation of Levels: Releases are fairly standard; if the dam is releasing then there is generally enough water.

Source of More Information: Adirondack Park, Department of Environmental Conservation, Rt. 86, Ray Brook, NY 12977; 518-891-1370.

Adirondack River Outfitters, PO Box 563, 143 Newell St., Watertown, NY 13601; 315-369-3536.

Adirondack Wildwaters, PO Box 801, Corinth, NY 12811; 518-696-2953.

Best Guidebooks Jamieson, *Adirondack Canoe Waters.*

Further Comments: Probable portages at Moody Falls and Jamestown Falls

SACANDAGA RIVER

Sections: (1) Middle Branch, Old Powerhouse to the junction of Routes 8 and 30 at the confluence of the East and Middle Branches, Class V
(2) East Branch, Griffin to the junction of Routes 8 and 30 at the confluence of the East and MiddleBranches, Class III-IV
(3) Great Sacandaga Section, Stewarts Dam on Great Sacandaga Lake near Hadley to the Hudson River, Class III

Length of Run: (1) Day trip, 3 miles
(2) Day trip, 4 miles
(3) Day trip, 3.5 miles

Location: Saratoga and Hamilton Counties, New York

Maps: USGS quads: Lake Luzerne, Wells, Griffin, Kunjamuk, Wells

Times Runnable: Releases on Section (3) usually provide sufficient water from the end of May to the first week of October. Releases occur every day but Sundays. Sections (1) and (2) are runnable only in early spring.

Permit: None required

Gauge: For Section (1), USGS Sacandaga River, release from Stewart's Dam

Source of Levels: National Weather Service, Albany, 518-869-6347.

How Reported: Cfs

Additional Gauge: For Section (2), Griffin Gauge, 100 feet upstream of the Highway 8 bridge

Source of Levels: Visual inspection only

How Reported: Feet

Additional Gauge: For Section (3), the flow is measured in terms of the number of inches coming over the old powerhouse dam at the put-in.

Source of Levels: Visual inspection only

How Reported: Inches

Interpretation of Levels: For Section (1), about 500 cfs is enough. For Section (2), interpretation of the Griffin gauge is unknown. However, if you use the W.D.S. method, about 300 cfs would be about minimum, and 1000-2000 cfs would be very high. For Section (3), between 1 and 4 inches coming over the dam is about right (200 to 300 cfs).

Source of More Information: Adirondack River Outfitters, PO Box 563, 143 Newell St., Watertown, NY 13601; 315-369-3536.

Adirondack Wildwaters, PO Box 801, Corinth, NY 12811; 518-696-2953.

Best Guidebooks: Connelly and Porterfield, *Appalachian Whitewater, Vol. III;* Proskine, *Adirondack Canoe Waters, South and West.*

Further Comments: On Section (1), be sure to portage Auger Falls. On Section (2), put in below the Class V and VI gorge at Griffin.

SALMON RIVER

(Not to be confused with the Salmon River, Idaho.)

Sections:	(1) Altman to Pulaski, Class II-III
	(2) Pulaski to Selkirk Shores State Park at Lake Ontario, Class II-III
Length of Run:	(1) Day trip, 9 miles
	(2) Day trip, 4 miles

Location: Oswego and Lewis Counties, New York

Maps USGS quads: Pulaski, Richland, Orwell, Redfield

Times Runnable: During releases for power production on weekdays, or after special releases for recreation during the summer.

Permit: None required

Gauge: Release from the Salmon River Reservoir

Source of Levels: Niagara-Mohawk Corporation, River Status Recording; 315-298-6531.

How Reported: Release schedule

Interpretation of Levels: Most releases provide enough water.

Source of More Information: Selkirk Shores State Park, Rt. 3, Pulaski, NY 13142; 315-298-5737.

Adirondack River Outfitters, PO Box 563, 143 Newell St., Watertown, NY 13601; 315-369-3536.

Adirondack Wildwaters, PO Box 801, Corinth, NY 12811; 518-696-2953.

Best Guidebooks: Proskine, *Adirondack Canoe Waters, South and West.*

GENERAL INFORMATION SOURCES FOR NEW YORK

The US Army Corps of Engineers and other managers of water projects coordinate many of the scheduled releases through the Appalachian Mountain Club. Call the office of the Appalachian Mountain Club in Boston; they should have a printed list they can mail out (I don't recommend that you call the New England Division of the Army Corps—they don't want to hear from you).

Appalachian Mountain Club, New England Rivers Center, Boston, 5 Joy St., Boston, MA; 617-523-0636.

The Connecticut Chapter of the Appalachian Mountain Club also maintains a river hotline which reports levels and events for Connecticut and surrounding areas: AMC Connecticut Chapter Whitewater Hotline, Hartford Recording; 203-582-6978.·

The Western New England Hydrological Service Area of the National Weather Service in Albany can provide gauge readings for eastern New York and Vermont. Call their forecast recording and stay on the line; someone will pick up: 717-234-6812.

They can report the following readings for New York:

Hudson River
    At North Creek
    At Hadley
Schoharie River, at Bertansville
Esopus Creek, at Mt. Tremper
Susquehanna River, at Unidillia
Fish Creek
    At Saratoga Lake
    At Boonville
Sacandaga River
    Release from Stewarts Pond
    At Hope

The Buffalo Forecast Office of the National Weather Service serves the Western New York Hydrological Service Area: 716-632-2223.

They can report the following stations:

Allegheny River
    At Olean
    At Salamanca
Black Creek, at Churchville
Black River
    Near Boonville
    At Watertown
Buffalo Creek, at Gardenville
Canacadea Creek, near Hornell
Canaseraga Creek, at Dansville

Jim Michaud in the first open boat descent of the 40-foot slide that begins the Class V Bottom Moose section. Photo by John Barry.

Canisteo River
    At Hornell
    At West Cameron
Cattaraugus Creek, at Gowanda
Cayuga Creek, at Lancaster
Cazenovia Creek, at Ebenezer
Chadakoin River, at Falconer
Chataugua Lake, at Bemus Pt.
Chemung River
    At Chemung
    At Corning
    At Elmira
Cohocton River, at Campbell
Conewango Creek, at Waterboro
Ellicott Creek, at Williamsville
Genesee River
    At Avon
    At Jones Bridge
    At Portageville
    At Wellsville

At Rochester
Mount Morris Lake
Oatka Creek
    At Garbutt
    At Warsaw
Scajaquada Creek, at Buffalo
Seneca River, at Baldwinsville
Tioga River
    At Erwins
    At Lindley
Tonawanda Creek at Batavia

The National Weather Service River Forecast Center in Harrisburg, PA acts as the hydrologic service office for the Delaware and Susquehanna River Basins: National Weather Service River Forecast Center, Harrisburg; 717-234-2251.

They can report readings for the following gauges located in New York (see the Pennsylvania summary for a more complete list of gauges reported by this office):

Delaware River Basin:
East Branch of the Delaware River, at Downsville
West Branch of the Delaware River, at Harvard
Callicoon Creek, at Callicoon Creek
Delaware River
    At Callicoon
    At Barryville
    At Port Jervis
Neversink River, at Woodbourne

Susquehanna River Basin
Ouleout Creek, at East Sidney
Susquehanna River
    At Unadilla
    At Bainbridge
    At Afton
Chenango River
    At Conklin
    At Sherbrune
    At Oxford
Tioughnioga River
    At Courtland
    At Lisle
Otselic River, at Cincinnatus

Tioughnioga River
    At Whitney Pt. Brook
    At Itsaka
Chenango River, at Chenango Forks
Susquehanna River
    At Binghamton
    At Vestal
Owego Creek, at Owego
Susquehanna River, at Waverly
Tioga River, at Lindley
Canacadea Creek, at Hornell
Canisteo River
    At Hornell
    At West Cameron
    At Addison
Tioga River, at Erwins
Cohocton River
    At Bath
    At Campbell
Chemung River
    At Corning
    At Hickling Station
    At Elmira
    At Chemung

The Philadelphia Forecast Office of the National Weather Service can report river stages for the Delaware River Basin: National Weather Service, Philadelphia; 215-627-5575.

They can report readings for the following gauges located in New York (see the Pennsylvania summary for a more complete list of gauges reported by this office):

West Branch of the Delaware River, at Hale-Eddy
East Branch of the Delaware River
    At Harvard
    At Cooks Falls
    At Fishs Eddy
Callicoon Creek, at Callicoon Creek
Delaware River
    At Callicoon
    At Woodbourne
    At Barryville

NORTH CAROLINA

BIG LAUREL CREEK

Sections: US 25-70 Bridge to confluence with the French Broad, and continuing to the Nantahala Outdoor Center take-out at Hot Springs, Class III-IV

Length of Run: Day trip, 7.5 miles, including 4 miles on French Broad

Location: Madison County, North Carolina; Pisgah National Forest

Maps: USGS quads: Hot Springs, White Rock

Times Runnable: Winter and spring after heavy rain

Permit: None required

Gauge: The paddlers' gauge is on the southeast side of the highway bridge, but is most easily seen from the northwest side

Source of Levels: Carolina Wilderness Adventures, 704-622-3535.

How Reported: Feet

Interpretation of Levels: Consider 0 feet to be minimum. Many folks consider 1 foot to be about optimum, and 2 feet and over to be high. A group of reasonably competent Atlanta boaters without prior experience on the creek tried it at two feet during the spring of 1987. They freaked out, abandoned their boats in the woods and hiked out. I've run Big Laurel as high as 3 feet, at which level it becomes Class IV+ and reminiscent of a steep, high-volume Western river, such as the Upper Crystal.

Source of More Information: Carolina Wilderness Adventures, PO Box 488, Hot Springs, NC 28743; 704-622-3535.

Nantahala Outdoor Center, US 19W, Box 41, Bryson City, NC 28713; 704-488-2175.

USDA Forest Service, French Broad Ranger District,

The author surfing on Big Laurel and keeping that smile. Photo by Anne Penny.

Pisgah National Forest, PO Box 128, Hot Springs, NC 28743; 704-622-3202.

Best Guidebooks: Nealy, *Whitewater Home Companion Vol. I*; Sehlinger et al., *Appalachian Whitewater Vol. I*.

FRENCH BROAD RIVER

Sections: County Road 1151 Bridge at Barnard to the Nantahala Outdoor Center take-out at Hot Springs; Class III-IV

Length of Run: Day trip, 7.5 miles

Location: Madison County, North Carolina; Pisgah National Forest

Maps: USGS quads: Hot Springs, Spring Creek

Times Runnable: Winter and spring after heavy rain

Permit: None required

Gauge: The paddlers' gauge is on the southeast side of the highway bridge, but is most easily seen from the northwest side.

Source of Levels: Tennessee Valley Authority, 615-632-6065.

How Reported: Cfs

Interpretation of Levels: Low water is about 1500 cfs; medium is about 2500, and high is 5000 or over. The best level for enders at Frank Bell's Rapid is between 1500 and 2000. I've run this section at high levels twice, at 10,000 and 30,000 cfs. Frank Bell's Rapid is pretty washed out at these very high levels and is actually easier than at lower levels around 3000 cfs. At 30,000 we did run left of the island (the Sneak) at Kayak Ledge.

Source of More Information: Carolina Wilderness Adventures, PO Box 488, Hot Springs, NC 28743; 704-622-3535.

Nantahala Outdoor Center, US 19W, Box 41, Bryson City, NC 28713; 704-488-2175.

USDA Forest Service, French Broad Ranger District, Pisgah National Forest, PO Box 128, Hot Springs, NC 28743; 704-622-3202.

Best Guidebooks: Nealy, *Whitewater Home Companion Vol. I*; Sehlinger et al., *Appalachian Whitewater Vol. I*.

HAW RIVER

Sections:
(1) Chicken Bridge (County Rd. 1545) to dam just upstream of US 15-501 Bridge, Class I-II
(2) US 15-501 Bridge, upstream of Bynum, NC to US 64 Bridge, Class I-II+ (III+ high)
(3) US 64 Bridge to Jordan Lake and continuing on Jordan Lake to the former site of County Rd. 1943 Bridge, Class II-III+ (to Class IV when very high) on the Haw, totally classless on the lake.

Length of Run:
(1) Day trip, 6.5 miles
(2) Day trip, 4 miles
(3) Day trip, 2 miles including about a mile of lake

Location: Chatham County, North Carolina

Maps: USGS quads: Bynum, New Hope Dam

Times Runnable: For good levels, only in winter and spring or after heavy rain; runnable at low levels well into the summer

Permit: None required

Gauge: USGS gauge at Bynum. Located in a pool on river-right between Bynum and Highway 64.

Source of Levels: Levels available from: National Weather Service, Raleigh; 919-860-1234 (recording, 7 to 9 a.m.), 919-840-0453 (answered number).

Other sources of Haw River levels include the *Raleigh News and Observer,* which publishes the level on Fridays in the weather section; the cable *Weather Channel,* which broadcasts the level around 7 a.m.; and the NAOA weather radio stations in Piedmont and Eastern North Carolina, which report the Haw level in the morning until 9 a.m.

How Reported: Feet

Additional Gauge: The paddlers' gauge is painted on a bridge abutment on the west side of the Highway 64 Bridge. Most paddlers discuss levels in terms of this gauge.

Source of Levels: Visual inspection only

How Reported: Feet

Interpretation of Levels: In terms of the paddlers' gauge, 6 inches is about minimum; 1-2 feet is medium, and 3 feet or higher is high. Above 4 or 5 feet is very high (extrapolated values; the paddlers' gauge only goes to 4 feet).

Source of More Information: River Runners Emporium, 201 Albemarle St., Durham, NC 27701; 919-688-2001.

Resource Manager, US Army Corps of Engineers, B. Everett Jordan Dam and Lake, PO Box 144, Moncure, NC 27559; 919-542-2227.

Best Guidebooks: Benner, *Carolina Whitewater;* Nealy, *Whitewater Home Companion Vol. I.*

Further Comments: Three points of warning: First, the Haw can be dangerous at high water. Large holes develop, and the tree-covered islands become giant strainers. Second, the paddlers' gauge only goes to four feet. If you can't see it, and the Haw is in flood, consider the possibility that the gauge is underwater. Some years ago several of us failed to figure this out and put on at a level (about 7 feet) that was a little too hard for us at the time. All three of us were separated. Convinced that the others were probably dead, each of us paddled to islands and climbed trees in a desperate search for survivors. When we spotted each other in our arboreal retreats we developed a belief in the miraculous. Third warning: the parts of the town of Bynum that take their drinking water from the Haw have one of the highest cancer rates in the nation. Don't drink the water.

Gauge Conversion: Subtract 5 from the Bynum USGS readings to roughly convert to the paddlers' gauge.

Conversion of the paddlers' gauge to Bynum and to cfs

Paddlers' Gauge	Bynum USGS	Cfs
0	5	1760
1	6	2980
2	7	4110
3	8	5180
4	9	6200
5	10	7440
6	11	9000
7	12	11,000
8	13	13,000
9	14	5,000
10	15	17,000

LITTLE TENNESSEE RIVER

Sections: Lost Bridge to Lake Fontana, Class III

Length of Run: Day trip, 13 miles

Location: Macon and Swain Counties, North Carolina; Nantahala National Forest

Maps: USGS quads: Franklin, Alarka, Wesser

Times Runnable: Best in winter when Fontana Lake is low, but runnable almost year-round

Permit: None required

Gauge: TVA gauge near Needmore, NC

Source of Levels: Tennessee Valley Authority, 615-632-6065.

How Reported: Cfs

Interpretation of Levels: Minimum is about 500 cfs, and high is 2500 cfs.

Source of More Information: Nantahala Outdoor Center, US 19W, Box 41, Bryson City, NC 28713; 704-488-2175.

USDA Forest Service, Wayah Ranger District, Nantahala National Forest, 8 Sloan Rd., Franklin, NC 28734; 204-524-6441.

Best Guidebooks: Benner, *Carolina Whitewater;* Sehlinger et al., *Appalachian Whitewater Vol. I.*

Further Comments: The Little Tennessee is a good alternative when the Nantahala is too crowded; however, the best rapids are uncovered only when Fontana Lake is low.

NANTAHALA RIVER

Sections: The Nantahala Gorge, Forest Service launch area to Nantahala Outdoor Center Take-out, Class II and III (plus one Class VI down stream of the takeout)

Length of Run: Day trip, 8 miles

Location: Macon and Swain Counties, North Carolina

Maps: USGS quads: Hewitt, Wesser

Times Runnable: The Nantahala can be run only when the power plant upstream of the take-out is operating. Releases can be expected from 8 a.m. to 5 p.m. on most weekdays. Water is also usually released on weekend days, but this is subject to change. You can check with the Nantahala Power Plant or with the NOC if you want to be sure.

Permit: Required for groups of 10 or more people. This does not just apply to clubs and so on—even a group of 10 friends who plan to paddle together.

Reservations: Although group permits are available from the ranger at the put-in, it's a good idea to apply ahead by mail (a letter is OK; there is no form) for a permit and reservations. Otherwise, if the river is very crowded, the ranger could decline to issue a permit or require your group to delay its put-in time. Contact: USDA Forest Service, Wayah Ranger District, Nantahala National Forest, 8 Sloan Rd., Franklin, NC 28734; 204-524-6441.

Gauge: Release from Nantahala Power Plant

Source of Levels: Release schedule is available from: Nantahala Power Plant, 704-321-4504.

How Reported: Times, cfs

Interpretation of Levels: The volumes released are fairly standard; not scrapey, not pushy, around 800-900 cfs.

Source of More Information: Nantahala Outdoor Center, US 19W, Box 41, Bryson City, NC 28713; 704-488-2175.

USDA Forest Service, Wayah Ranger District, Nantahala National Forest, 8 Sloan Rd., Franklin, NC 28734; 204-524-6441.

Best Guidebooks: Benner, *Carolina Whitewater;* Nealy, *Whitewater Home Companion Vol. I.*

Further Comments: In many regards the Nantahala River is the mother of whitewater boating in the Southeast. It was here in the early 70's that Payson Kennedy established the great Nantahala Outdoor Center.

The Nantahala flows through a deep and majestic gorge, filled with the dense, flowery rain forest characteristic of the coves, gullies, and gorges of the Smoky Mountains. Along its way it forms numerous fine Class II and III rapids, often obscured by the unusual fog that tends to hang just over the river.

During the summer the Nantahala is extremely popular, and on holiday weekends, as many as 2000 boaters a day descend this short stretch. Head somewhere else on Memorial Day, July the Fourth, and Labor Day!

Since I first paddled the Nantahala in 1974, I've seen this beautiful river greatly damaged by tacky development along its river-right shores and the expansion of a rock quarry on its left shore. The Nantahala desperately needs protection and restoration! You folks that boat the Nantahala, get active!

NOLICHUCKY RIVER

Sections: The Nolichucky Gorge, Poplar NC to the Nolichucky Expeditions Take-out near Erwin, TN, Class IV

Length of Run: Day trip, 8 miles

Location: Mitchell County, North Carolina and Unicoi County, Tennessee

Maps: USGS quads: Huntdale (NC), Chestoa (TN), Erwin (TN)

Times Runnable: December to June

Permit: None required

Gauge: Nolichucky at Embreeville

Source of Levels: Tennessee Valley Authority, 615-632-6065.

How Reported: Cfs

Additional Gauge: Staff gauge on river-right upstream of the put-in in Poplar. This gauge is a little tough to see from the bank—it's obscured by willows. Paddling back up from the put-in to see it is the best bet. Most paddlers like to check the gauge in Poplar before putting in, since it gives a reading of exactly how much water is available (the Embreeville gauge is far downstream, and so may not come up as fast).

Source of Levels: Visual inspection only.

How reported: Feet

Interpretation of Levels: Minimum for fun is about 500

cfs or about 1.6 feet on the Poplar gauge. About 1700 cfs is considered ideal (2.0 feet), and 2800 cfs (3.0 feet) is high. Expert boaters run the Nolichucky as high as 5000 cfs.

Source of More Information: Nolichucky Expeditions, PO Box 484, Erwin, TN 37650; 615-743-3221.

USDA Forest Service, Toecane Ranger District, Pisgah National Forest, PO Box 128, Burnsville, NC 28714; 704-682-6146.

USDA Forest Service, Nolichucky Ranger District, Cherokee National Forest, 504 Justis Dr., Greeneville, TN 37743; 615-638-4109.

USDA Forest Service, Unaka Ranger District, Cherokee National Forest, Erwin, TN 37650; 615-743-4452.

Best Guidebooks: Nealy, *Whitewater Home Companion Vol. I*; Sehlinger et al., *Appalachian Whitewater Vol. I*.

PIGEON RIVER

Sections:	Carolina Power and Light plant to Hartford, TN, Class III-IV
Length of Run:	Day trip, 4.5 miles

Location: Haywood County, North Carolina; Polk County, Tennessee; Pisgah and Cherokee National Forests

Maps: USGS quads: Waterville, Hartford

Times Runnable: When power plant is generating

Permit: None required

Gauge: Release from Carolina Power and Light plant on Waterville Lake

Source of Levels: Carolina Power and Light Co., 704-648-2485.

How Reported: Cfs. Release schedules also available.

Interpretation of Levels: Low runnable levels require one generator to be operating, producing 10,000 to 30,000 kw. High water is provided by two generators operating, producing 30,000 to 50,000 kw.

Source of More Information: USDA Forest Service, French Broad Ranger District, Pisgah National Forest, PO Box 128, Hot Springs, NC 28743; 704-622-3202.

USDA Forest Service, Nolichucky Ranger District, Cherokee National Forest, 504 Justis Dr., Greeneville, TN 37743; 615-638-4109.

Best Guidebooks: Benner, *Carolina Whitewater;* Sehlinger and Lantz, *A Canoeing and Kayaking Guide to Tennessee, Vol. II.*

WATAUGA RIVER

Sections:	Gorge, Guys Ford Bridge to Watauga Lake, Class IV-V+ (one at VI)
Length of Run:	Day trip, 6 miles

Location: Avery and Watauga Counties, North Carolina and Johnson County, Tennessee

Maps: USGS quads: Sherwood (NC) and Elk Mills (TN); Pisgah and Cherokee National Forests

Times Runnable: January to mid-April and after heavy rain

Permit: None required

Gauge: TVA gauge at Sugar Grove, about 15 miles upstream of the gorge

Source of Levels: Tennessee Valley Authority; 615-632-6065.

How Reported: Cfs

Additional Gauge: Painted paddlers' gauge on the Guys Ford Bridge at the put-in.

Source of Levels: Visual inspection only.

How reported: Feet

Interpretation of Levels: Minimum is about 150 cfs. Optimum is around 450 cfs, and 800 cfs is high. In terms of the paddlers' gauge at Guys Ford, -13 inches is bare minimum, -10 inches is a more realistic minimum, -8 to -2 inches is optimum. Anything over the top of the piling (0 and above) is high to very high.

Source of More Information: Cherokee Adventures, PO Box 666, Elwin, TN 37650; 615-743-7733.

USDA Forest Service, Grandfather Ranger District, Pisgah National Forest, PO Box 519, Marion, NC 28752; 704-652-2144.

USDA Forest Service, Watauga Ranger District, Cherokee National Forest, Rt. 9, Box 2235, Elizabethton, TN 37643; 615-638-4109.

High Mountain Expeditions, PO Box 1299, Blowing Rock, NC 28605; 704-295-4200.

Best Guidebooks: Sehlinger et al., *Appalachian Whitewater, Vol. I.*

Further Comments: The Watauga has long been known as *the* steep, expert run in North Carolina. I would never have expected it to happen, but it's now popular for commercial rafting. Watch out for "Tennessee Wrong Way," a 16-foot Class V-VI waterfall; you'll probably want to portage this one. My friend the renowned Oregon hair-boater, Jim Reed, punched a big hole in the nose of his Mirage when he ran this one by accident.

WILSON CREEK

Sections: Wilson Creek Gorge, beginning upstream of the Pisgah National Forest Boundary and continuing to Brown Mountain Beach, Class IV+ (V high)

Length of Run: Day trip, 2.5 miles

Location: Caldwell County, North Carolina

Maps: USGS quads: Chestnut Mountain, Colletsville

Times Runnable: February to May and after heavy rain

Permit: None required

Gauge: Paddlers' gauge at the County Road 1337 Bridge, downstream of the take-out.

Source of Levels: Visual inspection only.

How Reported: Inches and Feet

Additional Gauge: TVA Gauge on the Watauga River at Sugar Grove. Before you drive up to Wilson Creek, hoping for water, check the TVA reading for the Watauga, which drains the opposite side of Grandfather Mountain. If the Watauga is up, then Wilson Creek is likely to be up too!

Source of Levels: Tennessee Valley Authority; 615-632-6065.

Interpretation of Levels: The painted paddlers' gauge at the 1337 Bridge needs some explaining. The gauge has 6" high numerals for 0, 1, 2, and 3 feet, supplemented by hash marks placed every three inches. Please note that Wilson Creek is running at 0 feet when the water is even with the bottom of the 0, (not when the water is even with the middle of the 0, as is usually the case for paddlers' gauges), and the same is true for the 1, 2, and 3 feet levels. The fellow that painted the gauge screwed up a bit, and a lot of boaters have been fooled over the years into thinking that Wilson Creek is below minimum when it actually has plenty of water.

Minimum is about -4 inches; zero is medium; +4 inches is high, and +1 foot is extremely high. The highest I've run Wilson Creek is about +8 inches. At this level, if you descend to the last eddy above Razorback, you'll discover that you are irrevocably committed to running the drop—there is no way to get out of your boat! Make sure you know the route!

Source of More Information: USDA Forest Service, Toecane Ranger District, Pisgah National Forest, PO Box 128, Burnsville, NC 28714; 704-682-6146.

Best Guidebooks: Nealy, *Whitewater Home Companion, Vol. II;* Sehlinger et al., *Appalachian Whitewater, Vol. I.*

Further Comments: Wilson Creek! In the old days (circa 1975) we viewed Wilson Creek as the ultimate hair run, and boated it with extreme trepidation. Not so for the inner-tubers, who for some strange reason discovered the Wilson Creek Gorge before the kayakers did, and have ever since considered it as a safe and sane place to go tubing.

You still couldn't pay me enough to tube Wilson Creek Gorge, but in a decked boat, I see it now as a fun and challenging Class IV+ run, tight and technical, and chock full of more sheer ledges than I've ever seen on any other river.

GENERAL INFORMATION SOURCES FOR NORTH CAROLINA

The pleasant and helpful folks at the Tennessee Valley Authority can report levels for rivers throughout the Tennessee River watershed, including central and eastern Tennessee, northern Alabama and the western slope of the North Carolina mountains. Gauge readings are taken at 7 a.m. daily; all levels are reported in cfs. Dam releases are reported as average daily discharge in cfs; values are available for both the current day and for the following day. The TVA is also a source of a variety of other hydrologic data. The number is answered by human beings from 8:00 a.m. to 4:45 p.m., Monday through Friday.

Tennessee Valley Authority, 615-632-6065.

They can report the following river gauges and releases for North Carolina:

Watauga River, at Sugar Grove
Oconaluftee River, at Birdtown
Tuckasegee River, at Bryson City

The National Weather Service in Raleigh, NC can report levels for the following rivers and gauges in North Carolina. (A few are reported on a recording—sometimes—but generally you'll have to ask): 919-860-1234 (recording); 919-840-0453 (answered number).

Haw River
    At Haw River
    At Bynum
Deep River, at Moncure
Cape Fear River
    At Moncure
    Below B. E. Jordan Dam
    At Lillington
    At Fayetteville
    At W. O. Huske
    At Elizabethton
    Below Lock and Dam #1
Eno River, at Durham
Flat River, at Bahama
Neuse River
    Below Falls of the Neuse Dam
    At Clayton
    At Smithfield
    At Goldsboro

    At Kinston
Fishing Creek, at Louisburg
Tar River
    At Louisburg
    At Rocky Mount
    At Tarboro
    At Greenville
Roanoke River
    At Roanoke Rapids
    At Scotland Neck
    At Williamston
Smith River, at Eden
Yadkin River
    At High Rock
    At Patterson
    At Elkville
    At Wilkesboro
    At Elkin
    At Elon
    At Yadkin College
Lumber River, at Lumberton
South Fork of the Catwba River, at McAdenville
French Broad River
    At Rosman
    At Blantyre
    At Bent Creek
    At Asheville
    At Marshall
    At Hot Springs
North Fork of the French Broad River
    Near Pisgah
    At Davidson
Valley River, at Andrews
Hominy Creek, at Candler
Mud Creek, at East Flat Rock
Flat Creek, at Weaverville
Ivy Creek, at Barnardsville
Sandymush Creek, at Canto
Toe River, at Flat Top Mountain
Swannoa River, at Biltmore
Pee Dee River
    At Badin (Narrows)
    At Mt. Island
Catawba River
    At Hickory
    At Bridgewater
    At Rhodhiss
    At Oxford Shoals
    At Lake Norman (Cowen's Ford)

OHIO

CUYAHOGA RIVER, LOWER

Sections: Ohio Edison Dam to Peninsula, Class II-III (to III-IV very high)

Length of Run: Day trip, 12 miles, shorter sections possible

Location: Summit and Cuyahoga Counties, Ohio; Cuyahoga Valley National Recreation Area

Maps: USGS quads: Akron West, Peninsula, Northfield

Times Runnable: December to June

Permit: None required

Gauge: Release from Ohio Edison Dam

Source of Levels: Cuyahoga Valley National Recreation Area, 216-650-4414.

How Reported: Cfs

Interpretation of Levels: Minimum is about 250 cfs. A moderate level is about 550 cfs. Can be run by competent boaters to floodstage.

Source of More Information: Cuyahoga Valley National Recreation Area, 15610 Vaughn Rd., Brecksville, OH 44141; 216-650-4414.

Ohio Division of Watercraft, 3049 Akron-Peninsula Rd., Akron, OH 44313; 216-644-2265.

Best Guidebooks: Combs and Gillen, A *Canoeing and Kayaking Guide to the Streams of Ohio, Vol. II.*

Further Comments: Water quality is poor.

PAINT CREEK

Sections: Paint Creek Reservoir to Hwy. 41 Bridge, Class I-III

Length of Run: Day trip, 7.5 miles

Location: Ross County, Ohio

Maps: USGS quads: Greenfleld, Rainsboro, Bainbridge

Times Runnable: November to May after heavy rains resulting in dam releases

Permit: None required

Gauge: Release from Paint Creek Reservoir

Source of Levels: U.S. Army Corps of Engineers; 513-365-1167.

How Reported: Cfs

Interpretation of Levels: Minimum is about 250 cfs. At about 700 to 1100 cfs, two rapids approach Class III.

Source of More Information: Ohio Division of Watercraft, District III, 1225 Woodlawn Ave., Cambridge, OH 43725; 614-439-4076.

Paint Creek State Park, 7860 Upp Rd., Bainbridge, OH 45612; 513-981-7061.

Best Guidebooks: Combs and Gillen, A *Canoeing and Kayaking Guide to the Streams of Ohio, Vol. I.*

SANDUSKY RIVER

Sections: Tiffin to Fremont, Class I (to III high)

Length of Run: 2 days, 27 miles, shorter stretches possible

Location: Seneca and Sandusky Counties, Ohio

Maps: USGS quads: Tiffin South, Tiffin North, Fremont West, Fremont East

Times Runnable: Year-round, but best after heavy rains

Permit: None required

Gauge: None. But Portage Trail Canoe Livery has marks for too high and too low that they can check.

Source of Levels: Portage Trail Canoe Livery, 419-334-2988.

How Reported: Low, good or high

Interpretation of Levels: Runnable by competent boaters to floodstage.

Source of More Information: Portage Trail Canoe Livery, 1773 S. River Rd., Fremont, OH 43420; 419-334-8100.

Best Guidebooks: Combs and Gillen, *A Canoeing and Kayaking Guide to the Streams of Ohio, Vol. I.*

Further Comments: Portages at low-water dams.

WHITE OAK CREEK

Sections: Bethel-New Hope Road Bridge to Georgetown Dam, Class III (to IV high)

Length of Run: Day trip, 11.5 miles

Location: Brown County, Ohio

Maps: USGS quads: Hamersville, Higginsport

Times Runnable: Spring after heavy rain

Permit: None required

Gauge: Amount of water over Georgetown Dam

Source of Levels: Georgetown Waterworks, 513-378-6768.

How Reported: Inches or feet of water over the dam

Interpretation of Levels Minimum is about 8 inches over. Can be run by competent boaters to floodstage.

Source of More Information: Ohio Division of Watercraft, District III, 1225 Woodlawn Ave., Cambridge, OH 43725; 614-439-4076.

Best Guidebooks: Combs and Gillen, *A Canoeing and Kayaking Guide to the Streams of Ohio, Vol. I.*

Further Comments: A popular local creek run for Cincinnati boaters when it is up.

GENERAL INFORMATION SOURCES FOR OHIO

The National Weather Service Forecast Office in Cleveland gets daily readings for gauges on rivers in Ohio: 216-267-3900.

They can report readings for the following gauges:

Killbuck River, at Congress
Muskingum River, at Dresden
Scioto River, at Larue
Tiffin River, at Styker
St. Joseph River, at Montpelier
Blanchard River, at Findlay
Maumee River
    At Defiance
    At Waterville
Auglaize River, at Ft. Jennings
Sandusky River, at Upper Sandusky
Huron River, at Milan
Cuyahoga River
    At Old Portage
    At Akron
    At Independence
Olentangy River, at Claridon
Deer Creek, at Mt. Sterling
Darby Creek, at Darbyville
Scioto River
    At Prospect
    At Bellepoint
    At Worthington
    At Circleville
    At Piketon
Paint Creek, at Piketon
Scioto River
    At Columbus
    At Columbus/Morse Road
Alum Creek, at Killbourne

Deer Creek, at Williamsport
Scioto River, at Chillicothe
Paint Creek, at Bourneville
North Fork of the Licking River, at Newark
Wills Creek, at Drewent
Scioto River, at Higby
Little Miami River, at Milford
Walhonding River, at Walhonding
Muskingum River, at Zanesville
East Fork River, at Perintown
Muskingum River, at McConnelsville
Little Miami River
    At Harsha Dam
    At King Mills
Mad River, at Springfield
Great Miami River, at Hamilton
Little Miami River, at C. J. Brown Dam
Great Miami River
    At Dayton
    At Piqua
    At Franklin
    At Middletown
    At Tipp City
Ohio River
    At Marietta
    At Portsmouth
    At Fernbank
Mahoning River
    At Warren
    At Leavittsburg
Tuscarawas River, at Massillon
Killbuck Creek, at Killbuck
Tuscarawas River, at New Philadelphia
Stillwater River, at Tippecanoe
Tuscarawas River, at Uhrichsville
Walhonding River, at Mt. Vernon
Tuscarawas River, at Newcomerstown
Muskingum River, at Coshocton
Wills Creek, at Cambridge

OREGON

BLUE RIVER

Sections: Quentin Creek to Blue River Reservoir, Class IV (one at V)

Length of Run: Day trip, 4 miles

Location: Lane and Linn Counties, Oregon

Maps: USGS quads: Blue River (15')

Times Runnable: November to May after rain

Permit: None required

Gauge: Flow above Lookout Creek

Source of Levels: US Army Corps of Engineers, Lookout Point Dam; 503-937-2131.

How Reported: Cfs

Interpretation of Levels: Around 300 cfs is minimum, and 700-1000 is average high flow.

Source of More Information: Willamette Kayak and Canoe Club, PO Box 1062, Corvallis, OR 97331.

Sundance Expeditions, 14894 Galice Rd., Merlin, OR 97532; 503-479-8508.

USDA Forest Service, Blue River Ranger District, Willamette National Forest, Blue River, OR 97413; 503-822-3317.

Best Guidebooks: Willamette Kayak and Canoe Club, *Soggy Sneakers Guide.*

Further Comments: Watch for downed trees. In recent years, there have been as many as three to six spots that require portage.

CLACKAMAS RIVER
Wild and Scenic River

Sections:
(1) Seven miles above Collawash to Riverside Campground, Class III-IV
(2) Upper, Collawash River to Three Lynx Powerhouse, Class III-IV (plus one portage)
(3) Lower, McIver Park to mouth, Class II (one at IV)

Length of Run:
(1) Day trip, 7 miles
(2) Day trip, 17 miles
(3) Day trip, 20 miles

Location: Clackamas County, Oregon; Mt. Hood National Forest

Maps: USGS quads: High Rock (15'), Fish Creek Mtn. (15'), Colton (15'), Estacada, Redland, Damascus, Gladstone

Times Runnable: Year-round

Permit: None required

Gauge: For Sections (1) and (2), Clackamas River at Three Lynx

Source of Levels: National Weather Service, Portland; 503-249-0666.

How Reported: Cfs

Additional Gauge: For Section (3), Clackamas River at Estacada

Source of Levels: National Weather Service, Portland; 503-249-0666.

How Reported: Cfs

Interpretation of Levels: Minimum is about 1000 cfs; medium is 2000, and high is 5000. Experts have run this section as high as 20,000 to 30,000 cfs.

Source of More Information: USDA Forest Service, Estacada Ranger District, Mt. Hood National Forest, 200 SW Clubhouse Dr., Estacada, OR 97023; 503-630-6861.

Willamette Kayak and Canoe Club, PO Box 1062, Corvallis, OR 97331.

Sundance Expeditions, 14894 Galice Rd., Merlin, OR 97532; 503-479-8508.

Best Guidebooks: Willamette Kayak and Canoe Club, *Soggy Sneakers Guide;* Garren, *Oregon River Tours;* Interagency Whitewater Committee, *River Information Digest.*

Further Comments: There is a mandatory portage around Killer Fang on Section (2); watch for downed trees on all sections.

CROOKED RIVER
Wild and Scenic River

Sections:
(1) Lone Pine Bridge to Crooked River Ranch, Class IV (one at V)
(2) Crooked River Ranch to Lake Billy Chinnok, Class III-IV (one portage around dam)

Length of Run:
(1) Day trip, 18 miles
(2) Day trip, 9 miles with 2 miles on lake

Location: Jefferson and Deschutes Counties, Oregon

Maps: USGS quads: Redmond, Opal City, Steelhead

Times Runnable: Section (1) is runnable in spring after dam releases from the Prineville Reservoir; Section (2) is runnable year-round.

Permit: None required

Gauge: Crooked River, below Prineville Reservoir

Source of Levels: Ochoco Irrigation District, Prineville, OR; 503-447-6449.

National Weather Service, Portland; 503-249-0666. (Stay on the line and ask for this one after the recording.)

How Reported: Cfs

Interpretation of Levels: Minimum is about 250 cfs; medium is 2000-3500, and high is over 3500 cfs.

Source of More Information: Willamette Kayak and Canoe Club, PO Box 1062, Corvallis, OR 97331.

Sundance Expeditions, 14894 Galice Rd., Merlin, OR 97532; 503-479-8508.

Best Guidebooks: Willamette Kayak and Canoe Club, *Soggy Sneakers Guide.*

DESCHUTES RIVER
Wild and Scenic River

Sections:
(1) Wickiup Dam to Pringle Falls, Class I (one at IV)
(2) Pringle Falls to Big River Campground, Class I (one at II)
(3) Big River Campground to Benham Falls, Class I (one at V)

(4) Benham Falls to Dillon Falls, Class I
(one at VI, Dillon Falls)
(5) Dillon Falls to Lava Island Falls, Class III
(6) Bend to Tumalo State Park, Class IV
(7) Highway 26 to Sherer's Falls, Class III
(8) Below Sherer's Falls to the confluence with the Columbia River, Class III

Length of Run:
(1) Day trip, 9 miles
(2) Day trip, 16 miles
(3) Day trip, 18 miles
(4) Day trip, 2.5 miles
(5) Day trip, 2.5 miles
(6) Day trip, 5.5 miles
(7) 2-3 days, 54 miles
(8) 2-3 days, 44 miles

Location: Deschutes County, Oregon; Deschutes National Forest

Maps: USGS quads: Wickiup Dam, La Pine, Pistol Butte, Anns Butte, Benham Falls, Shevlin Park, Bend Tumalo, Forked Horn Butte, Cline Falls, Redmond, Steelhead Falls.

Times Runnable: Sections (1) to (6) are generally runnable from spring until fall; Wickiup Dam releases most days during this period. The flow on Sections (7) and (8) is controlled by Pelton Dam; these sections are runnable year-round.

Permit: A State of Oregon Boater's Pass is required for Sections (7) and (8). These are available from vendors throughout Oregon, including sporting goods stores and outfitters, for $1.75 per person, per day. The funds generated by the sale of these permits are used to benefit the Deschutes River. For more information, contact: Parks and Recreation Division, Department of Transportation, State of Oregon, 525 Trade St., SE, Salem, OR 97310; 503-378-6500.

Reservations: Not required

Restrictions: The Bureau of Land Management imposes the following restrictions: Open canoes are considered unsuitable craft. Fishing from floating craft is prohibited. Camping on islands is prohibited. From June 1 to October 1, charcoal fires and gas stoves are the only fires permitted. At other times, firepans are required, and you must bring your own wood. Burning of downed wood and driftwood is prohibited. Call 503-447-6845 for additional campfire information.

Gauge: For Sections (1) and (2), release from Wickiup

Source of Levels: Oregon State Water Resources Department, 503-388-6669.

How Reported: Cfs

Additional Gauge: For Sections (3), (4) and (5), Deschutes River at Benham

Source of Levels: Oregon State Water Resources Department, 503-388-6669.

How Reported: Cfs

Additional Gauge: For Section (6), Deschutes River at Bend

Source of Levels: Oregon State Water Resources Department, 503-388-6669.

How Reported: Cfs

Additional Gauge: For Sections (7) and (8), Deschutes River at Moody

Source of Levels: National Weather Service, Portland; 503-249-0666.

How Reported: Cfs

Interpretation of Levels: For Sections (1), (2), and (3), 500 cfs is minimum; the flow is dam-regulated, and the flow from spring to fall is usually between 1500 and 2500 cfs. For Sections (4) and (5), about 1000 cfs is minimum, and 3000 is high. For Section (6), about 500 cfs is minimum, and 1500 is high. For Sections (7) and (8), about 3000 cfs is minimum, and 8000 is high.

Source of More Information: District Manager, Bureau of Land Management, PO Box 550, Prineville, OR 97754; 503-447-4115.

Willamette Kayak and Canoe Club, PO Box 1062, Corvallis, OR 97331.

Sundance Expeditions, 14894 Galice Rd., Merlin, OR 97532; 503-479-8508.

Best Guidebooks: Willamette Kayak and Canoe Club, *Soggy Sneakers Guide;* Garren, *Oregon River Tours;* Bureau of Land Management, "Deschutes River Scenic Waterway" map/guide. (from BLM, address above); Interagency Whitewater Committee, *River Information Digest.*

FALL CREEK

Sections:
(1) Bedrock Campground to Fall Creek Reservoir, Class III (one at IV)
(2) Fall Creek Dam to Jasper Park, Class I-II.

Length of Run:
(1) Day trip, 10 miles
(2) Day trip, 7.5 miles

Location: Lane County, Oregon; Willamette National Forest

Maps: USGS quads: Hardesty Mtn., (15'), Lowell (15')

Times Runnable: November to May after rain

Permit: None required

Gauge: Discharge from Fall Creek Reservoir

Source of Levels: US Army Corps of Engineers, Lookout Point Reservoir; 503-937-2131.

How Reported: Cfs

Interpretation of Levels: About 800 or 1000 is minimum and 3000 is high. Experts have run this section as high as 18,000 cfs.

Source of More Information: Willamette Kayak and Canoe Club, PO Box 1062, Corvallis, OR 97331.

Sundance Expeditions, 14894 Galice Rd., Merlin, OR 97532; 503-479-8508.

USDA Forest Service, Willamette National Forest, 211 E. 7th Ave., Eugene, OR 97401; 503-687-6521.

Best Guidebooks: Willamette Kayak and Canoe Club, *Soggy Sneakers Guide.*

GRANDE RONDE RIVER
Wild and Scenic River

Sections:
(1) Tony Vey Meadows to Red Bridge State Park, Class III (one at IV)
(2) Red Bridge State Park to Riverside City Park, Class II
(3) Hilgard State Park to Riverside City Park, Class II-III (I at IV)
(4) Riverside City Park to Elgin, Class I
(5) Elgin to Palmer, Class II (I at IV)
(6) Minam (on the Wallowa River) to the confluence with the Grande Ronde and continuing to Powwatka Bridge, Class II
(7) Powwatka Bridge to Boggans Oasis, Class II
(8) Boggans Oasis to the confluence with the Snake River, and continuing to Hellers Bar, Class II (one at III, the Narrows)

Length of Run:
(1) 1-2 days, 17 miles
(2) Day trip, 8 miles
(3) Day trip, 9 miles
(4) 2 days, 29 miles
(5) Day trip, 13 miles
(6) 3 days, 37 miles
(7) 2 days, 26 miles
(8) 2 days, 26 miles

Location: Union and Wallowa Counties, Oregon; Asotin County, Washington; Umatilla National Forest

Maps: USGS quads: Fly Valley, Marley Creek, McIntyre Creek, Kamela SE, Hilgard, La Grande SE, Conley, Imbler, Elgin, Partridge Creek, Rondawa, Fry Meadow, Deep Creek, Elbow Creek, Promise, Eden, Troy, Sadde Butte, Mountain View, Field Spring, Black Butte, Limekiln Rapids

Times Runnable: Sections (1) through (4) are runnable in spring or early summer during runoff; the rest are runnable year-round.

Permit: None required

Gauge: Grande Ronde River at Lagrande

Source of Levels: National Weather Service, Portland; 503-249-0666. Stay on the line and ask for this one; it's not on the recording.

How Reported: Cfs

Additional Gauge: Grande Ronde River at Troy

Source of Levels: National Weather Service, Portland; 503-249-0666.

How Reported: Cfs

Interpretation of Levels: For Section (1), extrapolate from the gauge at Lagrande. About 900 to 1100 cfs there should be enough. For Sections (2), (3), (4), and (5), also use the gauge at Lagrande. About 1000 cfs is minimum; 4000-5000 is medium, and 8000 is high. For Sections (6), (7) and (8), use the gauge on the Grande Ronde at Troy. Minimum is 1200 to 1800 cfs; medium is 4000, and high is 8000 to 12,000.

Source of More Information: Bureau of Land Management, Baker Resource Area, PO Box 987, Baker, OR 97814; 503-523-6391; ext. 281.

Willamette Kayak and Canoe Club, PO Box 1062, Corvallis, OR 97331.

Sundance Expeditions, 14894 Galice Rd., Merlin, OR 97532; 503-479-8508.

Best Guidebooks: Williamette Canoe and Kayak Club, *Soggy Sneakers Guide;* Garren, *Oregon River Tours;* North, *Washington Whitewater 2.*

ILLINOIS RIVER
Wild and Scenic River

Sections: Miami Bar to Lower Oak Flat, Class IV+

Length of Run: 2-3 days, 34 miles

Location: Curry County, Oregon; Siskiyou National Forest

Maps: USGS quads: Selma (15'), Pearsoll Peak (15'), Collier Butte (15'), Agness (15')

Times Runnable: April and early May

Permit: Required between April 15 and June 30. Self-issuing at the Miami Bar put-in.

Reservations: Not required

Restrictions: Open canoes are not recommended by the Forest Service. The maximum size of party allowed is 12 (Anne and I had a lot more people than that at our last party, so it's a good thing we had it at home). Firepans required. Pack out all trash. You must also carry PFDs, a first aid kit, an extra set of oars, an air pump, and an inflatable repair kit. Members should stay in sight of each other while boating.

Gauge: Illinois River, near Kirby

Source of Levels: National Weather Service, Portland; 503-249-0666.

How Reported: Cfs

Interpretation of Levels: Minimum is 500 cfs, and high is 3000.

Source of More Information: USDA Forest Service, River Permits and Information, 14335 Galice Rd., Merlin, OR 97532; 503-479-3735.

Willamette Kayak and Canoe Club, PO Box 1062, Corvallis, OR 97331.

Sundance Expeditions, 14894 Galice Rd., Merlin, OR 97532; 503-479-8508.

Best Guidebooks: Willamette Kayak and Canoe Club, *Soggy Sneakers Guide,* Garren, *Oregon River Tours;* Interagency Whitewater Committee, *River Information Digest.*

JOHN DAY RIVER
Wild and Scenic River

Sections: (1) Service Creek to Clarno, Class I-II
(2) Clarno to Cottonwood, Class II-III

Length of Run: (1) 2-3 days, 44 miles
(2) 2-3 days, 70 miles

Location: Wheeler, Sherman, and Gilliam Counties, Oregon

Maps: USGS quads: Painted Hills, Clarno (15'), Chimney Springs, Shoestring Ridge, Horseshoe Bend, Indian Cove, Harmony, Esau Canyon, Devils Backbone, Turner Butte, McDonald

Times Runnable: April to May or June

Permit: None required

Gauge: John Day River, at Service Creek

Source of Levels: National Weather Service, Portland; 503-249-0666.

How Reported: Cfs

Interpretation of Levels: Minimum is about 1000 cfs; optimum is 2000 to 4000, and high is 5000 to 6000.

Source of More Information: District Manager, Bureau of Land Management, PO Box 550, Prineville, OR 97754; 503-447-4115.

Willamette Kayak and Canoe Club, PO Box 1062, Corvallis, OR 97331.

Sundance Expeditions, 14894 Galice Rd., Merlin, OR 97532; 503-479-8508.

Best Guidebooks: Willamette Kayak and Canoe Club, *Soggy Sneakers Guide;* Garren, *Oregon River Tours;* Interagency Whitewater Committee, *River Information Digest.*

Further Comments: While you're on the John Day, expect to enjoy an unmatched sense of isolated wilderness!

KLAMATH RIVER

See California.

LAKE CREEK

Sections: Deadwood Creek to Tide, Class III (IV high)

Length of Run: Day trip, 7 miles

Location: Lane County, Oregon

Maps: USGS quads: Mapleton (15')

Times Runnable: November to May after rain

Permit: None required

Gauge: Extrapolate from the Siuslaw at Mapleton Nearby.

Source of Levels: National Weather Service, Portland; 503-249-0666. Stay on the line and ask for this one.

How Reported: Cfs

Interpretation of Levels: The flow on Lake Creek is usually about a third of the flow on the Siuslaw. After conversion, minimum will be about 1600 cfs; medium is 8000, and high is 15,000-20,000 (Class IV)

Source of More Information: Willamette Kayak and Canoe Club, PO Box 1062, Corvallis, OR 97331.

Sundance Expeditions, 14894 Galice Rd., Merlin, OR 97532; 503-479-8508.

Best Guidebooks: Willamette Kayak and Canoe Club, *Soggy Sneakers Guide.*

MCKENZIE RIVER
Wild and Scenic River

Sections: Finn Rock to Leaburg Dam, Class II-III

Length of Run: Day trip, 18 miles

Location: Lane County, Oregon; Willamette National Forest

Maps: USGS quads: Blue River (15'), Leaburg (15')

Times Runnable: Year-round

Permit: None required

Gauge: McKenzie River at Vida

Source of Levels: National Weather Service, Portland; 503-249-0666.

How Reported: Cfs

Interpretation of Levels: Minimum is about 1000 cfs, and high is 5000.

Source of More Information: USDA Forest Service, McKenzie Ranger District, Willamette National Forest, McKenzie Bridge, OR 97413; 503-822-3381.

USDA Forest Service, Blue River Ranger District, Willamette National Forest, Blue River, OR 97413; 503-822-3317.

Willamette Kayak and Canoe Club, PO Box 1062, Corvallis, OR 97331.

Sundance Expeditions, 14894 Galice Rd., Merlin, OR 97532; 503-479-8508.

Best Guidebooks: Willamette Kayak and Canoe Club, *Soggy Sneakers Guide;* Interagency Whitewater Committee, *River Information Digest;* Garren, *Oregon River Tours.*

MCKENZIE RIVER, SOUTH FORK
Wild and Scenic River

Sections: Near French Pete to Cougar Reservoir, Class III-IV

Length of Run: Day trip, 8.5 miles

Location: Lane County, Oregon; Willamette National Forest

Maps: USGS quads: McKenzie Bridge (15')

Times Runnable: November to May after rain

Permit: None required

Gauge: Inflow to Cougar Reservoir

Source of Levels: US Army Corps of Engineers, Cougar Dam; 503-822-3344.

How Reported: Cfs

Interpretation of Levels: Minimum is 1500; medium is 2000 to 3000; high is 3500 to 4500.

Source of More Information: USDA Forest Service, McKenzie Ranger District, Willamette National Forest, McKenzie Bridge, OR 97413; 503-822-3381.

Willamette Kayak and Canoe Club, PO Box 1062, Corvallis, OR 97331.

Sundance Expeditions, 14894 Galice Rd., Merlin, OR 97532; 503-479-8508.

Best Guidebooks: Willamette Kayak and Canoe Club, *Soggy Sneakers Guide,* Interagency Whitewater Committee, *River Information Digest.*

OWYHEE RIVER
Wild and Scenic River
(See Idaho for additional sections upstream.)

| Sections: | (1) | Three Forks to Rome, Class IV (one at V) |
| | (2) | Rome to Leslie Gulch, Class III (one at IV) |

| Length of Run: | (1) | 2-3 days, 35 miles |
| | (2) | 4-5 days, 63 miles |

Location: Malheur County, Oregon

Maps: USGS quads: Three Forks, Whitehorse Butte, Skull Creek, Indian Fort, Little Grassy Mtn, Dry Creek Rim, Scott Reservoir, Owyhee Butte, Lambert Rocks, Rinehart Canyon, The Hole in the Ground, Jordan Craters North, Diamond Butte.

Times Runnable: Spring and early summer after snowmelt

Permit: You must register with the BLM before you put in. A registration form is included in Appendix One.

March 15 to June 15: Bureau of Land Management, Rome Launch Site, Box HC65, Jordan Valley, ID 97910; 503-586-2612.

Year-round: Bureau of Land Management, PO Box 700, Vale, OR 97918; 503-473-3144.

Reservations: Not required

Restrictions: The maximum party size is 15. Pack out your trash. Firepans are required. PFDs are required.

Gauge: Owyhee River, at Rome

Source of Levels: National Weather Service, Portland; 503-249-0666.

How Reported: Cfs

Interpretation of Levels: Minimum is 1200 cfs; medium is 3000 to 5000; high is 8000 cfs.

Source of More Information: For Section (1): Bureau of Land Management, PO Box 700, Vale, OR 97918; 503-473-3144.

For Sections (2) and (3): Bureau of Land Management, address and phone above. Or, from March 15 to June 15: Bureau of Land Management, Rome Launch Site, Jordan Valley, ID 97910; 503-586-2612.

Willamette Kayak and Canoe Club, PO Box 1062, Corvallis, OR 97331.

Sundance Expeditions, 14894 Galice Rd., Merlin, OR 97532; 503-479-8508.

Best Guidebooks: Willamette Canoe and Kayak Club, *Soggy Sneakers Guide*; BLM, "Owyhee River Boating Guide".

Further Comments: An isolated desert wilderness run, packed with fine whitewater.

ROGUE RIVER
Wild and Scenic River

| Sections: | Grave Creek to Foster Bar, Class III (1 at IV, Blossom Bar Rapid and 1 portage at Rainie Falls) |

| Length of Run: | 2-3 days, 35 miles |

Location: Josephine and Curry Counties, Oregon; Siskiyou National Forest

Maps: USGS quads: Galice (15'), Marial (15'), Agness (15')

Times Runnable: Year-round

Permit: Required from June 1 through September 15. Reservations are required at these times too; see below.

Reservations: From June 1 to September 15 permits are available on a call-in basis (503-479-3735). Out of 6,000

Blossom Bar Rapid, Rogue River. Photo by Curt Smith

private users each year, 3,000 get on through this call-in procedure (called the open pool or common pool). Otherwise, permits and reservations are awarded by lottery. Lottery applications are accepted from the first business day in January through the Friday nearest mid-February of each year. A fee of $2 must accompany your application (check payable to USDA Forest Service; not cash). Your application must be on a standard 3" x 5" card (does this sound like a contest from the back of a cereal box?) On your 3 x 5 card should be the intended launch date; the intended party size (20 or less, but the smaller you keep it, the better your chance of winning); the name, address, and phone of the trip leader; and the name, address, and phone of the alternate trip leader (optional; this leader is allowed to lead if the first leader drops out, otherwise it's a no-go); and the signature of the trip leader.

I show a sample application on a 3 x 5 card in Appendix One, so you'll know how to do it. Make sure to follow my example exactly; otherwise you get the booby prize. Don't make a photocopy of the one in the back; applicants using 3 x 5 sheets that aren't on standard card stock are disqualified (besides, I used my name, not yours). The Forest Service thinks it is O.K. for every member of a prospective party to submit an application to lead the trip, and doing so would increase your group's chances. However, you may submit only one application that lists you as a trip leader or alternate trip leader. Successful applicants are notified in mid-March. If you win you'll have to submit another $5 per person when you confirm your permit. Send your application to:

River Permits and Information, Siskiyou National Forest, 14335 Galice Rd., Merlin, OR 97532; 503-479-3735.

Restrictions: Maximum party size is 20. Only 120 persons are allowed to launch per day. Firepans are required. Pack out all trash.

Gauge: Rogue River, near Agness

Source of Levels: National Weather Service, Portland; 503-249-0666.

How Reported: Cfs

Additional Gauge: Rogue River near Grant's Pass.

Additional Source of Levels: National Weather Service, Portland; 503-249-0666.

Interpretation of Levels: About 1000-1500 cfs is minimum, and 6000 is high.

Source of More Information: River Permits and Information, address and phone above.

Willamette Kayak and Canoe Club, PO Box 1062, Corvallis, OR 97331.

Sundance Expeditions, 14894 Galice Rd., Merlin, OR 97532; 503-479-8508.

Best Guidebooks: Willamette Kayak and Canoe Club, *Soggy Sneakers Guide;* Interagency Whitewater Committee, *River Information Digest;* Garren, *Oregon River Tours.*

BLM and Forest Service, "The Wild and Scenic Rogue River" map/guide.

Further Comments: The Rogue is the most popular river in the Northwest, and justifiably so! The combination of warm water, dependable flow and a wide variety of rapids make it an ideal wilderness training-ground for intermediate boaters.

SANTIAM RIVER, MIDDLE

Sections:
    (1) Seven miles above Green Peter Reservoir to Green Peter Reservoir, Class IV
    (2) Green Peter Reservoir to Foster Reservoir, Class IV

Length of Run:
    (1) Day trip, 7 miles;
    (2) Day trip, 2.5 miles

Location: Linn County, Oregon

Maps: USGS quads: Quartzville (15'), Cascadia (15'), Sweet Home (15')

Times Runnable: Section (1) is runnable in winter after rain, or in spring and early summer after snowmelt. Section (2) is runnable year-round after dam releases for power generation at Foster Dam.

Permit: None required

Gauge: For Section (1), extrapolate from the South Santiam at Cascadia. The Middle Santiam will be running a few hundred cfs less.

Source of Levels: US Army Corps of Engineers, Foster Dam; 503-367-5124.

How Reported: Cfs

Additional Gauge: For Section (2), release from Green Peter Dam

Source of Levels: US Army Corps of Engineers, Foster Dam; 503-367-5124.

How Reported: Cfs, upcoming release schedule (in units). One unit releasing corresponds to 2000 cfs, and two units to 4000.

Interpretation of Levels: For Section (1), minimum is

about 900, and high is about 2000. For section (2), minimum is about 200 and high is about 4000. Experts have run this section at 10,000 cfs.

Source of More Information: Willamette Kayak and Canoe Club, PO Box 1062, Corvallis, OR 97331.

Sundance Expeditions, 14894 Galice Rd., Merlin, OR 97532; 503-479-8508.

Best Guidebooks: Willamette Kayak and Canoe Club *Soggy Sneakers Guide.*

SANTIAM RIVER, NORTH
Wild and Scenic River

Sections:	(1) Whispering Falls Campground to Detroit Reservoir, Class III
	(2) Big Cliff Dam to Packsaddle Park, Class III (one at IV-V plus portage of one dam)
	(3) Packsaddle Park to Mill City, Class II-`III
	(4) Mill City to Mehama, Class II-III
Length of Run:	(1) Day trip, 6 miles
	(2) Day trip, 5 miles
	(3) Day trip, 7 miles
	(4) Day trip, 7.5 miles

Location: Linn and Marion Counties, Oregon; Willamette and Mt. Hood National Forests

Maps: USGS quads: Detroit (15'), Quartzville (15'), Mill City (15'), Lyons (15')

Times Runnable: October to June

Permit: None required

Gauge: For Section (1), inflow to the Detroit Reservoir

Source of Levels: US Army Corps of Engineers, Detroit Dam, 503-897-2385.

How Reported: Cfs

Additional Gauge: For Sections (2)-(4), North Santiam at Mehema

Source of Levels: National Weather Service, Portland; 503-249-0666.

How Reported: Cfs

Interpretation of Levels: For Section (1), about 1000 cfs is minimum, and 2000 is high. For Sections (2)-(4), minimum is about 750 to 1000 cfs. Moderate flows are in the range from 2000 to 4000; high is 4000 to 6000, and very high is 6000 to 10,000 cfs.

Source of More Information: USDA Forest Service, Willamette National Forest, 211 E. 7th Ave., Eugene, OR 97401; 503-687-6521.

USDA Forest Service, Mt. Hood National Forest, 2955 NW Division St., Gresham, OR 97030; 503-667-0511.

Willamette Kayak and Canoe Club, PO Box 1062, Corvallis, OR 97331.

Sundance Expeditions, 14894 Galice Rd., Merlin, OR 97532; 503-479-8508.

Best Guidebooks: Willamette Kayak and Canoe Club, *Soggy Sneakers Guide.*

SANTIAM RIVER, SOUTH
Wild and Scenic River

Sections:	Mountain House to Foster Reservoir, Class IV (one at VI+)
Length of Run:	Day trip, 10 miles

Location: Linn County, Oregon; Willamette National Forest

Maps: USGS quads: Cascadia (15'), Sweet Home (15')

Times Runnable: In winter to spring after rain or in spring to summer after snowmelt.

Permit: None required

Gauge: South Santiam at Waterloo

Source of Levels: US Army Corps of Engineers, Foster Dam, Sweet Home, OR; 503-367-5124.

National Weather Service, Portland; 503-249-0666. Stay on the line and ask for this one.

How Reported: Cfs

Interpretation of Levels: About 800 cfs is minimum and 3000 is high.

Source of More Information: USDA Forest Service, Willamette National Forest, 211 E. 7th Ave., Eugene, OR 97401; 503-687-6521.

Willamette Kayak and Canoe Club, PO Box 1062, Corvallis, OR 97331.

Sundance Expeditions, 14894 Galice Rd., Merlin, OR 97532; 503-479-8508.

Best Guidebooks: Willamette Kayak and Canoe Club, *Soggy Sneakers Guide.*

Further Comments: As of this writing, the Class VI rapid on this section had been run three times. You'll probably want to portage it.

SNAKE RIVER, HELLS CANYON

See Idaho.

UMPQUA RIVER, NORTH
Wild and Scenic River

Sections:	(1) Boulder Flat to Horseshoe Bend, Class II-III
	(2 Horseshoe Bend to Steamboat, Class III-IV
	(3) Steamboat to Cable Crossing, Class III (one at IV)
	(4) Idleyld Park to Winchester, Class II+
	(5) Winchester to Umpqua Landing, Class II
Length of Run:	(1) Day trip, 7 miles
	(2) Day trip, 9 miles
	(3) Long day trip, 16 miles, shorter sections possible
	(4) 2 days, 26 miles, shorter sections possible
	(5) 1-2 days, 16 miles

Location: Douglas County, Oregon

Maps: USGS quads: Illahee Rock (15'), Mace (15'), Glide (15'), Sutherlin (15'), Tyee (15')

Times Runnable: Year-round

Permit: None required

Gauge: USGS gauge at Winchester

Source of Levels: National Weather Service, Portland; 503-249-0666. Stay on the line and ask for this one.

How Reported: Cfs

Interpretation of Levels: About 1000 is minimum, and 3000 is high.

Source of More Information: Willamette Kayak and Canoe Club, PO Box 1062, Corvallis, OR 97331.

Sundance Expeditions, 14894 Galice Rd., Merlin, OR 97532; 503-479-8508.

Cimarron Outdoors, HC60 Box 62, Idlewild, OR 97447; 503-498-2235.

Best Guidebooks: Willamette Kayak and Canoe Club, *Soggy Sneakers Guide.*

Further Comments: The North Umpqua is one of the most popular Class III rivers in Oregon. It's similar to the Tuolumne River of California, but not so difficult. If you run Section (3), be sure to take out at the cable crossing. Two Class V+ rapids are just downstream.

WHITE RIVER

Sections:	(1) Barlow Crossing to Victor Road Bridge, Class III-IV
	(2) Victor Road Bridge to Tygh Valley, Class II+ (one at III)
Length of Run:	(1) Day trip, 18 miles
	(2) Day trip, 11 miles

Location: Wasco County, Oregon

Maps: USGS quads: Mt. Hood South, Badger Lake, Mt. Wilson (15'), Rock Creek Reservoir, Wamac, Tygh Valley

Times Runnable: In spring or early summer after snowmelt

Permit: None required

Gauge: White River at Tygh Valley

Source of Levels: National Weather Service, Portland; 503-249-0666.

How Reported: Cfs

Interpretation of Levels: Minimum is about 500 cfs; 1000 is medium, and 2000 is high.

Source of More Information: Willamette Kayak and Canoe Club, PO Box 1062, Corvallis, OR 97331.

Sundance Expeditions, 14894 Galice Rd., Merlin, OR 97532; 503-479-8508.

Best Guidebooks: Willamette Kayak and Canoe Club, *Soggy Sneakers Guide.*

WILLAMETTE RIVER

Sections:	(1) Jasper Park on the Middle Fork to the confluence and continuing to Alton Baker Park, Class II-III
	(2) Alton Baker Park to Harrisburg, Class I-II

Length   (1) Day trip, 14 miles
of Run: (2) Day trip, 14 miles

Location: Lane County, Oregon

Maps: USGS quads: Lowell (15'), Springfield, Eugene East, Coburg, Junction City, Harrisburg

Times Runnable: Year-round

Permit: None required

Gauge: For the upper part of Section (1), Middle Fork of the Willamette at Jasper

Source of Levels: National Weather Service, Portland; 503-249-0666. Stay on the line and ask for this one.

How Reported: Cfs

Additional Gauge: Willamette River at Eugene

Source of Levels: National Weather Service, Portland; 503-249-0666. Stay on the line and ask for this one.

How Reported: Cfs

Interpretation of Levels: About 2000 is the minimum release on the Willamette; high is between 6000 and 10,000.

Source of More Information: Willamette Kayak and Canoe Club, PO Box 1062, Corvallis, OR 97331.

Sundance Expeditions, 14894 Galice Rd., Merlin, OR 97532; 503-479-8508.

Best Guidebooks: Willamette Kayak and Canoe Club, *Soggy Sneakers Guide.*

WILSON

Sections: (1) Jones Creek Forest Camp to Milepost 15, Class III
                  (2) Milepost 15 to boat ramp, Class II-III

Length   (1) Day trip, 8 miles
of Run: (2) Day trip, 8 miles

Location: Tillamook County, Oregon

Maps: USGS quads: Enright (15'), Blaine (15'), Tillamook (15')

Times Runnable: November to May after rain

Permit: None required

Gauge: Wilson River near Tillamook

Source of Levels: National Weather Service, Portland; 503-249-0666. You'll have to stay on the line and ask for this one.

How Reported: Cfs

Interpretation of Levels: Minimum is 1000; medium is 3500, and high is 7000.

Source of More Information: Willamette Kayak and Canoe Club, PO Box 1062, Corvallis, OR 97331.

Sundance Expeditions, 14894 Galice Rd., Merlin, OR 97532; 503-479-8508.

Best Guidebooks: Willamette Kayak and Canoe Club, *Soggy Sneakers Guide.*

GENERAL INFORMATION SOURCES FOR OREGON

Levels for rivers in Oregon can be obtained by calling the National Weather Service Forecast Office at the Portland Airport: 503-249-0666.

Calling this number accesses a 24-hour recording. From 8:30 a.m. to 2 p.m. during April through June, if you hold the line after the recording, a hydrologist will answer to provide further information. Gauge readings are reported for the following rivers:

Sandy River, near Bull Run
Clackamas River
    At Three Lynx
    At Estacada
North Santiam River, at Mehema
Mackenzie River, at Vida
Rogue River, near Agness
Grande Ronde River, at Troy
John Day River, at Service Creek
Deschutes River, at Moody
Illinois River, near Kirby
Owyhee River, at Rome

A forecast of future flows is also provided. Other gauges, for which readings can be obtained by asking the hydrologist, include:

Crooked River, below Prineville Reservoir
Nehalem River, at Foss

Mackenzie River, at Trail Bridge
South Santiam River, at Waterloo
Rogue River
    At Gold Ray
    At Grants Pass
North Umpqua River, at Winchester
Umpqua River, at Elkton
Imnaha River, at Imnaha
North Fork of the John Day River, at Monument
Hood River, near Hood River at Tucker Bridge
Breitenbush River, near Detroit
Grande Ronde River, at La Grande
Siuslaw at Mapleton
White River at Tygh Valley
Willamette River at Eugene
Middle Fork of the Willamette River at Jasper
Wilson River, near Tillamook

The Pacific Power and Light Company in Portland maintains a recording that reports reservoir levels and dam releases. Call them at 800-547-1501. They report the following releases:

Lewis River, North Fork, Release from Merwin Dam
Klamath River
    Release from Keno Dam
    Release from J.C. Boyle Powerhouse
    Release from Irongate Dam

PENNSYLVANIA

CASSELMAN RIVER

Sections: Markleton to Fort Hill, Class II-III

Length of Run: Day trip, 6 miles

Location: Somerset County, Pennsylvania

Maps: USGS quads: Markleton, Confluence

Times Runnable: Spring after snowmelt or after heavy rain

Permit: None required

Gauge: USGS gauge at Markleton

Source of Levels: National Weather Service, Pittsburgh; 412-644-2890.

National Weather Service, Washington; 703-260-0305.

How Reported: Feet

Interpretation of Levels: Minimum is about 2.5 feet (775 cfs). High is 5.0 feet (3900 cfs).

Source of More Information: Wildwater Designs, 230 Penllyn Pike, Penllyn, PA 19422; 215-646-5034.

Best Guidebooks: Gertler, *Keystone Canoeing.*

Gauge Conversion: USGS Casselman River at Markleton

Feet	Cfs	Feet	Cfs
2.4	775	5.0	3900
2.6	840	5.2	4240
2.8	1030	5.4	4610
3.0	1230	5.6	5020
3.2	1430	5.8	5440
3.4	1650	6.0	5860
3.6	1880	6.5	6970
3.8	2120	7.0	8190
4.0	2400	7.5	9630
4.2	2700	8.0	11200
4.4	3000	8.5	12920
4.6	3300	9.0	15020
4.8	3600	10.0	20300

DARK SHADE CREEK

Sections: Cairnbrook Bridge to confluence with Clear Shade Creek (to form Shade Creek), Class IV-V

Length of Run: Day trip, 2 miles

Location: Somerset County, Pennsylvania

Maps: USGS quads: Central City, Windber

Times Runnable: February to March during peak runoff or after heavy rain

Permit: None required

Gauge: None

Source of Levels: Guestimation only

Interpretation of Levels: Check the water at the take-out. If last rapid looks runnable, it is.

Source of More Information: Wildwater Designs, 230 Penllyn Pike, Penllyn, PA 19422; 215-646-5034.

Best Guidebooks: Grove et al., *Appalachian Whitewater, Vol. II.;* Gertler, *Keystone Canoeing.*

LEHIGH RIVER

Sections: Upper Gorge
(1) Francis Walter Dam to White Haven, Class II
(2) White Haven to Rockport, Class II-III

Lower Gorge
(3) Rockport to Jim Thorpe, Class II-III at low to moderate levels.

Length of Run:
(1) Day trip, 5.6 miles
(2) Day trip, 9.0 miles
(3) Day trip, 14.5 miles

Location: Luzerne and Carbon Counties, Pennsylvania; Lehigh River State Park

Maps: USGS quads: White Haven, Hickory Run, Pleasant View, Summit, Christmans, Lehighton, Weatherly, Hickory Run

Times Runnable: March through May and on special release days during June and the early fall.

Permit: None required

Gauge: Release from the Francis E. Walter Dam

Source of Levels: Whitewater Challengers, 717-443-8345.

How Reported: Releases in cfs and release schedules

Additional Gauge: USGS Lehigh River at White Haven, Pennsylvania

Source of Levels: National Weather Service, Harrisburg; 717-234-6812.

How Reported: Feet

Interpretation of Levels: Minimum is about 750 cfs; moderate is 1000 to 2000; high is over 2000, and extremely high (Class IV or IV+) is 5000 to 10,000.

Source of More Information: Whitewater Challengers, Star Route 6A1, White Haven, PA 18661; 717-443-8345.

Lehigh Gorge State Park, RFD 1, Box 284, Drums, PA 18222; 717-443-7348.

Lehigh River Rafting, PO Box 66, White Haven, PA 18661; 717-443-9777.

Best Guidebooks: Grove et al., *Appalachian Whitewater, Vol. II,* Gertler, *Keystone Canoeing.*

Further Comments: The Lehigh rivers cuts a splendid scenic gorge through the Pocono Mountains.

LOYALSOCK CREEK

Sections:
(1) Lopez to Rt. 220 bridge, Class II-III
(2) Rt. 220 bridge to Forksville, Class III (to IV high with one Class IV-V)

Length of Run:
(1) Day trip, 7 miles
(2) Day trip, 10 miles

Location: Sullivan County, Pennsylvania

Maps: USGS quads: Laporte, Eagles Mere

Janice Dunham and Fred Reinhall on the Loyalsock River in winter. Photo by Bob Hall.

Times Runnable: March to early May

Permit: None required

Gauge: Painted gauge at Rt. 87 at World's End Park

Source of Levels: World's End State Park, 717-924-3287.

How Reported: Feet

Additional Gauge: USGS Loyalsock Creek at Loyalsockville

Source of Levels: National Weather Service, Harrisburg; 717-234-6812.

How Reported: Feet

Interpretation of Levels: In terms of the World's End Gauge, low is 4 to 4.5; medium is 5; high is 6, and extremely high is 7 feet.

Source of More Information: Wildwater Designs, 230 Penllyn Pike, Penllyn, PA 19422; 215-646-5034.

World's End State Park, PO Box 62, Fortsville, PA 18616-0062; 717-924-3287.

Best Guidebooks: Grove et al., *Appalachian Whitewater, Vol. II*; Gertler, *Keystone Canoeing.*

Gauge Conversion: USGS Loyalsock Creek at Loyalsockville

Feet	Cfs	Feet	Cfs
4.0	512	6.2	4504
4.2	1035	6.4	5079
4.6	1165	6.6	5698
4.8	1457	6.8	6360
5.0	1795	7.0	7068
5.2	2145	7.5	9171
5.4	2535	8.0	11630
5.6	2969	8.5	14480
5.8	3446	9.0	17730
6.0	3970	10.0	25510

NESCOPECK CREEK

Sections: Rt. 93 bridge to last bridge above I-80, Class II

Length of Run: Day trip, 8.4 miles

Location: Luzerne County, Pennsylvania

Nescopeck Creek. Photo by Roger Corbett.

Maps: USGS quads: Seibertsville, Nurenburg, Berwick

Times Runnable: March to April and after heavy rain

Permit: None required

Gauge: A paddlers' gauge is on river-left at a bridge 100 yards below the put-in.

Source of Levels: Visual inspection only

How Reported: Feet

Interpretation of Levels: Low is about 1 foot; moderate is 2.5 feet; high is 3 feet (Class III); 4 feet is floodstage.

Source of More Information: Wildwater Designs, 230 Penllyn Pike, Penllyn, PA 19422; 215-646-5034.

Best Guidebooks: Grove et al., *Appalachian Whitewater, Vol. II;* Gertler, *Keystone Canoeing.*

PINE CREEK

Sections: (1) Grand Canyon Run, Ansonia to Blackwell, Class I (one at II-III)
(2) Blackwell to Waterville, Class I

Length of Run: (1) 1-2 days, 17 miles
(2) 2 days, 27 miles

Location: Tioga and Lycoming Counties, Pennsylvania

Maps: USGS quads: Tiadaghton, Cedar Run, Cammal, Slate Run, Jersey Mills

Times Runnable: March to May

Permit: None required

Gauge: Cedar Run Gauge, for Section (1)

Source of Levels: National Weather Service, Williamsburg; 717-368-8744.

National Weather Service, Harrisburg; 717-234-6812.

How Reported: Feet

Additional Gauge: Slate Run Gauge, for Section (2)

Source of Levels: National Weather Service, Williamsburg; 717-368-8744.

National Weather Service, Harrisburg; 717-234-6812.

How Reported: Feet

Interpretation of Levels: For Section (1), minimum is about 2 feet on the Cedar Run gauge; medium is 2.5 feet, and 3.5 feet is medium-high. For Section (2), minimum on the Slate Run gauge is about 2 feet, and optimum levels range from 2.5 to 3.5 feet.

Source of More Information: Pine Creek Outfitters, Rt. 4, Box 130B, Wellsboro, PA 16901; 717-724-3003.

Tiadaghton State Forest, 423 East Central Ave., S. Williamsport, PA 17701; 717-327-3450.

Best Guidebooks: Grove et al., *Appalachian Whitewater, Vol. II;* Gertler, *Keystone Canoeing.*

Gauge Conversion: USGS gauge Pine Creek at Cedar Run

Feet	Cfs	Feet	Cfs
2.0	376	4.0	2699
2.2	532	4.5	3595
2.4	708	5.0	4613
2.6	891	5.5	5757
2.8	1090	6.0	7054
3.0	1319	6.5	8496
3.2	1562	7.0	10070
3.4	1817	7.5	11780
3.6	2086	8.0	13620
3.8	2378	—	—

SHADE CREEK

Sections: From the confluence of Dark Shade and Clear Shade Creeks to the confluence with Stony Creek, Class III-IV

Length of Run: Day trip, 9.6 miles

Location: Somerset County, Pennsylvania

Maps: USGS quads: Windber, Hooversville

Times Runnable: March to April and after heavy rain

Permit: None required

Gauge: None

Source of Levels: Guestimation only

Additional Gauge: Extrapolate from the USGS Markleton gauge on the Casselman.

Source of Levels: National Weather Service, Pittsburgh, 412-644-2890; Washington, 703-260-0305.

How Reported: Feet

Interpretation of Levels: If the Markleton gauge reads over 3.5 feet then there should be enough water on Shade Creek. If it looks runnable at the take-out, then it probably is.

Source of More Information: Wildwater Designs, 230 Penllyn Pike, Penllyn, PA 19422; 215-646-5034.

Western Pennsylvania Whitewater School on Slippery Rock Creek. Photo by Tom Irwin.

Best Guidebooks: Grove et al., *Appalachian Whitewater, Vol. II;* Gertler, *Keystone Canoeing.*

SLIPPERY ROCK CREEK

Sections: Kennedy Mill to Connoquenessing Creek, Class III-IV

Length of Run: Day trip, 11 miles

Location: Lawrence County, Pennsylvania

Maps: USGS quads: Portersville, Zelienople, Beaver Falls

Times Runnable: March to May and after heavy rain

Permit: None required

Gauge: USGS at Slippery Rock

Source of Levels: National Weather Service, Pittsburgh; 412-644-2890.

McConnell's Mill State Park, 412-368-8091.

How Reported: Feet

Interpretation of Levels: Low is 0.5 feet; optimum is 2 feet; high is 3.0 feet (about Class IV), and extremely high is 5 feet (about Class V).

Source of More Information: Wildwater Designs, 230 Penllyn Pike, Penllyn, PA 19422; 215-646-5034.

McConnell's Mill State Park, Rt. 1, Portersville, PA 16051; 412-368-8091.

Best Guidebooks: Grove et al., *Appalachian Whitewater, Vol. II;* Gertler, *Keystone Canoeing.*

STONEY CREEK

Sections: Seanor to Rt. 55127 near Paint, PA, Class III-IV

Length of Run: Day trip, 4 miles

Location: Somerset County, Pennsylvania

Maps: USGS quads: Hooverville, Johnston

Times Runnable: February to May and after heavy rain

Permit: None required

Gauge: Painted gauge at Hollsopple Bridge, 2 miles upstream of the put-in, off Rt. 403

Source of Levels: Visual inspection only

How Reported: Feet

Additional Gauge: Extrapolate from the Markleton USGS gauge on the Casselman River.

Source of Levels: National Weather Service, Pittsburgh, 412-644-2890; Washington, 703-899-7378 (weekdays).

How Reported: Feet

Interpretation of Levels: In terms of the Hollsopple gauge, 1.5 feet is minimum; 3 is optimum, and 4 is high. If the Casselman is at least 3.5 feet then the Stony should at least be at minimum.

Source of More Information: Wildwater Designs, 230 Penllyn Pike, Penllyn, PA 19422; 215-646-5034.

Best Guidebooks: Grove et al., *Appalachian Whitewater, Vol. II;* Gertler, *Keystone Canoeing.*

Further Comments: Stoney Creek is similar in difficulty to the Lower Yough.

TOHICKON CREEK

Sections: (1) South Park Rd. to Ralph Stover State Park, Class I-II
                 (2) Ralph Stover State Park to Point Pleasant, Class III-IV

Length of Run: (1) Day trip, 7 miles
                      (2) Day trip, 4 miles

Tohickon Creek at release level (about 1.8 feet).
Photo by Robert Hall.

Location: Bucks County, Pennsylvania

Maps: USGS quads: Lumberville, Bedminster

Times Runnable: After scheduled releases from Lake Nockamixon on the last weekend in March and the first weekend in November, or after heavy rain.

Permit: None required

Gauge: USGS Tohickon Creek near Pipersville (downstream of Lake Nockamixon).

Source of Levels: Ralph Stover State Park, 215-982-5560.

How Reported: Feet

Additional Gauge: Paddlers' gauge at Stover Park Bridge

Source of Levels: Ralph Stover State Park, 215-982-5560.

Interpretation of Levels: For the Pipersville gauge, low is about 2 feet; moderate is 3.0 (Class IV on Section (2); high is 3.5 (Class IV+), and extremely high, experts only, is 6 feet. For the Stover Park gauge, low is 0 to 1 foot; moderate is 1 to 2.5 feet; high is 2.5 to 3.5 feet, and flood is over 5 feet (experts only).

Source of More Information: Ralph Stover State Park, Box 209-L, Rural Route 1, Pipersville, PA 18947; 215-982-5560.

Bucks County Park, 901 E. Bridgeton Rd., Langhorn, PA 19047; 215-751-0571.

Wildwater Designs, 230 Penllyn Pike, Penllyn, PA 19422; 215-646-5034.

Best Guidebooks: Grove et al., *Appalachian Whitewater, Vol. II*; Gertler, *Keystone Canoeing*.

Further Comments: Two dams to portage on the upper section.

Gauge Conversion: USGS Tohickon Creek near Pipersville

Feet	Cfs	Feet	Cfs
2.0	153	4.6	1837
2.2	215	4.8	2045
2.4	291	5.0	2266
2.6	385	5.5	2858
2.8	492	6.0	3515
3.0	615	6.5	4263
3.2	740	7.0	5104
3.4	860	7.5	6034
3.6	985	8.0	7053
3.8	1130	8.5	8166
4.0	1289	9.0	9376
4.2	1460	9.5	10680
4.4	1643	10.0	12090

WILLS CREEK

Sections: Fairhope to Hyndman, Class III-IV (low), Class IV (medium), or Class IV-V (high)

Length of Run: Day trip, 5.5 miles

Location: Somerset and Bedford Counties, Pennsylvania

Maps: USGS quads: Fairhope, Hyndman

Times Runnable: Winter and spring during snowmelt or after heavy rains

Permit: None required

Gauge: There is a painted paddlers' gauge at Hyndman on river-right side of bridge.

Source of Levels: Visual inspection only

How Reported: Feet

Additional Gauge: Extrapolate from the Kitzmiller or Cumberland USGS gauges on the North Branch of the Potomac or from the Markleton gauge on the Casselman.

Source of Levels: National Weather Service, Washington; 703-260-0305.

National Weather Service, Harrisburg; 717-234-6812.

How Reported: Feet

Interpretation of Levels: In terms of the Hyndman gauge, minimum is around 2.2 feet, and very high is around 3.5

or 4.0 feet. In terms of the Cumberland gauge, 3.5 to 4.5 feet suggests a minimum level on Wills Creek and 6 to 6.5 feet suggests high water. Readings at Kitzmiller of at least 5 feet and at Markleton of at least 3 feet suggest at least minimum levels at Wills.

Source of More Information: Wildwater Designs, 230 Penllyn Pike, Penllyn, PA 19422; 215-646-5034.

Best Guidebooks: Grove et al., *Appalachian Whitewater, Vol. II*; Gertler, *Keystone Canoeing.*

YOUGHIOGHENY RIVER, LOWER
(See Maryland for upper sections of the Youghiogheny.)

Sections: Ohiopyle to Stewarton, Class III+

Length of Run: Day trip, 7 miles

Location: Fayette County, Pennsylvania

Maps: USGS quads: Ohiopyle, Mill Run, Ft. Necessity

Times Runnable: Year-round when not frozen

Permit: Permits are required for all boaters. Shuttle tokens are required for everyone ($1.25).

Reservations: Reservations are required. Persons paddling hard boats may obtain reservations either by phone or on a first-come-first-served basis at the launch site. Folks paddling inflatables must apply ahead of time. The park personnel will issue you a launch time and a check-in time. If you launch before 7:45 AM or after 3:15 PM, then you won't need reservations; just self-register at the put-in. Applications for reservations can be made by telephone or mail (no special form is required) at anytime in the year.

Any group of 15 or more persons regardless of their craft must confirm their launch reservation on the sponsoring organization's letterhead stationary at least two weeks prior to the intended launch date.

Contact: Ohiopyle State Park, Box 105, Ohiopyle, PA 15470; 412-329-8591.

Restrictions: A maximum of 60 inflatable private boats is allowed to launch per hour. A maximum of 200 hard boats is allowed per day (the latter is increasingly reached before noon on summer weekends). Other restrictions on class of craft apply to inflatable craft, depending on water levels.

Gauge: USGS at Ohiopyle

Source of Levels: National Weather Service, Pittsburgh; 412-644-2890.

How Reported: Feet

Interpretation of Levels: Low is about 1.0 to 1.5 feet; 2.0 to 3.0 feet is optimum. High is from 4 to 8 feet; above 8 feet is extremely high.

Source of More Information: Ohiopyle State Park, Box 105, Ohiopyle, PA 15470; 412-329-8591.

Wildwater Designs, 230 Penllyn Pike, Penllyn, PA 19422; 215-646-5034.

Best Guidebooks: Grove et al., *Appalachian Whitewater, Vol. II;* Gertler, *Keystone Canoeing;* Nealy, *Whitewater Home Companion, Vol. I.*

Further Comments: The Lower Youghiogheny, because of its proximity to major urban areas, its fine rapids, and reliable summertime flows, is one of the most crowded rivers in the Eastern U.S. Savvy boaters like you will want to relieve the pressure a little by going there only when you can't find an alternative. The New, the Cheat, the Potomac, the James, and the Genesee all usually have water in the summer, and are nowhere near as overutilized.

GENERAL INFORMATION SOURCES FOR PENNSYLVANIA

The National Weather Service in Williamsport reports gauge readings: 717-368-8744.

Susquehanna River, Market Street gauge in Williamsport, Pennsylvania

Pine Creek, at Cedar Run, Pennsylvania

The National Weather Service in Pittsburgh reports gauge readings for the Monongahela River Basin in Pennsylvania and parts of Maryland and West Virginia: 412-644-2890.

They get gauge readings for the following Pennsylvania rivers:

Laurel Creek, at Ursina
Casselman River, at Markleton
Youghiogheny River
   At Confluence
   At Ohiopyle
Black Lake Creek, at Josephine
Slippery Rock Creek, at Slippery Rock
Loyalhayna Creek, at Kinston

The National Weather Service Washington, DC, District Office is responsible for the Potomac and Rappahannock River Basins. They prepare a recording, updated daily at 10 a.m. and 8 p.m. The 10 a.m. edition is more inclusive, with data for the Monongahela and James River basins.

National Weather Service, Washington; 703-260-0305.

They report the following Pennsylvania readings:

Monongahela River and Tributaries
   Youghiogheny River, at Confluence
   Casselman River, at Markleton

The National Weather Service River Forecast Center in Harrisburg, PA, acts as the hydrologic service office for the Delaware and Susquehanna River basins. They also receive information on the Potomac and James River basins relayed from the Washington, DC and Richmond, VA forecast offices. National Weather Service River Forecast Center, Harrisburg; 717-234-6812.

Dialing this line accesses a ring-through recording. Here's what you'll hear on the recording:

Susquehanna River Basin
   Susquehanna River, at Harrisburg
   Susquehanna River, at Wilkes-Barre
   Susquehanna River, at Sunbury
   West Branch of the Susquehanna River, at Carson

West Branch of the Susquehanna River, at Renovo
Pine Creek, at Cedar Run
Judiana River, at Newport
Condoquinet Creek, at Hoyestown
Yellow Breeches Creek, near Camp Hill
Swatara Creek, at Hershey

Other Stages:
   Swatara Creek, at Harpers Tavern
   Codorus Creek, near York
   Little Judiana River, at Spruce Creek
   Loyalsock Creek, at Loyalsockville
   Penns Creek, near Penns Creek
   Tioga River, at Mansfield
   Schuylkill River, at Fern
   Bushgill River, at Shoemaker
   Lehigh River, at Whitehaven
   Flow from Walter Dam, at Whitehaven

If you don't hear what you need on the recording, stay on the line and ask for it. The following is a complete list of the gauges that the National Weather Service in Harrisburg receives readings for daily:

Delaware River Basin
   West Branch of the Lackawaxen River, at Prompton
   Dyberry Creek, at Dyberry Creek
   Lackawaxen River
      At Honesdale
      At Hawley
   Delaware River, at Portland
   Lehigh River, at Stoddartsville
   Tobyanna Creek, at Blakeslee
   Lehigh River
      At White Haven
      At Lehighton
   Pohopoco Creek
      At Kresgeville
      At Parryville
   Lehigh River
      At Walnutport
      At Bethlehem
   Delaware River
      At Lumberville
      At New Hope
      At Yardley
   Neshaminy Creek, at Rushland
   Little Neshaminy Creek, at Jacksonville
   Neshaminy Creek, at Langhorne
   Schuylkill River, at Landingville
   Little Schuylkill River, at Tamaqua
   Schuylkill River, at Berne
   Tulpehocken Creek
      At Bernville
      At Tulpehocken Creek below dam
      At Tulpehocken Creek near Reading

Schuylkill River
   At Reading
   At Pottstown
Perkiomen Creek, at Graterford
Schuylkill River, at Fairmont Dam, Philadelphia
Chester Creek, at Chester
West Branch of the Brandywine Creek
   At Coatesville
   At Modena
Marsh Creek, at Glenmoore
East Branch of the Brandywine Creek
   At Downington, above dam
   At Downington, below dam
Brandywine Creek, at Chadds Ford

Susquehanna River Basin
Tioga River, at Mansfield
Crooked Creek, at Middlebury Center
Tioga River
   At Tioga
   At Tioga Junction
Cowanesque River
   At Elkland
   At Lawrenceville
Susquehanna River, at Towanda
Towanda Creek, at Monroeton
Susquehanna River
   At Meshoppen
   At Mehoopany
Tunkhannock Creek, at Tunkhannock
Lackawanna River
   At Forest City
   At Archbald
   At Old Forge
Susquehanna River, at Wilkes-Barre
Fishing Creek, at Bloomsburg
Susquehanna River, at Danville
West Branch of the Susquehanna River
   At Bower
   At Curwensville
   At Hyde
   At Clearfield
Clearfield Creek, at Dimeling
West Branch of the Susquehanna River, at Karthaus
Driftwood Branch of the South Creek, at Sterling Run
Sinnemahoning Creek, at Sinnemahoning
First Fork of the Sinnemahoning Creek
   At Wharton
   At Sinnemahoning
Kettle Creek
   At Cross Fork
   At Westport
West Branch of the Susquehanna River
   At Renovo
   At Lock Haven

Bald Eagle Creek
   At Milesburg
   At Blanchard
   At Beech Creek Station
Pine Creek
   At Cedar Run
   At Waterville
West Branch of the Susquehanna River
   At Jersey Shore
   At Williamsport
Loyalsock Creek, at Loyalsockville
West Branch of the Susquehanna River
   At Muncy
   At Milton
   At Lewisburg
Susquehanna River, at Sunbury
Penns Creek, at Penns Creek
Frankstown Branch of the Juniata River,
   at Williamsburg
Little Juniata River, at Spruce Creek
Juniata River, at Huntingdon
Dunning Creek, at Belden
Kishcoquillas Creek, at Reedsville
Juniata River, at Newport
Sherman Creek, at Shermansdale
Conodoguinet Creek, at Hogestown
Susquehanna River, at Harrisburg
Yellow Breeches Creek, at Camp Hill
Swatara Creek
   At Harper Tavern
   At Hershey
Codorus Creek
   At Spring Grove
   At York
Susquehanna River, at Marietta
Conestoga River, at Lancaster

The Philadelphia Forecast Office of the National Weather Service can report river stages for the Delaware River Basin: 215-627-5575.

They can report readings for the following Pennsylvania gauges:

Lackawaxen River, at Hawley
Lehigh River
   At Lehighton
   At Walnutport
   At Bethlehem
Neshaminy Creek, at Langhorne
Schuylkill River
   At Landingville
   At Berne
   At Tulpehocken

At Reading
At Pottstown
At Philadelphia
Perkiomen Creek, at Graterford
Chester Creek, at Chester
Brandywine Creek
    At Modena
    At Coatsville
Lehigh River
    At Kresgeville

At Stoddartsville
    At Blakeslee
Brandywine Creek
    At Downingtown
    At Chadds Ford
Delaware River
    At Easton-Phillipsburg
    At New Hope-Lambertville

PENNSYLVANIA

CONASAUGA RIVER

See Georgia.

CUMBERLAND RIVER, BIG SOUTH FORK
National Recreational River

Sections: (1) Gorge, Burnt Mill Bridge on Clear Creek to confluence with the Big South Fork and continuing to Leatherwood Ford, Class III-IV (IV to IV+ high)

(2) Leatherwood Ford to Lake Cumberland, Class II-III (two at III-IV)

Length of Run: (1) Day trip, 10.6 miles

(2) 2-3 days, 42 miles

Location: Scott County, Tennessee and McCreary County, Kentucky; Big South Fork National Area

Maps: USGS quads: Oneida South (TN), Honey Creek (TN), Oneida North (TN), Barthell (KY), Nevelsville (KY), Burnside (KY). Also: National Park Service Big South Fork National River and Recreation Area Map and TVA Big South Fork National River and Recreation Area Map.

Times Runnable: November to mid-May or during hurricane season

Permit: None required

Gauge: US Army Corps of Engineers gauge at Sterns

Source of Levels: US Army Corps of Engineers, Nashville District, Cumberland Basin Stream and Reservoir Recording; 615-736-5455.

How Reported: Cfs

Additional gauge: Staff gauge at the Leatherwood take-out

Source of Levels: National Park Service; 615-879-4890.

Double Falls, Big South Fork Gorge. Photo by Bill Millard.

How reported: Cfs

Interpretation of Levels: Low is about 1000 cfs; medium is 2000 cfs, and high is 3000 cfs or better. I've been on the Big South Fork at about 10,000 and about 14,000 cfs. At these levels the river becomes very big and Western, but visibility stays good and the major holes are easy to avoid. I'd rate the Gorge at these levels at about Class IV+ or maybe IV-V.

Source of More Information: National Park Service, Big South Fork National Recreational Area, PO Drawer 630, Oneida, TN 37841; 615-879-4890.

US Army Corps of Engineers, Nashville District, PO Box 1070, Nashville, TN 37202; 615-736-5455.

Sheltowee Trace Outfitters, 117 Hawkins Dr., Somerset, KY 42501; 606-679-5026.

Best Guidebooks: Nealy, *Whitewater Home Companion Vol. II;* Sehlinger et al., *Appalachian Whitewater Vol. I;* Sehlinger and Lantz, *Canoeing and Kayaking Guide to the Streams of Tennessee, Vol. II;* US Army Corps of Engineers and National Park Service, "River Guide to the Big South Fork and its Tributaries."

DOE RIVER

Sections:	(1) Roan Mountain to Blevins, Class II-III
	(2) Gorge, Blevins to Hwy. 19E Bridge at Hampton, Class IV to VI
Length of Run:	(1) Day trip, 7 miles
	(2) Day trip, 7 miles

Location: Carter County, Tennessee; Cherokee National Forest

Maps: USGS quads: White Rocks Mtn., Iron Mtn. Gap, Elizabethton

Times Runnable: January to April and after heavy rain

Permit: None required

Gauge: TVA gauge at Elizabethton

Source of Levels: Tennessee Valley Authority, 615-632-6065.

How Reported: Cfs

Additional Gauge: Paddlers' gauge on the Highway 19E Bridge

Source of Levels: Visual inspection only.

How Reported: Feet

Interpretation of Levels: The paddlers' gauge at Highway 19E is the most accurate measure. Use it when you get there. Around -1 inch is minimum, and +1 inch to +4 inches is optimum. Around +1 foot is very high!

The Elizabethton gauge can be used for a rough estimate. Minimum is about 200 cfs, with 600 cfs considered high. If the TVA doesn't have a recent Doe reading, check the Watauga and Nolichucky. If the Watauga is above 220 or the Nolichucky above 2300, then there should be water on the Doe.

Source of More Information: USDA Forest Service, Watauga Ranger District, Rt. 9, Box 352-B, Highway 91, Elizabethton, TN 37643; 615-542-2942.

Best Guidebooks: Sehlinger et al., *Appalachian Whitewater, Vol. I;* Sehlinger and Lantz, *Canoeing and Kayaking Guide to the Streams of Tennessee, Vol. I.*

Further Comments: The Doe Gorge is for aggro experts only. At least one unrunnable Class VI+ drop will have to be carried, and possibly others.

HIWASSEE RIVER

| Sections: | Powerhouse to Reliance, Class I-II |
| Length of Run: | Day trip, 5 5 miles |

Location: Polk County, Tennessee; Cherokee National Forest

Maps: USGS quads: McFarland, Oswald Dome

Times Runnable: Water is released by the TVA Lake Chatuge Plant on the Hiwassee most days.

Permit: None required

Gauge: Release from TVA Lake Chatuge Dam

Source of Levels: Tennessee Valley Authority Automated Dam Information Line; 615-632-2264.

How Reported: Release schedules and numbers of units operating

Interpretation of Levels: The TVA after 4 p.m. can provide a release schedule for the day following. For example, when I called on the day I wrote this, I was told that the plant would be off until noon, that one unit would operate for one hour, then two units for seven hours, and then one for two. Releases from one or two units provide adequate water.

Source of More Information: Tennessee Department of Conservation, Hiwassee/Ocoee Rivers, Box 255, Delano, TN 37325; 615-338-4133, 615-263-3182

Hiwassee Outfitters, Reliance, TN 37369; 615-338-8115.

Ocoee Outdoors, PO Box 72, Ocoee, TN 37361; 615-338-2438.

USDA Forest Service, Hiwassee Ranger District, Cherokee National Forest, South Tennessee Ave., Etowah, TN 37331; 615-263-5486.

The Hiwassee Market maintains a bulletin board message service to help you keep in touch with friends and family while you're at the river, 615-338-8467.

Best Guidebooks: Nealy, *Whitewater Home Companion, Vol. I;* Sehlinger et al., *Appalachian Whitewater, Vol. I;* Sehlinger and Lantz, *Canoeing and Kayaking Guide to the Streams of Tennessee, Vol. II.*

Further Comments: The Hiwassee is an easy but scenic stream, conveniently located within a half hour of the Ocoee. It's popular for family float-rafting and for open canoeing. It makes a fun and easy-to-get-to run for beginning and novice boaters who are camping with folks at the Ocoee.

LITTLE RIVER

Sections: The Sinks, Elkmont to Townsend, Class III-IV (one at IV-V)

Length of Run: 1-2 days, 21 miles (shorter sections are possible)

Location: Sevier, Blount Counties, Tennessee; Great Smoky Mountains National Park

Maps: USGS quads: Gatlinburg, Wear Cove

Times Runnable: After heavy rain

Permit: None required

Gauge: TVA gauge at Maryville

Source of Levels: Tennessee Valley Authority, 615-632-6065.

How Reported: Cfs

Interpretation of Levels: Minimum is about 400 cfs, with 1000 cfs often considered ideal, and 2000 cfs high.

Source of More Information: National Park Service, Great Smoky Mountains National Park, Gatlinburg, TN 37738; 615-436-5615.

Best Guidebooks: Sehlinger and Lantz, *Canoeing and Kayaking Guide to the Streams of Tennessee, Vol. II.*

NOLICHUCKY RIVER

See North Carolina.

OBED-EMORY RIVER SYSTEM
Wild and Scenic River

Sections:
(1) White Creek, Twin Bridge to Barnett Bridge, Class II-III
(2) Clear Creek, US 127 to confluence with the Obed River and continuing to Nemo at the confluence of the Obed and Emory, Class II-III (III-IV on Clear Creek below Lily)
(3) Daddy's Creek, Big Lick to Antioch Bridge, Class I-II
(4) Daddy's Creek, Canyon, Antioch Bridge to Devil's Breakfast Table, Class III-V
(5) Obed River, US 127 Bridge to Adams Bridge, Class II (three at IV)
(6) Obed River, Adams Bridge to the Emory River, Class II-III (one at IV)
(7) Emory River, Gobey Bridge to Oakdale, Class II-III (one at IV)
(8) Crab Orchard Creek, defunct ford to confluence with the Emory and continuing to Oakdale, Class III+
(9) Crooked Fork Creek, US 27 Bridge to Emory River and continuing to Camp

Austin, Class V (plus one portage at
lower Potters Falls)

**Length
of Run:**
(1) Day trip, 7 miles
(2) 2-3 days, 35.7 miles, shorter sections possible
(3) 2-3 days, 30.5 miles, shorter sections possible
(4) Day trip, 7 miles
(5) Day trip, 9.6 miles
(6) Day trip, 26 miles, shorter sections possible
(7) Day trip, 21.2 miles, shorter sections possible
(8) Day trip, 13.5 miles
(9) Day trip, 8 miles

(Some of these sections are outside the designated Wild and Scenic area.)

Location: Fentress, Morgan and Cumberland Counties, Tennessee; Catoosa Wildlife Management Area

Maps: USGS quads: (1) Twin Bridges, Herbertsville; (2) Herbertsville, Lancing, Clark Range, Jones Knob, Pilot Mtn.; (3) Dorton, Herbertsville, Ozone, Grassy Cove, Vandever; (4) Herbertsville; (5) Fox Creek, Isoline, Crossville; (6) Herbertsburg, Lancing; (7) Gobey, Camp Austin, Lancing, Harriman; (8) Cardiff, Lancing and Camp Austin; (9) Camp Austin. Also: TVA Emory River Watershed Map.

Times Runnable: December to April

Permit: None required

Gauge: TVA gauge on the Emory River at Oakdale

Source of Levels: Tennessee Valley Authority, 615-632-6065.

National Park Service, 615-346-6295.

How Reported: Cfs

Interpretation of Levels: Levels on all tributaries to the Obed-Emory system can be inferred from the Oakdale gauge on the Emory. Basically, the more water is on the Emory, the higher it is possible to move in the watershed. Guidebooks, especially M. D. Smith's *The Obed/Emory Watershed*, explain appropriate levels for the various tributaries in detail. 1500 cfs is enough water for the Obed anywhere below Adams Bridge and for the Emory from Nemo to Oakdale. Above 3000 there are plenty of opportunities higher in the watershed. A reading of 10,000 on the Oakdale gauge is often considered maximum for the lower Obed.

Source of More Information: National Park Ranger, Obed Wild and Scenic River, PO Box 429, Wartburg, TN 37887; 615-346-6295.

Obed Wild and Scenic River, PO Drawer 630, Oneida, TN 37841; 615-569-6389.

Catoosa Wildlife Management Agency, Tennessee Wildlife Resources Area, Region 3, 216 E. Penfield, Crossville, TN 38555; 615-484-9571.

Tennessee Wildlife Resources Agency, PO Box 40747, Nashville, TN 37204; 615-484-9571.

Best Guidebooks: Smith, *A Paddler's Guide to the Obed/Emory Watershed;* Waller, *A Canoeist's Guide to the Obed-Emory System;* TVA, "Obed-Emory Canoe Trails" map/guide; Sehlinger and Lantz, *Canoeing and Kayaking Guide to the Streams of Tennessee, Vol. II.*

Further Comments: The Obed-Emory system of rivers was one of the early members of America's Wild and Scenic Rivers system. Located on the Cumberland Plateau of Tennessee, the Emory River and its tributaries offer an incredible variety of whitewater in canyons cut through sandstone and limestone. As a rule, the most challenging sections, such as Daddy's Creek, are higher in the watershed. Within the river gorges, the lush Southern Appalachian foliage and giant sandstone boulders make for incredible scenery.

Away from the rivers, the view isn't so nice; clearcutting has devastated the area. Be forewarned too that crime and vandalism are such serious problems in the area that most folks hire someone to watch their autos during their runs.

At present, conflicting principles of management by government agencies interfere with recreation on the Obed-Emory system. The Catoosa Wildlife Management Area (CWMA) controls land and roads surrounding the National Wild and Scenic Rivers. During winter, the CWMA locks gates to many access roads. During spring turkey season, only turkey hunters are allowed to enter the CWMA by road. Dead turkeys are allowed to leave. Write to the governor of Tennessee or to your state legislator.

Daddy's Creek is for advanced and expert paddlers only; the Crooked Fork is only for hot experts who can really shred.

OCOEE RIVER

Sections: Tennessee State Parks ramp below Ocoee Dam No. 2 to Tennessee State Parks take-out below Ocoee Powerhouse No. 2, Class III-IV

**Length
of Run:**   Day trip, 5 miles

Location: Polk County, Tennessee; Cherokee National
Forest

Maps: USGS quads: Ducktown, Caney Creek

Times Runnable: Water is released on the Ocoee for 116
days a year (on weekends in spring and fall and during
much of the week in summer). The TVA will send you a
release schedule if you call and ask them.

Permit: None required

Gauge: Release from Ocoee Plant No. 3 (which passes to
Dam No. 2)

Source of Levels: Tennessee Valley Authority, 615-632-
2264.

How Reported: Cfs

Interpretation of Levels: The standard release is around
1200-1300 cfs. Larger or smaller releases are rare.

Source of More Information: Tennessee Department of
Conservation, Hiwassee/Ocoee Rivers, Box 255, Delano,
TN 37325; 615-338-4133, 615-263-3182.

Ocoee Outdoors, PO Box 172, Ocoee, TN 37361; 615-
338-2438.

Outdoor Sports Center, PO Box 19, Hwy. 64E, Ocoee,
TN 37361; 615-338-2147. Or: 8147 Savannah Hills Dr.,
Ooltewah, TN 37363; 615-238-4867.

USDA Forest Service, Ocoee Ranger District, Cherokee
National Forest, Route 1, Parksville, Highway 64,
Benton, TN 37307; 615-338-5201.

Best Guidebooks: Nealy, *Whitewater Home Companion,
Vol. I;* Sehlinger et al., *Appalachian Whitewater, Vol. I;*
Sehlinger and Lantz, *Canoeing and Kayaking Guide to
the Streams of Tennessee, Vol. II.*

Further Comments: The Ocoee! What an incredible
resource! The Ocoee may very well be the greatest play
river in the United States. Moreover, it has 116 days
during the spring, summer, and fall when you can count
on plenty of warm water! It's no wonder that there are so
many excellent boaters in the Southeast today.

The strange winter and spring of 1989-1990 brought
floods exceeding 40,000 cfs to the Ocoee, washing out
much of Highway 64 along the river's banks, destroying
the parking lot and put-in ramp at TVA's Ocoee Dam #2,
and seriously damaging Powerhouse #2 near the take-
out.

There were also many changes to the river. Many rocks

Richard Penny floating down the Tellico River. Photo by
Michael Sawyer.

that served as support at the bottom of Dam #2 were
washed into Grumpy Rapid (but I understand that the
TVA plans to remove them again). Sadly, the wonderful
surfing holes and waves at Double Trouble are no more
for this world; we wish them well wherever they have
gone. Happily, the flood restored Hell Hole to all its
former glory, and it now, once more, reigns supreme as
the primo Southeastern spot for hole-riding.

PIGEON RIVER

See North Carolina.

TELLICO RIVER

Sections: (1) The Ledges, Trout Hatchery to Bald
River Falls, Class III-IV (to Class IV+
high)
(2) Bald River Falls to Ranger Station,
Class III+

**Length
of Run:**   (1) Day trip, 10 miles
(2) Day trip, 5.4 miles

Location: Monroe County, Tennessee; Cherokee
National Forest

Maps: USGS quads: Bald River Falls

Times Runnable: January to April

Permit: None required

Upper Tellico River. Photo by Don Otey.

Gauge Conversions: Conversions to Cfs

Feet	Cfs	Feet	Cfs
1.2	102	3.2	858
1.3	123	3.5	998
1.5	173	3.7	1096
1.7	234	4.0	1250
1.8	268	4.5	1515
2.0	330	5.0	1800
2.3	442	5.5	2092
2.5	526	6.0	2400
2.7	618	8.0	4100
3.0	770	10.0	7308

WATAUGA RIVER

See North Carolina.

Gauge: Retired TVA Gauge at Tellico Plains

Source of Levels: Arrowhead Land Company; 615-253-7670.

How Reported: Feet

Interpretation of Levels: Low is about 250 cfs, high is about 500 to 1000 cfs, and very high is 1000 or above.

Source of More Information: USDA Forest Service, Tellico Ranger District, Cherokee National Forest, Route 3, Tellico Plains, TN 37385; 615-253-2520.

Best Guidebooks: Sehlinger et al., *Appalachian Whitewater, Vol. I;* Sehlinger and Lantz, *Canoeing and Kayaking Guide to the Streams of Tennessee, Vol. II.*

GENERAL INFORMATION SOURCES FOR TENNESSEE

The pleasant and helpful folks at the Tennessee Valley Authority can report levels for rivers throughout the Tennessee River watershed, including central and eastern Tennessee, Northern Alabama and the western slope of the North Carolina mountains. Gauge readings are taken at 7 a.m. daily; all levels are reported in cfs. The TVA is also a source of a variety of other hydrologic data. The TVA number is answered by human beings from 8:30 to 4:45, Monday through Friday.

Tennessee Valley Authority, 615-632-6065.

They can report the following readings for the following river gauges:

Little River, at Maryville TN
Sequatchie River, at Whitwell TN
French Broad River, at Newport TN
Doe River, at Elizabethton TN
Watauga River, at Sugar Grove NC
Nolichucky River, at Embreeville TN
Little Pigeon River, at Sevierville TN
Clinch River, at Cleveland TN
Clinch River, at Tazewell TN
Little Tennessee River, at Needmore TN
Oconaluftee River, at Birdtown NC
Emory River, at Oakdale TN
Toccoa River, at Dial TN
Collins River, at McMinnville TN
Buffalo River, at Lobelville TN
Harpeth River, at Kingston Springs TN

Rockcastle River, at Billows KY
Cumberland River, at Williamsburg KY
Powell River, at Arthur TN
Powell River, at Jonesville KY
Tuckaseegee River, at Bryson City NC

To get reports of dam releases from TVA reservoirs call the TVA automated information line at 615-632-2264. Using your touch-tone phone, you can get release schedules for reservoirs in the following river drainages:

1   Clinch River
2   Tennessee River
3   Holston and Watauga Rivers
4   Hiwassee River
5   Ocoee River
6   Little Tennessee River
7   French Broad River
8   Elk River
9   Cumberland River

The Nashville District Office of the U.S. Army Corps of Engineers maintains a recording that reports reservoir levels, releases and streamflows in the Cumberland River Basin. You can reach the recording at 615-736-5455. They include the following readings in near the end of the report:

Cumberland River, at Williamsburg KY
Rockcastle River, at Billows KY
South Fork of the Cumberland River, at Stearns KY

TEXAS

BRAZOS RIVER, MAIN

Sections: (1) Highway 16 to Highway 4, Class I
                  (2) Highway 4 to Highway 180, Class I

Length   (1) Day trip, 19.5 miles
of Run: (2) Day trip, 19 miles

Location: Palo Pinto County, Texas

Maps: USGS quad: Palo Pinto

Times Runnable: Winter and spring after releases

Permit: None required

Gauge: Release from Possum Kingdom Dam

Source of Levels: US Army Corps of Engineers, Possum Kingdom Dam; 817-779-2422.

National Weather Service, San Antonio; 512-826-4679.

Major city newspapers report river levels weekly.

How Reported: Cfs

Interpretation of Levels: Good levels are in the range from 600 to 2000 cfs. High is 3000, and over 5000 cfs is experts-only water.

Source of More Information: Mountain Sports, 2025 W. Pioneer Parkway, Arlington, TX 76013; 817-461-4503.

Rochelle's Canoe Rentals, Rt. I, Box 119, Grafford, TX 76045; 817-659-3341, 817-659-2581, 817-659-2425.

Texas Parks and Wildlife Department, 4200 Smith School Rd., Austin, TX 78744; 800-792-1112.

Best Guidebooks: Kirkley, *A Guide to Texas Rivers.*

BRAZOS RIVER, HIDAGALO FALLS

Sections: Hidagalo Falls, Class II-III

Length of Run: Play spot, 1.0 miles

Location: Grimes and Washington Counties, Texas

Maps: USGS quads: Washington, Millican

Times Runnable: Winter, spring and early summer

Permit: None required

Gauge: Gauge at Brazos River Resort

Source of Levels: Major newspapers report levels weekly.

How Reported: Feet

Interpretation of Levels: About 8 feet is minimum; 10 is medium and 14 high.

Source of More Information: Mountain Sports, 2025 W. Pioneer Parkway, Arlington, TX 76013; 817-461-4503.

Texas Parks and Wildlife Department, 4200 Smith School Rd., Austin, TX 78744; 800-792-1112.

Best Guidebooks: Kirkley, *A Guide to Texas Rivers.*

GUADALUPE RIVER

Sections:
(1) Comfort to Sultenfus Crossing, Class I-II
(2) Sultenfus Crossing to Rebecca Creek Crossing, Class I-II
(3) Canyon Dam to 14-mile Crossing, Class I-II (II-III high)
(4) 14-mile crossing to Cypress Bend Park, Class I-II

Length of Run:
(1) 2-3 days, 44.5 miles
(2) 1-2 days, 23 miles
(3) Very long day trip, 14 miles
(4) Day trip, 8 miles

Location: Kendall and Comal Counties, Texas

Maps: USGS quads: Comfort, Waring, Kendalia, Sisterdale, Anhalt, Spring Branch, Fischer, Sattler, New Braunfels East

Times Runnable: Winter and spring

Permit: None required

Gauge: For Sections (1) and (2), use the paddlers' gauge located at the bridge at the put-in.

Source of Levels: Guadalupe Canoe Livery, PO Box 8, Straight Branch, TX 78070; 512-885-4671.

Texas Canoe Trails, PO Box 310654, New Braunfels, TX 78130; 512-625-3375.

Major newspapers publish levels weekly.

How Reported: Feet

Additional Gauge: For Sections (1) and (2) you can also use the USGS gauge at Spring Branch.

Source of Levels: National Weather Service, San Antonio; 512-826-4679. Major newspapers publish levels weekly.

How Reported: Cfs

Additional Gauge: Sections (3) and (4) depend on releases from Canyon Dam.

Source of Levels: US Army Corps of Engineers, Canyon Dam; 512-964-3760.

National Weather Service, San Antonio; 512-826-4679.

How Reported: Cfs

Interpretation of Levels: For Sections (1) and (2), about 4 feet on the paddlers' gauge is low, and 7 is high. In terms of cfs for all sections, 400 cfs is low; 600-900 is medium; and above 1000 is high (experts only).

Source of More Information: Mountain Sports, 2025 W. Pioneer Parkway, Arlington, TX 76013; 817-461-4503.

Best Guidebooks: Kirkley, *A Guide to Texas Rivers.*

Further Comments: Watch out for dams and low-water bridges. Don't try to run this river in flood if you're not an expert boater; there have been many drownings of novices attempting high-water canoe runs. Never attempt crossings of flooded bridges in fully-packed school buses. Some Texas canoeists rate Sections (2) and (3) as Class IV at high water.

RIO GRANDE RIVER
Wild and Scenic River
(See New Mexico for upper sections of the Rio Grande.)

Sections: Big Bend, Class II-IV

Length of Run: 5-7 days, 94 miles

Location: Presidio, Brewster and Terrell Counties, Texas; Big Bend National Park

Maps: USGS quads: Lajitas, Mesa de Anguila, Castolon, Smoky Creek, Reed Camp, Mariscal Mountain, Solis, Boquillas, Ernst Valley, Stillwell Crossing

Times Runnable: November to March

Permit: Required. Obtain on site from: Big Bend National Park, Rio Grande Wild and Scenic River, Big Bend National Park, Texas; 915-477-2393, 915-477-2251.

Reservations: Not required

Restrictions: Rangers will inspect your equipment to make sure that you meet their requirements before launch. Canoes, kayaks, and heavy-duty rafts are all considered acceptable boats. You must have one PFD per person plus one extra PFD for the group. Bring one extra paddle or oar per boat, except for kayaks, which need only one extra paddle per party. You'll also need a patch kit for inflatables, a first aid kit, plastic trash bags, a safety rope, a bail bucket, water-tight containers for food and clothing, a porta-johnny, a flashlight and a small shovel.

Gauge: At Rio Grande Village

Source of Levels: Big Bend National Park, 915-477-2251.

How Reported: Feet

Additional Gauges: USGS gauges at Presidio (above the National Park) and at Boquillas (near the lower end of the park)

Source of Levels: National Weather Service, San Antonio; 512-826-4679.

How Reported: Cfs

Interpretation of Levels: In terms of the Rio Grande Village gauges, very low is considered 2.0. Low is from 2.5 to 4.0. Optimum is from 4.0 to 7.0. Above 7.0 is high. In terms of the USGS gauges at Presidio and at Boquillas, 300 cfs is minimum; 500 is low; 1000 is optimum, and 1200 to 1500 is high.

Source of More Information: Big Bend National Park, Rio Grande Wild and Scenic River, Big Bend National Park, Texas; 915-477-2393, 915-477-2251.

Big Bend Natural History Association, PO Box 68, Big Bend National Park, TX 79834; 915-477-2236.

Best Guidebooks: Humphrey, *Running the Rio Grande;* Big Bend Natural History Assoc., "Map-guides 1-4" (from Big Bend NHA, address above).

Further Comments: Forget what the Rio Grande looks like on TV Westerns. Through Big Bend National Park, the Rio Grande is a big, powerful, and muddy river that cuts a 1200 foot deep canyon through mesa country. The warm South Texas weather makes the Rio Grande a fine winter trip!

SAN MARCOS RIVER

Sections: San Marcos to Staples Dam, Class I-II

Length of Run: Day trip, 16.5 miles

Location: Hays, Guadalupe and Caldwell Counties, Texas

Maps: USGS quads: San Marcos North, San Marcos South, Martindale

Times Runnable: Year-round. Flow is from a constant flow spring.

Permit: None required

Gauge: USGS at San Marcos (below Blanco)

Source of Levels: National Weather Service, San Antonio; 512-826-4679. Major newspapers publish levels weekly.

How Reported: Cfs

Additional Gauge: None. Impression only.

Source of Levels: Goynes Canoe Livery, 512-357-6113.

How Reported: Goynes Canoe Livery can tell you if the flow is normal, low, or high. In terms of the San Marcos gauge, about 500 cfs is optimum. In terms of the USGS gauge at San Marcos (below Blanco), about 100 cfs is minimum; 150 is low; 300 optimum, and 700 to 1200 is high.

Source of More Information: Goynes Canoe Livery, Rt. 1, Box 55R, Martindale, TX 78655; 512-357-6113.

Mountain Sports, 2025 W. Pioneer Parkway, Arlington, TX 76013; 817-461-4503.

Texas Parks and Wildlife Department, 4200 Smith School Rd., Austin, TX 78744; 800-792-1112.

Best Guidebooks: Kirkley, *A Guide to Texas Rivers.*

GENERAL INFORMATION SOURCES FOR TEXAS

The National Weather Service Forecast Office in San Antonio can report river levels and three-day forecasts for south and southwest Texas: 512-826-4679.

They can report the following gauges on rivers that are commonly used for recreation (plus many others not listed here):

Brazos River
   Release from Possum Kingdom Dam
   At Dennis
   Release from Granbury Dam
   Release from Whitney Dam
Clear Fork of the Trinity River, release from
   Benbrook Dam
Denton Creek, release from Grapevine Dam
Elm Fork of the Trinity River, release from
   Lewisville Dam
Angelina River, release from Sam Rayburn Dam
Neches River, Town Bluff Dam
Village Creek, at Kountze

Sabine River, release from Toledo Bend Dam
Colorado River
   At San Saba
   At Austin
Frio River, at Garner State Park
Guadalupe River
   At Spring Branch
   Release from Canyon Dam
   At Cuero
Lampassas River, release from Stillhouse Hollow Dam
Llano River, at Llano
Perdernales River, at Johnson City
San Antonio River, at Falls City
San Marcos River, at San Marcos (below Blanco)
Trinity River, release from Livingston Dam
Rio Grande River
   At Presidio
   At Boquillas
Pecos River, at Pandale

The National Weather Service River Forecast Center in Fort Worth can provide the same information: 817-334-3833.

The Texas River Recreation Association, in conjunction with the Texas Parks and Wildlife Department, has developed the following guide to interpreting levels on Texas rivers. In this scheme, 1 indicates rock-bottom minimum; 2 is low; 3 is optimum; 4 is high, approaching dangerous; and 5 is for experts only. The River Forecast Center in Fort Worth uses these interpretations for developing the river recreation forecasts that they provide to the news media and the Weather Service offices.

	Levels				
	1	2	3	4	5
Neches River, at Alto	500	1000	1500	2000	5000
Sabine River, at Tatum	500	1000	1500	2000	5000
Brazos River, release from Possum Kingdom Dam	200	500	1200	3000	5000
Brazos River, at Highbank	200	500	1200	3000	5000
Brazos River, release from Granbury Dam	200	500	1200	3000	5000
Brazos River, release from Whitney Dam	200	500	1200	3000	5000
Clear Fork of the Trinity River, rel. fr. Benbrook Dam	70	140	280	500	1200
Denton Creek, release from Grapevine Dam	60	125	250	350	500
Elm Fork of the Trinity River, rel. fr. Lewisville Dam	100	400	700	1000	2000
Angelina River, release from Sam Rayburn Dam	500	1000	2000	5000	10000
Neches River, Town Bluff Dam	500	1000	2000	5000	10000
Village Creek, at Koontz	200	400	700	1500	2000
Sabine River, release from Toledo Bend Dam	500	1000	2000	5000	10000
Colorado River, at San Saba	100	250	750	2000	5000
Colorado River, at Austin	200	500	1000	3000	5000
Frio River, at Garner State Park	125	250	400	700	1000
Guadalupe River, at Spring Branch	125	250	450	750	1200
Guadalupe River, release from Canyon Dam	150	250	450	750	1200
Guadalupe River, at Cuero	200	800	1000	2000	3000
Lampassas River, rel. fr. Stillhouse Hollow Dam	100	200	300	700	1000
Llano River, at Mason	250	500	1000	2000	3000
Pedernales River, at Johnson City	125	250	400	700	1000
San Antonio River, at Falls City	250	450	600	1000	3000
San Marcos River, at San Marcos (below Blanco)	100	150	300	700	1200
San Marcos, at Luling	100	150	300	1000	1500
Trinity River, release from Livingston Dam	500	1000	2000	5000	10000
Rio Grande River, at Presidio	300	500	1000	1200	1500
Rio Grande River, at Boquillas	300	500	1000	1200	1500
Pecos River, at Pandale	125	300	500	900	1500

UTAH

COLORADO RIVER, WESTWATER CANYON

(See Colorado, Arizona, and the following entry for additional sections of the Colorado River.)

Sections: Westwater Canyon, Westwater Ranger Station to Cisco, Class III-IV (IV above 9000 cfs)

Length of Run: 1-2 days, 17 miles

Location: Grand County, Utah

Maps: USGS quads: Westwater 4SE, Westwater 4SW, Coates Creek

Times Runnable: Almost year-round

Permit: Permits are required year-round, but fees and reservations are required only from May 1 through September 30 (see below). Obtain a permit application by phone from the: Bureau of Land Management, Grand Resource Area, PO Box M, Moab, Utah 84532; 801-259-8193. A copy of the application form is included in Appendix One, but don't use it. All BLM offices like you to use fresh, new originals!

Reservations: Reservations are required from May 1 to September 30. To participate in the drawing for reservations, submit your application during January or February. The drawing is held on March 1. After March 21 you may call and draw a leftover launch date or request to be placed on the waiting list for specific dates. If you are assigned a launch date, you will have pay a fee of $2.25 per person. Your check for the fee must reach the BLM at least 2 weeks prior to the launch date; otherwise you forfeit your launch.

Bring your permit along to the ranger station at Westwater on your launch day. If it turns out you must cancel your trip, let the BLM know as soon as possible.

Restrictions: Every boater must be at least 18 years of age.

No more than 25 persons may be in your group. Rafts must be of decent quality, and each boat must have a competent, experienced boatman. Each raft or dory must have a spare oar, paddle, or motor as is appropriate. Each raft or dory must have a bail bucket, one spare PFD, and a throw bag.

Your group must bring a first aid kit, an air pump, repair kit, and a firepan. Overnight trips (other than kayak trips) must bring portable toilets. Have everyone urinate in the river, rather than on the land.

A river ranger will make a final inspection of your gear on your launch day.

Gauge: Colorado River at Westwater, near Westwater Ranch

Source of Levels: Bureau of Reclamation, Salt Lake City; 801-539-1311.

Bureau of Land Management, 801-259-8193.

How Reported: Cfs

Interpretation of Levels: Minimum is about 1000 cfs. Optimum is around 3000-10,000. High is over 10,000. Flows in May and June can reach 35,000.

Source of More Information: BLM, address and phone above. Also:

Bill Dvorak Kayak and Rafting Expeditions, 17921 US Highway 285, Nathrop, CO 81236; 717-539-6851.

Colorado Outward Bound School, 945 Pennsylvania St., Denver, CO 80203; 303-837-0880.

Best Guidebooks: Belknap and Belknap, *Canyonlands River Guide;* Bureau of Land Management, "Guide to Westwater: a Section of the Colorado River"

COLORADO RIVER, CATARACT CANYON

(See Colorado, Arizona, and the preceding entry for additional sections of the Colorado River.)

Sections: Cataract Canyon, Moab to Lake Powell, Class I-IV

Length of Run: 5-8 days, 112 miles

Location: Grand, Wayne, San Juan and Garfield Counties, Utah; Canyonlands National Park

Maps: USGS quads: Moab, Gold Bar Canyon, Shafer Basin, Musselman Arch, Lockart Basin, Monument Basin, The Loop, Spanish Bottom, Cross Canyon, Teapot Rock, Clearwater Canyon, Bowdie Canyon East, Bowdie Canyon West, Sewing Machine, Copper Point

Times Runnable: Year-round. Highest flows are in May and June

Permit: Required, and so are reservations. Apply to: Unit Coordinator, National Park Service, Canyonlands National Park, Moab, UT 84532; 801-259-7164.

Reservations: Required. Submit a permit form as your application. A copy is in Appendix One, but don't use it. Get a nice fresh one from the Park Service. Complete and sign the form and submit it after January 1. Applications are considered on a first-come, first-served basis, and permits are issued after March 1. The trip leader must submit a confirmation of the trip and the passengers by mail or phone at least 2 weeks prior to the departure date.

Applications that are received too late to receive a slot are placed on a waiting list. Sometime in early June a pool is used to assign empty slots to folks on the waiting list. During the off season, from October 15 through April 14 there are no use limits or allocations. You will still need to apply for a permit and reservations, but it should be possible to do so at any time.

Restrictions: Although still numerous, the restrictions that the Park Service applies at Cataract Canyon have been greatly improved and simplified since the first edition of the *Sourcebook* was published. I was especially pleased to discover that the prohibition of C-1s and open canoes has been lifted! My thanks to the river management team for their responsiveness!

Here's how the restrictions stand now: The gear for all trips will be inspected before launch. Approved watercraft are defined as rafts at least 13.5 by 6.5 feet in size, with at least three chambers. Dories may count, but they will have to be inspected. Other boats, including kayaks, whitewater canoes, funyaks, and small rafts are allowed only if accompanied by an approved craft (i.e. a big raft). Light-duty boats, either hard or inflatable, will not be permitted.

Boatmen must have previous experience on major Western whitewater rivers. The trip leader must be an especially experienced boatman. It is strongly recommended that at least one boatman have experience on Cataract Canyon. Additional restrictions on type of craft and on boatman qualifications may apply during periods of peak flow.

Upriver travel in Cataract Canyon by any watercraft is not permitted. Every boater must have a type I or V PFD. Kayakers and canoeists may wear type III PFDs, but during runs prior to July 15 they must also have a spare type I or V jacket aboard an approved watercraft (a big raft, remember?). Swimmers must wear PFDs. Every raft should have a spare PFD.

Every craft must have a spare oar, paddle or motor, except kayaks and canoes, which require only one spare paddle per group. If you have a motor, bring a fix-it-kit and a fire extinguisher. Patch kits, pumps, a signaling device, and a river guidebook are required. Every raft with a floor (except self-bailers) must have a bail bucket. Every party must have one major first aid kit plus a minor kit in every boat (except for kayaks, canoes and funyaks). The Park Service says every boat over 16 feet in length (except kayaks, but who paddles kayaks over 16 feet?) should have a throwable rescue device. *Only bureaucrats could come up with a rule like this! Let reason be your guide instead, and always carry a throw bag in every boat, everywhere you boat! Equip your rafts with flip lines, and bring one set of the gear you'll need in case you flip or pin a raft: a long static haul line and several biners, pulleys, and prussiks.*

You'll have to carry out all human waste and all garbage and trash. Bring firepans for campfires, and a drinking water purification system. Permitees are financially responsible for costs of a rescue. Leave your pets at home.

Gauge: Colorado River at Cataract Canyon

Source of Levels: Bureau of Reclamation, Salt Lake City; 801-539-1311.

How Reported: Cfs

Interpretation of Levels: Almost all flows on the Cataract Canyon are boatable if you are sufficiently competent. Peak flows in June this past season were between 45,000 and 50,000 cfs. A 60,000 peak is more common, and flows as high as 80,000 or 90,000 are not unheard of. In August, flows fall to around 5,000 cfs due to diversions for irrigation, and flows in fall and winter are generally around 5000 to 10,000 cfs. In general, the mid-30s are difficult; 40,000-50,000 cfs is easier; around 60,000 cfs is difficult, and 80,000 to 90,000 cfs is easier again. Special safety restrictions apply above 60,000 cfs.

Source of More Information: Bill Dvorak Kayak and Rafting Expeditions, 17921 US Highway 285, Nathrop, CO 81236; 717-539-6851.

Colorado Outward Bound School, 945 Pennsylvania St., Denver, CO 80203; 303-837-0880.

Best Guidebooks: Belknap and Belknap, *Canyonlands River Guide.*

Further Comments: Very big water, rivaling the Grand Canyon.

COTTONWOOD CREEK

Sections: Straight Canyon, along Highway 29, Class III, IV

Length of Run: Day trip, 8 miles

Location: Emery County, Utah; Manti-Lasal National Forest; Fishlake National Forest

Maps: USGS quads: Joe's Valley Reservoir, Mahogany Point, Red Point

Times Runnable: Dam-controlled. Best levels are in June.

Permit: None required

Gauge: Release from Joe's Valley Reservoir

Source of Levels: USDA Forest Service, Manti-Lasal National Forest, 599 West Price River Dr., Price, UT 84510; 801-637-2817.

How Reported: Cfs

Interpretation of Levels: About 300 cfs is about minimum. Peak flow is usually about 500 cfs. Flow rarely reaches 1000 cfs.

Source of More Information: USDA Forest Service, Manti-Lasal National Forest, 599 West Price River Dr., Price, UT 84510; 801-637-2817.

USDA Forest Service, Fishlake National Forest, PO Box 628, 170 North Main St., Richfield, UT 84701; 801-896-9233.

Best Guidebooks: Nichols, *River Runner's Guide to Utah.*

Further Comments: One of the best advanced kayak runs in Utah.

DOLORES RIVER

See Colorado.

DUCHESNE RIVER

Sections: (1) North Fork, Hades Campground to the confluence with the West Fork, Class I-III
           (2) Main River, confluence to Hanna, Class I-III

Length   (1) Day trip, 6.5 miles
of Run: (2) Day trip, 6.5 miles

Location: Duchesne County, Utah; Wasatch National Forest

Maps: USGS quads: Iron Mine Mtn., Granddaddy Lake, Hanna, Blacktail Mtn., Talmadge

Times Runnable: June

Permit: None required

Gauge: Staff gauge on bridge above the confluence

Source of Levels: Visual inspection only

How Reported: Feet

Interpretation of Levels: About 3.1 feet on the gauge is a good level (roughly 500 cfs).

Source of More Information: Wasatch National Forest, 8226 Federal Building, 125 South State St., Salt Lake City, UT 84109; 801-524-5030.

Best Guidebooks: Nichols, *River Runner's Guide to Utah.*

Further Comments: Watch for dams, low bridges, logs, fences, and diversions.

GREEN RIVER, LOWER RED CANYON
(Utah and Colorado)

Sections: Lower Red Canyon: Flaming Gorge Dam to Swallow Canyon ramp, Class I, II

Length of Run: 2 days, 27 miles

Location: Moffat County, Colorado and Unitah County, Utah; Flaming Gorge National Recreation Area

Maps: USGS quads: Dutch John, Goslin Mtn., Clay Basin, Warren Draw, Swallow Canyon

Times Runnable: May to August

Permit: None required

Restrictions: No fires or camping in the first 7 miles

Gauge: Release from Flaming Gorge Dam

Source of Levels: Bureau of Reclamation, Salt Lake City; 801-539-1311.

How Reported: Cfs

Interpretation of Levels: Low is from 700 to 2000 cfs. High flows in May to July can vary from 3000 to 6000 cfs. Levels can fluctuate widely.

Source of More Information: USDA Forest Service, Flaming Gorge Ranger District, Ashley National Forest, PO Box 157, Dutch John, UT 84023; 801-885-3315.

Best Guidebooks: Nichols, *River Runner's Guide Utah;* Hopkinson, *Rivers of the Southwest.*

Further Comments: This section of small, splashy rapids is the most popular on the entire Green River, and during the season is crowded with thousands of boaters in rental rafts.

GREEN RIVER, IN DINOSAUR
(Utah and Colorado)

Sections: Dinosaur National Monument; Lodore, Whirlpool and Split Mountain Canyons, Class II-III (a few at IV)

Length of Run: 2-4 days, 45 miles

Location: Moffat County, Colorado and Uintah County, Utah

Maps: USGS quads: Canyon of Lodore North, Canyon of Lodore South, Jones Hole, Island Park, Split Mtn., Dinosaur Quarry

Times Runnable: Almost all year

Permit: Required, and so are reservations!

Reservations: Required. A sample reservation application form is in Appendix One, but don't use it. Photocopies of applications are not accepted. Write or call to get a nice, fresh one:

River Office, National Park Service, PO Box 210, Dinosaur, CO 81610; 303-374-2468.

For multi-day trips, the high-use season begins the second Monday in May and continues to the second Friday in September. During this period, a total of 300 noncommercial trips are allowed to launch. Applications to the lottery are accepted from December 1 through January 15. You must specify the launch date you desire on your form, and chances are improved by choosing a less popular date. Selected permittees are notified by March 15. If you don't hear anything, that means you lose. After the lottery, folks may telephone and request unfilled slots whether or not they participated in the lottery. If you are a lucky winner, then you must submit a passenger list with names, addresses, and phone numbers for everyone no later than four weeks before the launch date. The low-use season begins the second

Friday in September and continues to the second Monday in May; one launch per day is available. Requests for permits to launch during this period are accepted after March 1, either by mail (postcards only), by phone, or in person. Permits are issued on a first-come, first-served basis. Permits for one day trips through Split Mountain Gorge are available on a first-come, first-served basis after March 1.

Restrictions: Groups must have at least 2 members and no more than 25. No permittees or trip leader may be under 18 (passengers or boatmen under 18 are okay). Rafts, canoes, and dories must bring an extra PFD and at least one spare oar or paddle. PFDs are required, and must be worn. Hard boaters must wear helmets. Decked boats must have sprayskirts and floatation. One major first aid kit is required for each group, and a minor first aid kit must be in every boat.

A dishwater strainer is required. Firepans and portable toilets are required. Maps are required.

There are no-show and late cancellation penalties.

Gauge: Release from Flaming Gorge Reservoir

Source of Levels: Bureau of Reclamation, Salt Lake City; 801-539-1311.

How Reported: Cfs

Interpretation of Levels: Low is from 700 to 2000 cfs. High is from 3000 to 6000 cfs. Levels fluctuate widely.

Source of More Information: Bureau of Land Management, Dinosaur National Monument (address and phone above).

Bill Dvorak Kayak and Rafting Expeditions, 17921 US Highway 285, Nathrop, CO 81236; 303-539-6851.

Colorado Outward Bound School, 945 Pennsylvania St., Denver, CO 80203; 303-837-0880.

Best Guidebooks: Evans and Belknap, *Dinosaur River Guide;* Nichols, *River Runners' Guide to Utah.*

Further Comments: One of the finest multi-day trips. It's tough to get permits.

GREEN RIVER, DESOLATION AND GRAY CANYONS

Sections: Desolation and Gray Canyons, Sand Wash to Green River, Utah, Class II-III

Length of Run: 5-10 days, 84 miles

Location: Unitah, Carbon and Emery Counties, Utah

Maps: USGS quads: Duches Hole, Nutters Hole, Firewater Canyon North, Cedar Ridge Canyon, Steer Ridge Canyon, Chandler Falls, Tiree Fords Canyon, Butler Canyon, Tusher Canyon, Blue Castle Butte

Times Runnable: Year-round; highest in May and June

Permit: Permits are required year-round, but fees and reservations are required only from May 1 through September 30 (see below). Obtain a permit application by phone from the: Bureau of Land Management, Grand Resource Area, PO Box M, Moab, UT 84532; 801-259-8193. A copy of the application form is included in Appendix One, but don't use it. All BLM offices like you to use fresh, new originals!

Reservations: Reservations are required from May 1 to September 30. To participate in the drawing for reservations, submit your application during January or February. The drawing is held on March 1. After March 21 you may call and draw a leftover launch date or request to be placed on the waiting list for specific dates. If you are assigned a launch date, you will have pay a fee of $2.25 per person. Your check for the fee must reach the BLM at least 2 weeks prior to the launch date; otherwise you forfeit your launch.

Bring your permit along to the ranger station at Westwater on your launch day. If it turns out you must cancel your trip, let the BLM know as soon as possible.

Restrictions: Every boater must be at least 18 years of age. No more than 25 persons may be in your group. Rafts must be of decent quality, and each boat must have a competent, experienced boatman. Each raft or dory must have a spare oar, paddle, or motor as is appropriate. Each raft or dory must have a bail bucket, one spare PFD, and a throw bag.

Your group must bring a first aid kit, an air pump, repair kit, and a firepan. Overnight trips (other than kayak trips) must bring portable toilets. Have everyone urinate in the river, rather than on the land.

A river ranger will make a final inspection of your gear on your launch day.

Gauge: Green River at Green River, Utah

Source of Levels: Bureau of Reclamation, Salt Lake City; 801-539-1311.

How Reported: Cfs

Interpretation of Levels: Flows rarely fall below 3000 cfs. Average flow in April is 6000, in May 12,000, June 14,000, and July 6000 cfs. Flow may peak from 20,000 to 48,000 cfs.

Source of More Information: Bill Dvorak Kayak and Rafting Expeditions, 17921 US Highway 285, Nathrop, CO 81236; 717-539-6851.

Colorado Outward Bound School, 945 Pennsylvania St., Denver, CO 80203; 303-837-0880.

Best Guidebooks: Belknap and Belknap, *Desolation River Guide.*

Further Comments: A true wilderness experience in an eerie world of desolate canyons.

LOGAN RIVER

Sections: Logan Canyon, Rick's Spring to Preston Valley Campground, Class II-V

Length of Run: Day trip, 8 miles

Location: Cache County, Utah; Wasatch National Forest

Maps: USGS quads: Tony Grove, Temple Peak, Mount Elmer, Logan Peak, Logan

Times Runnable: Mid-May to June

Permit: None required

Gauge: USGS on the Logan River above State Dam, near Logan, UT

Source of Levels: USGS, Salt Lake City; 801-524-5663.

How Reported: Cfs

Interpretation of Levels: Average peak is around 1000 cfs.

Source of More Information: USDA Forest Service, Logan Ranger District, Wasatch National Forest, 860 North, 1200 East, Logan, UT 84321; 801-753-2772.

Best Guidebooks: Nichols, *River Runner's Guide to Utah.*

Further Comments: Portage two dams. Watch for downed trees.

PRICE RIVER

Sections:
(1) Scofield Reservoir to picnic area above Price Canyon, Class I-III
(2) Price Canyon, picnic area to Castle Gate, Class III-V

Length of Run:
(1) Day trip, 15 miles
(2) Day trip, 8.5 miles

Location: Carbon and Utah Counties, Utah

Maps: USGS quads: Colton, Kyune, Standardville, Helper

Times Runnable: May and June

Permit: None required

Gauge: Release from the Scofield Reservoir

Source of Levels: Bureau of Land Management, Moab District, Price River Resource Area; 801-637-4584.

How Reported: Cfs

Interpretation of Levels: About 300-500 cfs should be enough.

Source of More Information: Bureau of Land Management, Moab District, Price River Resource Area, PO Drawer AB, Price, UT 84501; 801-637-4584.

Best Guidebooks: Nichols, *River Runner's Guide to Utah.*

SAN JUAN RIVER
(See New Mexico for additional sections.)

Sections:
(1) Sand Island launch point near Bluff, Utah to Mexican Hat, Class I-III
(2) Mexican Hat to Clay Hills boat ramp on Lake Powell, Class I-III

Length of Run:
(1) 2 days, 28 miles
(2) 3 days, 56 miles (when Lake Powell is at full capacity, the last 15 miles from Grand Gulch to Clay Hills is flatwater)

Location: San Juan County, Utah; Glen Canyon National Recreation Area; Navajo Indian Reservation

Maps: USGS quads: Bluff, Boundary Butte, Mexican Hat, Goulding, Grand Gulch and Clay Hills

Times Runnable: Almost year-round

Permit: Permits are required year-round, but fees and reservations are required only from May 1 through September 30 (see below). Obtain a permit application by phone from the: Bureau of Land Management, Grand Resource Area, PO Box M, Moab, UT 84532; 801-259-8193. A copy of the application form is included in Appendix One, but don't use it. All BLM offices like you to use fresh, new originals!

Reservations: Reservations are required from May 1 to September 30. To participate in the drawing for reservations, submit your application during January or February. The drawing is held on March 1. After March 21 you may call and request a leftover launch date or request to be placed on the waiting list for specific dates. If you are assigned a launch date, you will have pay a fee ($2.25 per person from Sand Island to Mexican Hat or $5.25 from Mexican Hat to Clay Hills). Your check for the fee must reach the BLM at least 2 weeks prior to the launch date; otherwise you forfeit your launch.

Bring your permit along to the ranger station at Westwater on your launch day. If it turns out you must cancel your trip, let the BLM know as soon as possible.

Restrictions: Every boater must be at least 18 years of age. No more than 25 persons may be in your group. Rafts must be of decent quality, and each boat must have a competent, experienced boatman. Each raft or dory must have a spare oar, paddle, or motor as is appropriate. Each raft or dory must have a bail bucket, one spare PFD, and a throw bag.

Your group must bring a first aid kit, an air pump, repair kit, and a firepan. Overnight trips (other than kayak trips) must bring portable toilets. Have everyone urinate in the river, rather than on the land.

A river ranger will make a final inspection of your gear on your launch day.

Gauge: San Juan River at Bluff (just above Mexican Hat Bridge)

Source of Levels: Bureau of Reclamation, Salt Lake City; 801-539-1311.

How Reported: Cfs

Interpretation of Levels: Low water is around 3000 cfs, and high is around 7000.

Source of More Information: BLM, address and phone above.

Holiday River Expeditions, 544 East 3900 St., Salt Lake City, UT 84107; 801-266-2087, 800-624-6323 (outside Utah).

Slickrock Kayak Adventures, PO Box 1400! Moab, UT 84532; 801-259-6996, 208-462-3639.

Best Guidebooks: Baers and Stevenson, *San Juan Canyons.*

Further Comments: The San Juan is the undiscovered Grand Canyon of the Southwest. These two sections have beauty that equals the more famous canyon of the Colorado River, without the cold water and intimidating rapids. Plenty of opportunity for whitewater fun remains, however; the surfing waves on the San Juan are unparalleled. Plus, getting permits is easy!

SAN RAFAEL RIVER

Sections:
(1) First Canyon, confluence of Ferron Creek, Cottonwood Creek and Hunting ton Creeks to bridge at San Rafael Campground, Class I,II.
(2) First Black Box, bridge at San Rafael Campground to below first box, Class III-IV.
(3) Second Black Box, from below the first black box to US Interstate 70, Class III-V (one unrunnable drop and one waterfall to portage).

Length of Run:
(1) Day trip, 23 miles
(2) Day trip, 22 miles
(3) Day trip, 20 miles

Location: Emery County, Utah

Maps: USGS quads: Hadden Holes, Wilsonville SE, Red Plateau SW, Red Plateau SE, The Wickiup, Beckwith Peak SW, Tidwell Bottoms

Times Runnable: May and June

Permit: None required

Gauge: None

Source of Levels: Inspection only. Use the W.D.S. method.

Interpretation of Levels: About 200 cfs is enough water; about 400 is high, and over 1000 is dangerously high.

Source of More Information: Bear River Canoe and Kayak School, 943 McClelland St., Salt Lake City, UT 84105; 801-485-3163.

Best Guidebooks: Nichols, *River Runner's Guide to Utah.*

Further Comments: One of the most difficult runs in Utah. Kids: never try this at home.

YAMPA RIVER, DINOSAUR NATIONAL MONUMENT

See Colorado.

GENERAL INFORMATION SOURCES FOR UTAH

Levels for rivers in Arizona and Utah can be obtained by calling Salt Lake City for the recorded Bureau of Reclamation River Observations: 801-539-1311.

Gauge readings updated daily at 4 AM are reported for the following rivers:

Colorado River Basin

Colorado River, at Westwater
Gunnison River, at Gun Summit
Dolores River, at Bedrock
Dolores River, near Cisco
Colorado River, near Cisco
Colorado River, Cataract Canyon
Colorado River, at Lees Ferry
Virgin River, near Littlefield
Muddy River, near Emory

Green River Basin

Yampa River, at Maybell
Little Snake River, near Lily
Yampa River, at the mouth
Green River, near Jensen
White River, near Watson
Green River, near Green River, Utah
San Rafael River, near Green River, Utah
Dirty Devil River, at Hanksville

Great Basin

Weaver River, near Oakley
Weaver River, below Echo
Sevier River, above Clear Creek

San Juan Basin

Animas, near Durango
San Juan River, near Bluff

Dam Releases

Flaming Gorge Dam, Green River
Glen Canyon Dam, Colorado River
Navaho Dam, San Juan River
McPhee Dam, Dolores River

Other sources of information on Utah's whitewater rivers include:

Grand County Travel Council, 805 North Main, Moab, UT 84532; 800-635-6622.

San Juan County Travel Council, 117 S. Main St., Monticello, UT 84535; 801-587-2231.

Canyonlands Natural History Association, 125 W. 200th St. South, Moab, UT 84532; 801-259-6003.

VERMONT

BATTEN KILL

Sections: Manchester to Arlington, Class I-II

Length of Run: Day trip, 10.5 miles

Location: Bennington County, Vermont

Maps: USGS quad: Equinox (15')

Times Runnable: Spring and early summer

Permit: None required

Gauge: A gauging rock is located upstream of Batten Kill Canoe

Source of Levels: Batten Kill Canoe, 802-375-9559.

How Reported: Low, medium, or high

Interpretation of Levels: If the rock is showing a foot or less, then the Batten Kill is too high for novice and beginning boaters. However, the best levels for intermediate or better boaters are from the rock showing 10 inches or less up to the rock just showing. To tell if the Batten Kill is too low, take a look from the Highway 313 bridge. If it looks too low, then it is.

Source of More Information: Batten Kill Canoe, Box N469, West Arlington, VT 05250; 802-375-9559.

Best Guidebooks: Appalachian Mountain Club, *AMC River Guide: New Hampshire and Vermont.*

Further Comments: A new gauge will be installed in Rochester soon. Check with Batten Kill Canoe for the interpretation. Watch for fallen trees on the upper reaches.

CLYDE RIVER

Sections: Salem Pond to Clyde Pond, Class I-II

Length of Run: Day trip, 6.5 miles

Location: Orleans County, Vermont

Maps: USGS quads: Memphremagog, (15')

Times Runnable: Spring and summer

Permit: None required

Gauge: None

Source of Levels: Batten Kill Canoe, 802-375-9559.

How Reported: Impression

Interpretation of Levels: If Batten Kill Canoe tells you there is enough water, then there is. Alternatively, you can check at the Route 105 bridge. If it looks high enough, then it is.

Source of More Information: Batten Kill Canoe, Box N469, West Arlington, VT 05250; 802-375-9559.

Best Guidebooks: Appalachian Mountain Club, *AMC River Guide: New Hampshire and Vermont.*

GREEN RIVER

See Massachusetts.

LAMOILLE RIVER

Sections: (1) Johnson to Fairfax Falls, Class I
(2) Fairfax Falls to Mita, Class I-II

Length of Run: (1) 2 days, 24.5 miles
(2) Day trip, 10 miles

Location: Lamoille and Franklin Counties, Vermont

Maps: USGS quads: Hyde Park (15'), Jeffersonville, Gilson Mtn.

Times Runnable: Spring and summer

Permit: None required

Gauge: USGS at Johnson

Source of Levels: Batten Kill Canoe, 802-375-9559.

How Reported: Feet

Interpretation of Levels: Minimum is around 200 or 300 cfs. Mean flow in March is 730 cfs; in April, 1300; May, 550; June, 330; and July, 200 cfs. Peak flows in March and April can reach 2800 cfs.

Source of More Information: Batten Kill Canoe, Box N469, West Arlington, VT 05250; 802-375-9559.

Best Guidebooks: Appalachian Mountain Club, *AMC River Guide: New Hampshire and Vermont.*

Further Comments: There is a dam to portage on Section (1), as well as a dam to portage immediately above the take-out on Section (2).

Gauge Conversion: USGS at Johnson

Feet	Cfs	Feet	Cfs	Feet	Cfs
2.5	200	4.2	1044	6.0	2010
2.6	242	4.4	1141	6.2	2126
2.8	336	4.6	1241	6.4	2244
3.0	440	4.8	1345	6.6	2364
3.2	548	5.0	1452	6.8	2486
3.4	649	5.2	1561	7.0	2610
3.6	747	5.4	1673	7.2	2740
3.8	846	5.6	1785	7.4	2872
4.0	950	5.8	1896	—	—

OTTAUQUECHEE RIVER

Sections: Quechee Gorge, Class IV (one Class VI usually portaged)

Length of Run: Day trip, 1.0 miles

Location: Windsor County, Vermont

Maps: USGS quads: Quechee, Hartland, North Hartland

Times Runnable: Releases are scheduled beginning in April and continuing through the summer.

Permit: None required

Gauge: Release from Long Lake

Source of Levels: Netam Corporation (hydro project management), 802-295-1490.

National Weather Service, Albany; 518-869-6347.

How Reported: Cfs

Interpretation of Levels: Releases range from 300 to 3000 cfs. Minimum is about 300. The Quechee gorge becomes continuous and difficult above 1500.

Source of More Information: Quechee Gorge State Park, White River Junction, VT 05001; 802-295-2990.

Rugged Vermont beauty is found deep within Quechee Gorge of the Ottaquechee River. Photo by John Porterfield.

Best Guidebooks: Connelly and Porterfield, *Appalachian Whitewater, Vol. III.*

Further Comments: This is a tough, continuous section. Partway down the run, Washermachine Rapid is considered Class VI and is generally portaged. *Scout from the bridge first.* If right side is barely underwater, don't run. If it is sufficiently deep, it can be run down the extreme right side.

WARDSBORO BROOK

Sections: Town of North Wardsboro to the confluence with the West River, Class III-IV

Length of Run: Day trip, 8 miles

Location: Windham County, Vermont; Green Mountains National Forest

Maps: USGS quads: Londonderry (15'), Saxton's River

Times Runnable: Brief runoff for a few days in March and during fall flooding

Permit: None required

Gauge: Painted paddlers' gauge on river-right at the confluence with the West River

Source of Levels: Visual inspection, but you might try: Merrimack Valley Paddlers' Recording, 603-432-6870

How Reported: Feet

Interpretation of Levels: Minimum is 0 feet. Optimum is around 2 feet. Can be run by sufficiently competent paddlers to floodstage.

Source of More Information: Jamaica State Park, Jamaica, VT 05343; 802-874-4600

Green Mountain National Forest, Federal Building, PO Box 519, Rutland, VT 05701; 802-773-2300

Best Guidebooks: Connelly and Porterfield, *Appalachian Whitewater, Vol. III.*

WEST RIVER

Sections: Jamaica Gorge, Ball Mountain Dam to Jamaica State Park, Class III-IV

Length of Run: Day trip, 2.5 miles

Sue Burgess on medium water on the turbulent last mile of Wardsboro Brook. Photo by Robert Hall.

Location: Windham County, Vermont

Maps: USGS quads: Londonderry (15')

Times Runnable: Releases are scheduled during the first two weekends in May and the first in October.

Permit: None required

Gauge: Release from Ball Mountain Dam

Source of Levels: US Army Corps of Engineers, Ball Mountain Dam; 802-874-4881

How Reported: Cfs

Interpretation of Levels: Normal releases are 1300 cfs; releases rarely exceed 2200 cfs.

Source of More Information: Jamaica State Park, Jamaica, VT 05343; 802-874-4600.

Green Mountain National Forest, Federal Building, PO Box 519, Rutland, VT 05701; 802-773-2300.

North American Whitewater Expeditions, 60C Skiff St., Suite 770, Hamden, CT 06518; 203-248-8924.

Best Guidebooks: Connelly and Porterfield, *Appalachian Whitewater, Vol. III.*

Further Comments: The West River in Jamaica Gorge flows through scenic pastoral country and past the pleasant villages of Jamaica and Kingsland. On its way, it creates the best rapids for play in the state of Vermont. The scheduled releases draw hundreds of boaters from around New England to enjoy this fine river.

WHITE RIVER

Sections: Rochester to Gaysville, Class I-II

Length of Run: 1-2 days, 16 miles

Location: Windsor County, Vermont; Green Mountains National Forest

Maps: USGS quads: Rochester, Randolph (15')

Times Runnable: Spring and early summer

Permit: None required

Gauge: USGS White River at West Hartford (far downstream)

Source of Levels: National Weather Service, Albany; 518-869-6347.

How Reported: Feet

Interpretation of Levels: Six feet (2420 cfs) is minimum.

Source of More Information: Green Mountains National Forest, Federal Building, PO Box 519, Rutland, VT 05701; 802-773-2300.

Best Guidebooks: Appalachian Mountain Club, *AMC River Guide: New Hampshire and Vermont;* Gabler, *New England Whitewater River Guide.*

Further Comments: Pleasant flatwater and easy whitewater in farm country.

Gauge Conversions:

Feet	Cfs	Feet	Cfs	Feet	Cfs
5.0	1300	6.4	2910	7.6	4670
5.2	1570	6.6	3170	7.8	5010
5.4	1770	6.8	3450	8.0	5360
5.6	1980	7.0	3740	8.5	6280
5.8	2200	7.2	4040	9.0	7280
6.0	2420	7.4	4350	9.5	8380
6.2	2660	—	—	—	—

WHITE RIVER, FIRST BRANCH

Sections: Chelsea Health Center to above Sawmill Dam, Class III-IV

Length of Run: Day trip, 6 miles

Location: Orange County, Vermont; Green Mountain National Forest

Maps: USGS quads: Strafford (15')

Times Runnable: In early spring

Permit: None required

Gauge: Extrapolate from the West Hartford gauge on the White River.

Source of Levels: National Weather Service, Albany; 518-869-6347.

How Reported: Feet

Interpretation of Levels: Extrapolating from the West Hartford gauge on the White River downstream, about 7.5 feet (4500 cfs) at West Hartford should provide enough water on the first branch.

Source of More Information: Green Mountains National Forest, Federal Building, PO Box 519, Rutland, VT 05701; 802-773-2300.

Best Guidebooks: Connelly and Porterfield, *Appalachian Whitewater, Vol. III.*

WINHALL RIVER

Sections: Grahamville School Road to Winhall Campground, Class III (with one Class IV, Londonderry Rapids, often portaged)

Length of Run: Day trip, 7 miles

Location: Bennington and Windham Counties, Vermont; Green Mountain National Forest

Maps: USGS quads: Londonderry (15')

Times Runnable: During a short season of peak runoff in March and April

Permit: None required

Gauge: Painted paddlers' gauge on river-left slightly upstream of the Rawsonville Rt. 100 Bridge gauge.

Source of Levels: Visual inspection only, but you might try: Merrimack Valley Paddlers' Recording, 603-432-6870.

How Reported: Feet

Additional Gauge: You might also check the outflow from the Ball Mountain Dam. If they are releasing water, then there is a good chance that water is entering the reservoir on the Winhall.

Source of Levels: US Army Corps of Engineers, Ball Mountain Dam; 802-874-4881.

How Reported: Cfs

Interpretation of Levels: On the paddlers' gauge, minimum is about 1 foot; optimum is 2.5 feet, and high is 3.5 feet. If the Ball Mountain Dam is releasing as much as 2500 cfs, then there is a good chance that the Winhall is running.

Source of More Information: Green Mountains National Forest, Federal Building, PO Box 519, Rutland, VT 05701; 802-773-2300.

Wildwater Outfitters, 20 Elliot St., Brattleboro, VT 05301; 802-254-4133.

Best Guidebooks: Connelly and Porterfield, *Appalachian Whitewater, Vol. III.*

WINOOSKI RIVER

Sections: Marchfield to Montpelier, Class II-III

Length of Run: Day trip, 24 miles

Location: Washington County, Vermont

Maps: USGS quads: Plainfield (15'), Barre (15'), Montpelier (15')

Times Runnable: April to May

Permit: None required

Gauge: Winooski at Montpelier

Source of Levels: National Weather Service, Albany; 518-869-6347.

How Reported: Feet

Interpretation of Levels: Around 200 to 300 cfs is minimum, and 1000 cfs is optimum.

Best Guidebooks: Appalachian Mountain Club, *AMC River Guide: New Hampshire and Vermont.*

Gauge Conversion: USGS Winooski at Montpelier

Feet	Cfs	Feet	Cfs	Feet	Cfs
3.5	214	5.2	1180	7.5	3312
4.0	403	5.4	1344	8.0	3800
4.2	500	5.6	1510	8.5	4243
4.4	602	5.8	1675	9.0	4700
4.6	720	6.0	1850	9.5	5192
4.8	862	6.5	2321	10.0	5700
5.0	1016	7.0	2832	—	—

**GENERAL INFORMATION SOURCES
FOR VERMONT**

The US Army Corps of Engineers and other managers of water projects coordinate many of the scheduled releases through the Appalachian Mountain Club. Call the office of the Appalachian Mountain Club in Boston; they should have a printed list they can mail out (I don't recommend that you call the New England Division of the Army Corps—they don't want to hear from you).

Appalachian Mountain Club, New England Rivers Center, Boston, 5 Joy St., Boston, MA; 617-523-0636.

The Merrimack Valley Paddlers have established a river phone line that reports upcoming trips and that may include levels on various rivers. Call 603-432-6870.

The Western New England Hydrological Service Area of the National Weather Service in Albany can provide gauge readings for eastern New York and Vermont. Call their forecast recording and stay on the line; someone will pick up: 518-869-6347.

They can report the following readings for Vermont:

White River, at West Hartford
Winooski River, at Montpelier
Battenkill River, at Battenville
West River, at Newfane
Ottaquechee, release from Long Lake
Black River, at Boonville

VERMONT

VIRGINIA/DISTRICT OF COLUMBIA

APPOMATTOX RIVER

Sections: Chesdin Dam to Rt. 36 in Petersburg, Class II and III

Length of Run: Day trip, 6.5 miles

Location: Chesterfield and Dinwiddie Counties, Virginia

Maps: USGS quads: Sutherland and Petersburg

Times Runnable: January through June

Permit: None required

Gauge: Flow over Chesdin Dam

Source of Levels: Appomattox River Water Authority, 804-590-1145.

How Reported: Inches over the Dam

Additional Gauge: USGS gauge on the Appomattox at Matoaca

Source of Levels: National Weather Service, Richmond Recording; 804-226-4423.

National Weather Service, Harrisburg; 717-234-2251.

How Reported: Feet

Interpretation of Levels: About 3 inches of flow over Chesdin Dam is minimum; 8 inches is optimum, and 16 inches is high. In terms of the Matoaca gauge, about 2 feet is minimum. Converted to cfs, about 500 cfs is minimum, and 1800 is high.

Source of More Information: Appomattox River Co., 610 N. Main St., Farmville, VA 23901; 804-392-6645.

Best Guidebooks: Grove et al., *Appalachian Whitewater, Vol. II;* Corbett, *Virginia Whitewater.*

Further Comments: Portage the dam located about 1 mile below the put-in. When the Appomattox is very high, watch out for a whirlpool that develops below the Highway 36 Bridge.

AQUIA CREEK

Sections: Rt. 610 to Rt. 1, Class II

Length of Run: Day trip, 10.5 miles

Location: Stafford County, Virginia

Maps: USGS quad: Stafford

Times Runnable: January through April

Permit: None required

Gauge: None. Extrapolate from the Remington gauge on the Rappahannock.

Source of Levels: National Weather Service, Washington; 703-260-0305.

National Weather Service, Harrisburg; 717-234-6812.

How Reported: Feet

Interpretation of Levels: If the Remington gauge is over 5 feet, then the Aquia may be runnable. If it looks runnable at the Rt. 610 put-in, then it is.

Source of More Information: Appomattox River Co., 610 N. Main St., Farmville, VA 23901; 804-392-6645.

Best Guidebooks: Grove et al., *Appalachian Whitewater, Vol. II;* Corbett, *Virginia Whitewater.*

Further Comments: Watch for downed trees.

JAMES RIVER

Sections:
(1) Pony Pasture to Reedy Creek, Class II III
(2) Reedy Creek to Reynolds plant, Class III-IV (Class IV-V high)

Length of Run:
(1) Day trip, 3.5 miles
(2) Day trip, 2 miles

Location: City of Richmond, Virginia; Henrico and Chesterfield Counties, Virginia

Maps: USGS quad: Richmond

Times Runnable: Essentially year-round, but levels are often high in late winter and spring.

Permit: Above 9 feet on the Westham gauge (very high, Class IV-V). The city of Richmond requires boaters to possess an "expert permit." An application form for an expert permit, good for two years, is in Appendix One. Apply to: Director of Public Safety, 501 North 94th St., Room 131, Richmond, VA; 804-780-8680 or 804-780-8621.

Restrictions: Boaters requiring rescue at high water levels by the Richmond Department of Public Safety are required to pay the costs. Be careful out there!

Gauge: USGS gauge at Westham

Source of Levels: National Weather Service, Richmond; 804-226-4423.

National Weather Service, Washington; 703-260-0305.

National Weather Service, Harrisburg; 717-234-6812.

How Reported: Feet

Interpretation of Levels: Low is 4 feet; medium is 6 feet; 8 feet is high, and 9 is very high.

Source of More Information: James River Park, 900 East Broad St., Richmond, VA 23219; 804-231-7411.

Appomattox River Co., 610 N. Main St., Farmville, VA 23901; 804-392-6645.

Richmond Raft Company, 4400 E. Main St., Richmond, VA 23231; 804-222-7238.

Best Guidebooks: Grove et al., *Appalachian Whitewater, Vol. II;* Nealy, *Whitewater Home Companion, Vol. II;* Corbett, *Virginia Whitewater;* James River Park, "Map of Rapids Through Richmond for Average-High Water" (from James River Park, address above).

Further Comments: I recommend that first-time boaters on the James run with someone who knows the way. Many of the drops are broken dams; it would be a drag to miss a slot and end up surfing a dam hydraulic.

Gauge Conversion: James River at Westham

Feet	Cfs	Feet	Cfs	Feet	Cfs
3.5	960	6.2	8250	10.0	26620
3.8	1660	6.4	8980	10.5	29700
4.0	2140	6.6	9740	11.0	32950
4.2	2620	6.8	10530	12.0	40100
4.4	3120	7.0	11340	13.0	48200
4.6	3620	7.2	12190	14.0	57000
4.8	4120	7.4	13080	15.0	66600
5.0	4620	7.6	14010	16	77200
5.2	5150	7.8	14960	17	88500
5.4	5720	8.0	15930	18	100500
5.6	6300	8.5	18430	19	115500
5.8	6910	9.0	20960	20	131000
6.0	7560	9.5	23700	—	—

JOHNS CREEK

Sections: Johns Creek Gorge, Rt. 311 Bridge to Rt. 615 Bridge at New Castle, Class IV (one at IV-V)

Length of Run: Day trip, 5.5 miles

Location: Craig County, Virginia; Jefferson National Forest

Maps: USGS quads: Potts Creek, New Castle
Also: Jefferson National Forest Visitor Map

Times Runnable: Winter, spring and after heavy rain

Permit: None required

Gauge: Paddlers' gauge at Rt. 615 in New Castle

Source of Levels: Visual inspection only

How Reported: Feet

Interpretation of Levels: Minimum is 0, and high is 1.5 feet.

Source of More Information: Appomattox River Co., 610 N. Main St., Farmville, VA 23901; 804-392-6645.

USDA Forest Service, New Castle Ranger District, Jefferson National Forest, Box 246, New Castle, VA 24127; 703-864-5195.

Best Guidebooks: Grove et al., *Appalachian Whitewater, Vol. II*; Corbett, *Virginia Whitewater*.

Further Comments: Johns Creek is the big dog of Virginia whitewater runs. Expect to find at least 4 miles of very continuous Class IV and at least one rapid harder than that!

MAURY RIVER

Sections: Goshen to Rockbridge Baths, Class III-IV

Length of Run: Day trip, 5.5 miles

Location: Rockbridge County, Virginia; George Washington National Forest

Maps: USGS quad: Goshen

Times Runnable: January to May or after a heavy rain. The Maury has an excellent watershed.

Permit: None required

Gauge: USGS at Buena Vista; paddlers' gauges at Rockbridge Baths (now repaired) and James River Basin Canoe Livery

Source of Levels: James River Basin Canoe Livery, 703-761-7334.

National Weather Service, Richmond; 804-226-4423.

National Weather Service, Washington; 703-260-0305.

National Weather Service, Harrisburg; 717-234-6812.

How Reported: Feet

Interpretation of Levels: Buena Vista gauge minimum is about 3 feet; 5 feet is high, and 7 feet or above is extremely high. Rockbridge Baths and James River Basin gauges have minimum at 1 foot; 3 feet is getting high, and 5 feet or above is extremely high.

Source of More Information: Appomattox River Co., 610 N. Main St., Farmville, VA 23901; 804-392-6645.

James River Basin Canoe Livery, RFD. No. 4, Box 125, Lexington, VA 24450; 703-261-7334.

USDA Forest Service, Warm Springs Ranger District, George Washington National Forest, Highway 220 South, Rt. 2, Box 30, Hot Springs, VA 24445; 703839-2521, 703-839-2442.

Best Guidebooks: Grove et al., *Appalachian Whitewater, Vol. II;* Corbett, *Virginia Whitewater;* Nealy, *Whitewater Home Companion, Vol. II.*

Further Comments: The Maury provides some of the most exciting and scenic whitewater in the Old Dominion. Don't forget to scout Devils Kitchen Rapid from the highway before you run.

Gauge Conversion: Maury River at Buena Vista

Feet	Cfs	Feet	Cfs	Feet	Cfs
2.0	388	4.8	2419	6.8	4728
2.5	638	5.0	2620	7.0	4995
3.0	939	5.2	2827	7.2	5268
3.2	1074	5.4	3041	7.4	5548
3.4	1216	5.6	3242	7.6	5833
3.6	1366	5.8	3490	7.8	6126
3.8	1523	6.0	3724	8.0	6424
4.0	1688	6.2	3965	8.5	7197
4.2	1860	6.4	4213	9.0	8007
4.4	2039	6.6	4467	9.5	8855
4.6	2226	—	—	10.0	9740

PASSAGE CREEK

Sections: Elizabeth Furnace Picnic Area near Front Royal on County Road 678 to the Highway 55 Bridge at Waterlick, Class II and III

Length of Run: Day trip, 6 miles

Location: Shenandoah and Warren counties, Virginia; George Washington National Forest

Maps: USGS quad: Strasburg

Times Runnable: January to May or after heavy rains

Permit: None required

Gauge: None. Extrapolate from the USGS Cootes Store gauge on the North Fork of the Shenandoah.

Source of Levels: National Weather Service, Washington; 703-260-0305.

National Weather Service, Harrisburg; 717-234-6812.

How Reported: Feet

Interpretation of Levels: About 3.5 feet on the North Fork of the Shenandoah at Cootes Store should provide minimum water. Once at the creek, use the old Randy Carter paddlers' gauge on the Rt. 55 bridge.

Source of More Information: Appomattox River Co., 610 N. Main St., Farmville, VA 23901; 804-392-6645.

USDA Forest Service, Lee Ranger District, Windsor Knit Rd., Rt. 1, Box 31A, Edinburg, VA 22824; 703-984-4101, 703-261-6106.

Best Guidebooks: Grove et al., *Appalachian Whitewater, Vol. II;* Corbett, *Virginia Whitewater.*

Further Comments: Portage the dam at the fish hatchery. Go somewhere else during peak trout season in early April.

POTOMAC RIVER
(Virginia, District of Columbia and Maryland)

Sections: Mather Gorge, below Great Falls to Little Falls, Class III-IV (Little Falls itself can vary from Class III to Class VI depending on water levels)

Length of Run: Day trip, 11.5 miles, shorter sections possible

Location: Montgomery County, Maryland, Fairfax and Arlington Counties, Virginia, and the District of Columbia

Maps: USGS quads: Falls Church, Washington West

Times Runnable: Year-round, except when it is too high for your skill and experience.

Permit: None required

Gauge: USGS at Little Falls

Source of Levels: National Weather Service, Washington; 703-260-0305.

National Weather Service, Harrisburg; 717-234-6812.

How Reported: Feet

Interpretation of Levels: Low is 3 feet; 3.5 feet is medium; 4 feet is high, and above 5 feet is extremely high.

Source of More Information: Canoe Cruisers of Greater Washington, Inc., PO Box 572, Arlington, VA 22016.

Great Falls National Recreational Area, c/o George Washington Memorial Parkway Turkey Run Park, McLean, VA 22101; 301-299-3613.

C&O Canal National Historic Park, PO Box 4, Sharpsburg, MD 21782; 301-739-4200.

Blue Ridge Outfitters, PO Box 750, Harpers Ferry, WV 25425; 304-725-3444.

Best Guidebooks: Grove et al., *Appalachian Whitewater, Vol. II;* Corbett, *Virginia Whitewater;* Nealy, *Whitewater Home Companion, Vol. II.*

Further Comments: Portage dangerous Brookmont Dam (next to Little Falls pumping station on river left). Avoid Little Falls at high water.

Gauge Conversion: Potomac River at Little Falls

Feet	Cfs	Feet	Cfs	Feet	Cfs
2.5	440	3.5	5700	6.5	46180
2.6	700	3.6	6523	7.0	56000
2.7	1050	3.7	7405	7.5	66590
2.8	1470	3.8	8344	8.0	78000
2.9	1940	3.9	9343	8.5	90570
3.0	2450	4.0	10400	9.0	104000
3.1	2988	4.5	15710	9.5	118600
3.2	3581	5.0	22000	10.0	134000
3.3	4231	5.5	29170	15.0	250000
3.4	4937	6.0	37230	20.0	363300

Gauge Conversion: Rappahannock River at Remington

Feet	Cfs	Feet	Cfs	Feet	Cfs
3.0	121	4.6	953	7.0	2626
3.5	295	4.7	1020	7.5	2998
4.0	566	4.8	1087	8.0	3387
4.1	633	4.9	1151	8.5	3795
4.2	707	5.0	1211	9.0	4208
4.3	766	5.5	1540	9.5	4616
4.4	827	6.0	1901	10.0	5053
4.5	889	6.5	2257	—	—

RAPPAHANNOCK RIVER

Sections: Highway 29 Bridge at Remington to Kellys Ford Bridge at Highway 620, Class II-III at moderate levels

Length of Run: Day Trip, 4.5 miles

Location: Culpeper and Fauquier Counties, Virginia

Maps: USGS quads: Remington, Germanna Bridge

Times Runnable: January to May

Permit: None required

Gauge: USGS at Remington

Source of Levels: National Weather Service, Washington; 703-260-0305.

National Weather Service, Harrisburg; 717-234-6812.

How Reported: Feet

Interpretation of Levels: 4 to 5 feet on Remington gauge is about right.

Source of More Information: Coastal Canoeists, PO Box 566, Richmond, VA 23204.

Best Guidebooks: Grove et al., *Appalachian Whitewater, Vol. II;* Corbett, *Virginia Whitewater.*

Further Comments: The Rappahannock is one of the most popular paddling rivers in Virginia. It is blessed both by dependable water levels and plenty of super rapids.

RUSSELL FORK OF THE LEVISA FORK OF THE BIG SANDY RIVER

See Kentucky.

SHENANDOAH RIVER, SOUTH FORK
(See Maryland for an additional section of the Shenandoah.)

Sections: Bixler Bridge to Karo Landing, Class I (one at II)

Length of Run: 3-4 days, 36.5 miles, shorter trips possible

Location: Page and Warren Counties, Virginia

Maps: USGS quads: Luray, Rileyville, Bentonville

Times Runnable: Year-round, except during dry summers

Permit: None required

Gauge: USGS at Front Royal

Source of Levels: National Weather Service, Washington; 703-260-0305.

National Weather Service, Harrisburg; 717-234-6812.

How Reported: Feet

Interpretation of Levels: Minimum is about 1.3 feet at Front Royal (639 cfs), and high is 3 feet (about 2500 cfs).

Source of More Information: Appomattox River Co., 610 N. Main St., Fannville, VA 23901; 804-392-6645.

Best Guidebooks: Grove et al., *Appalachian Whitewater, Vol. II;* Corbett, *Virginia Whitewater*

Further Comments: Portage at one low-water bridge.

Gauge Conversion: Shenandoah River at Front Royal

Feet	Cfs	Feet	Cfs	Feet	Cfs
1.0	409	1.7	997	2.4	1747
1.1	482	1.8	1095	2.5	1866
1.2	558	1.9	1196	2.6	1987
1.3	639	2.0	1300	2.7	2112
1.4	723	2.1	1408	2.8	2238
1.5	811	2.2	1518	2.9	2368
1.6	902	2.3	1631	3.0	2500

THORNTON RIVER

Sections: Fletchers Mill on Highway 620 to Rock Mills on Highway 626, Class II (one at III)

Length of Run: Day trip, 7 miles

Location: Rappahannock County, Virginia

Maps: USGS quads: Washington

Times Runnable: January to mid-April

Permit: None

Gauge: Extrapolate from the USGS gauge on the Rapidan at Culpeper

Source of Levels: National Weather Service, Washington; 703-260-0305.

National Weather Service, Harrisburg; 717-234-6812.

How Reported: Feet and cfs

Interpretation of Levels: If the Rapidan is over 2.0 feet, then there should be enough water on the Thornton. When you get there, use the paddlers' gauge at Fletcher's Mill Bridge on Rt. 620. Minimum (scrapey) is 0 on Fletcher's Mill gauge; high is 2 to 3 feet.

Source of More Information: Coastal Canoeists, PO Box 566, Richmond, VA 23204.

Best Guidebooks: Grove et al., *Appalachian Whitewater, Vol. II;* Corbett, *Virginia Whitewater.*

Further Comments: Watch for occasional strainers and fences.

TYE RIVER

Sections: Nash to Massies Mill, Class II-IV

Length of Run: Day trip, 8.5 miles

Location: Nelson County, Virginia; George Washington National Forest

Maps: USGS quad: Massies Mill

Times Runnable: January to April after heavy rain

Permit: None required

Gauge: Correlate to the Cootes Store gauge on the North Fork of the Shenandoah. There is also a paddlers' gauge at the bridge at Nash put-in.

Source of Levels: James River Basin Canoe Livery, 703-761-7334.

National Weather Service, Washington; 703-260-0305.

National Weather Service, Harrisburg; 717-234-6812.

How Reported: Feet

Interpretation of Levels: If the Cootes Store gauge is 4.5 or higher, then the Tye is probably running. Use the W.D.S. method when you get to the Tye. Minimum is about 200 cfs, and high is about 600. For the paddlers' gauge at the Nash put-in, 0 is low, and 2 feet is getting high.

Source of More Information: USDA Forest Service, Pedlar Ranger District, Jefferson National Forest, 2424 Magnolia Dr., Buena Vista, VA 24416; 703-261-6105, 703-261-6106.

James River Basin Canoe Livery, RFD No. 4, Box 125, Lexington, VA 24450; 703-261-7334.

Best Guidebooks: Grove et al., *Appalachian Whitewater, Vol. II;* Corbett, *Virginia Whitewater.*

Further Comments: The Tye River is probably the most beautiful whitewater river in Virginia.

GENERAL INFORMATION SOURCES FOR VIRGINIA/DISTRICT OF COLUMBIA

The National Weather Service Washington, DC District Office is responsible for the Potomac and Rappahannock River basins. They prepare a recording, updated daily at 10 a.m. and 8 p.m. The 10 a.m. edition is more inclusive, with data for the Monongahela and James River basins.

National Weather Service, Washington; 703-260-0305.

They report the following readings:

Rappahannock River Basin
Rapidan, at Culpeper, VA
Rappahannock, at Remington, VA

Potomac River Basin
North Branch of the Potomac River, at Kitzmiller, MD
Savage River, at Savage, MD
North Branch of the Potomac River, at Cumberland, MD
South Branch of the Potomac River
At Petersburg, WV
At Springfield, WV
Potomac River
At Paw Paw, WV
At Hancock, MD
At Williamsport, MD
At Shepardstown, WV
North Fork of the Shenandoah River
At Cootes Store, VA
At Strasburg, VA
South Fork of the Shenandoah River
At Lynnwood, VA
At Front Royal, VA
Shenandoah River, at Millville, WV
Potomac River
At Point of Rocks, MD
At Little Falls, DC/MD

James River and Tributaries
Maury River, at Buena Vista, VA
James River
At Bent Creek, VA
At Cartersville, VA
Westham gauge at Richmond, VA

Monongahela River and Tributaries
Tygart River, at Belington, WV
Cheat River, at Parsons, WV
Youghiogheny River, at Confluence, PA
Casselman River, at Markleton, PA
Upper Yough, Deep Creek Gauge (at Friendsville)
Big Sandy Creek, at Rockville, WV

The National Weather Service in Richmond reports levels for the James River, the Appomattox River, and tributaries on their recording: National Weather Service, Richmond, VA; 804-226-4423.

They report:

Maury River, at Buena Vista, VA
James River
At Bent Creek, VA
At Cartersville, VA
Westham gauge at Richmond, VA
Appomattox River at Matoaca

The National Weather Service River Forecast Center in Harrisburg, PA acts as the hydrologic service office for the Delaware and Susquehanna River basins: 717-234-6812.

Dialing this line accesses a ring-through recording. On the recording, you'll hear a bunch of Pennsylvania river stages, but if you stay on the line, you can ask the hydrologist for readings on any of the following Virginia rivers:

Potomac River Basin
South River, at Waynesboro
South Fork of the Shenandoah River
At Lynnwood
At Front Royal
North Fork of the Shenandoah River
At Cootes Store
At Strasburg
Shenandoah River, at Riverton
Goose Creek, at Leesburg
Rappahannock River, at Remington
Rapidan River
At Rapidan
At Culpeper
Rappahannock River, at Fredericksburg
Potomac River, at Colonial Beach
James River Basin
Jackson River
At Gathright Dam
At Covington
James River, at Lick Run
Craig River, at Parr
James River, at Buchanan
Maury River, at Buena Vista
James River
At Balcony Falls
At Holcombs Rock
At Lynchburg
At Bent Creek
At Scottsville
At Bremo Bluff
Rivanna River, at Palmyra

James River
  At Columbia
  At Cartersville
  At State Farm
  At Richmond (Westham gauge)
  At City Locks
Appomattox River Basin
Appomattox Rlver
  At Farmville
  At Matoaca
  At Petersburg

WASHINGTON STATE

CISPUS RIVER

Sections: (1) Upper, Road 23 Bridge to North Fork, Class III (one at IV)

             (2) Lower, Road 28 Bridge to Cowlitz River, Class II-III

Length of Run: (1) Day trip, 9 miles

             (2) Day trip, 12 miles

Location: Skamania and Lewis Counties, Gifford Pinchot National Forest

Maps: USGS quads: East Canyon Ridge, Blue Lake, Tower Rock, Greenhorn Buttes and Cowlitz Falls

Times Runnable: April through June

Permit: None required

Gauge: USGS Cispus River at Randle

Source of Levels: National Weather Service, Seattle, Whitewater Hotline; 206-526-8530.

How Reported: Cfs

Interpretation of Levels: On Section (1), you'll have about 70% of the flow at Randle. Minimum is around 1500 cfs, and high is around 2600. On Section (2), minimum is around 1400 cfs, and high is around 3500.

Source of More Information: USDA Forest Service, Randle Ranger District, Gifford Pinchot National Forest, Randle, WA 98377; 206-497-7565.

Best Guidebooks: North, *Washington Whitewater 2.*

Further Comments: Watch out for logjams.

COWLITZ RIVER

Sections: La Wis Wis Campground to Packwood, Class I-II

Length of Run: Day trip, 8 miles

Location: Lewis County, Washington; Gifford Pinchot National Forest

Maps: USGS quads: Packwood (15')

Times Runnable: From mid-April through July and again from November through January. However, the La Wis Wis Campground is closed from mid-November to Memorial Day. If you want to put in there during the winter or spring, you'll need to call the Packwood Ranger District to get access: 206-494-5515. Also, remember that Highways 410 and 123 through Cayuse Pass are often blocked by snow in winter—check with the Department of Transportation at 206-764-4097 before you go.

Permit: None required

Gauge: Cowlitz River at Packwood

Source of Levels: National Weather Service, Seattle, Whitewater Hotline (recording); 206-526-8530.

How Reported: Cfs

Interpretation of Levels: Minimum is about 1200 cfs, and optimum is around 1400 to 3200.

Source of More Information: USDA Forest Service, Gifford Pinchot National Forest, 500 W. 12th St., Vancouver, WA 98660; 206-696-7500.

Best Guidebook: North, *Washington Whitewater 1*.

ELWHA RIVER

Sections: Glines Canyon Dam to US 101, Class II-III (one at IV)

Length of Run: Day trip, 6 miles

Location: Clallam County, Olympic National Park

Maps: USGS quads: Elwha

Times Runnable: November through July

Permit: None required

Gauge: USGS Elwha River at McDonald Bridge

Source of Levels: National Weather Service, Seattle, Whitewater Hotline; 206-526-8530.

How Reported: Cfs

Interpretation of Levels: Optimum is between 1200 and 2600 cfs.

Source of More Information: Olympic National Park, 600 East Park Avenue, Port Angeles, WA 98362; 206-452-4501.

Best Guidebooks: North, *Washington Whitewater 2*.

GRANDE RONDE RIVER

See Oregon.

GREEN RIVER

Sections: Green River Gorge, Kanaskat-Palmer State Park to Flaming Geyser State Park, Class III-IV

Length of Run: Day trip, 14 miles

Location: King County, Washington

Maps: USGS quads: Cumberland, Black Diamond

Times Runnable: Mid-November to June

Permit: None required

Gauge: Green River, below Howard Hansen Dam

Source of Levels: National Weather Service, Seattle, Whitewater Hotline (recording); 206-526-8530.

US Army Corps of Engineers, Howard Hansen Dam; 206-764-3590.

How Reported: Cfs

Interpretation of Levels: Optimum is between 1100 and 2200 cfs.

Source of More Information: Flaming Geyser State Park, 23700 S.E. Flaming Geyser Road, Auburn, WA 98002; 206-931-3930

Kanaskat-Palmer State Park, 32101 Kanaskat-Cumberland Rd., Ravensdale, WA 98051; 206-886-0148.

Best Guidebook: North, *Washington Whitewater 1.*

Further Comments: The gorge of the Green River is the most scenic run in the state of Washington.

HOH RIVER

Sections: National Park Service ranger station to US 101, Class II

Length of Run: Day trip, 21.5 miles

Location: Jefferson County, Washington Mount Ranier National Park

Maps: USGS quads: Mt. Tom (15'), Spruce Mtn. (15')

Times Runnable: Spring and summer

Permit: None required

Gauge: Hoh River below Tom Creek

Source of Levels: National Weather Service, Seattle, Steelheaders' Hotline (recording); 206-526-6087.

How Reported: Cfs

Interpretation of Levels: Optimum is 1000 to 2000 cfs.

Source of More Information: Mount Ranier National Park, Tahoma Woods, Star Route, Ashford, WA 98304; 206-569-2211.

Best Guidebooks: Furrer, *Water Trails of Washington.*

Further Comments: Watch for logjams.

KLICKITAT RIVER
Wild and Scenic River

Sections: Gauging station to Dept. of Wildlife ramp at Leidl Bridge, Class II-III

Length of Run: Day trip, 18 miles

Location: Yakima and Klickitat Counties, Washington

Maps: USGS quads: Jungle Butte, Glenwood, Outlet Falls, Klickitat (15')

Times Runnable: December to June

Permit: The Washington Department of Wildlife requires that you have a conservation or fishing license in order to use their landing. Conservation licenses are available for $8 from bait shops and sporting goods stores.

Gauge: Klickitat River near Pitt

Source of Levels: National Weather Service, Seattle, Whitewater Hotline (recording); 206-526-8530.

How Reported: Cfs

Interpretation of Levels: Minimum is about 1500 cfs recorded at Pitt, and optimum is between 2000 and 3500 cfs. High is between 3200 and 5000. You'll actually have about one-half this flow at the put-in.

Source of More Information: Phil's Guide Service, Highway 141 at BZ Corners, White Salmon, WA 98672; 509-493-2641.

Best Guidebook: North, *Washington Whitewater 1.*

Further Comments: Watch for logjams.

METHOW RIVER

Sections: Carlton to Pateros, Class I-II

Length of Run: Day trip, 26 miles

Location: Okanogan County, Washington; Okanogan National Forest

Maps: USGS quads: Twisp East, Methow, Brewster (15')

Times Runnable: May to mid-July

Permit: The Washington Department of Wildlife requires that you have a conservation or fishing license in order to use their landing at Carlton. Conservation licenses are available for $8 from bait shops and sporting goods stores.

Gauge: Methow River near Pateros

Source of Levels: National Weather Service, Seattle, Whitewater Hotline (recording); 206-526-8530.

How Reported: Cfs

Interpretation of Levels: Optimum is 3000 to 11,000 cfs.

Source of More Information: Alta Lake State Park, 40 Star Route, Pateros, WA 98846; 509-923-2473.

USDA Forest Service, Okanogan National Forest, 1240 S. 2nd St., Okanogan, WA 98840; 509-422-2704.

Best Guidebook: North, *Washington Whitewater 1.*

Further Comments: The Methow is the best example of a big-water run in Washington.

NACHES RIVER

Sections:
(1) Sawmill Flat Campground along Highway 410 to Upper Nile Bridge, Class II (one at III)
(2) Upper Nile Bridge to the confluence with the Tieton River, Class II-III

Length of Run:
(1) Day trip, 13 miles
(2) Day trip, 13 miles

Location: Yakima County, Washington; Wenatchee National Forest

Maps: USGS quads: Manastash, Nile, Milk Canyon, Tieton Lake

Times Runnable: From mid-April through July. Remember that Highway 410 through Cayuse and Chinook Passes is often blocked by snow in winter—check with the Department of Transportation at 206-764-4097 before you go.

Permit: None required

Gauge: Naches River near Cliffdell

Source of Levels: National Weather Service, Seattle, Whitewater Hotline (recording); 206-526-8530.

How Reported: Cfs

Interpretation of Levels: Optimum is between 1200 and 2600 cfs.

Source of More Information: USDA Forest Service, Naches Ranger District, Wenatchee National Forest, 630 Highway 12, Naches, WA 9 8937; 509-653-2205.

Best Guidebook: North, *Washington Whitewater 1.*

NOOKSACK RIVER, NORTH FORK

Sections: Douglas Fir Camp to Maple Falls, Class II-III

Length of Run: Day trip, 9 miles

Location: Whatcom County, Washington; Mt. Baker-Snoqualmie National Forest

Maps: USGS quads: Mt. Baker (15'), Maple Falls

Times Runnable: Year-round unless it is too high

Permit: None required

Gauge: Nooksack River at Deming

Source of Levels: National Weather Service, Seattle, Whitewater Hotline (recording); 206-526-8530.

How Reported: Cfs

Interpretation of Levels: Optimum is between 600 and 1600 cfs. High is 3000.

Source of More Information: USDA Forest Service, Glacier Ranger District, Mount Baker-Snoqualmie National Forest, Glacier, WA 98244; 206-599-2714.

Best Guidebook: North, *Washington Whitewater 1.*

Further Comments: Watch for numerous logjams.

SAUK RIVER, UPPER

Sections: Bedal Campground to Whitechuck, Class I-II (one at III)

Length of Run: Day trip, 8 miles

Location: Snohomish County, Washington; Mount Baker-Snoqualmie National Forest

Maps: USGS quads: Bedal, Whitechuck

Times Runnable: Late May to early July

Permit: Not required

Gauge: Sauk River near Sauk

Source of Levels: National Weather Service, Seattle, Whitewater Hotline (recording); 206-526-8530.

How Reported: Cfs

Interpretation of Levels: Minimum for kayaks is about 4000 cfs at Sauk, and for rafts is 5500. Optimum is 6500, and 12,000 is very high. You'll be boating on about 25% of the water read at Sauk.

Source of More Information: USDA Forest Service, Darrington Ranger District, Mount Baker-Snoqualmie National Forest, Darrington, WA 98241; 206-436-1155.

Best Guidebook: North, *Washington Whitewater 1.*

SAUK RIVER, MIDDLE

Sections: (1) Whitechuck to Darrington, Class II-III (to IV high)
(2) Darrington to Skagit River, Class I-II

Length of Run: (1) Day trip, 11 miles
(2) Day trip, 16 miles

Location: Snohomish County, Washington; Mount Baker-Snoqualmie National Forest

Maps: USGS quads: Whitechuck, Silverton (15')

Times Runnable: May to July

Permit: Not required

Gauge: Sauk River, near Sauk

Source of Levels: National Weather Service, Seattle, Whitewater Hotline (recording); 206-526-8530.

How Reported: Cfs

Interpretation of Levels: Optimum is 4000 to 10,000 cfs.

Source of More Information: USDA Forest Service, Darrington Ranger District, Mount Baker-Snoqualmie National Forest, Darrington, WA 98241; 206-436-1155.

Best Guidebook: North, *Washington Whitewater 1.*

Further Comments: The Forest Service rates the first 7 miles of Section (1) as Class IV–V.

SKAGIT RIVER
Wild and Scenic River

Sections: Goodell Creek to Copper Creek, along Highway 20, Class I-II (one at III)

Length of Run: Day trip, 8 miles

Location: Skagit and Whatcom Counties, Washington; North Cascades National Park

Maps: USGS quads: Marble Mount (15')

Times Runnable: Year-round (dam-released)

Permit: Registration is required by the National Park Service. Fill out a self-issuing form at the put-in or at the Marblemount Ranger Station.

Reservations: Not required

Restrictions: Pack out trash (you should do this everywhere!). Fires are allowed only in designated areas. No camping on the river.

Gauge: Skagit River at Newhalem

Source of Levels: National Weather Service, Seattle, Whitewater Hotline (recording); 206-526-8530.

How Reported: Cfs

Interpretation of Levels: Optimum is between 1500 and 5500 cfs.

Source of More Information: District Manager, National Park Service, North Cascades National Park, Marblemount, WA 98267; 206-873-4590.

Best Guidebook: North, *Washington Whitewater 1.*

SKYKOMISH RIVER

Sections: (1) City of Skykomish to Money Creek, Class II+
(2) Index to Goldbar, Class III (one at IV-V)

Length of Run: (1) Day trip, 9 miles
(2) Day trip, 7 miles

Location: Snohomish County, Washington; Mount Baker-Snoqualmie National Forest

Maps: USGS quads: Index (15')

Times Runnable: Year-round, with the exception of August and September

Permit: The Washington Department of Wildlife requires that you have a conservation or fishing license in order to use their landing at Goldbar. Conservation licenses are available for $8 from bait shops and sporting goods stores.

Restrictions: The Forest Service requires boaters to wear helmets and PFDs. Seems reasonable to me.

Gauge: Skykomish near Goldbar

Source of Levels: National Weather Service, Seattle, Whitewater Hotline (recording); 206-526-8530.

How Reported: Cfs

Interpretation of Levels: Optimum is 2000 to 5000 cfs.

Source of More Information: USDA Forest Service, Skykomish Ranger District, Mount Baker-Snoqualmie National Forest, 1022 First Ave., Seattle, WA 98104; 206-442-5400.

Best Guidebook: North, *Washington Whitewater 1.*

Further Comments: There is one Class IV-V rapid on this section, Boulder Drop, that is considerably more difficult than the other rapids on this section. It is often portaged.

SKYKOMISH RIVER, NORTH FORK

Sections: Galena to Confluence, Class III-IV

Length of Run: Day trip, 11 miles

Location: Snohomish County, Mount Baker—Snoqualmie National Forest

Maps: USGS quads: Monte Cristo, Blanca Lake, and Index (15')

Times Runnable: May and June

Permit: None required

Gauge: USGS Skykomish River at Goldbar

Source of Levels: National Weather Service, Seattle, Whitewater Hotline; 206-526-8530

How Reported: Cfs

Interpretation of Levels: You'll find about 40% of the flow at Goldbar once you get up to the North Fork. For that reason, there'll need to be plenty of water at Goldbar. In terms of the Goldbar gauge, inimum for kayaks is 4000, and for rafts 6000. Optimum is between 6000 and 12,000.

Source of More Information: USDA Forest Service, Skykomish Ranger District, Mount Baker-Snolqualmie National Forest, 1022 First Ave., Seattle, WA 98104; 206-442-5400.

Best Guidebooks: North, *Washington Whitewater 2.*

SNOQUALMIE RIVER, MIDDLE FORK

Sections:
(1) Taylor River to Concrete Bridge, Class III
(2) Concrete Bridge to Tanner, Class III

Length of Run:
(1) Day trip, 7 miles
(2) Day trip, 7 miles

Location: King County, Washington

Maps: USGS quads: Mount Si (15'), Bandera (15')

Times Runnable: December and January, and May to June

Permit: None required

Gauge: Snoqualmie River, Middle Fork

Source of Levels: National Weather Service, Seattle, Whitewater Hotline (recording); 206-526-8530.

How Reported: Cfs

Interpretation of Levels: Optimum is between 1500 and 3000 cfs.

Source of More Information: USDA Forest Service North Bend Ranger District, Mount Baker-Snoqualmie National Forest, North Bend, WA 98045; 206-888-1421.

Best Guidebook: North, *Washington Whitewater 1.*

SNOQUALMIE RIVER, NORTH FORK

Sections: Deep Creek to Swinging Bridge, Class II and III

Length of Run: Day trip, 6 miles

Location: King County, Snoqualmie National Forest

Maps: USGS quads: Mount Si (15'), Snoqualmie

Times Runnable: April through June

Permit: None required

Gauge: USGS Snoqualmie River, North Fork

Source of Levels: National Weather Service, Seattle, Whitewater Hotline; 206-526-8530.

How Reported: Cfs

Interpretation of Levels: Between 600 and 1600 cfs is about right.

Source of More Information: USDA Forest Service, North Bend Ranger District, Mount Baker-Snoqualmie National Forest, North Bend, WA 98045; 206-888-1421.

Best Guidebooks: North, *Washington Whitewater 2.*

Further Comments: Its great diversity of whitewater rapids makes the Snoqualmie a favorite of University of Washington boaters.

SPOKANE RIVER

Sections: (1) Upper, Harvard Park to Walk-in-the-Wild Park, Class II
(2) Lower, T. J. Meenach Bridge to Plese Flat, Class II and III

Length of Run: (1) Day trip, 6 miles
(2 Day trip, 6 miles

Location: Spokane County

Maps: USGS Quads: Section (1): Liberty Lake, Greenacres; Section (2): Airway Heights, Spokane NW

Times Runnable: March through June

Permit: None required

Gauge: USGS Spokane River at Spokane

Source of Levels: National Weather Service, Seattle, Whitewater Hotline; 206-526-8530.

How Reported: Cfs

Interpretation of Levels: Minimum is 4000. Both runs are good anywhere between 4000 and 19,000. Above 19,000 the rapids begin to wash out and there are few places left to play.

Source of More Information: Riverside State Park, 4427 Aubrey Light Parkway, Spokane, WA 99205; 509-456-3964.

Best Guidebooks: North, *Washington Whitewater 2.*

Further Comments: A popular local river for Spokane area boaters.

SUIATTLE RIVER

Sections: Rat Trap Bridge to Sauk River Bridge, Class II-III

Length of Run: Day trip, 13 miles

Location: Skagit County, Washington; Mount Baker-Snoqualmie National Forest

Maps: USGS quads: Prairie Mtn., Darrington

Times Runnable: Year-round except September

Permit: None required

Gauge: Extrapolate from the Sauk River at Sauk (below the confluence of the Suiattle)

Source of Levels: National Weather Service, Seattle, Whitewater Hotline (recording); 206-526-8530.

How Reported: Cfs

Interpretation of Levels: Levels between 2500 and 9000 cfs on the Sauk should make for enough water on the Suiattle.

Source of More Information: USDA Forest Service, Darrington Ranger District, Mount Baker-Snoqualmie National Forest, Darrington, WA 98045; 206-888-1421

Best Guidebook: North, *Washington Whitewater 1.*

TIETON RIVER

Sections: Rimrock to Windy Point, Class II-III+

Length of Run: Day trip, 13 miles

Location: Yakima County, Washington; Wenatchee National Forest

Maps: USGS quads: Tieton Basin, Weddle Canyon

Times Runnable: After releases from Rimrock Dam in September for the salmon spawning run

Permit: None required

Gauge: Tieton River at Rimrock

Source of Levels: Bureau of Reclamation, Yakima Project Office; 509-575-5854.

How Reported: Cfs, schedule of releases

Interpretation of Levels: Minimum for kayaks is about 700 cfs. Optimum is between 1000 and 2000 cfs.

Source of More Information: Bureau of Reclamation, Yakima Project Office, PO Box 1749, 1917 March Rd., Yakima, WA 98907; 509-575-5848.

USDA Forest Service, Naches Ranger District, Wenatchee National Forest, 630 Highway 12, Natches, WA 98937; 509-653-2205.

Best Guidebook: North, *Washington Whitewater 1.*

Further Comments: There is one dangerous dam to portage. Watch for logjams.

TOUTLE RIVER

Sections: Toutle to Tower Road Bridge, Class III-IV

Length   Day trip, 10 miles
of Run:

Location: Cowlitz County

Maps: USGS quads: Silver Lake and Castle Rock (15')

Times Runnable: November through June

Permit: None required

Gauge: Extrapolate from the Kalama River at Kalama. The gauge on the Toutle at Tower Road is not too reliable due to tremendous amounts of silt being washed downstream from the Mt. St. Helens eruption.

Source of Levels: National Weather Service, Seattle, Whitewater Hotline; 206-526-8530.

How Reported: Cfs

Interpretation of Levels: Between 800 and 2000 cfs on the Kalama should make for enough water on the Toutle.

Source of More Information: Visitors' Center, Mt. St. Helens National Volcanic Monument, 309 Spirit Lake Highway, Castle Rock, WA 98611; 206-274-6644.

Best Guidebooks: North, *Washington Whitewater 2.*

Further Comments: Boating the Toutle is great way to view the incredible aftermath of the Mt. St. Helens eruption.

WASHOUGAL RIVER

Sections: (1) Dougan Falls to Salmon Falls, Class III (one at IV)
                    (2) Below Salmon Falls to above Washougal, Class III-IV

Length   (1) Day trip, 6 miles
of Run: (2) Day trip, 7 miles

Location: Skamania County, Washington

Maps: USGS quads: Washougal, Bridal Veil (15')

Times Runnable: November to May after rain

Permit: None required

Gauge: None

Source of Levels: None

Interpretation of Levels: Use the W.D.S. method. Around 1500 cfs should be about right.

Source of More Information: Willamette Kayak and Canoe Club, PO Box 1062, Corvallis, OR 97331.

Sundance Expeditions, 14494 Galice Rd., Merlin, OR 97532; 503-479-8508.

Best Guidebooks: Willamette Kayak and Canoe Club, *Soggy Sneakers Guide.*

Further Comments: Make sure to take out at the right spot for Section (1); a falls is downstream.

WENATCHEE RIVER

Sections: Leavenworth to Monitor, Class II-III

Length   Day trip, 22 miles
of Run:

Location: Chelan County, Washington; Wenatchee National Forest

Maps: USGS quads: Leavenworth (15'), Cashmere, Monitor

Times Runnable: Late April to mid-July

Permit: The Washington Department of Wildlife requires that you have a conservation or fishing license in order to use their landing in Peshastin at mile 4.5, but if you launch in Leavenworth and take out in Monitor you won't need it. Conservation licenses are available for $8 from bait shops and sporting goods stores.

Source of Levels: National Weather Service, Seattle, Whitewater Hotline (recording); 206-526-8530.

How Reported: Cfs

Interpretation of Levels: Minimum for kayaks is about 1500 cfs, and around 3000 is minimum for big rafts. Optimum is between 4000 and 13,000 cfs, and high is 20,000 cfs.

Source of More Information: USDA Forest Service, Leavenworth Ranger District, Wenatchee National Forest, 600 Sherbourne, Leavenworth, WA 98826; 509-782-1413.

USDA Forest Service, Lake Wenatchee Ranger District, Wenatchee National Forest, Star Route, Box 109, Leavenworth, WA 98826; 509-763-3211.

Best Guidebook: North, *Washington Whitewater 1.*

Further Comments: Portage the irrigation dam at Dryden.

WHITE RIVER

Sections: West Fork Road to Bridge Camp, Class II–III

Length of Run: Day trip, 13.5 miles

Location: King and Pierce Counties

Maps: USGS quads: Greenwater (15'), Enumclaw (15')

Times Runnable: December through July

Permit: None required

Gauge: Army Corps White River above Buckley

Source of Levels: National Weather Service, Seattle, Whitewater Hotline; 206-526-8530.

How Reported: Cfs

Interpretation of Levels: Optimum is between 1000 and 3400.

Source of More Information: Federation State Forest; 206-663-2207.

Best Guidebooks: North, *Washington Whitewater 2.*

Further Comments: A super play river, littered with holes!

WHITE SALMON RIVER
Wild and Scenic River

Sections:
(1) Indian reservation to fish hatchery, Class IV+ (plus one 14-foot waterfall, generally portaged)
(2) Green Truss Bridge to Zig-Zag Canyon, Class III+ (one at IV)
(3) Above BZ Corners to BZ Corners, Class II
(4) BZ Corners to Northwestern Lake, Class III-IV

Length of Run:
(1) Day trip, 2 miles
(2) Day trip, 5 miles
(3) Day trip, 2 miles
(4) Day trip, 7 miles

Location: Klickitat County, Washington

Maps: USGS quads: Trout Lake, Willard (15'), Hussum (15')

Times Runnable: Most of the year, except August through October

Permit: The launch site for Section (4) at BZ Corner is privately owned, and the folks there charge a fee for boaters to launch.

Gauge: White Salmon River near Underwood

Source of Levels: National Weather Service, Seattle, Whitewater Hotline (recording); 206-526-8530.

How Reported: Cfs

Interpretation of Levels: Minimum is about 500, and optimum is 1000 to 1500 cfs. Above 1500 is high (about Class IV overall).

Source of More Information: Phil's Guide Service, Highway 141, BZ Corners, White Salmon, WA 98672; 509-493-2641.

Best Guidebook: North, *Washington Whitewater 1.*

Further Comments: Hussum's Falls (8 feet) on Section (4) is rarely run by rafts.

WIND RIVER

Sections: Stabler to High Bridge, Class V

Length of Run: Day trip, 6 miles

Location: Skamania County, Washington; Gifford Pinchot National Forest

Maps: USGS quads: Wind River (15'), Carson

Times Runnable: Winter and spring after rain or snowmelt

Permit: None required

Gauge: None. Extrapolate from the Clackmas at Three Lynx

Source of Levels: National Weather Service, Seattle, Whitewater Hotline (recording); 206-526-8530.

How Reported: Cfs

Interpretation of Levels: If the Clackmas is over 900, then the Wind River is usually O.K.

Source of More Information: USDA Forest Service, Gifford Pinchot National Forest, 500 W. 12th St., Vancouver, WA 98660; 206-696-7500.

Best Guidebooks: Willamette Kayak and Canoe Club, *Soggy Sneakers Guide.*

GENERAL INFORMATION SOURCES
FOR WASHINGTON STATE

The National Weather Service River Forecast Center maintains two recordings that provide river levels for Washington rivers; both recordings report levels for all rivers in cfs; gauge height is reported for a few as well, for the convenience of fishermen: National Weather Service, Seattle, Whitewater Hotline (recording); 206-526-8530.

The first recording reports the following readings:

Satsop River, near Satsop
Elwha River, near McDonald bridge
Nisqually River, at McKenna
White River, below Clearwater
Green River, below Howard Hansen Dam
Cedar River, near Landsburg
Skykomish River, near Goldbar
Snoqualmie River, Middle Fork
Snoqualmie River, North Fork
Snoqualmie River, below the Falls
Stillagaumish River, South Fork
Skagit River, at Newhalem
Sauk River, near Sauk
Nooksack River, at Deming
Methow River, near Pateros
Wenatchee River, at Peshastin
Yakima River, at Ellensburg
Naches River, near Cliffdell
Klickitat River, near Pitt
White Salmon River, near Underwood
Cowlitz River, at Packwood
Cispus River, near Randle
Toutle River, at Tower Road

The following are reported in gauge height only:

Green River, near Auburn
Snoqualmie River, near Carnation
Stillaguamish River, North Fork

Skagit River, at Concrete
Lewis River, at Woodland
Kalama River, near Kalama
Cowlitz River, below Mayfield Dam

A second recording, maintained by the River Forecast Center in Seattle, is primarily for the convenience of fishermen, but it provides some useful information for paddlers, too. Most of these are reported in gauge height: National Weather Service River Forecast Center, Seattle, Steelheaders' Hotline; 206-526-6087.

They report the following:

Nooksack River, at Deming
Skagit River, near Concrete
Sauk River, at Sauk
Stillaguamish River, North Fork
Skykomish River, near Goldbar
Snoqualmie River, near Carnation
Tolt River, near Carnation
Cedar River, at Renton
Green River, near Auburn
Puyallup River, near Puyallup
Nisqually River, at McKenna
Satsop River, at Satsop
Comlitz River, below Mayfield Dam
Hoh River, below Tom Creek
Snoqualmie River
    North Fork
    Middle Fork
    South Fork
White River, above Mud Mt. Dam
Stillaguamish River, South Fork
Green River, below Howard Hansen Dam
Toutle River, at Tower Rd.
Kalama River, near Kalama

For further information on river flow, or for rivers not on the recordings, you can call the National Weather Service in Seattle at 206-526-6087.

WEST VIRGINIA

BIG SANDY CREEK

Sections: (1) Bruceton Mills to Rockville, Class II-IV
(2) Rockville to the Cheat River, Class IV–V, one VI

Length of Run: (1) Day trip, 6.0 miles
(2) Day trip, 5.5 miles

Location: Preston County, West Virginia

Maps: USGS quads: Bruceton Mills, Valley Point

Times Runnable: Winter and spring

Permit: Not required

Gauge: Rockville gauge

Source of Levels: National Weather Service, Pittsburgh; 412-644-2890.

How Reported: Feet

Additional Gauge: Paddlers' gauge painted on bridge at Bruceton

Source of Levels: Visual inspection only

Interpretation of Levels: In terms of the Rockville gauge, comfortable low for this run is about 5.8 feet; very high is 6.5 to 7 feet. In terms of the Bruceton gauge, 0 is low and 2 feet is very high.

Source of More Information: Precision Rafting, PO Box 185, Friendsville, MD 21531; 301-746-5290.

Upper Yough Whitewater Expeditions, PO Box 158, Friendsville, MD 21531; 301-746-5808.

Best Guidebooks: Davidson et al., *Wildwater West Virginia, Vol. I;* Grove et al., *Appalachian Whitewater, Vol. II.*

Further Comments: The lower Big Sandy is a tough expert run.

Diana Kendrick on Wonder Falls of the Big Sandy. Photo by Paul Marshall.

Gauge Conversion: The Rockville reading from the National Weather Service is approximately equal to (3/4 [Bruceton +1]) +5.

Big Sandy Creek at Rockville:

Feet	Cfs	Feet	Cfs
5.0	200	7.0	1120
5.2	250	7.2	1280
5.4	310	7.4	1440
5.6	375	7.6	1600
5.8	445	7.8	1770
6.0	530	8.0	1950
6.2	620	9.0	3000
6.4	720	9.5	3600
6.6	830	10.0	4250
6.8	960	—	—

BLACKWATER RIVER

Sections: North Fork Junction to Hendricks, Class IV-V (with several at VI)

Length of Run: Day trip, 7 miles

Location: Tucker County, West Virginia; Monongahela National Forest

Maps: USGS quads: Mozark Mtn. Also: Monongahela National Forest Visitor Map

Times Runnable: Early spring

Permit: None required

Gauge: None on the Blackwater. Extrapolate from the Parsons gauge on the Cheat.

Source of Levels: National Weather Service, Pittsburgh; 412-644-2890.

National Weather Service, Washington; 703-899-7378.

How Reported: Feet

Interpretation of Levels: A reading from Parsons between 4 and 5.5 suggests adequate water. When you get to Hendricks Bridge, look at the water. Very low but runnable is probably O.K., but apparently good water is probably too much.

Source of More Information: USDA Forest Service, Monongahela National Forest, Sycamore St., PO Box 1548, Elkins, WV 26241; 304-478-3251.

Blackwater Falls State Park, WV 32, Davis, WV 26260; 304-259-5216.

Best Guidebooks: Davidson et al., *Wildwater West Virginia. Vol. I;* Grove et al., *Appalachian Whitewater. Vol. II.*

BLUESTONE RIVER

Sections: (1) Spanishburg to Eads Mill, Class II-III.
(2) Eads Mill to Bluestone State Park, Class II-III.

Length of Run: (1) Day trip, 7 miles
(2) Day trip, 18 miles

Location: Mercer and Summers Counties, WV

Maps: USGS quads: Athens, Flat Top and Pipestem

Times Runnable: February to April

Permit: None required

Gauge: USGS Bluestone River at Pipestem

Source of Levels: US Army Corps of Engineers, Huntington; 304-529-5127.

US Army Corps of Engineers, Bluestone Dam; 304-466-0156.

National Weather Service, Charleston; 304-342-7771.

How Reported: Cfs

Additional Gauge: Paddlers' gauge at Eads Mill Bridge

Source of Levels: None

How Reported: Feet

Interpretation of Levels: Between 5' and 9' at the Eads Mill Bridge gauge is about right.

Source of More Information: Bluestone State Park, Box 3, Athens Star Route, Hinton, WV 25951; 304-466-1922.

Pipestem State Park, Pipestem WV 25979; 304-466-1800; 800-642-9058 (outside WV).

New River Scenic Whitewater Tours, PO Box 637, Hinton WV 25951; 304-466-2248; 800-292-0880 (outside WV).

Best Guidebooks: Davidson et al., *Wildwater West Virginia II.*

Further Comments: The Bluestone offers mile after mile of intermediate whitewater as it rushes through a spectacular chasm on its way to join the New River!

CACAPON RIVER

Sections: Capon Bridge to WV Rt. 127, Class I-III

Length   Day trip, 12 miles
of Run:

Location: Hampshire County, West Virginia

Maps: USGS quad: Capon Bridge

Times Runnable: Winter, spring, and after heavy summer rain

Permit: None required

Gauge: Extrapolate from the USGS Cootes Store gauge on the North Fork of the Shenandoah in Virginia.

Source of Levels: National Weather Service, Maryland; 301-260-0305.

National Weather Service, Harrisburg; 717-234-6812.

How Reported: Feet

Additional Gauge: Paddlers' gauge at Capon Bridge

Source of Levels: Visual inspection only.

How Reported: Feet

Interpretation of Levels: On the Capon Bridge gauge, minimum is zero and high is 3 to 4 feet. If the North Fork of the Shenandoah at Cootes Store is between 3 to 5 feet, then the Cacapon should be up.

Best Guidebooks: Davidson et al., *Wildwater West Virginia, Vol. I;* Grove et al., *Appalachian Whitewater,. Vol.II*

CHEAT RIVER

Sections: Narrows, below Rowlesburg to Lick Run, Class II-IV Canyon, WV 26 Bridge to Jenkinsburg Bridge, Class III-V

Length   (1) 5.0 miles
of Run: (2) 11.0 miles

Location: Preston County, West Virginia

Maps: USGS quads: Kingwood, Rowlesburg, Valley Point

Times Runnable: Almost all year

Permit: None required

Gauge: USGS gauge at the WV Route 26 Bridge in Albright.

Source of Levels: National Weather Service, Pittsburgh; 412-644-2890.

Cheat Canyon Campground; 304-329-1299.

How Reported: Feet

Interpretation of Levels: Minimum for run at Albright is about 1 foot; moderate is 2 to 3 feet; and high is 3 to 5 feet.

Source of More Information: Cheat River Outfitters, PO Box 134, Albright, WV 26519; 304-329-2024.

Best Guidebooks: Grove et al., *Appalachian Whitewater, Vol. II;* Davidson et al., *Wildwater West Virginia, Vol. I.*

Further Comments: Since the flood of 1985 the Cheat has become somewhat more difficult.

Gauge Conversion: Cheat River at Parsons

Feet	Cfs	Feet	Cfs
2.0	102	5.4	3280
2.5	255	5.6	3650
3.0	500	5.8	4050
3.2	620	6.0	4450
3.4	760	6.2	4900
3.6	900	6.4	5400
3.8	1080	6.6	5900
4.0	1280	6.8	6400
4.2	1500	7.0	6900
4.4	1750	7.2	7500
4.6	2020	7.4	8100
4.8	2300	7.6	8700
5.0	2600	7.8	9300
5 2	2940	8.0	9900

Cyclotron Rapid, Upper Coliseum, Cheat Canyon. Photo by Paul Marshall.

CHEAT RIVER, LAUREL FORK

Sections: US 33 Bridge to Jenningston, Class III-IV

Length of Run: Day trip, 13 miles

Location: Randolph and Tucker Counties, West Virginia; Monongahela National Forest

Maps: USGS quads: Harman. Also: Monongahela National Forest Map

Times Runnable: Late winter and spring

Permit: None required

Gauge: Parsons gauge

Source of Levels: National Weather Service, Pittsburgh; 412-644-2890.

How Reported: Feet

Additional Gauge: A paddlers' gauge is located on the right side of the Highway 33 bridge abutment.

Source of Levels: Visual inspection only.

Interpretation of Levels: In terms of the Parsons gauge, low for this run is about 5 feet, and high is about 7 feet. In terms of the Route 33 bridge gauge, low is 0.3 feet, and high is 1.5 feet.

Source of More Information: Cheat River Outfitters, PO Box 134, Albright, WV 26519; 304-329-2024.

USDA Forest Service, Monongahela National Forest, Sycamore St., PO Box 1548, Elkins, WV 26241; 304-478-3251.

Canaan Valley State Park, Rt 1, Box 39, Davis, WV 26260; 304-866-4121.

Best Guidebooks: Grove et al., *Appalachian Whitewater, Vol. II;* Davidson et al., *Wildwater West Virginia, Vol. I.*

THE CRANBERRY RIVER

Sections:
(1) Above Cranberry Recreation Area, Class II-IV
(2) Cranberry Recreation Area to Big Rock Campground, Class IV-V
(3) Webster County line to the Gauley, Class II-IV

Length of Run:
(1) Day trip, 15 miles
(2) Day trip, 6 miles
(3) Day trip, 7 miles

Location: Nicholas, Pocohontas, and Webster Counties, West Virginia; Monongahela National Forest

Maps: USGS quads: Webster Springs SE, Webster Springs SW, Lobelia, Camden on Gauley. Also: Monongahela National Forest Visitor Map.

Times Runnable: Late winter and spring after rain

Permit: None required

Gauge: A USGS gauge is located at the bridge leading across the Cranberry from Forest Service Road 76 to the Woodbine Recreation Area.

Source of Levels: US Army Corps of Engineers, Huntington; 304-529-5127.

How Reported: Feet

Interpretation of Levels: On the Woodbine Gauge, 3.5 feet is considered low, and 5 feet high.

Source of More Information: Class VI River Runners, PO Box 78, Lansing, WV 25862; 304-574-0704.

USDA Forest Service, Monongahela National Forest, Sycamore St., PO Box 1548, Elkins, WV 26241; 304-478-3251.

Best Guidebooks: Davidson et al., *Wildwater West Virginia, Vol. II.*

ELK RIVER, BACK FORK

Sections: Three Falls Section, Sugar Creek at Breece, Class III-IV

Length of Run: Day trip, 5.5 miles

Location: Webster County, West Virginia

Maps: USGS quads: Bergoo, Skelt, and Webster Springs

Times Runnable: Late winter and spring after rain

Permit: Not required

Gauge: Webster Springs gauge

Source of Levels: US Army Corps of Engineers, Huntington; 304-529-5127.

National Weather Service, Pittsburgh; 412-644-2890.

How Reported: Feet

Interpretation of Levels: Low is about 5.8 feet, and high is 6.1

Best Guidebooks: Grove et al., *Appalachian Whitewater, Vol. II;* Davidson et al., *Wildwater West Virginia, Vol. II.*

Gauge Conversion: Elk River below Webster Springs

Feet	Cfs	Feet	Cfs
5.4	1002	6.3	2017
5.5	1.100	6.4	2155
5.6	1 196	6.5	2300
5.7	1298	6.6	2443
5.8	1404	6.7	2591
5.9	1516	6.8	2744
6.0	1633	6.9	2902
6.1	1756	7.0	3095
6.2	1883	—	—

THE GAULEY RIVER

Sections:
    (1) Upper, Summersville Dam to Koontz Flume, Class IV-V
    (2) Lower, Koontz Flume to Swiss, Class III-IV
    (Other put-in and take-out options exist.)

Length of Run:
    (1) Day trip, 15 miles
    (2) Day trip, 10.5 miles

Location: Nicholas and Fayette Counties, West Virginia

Maps: USGS quads: (1) Summersville Dam and Ansted

Times Runnable: In October of 1986, as part of the Water Resources Development Act of 1986, Congress made whitewater recreation an official project purpose of the Summersville Dam, mandating a minimum of 20 days of recreational releases during the fall flood control drawdown. The release schedule for the following year is

An open boater takes on Pillow Rock. Photo by Anne Penny.

announced in January. Scheduled releases occur during 20 days in September and October. Schedules can be obtained from outfitters or the US Army Corps (see below). Unscheduled releases can occur after periods of heavy rain; check if you are in the area.

Permit: None required

Gauge: Belva gauge, below the confluence of the Meadow

Source of Levels: US Army Corps of Engineers, Huntington; 304-529-5127.

How Reported: Feet

Additional Gauge: Summersville gauge (release from dam)

Source of Levels: US Army Corps of Engineers, Huntington; 304-529-5127.

US Army Corps of Engineers, Summersville Dam; 304-872-5809.

How Reported: Feet and cfs

Interpretation of Levels: The National Weather Service at Charleston provides the Belva gauge reading, located downstream of the influx of the Meadow. The recording at the Summersville Dam separately reports the Summersville gauge, in feet and cfs, reflecting the amount of water being released at the dam and the Mount Lookout gauge, reflecting the amount of water on the Meadow in cfs. In terms of the Summersville release, minimum for the Gauley is about 700 cfs; standard fall release is about 2400 (plus the influx from the Meadow above Lost Paddle Rapid); high is 5000.

Source of More Information: Class VI River Runners, PO Box 78, Lansing, WV 25862; 304-574-0704.

Huntington District, US Army Corps of Engineers, 502 Eighth St., Huntington, WV 25701-2070; 304-529-5451.

Best Guidebooks: Grove et al., *Appalachian Whitewater, Vol. II;* Davidson et al., *Wildwater West Virginia, Vol. II.*

Further Comments: The Gauley River is the big-shouldered tough guy of Southeastern rivers. The rapids are long, wide, powerful, and complex. Plenty of strategically placed and undercut sandstone boulders add to the river's panache.

If you're a good boater you'll find the Gauley addictive; there's nothing else that matches it. But if you're not ready for it, you'll be in for an ugly time.

My memory of my first run down the Gauley is still acute. There were about 10 boaters in my group, from Kentucky, North Carolina, and Tennessee. About half had made the run before; the rest of us were first-timers. On that first run, Lost Paddle—the big dog of all the Gauley rapids—looked darn intimidating from the top. Drop after drop, boulder after boulder, and complex as all-get-out. About halfway down, the last three or four of us ended up in the same eddy, and the following desperate conversation ensued:

"Where do we go next?"

"Homeboy, I was following you. Haven't you run this before?"

"Nope."

"Anybody know where we are?"

"Nope. Haven't a clue. It all looks like certain death."

"We're doomed."

We eventually decided to hang out a while until another group passed, and then we followed them safely to the bottom. Since then, I've learned one route through Lost Paddle; there must be loads of other ways to go, but somehow I've never been interested in exploring.

Gauge Conversion: Conversions of the Belva gauge to cfs:

Feet	Cfs	Feet	Cfs
1	110	10	17000
2	570	11	20000
3	1500	12	23100
4	2900	13	26200
5	4540	14	29400
6	6400	15	32600
7	8500	16	35900
8	11000	17	39200
9	14000	18	42600

Entering Iron Ring on the Gauley. Photo by Dennis Rhodes.

LOST RIVER

Sections: Dry Gorge Section, WV 55 Bridge above Wardensville to WV 259 Bridge below Wardensville, Class II-IV

Length of Run: Day trip, 6.0 miles

Location: Hardy County, West Virginia

Maps: USGS quad: Wardensville

Times Runnable: November through April

Permit: None required

Gauge: Extrapolate from the Capon Bridge paddlers' gauge on the Cacapon River, downstream.

Source of Levels: Visual inspection only.

How Reported: Feet

Additional Gauge: Extrapolate from the USGS Cootes Store gauge on the North Fork of the Shenandoah.

Source of Levels: National Weather Service, Washington; 703-899-7378.

National Weather Service, Harrisburg; 717-234-2257.

How Reported: Feet

Additional Gauge: Paddlers' gauge on the Lost River at the WV 55 Bridge (at the put-in)

Source of Levels: None. Visual inspection only.

How Reported: Feet

Interpretation of Levels: The Capon Bridge gauge on the Cacapon should read about 2.5 feet for optimum levels on the Lost River; the North Fork of the Shenandoah should be almost 4 feet. In terms of the WV 55 bridge paddlers' gauge, minimum is about 0, and high is 3 or 4 feet.

Source of More Information: Lost River State Park, Mathias, WV 26812; 304-897-5372.

Best Guidebooks: Grove et al., *Appalachian Whitewater, Vol. II;* Davidson et al., *Wildwater West Virginia, Vol. I.*

MEADOW RIVER

Sections:	(1) Upper, East Rainelle to Russellville, Class III-V
	(2) Middle, Nallen to the US 19 Bridge, Class IV
	(3) Lower, US 19 Bridge to the confluence with the Upper Gauley, and continuing to Koontz Flume, Class V-VI (Class IV and V on the Gauley)
Length of Run:	(1) Day trip, 15 miles
	(2) Day trip, 5 miles
	(3) Day trip, 5 miles on Meadow and 4 more on Gauley

Location: Nicholas and Fayette Counties, West Virginia

Maps: USGS quads: Rainelle, Corliss, Winona, Summersville Dam

Times Runnable: Late winter and spring or after heavy rain

Permit: None required

Gauge: Mount Lookout gauge

Source of Levels: US Army Corps of Engineers, Huntington; 304-529-5127.

US Army Corps of Engineers, Summersville Dam; 304-872-5809.

How Reported: Feet and cfs

Interpretation of Levels: Minimum for the Middle or Upper Meadow is about 4.5 feet, and high is 7 feet. Minimum for the Lower Meadow is 4.2 feet, and high is 6 feet. In terms of cfs, about 1200 cfs is considered optimum, and 1600 is very high.

Source of More Information: Class VI River Runners, PO Box 78, Lansing, WV 25862; 304-574-0704.

Best Guidebooks: Grove et al., *Appalachian Whitewater, Vol. II;* Davidson et al., *Wildwater West Virginia, Vol. II.*

Further Comments: The Middle Meadow is a popular run, filled with challenging rapids, and appropriate for advanced and expert paddlers. The Lower Meadow, particularly at higher levels, defines the upper extreme of difficulty and danger associated with whitewater. During the 1989 season it claimed the lives of two fine boaters, Whitney Shields and John Dolbeare. Unless you're an expert of the first rank, don't try it. Even if you are, carefully consider the risk.

Gauge Conversion: Meadow River at Mt. Lookout

Feet	Cfs	Feet	Cfs
4.0	240	6.6	2120
4.2	320	6.8	2360
4.6	500	7.0	2620
5.0	720	7.2	2890
5.2	840	7.4	3170
5.4	980	7.6	3470
5.6	1140	7.8	3780
5.8	1310	8.0	4100
6.0	1500	9.0	5900
6.2	1700	10.0	8000
6.4	1900	—	—

MIDDLE FORK RIVER

Sections:	Audra State Park to confluence with the Tygart and continuing to Tygart Junction, Class IV
Length of Run:	Day trip, 7 miles, including 4 on the Tygart

Location: Barbour County, West Virginia

Maps: USGS quad: Audra

Times Runnable: Spring

Permit: None required

Gauge: Extrapolate from the Belington gauge on the Tygart.

Source of Levels: National Weather Service, Pittsburgh; 412-644-2890.

How Reported: Feet

Interpretation of Levels: About 5 feet at Belington should be enough for minimum here.

Source of More Information: Class VI River Runners, PO Box 78, Lansing, WV 25862; 304-574-0704.

Best Guidebooks: Grove et al., *Appalachian Whitewater, Vol. II;* Davidson et al., *Wildwater West Virginia, Vol. I.*

NEW RIVER GORGE

Sections: Gorge, Thurmond to Fayette Station, Class III-V (IV-V at high water)

Length of Run: Day trip, 14 miles

Location: Fayette County, West Virginia

Maps: USGS quads: Thurmond, Fayette

Times Runnable: Year-round

Gauge: US Army Corps of Engineers Gauge at Thurmond

Source of Levels: US Army Corps of Engineers, Huntington; 304-529-5127.

How Reported: Cfs

Additional Gauge: Fayette Station paddlers' gauge, on the New River near the take-out for the gorge

Source of Levels: Visual Inspection.

How Reported: Feet

Interpretation of Levels: Low for a run on the New River Gorge is about 2000 cfs (about 0.5 feet on the Fayette Station gauge), although it can be run lower. High is 6000 cfs (3 feet on the Fayette Station gauge). Above about 8000 cfs (4 or 5 feet at Fayette Station) is very high.

Source of More Information: Class VI River Runners, PO Box 78, Lansing, WV 25862; 304-574-0704.

Wildwater Unlimited, PO Box 55, Thurmond, WV 25936; 304-466-0595.

National Park Service, New River Gorge National River, PO Box 1189, Oak Hill, WV 25901; 304-465-0608.

Best Guidebooks: Davidson et al., *Wildwater West Virginia, Vol. II;* Grove et al., *Appalachian Whitewater, Vol. II;* Nealy, *Whitewater Home Companion, Vol. II.*

Further Comments: The New River Gorge is the great and unequalled big-water river of the East. The gorge is stunning, and the rapids are intoxicating. Don't miss it when you visit West Virginia.

Gauge Conversions:

Fayette Station Gauge to CFS Conversion:

Feet	Cfs	Feet	Cfs
1.0	3600	7.0	14,000
2.0	4800	8.0	16,000
3.0	6300	9.0	20,000
4.0	8000	10.0	25,000
5.0	10,000	11.0	28,000
6.0	12,000	12.0	33,000

Thurmond Gauge to CFS Conversion:

Feet	Cfs	Feet	Cfs
1.0	570	8.0	11400
2.0	1240	9.0	14400
3.0	2100	10.0	17800
3.5	2580	11.0	21800
4.0	3160	12.0	26800
4.5	3780	13.0	33200
5.0	4500	14.0	40500
5.5	5340	15.0	49000
6.0	6399	16.0	59999
6.5	7400	17.0	70000
7.0	8650	18.0	82400

POTOMAC RIVER, NORTH BRANCH

See Maryland.

SHENANDOAH RIVER

(See Virginia/District of Columbia for an additional section of the Shenandoah River.)

Sections: Bull Falls and the Staircase section, Bloomery Rd. in Millville, West Virginia to confluence with the Potomac River and continuing to Sandy Hook, Maryland, Class II-III

Length of Run: Day trip, 6.5 miles (including 2 miles on the Potomac River)

Location: Jefferson County, West Virginia and Washington County, Maryland

Maps: USGS quads: Charles Town, Harper's Ferry

Times Runnable: Most of the year, except when it's very dry

Permit: None required

Gauge: USGS gauge, Shenandoah at Millville, WV

Source of Levels: National Weather Service River Forecast Center, Harrisburg; 717-234-6812.

National Weather Service, Maryland; 301-260-0305.

How Reported: Feet

Interpretation of Levels: Low is 2.0 feet at Millville, and high is 5.5 feet.

Source of More Information: Harper's Ferry National Historic Park, PO Box 65, Harper's Ferry, WV 25425; 304-535-6371.

C&O Canal National Historic Park, PO Box 4, Sharpsburg, MD 21782; 301-739-4200.

Best Guidebooks: Grove et al., *Appalachian Whitewater, Vol. II.*

Further Comments: The Shenandoah is an alluring run through the scenic Blue Ridge Mountains; popular as a family rafting trip.

Gauge Conversions: USGS at Millville

Feet	Cfs	Feet	Cfs	Feet	Cfs
2.0	920	4.0	3550	5.8	7130
2.2	1100	4.2	3920	6.0	7600
2.4	1300	4.4	4300	6.5	8370
2.6	1510	4.6	4680	7.0	10300
2.8	1740	4.8	5060	7.5	11850
3.0	1990	5.0	5440	8.0	13510
3.2	2250	5.2	5840	8.5	15280
3.4	2530	5.4	6250	9.0	17120
3.6	2840	5.6	6680	10.0	21000
3.8	3190	-	-	-	-

TYGART RIVER, ARDEN SECTION

Sections: Arden to Cove Run, Class III-V

Length of Run: Day trip, 8 miles

Location: Barbour County, West Virginia

Maps: USGS quads: Phillipi, Nestorville

Times Runnable: All year except after drought

Permit: None required

Gauge: Phillipi gauge

Source of Levels: National Weather Service, Pittsburgh; 412-644-2890.

How Reported: Feet

Interpretation of Levels: Low for this run is about 2.5 feet, and high is 5 feet.

Source of More Information: Mountain Streams and Trails Outfitters, PO Box 106, Ohiopyle, PA 15470; 412-329-8810.

Rough Run Expeditions, PO Box 277, Rowlesburg, WV 26425; 304-454-2475.

Tygart Lake State Park, Rt. 1, Box 260, Grafton, WV 26354; 304-265-3383.

Best Guidebooks: Grove et al., *Appalachian Whitewater, Vol. II;* Davidson et al., *Wildwater West Virginia, Vol. I.*

Further Comments: The Arden Section, with over 25 major rapids packed into 8 miles, is one of the more popular rivers for commercial rafting in West Virginia.

Gauge Conversions: Tygart River at Phillipi

Feet	Cfs	Feet	Cfs
2.5	320	4.4	2100
2.6	460	4.6	2340
2.8	480	4.8	2580
3.0	620	5.0	2820
3.2	780	6.0	4020
3 4	960	7.0	5220
3.6	1160	8.0	6420
3.8	1380	9.0	7650
4.0	1620	10.0	8950
4.2	1860	—	—

TYGART RIVER GORGE

Sections: Belington to mouth of the Buckhannon, Class III-V

Length of Run: Day trip, 11 miles

Location: Barbour County, West Virginia

Maps: USGS quads: Audra and Belington. Also: Monongahela National Forest Visitor's Map.

Times Runnable: Spring and after extended summer rains

Permit: None required

Gauge: Belington gauge

Source of Levels: National Weather Service, Pittsburgh; 412-644-2890.

How Reported: Feet

Interpretation of Levels: Low for this run is 3 to 3.5 feet, and high is 7 feet.

Source of More Information: Audra State Park, Rt. 4, Box 564, Buckhannon, WV 26201; 304-457-1162.

Tygart Lake State Park, Rt. 1, Box 260, Grafton, WV 26354; 304-265-3883.

Mountain Streams and Trails Outfitters, PO Box 106, Ohiopyle, PA 15470; 412-329-8810.

Rough Run Expeditions, PO Box 277, Rowlesburg, WV 26425; 304-454-2475.

Best Guidebooks: Grove et al., *Appalachian Whitewater, Vol. II;* Davidson et al., *Wildwater West Virginia, Vol. 1.*

Gauge Conversions: Tygart River at Belington

Feet	Cfs	Feet	Cfs
3 5	410	6.0	1910
3.6	460	6.2	2050
3.8	565	6.4	2190
4 0	675	6.6	2330
4.2	785	6.8	2470
4-4	895	7.0	2610
4-6	1010	7.5	3000
4.8	1130	8.0	3400
5.0	1250	8.5	3820
5.2	1370	9.0	4270
5-4	1490	9.5	4770
5.6	1630	10.0	5270
5.8	1770	—	—

GENERAL INFORMATION SOURCES FOR WEST VIRGINIA

The National Weather Service in Pittsburgh reports gauge readings for the Monongahela River Basin (including the Tygart, Cheat, and Youghiogheny Rivers) in Pennsylvania and parts of Maryland and West Virginia: 412-644-2890.

They get readings for the following gauges in West Virginia:

Tygart River
    At Belington
    At Phillipi
Buckhannon River, at Buckhannon
Cheat River
    At Parsons
    At Albright
Big Sandy Creek, at Rockville

The US Army Corps of Engineers Office in Huntington, WV tracks gauges on rivers in the Kanawha Basin. Their recording reports the following readings:

Bluestone River, at Pipestem
Bluestone River, at Hilldale
New River, at Hinton
New River, at Thurmond
Meadow River, at Mt Lookout
Cranberry River
Gauley River, at Craigsville
Gauley River, at Belva
Elk River, at Webster Springs
Gauley River, release from Summersville Dam
Bluestone River, release from Bluestone Dam

The National Weather Service, Washington, DC, District Office is responsible for the Potomac and Rappahannock River basins. They prepare a recording, updated daily at 10 a.m. and 8 p.m. The 10 a.m. edition is more inclusive, with data for the Monongahela and James River basins.

National Weather Service, Washington; 703-260-0305.

They report the following readings:

Potomac River Basin
South Branch of the Potomac River
    At Petersburg, WV
    At Springfield, WV
Potomac River
    At Paw Paw, WV
    At Shepardstown, WV
Shenandoah River, at Millville, WV

Monongahela River and Tributaries
Tygart River, at Belington, WV
Cheat River, at Parsons, WV
Big Sandy Creek, at Rockville, WV

The National Weather Service in Charleston, WV, reports readings for gauges throughout West Virginia. They have no recording, so call between 7 a.m. and 4 p.m.: 304-342-7771.

They can report the following readings:

Little Kanawha River
    At Wildcat
    At Burnsville
    At Grantsville
    At Elizabeth
New River
    At Galax
    At Allisonia
    At Radford
    At Hinton
    At Thurmond
Bluestone River, at Pipestem
Greenbrier River
    At Durbin
    At Marlington
    At Renick
    At Alderson
Gauley River
    At Camden
    At Craigsville
Meadow River, at Mount Lookout
Guyandotte River
    At Baileysville
    At Man
    At Logan
    At Branchland
Tug Fork River
    At Welch
    At Bradshaw
    At Iaeger
    At Vulcan
    At Matwan
    At Williamson
    At Kermit
Elk River
    At Webster Springs
    At Guardian
    At Replete
    At Frametown
    At Clay
Twelve Pole River
    At Dunlow
    At Wayne

Coal River, at Tornado
West Fork River
    At Clarksburg
    At Weston
Cheat River
    At Parsons
    At Rolesburg
    At Albright
Tygart River
    At Dailey
    At Belington
    At Phillipi

Discharges from Reservoirs:
New River, release from Bluestone Dam
Twelve Pole River
    Release from East Lynn Dam
    Release from Beach Fork Dam
Guyandotte River, release from R. D. Bailey Dam
Elk River, release from Sutton Dam
Gauley River, release from Summersville Dam
Little Kanawha River, release from Burnsville Dam

The National Weather Service River Forecast Center in Harrisburg, PA, acts as the hydrologic service office for the Delaware and Susquehanna River Basins. They also receive information on the Potomac and James River basins relayed from the Washington, DC, and Richmond, VA, forecast offices: National Weather Service River Forecast Center, Harrisburg; 717-234-6812.

They report river stages at the following West Virginia stations:

Potomac River Basin
North Branch of the Potomac River, at Barnum/
    Bloomington
South Branch of the Potomac River
    At Petersburg
    At Moorefield
    At Springfield
Potomac River
    At Paw Paw
    At Shepardstown
Shenandoah River, at Millville
Potomac River, at Harpers Ferry

WISCONSIN

BOIS BRULE RIVER

(Not to be confused with the
Brule River at the Wisconsin-Michigan border)

Sections: Copper Range Campground to the
Highway 13 bridge, Class II–III

**Length
of Run:** Day trip, 8 miles

Location: Douglas County, Wisconsin

Maps: USGS quads: Brule, Oulu

Times Runnable: April to June, plus September and
October

Permit: None required

Gauge: USGS gauge near Brule

Source of Levels: Brule Ranger Station, Brule River State
Forest; 715-372-4866.

How Reported: Feet

Interpretation of Levels: Low is around 2 feet to 2.5 feet
(200 to 300 cfs), about Class I-II. Medium is 2.5 feet to
3.2 feet (about 300 to 500 cfs). High is over 3.2 feet (500
cfs). Flows rarely exceed 500 cfs.

Source of More Information: Brule Ranger Station, Brule
River State Forest, Brule, WI 54820; 715-372-4866.

Best Guidebooks: Palzer and Palzer, *Whitewater/
Quietwater*.

Gauge Conversion:

Feet	Cfs	Feet	Cfs
2 0	200	3.4	555
2.2	241	3.6	615
2.4	287	3.8	676
2.6	337	4.0	742
2.8	388	4.2	818
3.0	442	4.4	897
3.2	498	4.6	990

FLAMBEAU RIVER, NORTH FORK

Sections: (1) Mouth of Nine-Mile Creek to Highway 70 Bridge at Oxbo, Class I
(2) Highway 70 Bridge to Babbs Island Ranger Station, Class I
(3) Babbs Island Ranger Station to Hervas Landing, Class I-II

Length of Run: (1) Day trip, 9 miles
(2) Day trip, 7 miles
(3) Day trip, 14 miles

Location: Sawyer, Price and Rusk Counties, Wisconsin

Maps: USGS quads: Pike Lake SW, and Dover

Times Runnable: Almost year-round

Permit: None required

Gauge: Release from Crowley Dam

Source of Levels: Nine-Mile Tavern, Canoe Livery, 715-762-3174.

How Reported: Feet

Interpretation of Levels: Minimum is about 1.5 feet; medium is about 1.5 to 4 feet; and high is above 4 feet.

Source of More Information: Nine-Mile Tavern, Canoe Livery, Rt. 1, Highway 70, Park Falls, WI 54552; 715-762-3174.

Fort Flambeau Resort, Rt. 2, Box 90, Butternut, WI 54514; 715-476-2510.

Flambeau River State Forest, Star Route, Winter, WI 54896; 715-332-5271.

Best Guidebooks: Palzer and Palzer, *Whitewater/ Quietwater.*

Further Comments: Exceptionally beautiful.

LITTLE WOLF RIVER

Sections: Mud Lake Road Bridge to County Highway C Bridge at town of Big Falls, Class I-II (one at III high). (In the town Big Falls, below the dam, is a Class IV rapid, not usually run.)

Length of Run: Day trip, 8 miles

Location: Waupaca County, Wisconsin

Maps: USGS quads: Tigerton, Big Falls

Times Runnable: October to May. High-water months include November (average flow 1039 cfs), March (1242 cfs), April (1033 cfs), and October (823 cfs). Average flow in summer from June through September is around 300 cfs.

Permit: None required

Gauge: USGS Little Wolf at Royalton

Source of Levels: National Weather Service, Minneapolis; 612-725-6090.

How Reported: Feet

Interpretation of Levels: Minimum is about 1.4 feet (300 cfs). Low is 1.5 to 2.6 feet (300 to 1000 cfs). Medium is 2.6 to 4.6 feet (1000 to 3000 cfs). High is above 4.6 feet (3000 cfs).

Source of More Information: Wolf River Trips and Campground, Rt. 3, Box 122, Highway X, New London, WI 54961; 414-982-2458.

Best Guidebooks: Palzer and Palzer, *Whitewater/ Quietwater.*

Gauge Conversion: Little Wolf at Royalton

Feet	Cfs	Feet	Cfs
1.4	290	3.8	2077
1.6	370	4.0	2283
1.8	470	4.2	2494
2.0	579	4.4	2711
2.2	699	4.6	2932
2.4	829	4.8	3157
2.6	979	5.0	3387
2.8	1143	5.2	3622
3.0	1313	5.4	3860
3.2	1492	5.6	4103
3.4	1681	5.8	4350
3.6	1876	—	—

MENOMINEE RIVER

Sections: Little Quinnesee Falls Dam to US Highway 8 bridge, Class II-IV.

Length of Run: Day trip, 4 miles

Location: Marinette County, Wisconsin and Dickinson County, Michigan

Maps: USGS quads: Norway

Times Runnable: Year-round, except when too high

Permit: None required

Gauge: Release from the Little Quinnesee Falls Dam

Source of Levels: Bill Roberts, Niagra Paper Co.; 715-251-3151.

How Reported: Cfs

Interpretation of Levels: About 500 cfs is minimum, and optimum is 1000 to 2000.

Source of More Information: Kosir's Rafting Co., Box 72A, Highway C, Athelstane, WI; 715-757-3431.

Best Guidebooks: Dennis and Date, *Canoeing Michigan Rivers.*

Further Comments: Misicot Falls, 9 feet, at mile 2.4, rates Class III. The Menominee is the Midwest big-water run, often used as a training ground for advanced kayakers and canoeists. The gorge and falls together approach Class IV. A surprise hole is located 0.5 miles below the gorge.

MONTREAL RIVER

Sections: (1) US 2 Bridge on the West Branch, and continuing to the confluence with the main Montreal, and continuing to Saxon Falls Dam, Class II

(2) Below Saxon Falls Dam to Lake Superior Rd. (Highway 505) bridge, Class II (to III high)

Length of Run: (1) Day trip, 13 miles
(2) Day trip, 3.5 miles

Location: Iron County, Wisconsin and Gogebic County, Michigan

Maps: USGS quads: Iron Belt and Oronto Bay

Times Runnable: February to June. Average flow in February and March is about 205 cfs. In April, it's 605 cfs, in May 591, and in June 258. The rest of the year, flows are between 100 and 200 cfs.

Permit: None required

Gauge: Release from Saxon Falls Dam

Source of Levels: Lake Superior District Power Co., Saxon Falls Dam; 715-893-2213.

How Reported: Cfs

Additional Gauge: USGS Montreal River near Saxon (located on right bank, 1.5 miles downstream of the powerhouse)

How Reported: Visual inspection

Interpretation of Levels: About 2.35 feet (250 cfs) on the gauge at Saxon is low, but runnable.

Source of More Information: Trek and Trail, US Route 2, Bessemer, MI 49911; 906-663-4791.

Department of Natural Resources, State of Michigan, Wakefield Field Office, US Route 2, Wakefield, MI 49968; 906-224-2771.

USDA Forest Service, Bessemer Ranger District, Ottawa National Forest, Bessemer, MI 49911; 906-667-0261.

Best Guidebooks: Dennis and Date, *Canoeing Michigan Rivers.*

Further Comments: Section (1) is only rarely run. Shuttle around the one mile of dams and falls at Saxon Falls. Section (2) is a popular and beautiful whitewater stretch.

Gauge Conversion: USGS Montreal River near Saxon

Feet	Cfs	Feet	Cfs
2.3	240	3.0	600
2.4	280	3.2	735
2.5	324	3.4	894
2.6	372	3.6	1080
2 7	425	4.0	1520
2.8	481	4.2	1760
2.9	539	—	—

PESHTIGO RIVER

Sections: (1) Forest Service 2131 Bridge to Burnt Bridge Campground, Class II-II+

(2) Burnt Bridge Campground to Forest Service 2136 bridge, Class II-III.

(3) Roaring Rapids section, dam at town of Silver Cliff to County Highway C bridge, Class III (IV high)

**Length
of Run:** (1) Day trip, 9 miles
(2) Day trip, 7 miles
(3) Day trip, 4 miles

Location: Forest and Marinette Counties, Wisconsin;
Nicolet National Forest

Maps: USGS quads: Blackwell, Goodman SW, Roaring
Rapids

Times Runnable: (1), (2) Spring and after heavy rains
(3) Spring, summer and fall, but best when high

Permit: None required

Gauge: Painted stage marker on County Highway C
bridge, the take-out for Section (3).

Source of Levels: Kosir's Rafting Co., 715-757-3431.

Whitewater Specialties, 715-882-5400.

How Reported: Inches

Interpretation of Levels: For Sections (1) and (2),
minimum is about 10 inches. Low is from 10 to 20
inches, about Class II. Optimum is from 20 to 40 inches,
about Class II-III. For Section (3), minimum is about 5
inches. Low is from 5 to 10 inches, about Class II-III; 10
to 20 inches is medium, Class III; 20 to 40 is high, about
Class III-IV. Above 40 inches is extremely high.

On Section (2), Michigan Rapids and Railton's Rips
become Class III at higher flows. Section (3), the
Roaring Rapids Section, is very continuous. At levels
between 18 and 24 inches, it includes six Class II rapids.
At higher flows the section reaches Class IV, and over
40 inches it is for experts only.

Source of More Information: USDA Forest Service,
Lakewood Ranger District, Nicolet National Forest,
Lakewood, WI 54138; 715-276-6333.

Whitewater Specialties, N3894 Highway 55, Whitelake,
WI 54491; 715-882-5400.

Best Guidebooks: Palzer and Palzer, *Whitewater/
Quietwater.*

Further Comments: The Peshtigo has the best, most
continuous whitewater in the North-Central U.S.

PIKE RIVER

Sections: (1) US Highway 141 bridge to County
Highway K bridge, Class II
(2) County Highway K bridge to take-out
below Yellow Bridge Rapids, Class II-
III.

**Length
of Run:** (1) Day trip, 6 miles
(2) Day trip, 3 miles

Location: Marinette County, Wisconsin

Maps: USGS quads: Amberg, Wausaukee North

Times Runnable: Almost always

Permit: None required

Gauge: Stage marker at US Highway 141 bridge

Source of Levels: Visual inspection only

How Reported: Feet

Interpretation of Levels: Around 2.5 feet is minimum. If
you apply the W.D.S. method, 150 cfs is minimum, 200-
500 is low, and 600 to 1000 is optimum.

Best Guidebooks: Palzer and Palzer, *Whitewater/
Quietwater.*

POPPLE RIVER

Sections: (1) Forest Service 2378 bridge to Forest
Service 2159 bridge, Class II
(2) Forest Service 2159 bridge to
confluence with the Pine River, Class
II-III

**Length
of Run:** (1) Day trip, 9 miles
(2) Day trip, 10 miles

Location: Florence County, Wisconsin

Maps: USGS quads: Florence SW, Florence SE

Times Runnable: Spring and after heavy rains

Permit: None required

Gauge: Stage marker at the Hwy. 101 bridge

Source of Levels: Visual inspection only

How Reported: Feet

Interpretation of Levels: About 2 feet is minimum
(around 150 cfs) .

Best Guidebooks: Palzer and Palzer, *Whitewater/
Quietwater.*

ST. CROIX RIVER

See Minnesota.

WOLF RIVER
Wild and Scenic River

Sections:
(1) Highway 55 bridge to Hollister, Class II
(2) Hollister to Highway 64 bridge in Langlade, Class II
(3) Highway 64 bridge in Langlade to Menominee County Highway WW Bridge, Class II-III (III high)

Length of Run:
(1) Day trip, 7 miles
(2) Day trip, 8 miles
(3) Day trip, 14 miles

Location: Langlade and Menominee Counties, Wisconsin

Maps: USGS quads: Lily, White Lake, Langlade, Markton

Times Runnable: Almost year-round, except August and September

Permit: None required

Gauge: USGS gauge at the Highway 64 Bridge in Langlade

Source of Levels: USGS Field Office, Merrill, WI; 715-536-2200.

Whitewater Specialties, 715-882-5400.

How Reported: Cfs

Interpretation of Levels: About 300 cfs is minimum, from 300 to 800 is medium-low, and 800 to 1400 is medium-high (about Class II-III+)

Source of More Information: USGS Field Office, PO Box 151, Merrill, WI 54452; 715-536-2200.

Whitewater Specialties, N3894 Highway 55, Whitelake, WI 54491; 715-882-5400.

Best Guidebooks: Palzer and Palzer, *Whitewater/Quietwater.*

Further Comments: The Wolf River is tops; it can't be matched in the northern Midwest for scenery and excellent novice to intermediate whitewater.

GENERAL INFORMATION SOURCES
FOR WISCONSIN

The National Weather Service Forecast Office in Minneapolis can report river stages for rivers in Minnesota and Wisconsin: 612-725-6090.

They receive the following readings daily:

Mississippi River
    At Ft. Ripley, MN
    At Minneapolis, MN
    At St. Paul, MN
    At Hastings, MN
    At Red Wing, MN
    At Lake City, MN
    At Wabasha, MN
    At Alma, WI
    At La Crosse, WI
    At Lansing, IA
    At Prairie Du Chien, WI
    At Guttenburg, IA
    At Dubuque, IA
Minnesota River
    At Montevido, MN
    At Mankato, MN
    At Jordan, MN
    At Savage, MN
St. Croix River, at Stillwater, MN
Chippewa River, at Durand, MN
Zumbro River, at Zumbro Falls, MN
Trempealeau River, at Dodge, WI
Black River, at Galesville, WI
Root River, at Houston, MN
Wisconsin River
    At Merrill, WI
    At Wisconsin Rapids, WI
    At Muscoda, WI
Kickapoo River
    At La Farge, WI
    At Steuben, WI
Crow River, at Rockford, MN

WYOMING

GREEN RIVER

Sections: Highway 189 at Warren Bridge to Daniel, Class II

**Length
of Run:**   Day trip, 16 miles

Location: Sublette County, Wyoming

Maps: USGS quads: Warren Bridge, Daniel Junction

Times Runnable: June and July

Permit: None required

Gauge: USGS Green River near La Barge

Source of Levels: National Weather Service, Cheyenne; 307-635-9901.

How Reported: Cfs

Interpretation of Levels: About 500 cfs is enough.

Source of More Information: Green River Outfitters, PO Box 727, Pinedale, WY 82941; 307-367-2416.

Best Guidebooks: None.

GREYS RIVER

Sections: Corral Creek Fire Guard Station to Lynx Creek Campground, Class I-II. There are other very difficult sections higher in the watershed. Check with the Snake River Kayak School.

**Length
of Run:**   2-4 days, 43 miles

Location: Lincoln County, Wyoming; Bridger-Teton National Forest

Maps: USGS quads: Poison Meadows, Box Canyon Creek, Pink Creek, Blind Bull Creek, Deer Creek

Times Runnable: April to May

Permit: None required

Gauge: None

Source of Levels: USDA Forest Service, Greys Ranger District, Bridger-Teton National Forest; 307-733-2752.

How Reported: Impression only

Interpretation of Levels: If the Forest Service says there is enough water, then there is.

Source of More Information: USDA Forest Service, Greys Ranger District, Bridger-Teton National Forest, PO Box 339, Aston, WY 83116; 307-733-2752.

Snake River Kayak School, Box 3482, Jackson, WY 83001; 307-733-3127.

Best Guidebooks: Jenkins, *Wild Rivers of North America.*

Further Comments: Watch for downed trees.

HOBACK RIVER

Sections: Stinking Springs to the confluence with the Snake River, Class II-III

Length of Run: Day trip, 7 miles

Location: Teton County, Wyoming; Bridger-Teton National Forest; Shoshone National Forest

Maps: USGS quads: Bull Creek, Camp Davis

Times Runnable: June to July

Permit: None required

Gauge: Extrapolate from the Forest Service gauge on the Snake River at Wolf Creek

Source of Levels: USDA Forest Service, Jackson Ranger District, Bridger-Teton National Forest; 307-733-4755.

How Reported: Cfs

Interpretation of Levels: If the Snake is running 10,000 to 20,000, then the Hoback should be up.

Source of More Information: USDA Forest Service, Jackson Ranger District, Bridger-Teton National Forest, PO Box 1689, Jackson, WY 83301; 307-733-4755.

Shoshone National Forest, W. Yellowstone Highway, PO Box 2140, Cody, WY 82414; 307-527-6241.

Snake River Kayak School, Box 3482, Jackson, WY 83001; 307-733-3127.

Best Guidebooks: None

NORTH PLATTE RIVER

Sections: (1) Northgate Canyon, Routt launch site to Pickaroon Campground, Class III-IV (IV above 1000 cfs)
                 (2) Pickaroon Campground to Bennett Peak Campground, Class I-II

Length of Run: (1) Day trip, 18 miles
                    (2) 2-3 days, miles

Location: Carbon County, Wyoming and Jackson County, Colorado; Routt and Medicine Bow National Forests

Maps: USGS quads: Northgate, Horatio Peak, Elkhorn Point, Como E, Como W, Overlook Hill, Barcus Peak, Ryan Park, Cow Creek, Finley Reservoir, Saratoga, Overland, Overland Crossing, Savage Ranch

Times Runnable: May to July

Permit: None required

Gauge: North Platte at Northgate (or Gateway)

Source of Levels: Colorado Dept of Water Resources, Watertalk Station; 303-831-7135

National Weather Service, Cheyenne; 307-635-9901

USDA Forest Service, North Park Ranger District, Routt National Forest; 303-723-4505

How Reported: Cfs

Interpretation of Levels: Minimum is about 1000 cfs, and optimum is about 3000.

Source of More Information: For Section (1): USDA Forest Service, North Park Ranger District, Routt National Forest, PO Box 158, Walden, CO 80480; 303-723-4505.

For Sections (2)-(6): Bureau of Land Management, Rawlins District Office, 1300 N. 3rd St., PO Box 670, Rawlins, WY 82301; 307-324-7171.

Bill Dvorak Kayak and Rafting Expeditions, 17921 US Highway 285, Nathrop, CO 81236; 719-539-6851.

Great Rocky Mountain Outfitters, Box 188, Saratoga, WY 82331; 307-326-8750.

Best Guidebooks: Interagency Whitewater Committee, *River Information Digest*. Stohlquist, *Colorado Whitewater;* Wheat, *Floater's Guide to Colorado*.

SHOSHONE RIVER, NORTH FORK

Sections: Wapiti to Buffalo Bill Reservoir, Class II

Length of Run: Day trip, 9.5 miles

Location: Springs County, Wyoming

Maps: USGS quads: Wapiti, Castle Rock Creek

Times Runnable: June to early August

Permit: None required

Gauge: USGS North Fork of the Shoshone River, near Wapiti

Source of Levels: National Weather Service, Cheyenne; 307-635-9901.

How Reported: Cfs

Interpretation of Levels: Minimum is about 1000 cfs. Peak flow in June or July is about 4000.

Source of More Information: USDA Forest Service, Wapiti Ranger District, Shoshone National Forest, PO Box 2140, Cody,. WY 82414; 307-527-6921.

Wyoming River Trips Inc., Box 9541, Cody, WY 82414; 307-587-6661.

Snake River Kayak School, Box 3482, Jackson, WY 83001; 307-733-3127.

Best Guidebooks: Interagency Whitewater Committee, *River Information Digest*.

SNAKE RIVER
(See Idaho for sections downstream)

Sections:
(1) Moran to Deadman's Bar, Class I-III
(2) Deadman's Bar to Schwabacher's Lodge, Class I-III
(3) Schwabacher's Lodge to Moose, Class I-III
(4) Moose to Wilson Bridge, Class I-III
(5) Wilson Bridge to South Park Bridge, Class I-III
(6) South Park Bridge to Astoria Hot Springs, Class I-III
(7) Astoria to West Table Creek, Class I-III
(8) Grand Canyon of the Snake, West Table Creek to Sheep Gulch, Class III-IV +

Length of Run:
(1) 1-2 days, 26 miles
(2) 1-2 days, 26 miles
(3) 1-2 days, 26 miles
(4) Day trip, 12 miles
(5) Day trip, 12 miles
(6) Day trip, 9 miles
(7) Day trip, 10 miles
(8) Day trip, 10 miles

Location: Teton and Lincoln Counties, Wyoming; Sections (1)-(5) in Grand Teton National Park; Sections (6)-(8) in Bridger-Teton National Forest

Maps: USGS quads: Moran, Jenny Lane, Moose, Gros Ventre Junction, Jackson, Cache Creek, Camp Davis, Munger Mtn., Pine Creek, Ferry Peak

Times Runnable: June to July

Permit: A fee and boating permit is required for the sections in Grand Teton National Park. Check with them prior to paddling (no application form is reproduced in the Appendix): Buffalo Forks District Ranger, Grand Teton National Park, Moran, WY 83013; 307-543-2532. Voluntary registration is requested by the Forest Service at the launch site for Section (8), the Grand Canyon section.

Reservations: None required

Restrictions: National Park sections: PFDs must be worn. Spare oar or paddle must be carried. No motors. Other park rules and regulations apply.

National Forest sections: No motors larger than 35 horsepower. No fires on the south side of the river, below Elbow Campground. PFDs are required. No parking at the Sheep Gulch access site.

Gauge: Forest Service gauge: Snake River at Wolf Creek

Source of Levels: USDA Forest Service, Jackson Ranger District, Bridger-Teton National Forest; 307-733-4755.

How Reported: Cfs

Interpretation of Levels: Minimum is around 2000 cfs. Peak flows range from 17,000 to 30,000 cfs. High flows are from 25,000 to 30,000 cfs; these are still boatable by sufficiently competent paddlers.

Source of More Information: Grand Teton National Park, address and phone above.

USDA Forest Service, Jackson Ranger District, Bridger-Teton National Forest, PO Box 1689, Jackson WY 83301; 307-733-4755.

Snake River Kayak School, Box 3482, Jackson, WY 83001; 307-733-3127.

Best Guidebooks: None

GENERAL INFORMATION SOURCES FOR WYOMING

The National Weather Service Forecast Office can provide the public with levels for Wyoming rivers: National Weather Service, Cheyenne; 307-635-9901.

Bull Lake Creek, near Lenore
Wind River
   Near Crowheart
   Below Boysen Dam near Shoshone
Little Wind River, near Riverton
Big Horn River, at Kane near Lovell
North Fork of the Shoshone River, near Wapiti
South Fork of the Shoshone River, above Buffalo Bill
   Reservoir
Shoshone River, below Buffalo Bill Reservoir at Cody
Little Laramie River, at Wood's Landing
Tongue River, near Dayton

North Platte River
   Near Northgate
   Near Glenrock
Laramie River
   Near Fort Laramie
   Near Bosler
North Platte River, at Wyoming-Nebraska State Line
Green River
   Near La Barge
   Below Fontenelle Reservoir near La Barge
Big Sandy River, near Farson
Green River, near Green River
Hams Fork of the Bel Pole Creek, near Frontier
Blacks Fork, near Little America
Henry's Fork, near Manila near Lonetree
Little Snake River, near Dixon
New Fork River, near Big Piney
Crow Creek, near Cheyenne

PART II

THE
WILD AND
SCENIC
RIVER
SYSTEM

The Wild and Scenic Rivers Act, enacted as Public Law 90-542 in 1968, was a landmark achievement by the American people and their government. This legislation created a means to identify and protect the best of our rivers. The law specifies that rivers in the system be classified as *wild, scenic,* or *recreational.*

Rivers can be included under the Act by one of two mechanisms: the first, an act of Congress. Congress can either directly include a river, or can designate a river as a Wild and Scenic Study River. The Department of the Interior undertakes the job of preparing a report on study rivers, and forwards their report to the President. The President then returns a recommendation to Congress for action. Under the second mechanism, the governor of a state may apply to the Secretary of the Interior to include a river in the system, provided the legislature of that state has designated the river as wild, scenic, or recreational.

Rivers in the Wild and Scenic River System include:

ALASKA

Alagnak River
Andreafsky River
Aniakchak River
Atltna River
Beaver River
Birch Creek
Charley River
Chilikadrotna River
Delta River
Fortmile River
Gulkana River
Ivishak River
John River
Kobuk River
Mulchatna River
Noatak River
North Fork of the Koyukuk River
Nowitna River
Salmon River
Selawik River
Sheenjek River
Tinayguk River
Tlikakila River
Unalakleet River
Wind River

ALABAMA

Sipsey Fork of the West Fork

ARIZONA

Verde River

CALIFORNIA

American River
Eel River
Feather River
Kern River
Kings River
Klamath River
Merced River
North Fork of the American River
Smith River
Trinity River
Tuolumne River

COLORADO

Cache la Poudre River

FLORIDA

Loxahatchee River

GEORGIA

Chattooga River

IDAHO

Middle Fork of the Clearwater River
Middle Fork of the Salmon River
Rapid River
Saint Joe River
Salmon River
Snake River
Middle Fork of the Vermillion River

LOUISIANA

Saline Bayou

MAINE

Allagash Wilderness Waterway

MICHIGAN

Au Sable River
Pere Marquette River

MINNESOTA

St. Croix River

MISSOURI

Eleven Point River

MISSISSIPPI

Black Creek

MONTANA

Flathead River
Missouri River

NEBRASKA

Missouri River
New Hampshire
Wildcat Creek
New Jersey
Delaware River
New Mexico
Rio Chama River
Rio Grande River
New York
Delaware River
North Carolina
Chattooga River
Horsepasture River
New River

OHIO

Little Beaver River
Little Miami River

OREGON

Big Marsh Creek
Chetco River
Clackamas River
Crescent Creek
Crooked River
Deschutes River
Donner und Blitzen River
Eagle Creek
Elk River
Grande Ronde River
Illinois River
Imnaha River
John Day River
Joseph Creek
Little Deschutes River
Lostine River
Malheur River
McKenzie River
Metolius River
Minam River
North Fork of the Crooked River
North Fork of the John Day River
North Fork of the Malheur River

North Fork of the Middle Fork of the
   Willamette River
North Fork of the Owyhee River
North Fork of the Smith River
North Fork of the Sprague River
North Powder River
North Umpqua River
Owyhee River
Powder River
Quartzville Creek
Roaring River
Rogue River
Salmon River
Sandy River
South Fork of the John Day River
Squaw Creek
Sycan River
Upper Rogue River
Wenaha River
West Little Owyhee River
White River

PENNSYLVANIA

Delaware River
South Carolina
Chattooga River
South Dakota
Missouri River

TENNESSEE

Obed River

TEXAS

Rio Grande River

WASHINGTON

Klickitat River
Skagit River
White Salmon River
West Virginia
Bluestone River

WISCONSIN

St. Croix River

The above list does not include rivers designated as *recreational.* Many other rivers are presently designated as wild and scenic study rivers. Hope they make it.

PART III

SOURCES OF MAPS AND INFORMATION

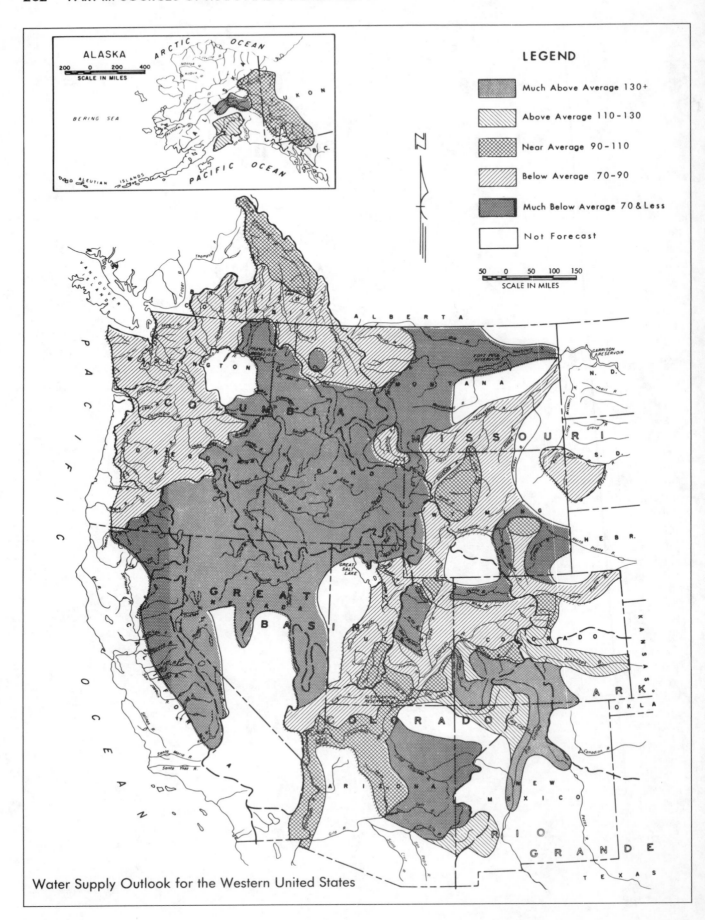

Water Supply Outlook for the Western United States

HYDROLOGIC INFORMATION

In the state-by-state river descriptions and the General Information Sources, a number of specific sources for river gauge readings were listed. In the sections that follow are listed additional general sources of hydrologic information.

Streamflow Predictions

The National Weather Service, in cooperation with the Soil Conservation Service, publishes streamflow predictions solely for Western rivers under the title *Water Supply Outlook for the Western United States.* Based on snowpack accumulation in addition to expected weather, runoff for rivers in this region is predicted in terms of percent of average runoff for each gauging station. For example, in an average year, the Snake River at Hells Canyon would be expected to have a forecast of 100 percent; during a low-water year the forecast might be 50 percent; and during a high-water year the forecast might be 150 percent. The predicted relative flow will predict not only the peak volume but also the length of the boating season; high flows make for long seasons. The following map shows the prediction for July of 1987. The *Water Supply Outlook for the Western United States* is prepared and updated on the tenth of each month from January through June. More detailed and voluminous versions are prepared each month for individual western states; for example, *The Water Supply Outlook for Oregon.* These

documents are available free of charge from:

Soil Conservation Service, West Technical Service Center, Room 510, 511 NW Broadway, Portland, OR 97209; 503-221-2843.

National Weather Service, National Oceanic and Atmospheric Administration, Department of Commerce, 8060 13th St., Silver Spring, MD 20910; 301-427-7622.

National Weather Service

The National Weather Service accepts the main federal responsibility for disseminating current and forecast hydrologic information to the public. The main office in Maryland operates a system of satellites that accepts gauge readings from USGS gauges. The regional river forecast centers collect information from local offices and distribute forecasts and warnings. Local offices are responsible for maintaining a river and rainfall reporting network within their hydrologic service area and for local distribution of information. These offices are of two types. The Weather Service Forecast Offices (WSFOs) have a dedicated professional hydrologist; the smaller Weather Service Offices (WSOs) do not.

River Forecast Centers

National Weather Service, River Forecast Center, Federal Building and Courthouse, 701 C Street, Box 23, Anchorage, AK 99513.

National Weather Service, River Forecast Center, 1641 Resource Building, 1416 9th St., Sacramento, CA 95814; 916-4421468.

National Weather Service, River Forecast Center, 707 Bloomfield Ave., Bloomfield, CN 06002; 203-722-2014.

National Weather Service, River Forecast Center, 1001 International Blvd., Atlanta, GA 30353.

National Weather Service, River Forecast Center, 1120 Old Spanish Trail, Slidel, LA 70458.

National Weather Service, River Forecast Center, Federal Aviation Building, 6301 34th Ave. S., Minneapolis, MN 55950.

National Weather Service, River Forecast Center, Rm. 1715A, 601 E. 12th St., Kansas City, MO 64106.

National Weather Service, River Forecast Center, John W. Peck Building, 550 Main St., Cincinnati, OH 45202-3256.

National Weather Service, River Forecast Center, Room 201, General Aviation Building, International Airport, Tulsa, OK 74115.

National Weather Service, River Forecast Center, 121 Customhouse, Portland, OR 97209; 503-221-3611.

National Weather Service, River Forecast Center, Federal Building, 228 Walnut St., PO Box 1185, Harrisburg, PA 17108; 717-234-6812.

Map Not to Scale

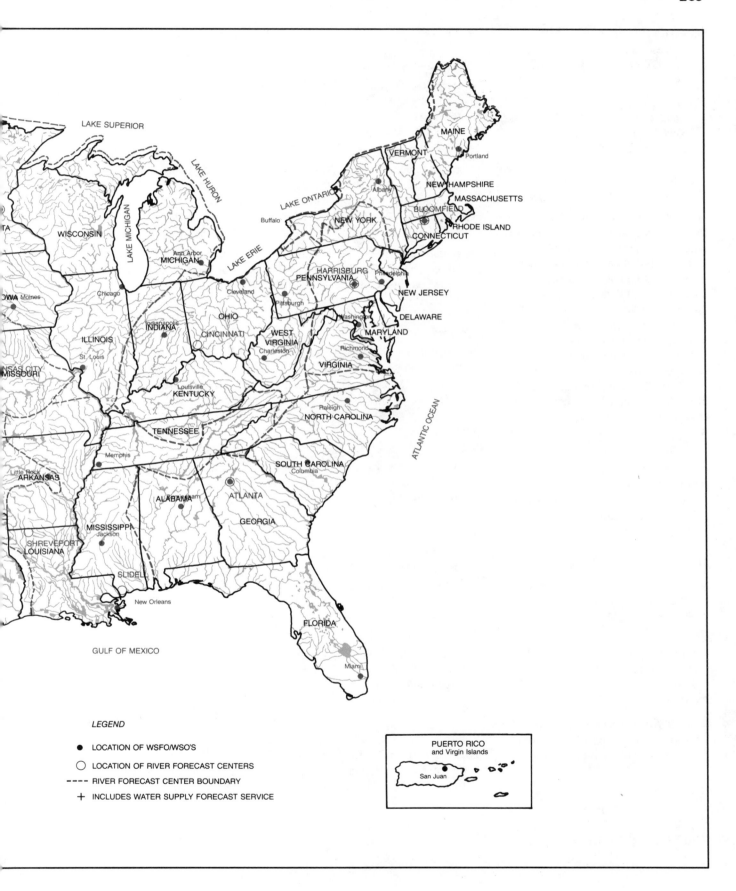

LEGEND

● LOCATION OF WSFO/WSO'S

○ LOCATION OF RIVER FORECAST CENTERS

---- RIVER FORECAST CENTER BOUNDARY

+ INCLUDES WATER SUPPLY FORECAST SERVICE

PUERTO RICO
and Virgin Islands

San Juan

National Weather Service, River Forecast Center, 819 Taylor St., Rm. 10A02, Fort Worth, TX 76102; 817-334-3833.

National Weather Service, River Forecast Center, 337 No. 2730 West, Executive Terminal Building, Salt Lake City, UT 84116.

Weather Service Offices and Weather Service Forecast Offices

For each of the following offices, I have included a telephone number. Numbers with the abbreviation **(AD)** following them are administrative, answered directly by a human. Numbers with the abbreviation **(RT)** after them are ring-through recordings, answered initially by a forecast recording, and later picked up by a human. Numbers with the abbreviation **(R)** after them are forecast recordings only. Be forewarned that if NWS offices receive too many calls on their administrative lines, they are apt to change them. The numbers listed here were current at the time of this writing.

Alabama

National Weather Service, Forecast Office, NOAA, 11 W. Oxmoor Rd., Suite 417, Birmingham, AL 35209; 205-942-1811.

Alaska

National Weather Service, Forecast Office, NOAA, 701 C. Street, Box 23, Anchorage, AK 99513; 907-271-5102 (AD).

National Weather Service, Forecast Office, NOAA, 101 12th St., Box 21, Fairbanks, AK 99701-6266; 907-456-0247 (AD).

National Weather Service, Forecast Office, NOAA, Box 1547, Juneau, AK 99802; 907-456-0247 (AD).

Arizona

National Weather Service, Forecast Office, NOAA, 2633 E. Buckeye Rd., Phoenix, AZ 85034; 602-261-4000 (AD).

Arkansas

National Weather Service, Forecast Office, NOAA, North Little Rock Airport, 8400 Remount Rd., North Little Rock, AR 72118; 501-834-0308 (AD).

California

National Weather Service, Forecast Office, NOAA, 11102 Federal Building, 1000 Wilshire Blvd., Los Angeles, CA 90024-5870; 213-209-7211 (AD).

National Weather Service, Forecast Office, NOAA, 660 Price Ave., Redwood City, CA 94063; 415-364-4610 (AD).

Colorado

National Weather Service, Forecast Office, NOAA, 10230 Smith Rd., Denver, CO 80239; 303-361-0661 (AD).

Georgia

National Weather Service, Forecast Office, NOAA, Airport International Center, Atlanta, GA 30354; 404-762-1186 (RT).

Idaho

National Weather Service, Forecast Office, NOAA, 3905 Vista Ave., Boise, ID 83705; 208-334-9863 (AD).

Kentucky

National Weather Service, Forecast Office, NOAA, FAA NWS Building, 1020 Standiford Lane, Louisville, KY 40213; 502-363-9655 (RT).

Maine

National Weather Service, Forecast Office, NOAA, Federal Building, PO Box 3563, Portland, ME 0404; 207-773-0352 (AD).

Massachusetts

National Weather Service, Forecast Office, NOAA, Edson Building, East Boston, MA 02128; 617-567-4670 (RT).

Michigan

National Weather Service, Forecast Office, NOAA, 200 E. Liberty St., Ann Arbor, MI 48107; 313-668-2220 (AD).

Minnesota

National Weather Service, Forecast Office, NOAA, Federal Aviation Building, 2nd Floor, 6301 34th Ave. S., Minneapolis, MN 55450; 612-725-6090 (RT).

Missouri

National Weather Service, Forecast Office, NOAA, 4100 Mexico Rd., St. Charles, MO 63305; 314-923-1197 (AD).

Montana

National Weather Service, Forecast Office, NOAA, Rural Route 4034, Great Falls, MT 59401; 406-453-2081 (AD).

Nevada

National Weather Service, Forecast Office, NOAA, 601 South Rock Blvd., Reno, NV 89502; 702-784-5402 (AD).

New Mexico

National Weather Service, Forecast Office, NOAA, PO Box 9025, Municipal Airport, Albuquerque, NM 87119; 505-243-1371 (RT).

New York

National Weather Service, Forecast Office, NOAA, 30 Rockefeller Plaza, New York, NY 10112; 212-315-2705 (RT).

National Weather Service, Forecast Office, NOAA, Albany County Airport, Albany, NY 12211; 518-869-6347 (RT).

National Weather Service, Forecast Office, NOAA, Greater Buffalo International Airport, East Terminal, Buffalo, NY 14225; 716-632-1319 (AD).

North Carolina

National Weather Service, Forecast Office, NOAA, Raleigh-Durham Airport, PO Box 165, Morrisville, NC 27560; 919-840-0453 (AD).

Ohio

National Weather Service, Forecast Office, NOAA, Cleveland Hopkins International Airport, Federal Facilities Building, Cleveland, OH 44135; 216-267-3900 (AD).

Oregon

National Weather Service, Forecast Office, NOAA, Airport, Portland, OR; 503-221-3611 (AD).

Pennsylvania

National Weather Service, ForecastOffice, NOAA, 192 Schaffer Rd., Corapolis, PA 15108; 412-644-2881 (R).

National Weather Service, Forecast Office, NOAA, Federal Building, Rm. 9258, 600 Arch St., Philadelphia, PA 19106; 215-627-5575 (RT).

South Carolina

National Weather Service, Forecast Office, NOAA, 2909 Aviation Way, West Columbia, SC 29169-2102; 803-822-8135 (RT).

Tennessee

National Weather Service, Forecast Office, NOAA, 7777 Walnut Grove, Memphis, TN 38119-2198; 901-757-6400 (AD).

Texas

National Weather Service, Forecast Office, NOAA, 819 Taylor St., Rm.1OA44, Fort Worth, TX 76102; 817-429-2631 (AD).

National Weather Service, Forecast Office, NOAA, 830 NE Loop 410, North Crown Building, Suite 300, San Antonio, TX 78209; 512-826-4679 (AD).

National Weather Service, Forecast Office, NOAA, RFD 3, Box 26, Lubbock, TX 79401; 806-762-4647 (AD).

Utah

National Weather Service, Forecast Office, NOAA, Executive Terminal Building, 337 North 2370 West, Salt Lake City, UT 84116; 801-524-5133 (AD).

Virginia/Maryland/District of Columbia of Columbia

National Weather Service, Forecast Office, NOAA, World Weather Bldg., 5200 Auth Rd., Washington, DC 20233; 301-899-3154 (RT).

Washington State

National Weather Service, Forecast Office, NOAA, 7600 Sand Point Way, NE, BIN C15700, Seattle, WA 98115; 206-526-6087 (AD).

West Virginia

National Weather Service, Forecast Office, NOAA, Kanawha Airport, 501 Eagle Mountain Rd., Charleston, WV 25311; 304-344-1961 (RT).

Wisconsin

National Weather Service, Forecast Office, NOAA, 5300 S. Howell Ave., Milwaukee, WI 55450; 612-725-6090 (RT).

Wyoming

National Weather Service, Forecast Office, NOAA, 4000 Morrie Ave., Cheyenne, WY 82001; 307-635-9901 (RT).

Soil Conservation Service Water Supply Specialists

The Soil Conservation Service of the Department of Agriculture maintains a system of automated snowpack depth transducers, the SNOTEL network. Using this information, the Soil Conservation Service cooperates with the National Weather Service to prepare water supply forecasts for the Western United States (see **Streamflow Predictions** above). Soil Conservation offices can provide information on present and future streamflow potentials.

Soil Conservation Service, Water Supply Specialist, 201 East 9th Ave., Suite 300, Anchorage, AK 99501; 907-271-2424.

Soil Conservation Service, Water Supply Specialist, 201 E. Indianola, Suite 200, Phoenix, AZ 85012; 602-241-2247.

Soil Conservation Service, Water Supply Specialist, 2490 W. 26th Ave., Bldg. A., 3rd Floor, Denver, CO 80211; 303-964-0292.

Soil Conservation Service, Water Supply Specialist, Room 345, 304 N. 8th St., Boise, ID 83702; 208-334-1601.

Soil Conservation Service, Water Supply Specialist, 10 E. Babcock, Room 443, Federal Building, Bozeman, MT 59715; 406-587-6813.

Soil Conservation Service, Water Supply Specialist, 1201 Terminal Way, Room 219, Reno, NV 89502; 702-784-5863.

Soil Conservation Service, Water Supply Specialist, 517 Golden Ave., SW, Albuquerque, NM 87102; 505-766-2173.

Soil Conservation Service, Water Supply Specialist, 1220 SW Third Ave., Room 1640, Portland, OR 97204; 503-221-2751.

Soil Conservation Service, Water Supply Specialist, 4420 Federal Bldg., 125 South State St., Salt Lake City, UT 84138; 801-524-5050.

Soil Conservation Service, Water Supply Specialist, West 920 Riverside, Room 360, Spokane, WA 99201; 509-456-3711.

Soil Conservation Service, Water Supply Specialist, 100 East "B" St., Casper, WY 82601; 307-261-5201.

Hydrologic Information Unit of the USGS

The Hydrologic Information Unit (HIU) of the United States Geological Survey (USGS) answers general questions on hydrology, water as a resource, hydrologic mapping, and the products, projects, and services of the Water Resources Division of the USGS. The HIU also provides information and material for specific needs. HIU offers free subscriptions to "National Water Conditions," a monthly summary of water resource conditions in the United States and Canada.

Hydrologic Information Unit, US Geological Survey, 419 National Center, Reston, VA 22092; 703-860-7531.

National Water Data Exchange

The National Water Data Exchange (NAWDEX) is a confederation of organizations working to improve access to water data. Its primary objective is to help identify, locate, and gather water data:

USGS Gauging Station

National Water Data Exchange, US Geological Survey, 421 National Center, Reston, VA 22092; 703-860-6031.

USGS Water Resource Division District Offices

The United States Geological Survey A is the principal supplier of hydrologic information in the United States; it is the agency that maintains the system of automated gauges reporting river stages (often via satellite) to the NWS and other agencies.

The Water Resource Division District Offices of the United States Geological Survey are NAWDEX assistance centers that can provide the public with water data and answer questions on the water resources of their specific regions. To quote the Chief of the Office of Surface Water, "Personnel from any of those offices would be happy to provide available information on river levels." The Water Resource Division District Offices are listed below:

Alabama

Water Resources Division District Office, US Geological Survey, 520 19th Ave., Tuscaloosa, AL 35401; 205-752-8104.

Alaska

Water Resources Division District Office, US Geological Survey, 4230 University Dr., Suite 201, Anchorage, AK 9958-4664; 907-271-4138.

Arizona

Water Resources Division District Office, US Geological Survey, Federal Building, FB 44, 301 West Congress St., Tucson, AZ 85701-1393; 602-629-6671.

Arkansas

Water Resources Division District Office, US Geological Survey, 2301 Federal Office Building, 700 West Capitol Ave., Little Rock, AR 72201; 501-378-6391.

California

Water Resources Division District Office, US Geological Survey, Federal Building, Room W-2235, 2800 Cottage Way, Sacramento, CA 95825; 916-484-4606.

Colorado

Water Resources Division District Office, US Geological Survey, Box 25046, Federal Center, Mail Stop 415, Denver, CO 80225; 303-236-4882.

Connecticut

Connecticut Office, Water Resources Division, US Geological Survey, 525 Ribicott Federal Building, 450 Main Street, Hartford, CT 06103; 203-244-2528.

Delaware

Delaware Office, Water Resources Division, US Geological Survey, 1201 Federal Building, 300 S. New St., Dover, DE 19901; 302-734-2506.

District of Columbia: See Maryland.

Georgia

Water Resources Division District Office, US Geological Survey, 6481 Peachtree Industrial Blvd., Suite B, Doraville, GA 30360; 404-331-4858.

Idaho

Water Resources Division District Office, US Geological Survey, 230 Collins Road, Boise, ID 83702; 208-334-1750.

Kentucky

Water Resources Division District Office, US Geological Survey, 2301 Bradley Ave., Louisville, KY 40217; 502-582-5241.

Maine

Water Resources Division District Office, US Geological Survey, 26 Gameston Dr., Augusta, ME 04330; 207-622-8208.

Maryland

Water Resources Division District Office, US Geological Survey, 208 Carroll Building, 8600 LaSalle Road, Towson, MD 21204; 301-828-1535.

Massachusetts

Water Resources Division District Office, US Geological Survey, 150 Causeway St., Suite 1309, Boston, MA 02114; 617-223-2822.

Michigan

Water Resources Division District Office, US Geological Survey, 6520 Mercantile Way, Suite 5, Lansing, MI 48910; 517-377-1608.

Minnesota

Water Resources Division District Office, US Geological Survey, 702 Post Office Building, St. Paul, MN 55101; 612-725-7841.

Missouri

Water Resources Division District Office, US Geological Survey, Mail Stop 200, 1400 Independence Rd., Rolla, MO 65401; 314-341-0824.

Montana

Water Resources Division District Office, US Geological Survey, 301 South Park Avenue, 428 Federal Building, Drawer 10076, Helena, MT 59626-0076; 406-449-5302.

Nevada

Nevada Office, Water Resources Division, US Geological Survey, 229 Federal Building, 705 North Plaza St., Carson City, NV 89701; 702-882-1388.

New Hampshire

New Hampshire Office, Water Resources Division, US Geological Survey, 525 Clinton St., RFD 2, Bow, NH 03301; 603-225-4681.

New Mexico

Water Resources Division District Office, 720 Western Bank Building, 505 Marquette, NW, Albuquerque, NM 87102; 505-766-2246.

New York

Water Resources Division District Office, US Geological Survey, PO Box 1669, 343 US Post Office and Courthouse Building, Albany, NY 12201; 518-472-3107.

North Carolina

Water Resources Division District Office, US Geological Survey, PO Box 2857, Raleigh, NC 27602; 919-755-4510.

North Dakota

Water Resources Division District Office, US Geological Survey, 821 East Interstate Ave., Bismarck, ND 58501; 701-255-4011, ext. 601.

Ohio

Water Resources Division District Office, US Geological Survey, 975 West Third Ave., Columbus, OH 43212; 614-469-5553.

Oklahoma

Water Resources Division District Office, US Geological Survey, Room 621, 215 Dean A. McGee Ave., Oklahoma City, OK 73102; 405-231-4256.

Oregon

Water Resources Division District Office, US Geological Survey, 847 NE 19th Ave., Suite 300, Portland, OR 97232; 503-231-2009.

Pennsylvania

Water Resources Division District Office, US Geological Survey, PO Box 1107, Federal Building, Fourth Floor, 228 Walnut St., Harrisburg, PA 17108; 717-782-4514.

South Carolina

Water Resources Division District Office, US Geological Survey, Suite 658, 1835 Assembly St., Columbia, SC 29201; 803-765-5966.

Tennessee

Water Resources Division District Office, US Geological Survey, A-413 Federal Building and US Courthouse, Nashville, TN 37203; 615-251-5424.

Texas

Water Resources Division District Office, US Geological Survey, 649 Federal Building, 300 East Eighth St., Austin, TX 78701; 512-482-5766.

Utah

Water Resources Division District Office, US Geological Survey, Room 1016 Administration Building, 1745 West 1700 South, Salt Lake City, UT 84104; 601-525663.

Vermont: See Massachusetts.

Virginia

Virginia Office, Water Resources Division, US Geological Survey, 3600 Broad St., Rm. 606, Richmond, VA 23230; 804-771-2427.

Washington

Water Resources Division District Office, US Geological Survey, 1201 Pacific Ave., Suite 600, Tacoma, WA 23220; 206-593-6510.

West Virginia

Water Resources Division District Office, US Geological Survey, 603 Morris St., Charleston, WV 25301; 304-347-5130.

Wisconsin

Water Resources Division District Office, US Geological Survey, 1815 University Ave., Madison, WI 53705; 608-262-2488.

Wyoming

Water Resources Division District Office, US Geological Survey, PO Box 1125, 4007 J. C. O'Mahoney Federal Center, 2120 Capitol Ave., Cheyenne, WY 82003; 307-772-2153.

US Army Corps of Engineers Offices

The Army Corps of Engineers builds and operates most public dams and water projects in the United States. Information on Corps projects, dam release schedules, and current releases can be obtained from Army Corps district offices.

National

Public Affairs Office, US Army Corps of Engineers, 20 Massachusetts Ave., NW, Washington, DC 20314-1000; 202-272-0010

Division and District

Huntsville Division

US Army Corps of Engineers, PO Box 1600, Huntsville, AL 35807-4301; 205-895-5740

Lower Mississippi Valley Division

US Army Corps of Engineers, PO Box 80, Vicksburg, MS 39180-0080; 601-634-5757

Memphis District

US Army Corps of Engineers, B202 Clifford Davis Federal Building, Memphis, TN 38134-1849; 901-521-3348.

New Orleans District

US Army Corps of Engineers, PO Box 60267, New Orleans, LA 70160-0267; 504-862-2201.

St. Louis District

US Army Corps of Engineers, 210 N. Tucker Blvd., St. Louis, MO 63101-1986; 314-263-5662.

Vicksburg District

US Army Corps of Engineers, PO Box 60, Vicksburg, MS 391800060; 601-634-5052.

Missouri River Division

US Army Corps of Engineers, PO Box 103, Downtown Station, Omaha, NB 68101-0103; 402-221-7208.

Kansas City District

US Army Corps of Engineers, 601 E. 12th St., Kansas City, MO 64106-2896; 816-374-5241.

Omaha District

US Army Corps of Engineers, 215 N. 17th St., Omaha, NB 681024910; 402-221-3916.

New England Division

US Army Corps of Engineers, 424 Trapelo Rd., Waltham, MA 02254-9149; 617-647-8778.

North Atlantic Division

US Army Corps of Engineers, 90 Church St., New York, NY 10007-9998; 212-264-7500.

Baltimore District

US Army Corps of Engineers, PO Box 1715, Baltimore, MD 21203-1715; 301-962-4616.

New York District

US Army Corps of Engineers, 26 Federal Plaza, New York, NY 10728-0090; 212-264-9113.

Norfolk District

US Army Corps of Engineers, 803 Front St., Norfolk, VA 23510-1096; 804-441-3606.

Philadelphia District

US Army Corps of Engineers, US Custom House, 2nd and Chestnut Sts., Philadelphia, PA 19106-2991; 215-597-4802.

North Central Division

US Army Corps of Engineers, 536 S. Clark St., Chicago, IL 60605-1592; 312-353-6319.

Buffalo District

US Army Corps of Engineers, 1776 Niagra St., Buffalo, NY 14207-3199; 716-876-5454.

Chicago District

US Army Corps of Engineers, 219 S. Dearborn St., Chicago, IL 60604-1797; 312-353-6412.

Detroit District

US Army Corps of Engineers, PO Box 1027, Detroit, MI 482311027; 313-226-4680.

Rock Island District

US Army Corps of Engineers, Clock Tower Building, Box 2004, Rock Island, IL 61204-2004; 309-788-6361.

North Pacific Division

US Army Corps of Engineers, PO Box 2827, Portland, OR 97208-2870; 503-221-3768.

Alaska District

US Army Corps of Engineers, PO Box 898, Anchorage, AK 99506-0898; 907-753-2520.

Portland District

US Army Corps of Engineers, PO Box 2946, Portland, OR 97208-2946; 503-221-6005.

Seattle District

US Army Corps of Engineers, PO Box C-3755, Seattle, WA 98124-2255; 206-764-3750.

Walla Walla District

US Army Corps of Engineers, Building 602, City-County Airport, Walla Walla, WA 99362-9265; 509-522-6660.

Ohio River Division

US Army Corps of Engineers, PO Box 1159, Cincinnati, OH 45201-1159; 513-684-3010.

Huntington District

US Army Corps of Engineers, 502 Eighth St., Huntington, WV 25701-2070; 304-529-5451.

Louisville District

US Army Corps of Engineers, PO Box 59, Louisville, KY 40201-0059; 502-582-5736.

Nashville District

US Army Corps of Engineers, PO Box 1070, Nashville, TN 37202-1070; 615-736-7161.

Pittsburgh District

US Army Corps of Engineers, Federal Building, 1000 Liberty Ave., Room 1802, Pittsburgh, PA 15222-4186; 412-644-4130.

South Atlantic Division

US Army Corps of Engineers, 510 Title Building, 30 Pryor St., SW, Atlanta, GA 30335-6801; 404-331-6715.

Charleston District

US Army Corps of Engineers, PO Box 919, Charleston, SC 29402-0019; 803-724-4201.

Mobile District

US Army Corps of Engineers, PO Box 2288, Mobile, AL 36628-0001; 205-690-2505.

Savannah District

US Army Corps of Engineers, PO Box 889, Savannah, GA 31402-0889; 912-944-5279.

Wilmington District

US Army Corps of Engineers, PO Box 1890, Wilmington, NC 28402-1890; 919-343-4625.

South Pacific Division

US Army Corps of Engineers, 630 Sansome St., San Francisco, CA 94111-2325; 415-556-5630.

Los Angeles District

US Army Corps of Engineers, PO Box 2711, Los Angeles, CA 90053-2325; 213-894-5320.

Sacramento District

US Army Corps of Engineers, 650 Capital Mall, Sacramento, CA 95814-4794; 916-551-2526.

San Francisco District

US Army Corps of Engineers, 211 Main St., San Francisco, CA 94105-1905; 415-974-0355.

Southwestern Division

US Army Corps of Engineers, 1114 Commerce St., Dallas, TX 75242-0216; 214-767-2510.

Albuquerque District

US Army Corps of Engineers, PO Box 1580, Albuquerque, NM 87103-1580; 505-766-2738.

Fort Worth District

US Army Corps of Engineers, PO Box 17300, Fort Worth, TX 76102-0300; 817-334-2150.

Galveston District

US Army Corps of Engineers, PO Box 1229, Galveston, TX 7 7553-1229; 409-766-3004.

Little Rock District

US Army Corps of Engineers, PO Box 867, Little Rock, AR 72203-0867; 501-378-5551.

Tulsa District

US Army Corps of Engineers, PO Box 61, Tulsa, OK 74121-0061; 918-581-7307.

Bureau of Reclamation Offices

The Bureau of Reclamation of the Department of the Interior constructs and manages dams and other water projects in the 17 Western states, primarily for agricultural, industrial, and municipal water supply (as opposed to the Army Corps, whose dams are primarily for flood control). Write to the Bureau of Reclamation Washington office for their nifty series of four recreation area maps of the West. Information about the operation of these

dams and about water releases can be obtained from the Bureau of Reclamation offices listed below.

Commissioner's Office, Bureau of Reclamation, Department of the Interior, C St. between 18th and 19th Sts., Washington, DC 20240; 202-343-1100.

Engineering and Research Center, Bureau of Reclamation, Department of the Interior, PO Box 25007, Denver Federal Center, Denver, CO 80225; 303-236-3131.

Pacific Northwest Region (Idaho, Oregon and Washington)

Regional Office, Bureau of Reclamation, Department of the Interior, Federal Building, US Court House, Box 043, 550 W. Fort St., Boise, ID 83724; 208-554-1153.

Mid-Pacific Region (Most of California and Nevada, and a little of Oregon)

Regional Office, Bureau of Reclamation, Department of the Interior, Federal Office Building, 2800 Cottage Way, Sacramento, CA 95825; 916-978-5040.

Lower Colorado Region (Arizona, southern California, southern Nevada, and a little of New Mexico and Utah)

Regional Office, Bureau of Reclamation, Department of the Interior, PO Box 427, Nevada Highway and Park St., Boulder City, NV 89005; 702-293-8000.

Upper Colorado Region (Utah and some of Arizona, Colorado, Idaho, New Mexico and Wyoming)

Regional Office, Bureau of Reclamation, Department of the Interior, PO Box 11568, 125 State St., Salt Lake City, UT 84147; 801-524-5438.

Southwest Region (New Mexico, Oklahoma, Texas and some of Colorado and Kansas)

Regional Office, Bureau of Reclamation, Department of the Interior, Commerce Building, 714 S. Tyler, Suite 201, Amarillo, TX 79101; 806-378-5426.

Missouri Basin Region (Montana, Nebraska, North Dakota, South Dakota, and some of Colorado, Kansas, and Wyoming)

Regional Office, Bureau of Reclamation, Department of the Interior, 316 N. 26th St., Billings, MT 59107-6900; 406-657-6411.

River Services, Inc.

A private company, River Services, Inc., offers a real-time, computer-based hydrologic information service:

River Services, Inc., 3414 Morningwood Dr., Suite 11, Olney, MD 20832; 301-774-1616.

Although the cost of this information service is probably out of the reach of individuals (currently a minimum of $100 per month, including one hour a month of connect time), clubs and outfitters might be interested. Using your own personal computer with a modem, and a toll-free number and access code provided by River Services, Inc., you can access a customized computer database of river forecasts and river levels (as well as a wide variety of other information). You should be able to get current readings for every USGS gauge that sends data to the National Weather Service satellite system.

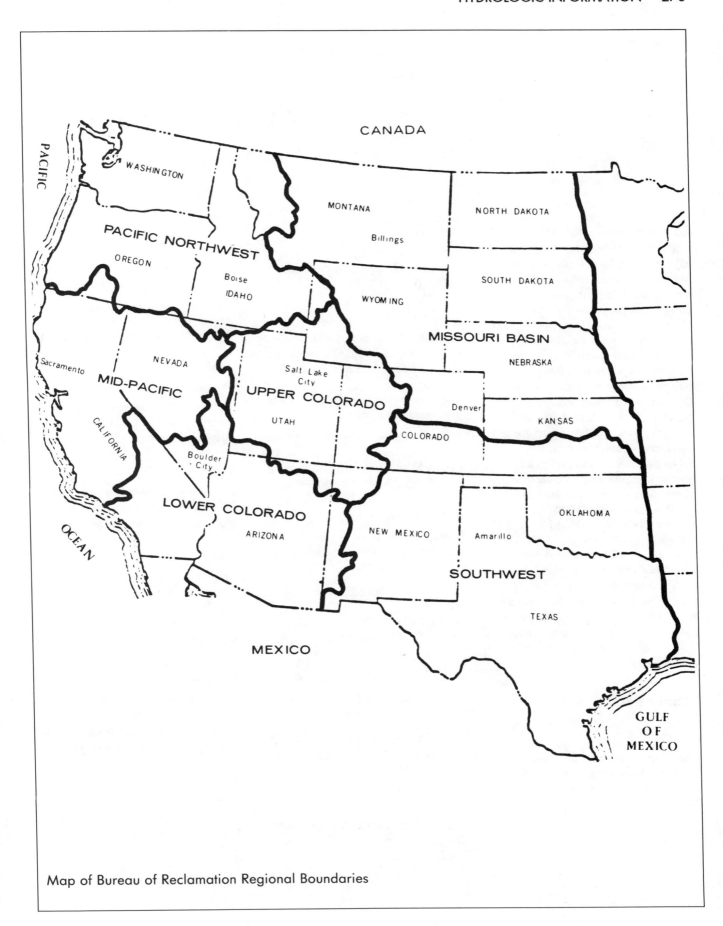

Map of Bureau of Reclamation Regional Boundaries

MAPS AND LITERATURE

Good maps are essential to the whitewater paddler who wants to run any river other than the most standard. Because state maps rarely show the minor secondary roads that almost always form the basis of shuttles, a set of county road maps is an essential tool. Until recently, county maps for most states have been available only through the state's department of transportation, and only as large individual sheets. Commercial cartographers are now beginning to make bound versions available, which are less expensive and easier to store and transport.

For paddlers with an exploratory bent, topographic maps are the ticket. These maps are available from the USGS for the entire country, or alternatively from the TVA for the Tennessee Valley area. A variety of scales are available, but the standard 7.5-minute series with 40-foot contours are best for planning descents of steep creeks. Other useful maps showing a variety of features include National Forest Visitor Maps and the Tennessee Valley Authority series of lake and watershed maps.

County Road Maps

Alabama

Attn: Map Room, State of Alabama Highway Department, Bureau of State Planning, Montgomery, AL 36130; 205-832-5637.

Arizona

Arizona State Transportation Department, 206 17th Ave., Phoenix, AZ 85007; 602-261-7011.

Arkansas

Arkansas State Highway and Transportation Department, Map Sales,~Room 203, PO Box 2261, Little Rock, AR 72203.
They can be purchased individually or in a complete set of 75.

A bound volume can be obtained from a commercial vendor:
County Maps, 50 Puetz Place, Lyndon Station, WI 53944; 608-666-3331.

California

California State Transportation Department, 1120 N St., Sacramento, CA 95814; 916-445-7011.

Or one of the following commercial publishers:
Erickson Maps, 337 17th St., Oakland, CA 94612; 415-893-3685.

Compass Maps, Inc., PO Box 4369, Modesto, CA 95352; 209-529-5017.

Rand-McNally, PO Box 7600, Chicago, IL 60680; 312-673-9100.

DeLorme Publishing Co., PO Box 298, Freeport, ME 04032; 207-865-4171 or 800-227-1656.

Colorado

Colorado State Highways Department, 4201 East Arkansas Ave., Denver, CO 80222; 303-757-4616.

Connecticut

State of Connecticut, Department of Transportation, PO Drawer A, Wethersfield, CT 06109-0801.

Or from a commercial vendor:
Marshall Penn York, Inc., 1538 Erie Blvd., West Syracuse, NY 13204; 315-422-2162.

Delaware

Delaware State Department of Transportation, Division of Highways, PO Box 778, Dover, DE 19901.

Georgia

Department of Transportation, Map Room, Room 10, Number 2, Capitol Square, Atlanta, GA 30334.

Idaho

Idaho State Transportation Department, 3311 West State St., Boise, ID 83720; 208-334-3664.

Kentucky

Map Sales, Department of Commerce, Frankfort, KY 40601.

Or a bound volume can be obtained from a commercial vendor:
County Maps, 50 Puetz Place, Lyndon Station, WI 53944; 608-666-3331.

Maine

Maine Department of Transportation, Special Services Division, State House, No. 16, Augusta, ME 04333.

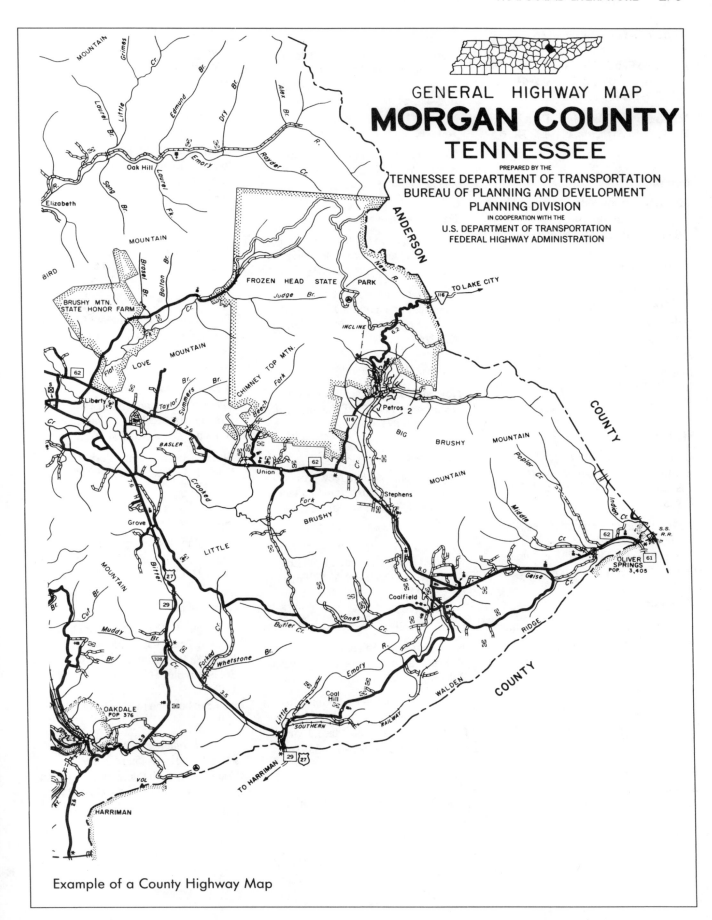

Example of a County Highway Map

Or from one of these commercial vendors:
DeLorme Publishing Co., PO Box 298, Freeport, ME 04032; 207-865-4171 or 800-227-1656.

Marshall Penn York, Inc., 1538 Erie Blvd., West Syracuse, NY 13204; 315-422-2162.

Maryland

Map Distribution Sales, Maryland State Highway Administration, Brooklandville, MD 21022.

Massachusetts

The Commonwealth of Massachusetts, 10 Park Plaza, Room 4150, Massachusetts Department of Public Works, Boston, MA 02116.

Or from a commercial vendor:
Marshall Penn York, Inc., 1538 Erie Blvd., West Syracuse, NY 13204; 315-422-2162.

Michigan

Information Service Center, State of Michigan, Department of Natural Resources, Box 30028, Lansing, MI 48933.

A bound volume can be obtained from a commercial vendor:
County Maps, 50 Puetz Place, Lyndon Station, WI 53944; 608-666-3331.

Minnesota

Minnesota Department of Transportation, Room B-20, Transportation Bldg., St. Paul, MN 55155; 612-296-2216.

Missouri

Division of Surveys and Maps, Missouri Highway and Transportation Department, PO Box 270, Jefferson City, MO 65102; 314-751-2557.
You can buy one copy or the whole set of 114.

Montana

Department of Highways, State of Montana, Mapping Section, 2701 Prospect Ave., Helena, MT 59620; 406-444-6119.

Nevada

Nevada State Transportation Department, 1263 S St., Carson City, NV 89712; 702-885-5440.

New Hampshire

New Hampshire Public Works and Highways Department, Map Division, Hazen Dr., Concord, NH 03301.

Or from a commercial vendor:
Marshall Penn York, Inc., 1538 Erie Blvd., West Syracuse, NY 13204; 315-422-2162.

New Mexico

New Mexico State Transportation Department, Pera Blvd., Santa Fe, NM 87501; 505-827-3170.

New York

Map Information Unit, New York State Department of Transportation, Planning Division, 133 State St., Montpelier, VT 05602.

Or from a commercial vendor:
Marshall Penn York, Inc., 1538 Erie Blvd., West Syracuse, NY 13204; 315-422-2162.

North Carolina

Attn: Map Sales, Department of Transportation, Division of Highways, Raleigh, NC 27611.

A bound volume can be obtained from a commercial vendor:
County Maps, 50 Puetz Place, Lyndon Station, WI 53944; 608-666-3331.

Ohio

Ohio State Transportation Department, 25 South Front St., Columbia, OH 43215; 614-466-2335.

A bound volume can be obtained from a commercial vendor:
County Maps, 50 Puetz Place, Lyndon Station, WI 53944; 608-666-3331.

Oregon

Department of Transportation, Map Distribution Unit, Room 17, Transportation Building, Salem, OR 97310; 503-378-6524.
You can buy a single map or a bound set with covers.

Or try this commercial vendor:
Pittman Map Co., 930 SE Sandy Blvd., Portland, OR 97214; 503-2321 161 .

Pennsylvania

Pennsylvania Department of Transportation, Publication Sales, Room 110 T & SB, Harrisburg, PA 17120; 717-787-6746.

A bound volume can be obtained from a commercial vendor:
County Maps, 50 Puetz Place, Lyndon Station, WI 53944; 608-666-3331.

Or try: Marshall Penn York, Inc., 1538 Erie Blvd., West Syracuse, NY 13204; 315-422-2162.

South Carolina

Attn: Map Sales, Department of Highway and Public Transportation, PO Box 191, Columbia, SC 29202.

Tennessee

Map Sales Office, Tennessee Department of Transportation, Suite 1000, James K. Polk Building, 505 Deaderick St., Nashville, TN 37219; 615-741-2195.
You can buy one map or a complete set of 95.

A bound volume can be obtained for $10.90 from a commercial vendor:
County Maps, 50 Puetz Place, Lyndon Station, WI 53944; 608-666-3331.

Texas

Department of Highways and Public Transportation, State of Texas, Attn: File D-10, PO Box 5051, West Austin Station, Austin, TX 78763-5051; 512-465-7397.

Utah

Utah State Transportation Department, 4501 South W St., Salt Lake City, UT 84114; 801-533-5933.

Vermont

Vermont Agency of Transportation, Planning Division, 133 State St;, Montpelier, VT 05602.

Or from a commercial vendor:
Marshall Penn York, Inc., 1538 Erie Blvd., West Syracuse, NY 13204; 315-422-2162.

Virginia

Attn: Map Sales, Department of Highways and Transportation, 1221 East Broad St., Richmond, VA 23219.

A bound volume can be obtained from a commercial vendor:
County Maps, 50 Puetz Place, Lyndon Station, WI 53944; 608-666-3331.

Washington

Washington State Transportation Department, Highway Administration Building, Olympia, WA 98501; 206-753-6005.

Or try this commercial vendor:
Pittman Map Co., 930 SE Sandy Blvd., Portland, OR 97214; 503-232-1161.

West Virginia

West Virginia Department of Highways, Planning Division, Map Sales, 1900 Washington St. East, Charleston, WV 25305.

Wisconsin

Wisconsin Department of Transportation, Document Sales, 3617 Pierstorff St., Madison, WI 53704; 608-246-3265.

A bound volume can be obtained from a commercial vendor:
County Maps, 50 Puetz Place, Lyndon Station, WI 53944; 608-666-3331.

Wyoming

Wyoming State Highway Department, 5300 Bishop Ave., Cheyenne, WY 82009; 307-778-7475.

National Forest Maps

The Forest Service of the Department of Agriculture produces a fairly standard set of maps. Their series of National Forest Visitor Maps covers the entire National Forest System. Individual maps will show either a single National Forest, or one or two Ranger Districts within that forest. Roads, rivers, lakes and other cartographic features are clearly indicated in color, making the National Forest Visitor Maps very easy to read. For that reason, when I can I prefer to use National Forest Visitor Maps rather than the more difficult-to-read county maps. Some National Forest Visitor Maps show contour lines, but most do not. Other, more specialized and detailed maps and brochures are often available (see below). Almost all National Forest Visitor Maps cost about $1, and there is no charge for postage. Make sure to ask for the *visitor* maps; the *travel* maps are not as good.

To find the maps and literature you need it is necessary to understand the organization of the Forest Service. The Forest Service is administratively divided into regions, each consisting of several states, often then into state offices, and then by forests, and then by ranger districts. Visitor maps can generally be obtained from the regional office. More specific maps, brochures and information can generally be obtained only from the state or forest offices. Listed below are National Forest Visitor Maps available from the regional offices (a more extensive listing of Forest Service offices within the individual states is in the next chapter).

For states in the **Northern Region** (Region 1, including northern Idaho and Montana), National Forest Visitor Maps are available from:

Regional Forester, Northern Region, Forest Service, Federal Building, PO Box 7669, Missoula, MT 59807; 406-329-3011.
A list of Northern Region National Forest Visitor Maps follows:

Idaho

Clearwater National Forest Map
Coeur d' Alene National Forest Map
Kaniksu National Forest Map
St. Joe National Forest Map
Nez Perce National Forest Map

Montana

Beaverhead National Forest Map
Bitterroot National Forest Map
Custer National Forest Map
Deerlodge National Forest Map
Flathead National Forest Map
Gallatin National Forest Map
Helena National Forest Map
Kootenai National Forest Map
Lewis and Clark National Forest Map
Lolo National Forest Map

For states in the **Rocky Mountain Region** (Region 2, including Colorado, Nebraska, South Dakota and Wyoming), National Forest Visitor Maps are available from: Regional Forester, Rocky Mountain Region, Forest Service, 11177 West 8th Ave., Lakewood, CO 80225; 303-234-4185. A list of Rocky Mountain Region National Forest Visitor Maps follows:

Colorado

Arapaho National Forest Map
Colorado Wilderness Map
Grand Mesa National Forest Map (travel, not visitor map)
Gunnison Basin Map
Pike National Forest Map
Roosevelt National Forest Map
Rio Grande National Forest Map
Routt National Forest Map
San Isabel National Forest Map
San Juan National Forest Map
Uncompahgre National Forest Map
White River National Forest Map

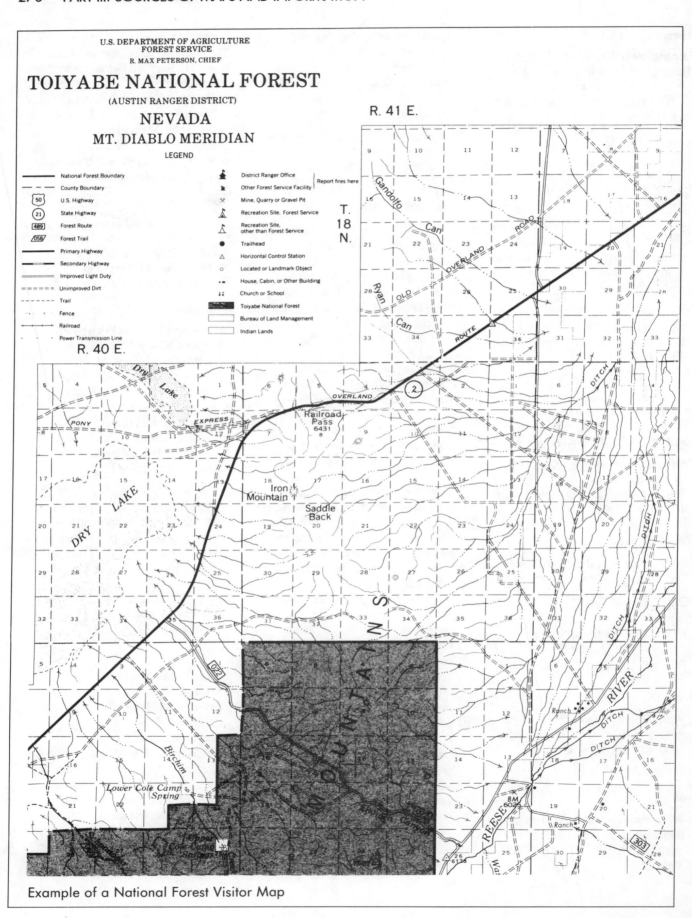

Example of a National Forest Visitor Map

Nebraska

Nebraska, Samuel McKelvie, and Ogala National Grassland Map

South Dakota

Black Hills National Forest Map

Wyoming

Bighorn National Forest Map
Medicine Bow National Forest Map
Shoshone National Forest Map - (North Half)
Shoshone National Forest Map (South Half)
Wyoming Wilderness Map

For states in the **Southwestern Region** (Region 3, including Arizona and New Mexico), National Forest Visitor Maps are available from:
Regional Forester, Southwestern Region, Forest Service, 517 Gold Ave., SW, Albuquerque, NM 87102; 505-766-2444.
A list of Southwestern Region National Forest Visitor Maps follows:

Arizona

Apache-Sitgraves National Forests Map
Coconino National Forest Map
Coronado National Forest Map (North)
Coronado National Forest Map (South)
Coronado National Forest Map (Douglas Ranger District)
Kaibab National Forest Map (North)
Kaibab National Forest Map (South)
Prescott National Forest Map
Tonto National Forest Map

New Mexico

Carson National Forest Map
Carson National Forest Map (Valle Vidal Unit)
Cibola National Forest Map (Magdelena Ranger District)
Cibola National Forest Map (Mt. Taylor Ranger District)
Cibola National Forest Map (Mountaineer Ranger District)
Cibola National Forest Map (Sandia Ranger District)

Kiowa-Rita Blanca National Grassland Map
Black Kettle National Grassland Map
Gila National Forest Map
Lincoln National Forest Map
Lincoln National Forest Map (Guadalupe Ranger District)
Santa Fe National Forest Map

For states in the **Intermountain Region** (Region 4, including southern Idaho, Nevada, Utah and Wyoming), National Forest Visitor Maps are available from:
Regional Forester, Intermountain Region, Forest Service, Federal Building, 324 25th St., Ogden, UT 84401; 801-625-5182 .
Ask these folks to send you the map and pamphlet, "National Forests of the Intermountain Region." A list of Intermountain Region National Forest Visitor Maps follows:

Idaho

Boise National Forest Map
Caribou (West) National Forest Map
Caribou (East) National Forest Map
Challis (West) National Forest Map
Challis (East) National Forest Map
Frank Church-River of No Return Wilderness (North)
Frank Church-River of No Return Wilderness (South)
Middle Fork of the Salmon Map and Booklet
Payette National Forest Map
Salmon National Forest Map
Sawtooth National Forest Map (North)
Sawtooth National Forest Map (South)
Targhee National Forest Map (West)
Targhee National Forest Map (East)

Nevada

Humboldt National Forest Map (Ruby Mountain Ranger District)
Humboldt National Forest Map (Santa Rosa Ranger District)
Humboldt National Forest Map (White Pine and Ely Ranger Districts)
Humboldt National Forest Map (Wheeler Peak Scenic Area)

Toiyabe National Forest Map (Brideport Ranger District)
Toiyabe National Forest Map (Carson Ranger District)
Toiyabe National Forest Map (Central Nevada Division)
Toiyabe National Forest Map (Las Vegas Ranger District)
Toiyabe National Forest Map (Austin Ranger District)
Toiyabe National Forest Map (Tonopah Ranger District)
Toiyabe National Forest Map (Hoover Wilderness)

Utah

Ashley National Forest Map
Dixie National Forest Map (Pine Valley and Cedar City Ranger Districts)
Dixie National Forest Map (Powell, Escalante, and Teasdale Ranger Districts)
Fishlake National Forest Map
Manti-LaSal National Forest Map (Manti Division)
Manti-LaSal National Forest Map (Lasal Division)
Uinita National Forest Map
Utah Wilderness Map
High Unitas Primitive Area
Wasatch-Cache National Forest Map

Wyoming

Bridger-Teton National Forest Map (Pinedale Ranger District)
Bridger-Teton National Forest Map (Gros Ventre and Teton Wilderness Ranger Districts)
Bridger-Teton National Forest Map (West Division)
Wyoming Wilderness Map

For states in the **Pacific Southwest Region** (Region 5, consisting of California), National Forest Visitor Maps are available from:
Regional Forester, Pacific Southwest Region, Forest Service, 630 Sansome St., San Francisco, CA 94111; 415-556-0122.
A list of Pacific Southwest Region National Forest Visitor Maps follows:

California

Angeles National Forest Map
Cleveland National Forest Map
Eldorado National Forest Map
Inyo National Forest Map
Klamath National Forest Map
Lassen National Forest Map
Los Padres National Forest Map
Mendocino National Forest Map
Modoc National Forest Map
Plumas National Forest Map
San Bernardino National Forest Map
Sequoia National Forest Map
Shasta-Trinity National Forest Map
Sierra National Forest Map
Six Rivers National Forest Map
Stanislaus National Forest Map
Tahoe National Forest Map
Lake Tahoe Basin Management Unit
    Map
Emigrant Wilderness Map
Golden Trout Wilderness and South
    Sierra Wilderness Map
Marble Mountain Wilderness Map
Minarets Wilderness Map
John Muir Wilderness and Sequoia
    Kings Canyon National Park
South Warner Wilderness
Trinity Alps Wilderness
Yolla Bolly Middle Eel Wilderness

For states in the **Pacific Northwest Region** (Region 6, including Oregon and Washington), National Forest Visitor Maps are available from:
    Regional Forester, Pacific Northwest Region, 319 SW Pine St., Portland, OR 97208; 503-221-2877.
A list of Pacific Northwest Region National Forest Visitor Maps follows:

Oregon

Deschutes National Forest Map
Fremont National Forest Map
Malheur National Forest Map
Mt. Hood National Forest Map
Ochoco National Forest Map
Rogue River National Forest Map
Siskiyou National Forest Map
Siuslaw National Forest Map
Umatilla National Forest Map
Umpqua National Forest Map

Wallowa-Whitman National Forest
    Map (North)
Wallowa-Whitman National Forest
    Map (South)
Willamette National Forest Map
Winema National Forest Map
Diamond Peak Wilderness Map
Eagle Cap Wilderness Map
Gearhart Mountain Wilderness Map
Kalmiopsis Wilderness-Wild Rogue
    Wilderness Map
Mt. Hood Wilderness Map
Mt. Jefferson Wilderness Map
Mountain Lakes Wilderness Map
Oregon Dunes National Recreation
    Area Map
Sky Lakes Wilderness Map
Strawberry Mountain Wilderness Map
Three Sisters Wilderness Map
Wenaha-Tucannon Wilderness Map
The Wild and Scenic Rogue River Map
The Wild and Scenic Snake River Map

Washington

Colville National Forest Map
Gifford Pinchot National Forest Map
Mt. Bake-Snoqualmie National
    Forest Map
Okanogan National Forest Map
Olympic National Forest Map
Wentchee National Forest Map
Glacier Peak Wilderness Map
Goat Rocks Wilderness Map
Mt. Adams Wilderness Map
Mt. St. Helens National Volcanic
    Monument Map
Pasayten Wilderness Map

For states in the **Southern Region** (Region 8, including Alabama, Arkansas, Florida, Georgia, Kentucky, Louisiana, Mississippi, North Carolina, Puerto Rico, South Carolina, Tennessee, Texas and Virginia), National Forest Visitor Maps are available from:
    US Forest Service Information Center, Southern Region, 1720 Peachtree Rd., NW, Room 8505, Atlanta, GA 30367; 404-347-2384.
    Ask these folks to send you the three-page list, "National Forest Maps for Sale," and the excellent color map, "National Forests of the South." A list

of Southern Region National Forest Visitor Maps follows:

Alabama

Bankhead National Forest Map
Conecuh National Forest Map
Talledega National Forest Map
Tuskegee National Forest Map

Arkansas

Ouachita National Forest Map
Ozark National Forest Map

Georgia

Chattahoochee National Forest Map
Chattooga National Wild and Scenic
    River Map

Kentucky

Daniel Boone National Forest Map,
    North Half
Daniel Boone National Forest Map,
    South Half
Daniel Boone National Forest Map,
    Redbird District

North Carolina

Pisgah National Forest Map
Pisgah National Forest Map, Pisgah
    Ranger District
Nantahala National Forest Map

South Carolina

Sumter National Forest Map, Andrew
    Pickens Ranger District

Tennessee

Cherokee National Forest Map,
    Nolichucky Ranger District
Cherokee National Forest Map,
    Unaka and Watauga Districts
Cherokee National Forest Map,
    Ocoee, Hiawasee, and Tellico

Texas

Angelina National Forest Map
Caddo-Lyndon Johnson National
    Grasslands
Davy Crockett National Forest
Sam Houston National Forest
Sabine National Forest

Virginia

Jefferson National Forest Map
Jefferson National Forest Map,
 Clinch Ranger District
George Washington National Forest
 Map

For states in the **Eastern Region** (Region 9, including Missouri, Pennsylvania, and West Virginia), National Forest Visitor Maps are available from:
 Attn: Maps, Regional Forester, Eastern Region, 310 W. Wisconsin Ave., Room 500, Milwaukee, WI 53203; 414-291-3693.
A list of Eastern Region National Forest Visitor Maps follows:

Michigan

Hiawatha National Forest Map
Huron-Manitistee National Forest
 Map
Ottawa National Forest Map

Minnesota

Chippewa National Forest Map
Superior National Forest Map

Missouri

Mark Twain National Forest Map
New Hampshire and Maine
White Mountain National Forest Map

Pennsylvania

Allegheny National Forest Map
Vermont and New York
Green Mountain National Forest Map

West Virginia

Monongahela National Forest Map

Wisconsin

Chequamegon National Forest Map
Nicolet National Forest Map

For additional sources of information from the Forest Service, see the listing of National Forest offices by state in the next chapter.

Bureau of Land Management Maps

The Bureau of Land Management of the Department of the Interior controls most federally owned western land outside the National Forests and National Parks. They prepare an excellent and useful series of surface ownership status maps of the Western United States. Surface ownership status maps are based on the USGS metric series of 1:100,000 intermediate scale maps, and are modified to show control by federal and state agency, as for example, BLM land, state land, Bureau of Reclamation land, and so on. The BLM surface ownership status maps are referred to by the same names as the USGS maps from which they are derived, so use the USGS *Index to Topographic and Other Map Coverage* and the companion *Catalog of Topographic and Other Published Maps* for the state in which you are interested to choose the BLM maps (see the following section on USGS maps for further explanation). Don't order your BLM maps from the USGS, though; that won't work. You have to order them from the BLM office for the appropriate states. Prices are the same as for the equivalent USGS maps.

Individual state offices may have other specialty maps available; for example, BLM offices managing popular recreational rivers will often prepare a map/guide. Inquire.

Alaska State Office, Bureau of Land Management, 222 W. 7th Avenue, Box 13, Anchorage, AK 99513; 907-271-5076.

Arizona State Office, Bureau of Land Management, 3707 North 7th St., PO Box 16563, Phoenix, AZ 85011; 602-241-5501.

California State Office, Bureau of Land Management, Federal Building, E-2841, 2800 Cottage Way, Sacramento, CA 95825; 916-978-4743.

Colorado State Office, Bureau of Land Management, 2850 Youngfield St., Denver, CO 80215; 303-236-1721.

Eastern States Office (covers states east of the Mississippi and those bordering its west bank), Bureau of Land Management, 350 South Pickett St., Alexandria, VA 22304; 703-274-0180.

Idaho State Office, Bureau of Land Management, Federal Building, Room 398, 3380 Americana Terrace, Boise, ID 83706; 208-334-1401.

Montana State Office (also covers North and South Dakota), Bureau of Land Management, 222 N. 32nd St., PO Box 36800, Billings, MT 59107; 406-657-6461.

Nevada State Office, Bureau of Land Management, 850 Harvard Way, PO Box 12000, Reno, NV 89520; 702-784-5311.

New Mexico State Office (also covers Oklahoma and Texas), Bureau of Land Management, Joseph M. Montoya Federal Building, PO Box 1449, South Federal Place, Santa Fe, NM 87501-1449; 505-988-6030.

Oregon State Office (also covers Washington), Bureau of Land Management, 81235 NE 47th St., Portland, OR 97213; 503-231-6274.

Utah State Office, Bureau of Land Management, Coordinated Financial Center Building, 324 South State St., Suite 301, Salt Lake City, UT 84111-2303; 801-524-5311.

Wyoming State Office, Bureau of Land Management, 2515 Warren Avenue, PO Box 1828, Cheyenne, WY 82003; 307-772-2326.

Other Maps and Literature

USGS Topographic Maps

Topographic maps are available at many outdoor shops and from other commercial vendors, but for the best prices and selection, you should order directly from the USGS of the Department of the Interior (but see TVA description below). They sell the topographic maps in the standard 7.5-minute (1:24,000) series of quadrangles and in a variety of other sizes as well. Write for the *Index to Topographic and*

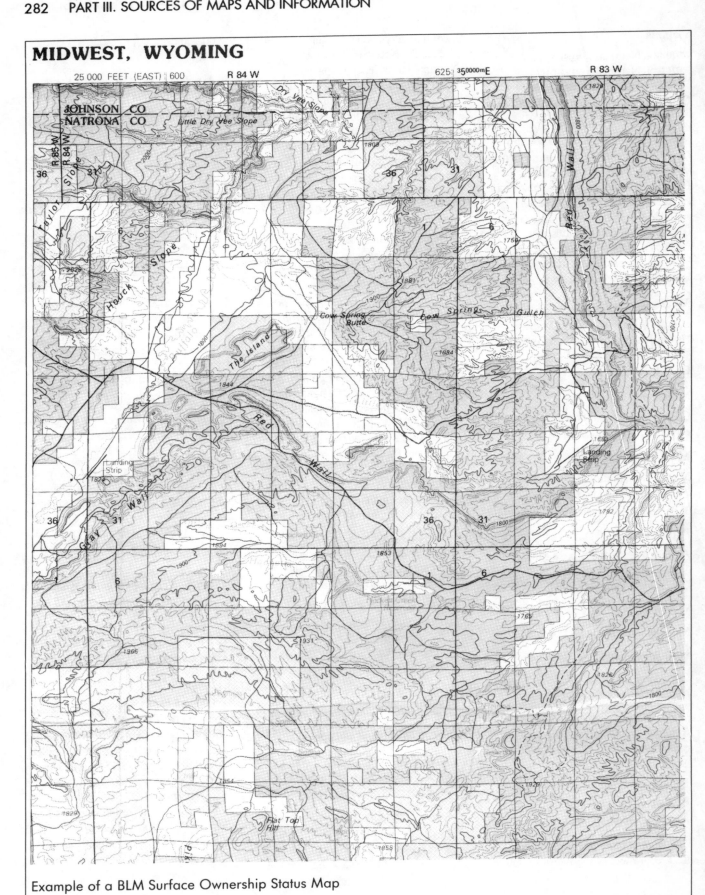

MIDWEST, WYOMING

Example of a BLM Surface Ownership Status Map

Other Map Coverage and the companion *Catalog of Topographic and Other Published Maps* for each state in which you are interested:

> Mapping Distribution, US Geological Survey, Box 25286 Federal Center, Building 41, Denver, CO 80225; 303-236-7477.

(Some of you will remember that the USGS used to have an Eastern and a Western Distribution Branch—that's no longer true.)

National Cartographic Information Center

The National Cartographic Information Center of the USGS is the best all-around source for information on maps produced or distributed by the Federal Government:

> National Cartographic Information Center, 507 National Center, 12201 Sunrise Valley Dr., Reston, VA 22092; 703-860-6045.

TVA Maps

The Tennessee Valley Authority publishes a variety of useful maps, the handiest of which are their series of watershed maps. Some TVA maps are free and others are available at reasonable cost. The TVA also sells standard USGS topographic maps for the entire Tennessee Valley system (including Tennessee, northern Alabama, northern Mississippi, southern Kentucky, southwestern Virginia, western North Carolina, and western South Carolina). They give faster service and better prices than the USGS, and you can order them by telephone. To ask them to send the *TVA Maps Price Catalog* and the *Index to Topographic Maps Currently Available Through TVA,* call the following number:

615-751-MAPS

Or write: Tennessee Valley Authority, Mapping Services Branch, 200 Haney Building, Chattanooga, TN 37401; 615-751-MAPS.

Some especially useful TVA maps are the Big South Fork National River and Recreation Area Map, the Emory River Watershed Map, and the Great Smoky Mountains 1:125,000 series map. Forget the Catoosa Wildlife Management Area Map (showing the Obed-Emory system); the quality of its reproduction is too poor for it to be of use.

Tennessee Division of Geology Maps

If you spend a lot of time paddling or exploring in Tennessee, you may want to write away for the Tennessee Division of Geology's "List of Publications." The Division of Geology stocks topographic maps, geological maps, hydrographic maps, and a variety of other maps, books, and publications.

> Tennessee Division of Geology, 701 Broadway, Nashville, TN 37219-5237.

William Nealy Maps

William Nealy has prepared a series of informative and entertaining river maps for many popular rivers, including:

South Fork of the American River, Chili Bar to Camp Lotus, CA
South Fork of the American River, Camp Lotus to Folsum Lake, CA
Arkansas River, Browns Canyon, CO
Upper Chattahoochee River, GA
Lower Chattahoochee River, GA
Youghiogheny River, Lower PA
French Broad River and Big Laurel Creek, NC
Haw River, NC
Nantahala River, NC
Nolichucky River, NC/TN
Ocoee River, TN
Shenandoah River, VA
Cheat River Canyon, WV
Gauley River, WV
New River Gorge, WV

Write to: William Nealy Maps, Menasha Ridge Press, PO Box 59257, Birmingham, AL 35259-9257; 205-991-0373.

Assorted Maps, by State

U.S.

A map of the National Wild and Scenic Rivers System, prepared by the National Park Services, is available from:

> Superintendent of Documents, US Government Printing Office, Washington, DC 20402.

A map of the National Wild and Scenic Rivers System, prepared by the National Geographic Society, as well as a complete list of maps for sale by the Society, is available from:

> National Geographic Society, 17th and M St., NW, Washington, DC 20036; 202-857-7000.

A map of American National Forests (Map FS 379) is available from the Forest Service:

> Information Office, National Forest Service, Department of Agriculture, PO Box 2417, Washington, DC 20013; 202-447-3760.

A very informative brochure, entitled "The Bureau of Land Management's Recreational Rivers," is available from:

> Office of Public Affairs, Bureau of Land Management, Department of the Interior, Washington, DC 20240; 202-343-9435.

A handy booklet, entitled "National Park Visitor Facilities and Services" is available from:

> Garner B. Hanson, Conference of National Park Concessioners, Mammoth Cave, KY 42259.

Other Maps, Individual States:

Arizona

The National Geographic Society publishes a variety of useful maps and publications, including a map entitled "The Heart of the Grand Canyon." Write for their publications order list:

> National Geographic Society, 17th and M St., NW, Washington, DC 20036; 202-857-7000.

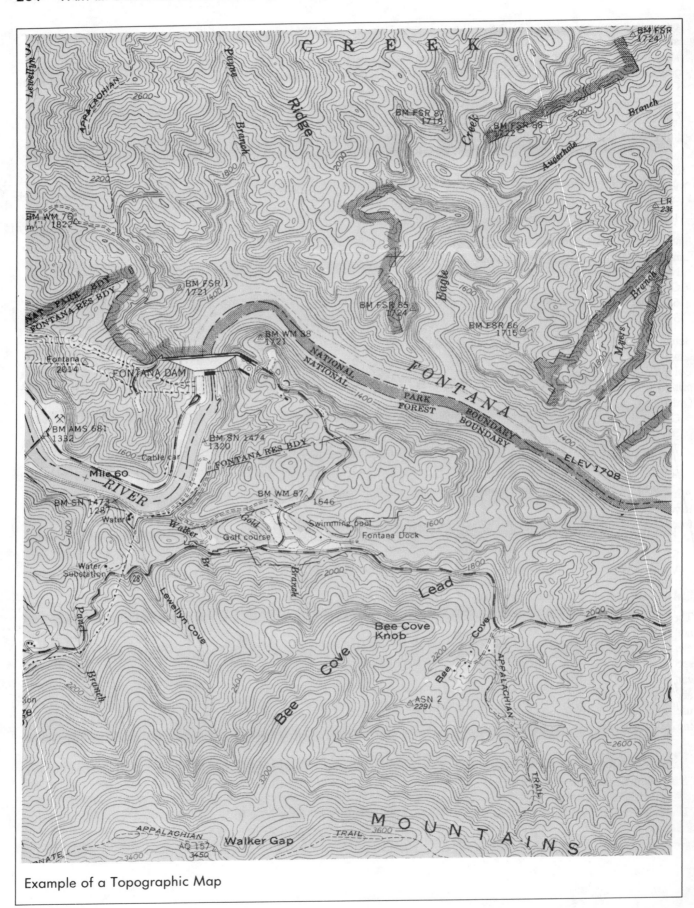

Example of a Topographic Map

The Grand Canyon Natural History Association sells maps, Colorado river guides, natural history guides, and geology guides for Grand Canyon

> Grand Canyon Natural History Association, PO Box 399, Grand Canyon, AZ 86023; 602-638-2771.

A variety of different maps for the Grand Canyon are available from Westwater:

> Westwater Books, PO Box 365, Boulder City, NV 89005; 702-293-1406.

A stripmap of the Grand Canyon by Larry Stevens is available from NORS:

> NORS Resource Center, National Organization for River Sports, Box 6847, Colorado Springs, CO 80934; 303-473-2466.

Beth Rundquist of Rivers and Mountains has prepared a map of the Colorado River in the Grand Canyon printed on teeshirts and bandanas. Order them from:

> Cascade Outfitters, PO Box 209, Springfield, OR 97477; 800-223-7238.

Arkansas

A map/guide for the Buffalo National River by Fogle C. Clark is available from the American Canoe Association:

> American Canoe Association Book Service, PO Box 1190, Newington, VA 22122; 703-550-7495.

California

The California Department of Boating and Waterways serves as a cheerful clearinghouse of information on recreational rivers in California. They can answer your questions by phone and can provide you with a variety of useful literature, including the following:

"Rafting on the South Fork of the American River"
"State of California River Flow Information Service: Flow Fone"
"List of River Contacts for Additional Information"

"River Running the American River Parkway"
"The South Yuba River Canyon: Public Resource Access Guide"
"The Mokelumne River Canyon: Public Resource Access Guide"
"The Merced River Canyon: Public Resource Access Guide"
"California Water Supply Outlook for Recreation at Selected Lakes and Reservoirs"
"California Water Supply Outlook for Boaters"
"A Boating Trail Guide to the Colorado River"

> Write to: California Department of Boating and Waterways, 1629 "S" St., Sacramento, CA 95814; 916-445-2085.

The following California river maps are available from the ACA and NORS:

Quinn, "Hell's Corner Gorge of the Klamath"
Cassady and Calhoun, "Tuolumne River"
Cassady and Calhoun, "South Fork of the American River"
Cassady and Calhoun, "Forks of the Kern"
Cassady and Calhoun, "Upper Kern River"
Cassady and Calhoun, "Lower Kern River"

> Write to: American Canoe Association Book Service, PO Box 1190, Newington, VA 22122; 703-550-7495.

NORS Resource Center, National Organization for River Sports, Box 6847, Colorado Springs, CO 80934; 303-473-2466.

The Friends of the River publish a map/guide to the American River Recreation Area. Write to:

> Friends of the River, Building C, Fort Mason Center, San Francisco, CA 94123-1382; 415-441-8778.

Beth Rundquist of Rivers and Mountains has prepared a series of river maps printed on teeshirts and bandanas for

California rivers. These include the North and Middle Forks of the American River, the South Fork of the American River, the Lower Kern, the Upper Kern, and the Tuolumne. Order them from:

> Cascade Outfitters, PO Box 209, Springfield, OR 97477; 800-223-7238.

Colorado See also Wyoming.

The Cassady and Calhoun waterproof river maps of the upper Arkansas River and the lower Arkansas River are available from NORS:

> NORS Resource Center, National Organization for River Sports, Box 6947, Colorado Springs, CO 80934; 303-473-2466.

Beth Rundquist of Rivers and Mountains has prepared a series of river maps printed on teeshirts and bandanas. Her maps for Colorado include the Granite to Canon City and Nathrop to Canon City sections of the Arkansas River. Order them from:

> Cascade Outfitters, PO Box 209, Springfield, OR 97477; 800-223-7238.

Georgia/South Carolina

A map of the Chattooga National Wild and Scenic River is available from:

> US Forest Service, Andrew Pickens Ranger District, Sumter National Forest, Star Route, Walhalla, SC 29691.

A waterproof scroll map entitled, "The River Runner's Guide to the Chattooga River" is available from:

> American Canoe Association Book Service, PO Box 1190, Newington, VA 22122; 703-550-7495.

And:

> NORS Resource Center, National Organization for River Sports, Box 6947, Colorado Springs, CO 80934; 303-473-2466.

A waterproof flip map of the Chattooga Section 4 by Ron Rathnow is available from:

Menasha Ridge Press
3169 Cahaba Heights Road
Birmingham, AL 35243

Idaho

Waterproof maps of the Middle Fork of the Salmon and the Main Stem of the Salmon River are available from CKS:
Colorado Kayak Supply, PO Box 3059, Buena Vista, CO 81211; 303-395-2421 or 800-535-3565.

Waterproof maps of the Snake River in Hells Canyon (by either Backeddy Books or by Quinn), the Main Salmon, River of No Return section (by Backeddy), and the Middle Fork of the Salmon (by Backeddy) are available from:
NORS Resource Center, National Organization for River Sports, Box 6947, Colorado Springs, CO 80934; 303-473-2466.

Several different maps of the Snake and Salmon rivers are available from Westwater:
Westwater Books, PO Box 365, Boulder City, NV 89005; 702-293-1406.

The Idaho Department of Parks and Recreation can provide a variety of information on river recreation:
Idaho Department of Parks and Recreation, Statehouse Mail, Boise, ID 83720; 208-334-2284.

Beth Rundquist of Rivers and Mountains has prepared a fine series of river maps printed on teeshirts and bandanas. Her maps for Idaho rivers include the Main Salmon, the Middle Salmon, the Lower Salmon, and the Snake River in Hells Canyon. Order them from:
Cascade Outfitters, PO Box 209, Springfield, OR 97477; 800-223-7238.

Maine

A map of the Allagash and St. John rivers is available from the ACA:
American Canoe Association Book Service, PO Box 1190, Newington, VA 22122; 703-550-7495.

Maryland/DC

The *Hiker's Guide to the C&O Canal is* crammed with useful information for the Potomac River paddler. It is available from:
Mason-Dixon Council of the Boy Scouts, 1200 Crestwood Dr., Hagerstown, MD 21740.

A flip map of the Lower Youghiogheny by Ron Rathnow is available from:
Menasha Ridge Press, PO Box 59257, Birmingham, AL 352599257; 205-991-0373.

Guide maps by River Maps, Ltd. to the Harper's Ferry Rapids at the confluence of the Potomac and Shenandoah rivers and to the Potomac Fall Line Rapids are available from ACA:
American Canoe Association Book Service, PO Box 1190, Newington, VA 22122; 703-550-7495.

Minnesota

The Division of Trails and Waterways of the Department of Natural Resources acts as a clearinghouse of information on paddling rivers in Minnesota. They can answer most questions. Publications available from these folks include:
A Gathering of Waters: A Guide to Minnesota's Rivers
"Minnesota's Trails and Waterways"
"Explore Minnesota: Canoeing, Hiking and Backpacking"
"River Level Gauges"
"River Level Inventory" (reproduced in Appendix Three)
Numerous, very complete canoe route maps and guides are available.

Write or call: Department of Natural Resources, Division of Trails and Waterways, 500 Lafayette Rd., St. Paul, MN 55155-4001; 612-296-6699 or 800-652-9747 (within Minnesota).

Missouri

A map of the St. Francis River is available from:
Liquid Pleasure Press, Inc., 6633 San Bonita Dr., St. Louis, MO 63105.

The "Ozark Scenic Riverways Guide," a pamphlet and map describing the Current, Jacks Fork, and Eleven Point Rivers by Fogle C. Clark (1977) is available from:
American Canoe Association Book Service, PO Box 1190, Newington, VA 22122; 703-550-7495.

New Mexico

A river poster map of the Rio Grande in northern New Mexico by John Lopez is available from CKS:
Colorado Kayak Supply, PO Box 3059, Buena Vista, CO 81211; 303-395-2421 or 800-535-3565.

A waterproof map and river guide to the upper Rio Grande by Cassady and Calhoun is available from NORS:
NORS Resource Center, National Organization for River Sports, Box 6947, Colorado Springs, CO 80934; 303-473-2466.

The Bureau of Land Management, the Forest Service and the US Army Corps of Engineers jointly publish a map/guide titled "Rio Chama: Wild and Scenic River". Order it from:
Coyote Ranger Station, Santa Fe National Forest, Coyote, NM 87012; 505-638-5526; or from Taos Resource Area, Bureau of Land Management, PO Box 1045, Taos, NM 87571; 505-758-8851.

Beth Rundquist of Rivers and Mountains has prepared a map of the Rio Grande River from the Red River confluence to Velarde, printed on teeshirts and bandanas. Order them from:
Cascade Outfitters, PO Box 209, Springfield, OR 97477; 800-223-7238.

New York

The New York State Department of Environmental Conservation has mapped canoe routes for portions of the Adirondack Park:

New York State Department of Environmental Conservation, 50 Wolf Rd., Albany, NY 12233.

The New York State Department of Transportation publishes several maps, including maps of the Barge Canal System that also includes many rivers:
New York State DOT, Waterways Maintenance Division, 5 Governor Harriman State Campus, Albany, NY 12232.

A map/guide titled "The Delaware and Outdoor Recreation" is available from the ACA book service:
American Canoe Association Book Service, PO Box 1190, Newington, VA 22122; 703-550-7495.

North Carolina

A map of the B. Everett Jordan Dam and Lake of the Haw and New Hope Rivers (showing the shuttle for the Haw) is available from:
Resource Manager, US Army Corps of Engineers, B. Everett Jordan Dam and Lake, PO Box 144, Moncure, NC 27559; 919-542-2227.

A map of the French Broad River is published by:
River Guide, Land of Sky Regional Council, PO Box 2175, Asheville, NC 28802.

A waterproof flip map of the Nantahala by Ron Rathnow is available from:
Menasha Ridge Press, PO Box 59257, Birmingham, AL 352599257; 205-991-0373.

Guide maps by River Maps, Ltd. of the French Broad River Gap rapids and the Nolichucky Gap rapids are available from the ACA:
American Canoe Association Book Service, PO Box 1190, Newington, VA 22122; 703-550-7495.

Beth Rundquist of Rivers and Mountains has prepared a map of the Nantahala River printed on teeshirts and bandanas. Order them from:
Cascade Outfitters, PO Box 209, Springfield, OR 97477; 800-223-7238.

Ohio

The Ohio Division of Watercraft offers resources and information for paddlers:
Ohio Division of Watercraft, Fountain Square, Building C/2, Columbus, OH 43224; 614-466-3686 or 614-466-7806.

Oregon

A color map/booklet of Hell's Corner Gorge of the Klamath is available from CKS:
Colorado Kayak Supply, PO Box 3059, Buena Vista, CO 81211; 303-395-2421 or 800-535-3565.

The Bureau of Land Management and the Forest Service jointly publish a map/guide to the Rogue, titled "The Wild and Scenic Rogue River". Order it from:
Siskiyou National Forest, 1504 NW Sixth St., PO Box 440, Grants Pass, OR 97526

Beth Rundquist of Rivers and Mountains has prepared a fine series of river maps printed on teeshirts and bandanas. Her maps for Oregon rivers include the Deschutes River, the McKenzie River, and the Rogue River. Order them from:
Cascade Outfitters, PO Box 209, Springfield, OR 97477; 800-223-7238.

Pennsylvania

A map of the lower Youghiogheny by Rich Harding is available from:
ACA Book Service, American Canoe Association, PO Box 1190, Newington, VA 22122; 703-550-7495.

A flip map of the Lower Youghiogheny by Ron Rathnow is available from:
Menasha Ridge Press, PO Box 59257, Birmingham, AL 35259-9257; 205-991-0373.

Beth Rundquist of Rivers and Mountains has prepared a map of the Lower Youghiogheny printed on teeshirts and bandanas. Order them from:
Cascade Outfitters, PO Box 209, Springfield, OR 97477; 800-223-7238.

Tennessee

A map of the Big South Fork National River and Recreation Area is available free of charge, and a River Guide is available from:
Superintendent, Big South Fork National River and Recreation Area, PO Drawer 630, Oneida, TN 32841; 615-569-6389.

An excellent series of combination river guides and maps is available from the TVA:
"Tennessee Valley Canoe Trails"
"The Little Bear Creek Canoe Trails"
"Obed-Emory Canoe Trails"
"Little Tennessee Valley Canoe Trails"

"Elk River Canoe Trails"
Write to: Information Office, Tennessee Valley Authority, Knoxville, TN 37902.

A waterproof flip map of the Ocoee by Ron Rathnow is available from:
Menasha Ridge Press, PO Box 59257, Birmingham, AL 352599257; 205-991-0373.

Beth Rundquist of Rivers and Mountains has prepared a map of the Ocoee printed on teeshirts and bandanas. Order them from:
Cascade Outfitters, PO Box 209, Springfield, OR 97477; 800-223-7238.

Texas

The Big Bend Natural History Association sells maps, Rio Grande River guides, natural history guides, and geology guides for the Big Bend and other areas in the Southwest. These include the strip map booklets:
"Colorado Canyon through Santa Elena Canyon"
"Mariscal Canyon Through Boquillas Canyon" "The Lower Canyon"
"General Information"
Their address is: Big Bend Natural History Association, PO Box 68, Big Bend National Park, TX 79834.

The Natural History Association strip maps listed above are also available from NORS:

Federal Lands

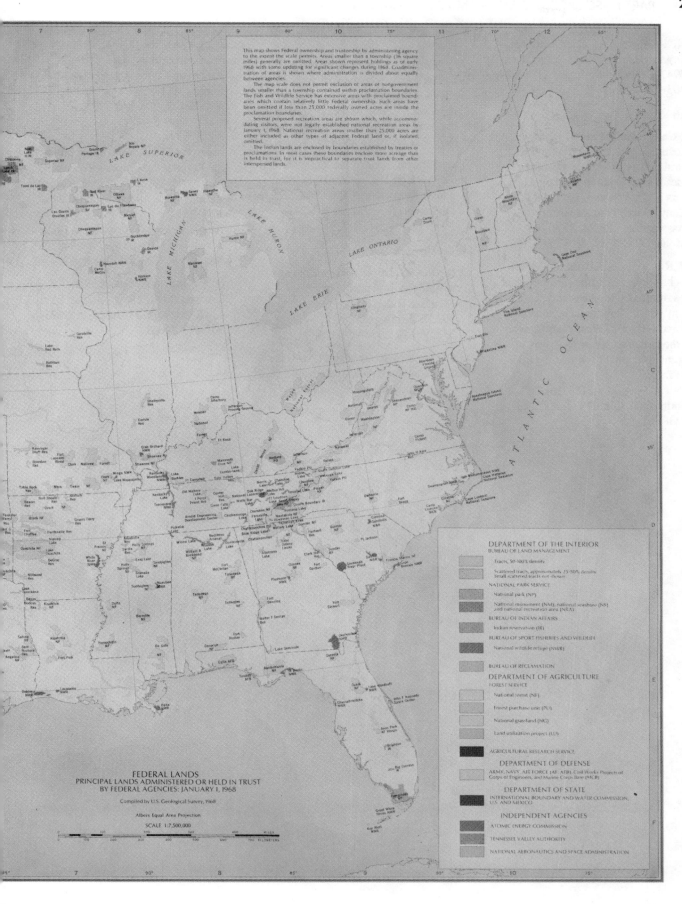

This map shows Federal ownership and trusteeship by administering agency to the extent the scale permits. Areas smaller than a township (36 square miles) generally are omitted. Areas shown represent holdings as of early 1968 with some updating for significant changes during 1968. Coadministration of areas is shown where administration is divided about equally between agencies.

The map scale does not permit exclusion of areas of nongovernment lands smaller than a township contained within proclamation boundaries. The Fish and Wildlife Service has extensive areas with proclaimed boundaries which contain relatively little Federal ownership. Such areas have been omitted if less than 25,000 federally owned acres are inside the proclamation boundaries.

Several proposed recreation areas are shown which, while accommodating visitors, were not legally established national recreation areas by January 1, 1968. National recreation areas smaller than 25,000 acres are either included as other types of adjacent Federal land or, if isolated, omitted.

The Indian lands are enclosed by boundaries established by treaties or proclamations. In most cases these boundaries enclose more acreage than is held in trust, for it is impractical to separate trust lands from other interspersed lands.

FEDERAL LANDS
PRINCIPAL LANDS ADMINISTERED OR HELD IN TRUST
BY FEDERAL AGENCIES: JANUARY 1, 1968

Compiled by U.S. Geological Survey, 1968

Albers Equal Area Projection

SCALE 1:7,500,000

DEPARTMENT OF THE INTERIOR
BUREAU OF LAND MANAGEMENT

Tracts, 50-100% density

Scattered tracts, approximately 25-50% density. Small scattered tracts not shown

NATIONAL PARK SERVICE

National park (NP)

National monument (NM), national seashore (NS) and national recreation area (NRA)

BUREAU OF INDIAN AFFAIRS

Indian reservation (IR)

BUREAU OF SPORT FISHERIES AND WILDLIFE

National wildlife refuge (NWR)

BUREAU OF RECLAMATION

DEPARTMENT OF AGRICULTURE
FOREST SERVICE

National forest (NF)

Forest purchase unit (PU)

National grassland (NG)

Land utilization project (LU)

AGRICULTURAL RESEARCH SERVICE

DEPARTMENT OF DEFENSE

ARMY, NAVY, AIR FORCE (AF, AFB), Civil Works Projects of Corps of Engineers, and Marine Corps Base (MCB)

DEPARTMENT OF STATE

INTERNATIONAL BOUNDARY AND WATER COMMISSION, U.S. AND MEXICO

INDEPENDENT AGENCIES

ATOMIC ENERGY COMMISSION

TENNESSEE VALLEY AUTHORITY

NATIONAL AERONAUTICS AND SPACE ADMINISTRATION

NORS Resource Center, National Organization for River Sports, Box 6947, Colorado Springs, CO 80934; 303-473-2466.

Utah

The Canyonlands Natural History Association sells maps, river guides, natural history guides, and geology guides for the Colorado and Green Rivers in Canyonlands National Park.

Canyonlands Natural History Association, 125 W. 200th St., Moab, UT 84532; 801-259-8163.

Beth Rundquist of Rivers and Mountains has prepared a fine series of river maps printed on teeshirts and bandanas. Her maps for Utah rivers include the Colorado River in Westwater Canyon and the Green and Yampa Rivers in Dinosaur National Monument. Order them from:

Cascade Outfitters, PO Box 209, Springfield, OR 97477; 800-223-7238.

Virginia

A guide/map to the upper New River in Virginia by River Maps, Ltd. is available from the ACA:

American Canoe Association Book Service, PO Box 1190, Newington, VA 22122; 703-550-7495.

Two different maps of the James River through Richmond are available from:

James River Park, 900 E. Broad St., Richmond, VA 23219; 804-231-7411.

West Virginia

A flip map of the New River Gorge by Ron Rathnow is available from:

Menasha Ridge Press, PO Box 59257, Birmingham, AL 352599257; 205-991-0373.

Guide maps by River Maps, Ltd. to the Gauley Canyon rapids, to the New River to Bluestone Lake, and to the lower gorge of the New River are available from the ACA:

American Canoe Association Book Service, PO Box 1190, Newington, VA 22122; 703-550-7495.

Wyoming

A waterproof map of the upper North Platte River at the Colorado/Wyoming border by the Wyoming Game and Fish Department is available from the ACA and NORS:

American Canoe Association Book Service, PO Box 1190, Newington, VA 22122; 703-550-7495.

NORS Resource Center, National Organization for River Sports, Box 6847, Colorado Springs, CO 80934; 303-473-2466.

SOURCES: FURTHER INFORMATION

The federal government serves as the (usually) benevolent landlord for most wild lands and wild rivers in the U.S., and it is to the various agencies of the government that we turn for information on those lands and rivers:

Bureau of Land Management Offices

The Bureau of Land Management of the Department of the Interior controls most federally owned western land outside the national forests and parks. The main offices of the BLM in Washington and Denver can answer general questions and can direct you to additional information sources. State offices can answer many more specific questions and can refer you to BLM district offices if necessary.

Office of Public Affairs, Bureau of Land Management, Department of the Interior, Washington, DC 20240; 202-343-9435.

Denver Service Center, Bureau of Land Management, Denver Federal Center, Building 50, PO Box 25047, Denver, CO 80225-0047; 303-236-6452.

State Offices

Alaska State Office

Bureau of Land Management, 222 W. 7th Avenue, Anchorage, AK 99513; 907-271-5076.

Arizona State Office

Bureau of Land Management, 3707 North 7th St., PO Box 16563, Phoenix, AZ 85011; 602-241-5501.

California State Office

Bureau of Land Management, Federal Building, E-2841, 2800 Cottage Way, Sacramento, CA 95825; 916-978-4743.

Colorado State Office

Bureau of Land Management, 2850 Youngfield St., Lakewood, CO 80215; 303-236-1700.

Eastern States Office (covers states east of the Mississippi and those bordering its west bank)

Bureau of Land Management, 350 South Pickett St., Alexandria, VA 22304; 703-461-1300.

Idaho State Office

Bureau of Land Management, 3380 Americana Terrace, Boise, ID 83706; 208-334-1771.

Montana State Office (also covers North and South Dakota)

Bureau of Land Management, P.O. Box 36800, 222 N. 32nd St., Billings, MT 59107; 406-6576561 .

Nevada State Office

Bureau of Land Management, 850 Harvard Way, PO Box 12000, Reno, NV 89520; 702-784-5311.

New Mexico State Office (also covers Oklahoma and Texas)

Bureau of Land Management, Joseph M. Montoya Federal Building, South Federal Place, PO Box 1449, Santa Fe, NM 87501-1449; 505-988-6030.

Oregon State Office (also covers Washington)

Bureau of Land Management, 1235 NE 47th St., Portland, OR 97213; 503-231-6274.

Utah State Office

Bureau of Land Management, Coordinated Financial Center Building, 324 S. State St., Suite 301, Salt Lake City, UT 84111-2303; 801-524-5311.

Wyoming State Office

Bureau of Land Management, 2515 Warren Ave., PO Box 1828, Cheyenne, WY 82003; 307-7722326.

District Offices

Anchorage District Office

Bureau of Land Management, 6881 Abbott Loop, Anchorage, AK 99507; 907-267-1246.

Arctic District Office

Bureau of Land Management, 1541 Gaffney Rd., Fairbanks, AK 99703; 907-356-5130.

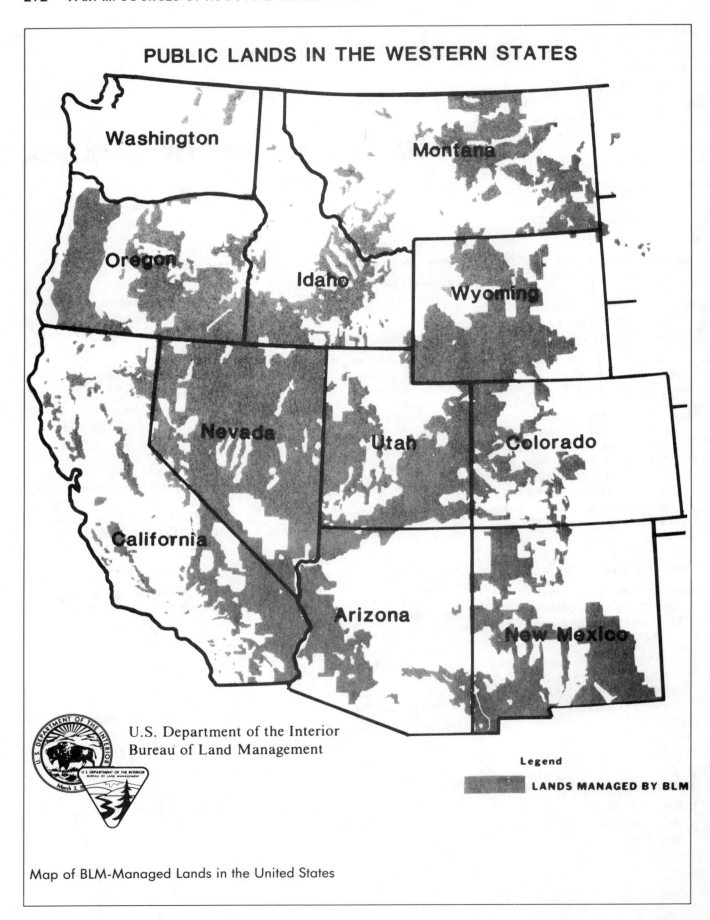

PUBLIC LANDS IN THE WESTERN STATES

U.S. Department of the Interior
Bureau of Land Management

Legend

LANDS MANAGED BY BLM

Map of BLM-Managed Lands in the United States

Arizona Strip District Office

Bureau of Land Management, 390 North, 3050 East, Saint George, UT 84770; 801-673-3545.

Phoenix District Office

Bureau of Land Management, 2015 West Deer Valley Rd., Phoenix, AZ 85027; 602-863-4464.

Safford District Office

Bureau of Land Management, 425 East 4th St., Safford, AZ 85546; 602-428-4040.

Yuma District Office

Bureau of Land Management, 3150 Windsor Ave., PO Box 5680, Yuma, AZ 85364; 602-726-6300.

Bakersfield District Office

Bureau of Land Management, 800 Truxton Ave., Room 302, Bakersfield, CA 93301; 805-861-4191.

Susanville District Office

Bureau of Land Management, 705 Hall St., Susanville, CA 96130; 916-257-5381.

Ukiah District Office

Bureau of Land Management, 555 Leslie St., Post Office Box 940, Ukiah, CA 95482; 707-462-3873.

California Desert District Office

Bureau of Land Management, 1695 Spruce St., Riverside, CA 92507; 714-351-6386.

Canon City District Office

Bureau of Land Management, 3170 East Main St., PO Box 311, Canon City, CO 81212; 303-275-0631.

Grand Junction District Office

Bureau of Land Management, 764 Horizon Dr., Grand Junction, CO 81506; 303-243-6552.

Montrose District Office

Bureau of Land Management, 2465 South Townsend, Montrose, CO 81401; 303-249-7791.

Jackson District Office

Bureau of Land Management, PO Box 11248, Delta Station, Jackson, MS 39213; 601-965-4405.

Milwaukee District Office

Bureau of Land Management, PO Box 631, Milwaukee, WI 53201; 414-291-4400.

Boise District Office

Bureau of Land Management, 3948 Development Ave., Boise, ID 83705; 208-334-1582.

Burley District Office

Bureau of Land Management, Route 3, Box 1, Burley, ID 83318; 208-678-5514.

Coeur d'Alene District Office

Bureau of Land Management, 1808 N. Third St., Coeur d'Alene, ID 83814; 208-765-7356.

Idaho Falls District Office

Bureau of Land Management, 940 Lincoln Rd., Idaho Falls, ID 83401; 208-529-1020.

Salmon District Office

Bureau of Land Management, PO Box 430, Salmon, ID 83467; 208756-5401.

Shoshone District Office

Bureau of Land Management, 400 West "F" St., PO Box 2B, Shoshone, ID 83352; 208-886-2206.

Butte District Office

Bureau of Land Management, 106 North Parkmont, PO Box 3388, Butte, MT 59702; 406-494-5059.

Miles City District Office

Bureau of Land Management, PO Box 950, Miles City, MT 59301; 406-232-4331.

Dickinson District Office

Bureau of Land Management, PO Box 1229, Dickinson, ND 58602; 701-225-9148.

Lewiston District Office

Bureau of Land Management, Airport Rd., Lewiston, MT 59457; 406-538-7461.

Battle Mountain District Office

Bureau of Land Management, PO Box 1420, N. 2nd and Scott Sts., Battle Mountain, NV 89820; 702-635-5181.

Carson City District Office

Bureau of Land Management, Suite 300, 1535 Hot Springs Rd., Carson City, NV 89701; 702-8821631.

Elko District Office

Bureau of Land Management, PO Box 831, Elko, NV 89801; 702-738-4071.

Ely District Office

Bureau of Land Management, Star Route 5, Box 1, Ely, NV 89301; 702-289-4865.

Las Vegas District Office

Bureau of Land Management, PO Box 26569, 4765 Vegas Dr., Las Vegas, NV 89126; 702-388-6627.

Winnemucca District Office

Bureau of Land Management, 705 East 4th St., Winnemucca, NV 89445; 702-623-3676.

Albuquerque District Office

Bureau of Land Management, 435 Montano Rd. NE, Albuquerque, NM 87107; 505-761-4504.

Roswell District Office

Bureau of Land Management, Featherstone Farms Bldg., PO Box 1397, Roswell, NM 88201; 505-622-9042.

Tulsa District Office

Bureau of Land Management, 9522H East 47th Place, Tulsa, OK 74145; 918-581-6480.

Roswell District Office

Bureau of Land Management, Featherstone Farms Building, PO Box 1397, Roswell, NM 88201; 505-622-9042.

Burns District Office

Bureau of Land Management, 74 South Alvord St., Burns, OR 97720; 503-573-5241.

Coos Bay District Office

Bureau of Land Management, 333 South Fourth St., Coos Bay, OR 97420; 503-269-5880.

Eugene District Office

Bureau of Land Management, 1255 Pearl St., PO Box 10226, Eugene, OR 97401; 503-687-6651.

Lakeview District Office

Bureau of Land Management, 1000 Ninth St. S., PO Box 151, Lakeview, OR 97630; 503-947-2177.

Medford District Office

Bureau of Land Management, 3040 Biddle Rd., Medford, OR 97504; 503-776-4173.

Prineville District Office

Bureau of Land Management, 185 East Fourth St., PO Box 550, Prineville, OR 97754; 503-447-4115.

Roseburg District Office

Bureau of Land Management, 777 NW Garden Valley Blvd., Roseburg, OR 97470; 503-672-4491.

Salem District Office

Bureau of Land Management, 1717 Fabry Rd., SE, Salem, OR 97302; 503-399-5643.

Spokane District Office

Bureau of Land Management, East 4217 Main Ave., Spokane, WA 99202; 509-456-2570.

Vale District Office

Bureau of Land Management, 100 Oregon St., PO Box 700, Vale, OR 97918; 503-473-3144.

Salt Lake District Office

Bureau of Land Management, 2370 South 2300 West, Salt Lake City, UT 84119; 801-524-5348.

Cedar City District Office

Bureau of Land Management, 176 East D. L. Sargent Dr., PO Box 724, Cedar City, UT 84720; 801-586-2401.

Richfield District Office

Bureau of Land Management, 150 East 900 North, PO Box 768, Richfield, UT 84701; 801-259-6111.

Moab District Office

Bureau of Land Management, 82 East Dogwood, PO Box 970, Moab, UT 84532; 801-259-6111.

Vernal District Office

Bureau of Land Management, 170 South 500 East, Vernal, UT 84078; 801-789-1362.

Casper District Office

Bureau of Land Management, 951 North Poplar Rd., Casper, WY 82601; 307-261-5101.

Rawlins District Office

Bureau of Land Management, PO Box 670, 1300 Third St., Rawlins, WY 82301; 307-324-7107.

Rock Springs District Office

Bureau of Land Management, Hwy. 191 North, PO Box 1869, Rock Springs, WY 82902; 307-382-5350.

Worland District Office

Bureau of Land Management, 101 South 23rd, PO Box 119, Worland, WY 82401; 307-347-9871.

National Forest Offices, by State

For specific information on National Forests, contact the Forest Service offices within the individual states. (For general sources of National Forest Visitor Maps, see the chapter, "Maps and Literature," earlier in this book.)

Alabama

National Forests in Alabama, 1765 Highland Ave., Montgomery, AL 36107; 205-832-7630.

Arizona

Apache-Sitgraves National Forests, South Mountain Ave., Highway 180, PO Box 640, Springerville, AZ 85938; 602-333-4301.

Cocino National Forest, 2323 E. Greenlaw Lane, Flagstaff, AZ 86004; 602-527-7400.

Coronado National Forest, Federal Building, 300 West Congress, Tucson, AZ 85701; 602-629-6483.

Kaibab National Forest, 800 S. 6th St., Williams, AZ 86046; 602-635-2681.

Prescott National Forest, 344 South Cortez St., Prescott, AZ 86303; 602-445-1762.

Tonto National Forest, 2324 East McDowell Rd., PO Box 5348, Phoenix, AZ 85010; 602-225-5200.

Arkansas

Ouachita National Forest, Box 1270 Federal Building, Hot Springs, AR 71902; 501-321-5202.

Ozark-St. Francis National Forests, 605 West Main, Box 1008, Russellville, AR 72801; 501-968-2354.

California

Angeles National Forest, 701 North Santa Anita Ave., Arcadia, CA 91006; 818-574-5200.

Cleveland National Forest, 880 Front St., Rm. 5-N-14, San Diego, CA 92188; 619-505-0557.

Eldorado National Forest, 100 Forni Rd., Placerville, CA 95667; 916-622-5061.

Inyo National Forest, 873 N. Main St., Bishop, CA 93514; 619-8735841 .

Klamath National Forest, 1312 Fairlane Rd., Yreka, CA 96097; 916-842-6131.

Lake Tahoe Basin Management Unit, PO Box 731002, 870 Emerald Bay Rd., South Lake Tahoe, CA 95731-7302; 916-573-2600.

Lassen National Forest, 55 South Sacramento St., Susanville, CA 96130; 916-257-2151.

Los Padres National Forest, 6144 Calle Real, Goleta, CA 93117; 805-683-6711.

Mendocino National Forest, 420 E. Laurel St., Willows, CA 95988; 916-934-3316.

Modoc National Forest, 441 N. Main St., Alturas, CA 96101; 916-233-5811.

Plumas National Forest, PO Box 1500, 159 Laurence St., Quincy, CA 95971; 916-282-2050.

San Bernardino National Forest, 1824 Commercenter Circle, San Bernardino, CA 92408-3230; 714-383-5588.

Sequoia National Forest, 900 W. Grand Ave., Porterville, CA 93257; 209-784-1500.

Shasta-Trinity National Forests, 2400 Washington Ave., Redding, CA 96001; 916-246-5222.

Sierra National Forest, Federal Building, 1130"0" St., Fresno, CA 93721; 209-487-5155.

Six Rivers National Forest, 507 F St., Eureka, CA 95501; 707-442-1721.

Stanislaus National Forest, 19777 Greenley Rd., Sonora, CA 95370; 209-532-3671.

Tahoe National Forest, Highway 49 and Coyote St., Nevada City, CA 95959; 916-265-4531.

Colorado

Arapaho and Roosevelt National Forests, 240 W. Prospect Rd., Fort Collins, CO 80526-2098; 303-224-1277.

Grand Mesa-Uncompahgre and Gunnisson National Forests, 2250 Highway 50, Delta, CO 81416-8723; 303-874-7691.

Pike and Isabel National Forests, 1920 Valley Dr., Pueblo, CO 81008; 303-545-8737 or 303-545-4328 (recording).

Rio Grande National Forest, 1803 West Highway 60, Monte Vista, CO 80225; 303-236-7386 or 303-236-0900 (recording).

Routt National Forest, 29587 West US 40, Suite 20, Steamboat Springs, CO 80487; 303-879-1722.

San Juan National Forest, 701 Camino del Rio, Rm. 301, Durango, CO 81301; 303-247-4874.

White River National Forest, 9th and Grand, PO Box 948, Glenwood Springs, CO 81602; 303-945-2521.

Georgia

Chattahoochee-Oconee National Forests, 508 Oak St., N.W., Gainesville, GA 30501; 404-536-0541 .

Idaho

Boise National Forest, 1750 Front St., Boise, ID 83702; 208-334-1516.

Caribou National Forest, Federal Building, Suite 294, 250 South 4th Ave., Pocatello, ID 83201; 208-236-6700.

Challis National Forest, Highway 93, PO Box 404, Challis, ID 83226; 208-879-2285.

Clearwater National Forest, Highway 93, PO Box 404, Challis, ID 83226; 208-879-2285.

Idaho Panhandle National Forests, (Coeur d'Alene, Kaniksu, St. Joe), 1201 Ironwood Dr., Coeur d'Alene, ID 83814; 208-765-7223.

Nez Perce National Forest, PO Box 1026, Route 2, Box 475, Grangeville, ID 83830.

Payette National Forest, 106 Park St., PO Box 1026, McCall, ID 83638; 208-634-2255.

Salmon National Forest, Forest Service Building, Highway 93 North, PO Box 729, Salmon, ID 83467; 208-756-2215.

Sawtooth National Forest, 1525 Addison Ave. East, Twin Falls, ID 83467; 208-733-3698.

Targhee National Forest, 420 North Bridge St., PO Box 208, St. Anthony, ID 83445; 208-624-3151.

Kentucky

Daniel Boone National Forest, 100 Vaught Rd., Winchester, KY 40391; 606-745-3100.

Maine

See New Hampshire.

Michigan

Hiawatha National Forest, 2727 North Lincoln Rd., Escanaba, MI 49829; 906-786-4062.

Huron-Mantistee National Forests, 421 South Mitchell St., Cadillac, MI 49601; 616-775-2421.

Ottawa National Forest, Ironwood, MI 49938; 906-932-1330.

Minnesota

Chippewa National Forest, Cass Lake, MN 56633; 218-335-2226.

Superior National Forest, Federal Building, PO Box 338, Duluth, MN 55801; 218-727-6692.

Missouri

Mark Twain National Forest, 3003 East Trafficway, Springfield, MO 65802; 314-783-7225.

Montana

Beaverhead National Forest, Montana 41 and Skiki St., Dillon, MT 59725; 406-683-2312.

Bitterroot National Forest, 316 N. 3rd St., Hamilton, MT 59840; 406-363-3131.

Custer National Forest, PO Box 2556, Billings, MT 59103; 406-657-6361.

Deerlodge National Forest, Federal Building, Box 400, Butte, MT 59701; 406-496-3400.

Flathead National Forest, PO Box 147, 1935 3rd Ave., E., Kalispell, MT 59901; 406-755-5401.

Gallatin National Forest, Federal Building, Box 130, Bozeman, MT 59715; 406-587-5271.

Helena National Forest, Federal Building, Drawer 10014, Helena, MT 59601; 406-449-5201.

Kootenai National Forest, PO Box AS, W. Highway 2, Libby, MT 59923; 406-293-6211.

Lewis and Clark National Forest, Box 871, 1601 2nd Ave., N.,Great Falls, MT 59403; 406-727-0901.

Lolo National Forest, Building 24, Fort Missoula, Missoula, MT 59801; 406-329-3557.

Nevada

Humboldt National Forest, 976 Mountain City Highway, Elko, NV 89801; 702-738-5171.

Toiyabe National Forest, 111 North Virginia St., Room 601, Reno, NV 89501; 702-784-5331.

New Hampshire and Maine

White Mountain National Forest, Federal Building, 719 Main St., Laconia, NH 03246; 603-524-6450.

New Mexico

Carson National Forest, Forest Service Building, PO Box 558, 112 Cruz Alta Rd., Taos, NM 87571; 505-758-6200.

Cibola National Forest, 10308 Candelaria NE, Albuquerque, NM 87112; 505-275-5207.

Gila National Forest, 2610 North Silver St., Silver City, NM 88061; 505-388-8201.

Lincoln National Forest. Federal Building, 11th and New York, Alamagordo, NM 88310; 505-437-6030.

Santa Fe National Forest, 120 St. Francis Dr., PO Box 1689, Santa Fe, NM 87504; 505-988-6940.

New York

See Vermont.

North Carolina

National Forests in North Carolina, Post and Otis Street, Asheville, NC 28801; 704-257-4200.

Ohio

Wayne-Hoosier National Forests, 3527 Tenth St., Bedford, IN 47421; 812-275-5987.

Oregon

Deschutes National Forest, 1645 Hwy. 20 E., Bend, OR 97701; 509-684-3711.

Fremont National Forest, 34 North G. St., PO Box 551, Lakeview, OR 97630; 503-947-2151.

Mt. Hood National Forest, 2955 NW Division, Gresham, OR 97023; 503-666-0700.

Ochoco National Forest, 155 North Court, PO Box 490, Prineville, OR 97754; 503-447-6247.

Rogue River National Forest, Federal Building, 333 West 8th St., PO Box 520, Medford, OR 97501; 503-776-3600.

Siskiyou National Forest, 200 NE Greenfield Rd., PO Box 440, Grant's Pass, OR 97526; 503-479-5301.

Siuslaw National Forest, 4077 Research Way, PO Box 1148, Corvallis, OR 97333; 503-757-4480.

Umatilla National Forest, 2517 SW Hailey Dr., Pendleton, OR 97801; 503-276-3811.

Umpqua National Forest, 2900 NW Stewart Parkway, PO Box 1008, Roseburg, OR 97470; 503-676-6601.

Wallowa-Whitman National Forests, 1550 Dewey Ave., PO Box 907, Baker, OR 97814; 503-523-6391.

Willamette National Forest, Federal Building, 211 East 7th Ave., PO Box 10607, Eugene, OR 97440; 503-662-4335.

Winema National Forest, Post Office Building, 2nd Floor, 7th and Walnut Sts., PO Box 1390, Klamath Falls, OR 97601; 503-883-6714.

Pennsylvania

Allegheny National Forest, Spiridon Building, Box 847, Warren, PA 16365; 814-726-1291.

South Carolina

Francis Marion-Sumter National Forests, 1805 Assembly St., Rm. 333, PO Box 2227, Columbia, SC 29202; 803-765-5222.

Tennessee

Cherokee National Forest, 2800 N. Ocoee St., Box 2010, Cleveland, TN 37311; 615-476-9700.

Texas

National Forests in Texas, Homer Garrison Federal Building, 701 N. First St., Lufkin, TX 75901; 409-639-8501.

Utah

Ashley National Forest, 437 East Main, Vernal, UT 84078; 801-789-1181.

Dixie National Forest, 82 North 100 East, PO Box 580, Cedar City, UT 84720; 801-586-2421.

Fishlake National Forest, 170 North Main St., PO Box 628, Richfield, UT 84701; 801-896-4491.

Manti-Lasal National Forest, 599 West Price River Dr., Price, UT 84501; 801-637-2817.

Unita National Forest, 88 West 100 North, PO Box 1428, Provo, UT 84603; 801-377-5780.

Wasatch National Forest, 8226 Federal Bldg., 125 South State Street, Salt Lake City, UT 84109; 801-524-5030.

Vermont and New York

Green Mountain National Forest, Federal Building, PO Box 519, Rutland, VT 05701; 802-773-2300.

Virginia

George Washington National Forest, Harrison Plaza, PO Box 233, North Main St., Harrisonburg, VA 22801; 703-433-2591.

Jefferson National Forest, 210 Franklin Rd., S.W., Roanoke, VA 24001; 703-982-6270.

Washington

Colville National Forest, Federal Building, 695 South Main St., Colville, WA 99114; 509-684-3711.

Gifford Pinchot National Forest, 500 West 12th St., Vancouver, WA 98660; 206-696-7500 or 503-285-9823.

Mt. Baker-Snoqualmie National Forest, 1022 First Ave., Seattle, WA 98104; 206-442-5400.

Okanogan National Forest, 1240 Second Ave. S., PO Box 950, Okanogan, WA 98840; 509-422-2704.

Olympic National Forest, 801 Capitol Way, PO Box 2288, Olympia, WA 98507; 206-753-9535.

Wenatchee National Forest, 301 Yakima St., PO Box 811, Wenatchee, WA 98801; 509-662-4335.

West Virginia

Forest Supervisor, Monongahela National Forest, Sycamore St., Box 1548, Elkins, WV 26241; 304-478-3251.

Wisconsin

Chequamegon National Forest, Federal Building, Park Falls, WI 54552; 715-762-2462.

Nicolet National Forest, Federal Building, Rhinelander, WI 54501; 715-362-3415.

Wyoming

Bighorn National Forest, 1969 S. Sheridan Ave., Sheridan, WY 82801; 307-672-0751.

Black Hills National Forest, Forest Service Office Building, PO Box 680, Sundance, WY 82729; 307-283-1361.

Bridger-Teton National Forest, Forest Service Building, 340 North Cache, PO Box 1888, Jackson, WY 83001; 307-733-2752.

Medicine Bow National Forest, 605 Skyline Dr., Laramie, WY 82070; 307-745-8971.

Shoshone National Forest, 225 W. Yellowstone, PO Box 2140, Cody, WY 82414.

National Park Service Offices

Chief of Public Affairs, National Park Service, Department of the Interior, PO Box 37127, Washington, DC 20013-7127; 202-343-7394.

The following two offices of the National Park Service give assistance and advice to individuals and organizations interested in protecting rivers and trails, whether or not these natural resources are part of the National Park System. Contact:

National Program Office, Rivers and Trails Conservation Assistance, National Park Service, Division of

Recreation Resources Assistance, PO Box 37127, Washington, DC 20013; 202-343-3775.

Western Regional Office, Rivers and Trails Conservation Assistance, National Park Service, Division of Recreation Resources Assistance, 450 Golden Gate Avenue, San Francisco, CA 94102; 415-556-5751.

Park Service Offices for the individual parks include:

Arcadia National Park, Rt. 1, Box 1, Bar Harbor, ME 04609; 207-288-3338.

Badlands National Park, PO Box 6, Interior, SD 57750; 605-433-5361.

Big Bend National Park, Big Bend National Park, TX 7 9834; 915-477-2251.

Bighorn Canyon National Recreation Area, PO Box 458, Hardin, MT 59035; 406-666-2412.

Bryce Canyon National Park, Bryce Canyon, UT 84717; 801-834-5322.

Canyonlands National Park, First Western Building, 72 South Main, Moab, UT 84532; 801-259-7164.

Chesapeake and Ohio Canal National Historical Park, Box 158, Sharpesburg, MD 21782; 301-739-4200.

Crater Lake National Park, PO Box 7, Crater Lake, OR 97604; 503-594-2211.

Dinosaur National Monument, PO Box 101, Dinosaur, CO 81610; 303-374-2216.

Glacier National Park, West Glacier, MT 59936; 406-888-5441.

Glen Canyon National Recreation Area, PO Box 1507, Page, AZ 86040; 801-684-2212.

Grand Canyon National Park and Grand Canyon National Monument, PO Box 129, Grand Canyon, AZ 86023; 602-638-2411.

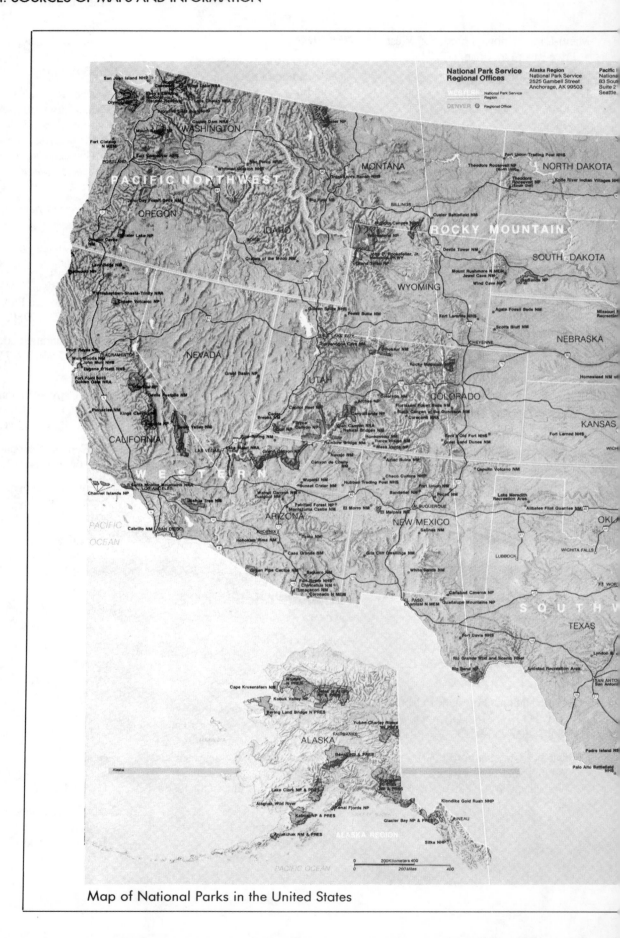

Map of National Parks in the United States

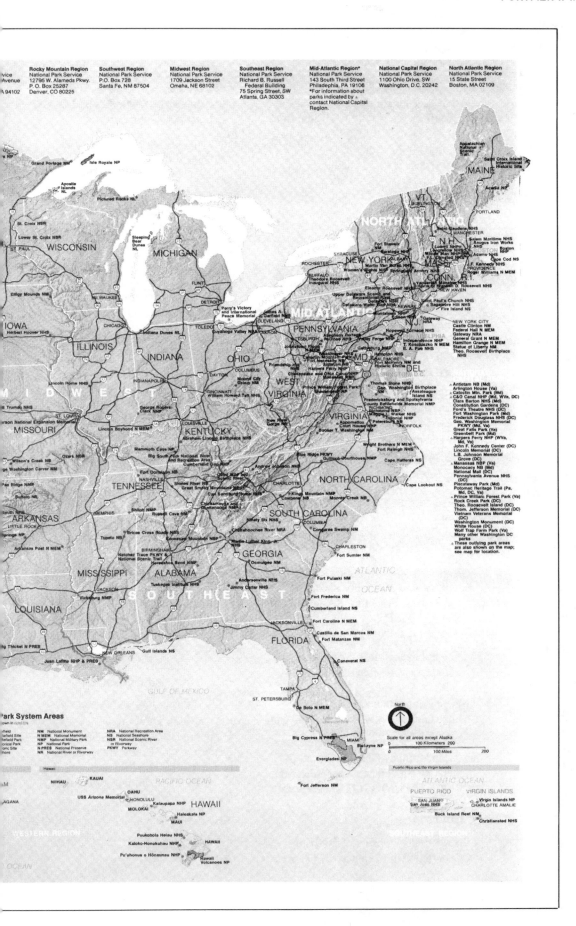

Rocky Mountain Region
National Park Service
12795 W. Alameda Pkwy.
P. O. Box 25287
Denver, CO 80225

Southwest Region
National Park Service
P.O. Box 728
Santa Fe, NM 87504

Midwest Region
National Park Service
1709 Jackson Street
Omaha, NE 68102

Southeast Region
National Park Service
Richard B. Russell
Federal Building
75 Spring Street, SW
Atlanta, GA 30303

Mid-Atlantic Region*
National Park Service
143 South Third Street
Philadelphia, PA 19106
*For information about
parks indicated by △
contact National Capital
Region.

National Capital Region
National Park Service
1100 Ohio Drive, SW
Washington, D.C. 20242

North Atlantic Region
National Park Service
15 State Street
Boston, MA 02109

Grand Teton National Park, PO Drawer 170, Moose, WY 83012; 307-733-2880.

Great Smoky Mountains National Park, Gatlinburg, TN 37738; 615-436-5615.

Isle Royale National Park, 87 North Ripley St., Houghton, MI 49931; 906-482-3310.

Lake Mead National Recreation Area, 601 Nevada Highway, Boulder City, NV 89005; 702-293-4041.

Lassen Volcanic National Park, Mineral, CA 96063; 916-5995-4444.

Lava Beds National Monument, PO Box 867, Tulelake, CA 96134; 916-667-2282.

Mount Rainier National Park, Tahoma Woods, Star Route, Longmire, WA 98397; 206-569-2211.

North Cascades National Park with Lake Chelan and Ross Lake National Recreation Areas, 800 State St., Sedro Woolley, WA 98284; 206-855-1331.

Olympic National Park, 600 East Park Ave., Port Angeles, WA 9 8362; 206-452-4501.

State Tourism Offices

Most of these offices are sources of useful information that include campground guides, state outdoors guides, and high-quality (free!) state maps. Tourism offices are also always good first eddies before descending into the state bureaucracy mainstream in search of information. Listed below are state tourism offices; titles of especially relevant available documents are below each address.

Alabama Bureau of Tourism and Travel, 532 S. Perry St., Montgomery, AL 36104; 800-392-8096 (in state), 800-ALABAMA (out of state).

Arizona Office of Tourism, 1480 East Bethany Home Rd., Phoenix, AZ 85014; 602-255-3618.
"Arizona River Rafters"

Arkansas Department of Parks and Tourism, 1 Capitol Mall, Little Rock, AR 72201; 800-482-8999 (in state), 800-643-8383 (out of state).
"State Park Fees and Facilities and Arkansas Campers' Guide"

California Office of Tourism, 1122 L St., 1st Floor, Sacramento, CA 95814; 800-862-2553.

Colorado Tourism Board, PO Box 38700, Dept. RMA, Denver, CO 80238; 800-255-5550.

Connecticut Vacations, Dept. of Economic Development, 210 Washington St., Hartford, CT 06106; 800-842-7492 (in state), 800-243-1685 (northeast), 203-566-3385.

Delaware Tourism Office, PO Box 1401, 99 Kings Highway, Dover, DE 19903; 800-282-8667 (in state), 800-441-8846.

Tour Georgia, PO Box 1776, Atlanta, GA 30301; 404-656-3590.

Idaho Tourism, Statehouse, Room 108, Boise, ID 83720; 800-635-7820.
"Idaho Vacation Planner" (lists parks, forests, campgrounds, outfitters and guides).

Kentucky Travel, Capitol Plaza Tower, 22nd Floor, Frankfort, KY 40601; 800-225-TRIP.
"Kentucky Outdoor Recreation Guide"

Maine Publicity Bureau, 97 Winthrop St., Hallowell, ME 04347; 207-289-2423.
"Maine Canoe Rentals"
"Maine Guided Whitewater Rafting and Canoe Trips"

Maryland Office of Tourist Development, 45 Calvert St., Annapolis, MD 21401; 301-269-3517.
"Maryland Outdoor Guide" (lists outfitters).

Massachusetts Division of Tourism, Department of Commerce, PO Box 30226, Boston, MA 02202; 617-727-3201.

Michigan Travel Bureau, Department of Commerce, PO Box 30226, Lansing, MI 48909; 800-543-2YES.
"Michigan Canoeing Directory"

Minnesota Office of Tourism, 240 Bremer Building, St. Paul, MN 55101; 800-328-1461.

Missouri Division of Tourism, Truman Building, PO Box 1055, Jefferson City, MO 65102; 314-751-4133.

Montana Promotional Division, Department of Commerce, 1424 Ninth Ave., Helena, MT 5 9620.
"The Montana Accommodations Guide" (lists outfitters and guides).

Nevada Commission of Tourism, Capitol Complex, Carson City, NV 89710; 702-885-4322.

New Hampshire Office of Vacation Travel, PO Box 856, Concord, NH 03301; 603-271-2666.
"Summer Canoeing and Kayaking in The White Mountains of New Hampshire"
"About Stream Canoeing in New Hampshire"

New Mexico Travel Division, Economic Development and Tourism Department, 1100 St. Francis Dr., Room 1057, Santa Fe, NM 87503; 800-545-2040.

Division of Tourism, New York State Department of Commerce, I Commerce Place, Albany, NY 12245; 800-225-5697.
"Camping and Outdoor Adventures" (lists rivers, outfitters and campgrounds).

North Carolina Travel and Tourism Director, 430 North Salisbury, Department of Commerce, Raleigh, NC 27611; 800-VISIT-NC.
"North Carolina Camping and Outdoors Directory"

Ohio Office of Travel and Tourism, PO Box 1001, Columbus, OH 43216; 1-800-BUCKEYE.

Oregon Economic Development Department, Tourism Division, 596 Cottage St., NE, Salem, OR 97310; 800-547-7842.
"A Guide to Oregon Boating Facilities"
"Oregon Outdoor Recreation: Fishing, Hunting, River Running"

Pennsylvania Bureau of Travel Development, Department of Commerce, 416 Forum Building, Harrisburg, PA 17120; 800-VISIT-PA

South Carolina Department of Parks, Recreation and Tourism, PO Box 71, Columbia, SC 29202; 803-758-8735.

Tennessee Tourist Development, PO Box 23170, Nashville, TN 37202; 615-741-2158.
"Outdoors in Tennessee" (lists whitewater rivers, canoe liveries, and rafting outfitters).

Travel and Information Division, Texas Department of Highways and Public Transportation, PO Box 5064, Austin, TX 78763; 512-465-7401.

Utah Travel Council, Council Hall, Capitol City, Salt Lake City, UT 84114; 801-533-5681.
"Tour Guide to Utah: 1987 Operators and Packages" (lists rivers and outfitters).
"Utah Travel Guide" (lists parks, forests, and campgrounds).

Vermont Travel Division, 134 State St., Montpelier, VT 05602; 802-828-3236.
"Vermont Guide to Fishing Map" (shows canoeable streams and danger spots).

Virginia Division of Tourism, 101 N. Ninth St., Bell Tower, Richmond, VA 23219; 800-VISIT-VA.

Tourism Development Division, Washington State Department of Trade and Economic Development, 101 General Administration Building, Olympia, WA 98504-0613; 800-562-4570 (in state), 800-541-WASH (out of state).

Travel West Virginia, Capitol Complex, Charleston, WV 25305; 800-CALL-WVA.
"Outdoor Recreation Guide" (lists parks, forests, clubs, rivers, and outfitters).
"Your Guide to Who Does What on Which of West Virginia's Rivers" (lists rivers and outfitters).

Wisconsin Department of Tourism, PO Box 7606, Madison, WI 53707; 608-266-2161.
"Wisconsin's Greatest Hits: Attraction and Recreation Guide" (lists outfitters and canoe liveries).
"Wisconsin Spring and Summer Escapes" (lists popular canoeing rivers, and provides an awesome list and map of waterfalls, handy for addicts of the big plunge).

Wyoming Travel Commission, Interstate 25 at College Dr., Cheyenne, WY 82002; 800-CALL-WYO.
"Wyoming's Family Water Sports"

Offices of Federal Agencies

Office of Public Affairs, Bureau of Land Management, Department of the Interior, Washington, DC 20240; 202-343-9435.

Office of Public Affairs, Bureau of Reclamation, Department of the Interior, C Street between 18th and 19th Sts., Washington, DC 20240; 202-343-1100.

Office of Public Affairs, National Oceanic and Atmospheric Administration, Department of Commerce, Washington, DC 20230; 202-377-4190.

National Weather Service, National Oceanic and Atmospheric Administration, Department of Commerce, 8060 13th St., Silver Spring, MD 20910; 301-427-7622.

Information Office, National Forest Service, Department of Agriculture, PO Box 2417, Washington, DC 20013; 202-447-3760.

Public Affairs Office, Office of the Chief of Engineers, US Army Corps of Engineers, Washington, DC 20314-1000; 202-272-0010.

Chief of Public Affairs, National Park Service, Department of the Interior, PO Box 37127, Washington, DC 20013-7127; 202-343-7394.

Public Affairs Office, United States Geological Survey, Department of the Interior, 119 National Center, Reston, VA 22092; 703-648-4460.

Central Region, United States Geological Survey, Department of the Interior, Denver Federal Center, Denver, CO 80225; 303-234-3661.

Eastern Region, United States Geological Survey, Department of the Interior, 12201 Sunrise Valley Dr., Reston, VA 22092; 703-860-7414.

Western Region, United States Geological Survey, Department of the Interior, 345 Middle Field Rd., Menlo Park, CA 94025.

Superintendent of Documents (central source of all government documents), US Government Printing Office, Washington, DC 204029325; 202-783-3238.

PART IV

ORGANIZATIONS AND SCHOOLS

ORGANIZATIONS

Conservation Groups

National and International

American Rivers (formerly American Rivers Conservation Council), 800 Pennsylvania Ave., SE, Suite 303, Washington, DC 20003; 202-547-6900.

Environmental Defense Fund, 2728 Durant, Berkeley, CA 94704.

Friends of the Earth, 530 7th Street, SE, Washington, DC 20003; 202-543-4312.

International Rivers Network, 301 Broadway, Suite B, San Francisco, CA 94133; 415-986-4694.

National Audubon Society, 950 Third Avenue, New York, NY 10022.

The Nature Conservancy, 1800 North Kent Street, Arlington, VA 22209; 703-841-5300.

The River Conservation Fund, 323 Pennsylvania Ave., NE, Washington, DC 20003; 202-547-6900.

River Watch, c/o American Rivers, 800 Pennsylvania Ave., SE, Suite 303, Washington, DC 20003; 202-547-6900.

The Sierra Club, 730 Polk St., San Francisco, CA 94109.

The Trust for Public Land, 116 New Montgomery, Third Floor, San Francisco, CA 94105; 415-495-5660.

Wilderness Society, Suite S-176, 3900 Wisconsin Ave., NW, Washington, DC 20016.

Regional and Local

American River Coalition, 909 12th St., Suite 207A, Sacramento, CA 95814; 916-448-1045.

California Natural Resources Federation, 2830 Tenth St., Berkeley, CA 94710; 415-848-2211.

California Wilderness Coalition, 2655 Portage Bay East, Suite 5, Davis, CA 95616; 916-758-0380.

Clavey River Preservation Coalition, PO Box 455, Sonora, CA 95370.

Friends of the River, Fort Mason, Building C, San Francisco, CA 94123; 415-771-0400.

Grand Canyon Trust, 1400 16th St. NW, Suite 300, Washington, DC 20036.

Lower Kern Recreation Association, 2118 Chester Lane, Bakersfield, CA 93304.

Northwest Rivers Council, PO Box 88, Seattle, WA 98111.

Oregon Rivers Council, PO Box 309, Eugene, OR 97440; 503-345-0119.

Savage River Defense Fund, c/o Mac Thornton, 322 Tenth St. SE, Washington, DC 20003.

Save the American River Association, PO Box 19496, Sacramento, CA 95819.

Southern Utah Wilderness Alliance, PO Box 518, Cedar City, Utah 84720; 801-586-8242.

South Yuba River Citizens League, PO Box 841, Nevada City, CA 95959; 916-265-5962.

The Wilderness Public Rights Club, PO Box 5791, Portland, OR 97228.

Professional Organizations

Forest and Park Rangers and other governmental river management officials belong to this organization:

American Rivers Management Society, Western Region, 7348 Sheephorn Mountain, Littleton, CO 80123

or, in the East,

American Rivers Management, Eastern Region, c/o Stuart Lewis, Administrator Ohio Scenic Rivers, Ohio Department of Natural Resources, 1889 Fountain Square, Columbus, OH 43224

A professional organization for both retailers, manufacturers, and outfitters is the North American Paddlesports Association. The principal goal of this group is to promote participation in Paddlesports:

North American Paddlesports Association, 715 Boylston, Boston, MA 02116; 617-266-6800.

The U.S. Inflatable Boat Manufacturers Association, 1800 K St., Suite 1000, Washington, DC 20006.

Rescue and Wilderness Medicine Organizations

National Association for Search and Rescue, PO Box 3709, Fairfax, VA 22038; 702-352-1349.

Wilderness Medical Society, PO Box 397, Point Reyes Station, CA 94956. 415-663-9107.

Outfitters' Organizations

The easiest way to locate outfitters is through their professional organizations. In the West, usually both the guides themselves and the outfitting companies are members of the organizations (the Idaho Outfitters and Guides Association, the Montana Outfitters and Guides Association, the Oregon Guides and Packers, and the Western River Guides Association). In the East the companies alone are associated with the Eastern Professional River Outfitters Association. To rent canoes and the like, turn to members of the National Association of Canoe Liveries and Outfitters. Each of these organizations is glad to provide you with a list of their members' addresses and telephone numbers.

Colorado River Outfitters Association, PO Box 502, Westminister, CO 80030; 303-220-8640.

Eastern Professional River Outfitters Association, 530 South Gay St., Suite 222, Knoxville, TN 37902; 615-524-1045.

Idaho Outfitters and Guides Association, Inc., PO Box 95, Boise, ID 83701; 208-342-1438.

Montana Outfitters and Guides Association, PO Box 631, Hot Springs, MT 59845.

National Association of Canoe Liveries and Outfitters, PO Box 1405, 225 East North St., Suite A, Indianapolis, IN 46202; 317-637-3564.

National Association of Canoe Liveries and Outfitters, California Division, c/

o Jim Sughrue, 3213 Sierra St., Riverbank, CA 95637.

Oregon Guides and Packers, Inc., PO Box 132, Sublimity, OR 93785.

Western River Guides Association,

Inc., 4260 E. Evans, Suite 8, Denver, CO 80222; 303-771-0389.

Whitewater Outfitters Association of Maine, Inc., P.O. Box 80, West Forks, ME 04985.

Worldwide Outfitter and Guides Association, PO Box 520400, Salt Lake City, UT 84152; 801-942-7863.

Private Boaters' Organizations

INTERNATIONAL

Project Raft is concerned with fostering international fellowship by means of cooperative international boating festivals and expeditions:

Project Raft, Russians and Americans for Teamwork, 209 Douglas Lane, Pleasant Hill, CA 94523; 415-935-4528.

NATIONAL

American Canoe Association, 8580 Cinderbed Rd., Suite 900, Newington, VA 22122; 203-550-7523.

American Whitewater Affiliation, 146 N. Broadway, Palatine, IL 60067.

National Organization for River Sports, PO Box 6847, 314 N. 20th Street, Colorado Springs, CO 80934.

United States Canoe Association, PO Box 5743, Lafayette, IN 47903; 317-474-9391.

REGIONAL

Alabama

Birmingham Canoe Club, Box 951, Birmingham, AL 35201.

Gunwale Grabbers, PO Box 19913, Birmingham, AL 35219.

Alaska

Juneau Kayak Club, 2725 John St., Juneau, AK 99801.

Valdez Alpine Club, c/o Andrew Embick, PO Box 1889, Valdez, AK 99686.

Arkansas

Arkansas Canoe Club, 1221 Reservoir Road #257, Little Rock, AR 72207; 501-521-5672.

Arizona

Arizona River Runners, 25 S. Lazona Dr. #26, Mesa, AZ 85204.

Central Arizona Paddlers Club, c/o Roger Seba, 18 W. Main St., Mesa, AZ 85201.

Northern Arizona Paddlers Club, c/o Michael E. Baron, 611 N. San Francisco Street, Flagstaff, AZ 86001; 602-774-0844.

California

California Kayak Friends, 14252 Culver Drive, A-199, Irvine, CA 92714.

Canoe Section of the San Francisco Chapter of the Sierra Club, c/o Eunice Vander Meer, 19027 Mayberry Drive, Castro Valley, CA 94546; 415-582-6898.

Friends of the River Rafting Chapter, c/o Friends of the River, Building C, Fort Mason Center, San Francisco, CA 94123-1382; 415-441-8778.

Haystackers, PO Box Y, Kernville, CA 93238.

National Outdoor College Paddling Club, 11383 Pyrites Way #A, Rancho Cordova, CA 95670.

Redlands High School Rafters, c/o Doug Chambers and Andy Reese, Redlands High School, 840 E. Citrus, Redlands, CA 92374.

Redwood Empire Paddlers' Section of the Sierra Club, c/o Nancy Gunn, 543 Mountain View Avenue, Santa Rosa, CA 95404; 707-546-5951.

River City Paddlers, 2524 Marshall Way, Sacramento, CA 95818; 916-361-3133.

River City Whitewater Club, 5441 10th Avenue, Sacramento, CA 95820; 916-371-3153.

San Francisco Bay River Touring Section of the Sierra Club, c/o Bill Brendt, 1544 Loganberry Way, Pleasanton, CA 94566.

Santa Cruz Kayak Club, P.O. Box 7228, Santa Cruz, CA 95061-7228.

Sequoia Canoe Club, Section of the Redwood Chapter of the Sierra Club, c/o Tom Meldau, PO Box 1164, Windsor, CA 95492; 707-526-0540.

Shasta Paddlers, c/o Mark Twitchel, 3330 Oakwood Pl., Redding, CA 96001.

Sierra Club, Angeles Chapter, River Touring Section, c/o Tom Church, PO Box 3397, Quartz Hill, CA 93536.

Sierra Club, Loma Prieta Chapter, Paddlers Section, c/o Ken Brunton, 525 Bonnie View Court, Morgan Hill, CA 95037; 408-779-2867.

Southern California Canoe Association, c/o Norm Malin, 8665 Nagle Avenue, Panorama City, CA 91402.

Western Waters Canoe Club, c/o Rich Burchby, 840 Town and Country Village, San Jose, CA 95128; 408-298-6300.

Colorado

Colorado Animas River Days Club, PO Box 379, Durango, CO 81302.

Colorado Rocky Mountain School, c/o Bob Campbell, 1493 County Road, Carbondale, CO 81623.

Colorado Whitewater Association, 7600 East Arapahoe Road, Englewood, CO 80112; 303-770-0515.

Confluence Club, PO Box 4167, Aspen, CO 81612.

High Country River Rafters, c/o Kathy and Roy Dvorak, 4665 W. 102nd. Pl., Westminister, CO 80960.

Pikes Peak Whitewater Club, c/o Kathleen M Laurin, 1814 W. Boulder, Colorado Springs, CO 80904; 719-471-2640.

Rocky Mountain Canoe Club, c/o Sandy Horn, 25074 N. Turkey Creek Road, Evergreen, CO 80439.

W.A.T.E.R., PO Box 3131, Grand Junction, CO 81502.

Connecticut

Columbia Canoe Club, c/o Charles Herrick, 38 Hunt Road, Columbia, CT 06237.

Connecticut Canoe Racing Association, 785 Bow Lane, Middletown, CT 06457; 203-346-0068.

Connecticut Chapter, Appalachian Mountain Club, c/o Richard Ploski, 29 Hardwich Rd., Forestville, CT 06010.

Connecticut River, Oar and Paddle Club, 18 Riverside Ave., Old Saybrook, CT 06475; 203-388-2343.

Farmington River Club, PO Box 475, Canton, CT 06019.

Hong Kong Snakes Kayak Club, 22 Bushy Hill Road, Simsbury, CT 06070.

Housatonic Area Canoe and Kayak Squad, c/o Douglas Gordon, RR Box #307, West Cornwall, CT 06796.

District of Columbia

See: Maryland/DC Area.

Florida

Florida Canoe and Kayak Association, c/o Butch Horn, PO Box 837, Tallahassee, FL 32302.

Georgia

Atlanta Whitewater Club, PO Box 33, Clarkston, GA 30021; 404-422-2643.

Canoocochee Canoe Race Association, c/o Dale Todd, Route 2, Box 179H, Claxton, GA 30417.

Central Georgia River Runners, c/o Richard Burnes, PO Box 6563, Macon, GA 31208.

Coastal Georgia Paddling Club, c/o Andrew Rea, 615 E. 44th St., Savannah, GA 31405.

Columbus College Canoe Club, 004C Woodruff Gyn College, Columbus, GA 31907.

Georgia Canoeing Association, Box 7023, Atlanta, GA 30357.

Ohoopee Canoe Club, PO Box 1186, Vidalia, GA 30474.

Idaho

Idaho Whitewater Assoc., c/o Grant Amaral, PO Box 721, Boise, ID 83701; 208-726-5244.

R.A.F.T. (River Access for Tomorrow), PO Box 1666, Lewiston, ID 83501.

Illinois

American Youth Hostels, c/o Anne Findeis, 3712 North Clark, Chicago, IL 60613; 312-327-8114.

Central Illinois Whitewater Club, c/o Roy Johnson, 2502 Willow St., Pekin, IL 61554.

Chicago Whitewater Association, 1343 No. Portage, Palantine, IL 60067; 312-359-5947.

Decatur Paddlers, 32 Whippoorwill Drive, Decatur, IL 62526.

G.L.O.P., c/o James Tibenski, PO Box 2576, Chicago, IL 60014.

Lincoln Park Boat Club, c/o Bill Thompson, 2631 N. Richmond, Chicago, IL 60647; 312-278-5539.

Middle Fork Paddling Group, c/o C.E. Wilson, PO Box 8, Urbana, IL 61801; 217-328-6666.

Prairie State Canoeists, c/o Ken Beck, 570 Webford, Des Plaines, IL 60016; 708-299-3977.

Pontiac Paddlers, c/o Janeen Pfaff, Rt. 4, Box 30, Pontiac, IL 61764.

St. Charles Canoe Club, c/o Gustave Lamperez, 24 Roosevelt St., St. Charles, IL 60174.

Indiana

Hoosier Canoe Club, c/o Dennis Kirkman, 6212 Furnas Road, Indianapolis, IN 46241.

Michiana Watershed Ind., PO Box 1284, Marion, IN 46952.

Mississinewa Canoe Club, c/o Jim Hensley, 2016 W. Walnuts, Marion, IN 46952.

South Bend Moving Water Club, c/o Jim Wagner, 3220 E. Jefferson Blvd., South Bend IN 46615; 219-234-0191.

Whitewater Valley Canoe Club, c/o Larry Sintz, 8157 Highway 52, Brookville, IN 47012.

Wildcat Canoe Club, c/o Lance Shelby, PO Box 6232, Kokomo, IN 46904.

Kansas

Kansas Canoe Association, c/o Sam Segraves, Box 2885, Wichita, KS 67201.

Kentucky

Bluegrass Pack and Paddle Club, 216 Inverness Dr., Lexington, KY 40503.

Bluegrass Wildwater Association, PO Box 4231, Lexington, KY 40504; Home of the Women in Rubber!

Elkhorn Paddlers, c/o Harold and Sue Jeffers, 1310 Deerfield Dr., Frankfort, KY 40601.

Four Corners Canoe Club, 523 Ilsen Barkley Dr., Paduce, KY 42021.

Kentucky Canoe Association, 2006 Marilee Dr., Louisville, KY 40272.

Southern Kentucky Paddlers Society, PO Box 265, Bowling Green, KY 42102.

Viking Canoe Club, PO Box 32263; Louisville, KY 40232.

Maine

Bangor Parks and Recreation Department, c/o Dale W. Theriauli, 100 Dutton Street, Bangor, ME 04401.

Bowdoin Outing Club, c/o J. Lentz, Sargent Gym, Bowdoin College, Brunswick, ME 04011.

Hebron Academy Outing Club, Hebron, ME 04238.

Kennebeck Sewer Runners, c/o Paul Reinstein, RFD 31, PO Box 5240, Skowhegan, ME 04976.

Maine Canoe/Kayak Racing Organization, c/o Earl H. Baldwin, RFD. 2, PO Box 268, Orrington, ME 04474; 207-825-4439.

Penobscot Paddle and Chowder Society, c/o Diane Laing, RFD 3, PO Box 840, Pittsfield, ME 04967.

UMM Outing Club, c/o Richard Scribner, 9 O'Brien Avenue, Machias, ME 04654.

York Hospital Canoe Club, c/o Don Delozier, PO Box 643, York, ME 03909.

Maryland/DC Area

Canoe Cruisers of Greater Washington DC, Inc., PO Box 572, Arlington, VA 22216.

Greater Baltimore Canoe Club, c/o Norm Fairhurst, PO Box 1841, Ellicott, MD 21043.

Mason-Dixon Canoe Cruisers, c/o Ron Shanholtz, 222 Pheasant Trail, Hagertown, MD 21740; 301-790-2622.

Potomac Boat Club, 3520 Water St., NW, Washington, DC 20007.

Washington Canoe Club, c/o Roy Jobber, 333 South Glebe Road, Apt. #212, Arlington, VA 22204; 703-521-7069

See also: Virginia

Massachusetts

Appalachian Mountain Club-Berkshire, c/o William T. Cushwa, 63 Silver Street, So. Hadley, MA 01075; 413-536-1347.

Birch Hill Paddlers, c/o Ruby Menard, PO Box 84, Winchendon, MA 01475

Brothers of the Foam, c/o Brian Chabot, 1195 Victoria Street, New Bedford, MA 02745.

Foxboro County Canoe Club, c/o Dean Ellis, Dept. 852, Building 57, Foxboro, MA 02035; 617-549-6543.

Hampshire College Kayak Program, Amherst, MA 01002.

New Hampshire Canoe Chapter AMC, c/o Bruce Healey, 1006 Broughton Drive, Beverly, MA 01915.

Westfield River Wildwater Club, c/o J. Defeo, Ingell Road, Chester, MA 01011; 413-354-9684.

Upper Housatonic Canoe Race Club, c/o George Wislocki, 8 Bank Row, Pittsfield, MA 01201; 413-443-0596.

Wilderness Experiences Unlimited, 194 Woodmont Street, W. Springfield, MA 01089.

Michigan

Kalamazoo WW Club, c/o Chuck Andrews, 3102 Woodhams, Portage, MI 49002.

Lansing Oar Paddle Club, c/o Jay Harks, PO Box 26254, Lansing, MI 48909.

Michigan Canoe Racing Assoc., c/o Lynne Witte, 58 Union Street, Mount Clemens, MI 48043; 313-469-3694.

Raw Strength and Courage Kayaks, c/o Jerry Gluck, 1230 Astro Drive, # 82922, Ann Arbor, MI 48103-6165.

St. Joseph Valley Paddlers, c/o Jim Korf, 23311 River Run Road, Mendon, MI 49072; 616-467-7920.

Minnesota

3M Canoe Club, c/o Martin Kubik, 518-1-1, 3M Center, St. Paul, MN 55144.

Boat Busters Anonymous, 2961 Hemingway Ave., St. Paul, MN 55119.

Cascaders Canoe and Kayak Club, PO Box 61, Minneapolis, MN 55440.

Minnesota Canoe Association, Inc., Venice Barsness, PO Box 13567 Dinkeytown Station, Minneapolis MN 55414; 612-725-4142.

Missouri

Kansas City Whitewater Club, c/o Bob Behrends, 3727 Jefferson, Kansas City, MO 64111; 816-753-5297.

Mermec River Canoe Club, c/o Earl C. Biffle, 26 Lake Road, Fenton, MO 63026.

Missouri Whitewater Association, c/o Stan Stoy, 308 Argent, Ferguson, MO 63135; 314-521-4003.

Ozark Wilderness Waterways Club, PO Box 16032, Kansas City, MO 64112.

Montana

Beartooth Paddlers' Society, PO Box 20432, Billings, MT 59104.

Farmington Hills Canoe and Kayak Club, c/o David Justis, 31555 Eleven Mile Road, Farmington Hills, MT 48018.

Glacier Kayak Club, c/o Jim Stack, 2472 Birch Glen, Whitefish, MT 59937.

Headwaters Paddling Association, PO Box 1392, Bozeman, MT 59715; 406-586-7682.

Ravall River Runners, c/o Ken Locks, 984 Skalkaho Road, Hamilton, MT 59840.

Nebraska

Midwest Canoe Association, 3019 S. 44th St., Lincoln, NE 68506.

Nevada

Sierra Nevada Whitewater Club, c/o Charles Albright, 7500 Gladstone Dr., Reno, NV 89506; 702-677-0164.

New Hampshire

Ledyard Canoe Club, c/o Cynthia Lynch, PO Box 9, Hanover, NH 03755; 603-646-2753.

New Jersey

Garden State Canoe Club, c/o Harry Levy, 142 Church Road, Millington, NJ 07946.

Inwood Canoe Club, c/o Elizabeth E. Sheppard, 186 Hackensack Street, E. Rutherford, NJ 07073; 201-935-1353.

Mohawk Canoe Club, c/o James M. Howie, RD. 2, Lebanon, NJ 08833; 201-832-2570.

Monoco Canoe Club, Inc., c/o Frank Cancellieri, 861 Colts Neck Road, Freehold, NJ 07728; 201-431-5678.

Wanda Canoe Club, PO Box 723, Ridgefield, NJ 07660.

New Mexico

Adobe Whitewater Club of New Mexico, PO Box 926, Albuquerque, NM 87103.

Three Rivers Whitewater Club, PO Box 173, Farmington, NM 87499.

New York

Adirondack Mountain Club, c/o Keith Robbins, 21 Beechwood Drive, Burnt Hills, NY 12002.

Appalachian Mountain Club, c/o D. Pratt, 56 Sandra Lane, Pearl River, NY 10965.

Association of North Atlantic Kayakers, 14 Heather Drive, Suffern, NY 10901.

Champaign Canoeing, c/o Keech LeClair, Brayton Park, Ossining, NY 10562.

Heuvelton Canoe Club, c/o Howard Friot, 7 York St., Heuvelton, NY 13654.

Hilltop Hoppers Canoe/Kayak, c/o Jill Noray, 2323 Pleasant Valley Road, Berne, NY 13654.

International Canoe and Kayak Club of Oneonta, PO Box 163, Davenport, NY 13750; 607-278-5990.

Inwood Canoe Club, c/o Elizabeth Shepard, 240 Sullivan St., #5, New York, NY 10012.

Ka-Na-Wa-Ke Canoe Club, 138D Lake Road, Tully NY 13159.

Kayak and Canoe Club of New York, c/o Phyllis Horowitz, PO Box 329, Phoenicia, NY 12464.

Mark Defley Whitewater Chapter, Ski Lodge, Skytop Road, Syracuse, NY 13210.

Metropolitan Canoe and Kayak Club, c/o Jane Alquist, PO Box 021868, Brooklyn, NY 11202, 516-482-2752.

Niagra Gorge Kayak Club, c/o Douglas Bushnell, 7661 Tonawanda Creek Road, Lockport, NY 14090.

Nissequogue River Canoe Club, c/o John Spahalski, 12 Hughes Lane, North Babylon, NY 11703.

North Country Whitewater, c/o T.P. Alton, RD 2, Winthrop Road, Potsdam, NY 13676; 315-268-6693

Northern New York Paddlers, c/o Thomas Giminiani, 19 Kelly Avenue, Albany, NY 12203.

New York State Canoe Racing Association, c/o Roberta Shapiro, 18 Cherlton Drive, Whitesboro, NY 18492.

Plainview River Rats, c/o Steven Rosenbaum, 6 Nora Lane, Plainview NY 11803.

Rockaway Olympic Canoe and Kayak 138 133rd St., Belle Harbor, NY 11694.

Sebago Canoe Club, c/o Richard Schneider, 1751 67th St., Brooklyn, NY 11204; 718-331-8577.

Schnectady Club, Northern New York Paddlers, c/o Edward Miller, PO Box 228, Schnectady, NY 12301.

Suffolk County Canoe Club, James T. Beck, PO Box 114, Blue Point, NY 11715.

Tenandeho Canoe Association Inc., c/o John Frano, 718B Bruno Road, Clifton Park, NY 12065; 518-877-6277.

Wildwaters, c/o Douglas R. Azaert, Rt. 28 At The Glen, Box 157, Warrensburg, NY 12885

North Carolina

Asheville YMCA Kayak Club, c/o Charles Hines, 30 Woodfin St., Asheville, NC 28801.

Blue Ridge Canoe Club, PO Box 1938, Morganton, NC 28655.

Catawba Valley Outing Club, c/o Jay Bajorek, 774 4th St., Hickory, NC 28602.

Carolina Canoe Club, PO Box 12932, Raleigh, NC 27605.

East Carolina Paddlers Club, c/o Jim Hix, 107 Hertage St., Greenville, NC 27858.

Eastern North Carolina Canoe Club, c/o Ben Eping, 4715 Carolina Ave., New Bern, NC 28562.

Nantahala Racing Club, c/o Mike Hipsher, US Highway 19W, PO Box 41, Bryson City, NC 28713; 704-488-9017.

Northwest Outing Club, c/o R.G. Absher, PO Box 1004, Wilkesboro, NC 28697.

Piedmont Paddlers, 3512 Tilley Morris Rd., Matthews, NC 28105.

Triad River Runners, PO Box 11283, Bethabara Station, Winston-Salem, NC 27116.

Triangle Paddlers Inc., c/o Thomas Anderson, PO Box 20902, Raleigh, NC 27619.

Watauga Whitewater Club, State Farm Rd., Boone, NC 28607.

Western Carolina Paddlers, PO Box 8153, Asheville, NC 28814.

Ohio

Buckeye Canoe Club, c/o Jim Hornbrook, 12338 Ledgeview Dr., Canal Fulton, OH 44614.

Dayton Canoe Club, 1020 Riverside Dr., Dayton, OH 45405; 513-222-9392.

Keel Haulers Canoe Club, c/o John Kobak, 1649 Allen Drive, Westlake, OH 44145; 216-871-1758.

Madhatters Canoe Club, 7690 Marylane, Mentor, OH 44060; 216-255-8356.

Merrimack Valley Paddlers, c/o Paul Jonas, Ridgeview Road, Weare, OH 43281.

New World River Runners, 215 Xenia Ave., Yellow Springs, OH 45387.

Ohio Historical Canoe Association, c/o Paul Wood, 914 June St., Fremont, OH 43420.

Scenic Scioto Canoe Club, c/o Mike Doyle, 1720 Coyles Blvd., Portsmouth, OH 45662

Toledo River Gang, c/o Mike Sidell, 626 Louisiana Avenue, Perrysburg, OH 43551; 419-874-9782.

Oregon

Lower Columbia Canoe Club, c/o Janice Stuart, 14490 N.W. Hunters Drive, Beaverton, OR 97006; 503-629-8124.

Northwest Rafters Association, PO Box 20384, Portland, OR 97220; 503-644-7969.

Oregon Kayak and Canoe Club, c/o Bill Bowey, PO Box 692, Portland, OR 97207; 503-629-1863.

Soak-Float, c/o Mel Bailey, 1021 Clay St., Ashland, OR 97520.

South Oregon Association of Kayakers, c/o Richard B. Haynes, 5168 Glen Echo Way, Central Point, OR 97502; 503-664-5669.

Willamette Kayak and Canoe Club, PO Box 1062, Corvallis, OR 97331.

Pennsylvania

Allegheny Canoe Club, c/o Walt Pilewski, 755 W. Spring St., Titusville, PA 16354.

Benscreek Canoe Club, PO Box 2, Johnstown, PA 15907.

Bucks County Whitewater Club, c/o Ray Curran, 3241 Lower Mountain Rd., Furlong, PA 18925.

Conewago Canoe Club, c/o Nany Putt, 113 Harrisburg Pike, Dillsburg, PA 17019.

Canoe Club of Greater Harrisburg, c/o John Ressler, 180 Andersontown Road, Dover, PA 17315.

D & P Rivers Paddling Association, c/o David T. Buyer, 2700 Cresmont Ave., Easton, PA 18402.

Keystone Canoe Club, c/o Daniel L. Fick, PO Box 377, Blandon, PA 19510; 215-670-0829.

Keystone River Runners, c/o Donald B. Frew, Rd. 6, PO Box 359, Indiana, PA 15701; 412-349-2805.

Lancaster Canoe Club, c/o Michelle McCann, 339 N. George St., Millersville, PA 17551; 717-872-4413.

Lehigh Valley Canoe Club, c/o Eugene Gallagher, 42 North Canal Street, Walnutport, PA 18088; 215-559-9595.

Philadelphia Canoe Club, 4900 Ridge Ave., Phildelphia, PA 19128; 215-668-8140.

Raystown Canoe Club Inc., c/o George England, Box 112, Everett, PA 15537; 814-652-5014.

Three Rivers Paddling Club, c/o Paul Kammer, 400 6th Street, Patterson Heights, Beaver Falls, PA 15010; 412-843-5152.

Western Pennsylvania Paddle Sport Association, c/o Rebekah Sheeler, RD #1 Box 358-D, Ellwood City, PA 16117; 412-924-9314.

Rhode Island

Rhode Island Canoe Association, 193 Pettaconsett Avenue, Warwick, RI 02888; 401-781-5187.

Westerly YMCA Canoe & Kayak Club c/o Scott McLeod, 95 High Street, Westerly, RI 02871; 401-596-2894.

South Carolina

Carolina Paddlers, 112 Pine St., Waterboro, SC 29488.

Carolina Whitewater Canoeing Association, 3412 Harvard Ave., Columbia, SC 29205.

Foothill Canoe Club, PO Box 10664, Greenville, SC 29603.

Palmetto Kayakers, 210 Irene St., N. Augusta, SC 29381.

Palmetto Paddlers Inc., c/o Tim Burke, 233 Edgewater Lane, West Columbia, SC 29169.

Savannah River Paddlers, 1211 Woodbine Rd., Aiken, SC 29801.

South Dakota

South Dakota Canoe Association, c/o Dick Davidson, PO Box 403, Sioux Falls, SD 57101.

Tennessee

Appalachian Paddling Enthusiasts, c/o Charles McNabb, PO Box 60, Erwin, TN 37650.

Bluff City Canoe Club, PO Box 40523, Memphis, TN 38104; 901-795-3988.

Carbide Canoe Club, 104 Ulena Dr., Oak Ridge, TN 37880.

Chota Canoe Club, PO Box 870, University Station, Knoxville, TN 37916; 615-573-5946.

East Tennessee Whitewater Club, PO Box 3074, Oak Ridge, TN 37830; 615-483-4800.

GDI Canoe Club, c/o Lynne Shaw, Rt. 1, Box 302, Jones Rd., Lenoir City, TN 37771.

Jackson Rapids Transit Canoe, PO Box 3034, Jackson, TN 38303.

Sewannee Canoe and Outing Club, The University of the South, Sewannee, TN 37375.

Tennessee Scenic Rivers Association, PO Box 15041, Nashville, TN 37215-9041.

Tennessee Valley Canoe Club, PO Box 11125, Chattanooga, TN 37401.

Texas

Aggieland Canoe Club, c/o Retha Groom, 703 Gilchrist, College Station, TX 77840.

Bayou City Whitewater Club, PO Box 980782, Houston, TX 77098.

Dallas Downriver Club, PO Box 595128, Dallas, TX 75259.

Houston Canoe Club, c/o Bob Arthur, PO Box 500582, Houston, TX 77250; 713-467-8857.

North Texas River Runners, c/o Billie McCallon, 215 Lakeshore Drive, Waxahachie, TX 75165, 214-937-8835.

Texas Canoe Racing Association, c/o Kevin Bradley, 9706 Brookshire, Houston, TX 77041, 713-939-7159.

Texas River Recreation Association, PO Box 12734, Austin, TX 78763.

Texas Whitewater Association, Box 5429, Austin, TX 78763.

Utah

Wasatch Mountain Club, 888 S. 200th, Ste. 11, Salt Lake City, UT 84111.

Vermont

Cochituate Canoe Club, c/o Barbara Rogers, Box 2805 RD#1, Wolcott, VT 05680.

Club Adventure, c/o Peter Kennedy, PO Box 184, Woodstock, VT 05091.

Northern Vermont Canoe Cruisers, c/o Sheri Larsen, 11 Discovery Road, Essex Junction, VT 05452; 802-878-6828.

West River Whitewater Association, c/o Kenneth Fisher, RD #4, Box 661, West Brattleboro, VT 05301.

Virginia

Blue Ridge River Runners, 120 Kenwood Dr., Lynchburg, VA 24052.

Blue Ridge Voyagers, 1610 Woodmoor Lane, McLean, VA 22101.

Coastal Canoeists, PO Box 566, Richmond, VA 23204.

Greater Rapppahannock Whitewater Canoe Racing, 3219 Fall Hill Ave., Fredericksburg, VA 22401.

Mid-Atlantic Paddlers Association, Kirk Havens, 154 Pacific Drive, Hampton, VA 23666; 804-838-8998.

Shenandoah River Canoe Club, PO Box 1423, Front Royal, VA 22630.

Virginia Canoe Racing Association, 111 South Witchduck Road, Virginia Beach, VA 23462; 804-497-4890.

See Also: Maryland/DC Area.

Washington

Paddle Trails Canoe Club, c/o Kathy McMonagle, PO Box 24932, Seattle, WA 98124.

Puget Sound Paddle Club, c/o Paul Shell, PO Box 22, Puyallup, WA 98371.

Spokane Canoe and Kayak Club, c/o Robbi Castleberry, West 4625 Bonnie Drive, Spokane, WA 99204; 509-624-8384.

Southwest Washington Canoe Club, c/o Gordon Sondker, 2537 Northlake, Longview, WA 98632; 206-425-3641.

University Kayak club, c/o John Hokanson, Intramural Act., Bldg. GD-10, Seattle, WA 98195; 206-524-7426.

Washington Kayak Club, c/o Fran Traje, 123rd Ave. SE, Bellevue, WA 98005.

Whatcom Association of Kayak Enthusiasts, PO Box 1952, Bellingham, WA 98227.

Washington Recreational River Runners Association, 1012 S. 30th Court, Renton, WA 98055.

West Virginia

Canoe Association of West Virginia, 111 8th St. East, Wheeling, WV 26003.

West Virginia Wildwater Association, c/o Idair Smookler, PO Box 8413, South Charleston, WV 25303; 304-744-8078.

Wisconsin

Badger State Boating Society, c/o Mark Budnik, 10920 W. Langlade St., Milwaukee, WI 53225.

Federation of United Canoes and Kayaks, c/o Terry Thorud, 2515 Western Ave., Eau Claire, WI 54703.

Green Bay Paddlers United, c/o Greg Gauthier, 13601 Marshek Rd., Maribel, WI 54227.

Hoofers Outing Club, c/o Jon McAnulty, Wisconsin Memorial Union, Madison, WI 53706.

River City Paddlers of Wisconsin, c/o John Mundahl, Box 340, Osseo, WI 54758.

Rock River Canoe Association, c/o Ray Hahn, PO Box 691, Janesville, WI 53547; 608-362-8751.

University of Wisconsin Hoofers Club, c/o Mike Sklavos, 329N Jackson #3, Janesville, WI 53545; 608-262-1630.

Wisconsin Canoe Association, c/o Neil Weisner-Hanks, 1630 West Lawn Ave., Milwaukee, WI 53209.

Wyoming

Beartooth Paddlers' Society, c/o Keith Thompson, 1171 N. 10th St., Laramie, WY 82070.

New Waves Kayaks Club, c/o Morgan Smith, 2644 Bonnie Brae, Casper, WY 82601.

WHITEWATER SCHOOLS

Kayak and Canoe

The following list includes many of the nation's leading whitewater schools of instruction.

California

Adventure Canoes and Kayaks, 11383 Pyrites Way #A, Rancho Cordova, CA 95670; 916-638-7900

Otter Bar Kayak School, Box 120, Forks of Salmon, CA 96031; 916-462-4772.

Sierra Kayak School, c/o California Canoe and Kayak, 229 Tewksbury Ave., Point Richmond, CA 94801; 800-366-9804.

Sierra South, 11306 Kernville Road, PO Box Y, Kernville, CA 93238; 619-376-3745.

Colorado

Bill Dvorak's Kayak and Rafting Expeditions, 17921 US Highway 285, Nathrop, CO 81236; 719-539-6851 or 800-824-3795 (from Colorado).

Aspen Kayak School, PO Box 1520, Aspen, CO 81612; 305-925-6248.

Maine

Unicorn Expeditions, PO Box T, Dept. 45, Brunswick, ME 04011; 207-725-2255.

Massachusetts

Outdoor Centre of New England, 8 Pleasant Dr., Millers Falls, MA 01349; 413-659-3926.

Minnesota

Kayak and Canoe Institute, 108 Kirby Student Center, 10 University Drive, Duluth, MN 55812; 218-726-7170.

New Hampshire

Saco Bound, Box 113, Center Conway, NH 03813; 603-447-2177.

New York

Wild Waters, PO Box 157, Route 28 at the Glen, Warrensburg, NY 12885; 518-494-3393.

North Carolina

Nantahala Outdoor Center, US 19 West, Box 41, Bryson City, NC 28713; 704-488-2175.

Oregon

Sundance Expeditions, 14894 Galice Road, Merlin, OR 97532; 503-479-8508.

Pennsylvania

Riversport School of Paddling, 213 Yough St., Confluence, PA 15424; 814-395-5744.

Rhode Island

Everett River and Mountain, PO Box 723, Wakefield, RI 02879; 401-783-4547.

Utah

Slickrock Kayak Adventures, PO Box 1400, Moab, UT 84532; 801259-6996 (winter), 208-462-3639 (summer).

Vermont

Adventure Quest, PO Box 184, Woodstock, VT 05091; 802-457-3257.

Virginia

Bob Taylor's Appomattox River Co., 610 N. Main St., Farmville, VA 23901; 804-392-6645.

Washington

Northwest Outdoor Center, Sea Kayaking and Whitewater School, 2100 Westlake Ave., Seattle, WA 98109; 206-281-9694.

Wisconsin

American Outdoor Learning Center, Box 133, Star Route, Athelstane, WI 54104; 715-757-3811.

Whitewater Specialty, Star Route, White Lake, WI 54491; 715-882-5400.

Wolf River Lodge Canoe School, White Lake, WI 54491; 715-882-2182.

Wyoming

Snake River Kayak and Canoe, PO Box 3482, Jackson Hole, WY 83001; 307-733-3127.

Rafting

The American River Touring Association, 445 High Street, Oakland, CA 94601; 415-465-9355

Echo, The Wilderness Company, 6529 Telegraph Avenue, Oakland, CA

94609; 415-652-1600; 800-652-ECHO (from California only)

Friends of the River, Rafting Chapter, c/o Friends of the River, Building C, Fort Mason Center, San Francisco, CA 94123-1382; 415-441-8778.

Bill Dvorak's Kayak and Rafting Expeditions, 17921 US Highway 285, Nathrop, CO 81236; 719-539-3795.

Nantahala Outdoor Center, US 19 West, Box 41, Bryson City, NC 28713; 704-488-2175.

Rivers Edge Guide School, 2459 S. York St., Denver, CO 80210; 303-733-0841.

Rescue and Wilderness Medicine

Les Bechdel, c/o Canyons Inc., PO Box 823, McCall, ID 83638; 208-634-4303. (*River Rescue*).

Canyonlands Field Institute, PO Box 68, Moab, UT 84532; 801-259-7750. (*River Safety and Rescue*).

Friends of the River Rafting Chapter, c/o Friends of the River, Building C, Fort Mason Center, San Francisco, CA 94123-1382; 415-441-8778. (*Swiftwater River Rescue*).

International Alpine School, PO Box 3037, Eldorado Springs, CO 80025; 303-494-4904. (*Wilderness EMT*).

Mountain Medicine Institute, 211 E. 14th Street, Oakland, CA 94606; 415-534-2086 (*Mountain Medicine and Medical Aspects of Foreign Travel*).

Nantahala Outdoor Center, US 19 West, Box 41, Bryson City, NC 28713; 704-488-2175 (*Standard First Aid and CPR, Wilderness First Responder, Emergency Medical Technician, EMT-Wilderness, Basic River Rescue, Standard River Rescue*).

National Association for Search and Rescue, PO Box 3709, Fairfax, VA

22038; 702-352-1349 (*EMT-Wilderness, Emergency Operations, Search and Rescue, Basic Water Rescue*).

Ohio Department of Natural Resources, Division of Watercraft, Fountain Square, Columbus, OH 43224; 615-265-6504. (*Swiftwater Rescue*)

Professional Emergency Programs, 3037 Grass Valley Highway, Suite 8165, Auburn, CA 95603; 916-889-8737. (*CPR, First Aid and Advanced First Aid for Paddlers*)

Rescue 3, PO Box 4686, Sonora, CA 95370; 209-532-7915. (*Swiftwater Rescue* and *Wilderness Evacuation*).

Sheriff's Department, El Dorado County, 300 Fair Lane, Placerville, CA 95667; 916-621-5353. (*Swiftwater Rescue*).

Sierra South, PO Box Y, Kernville, CA 93238; 619-376-3745. (*River Rescue*).

Eric Wiess, M.D. , Adventure Medical Kits, PO Box 2586; Berkeley, CA 94702. (*Wilderness Medicine*).

Festivals, Meetings, Rendezvous, and Rodeos

International

The *International Safety Symposium* is held every two years in a different country, and highlights issues of river safety of worldwide concern. Previous meetings have been held in Switzerland, Germany, Austria, England, and the 1990 meeting is scheduled to be held at the Nantahala Outdoor Center. For future meeting sites, contact: Betsy Lewis, c/o the Nantahala Outdoor Center, US 19W Box 41, Bryson City, CA 28713.

National

The American Canoe Association holds its *Annual Meeting* during November of each year. Contact: American Canoe

Association, PO Box 1190, Newington, VA 22122-1190; 703-550-7495.

The National Association for Search and Rescue holds its annual meeting, *Response,* in May of each year. Contact: National Association for Search and Rescue, PO Box 3709, Fairfax, VA 22038; 702-352-1349.

The North American Paddlesports Association coordinates *Paddle America Week*, during June of each year. An event which includes demonstrations, clinics, races and other activities in cities and parks nationwide. Contact: Paddle America Week, c/o ICS Books Inc., 107 East 89th Ave., Merrillville, IN 46410; 219-769-0585.

The North American Paddlesports Association coordinates a trade show that goes by the name *Canoecopia*, in conjunction with its annual meeting at the end of March of each year. Contact: Gordy Sussman, 820 S. Park St., Madison, WI 53715; 608-256-4303.

During December of each year, the Western River Guides and the Eastern Professional River Outfitters hold a joint meeting that is called the *Confluence*. Contact: David Brown, 531 S. Gay Street, Suite 600, Knoxville, TN 37902; 615-524-1045.

California

The *American River Festival* is held on the South Fork of the American River in May of each year. Contact: American River Festival, c/o California Canoe and Kayak, 249 Tewksbury Avenue, Pt. Richmond, CA 94801; 415-234-0929.

The American Canoe Association Pacific Division sponsors an *Encampment and Bigfoot Whitewater Rodeo* during May of each year on the Klamath River in California. Contact: Wayne Marks, Bigfoot Recreation; 916-496-3313.

Sierra South sponsors an annual *Kern River Slalom Raft Race*, a popular May get-together for the many professional guides and amateur rafters in California and the Southwest. Contact: Tom

Moore, Sierra South, PO Box Y, Kernville, CA 93238; 619-376-3745.

A *River Conference and Festival* is held by the Friends of the River Foundation in March of each year at the Dominican College in San Rafael, California. Contact: Friends of the River, Building C, Fort Mason, CA 94123; 415-771-0400.

Colorado

The *Animas River Days* rodeo, slalom race and downriver race is held annually in June in Durango. Contact: Nancy Wiley, PO Box 379, Durango, CO 81302; 303-259-3893.

The *Aspen River Daze* is held in Aspen during July of each year. Contact: Dianna Garzoli, The Confluence Club, PO Box 4167; Aspen, CO 81612; 303-925-1796.

The Colorado Rivers Outfitters Association holds its *Annual Meeting* in Vail during November of each year. Contact: Colorado Rivers Outfitters Association, PO Box 502, Westminister, CO 80030; 303-220-8040.

Fibark, a whitewater festival, rodeo, downriver race and slalom is held annually during June on the Arkansas River. Contact: Ed Loeffel, 422 D Street, Salida, CO 81201; 719-539-6478.

The *Yampa River Festival* is held during June of each year in Steamboat Springs. Contact: Nancy Wiley, PO Box 379, Durango, CO 81302; 303-259-3893.

Kentucky

The Bluegrass Wildwater Association and Menasha Ridge Press jointly sponsor an annual *National Paddling Film Festival*, held in Lexington, during February of each year. Contact: National Paddling Film Festival, c/o Bluegrass Wildwater Association, PO Box 4231, Lexington, KY 40504.

Michigan

The Valentine Recreation Center holds an *Annual Canoe Rendezvous* in Battle Creek Michigan during May of each year. Contact: Mark Stuart, Valentine Recreation Center: 616-781-3928.

Montana

The *Gallatin Whitewater Festival* is held each year during July, and features races, clinics and entertainment. Contact: Headwaters Padding Association, PO Box 1392, Bozeman, MT 59715; 406-586-7682.

The University of Montana hosts the annual *Blackfoot Whitewater Weekend* in June of each year. Contact: Joel Meier, University of Montana, Missoula, MT 59812; 406-243-6459.

Oregon

The Northwest Rafters' Association holds an annual *Upper Clackmas Whitewater Festival* during May of each year, featuring races, clinics and entertainment. Contact: Northwest Rafters' Association, PO Box 20384, Portland, OR 97220; 503-644-7969.

The *Nugget Whitewater Roundup* is held annually during July on the Rogue River in Oregon. Contact: Kirby at 503-535-2116, or Mel at 503-482-1530.

Tennessee

The American Whitewater Affiliation sponsors the annual Ocoee Rodeo. Contact: Risa Shimoda Calloway, American Whitewater Affiliation, PO Box 375, Denver, CO 28037; 704-483-5049.

The Tennessee Scenic Rivers Association holds a *Whitewater Rendezvous* on the Cumberland Plateau or in the Great Smoky Mountains during April of each year. Contact: Tennessee Scenic Rivers Association, PO Box 14051, Nashville, TN 37215-9041.

Texas

The *Southwest Canoe Rendezvous* is held during October of each year at Chain o' Lakes in Houston Texas. Contact: Bob Arthur, PO Box 500582, Houston, TX 77250; 713-895-7278.

Washington

The Northwest Rivers Council holds an annual *River Conference* dealing with river conservation issues during November of each year. Contact: Peggy Bartels, Northwest Rivers Council, PO Box 88, Seattle, WA 98111; 206-547-7886.

The *Wenatchee Whitewater Rodeo*, with competition in both freestyle and squirt categories, is held annually during the month of June. Contact: Frank Meyer, 6812 Phinney Avenue North, Seattle, WA 98103; 206-783-7107.

West Virginia

For Eastern Paddlers, the *Gauley River Festival* is the event of the year! They have entertainment, auctions, raffles, contests and more. The Gauley Festival is held in September, usually on the first weekend of the Gauley release. Contact: Risa Shimoda Calloway, PO Box 375, Denver, CO 28037; 704-483-5049.

PART V

BOOKS
AND
PERIODICALS

The suppliers that are listed below all stock a wide variety of books on whitewater. Write or call to get their latest catalogs.

American Canoe Association Book Service, 8580 Cinderbed Rd., Suite 1900, PO Box 1190, Newington, VA 22122; 703-550-7475.

Colorado Kayak Supply, PO Box 3059, Buena Vista, CO 81211; 800-535-3565 or 303-395-2421.

Four Corners Marine, PO Box 379, Durango, CO 81302; 800-426-7637 or 800-492-8080.

Menasha Ridge Press, PO Box 59257, Birmingham, AL 35259-9257; 205-991-0373.

Nantahala Outdoor Center, US 19 Box 41, Bryson City, NC 28713; 800-367-3521 or 704-488-2175.

NORS Resource Center, National Organization for River Sports, Box 6847, Colorado Springs, CO 80934; 303-473-2466.

Northwest River Supplies, Inc., PO Box 9186, Moscow, ID 83843-9186; 800-635-5202 or 208-882-2383.

Wildwater Designs, 230 Penllyn Pike, Penllyn, PA 19422; 215-646-5034.

Westwater Books, Box 365, Boulder City, NV 89005; 702-293-1406.

Regional, National, and International Whitewater Guidebooks

Armstead, L.D. *Whitewater Rafting in Eastern North America. 2nd. Edition.* Globe Pequot Press: Chester, Connecticut, 1989.

Armstead, L.D. *Whitewater Rafting in Western North America.* Globe Pequot Press: Chester, Connecticut, 1989.

Arighi, S. and M. S. Arighi. *Wildwater Touring.* MacMillan: New York, 1974.

Bangs, R. and C. Kallen. *Rivergods: Exploring the World's Wild Rivers.* Sierra Club Books: San Francisco, California, 1985.
A fantastic pictorial.

Cassidy, J., F. Calhoun and B. Cross. *Western Whitewater: From the Rockies to the Pacific Ocean.* North Fork Press: Berkeley, California, 1990.
Keep your eye out for this comprehensive guide to California, Colorado, Idaho, the Canyon Country and the Pacific Northwest. It's going to be a blockbuster!

Crump, D. (Ed.) *America's Wild and Scenic Rivers.* National Geographic Society: Washington, DC, 1983.

Essler, R. *Back to Nature in Canoes: A Guide to American Waters, 2nd Ed.* Vanguard Press, Inc.: New York, 1985.
Very hit-or-miss.

Interagency Whitewater Committee. *River Information Digest: For Popular Western Boating Rivers Managed by Federal Agencies, 3rd Ed.* US Government Printing Office: Washington, DC, 1985.
This book is a gold mine.

Jackson, B. *Whitewater: Running Wild Rivers of North America.* Walker Press: New York, 1979.
Describes a variety of rivers throughout North America, but is not entirely accurate. For example, a description of Little River Canyon in Alabama is incorrectly identified as being of the Locust Fork. This mistake was recently repeated by *Outside* magazine. *Out of Print.*

Jenkins, M. *Wild Rivers of North America. E. P.* Dutton: New York, 1973. *Out of Print.*

Makens, J. C. *Canoe Trails Directory.* Doubleday: Garden City, New York, 1979. Covers easy canoe outings around the United States. Entries are very brief. *Out of Print.*

Malo, J. W. *Midwest Canoe Trails.* Contemporary Books: Chicago, Illinois, 1978. Family canoe outings. *Out of Print.*

McGinnis, W. *Whitewater Rafting.* Times Books (Random House): New York, 1975.
Includes river descriptions for popular rivers in the East, Midwest, Northwest, California, and Southwest. *Out of Print.*

Penny, R. *The Whitewater Sourcebook: A Directory of Information on American Whitewater Rivers.* Menasha Ridge Press: Birmingham, Alabama, 1989.
That's this book in your hand. I want you to buy more copies.

Whitewater Guidebooks for each State

In the case of guidebooks that cover several states, a complete listing appears under the primary state (or the first state by alphabet), and secondary references will appear under the other states.

Alabama

Foshee, J. *Alabama Canoe Rides and Float Trips.* Strode Press: Huntsville, Alabama, 1975.
Now rather out of date, but Alabama calm-water boaters will want a copy.

Nealy, W. *Whitewater Home Companion, Vol. I. Southeastern Rivers.* Menasha Ridge Press: Birmingham, Alabama, 1981.
Buy this book; it's a modern classic.

Sehlinger, B., D. Otey, B. Benner, W. Nealy, and B. Lantz. *Appalachian Whitewater, Vol. I. The Southern Mountains: The Premier Canoeing and Kayaking Streams of Kentucky, Tennessee, Alabama, Georgia, North Carolina, and South Carolina.* Menasha Ridge Press: Birmingham, Alabama, 1986.
The classic Southeastern whitewater runs.

Arizona

Anderson, F. and A. Hopkinson. *Rivers of the Southwest: A Boater's Guide to the Rivers of Colorado, New Mexico, Utah and Arizona. 2nd Ed.* Pruett: Boulder, Colorado, 1987.
A super book, full of photographs, maps, and gripping stories. Some paddlers might find that they would sometimes assign more difficult ratings to rapids than those assigned by these authors.

Belknap, B. and L. Evans. *Belknap's Waterproof Grand Canyon River Guide.* Westwater: Boulder City, Nevada, 1989.
A superb work, one of the two best of the Grand Canyon guides.

Cassidy et al. *Western Whitewater.* See Regional, National and International.

Crumbo, K. *History of the Grand Canyon: A River Runner's Guide.* Johnson: Boulder, Colorado, 1981.

Hamblin, W. K. and J. K. Rigby. *Guidebook to the Colorado River, Part I: Lee's Ferry to Phantom Ranch in Grand Canyon National Park. 2nd Ed..* Brigham Young University: Salt Lake City, Utah, 1969.

Hamblin, W. K. and J. K. Rigby. *Guidebook to the Colorado River, Part II: Phantom Ranch in Grand Canyon National Park to Lake Mead, Arizona-Nevada.* Brigham Young University: Salt Lake City, Utah, 1969.

Hollister, D. *A Riverrunner's Guide to the Salt River.* Salt River Guide: Phoenix, Arizona, no date of publication.
A homemade waterproof flip map to the Salt River between Highway 60 and the Roosevelt Reservoir.

Linderman, L.L. *Colorado River Briefs for a trip through the Grand Canyon.* Lundquist Press: Tucson, Arizona, 1984.
A set of colorful historical notes keyed to locations along the canyon. Useful as supplement to a standard guidebook, such as Stevens or Belknap.

Simmons, G. C. and D. L. Gaskill. *River Runner's Guide to the Green and Colorado Rivers with Emphasis on Geologic Features, Vol. III. River Runner's Guide: Marble Gorge and Grand Canyon.* Powell Society: Denver, Colorado, 1969.

Stevens, L. *The Colorado River in the Grand Canyon: A Guide. 3rd Edition (Waterproof).* Red Lake Books: Flagstaff, Arizona, 1987.
Very nicely done. If you're going to do the Grand, take either this one or Belknap's.

Arkansas

Bluff City Canoe Club. *Mid-South Canoe Guide.* Bluff City Canoe Club: Memphis, Tennessee, no date of publication.
This small volume mostly describes easy family canoe outings in the Ozarks.

Kennon, T. *Ozark Whitewater: A Paddler's Guide to the Mountain Streams of Arkansas and Missouri.* Menasha Ridge Press: Birmingham, Alabama, (in press).
The authoritative guide to Arkansas. This is the revised, much expanded edition of Kennon's earlier book, *Arkansas Whitewater Rivers,* which is now out of print.

California

Cassidy, Jim and F. Calhoun. *California Whitewater: A Guide to the Rivers. New Revised Edition.* Cassady and Calhoun: Berkeley, California. 1990.
California is the only state that can claim two comprehensive and well-written guidebooks. I use them both.

Cassidy et al. *Western Whitewater.* See Regional, National and International.

Holbeck, L. and C. Stanley. *A Guide to the Best Whitewater in the State of California.* Friends of the River Books: San Francisco, California, 1989 *2nd. Edition.*
This book is filled with wonderfully hairy tales of descents of the most gnarly stuff around. Great reading for everyone, but most useful as a guidebook by advanced and expert boaters. Super photos, too.

Margulis, R. K. *The Complete Guide to Whitewater Rafting Tours: Califor-*

nia Edition 1986. Aquatic Adventure Publications: Palo Alto, California, 1986.

Martin, C. *Sierra Whitewater.* Fiddleneck Press: Sunnyvale, California, 1974.
Good, but now somewhat dated. *Out of Print.*

Mandel, S. et al. *The American River: North, Middle and South Forks.* Protect America's River Canyons: Auburn, California, 1989.
A comprehensive guide to the river, the rapids, the natural history, and the history of the entire American River watershed.

Quinn, J. M. and J. W. Quinn. *Handbook to the Klamath River Canyon.* Educational Adventures Inc.: Medford, Oregon, 1983. Pricey.

Robinson, K. and F. Lehman. *South Fork of the American River: From Chili Bar Dam to Salmon Forks Road.* Lore Unlimited: Fremont, California, 1982.
Out of Print.

Robinson, K. and F. Lehman. *Stanislaus River: From Camp Nine to Parrots Ferry.* Lore Unlimited: Fremont, California, 1982.
Out of Print.

Robinson, K. and F. Lehman. *Tuolumne River: From Lumsden Bridge to Ward's Ferry.* Lore Unlimited: Fremont, California, 1982.
Out of Print.

Colorado

Anderson. Hopkinson. *Rivers of the Southwest.*
See Arizona.

Cassidy et al. *Western Whitewater.*
See Regional, National and International.

Evans, L. and Buzz Belknap. *Dinosaur River Guide.* Westwater: Boulder City, Nevada, 1985.

Hayes, P. T. and G. C. Simmons. *River Runner's Guide to the Green and Colorado Rivers with Emphasis on Geologic Features, Vol. I River Runner's Guide to Dinosaur National Monument and Vicinity, with Emphasis on Geologic Features.* Powell Society: Denver, Colorado, 1973.

Staub, F. *The Upper Arkansas River: Rapids, History and Nature Mile by Mile.* Fulcrum Inc: Golden, Colorado, 1988.
A nicely detailed guide to one of my favorite rivers. Buy this book, and get there when you can!

Stohlquist, J. R. *Colorado Whitewater.* Colorado Kayak Supply: Buena Vista, Colorado, 1982.
An excellent book, except that the glue in the binding is lousy. Essential for Colorado paddlers. Keep the pages in a paper bag.

Wheat, D. *The Floater's Guide to Colorado.* Falcon Press: Helena, Montana, 1983.
An excellent guidebook with emphasis on more than whitewater. Superlative discussions of geology and history.

Connecticut

AMC Appalachian River Guide Committee (R. Schweiker, Ed). *River Guide, Vol. III. Massachusetts, Connecticut and Rhode Island.* Appalachian Mountain Club: Boston, Massachusetts, 1985.
Similar to the Maine Guide. *Out of Print.*

Connelly, J. and J. Porterfield. *Appalachian Whitewater, Vol. III The Northern Mountains: The Premier Canoeing and Kayaking Streams of Connecticut, Massachusetts, Eastern New York State, Vermont, New Hampshire, and Maine.* Menasha Ridge Press: Birmingham, Alabama, 1987.
Up-to-date descriptions of classic runs for intermediate, advanced, and expert paddlers.

Detels, P. and J. Harris. *Canoeing: Trips in Connecticut.* Birch Run Publishing: Madison, Connecticut, 1977.
Flatwater only.

Farmington River Watershed Association. *The Farmington River and Watershed Guide.* Farmington River Watershed Association: Avon, Connecticut, 1970 (Rpt. 1984).
A nice little guide written by local folks interested in protecting their river.

Gabler, R. *New England Whitewater River Guide.* Appalachian Mountain Club: Boston, Massachusetts, 1981.
Well-illustrated, and great tables of information.

Delaware

Burmeister, W. F. *Appalachian Waters, I: The Delaware River and Its Tributaries.* Appalachian Books: Oakton, Virginia, 1974.
The first volume of an incredibly comprehensive study. These four volumes are now somewhat dated, but remain a treasure-trove of information.

Falcomer, K. and R. Corbett. *The Delaware River.* Appalachian Books: Oakton, Virginia, 1981.

Gertler, Ed. *Maryland and Delaware Canoe Trails.* Seneca Press: Silver Spring, Maryland, 1979.

Grove, E., B. Kirby, C. Walbridge, W. Eister, P. Davidson, and D. Davidson. *Appalachian Whitewater. Vol. II. The Central Mountains: The Premier Canoeing and Kayaking Streams of Pennsylvania, West Virginia, Maryland, Delaware, and Virginia.* Menasha Ridge Press: Birmingham, Alabama, 1987. Classic runs for Eastern paddlers.

Letcher, G. *Canoeing the Delaware: A Guide to the River and Shore.* Rutgers University Press: New Brunswick, New Jersey, 1985.

Florida

Burmeister, W. F. *Appalachian Waters, IV: Southeastern U.S. Rivers.* Appalachian Books: Oakton, Virginia, 1974.

Carter, E. F. and J. L. Pearce. *A Canoeing and Kayaking Guide to the Streams of Florida, Vol. I: North Central Peninsula and Panhandle.* Menasha Ridge Press: Birmingham, Alabama, 1986.
I suppose you've guessed that this is about flatwater.

Glaros, L. and D. Sphar. *A Canoeing and Kayaking Guide to the Streams of Florida, Vol. II: Central and South Peninsula.* Menasha Ridge Press: Birmingham, Alabama, 1987.

Georgia

Burmeister. *Appalachian Waters, IV.* See Florida.

Nealy. *Whitewater Home Companion, Vol. I.* See Alabama.

Nealy, W. *Whitewater Home Companion, Vol. II: Southeastern Rivers.* Menasha Ridge Press: Birmingham, Alabama, 1984.
Another revolution in whitewater guidebooks by William Nealy. If you don't paddle in the Southeast, get it for coffee-table entertainment.

Sehlinger, B. and D. Otey. *Northern Georgia Canoeing.* Menasha Ridge Press: Birmingham, Alabama, 1980.
The most complete and authoritative guide to Georgia whitewater.

Sehlinger, B. and D. Otey. *Southern Georgia Canoeing.* Menasha Ridge Press: Birmingham, Alabama, 1986.
Mostly calm-water canoe tours here.

Sehlinger et al. *Appalachian Whitewater, Vol. I.* See Alabama.

Idaho

Conley, C. and J. Carrey. *The Middle Fork and Sheepeater War.* Backeddy Books: Cambridge, Idaho, 1977.

This volume is a guide to the rapids and the history of the Middle Fork of the Salmon.

Conley, C. and J. Carrey. *River of No Return.* Backeddy Books: Cambridge, Idaho, 1978.
This volume is a guide to the rapids and the history of the Main Salmon.

Conley, C. and J. Barton. *Snake River of Hell's Canyon.* Backeddy Books: Cambridge, Idaho, 1979.

Garren, J. *Idaho River Tours.* Touchstone Press: Beverton, Oregon, 1980.

Graeff, T. *River Runner's Guide to Idaho.* Idaho Department of Parks and Recreation: Boise, Idaho, 1986. Out of Print.

Moore, G. and D. McClaren. *Idaho Whitewater.* Class VI: McCall, Idaho, 1989.
The long-awaited authoritative guide to the best whitewater in the U.S.

Quinn, J. M., T. L. Quinn, J. W. Quinn and J. G. King. *Handbook to the Middle Fork of the Salmon,* Educational Adventures Inc: Medford, Oregon, 1979.
Expensive.

Wilderness Public Rights Fund. *Whitewater Primer: Including Selway and Illinois Rivers.* Wilderness Public Rights Fund: Portland, Oregon, no date of publication.
Includes John Garren's descriptions of Idaho's Selway and Oregon's Illinois River. The rest of the book deals with issues of permit allocation on Western rivers. The description of the Illinois duplicates that found in Garren's *Oregon River Tours.*

Kentucky

Burmeister, W. F. *Appalachian Waters, V: The Upper Ohio and Its Tributaries.* Appalachian Books: Oakton, Virginia, 1974.

Nealy. *Whitewater Home Companion, Vol. II.* See Georgia.

Sehlinger, B. *A Canoeing and Kayaking Guide to the Streams of Kentucky.* Menasha Ridge Press: Birmingham, Alabama, 1978.
A comprehensive guide to Kentucky. A new edition of this one will appear soon.

Sehlinger et al. *Appalachian Whitewater, Vol. I.* See Alabama.

Maine

AMC Appalachian River Guide Committee (R. Schweiker, Ed). *River Guide, Vol. I: Maine.* Appalachian Mountain Club: Boston, Massachusetts, 1986.
Comprehensive, but the short entries lack maps, shuttle directions, and gauge or level information. The International Scale of River Difficulty is not always used to describe rapids. Includes both whitewater and flatwater rivers.

Connelly and Porterfield. *Appalachian Whitewater, Vol. III.* See Connecticut.

Gabler. *New England Whitewater River Guide.* See Connecticut.

Huber, J. P. *The Wildest Country: A Guide to Thoreau's Maine.* Appalachian Mountain Club: Boston, 1982.
A collection of routes and portages in the Penobscot backcountry.

Kellogg, Z. *Canoeing, Vol. I: Coastal and Eastern Rivers* (Maine Geographic Series). DeLorme Press: Freeport, Maine, 1983.

Kellogg, Z. *Canoeing, Vol. II: Western Rivers* (Maine Geographic Series). DeLorme Press: Freeport, Maine, 1983.

Kellogg, Z. *Canoeing, Vol. III: Northern Rivers* (Maine Geographic Series). DeLorme Press: Freeport, Maine, 1983.

Maryland

Burmeister, W. F. *Appalachian Waters, III: The Susquehanna River and Its Tributaries.* Appalachian Books: Oakton, Virginia, 1974.

Burmeister. *Appalachian Waters, IV.* See Florida.

Burmeister. *Appalachian Waters, V.* See Kentucky.

Gertler. *Maryland and Delaware Canoe Trails.* See Delaware.

Gilbert, D. T. *Rivers and Trails: Bicycle Touring, Backpacking and Canoeing in the Mid-Atlantic States.* Outdoor Press: Knoxville, Maryland, 1978. Covers calm water, primarily.

Grove et al. *Appalachian Whitewater, Vol. II.* See Delaware.

Nealy. *Whitewater Home Companion, Vol. II.* See Georgia.

Massachusetts

AMC Appalachian River Guide Committee. *River Guide: Massachusetts, Connecticut and Rhode Island.* See Connecticut.

Burmeister, W. F. *Appalachian Waters, II: The Hudson River and Its Tributaries.* Appalachian Books: Oakton, Virginia, 1974.

Connelly and Porterfield. *Appalachian Whitewater, Vol. III.* See Connecticut.

Farmington River Watershed Association. *The Farmington River and Watershed Guide.* See Connecticut.

Gabler. *New England Whitewater River Guide.* See Connecticut.

Thomas, D. and S. Clauser. *Canoeing: Trips in Western Massachusetts.* Birch Run Publishing: Madison, Connecticut, 1979.

Weber, K. *Canoeing Massachusetts, Rhode Island and Connecticut.* Backcountry Publications: Woodstock, Vermont, 1983. Mostly flatwater.

Michigan

Dennis, J. and C. Date. *Canoeing Michigan Rivers.* Friede Publications: Davison, Michigan, 1986.

Palzer and Palzer. *Whitewater/ Quietwater.* See Wisconsin.

Minnesota

Beymer, R. *Boundary Waters Canoe Area, Vol. I: The Western Region. 3rd Ed.* Wilderness Press: Berkeley, California, 1986.

Beymer, R. *Boundary Waters Canoe Area, Vol. II: The Eastern Region. 2nd Ed.* Wilderness Press: Berkeley, California, 1985.

Breining, G. and L. Watson. *A Gathering of Waters: A Guide to Minnesota's Rivers.* Minnesota Dept. of Natural Resources: St. Paul, Minnesota, 1977.

DuFresne, J. *Voyageurs National Park: Water Routes, Foot Paths and Ski Trails.* Mountaineers: Seattle, Washington, 1986. Jim DuFresne is a prolific and excellent outdoor author; all of his books are recommended. *Out of Print.*

Duncanson, M. E. *A Paddler's Guide to the Boundary Waters Canoe Area.* W. A. Fisher: Richmond, Virginia, 1976.

Palzer and Palzer. *Whitewater/ Quietwater.* See Wisconsin.

Sreasau, M. *Canoeing the Boundary Waters: The Account of One Family's Explorations.* Signpost Books: Edmonds, WA, 1979.

Missouri

Bluff City Canoe Club. *Mid-South Canoe Guide.* See Arkansas.

Hawksley, 0. *Missouri Ozark Waterways.* Missouri Conservation Commission: Jefferson City, Missouri, 1964 (rev. 1981). The emphasis of this book is on rivers appropriate for family canoe outings.

Kennon. *Ozark Whitewater.* See Arkansas.

Pemberton, M. A. *Canoeing in Northern Missouri: An Introduction to Floatable Streams Above the Missouri River.* Missouri Dept. of Natural Resources: Jefferson City, Missouri, 1982. Easy canoe outings.

Montana

Cassidy et al. *Western Whitewater.* See Regional, National and International.

Fischer, H. *The Floater's Guide to Montana. 2nd Ed.* Falcon Press: Helena, Montana, 1986. This guide is the most complete for Montana, and is primarily written for rafters and open canoeists. The emphasis is on easier streams, with limited coverage of more serious whitewater. The AWA International Scale of River Difficulty is used only occasionally.

Huser, V. and Buzz Belknap. *Snake River Guide: Grand Teton National Park.* Westwater: Boulder City, Nevada, 1972.

Nevada

Cassady and Calhoun. *California Whitewater: A Guide to the Rivers.* See California.

Holbeck and Stanley. *A Guide to the Best Whitewater in the State of California.* See California.

Margulis. *The Complete Guide to Whitewater Rafting Tours.* See California.

Martin. *Sierra Whitewater.* See California.

New Hampshire

AMC Appalachian River Guide Committee (R. Schweiker, Ed). *River Guide, Vol. II: New Hampshire and Vermont.* Appalachian Mountain Club: Boston, Massachusetts, 1986. Similar to the Maine Guide.

Connelly and Porterfield. *Appalachian Whitewater, Vol. III.* See Connecticut.

Gabler. *New England Whitewater River Guide.* See Connecticut.

Schweiker, R. *Canoe Camping Vermont and New Hampshire Rivers,* 1985.

New Jersey

Burmeister. *Appalachian Waters, I* See Delaware.

Burmeister. *Appalachian Waters, II.* See Massachusetts.

Cawley, M. and J. Cawley. *Exploring the Little Rivers of New Jersey.* Rutgers University Press: New Brunswick, New Jersey, 1971.

Falcomer and Corbett. *The Delaware River.* See Delaware.

Letcher. *Canoeing the Delaware.* See Delaware.

New Mexico

Anderson and Hopkinson. *Rivers of the Southwest.* See Arizona.

Cassidy et al. *Western Whitewater.* See Regional, National and International.

Maurer, S. G. *A Guide to New Mexico's Popular Rivers and Lakes.* Heritage Associates Inc: Albuquerque, New Mexico, 1983. 2nd Edition. Out of Print.

New Mexico State Park Division. *New Mexico Whitewater: A Guide to River Trips.* Santa Fe, New Mexico, 1983.

New York

Burmeister. *Appalachian Waters, I.* See Delaware.

Burmeister. *Appalachian Waters, II.* See Massachusetts.

Burmeister. *Appalachian Waters, III.* See Maryland.

Burmeister. *Appalachian Waters, V.* See Kentucky.

Connelly and Porterfield. *Appalachian Whitewater, Vol. III.* See Connecticut.

Ehling, W. P. *Canoeing Central New York.* Backcountry Publications: Woodstock, Vermont, 1982.

Falcomer and Corbett. *The Delaware River.* See Delaware.

Gabler, R. *New England Whitewater River Guide.* See Connecticut.

Jamieson, P. *Adirondack Canoe Waters: North Flow, 2nd Rev. Ed.* Adirondack Mountain Club: Glens Falls, New York, 1986.

Ka-na-wa-ke Canoe Club. *Central New York Canoe Routes.* Ka-na-wa-ke Canoe Club: Syracuse, New York, 1981.
Not very useful. The descriptions are extremely terse, and there are no river difficulty ratings.

Letcher. *Canoeing the Delaware.* See Delaware.

Proskine, A. C. *No Two Rivers Alike: Fifty Canoeable Rivers in New York and Pennsylvania.* Crossing Press: Trumansburg, New York, 1980. Flatwater.

Proskine, A. C. *Adirondack Canoe Waters: South and West.* Adirondack Mountain Club: Glen Falls, New York, 1985.

North Carolina

Benner, B. *Carolina Whitewater: A Canoeist's Guide to the Western Carolinas, 5th Ed.* Menasha Ridge Press: Birmingham, Alabama, 1987. An earlier version of this book was the first guidebook I ever read or owned. Most North Carolina paddlers will want the most current edition.

Benner, B. and T. McCloud. *A Paddler's Guide to Eastern North Carolina.* Menasha Ridge Press: Birmingham, Alabama, 1987.

Burmeister. *Appalachian Waters, IV.* See Florida.

Burmeister. *Appalachian Waters, V.* See Kentucky.

Carter. *Canoeing Whitewater.* See Virginia.

Nealy. *Whitewater Home Companion, Vol. I* See Alabama.

Nealy. *Whitewater Home Companion, Vol. II.* See Georgia.

Sehlinger et al. *Appalachian Whitewater, Vol. I.* See Alabama.

Ohio

Burmeister. *Appalachian Waters, V.* See Kentucky.

Combs, R. and S. E. Gillen. *A Canoeing and Kayaking Guide to the Streams of Ohio, Vol. I.* Menasha Ridge Press: Birmingham, Alabama, 1983.

Combs, R. and S. E. Gillen. *A Canoeing and Kayaking Guide to the Streams of Ohio, Vol. II.* Menasha Ridge Press: Birmingham, Alabama, 1983.

Oregon

Campbell, A. *John Day River: Drift and Historical Guide.* Frank Amato Pubs: Portland, Oregon, 1980.

Cassidy et al. *Western Whitewater.* See Regional, National and International.

Garren, J. *Oregon River Tours.* Garren Publishing: Portland, Oregon. No date of publication.

Jones, P. N. *Canoe Routes: Northwest Oregon.* Mountaineers: Seattle, Washington, 1982. Flatwater touring.

Quinn and Quinn. *Handbook to the Klamath River Canyon.* See California.

Quinn, J. M., J. W. Quinn, and J. G. King. *Handbook to the Illinois River Canyon.* Educational Adventures, Inc: Medford, Oregon, 1979. Expensive.

Quinn, J. M., J. W. Quinn, and J. G. King. *Handbook to the Rogue.* Educational Adventures, Inc: Medford, Oregon, 1979. Expensive.

Quinn, J. W., J. M. Quinn, and J. G. King. *Handbook to the Deshutes River Canyon.* Educational Adventures, Inc: Medford, Oregon, 1979. Expensive.

Willamette Kayak and Canoe Club. *Soggy Sneakers Guide to Oregon, 2nd Rev. Ed.* Willamette Kayak and Canoe Club: Corvallis, Oregon, 1986. The standard for Oregon.

Wilderness Public Rights Fund. *Whitewater Primer: Including Selway and Illinois Rivers.* See Idaho.

Pennsylvania

Burmeister. *Appalachian Waters, I.* See Delaware.

Burmeister. *Appalachian Waters, III.* See Maryland.

Burmeister. *Appalachian Waters, V.* See Kentucky.

Falcomer and Corbett. *The Delaware River.* See Delaware.

Gertler, Ed. *Keystone Canoeing: A Guide to Canoeable Waters of Eastern Pennsylvania.* SenecaPress: Silver Spring, Maryland,1985.

Grove et al. *Appalachian Whitewater, Vol. II.* See Delaware.

Letcher. *Canoeing the Delaware.* See Delaware.

Nealy. *Whitewater Home Companion, Vol. I.* See Alabama.

Palmer, T. *Rivers of Pennsylvania.* Pennsylvania State University Press: University Park, Pennsylvania, 1980. Stories, history and exploration of Pennsylvania rivers. Very readable.

Pennsylvania Fish Commission. *Paddle Pennsylvania.* Pennsylvania Fish Commission: Harrisburg, Pennsylvania, 1984. Reminiscent of the 1960s. Buy Ed Gertler's book instead.

Proskine. *No Two Rivers Alike.* See New York.

Weil, R. and M. Shaw. *Canoeing Guide to Western Pennsylvania and Northern West Virginia. 7th Ed.* American Youth Hostels Pittsburgh Council: Pittsburgh, Pennsylvania, 1983.

Rhode Island

AMC Appalachian River Guide Committee. *River Guide: Massachusetts, Connecticut and Rhode Island.* See Connecticut.

South Carolina

Burmeister. *Appalachian Waters, IV.* See Florida.

Nealy. *Whitewater Home Companion, Vol. I.* See Alabama.

Sehlinger et al. *Appalachian Whitewater, Vol. I.* See Alabama.

Tennessee

Bluff City Canoe Club. *Mid-South Canoe Guide.* See Arkansas.

Mayfield, M. W. *Tennessee Whitewater.* Southeastern Brochure and Book Press: Knoxville, Tennessee, 1979. Out of Print.

Nealy. *Whitewater Home Companion, Vol. I.* See Alabama.

Nealy. *Whitewater Home Companion, Vol. II.* See Georgia.

Sehlinger, B. and B. Lantz. *A Canoeing and Kayaking Guide to the Streams of Tennessee, Vol. I.* Menasha Ridge Press: Birmingham~ Alabama, 1981. With its companion Volume II, the complete and authoritative guide to Tennessee.

Sehlinger, B. and B. Lantz. *A Canoeing and Kayaking Guide to the Streams of Tennessee, Vol. II.* Menasha Ridge Press: Birmingham, Alabama, 1983.

Sehlinger et al. *Appalachian Whitewater, Vol. I.* See Alabama.

Smith, M. *A Paddler's Guide to the Obed-Emory Watershed.* Menasha Ridge Press: Birmingham, Alabama (in press). This excellent book is the second edition of *The Obed-Emory Watershed.*

U.S. Army Corps of Engineers. *Cumberland River Basin: Canoe Trail Guide.* U.S. Army Corps of Engineers: Nashville, Tennessee. No date of publication. Includes rivers of all levels of difficulty, even some hairy stuff that appears nowhere else.

Waller, G. D. *A Canoeist's Guide to the Obed-Emory River System.* Tennessee Scenic Rivers Association: Nashville, Tennessee. No date of publication. This is a small photocopied document, but it's inexpensive.

Texas

Aulback, L.F. and J. Butler. *The Lower Canyons of the Rio Grande.* Wilderness Area Map Service: Houston, Texas. 1988.

Humphrey, M. *Running the Rio Grande: A Floater's Guide to the Big Bend.* AAR/Tantalus: Austin, Texas, 1981.

Now out of print, but I understand that it is soon to be reissued by a new publisher.

Kirkley, G. *A Guide to Texas Rivers and Streams*. Lone Star Books: Houston, Texas, 1983.
This well-illustrated book emphasizes streams appropriate for family canoe outings and float fishing. A striking omission is failure to use a rating system (such as the international scale of I to VI) to rate rapid or river difficulty, making it difficult to match paddler skill to river difficulty.

Nolen, B. M. and R. E. Narramore. *Texas Rivers and Rapids, Vol. VI.* Ben Nolen Graphics: Bandera, Texas, 1983.
This unfortunately garish volume is aimed at the rental canoe, cooler and beer crowd. It includes bizarre and dangerous safety advice, including, "If you must rescue your boat, be belayed from upstream with a rope," and instructions on how to run a dam: "If necessary." A striking omission is failure to use a rating system (such as the international classes I to VI) to rate rapid or river difficulty, making it difficult to match paddler skill to river difficulty. On the plus side, the book is packed with excellent information for finding out river levels and for connecting with outfitters.

Pearson, J. R. *River Guide to the Rio Grande: General Information.* Big Bend Natural History Assoc.: Big Bend National Park, Texas, 1982.

Pearson, J. R. *River Guide to the Rio Grande, Vol. I: Colorado and Santa Elena Canyons.* Big Bend Natural History Assoc.:.Big Bend National Park, Texas, 1982.

Pearson, J. R. *River Guide to the Rio Grande, Vol. II: Mariscal and Boquillas Canyons.* Big Bend Natural History Assoc.: Big Bend National Park, Texas, 1982.

Pearson, J. R. *River Guide to the Rio Grande, Vol. III: The Lower Can-*

yons. Big Bend Natural History Assoc.: Big Bend National Park, Texas, 1982.

Utah

Aitchison. *A Naturalist's San Juan River Guide.* See New Mexico.

Anderson and Hopkinson. *Rivers of the Southwest.*
See Arizona.

Baars, D. *A River Runner's Guide to Cataract Canyon and Approaches.* Waterproof Edition. Canon Publishers Ltd. Evergreen, Colorado, 1987.
A nice waterproof flip-map book, with a little history and natural history thrown in.

Baars, D. and G. Stevenson. *San Juan Canyons: A River Runner's Guide.* Westwater: Boulder City, Nevada, 1986.

Belknap, Bill and Buzz Belknap. *Canyonlands River Guide.* Westwater: Boulder City, Nevada, 1974.

Cassidy et al. *Western Whitewater.* See Regional, National and International.

Evans, L. and Buzz Belknap. *Desolation River Guide.* Westwater: Boulder City, Nevada, 1969.

Evans and Belknap. *Dinosaur River Guide.*
See Colorado.

Hayes and Simmons. *River Runner's Guide to the Green and Colorado Rivers, Vol. I.*
See Colorado.

Mutschler, F. E. *River Runner's Guide to the Green and Colorado Rivers with Emphasis on Geologic Features, Vol. II: River Runner's Guide to Canyonlands National Park and Vicinity with Emphasis on Geologic Features.* Powell Society: Denver, Colorado, 1977.

Mutschler, F. E. *River Runner's Guide to the Green and Colorado Rivers with Emphasis on Geologic Fea-*

tures, Vol. IV: River Runner's Guide to Desolation and Gray Canyons with Emphasis on Geologic Features. Powell Society: Denver, Colorado, 1972.

Nichols, G. C. *River Runner's Guide to Utah and Adjacent Areas, 2nd Ed.* Univ. of Utah Press: Salt Lake City, Utah, 1986.
Good, thorough coverage of Utah's canyon whitewater.

Rigby, J. K., W. H. Hamblin, R. Matheny, and S. L. Welsh. *Guidebook to the Colorado River, Part 3: Moab to Hite, Utah, Through Canyonlands National Park.* Brigham Young Univ. Press: Salt Lake City, Utah, 1969.

Vermont

AMC Appalachian River Guide Committee. *River Guide, New Hampshire and Vermont.* See New Hampshire.

Burmeister. *Appalachian Waters, II* See Massachusetts.

Connelly and Porterfield. *Appalachian Whitewater, Vol. III.* See Connecticut.

Gabler. *New England Whitewater River Guide.* See Connecticut.

Schweiker. *Canoe Camping Vermont and New Hampshire Rivers.* See New Hampshire.

Virginia/District of Columbia

Burmeister. *Appalachian Waters, IV.* See Florida.

Burmeister. *Appalachian Waters, V.* See Kentucky.

Carter, R. *Canoeing Whitewater, 8th Rev. Ed.* Appalachian Books: Oakton, Virginia, 1974.
Randy Carter was the great forerunner of Southeastern paddlers. His guidebook served as the model for many that came later, as did his system of painted paddlers' gauges. His book is now primarily of historical interest.

Corbett, H. R. *Virginia Whitewater.* Seneca Press: Springfield, Virginia, 1988. 2nd Edition.

Corbett, H. R. and L. J. Matacia. *Blue Ridge Voyages, Vol. I: An Illustrated Guide to Ten Beginning and Intermediate Canoe Outings.* Blue Ridge Voyagers: Oakton, Virginia, 1968.

Corbett, H. R. and L. J. Matacia. *Blue Ridge Voyages, Vol. II, 2nd Ed.* Appalachian Books: Oakton, Virginia, 1968. Out of print.

Gilbert. *Rivers and Trails: Bicycle Touring, Backpacking, and Canoeing in the Mid-Atlantic States.* See Maryland.

Grove et al. *Appalachian Whitewater, Vol. II.* See Delaware.

Matacia, L. J. and D. Cecil. *Blue Ridge Voyages, Vol. IV: The Shenandoah River.* Matacia: Oakton, Virginia, 1974.

Matacia, L. J. and R. Corbett. *Blue Ridge Voyages, Vol. III: An Illustrated Guide to Ten Whitewater Canoe Trips.* Matacia: Oakton, Virginia, 1972.

Nealy. *Whitewater Home Companion, Vol. II.* See Georgia.

Washington State

Cassidy et al. *Western Whitewater.* See Regional, National and International.

Furrer, W. *Water Trails of Washington.* Signpost: Edmonds, Washington, 1979.

North, D. *Washington Whitewater 1 2nd. Edition.* The Mountaineers: Seattle, Washington. 1988.

North, D. *Washington Whitewater, 2.* Mountaineers: Seattle, Washington, 1987. Covers 17 more whitewater rivers in Washington and includes more strip maps.

West Virginia

Burmeister. *Appalachian Waters, V.* See Kentucky.

Carter. *Canoeing Whitewater.* See North Carolina.

Davidson, P. and W. Eister, with D. Davidson. *Wildwater West Virginia, Vol. I: The Northern Streams, 3rd Ed.* Menasha Ridge Press: Birmingham, Alabama, 1985. Together with its companion Vol. II, this is the complete and authoritative guide to West Virginia.

Davidson, P. and W. Eister, with D. Davidson. *Wildwater West Virginia, Vol. II: The Northern Streams, 3rd Ed.* Menasha Ridge Press: Birmingham, Alabama, 1985.

Gilbert. *Rivers and Trails: Bicycle Touring, Backpacking, and Canoeing in the Mid-Atlantic States.* See Maryland.

Grove et al. *Appalachian Whitewater, Vol. II.* See Delaware.

Nealy. *Whitewater Home Companion, Vol. I.* See Alabama.

Nealy. *Whitewater Home Companion, Vol. II.* See Georgia.

Weil and Shaw. *Canoeing Guide to Western Pennsylvania and Northern West Virginia.* See Pennsylvania.

Wisconsin

Duncanson, M. E. *Canoeing Guide to the Indian Head Rivers of West Central Wisconsin.* W. A. Fisher: Richmond, Virginia, 1976.

Duncanson, M. E. *Canoe Trails for Southern Wisconsin.* W. A. Fisher: Richmond, Virginia, 1976.

Palzer, B. and J. Palzer. *Whitewater/ Quietwater: A Guide to the Rivers of Wisconsin, Upper Michigan and NE Minnesota. 6th ed.* Evergreen Paddlers: Two Rivers, Wisconsin, 1989. The most complete guide to the area, but in need of revision. (It was

recently acquired by Menasha Ridge Press, which plans to issue a revised edition.)

Selin, S. and J. Selin. *Best Canoe Trails of Northern Wisconsin.* Tamarack Press: Madison, Wisconsin, 1984. Out of print.

Wyoming

As far as I know, there is no whitewater guidebook for Wyoming.

Instruction
Boating Technique

Canoeing

Mason, B. *Path of the Paddle.* Northword Press: Minocqua, Wisconsin, 1987.

Kayaking

Tejada-Flores, Lito. *Wildwater: The Sierra Club Guide to Kayaking and Whitewater Boating.* Sierra Club Books: San Francisco, California, 1978. *Wildwater* is an excellent introduction to the sport of kayaking. Surprisingly, despite its 1978 publication, it is not too dated.

Nealy, W. *Kayak.* Menasha Ridge Press: Birmingham, Alabama, 1986. *Kayak* is an ingenious book covering a variety of principles and skills for the advanced and expert kayaker. The illustrations are fantastic.

Rowe, R. *White Water Kayaking.* Stackpole Books: Harrisburg, Pennsylvania, 1988. A thorough, excellent and abundantly illustrated text on the technique of kayaking. Beginning boaters may, however, find the numerous photographs of European boaters running extreme rapids and waterfalls intimidating.

Snyder, J.E. *The Squirt Book: A Manual of Squirt Kayaking Tech-

nique. Menasha Ridge Press: Birmingham, Alabama, 1987.
A fantastic excursion into the strange world of zen and squirt boating by a witty and warm writer and teacher.

U'ren, S. B. *Performance Kayaking.* Stackpole Books: Harrisburg, Pennsylvania, 1990.
A modern discussion of basic and advanced whitewater kayaking technique. Plenty of excellent illustrations:

Rafting

McGinnis, William. *Whitewater Rafting.* Times Books: New York, 1975.
The standard and still the best. A new edition is in the works!

First Aid and Rescue

Bechdel, L. and S. Ray. *River Rescue. 2nd Edition.* Appalachian Mountain Club: Boston, Massachusetts, 1988.
Don't consider yourself an advanced paddler until you know the stuff in *River Rescue.*

Grant, H. D., R. H. Murray, and J. D. Bergeron. *Emergency Care. 4th Ed.* Prentice-Hall: Englewood Cliffs, New Jersey, 1986.
This standard EMT text describes just about everything you need to know for emergency treatment in a situation where you are within hours of help. For situations where help is further away, *Medicine for Mountaineering* fits the bill.

Loughman, M. *Learning to Rock Climb.* Sierra Club Books: San Francisco, California, 1981.
A little theory and practice in rock climbing makes a paddler a lot more confident with rope-based rescue systems.

Patient Care Publications with Benner, G. A., R. E. Church, and L. Feild. *Emergency Medical Procedures for the Outdoors.* Menasha Ridge Press: Birmingham, Alabama, 1987 Reprint.

This compact book is organized as a decision tree, making for amazingly quick reference. It might be a good choice as a carry-along guide for persons with limited training, or who might find *Medicine for Mountaineering* too complex or too wordy for quick reference.

Rose, S. R. *1990 International Travel Health Guide.* Travel Medicine Inc: Northampton, Massachusetts, 1990.
A fantastic resource for anyone planning a long expedition or an overseas paddling trip. Covers vaccinations, prophylaxis against tropical diseases, water purification, emergency evacuation, and insurance considerations. Revised annually.

Setnicka, T. J. *Wilderness Search and Rescue.* Appalachian Mountain Club: Boston, Massachusetts, 1980.
If you want to go beyond the skills described in *River Rescue,* here is the place to start.

Walbridge, C. *The Best of the River Safety Task Force Newsletter: 19761982.* American Canoe Association River Safety Task Force: Lorton, Virginia, 1983.
Chilling tales to take your breath away. Read and learn.

Walbridge, C. *The American Canoe Association River Safety Report: 1982-1985.* American Canoe Association River Safety Task Force: Lorton, Virginia, 1986.
More chilling tales.

Wilkerson, J. A. (Ed.) *Medicine for Mountaineering. 3rd Ed.* The Mountaineers: Seattle, Washington, 1985.
This is the classic text for learning wilderness care. Read it and take it along on your next expedition. It is, however, a little weak on first aid; an EMT text, such as *Emergency Care* (above) provides a better description of what to do.

Wilkerson, J. A., C. C. Bangs, and J. S. Hayward. *Hypothermia, Frostbite and Other Cold Injuries: Prevention,* *Recognition and Prehospital Treatment.* The Mountaineers: Seattle, Washington, 1985.
Intense, but if you are planning to get really cold, read this first.

REFERENCE

Barrow, P. (Ed.). *Nationwide Whitewater Inventory.* American Whitewater Affiliation: Washington, DC, 1989.
An incredibly complete listing of whitewater rivers in the United States by location, length and difficulty. Intended for use by conservationists and governmental organizations.

Crump, D. J. (Ed.). *A Guide to Our Federal Lands.* National Geographic Society: Washington, DC, 1984.

Griffin, R.A. and D.O. Parking. *Celebrate American Rivers: A River Conservation Agenda: 1990 and Beyond.* American Rivers: Washington, DC. 1989.

Landi, H. *The Bantam Great Outdoors Guide: The Complete Travel Encyclopedia and Wilderness Guide.* Bantam: New York, 1978. *Out of print.*

Makower, J. and L. Bergher (Eds.). *The Map Catalog: Every Kind of Map and Chart on Earth and Even Some Above It.* Vintage Books (Random House): New York, 1986.

National Park Service. *Riverwork Book.* U.S. Department of the Interior. National Park Service: Washington, DC. 1988.
A guide to conservation action by local groups interested in protecting rivers. Incredibly valuable. The very existence of this book reveals that government is not a monolith! The various agencies have conflicting agendas and priorities; luckily, the Park Service is filled with right-thinking people.
Source: National Program Office, Rivers and Trails Conservation Assistance, National Park Service,

Division of Recreation Resources Assistance, PO Box 37127, Washington, DC 200013; 202-343-3775.

Olson, W.K. *National Rivers and the Public Trust.* American Rivers: Washington, DC: 1989.
Source: American Rivers, 800 Pennsylvania Ave., SE, Suite 303, Washington, DC 20003; 202-547-6000.

Painter, Bill. *Flowing Free: A Citizen's Guide to Protecting Wild and Scenic Rivers.* The River Conservation Fund: Washington, DC, 1977. Update 1980.

Perrin, A. T. (Ed.). *The Explorers Ltd. Source Book.* Harper and Row: New York, 1973.
Out of print.

Rand-McNally. *Campground and Trailer Park Directory: East.* Rand McNally: Skokie, Illinois, 1986.

Rand-McNally. *Campground and Trailer Park Directory: West.* Rand McNally: Skokie, Illinois, 1986.

Sutton, A. and M. Sutton. *Wilderness Areas of North America.* Funk and Wagnalls: New York, 1974.
Out of print.

PERIODICALS

Adventure Travel

Each semiannual issue contains several whitewater articles. These serve primarily as promotion for outfitters, and may have factual errors, but occasionally an excellent piece appears. *Source: Adventure Travel,* 1515 Broadway, New York, NY 10036.

American Whitewater

American Whitewater is published bimonthly by the American Whitewater Affiliation and is aimed exclusively at whitewater paddlers. This periodical is the principal journal of record for hardcore whitewater activity. *American Whitewater* accepts many articles and news items submitted by its readership.
Source: American Whitewater, American Whitewater Affiliation, 146 N. Brockway, Palatine, IL 60067.

Canoe

This glossy bimonthly magazine is endorsed by the American Canoe Association. It tries to cover the full spectrum of canoe and kayak sport, including flatwater, whitewater, and sea. The professional staff provides a quality of writing, layout, and illustration not possible for the other smaller periodicals, but the coverage of whitewater is sometimes spotty.
Source: Canoe, PO Box 10748, Des Moines, IA 50349; 800-2475470.

Canoe and Kayak Racing News

Covers the broad spectrum of the racing scene, including profiles of racers, world news, training and racing advice, and race results. Published by the publisher of *Canoe.*
Source: Canoe and Kayak Racing News, PO Box 3146, Kirkland, WA 98083

Currents

The publication of the National Organization for River Sports (NORS). The emphasis is on river conservation and on permit policy.
Source: National Organization for River Sports, PO Box 6847, Colorado Springs, CO 80934.

Outside

Despite the fact that *Outside* provides general coverage of outdoor sports, it consistently contains excellent whitewater articles, often including reports of significant first descents.
Source: Outside, PO Box 54729, Boulder, CO 80322-4729.

River Runner

River Runner is a glossy bimonthly with a distinctly Western flavor, in contrast to the more Eastern *Canoe.* It includes articles on rafting as well as hard boats. The theme is definitely whitewater, especially raft-supported, multi-day tripping.
Source: RiverRunner, 621 E. Alvarado St., Fallbrook, CA 92028; 619-723-3639.

World Rivers Review

Bimonthly newsletter that highlights conservation issues for rivers worldwide.
Source: International Rivers Network, 301 Broadway, Suite B, San Francisco, CA 94133; 415-986-4694.

PART VI

TOOLS

The W.D.S. Method for River Volume Estimation

In many cases, especially in the West or on exploratory runs, the Randy Carter-type gauge may not be available for measuring flow volume. In such cases, it is possible to estimate volume of flow in cfs by **the W.D.S. Method** (Width x Depth x Speed).

To apply this method, first choose a convenient point on the stream and estimate its **width.** Next, estimate the average **depth** of the stream at that point. Finally, measure the **speed** of the current in feet per second. Do this by tossing a small stick into the water, allow it to accelerate to the water velocity, and then estimate the distance it travels over a timed interval (five seconds usually works well). Now, divide the distance traveled by the stick by the interval in order to get the speed in feet per second. Finally, multiply the width by the depth by the speed to get the volume of flow in cubic feet per second.

For example, suppose we choose to measure the flow on Big Laurel Creek, NC at three feet on the Randy Carter gauge. The river is about 60 feet wide at the put-in bridge and about 4 feet deep. A stick tossed into the water travels about 30 feet in 5 seconds. The speed, therefore, is 30/5 or 6 feet per second. The volume of flow is 60 x 4 x 6, or 1440 cfs, approximately.

The International Scale of River Difficulty

The following system of six classes is generally accepted to rate rapid and overall river difficulty (although big-water boaters in the Southwest may use the ten-class Deseret system). Definitions are according to the American Whitewater Association. Finer distinctions can be made by subdividing the range between two major classes as follows: Class II, Class II+, Class II-III, Class III- and Class III.

Unfortunately, the International Scale is close-ended. As boaters have gotten better over the years, the scale has been forced to slide to accommodate more difficult rapids. The result has been that the more standard rapids have been downgraded every few years, and wide ranges of difficulty have been lumped into single categories. Beginning and intermediate paddlers suffer especially from this state of affairs, as the advanced and expert paddlers hog more of the scale in order to obtain a sufficient range of distinction. Beginning and intermediate runs are now entirely lumped into Classes I and II. Class III can now get fairly difficult (most of the rapids on the Ocoee River in Tennessee are Class III, for example), and intermediate paddlers may need considerable support in order to paddle continuous Class III. Guidebook writers, often being expert paddlers (or at least believing so), are much to blame for this sorry state of affairs.

Rock climbers have a better solution; they have an open-ended scale for rock difficulty ranging from 5.0 through 5.13 or so. A new category is added when someone climbs something harder.

Anyway, the International Scale, with its faults, is still a radically handy instrument. Learn it and use it either to assess difficulty and risk or to start arguments.

Class I
Moving water with a few riffles or small waves; few or no obstructions.

Class II
Easy rapids with waves up to three feet and wide, clear channels that are obvious without scouting; some maneuvering required.

Class III
Rapids with high, irregular waves that can often swamp an open canoe; narrow passages that often require complex maneuvering; may require scouting from shore.

Class IV
Long, difficult rapids with constricted passages that often require precise maneuvering in very turbulent waters. Scouting from shore is often necessary, and conditions make rescue difficult. Generally not possible for open canoes. (*Author's note: This no longer applies to many contemporary expert canoeists.*) Boaters in decked boats should be able to roll.

Class V
Extremely difficult, long, and very violent rapids with highly congested routes that nearly always must be

scouted from shore. Rescue conditions are difficult and there is significant hazard to life in event of a mishap. Ability to roll is essential for decked boaters.

Class VI
Difficulties of Class V carried to the extreme of navigability. Nearly impossible and very dangerous. For teams of experts only, after.close study and with all precautions taken.

Expert boaters avoid straining their intellects by remembering the following: "IIIs are too easy; IVs are fun; Vs are kind of scary; VIs I don't run."

APPENDICES

SUPPLEMENTARY TABLE OF CONTENTS TO THE APPENDICES

APPENDIX ONE: PERMIT AND RESERVATION APPLICATION FORMS

NON-COMMERCIAL RIVER TRIP APPLICATION AND PERMIT

UT-060-8372-1
Oct: 88

U.S. Department of the Interior
Bureau of Land Management
Moab District - Utah

No. _____

Group Name (if applicable) _____

1. _____
   Name of Trip Leader

   _____
   Street or Box No.

   _____
   City, State and Zip Code

   Day Phone # (8 am-4:30 pm MT) (Collect)
   _____

   Name of River Segment
   _____

2. Launch Point   Requested Dates   Takeout Point   Dates

   _____ (1st)_____   _____   _____
                       (2nd)_____   _____
                       (3rd)_____   _____

3. Number of Persons in Group: _____

4. Expected Make and Model of Boat(s): Number of Each:

   _____   _____   _____

   _____   _____   _____

   _____   _____   _____

5. Proposed Campsites: (Permit approval does not guarantee campsites)

   1st Night _____   5th Night _____

   2nd Night _____   6th Night _____

   3rd Night _____   7th Night _____

   4th Night _____   8th Night _____

6. I hereby agree to abide by the conditions and stipulations attached to this permit. I
   understand that the permit is revocable due to any violation of the stipulations hereof
   or at the discretion of an authorized officer of BLM.

   _____   _____
   Date   Signature of Applicant

This permit is:
_____ Approved subject to final approval by a BLM Ranger, after prelaunch check for compliance
        with the attached stipulations.
_____ Rejected: _____

_____   _____
Date   Authorized Officer

_____   _____
Date   Approving Ranger

BLM-UT-GI-89-002-4333

DINOSAUR NATIONAL MONUMENT-1991 RIVER RUNNING NEWS

1. The Environmental Assessment for human waste disposal on river
    trips was completed in the spring of 1990. During the 1990
    season all pit toilet facilities were removed from the river
    camps in Dinosaur. Picnic tables and metal fire pan "locators"
    were also removed. River runners are now required to use
    portable toilets and pack out all solid human waste. A
    disposal tank has been placed at the Split Mountain ramp.

2. A standard sized envelope (9 1/2" X 4"), with first class
    postage is required to request an application for the lottery.

3. River flows were below average again in 1990. The Yampa peaked
    at about 8700 CFS on June 16. Releases from Flaming Gorge dam
    averaged around 800 CFS during the entire boating season, with
    the exception of a few days of short-term higher releases.

APPLICATION/PERMIT DEADLINES FOR 1991

November 20 - January 10 - High-use lottery applications mailed out

December 1 - January 15 - High-use lottery applications accepted

March 1 - Permitees selected in lottery notified by this date

March 1 and after - Low-use and one-day reservation requests
                    accepted by mail or phone
                  - Available high-use trips filled by phone-in

Telephone calls for river information, reservations, cancellations
and changes must be made between 8:00 am and 12:00 noon, Monday
through Friday on the river phone only at 303-374-2468. Boating
calls cannot be accepted at other times or Monument phone numbers.

DINOSAUR NATIONAL MONUMENT RIVER PERMIT APPLICATION - 1991

APPLICANT:_____   Applicant must be at least
                                           18 years old. Applicant
ADDRESS: _____   or trip leader must have
                                           operated boats on rivers
_____ ZIP_____   Class III or greater.

LAUNCH DATE_____ (one only, must be between 5/13/91-9/13/91)
RIVER: GREEN____YAMPA____
SUBMIT ONLY ONE APPLICATION Applications must be received between
12/1/90 and 1/15/91. **NO DUPLICATIONS OF THIS FORM WILL BE
ACCEPTED.** Those selected will be notified by March 1. Cancelled
and unfilled launches will be filled by call-in starting March 1.

APPLICANT SIGNATURE_____DATE_____

Return application to: River Ranger, Dinosaur National Monument
               P.O. Box 210, Dinosaur, CO 81610

1990 HIGH USE SEASON LAUNCH STATISTICS

The following information is provided to assist you in acquiring a river permit in Dinosaur National Monument

<u>THE LOTTERY</u>

2440 applications received

390 rejected because of: sending in more than one application, not applying for a specific launch date, applying for a launch date outside the high-use season, using a duplicated application form.

2050 applications entered into lottery

25 launch dates not applied for - 7/19, 7/22, 7/28, 8/4, 8/8, 8/12, 8/13, 8/26, 8/28, 8/29, 8/30, 8/31, 9/1-10, 9/12-14.

246 awarded trips
105 lottery trips cancelled
141 lottery trips used

<u>CALL-IN PROCEDURE</u>

126 launches used

<u>PERMIT PROFILE</u>

141 lottery
126 call in
 33 not filled
  0 no show
300 trips available

PROBABILITY OF BEING DRAWN IN THE LOTTERY

WEEK	LAUNCHES AVAILABLE/REQUESTS	PERCENTAGE
5/14 - 5/20	13/166	8
5/21 - 5/27	15/318	5
5/28 - 6/03	20/134	15
6/04 - 6/10	20/342	6
6/11 - 6/17	20/211	10
6/18 - 6/24	20/153	13
6/25 - 7/01	20/110	18
7/02 - 7/08	20/95	21
7/09 - 7/15	18/35	51
7/16 - 7/22	13/34	38
7/23 - 7/29	13/43	30
7/30 - 8/05	13/9	100
8/06 - 8/13	13/16	81
8/14 - 8/20	14/18	78

(From 8/21 to 9/14 only 10 people applied for 50 available launches.)

U.S. Department of Agriculture
Forest Service
FORM APPROVED OMB No.40
R 3857 (Rev.)

CHATTOOGA
WILD and SCENIC RIVER
SELF-REGISTRATION PERMIT

When signed, this single-visit permit authorizes:

Do Not Write in Shaded Areas

Name _____

Address _____

City _____ State ____ Zip ____

To visit **CHATTOOGA RIVER** | 1 | 2 | 3 |

and to build campfires in accordance with regulations | R | C | P |

Give best estimate of start   FROM MO./DAY

and finish dates   THROUGH MO./DAY

Location of entry _____

Location of exit _____

NUMBER OF PEOPLE

The visitor must have this permit in possession during the river visit. One permit per group.

I agree to abide by all laws, rules, and regulations which apply to this area. [See Reverse Side]

I will do my best to see that everyone in my group does likewise.

Number of Watercraft in Party

| Rafts |
| Canoes |
| Kayaks |
| Innertubes |
| Other |

Time of Launch

Remarks   MD

Visitor Signature _____

DEPOSIT WHITE COPY IN BOX   FM & S N0. 2300-30 2 74 Rev. 12 80

Form I-01-6223-1
November 1982

BRUNEAU-JARBIDGE RIVER BOATER REGISTRATION
(ONLY ONE PERSON PER PARTY NEED REGISTER)

NAME _____

ADDRESS _____

TELEPHONE (in case of emergency) _____

DATES OF TRIP _____

NUMBER OF PEOPLE IN PARTY _____

HOMETOWN OF PARTY MEMBERS _____

NUMBER AND TYPES OF BOATS

    Raft   Kayak   Canoe   Motor Boat   Other

PUT-IN POINT _____

TAKE-OUT POINT _____

WILL YOU FILL OUT A POST-USE QUESTIONNAIRE (circle)

                                    yes   no

Please read the enclosed information and please practice low impact camping techniques while on the river.

(Space on back for your comment and/or suggestions)

Bureau of Land Management
3948 Development Avenue
Boise, Idaho 83705

BLM Permit Application Form, Jarbridge and Bruneau Rivers, ID

CNP-71
10/89

UNITED STATES DEPARTMENT OF THE INTERIOR
NATIONAL PARK SERVICE
CANYONLANDS NATIONAL PARK
MOAB, UTAH 84532

PERMIT NUMBER

NONCOMMERCIAL BOATING PERMIT

Pursuant to Section 3.2, Title 36 of the C.F.R., permission is hereby granted:

_____   (____)_____   (____)_____

Trip Leader (Print Name)   Daytime Telephone Number   Other

_____   _____

Address   City   State   Zip Code

to traverse Cataract Canyon within Canyonlands National Park and Glen Canyon NRA with the indicated numbers and types of craft (rafts, kayaks, etc.) as follows:

_____   _____   _____   _____

(Number)   (Brand Name)   (Number)   (Brand Name)   (Number)   (Brand Name)   (Number)   (Brand Name)

WITH _____ TOTAL persons (incl. leader, boatmen)

Trip will begin on _____/_____/_____ and end at Hite Marina on _____/_____/_____
                   Month   Day   Year   Month   Day   Year

Trip leader will have boating equipment available for inspection on: _____ at _____
                                                                    (Month/Day)   (Time - between 9 am and 4 pm)

at the following launch site:

   COLORADO RIVER   GREEN RIVER

   ___ Moab Dock   ___ Potash   ___ Green River State Park   ___ Mineral Bottom

OTHER: _____

If motors will be used, indicate location:

   ___ Entire Trip   ___ Flat Water Colorado   ___ Flat Water Green   ___ Cataract Canyon   ___ Lake Powell

All trips must be inspected prior to launch. However, if a ranger is not present at your launch site at the time specified in the permit, the inspection has been waived and you may proceed without delay.

This permit is revocable at the discretion of the Superintendent. It is issued on the basis of information provided in the application which has been made a part of this permit. The permit is subject to the special requirements and conditions of the Noncommercial Boating Permit Provisions, Cataract Canyon (Appendix A). Incorrect information given on the permit or application renders this permit null and void and applicants subject to prosecution.

THIS PERMIT MUST ACCOMPANY THE PARTY AND BE AVAILABLE FOR DISPLAY UPON REQUEST OF ANY AUTHORIZED PERSON.

RECOMMENDED: _____   DATE: _____

APPROVED: _____   DATE: _____

I. **APPROVED WATERCRAFT INCLUDES** rafts and pontoons of size 13 1/2'x6 1/2' or larger. All inflatables must have at least 3 chambers — not counting cross tubes. Kayaks or rafts smaller than 13 1/2'x6 1/2' will normally be accompanied by an approved watercraft. Dories will be evaluated on a case by case basis. In the spaces provided below, indicate the brand name and model of the types of craft you plan to use. For an inflatable craft, show the length, width, and tube diameter when inflated.

(CIRCLE ONE)

1. _____   _____   Oars/Paddles/Motors
        (Brand Name/Model)   (Size/Specifications)

2. _____   _____   Oars/Paddles/Motors
        (Brand Name/Model)   (Size/Specifications)

3. _____   _____   Oars/Paddles/Motors
        (Brand Name/Model)   (Size/Specifications)

4. _____   _____   Oars/Paddles/Motors
        (Brand Name/Model)   (Size/Specifications)

5. _____   _____   Oars/Paddles/Motors
        (Brand Name/Model)   (Size/Specifications)

6. _____   _____   Oars/Paddles/Motors
        (Brand Name/Model)   (Size/Specifications)

7. _____   _____   Oars/Paddles/Motors
        (Brand Name/Model)   (Size/Specifications)

8. _____   _____   Oars/Paddles/Motors
        (Brand Name/Model)   (Size/Specifications)

II. **AS THE COLORADO RIVER PASSES THROUGH CATARACT CANYON, IT TRAVERSES SOME OF THE MOST TREACHEROUS WHITEWATER IN THE UNITED STATES.** Experience on one or more of the major western rivers is mandatory. As trip leader, indicate in detail your experience and the experience of each person who will act as boatman. The experience listed MUST show the canyons or sections of rivers run, the number of times through each one, and how the experience was gained (oars/paddles/motors/kayaks). All persons operating kayaks are considered to be boatmen and must show the rivers they have previously kayaked. If a boatman has a valid state Boatman's Permit, the number should be shown in the experience section. EXPERIENCE GAINED AS A PASSENGER IS NOT QUALIFYING.

1. _____ _____ _____
   Trip Leader   Craft   Experience - list canyons or parts of rivers you have led and/or operated trips on

   _____

2. _____ _____ _____
   Boatman   Craft   Experience - list canyons/rivers, number of times, and type of experience (O,P,M,K)

   _____

3. _____ _____ _____
   Boatman   Craft   Experience

   _____

4. _____ _____ _____
   Boatman   Craft   Experience

   _____

5. _____ _____ _____
   Boatman   Craft   Experience

   _____

6. _____   _____   _____
   Boatman   Craft   Experience

   _____

7. _____   _____   _____
   Boatman   Craft   Experience

   _____

8. _____   _____   _____
   Boatman   Craft   Experience

   _____

9. _____   _____   _____
   Boatman   Craft   Experience

   _____

10. _____   _____   _____
    Boatman   Craft   Experience

    _____

III. **EMERGENCY EQUIPMENT MUST MEET THE GUIDELINES SET FORTH IN THE** "Noncommercial Boating Permit Provisions, Cataract Canyon" which is attached as Appendix A.

IV. **A WARNING SIGN** is located below the Confluence on the west bank. At the sign is a campsite information and registration station. The purpose of the station is to assist you in planning overnight stops in Cataract Canyon where there are a limited number of campsites. We also hope to gain valuable information about river use. **PLEASE STOP** and fill in the information requested on the river record at the station.

V. **IF THE TRIP MUST BE CANCELLED OR IF ANY CHANGES IN THE INFORMATION PROVIDED ARE MADE FOR ANY REASON, YOU MUST NOTIFY US AS SOON AS POSSIBLE BEFORE YOUR TRIP LEAVES.** Telephone: (801) 259-7164, Monday through Friday, 8 am - 4:30 pm or (801) 259-5277, Sat., Sun., or holidays, 8 am to 5 pm (if no answer, please call (801) 259-8161). Failure to notify of cancellation or change in date/time may cost another party a trip permit because of use limits, and may jeopardize **YOUR** chances for a future permit.

VI. **COMMERCIAL USE OF THIS PERMIT IS PROHIBITED.** Your signature on this application form will be our assurance that you have considered the following conditions and that your trip is organized to meet the spirit as well as the intent of all three of these conditions:

A.   A river trip is not commercial if there is a bona fide sharing of all expenses of any nature.
B.   The costs shared do not include any costs for payment of salaries or expenses of any person to guide, outfit, lead, assist, or help with the logistics of the trip.
C.   Costs shared by trip members may include the cost of damaged or lost equipment, renting or buying minor equipment needed for the trip, etc., but will not result in amortization of equipment or acquiring new equipment to the advantage of an individual or an organization.

****

In consideration for obtaining the privileges granted herein, permittee agrees to indemnify and save harmless the United States from any loss to it, including not only damage to government property and injury to government employees, but also judgments, settlements, or compromises for property damage or injury to all persons for which the United States may be liable resulting from the exercise by the permittee and his associates on the trip of the privileges granted herein.

I have given complete and accurate descriptions and answers to all questions asked. I agree to comply with all Park rules and regulations, and assume full responsibility for the conduct of my entire party in obeying these rules and regulations. I understand that any false or incorrect information given in this application renders any permit obtained null and void and may subject me to criminal prosecution. I have read and understand all requirements and conditions of this permit and attachments and agree to abide by them.

Signed: _____   _____
                        (Trip Leader)   (Date)

Form 8370-1
(November 1985)

**UNITED STATES
DEPARTMENT OF THE INTERIOR
BUREAU OF LAND MANAGEMENT**

SPECIAL RECREATION APPLICATION AND PERMIT
(43 U.S.C. 1201; 43 U.S.C. 1701; 16 U.S.C. 460 L—6(a); and 43 CFR Group 8300)

FORM APPROVED
OMP NO. 1004-0119
Expires: July 31, 1988

Permit No.

Instructions: Complete Items 1 through 8, and return to appropriate BLM Office. *(Use additional sheets, if necessary.)*

(Type Or Print Plainly In Ink)

WHEN SIGNED BY AUTHORIZED BLM OFFICIAL, THIS PERMIT AUTHORIZES

1. Name of person and/or organization

    Address *(include zip code)*

    Telephone No. *(include area code)* Business

    Residence

2. To use the following public lands *(provide name and legal description, or attach map).*

3. For the following purpose *(provide full description of activity or event including number of anticipated participants and spectators).*

4. During the following times and dates *(specify below)*

ARRIVAL			DEPARTURE		
DATE *(Mon., Day, Yr.)*	TIME		DATE *(Mon., Day, Yr.)*	TIME	
	AM	PM		AM	PM

5a. Type of permit: or *Free Use*   ☑ Commercial   ☐ Other ORV events with 50 or more vehicles

☑ Competitive   ☐ Individual/Private *(if "checked," skip to item 8)*

b. ~~A $10 nonrefundable filing fee must accompany all commercial and competitive permit applications.~~

c. ~~If you request a waiver of filing and use fees for educational, scientific, or therapeutic purposes which are non-commercial you must attach proof of eligibility (see 43 CFR 8372.4(d)).~~

6. Facilities *(describe facilities including water and sanitation facilities you intend to provide, attach plans and location maps).*

7a. Previous permits: Have you been issued a permit for a previous event or activity? *(If "yes," answer the following.)*

b. BLM Office issuing permit

c. Date of latest permit

d. Have you, or your organization, forfeited any portion of any previous permit, bond, or surety submitted for use of public lands, or is any investigation or legal action pending against you or your organization for use of public lands? ☐ Yes ☐ No *(if "yes," attach details on separate sheet.)*

8. Certification of Information: I CERTIFY That the information given by me in this application is true, complete, and correct to the best of my knowledge and belief and is given in good faith. I acknowledge that I (we) am (are) required to comply with any conditions or stipulations that are required by the authorized officer when the permit is issued.

_____

(Signature of Applicant)   *(Date)*

Title 18 U.S.C. Section 1001, makes it a crime for any person knowingly and willfully to make to any department or agency of the United States any false, fictitious, or fraudulent statements or representations as to any matter within its jurisdiction.

This application is hereby approved subject to the conditions and special stipulations on reverse and any attachments.

_____

(Signature of Authorized Official)   *(Date)*

PERMITTEE MUST HAVE THIS PERMIT *(OR LEGIBLE COPY)* IN POSSESSION DURING USE IN PERMITTED AREAS.

SPECIAL STIPULATIONS
*(The conditions and stipulations required by the
authorized officer are checked below.)*

The following *must* be submitted before an application is approved and a permit issued. This information *must* be submitted within ____ days after the date of application:

[ ] a. A topographic map, showing area of proposed use with routes, parking, staging areas, proposed improvements, and other points of intensive use specifically identified. U.S. Geological Survey topographic quadrangle maps are available from U.S.G.S. offices and from numerous private concerns. *Planning unit maps* are also available at most BLM District Offices to help determine land ownership patterns in planning your use.

[ ] b. List all private landowners whose property is affected by the event, route, access, pits, parking areas or any other action associated with the event or use and show evidence that permission to use this property has been obtained.

[ ] c. Applicant also *must* inform other pertinent public agencies *(law enforcement, highway, fish and game, etc.)*. Bureau of Land Management will contact other authorized users of public lands, etc.

[ ] d. A certificate from an insurer that comprehensive insurance has been obtained for this use or event in the minimum amount of (1) $ *100,000.00* for bodily injury for any one person; $ *300,000.00* for any one occurrence; and (2) $ *10,000.00* property damage for any one occurrence. The certificate *must* also state that such insurance is in force and that the insurer will give BLM thirty (30) days notice prior to cancellation or modification of such insurance.

[ ] e. An acceptable bond, surety, cash deposit, or other acceptable guarantee of payment in amount of $ ____ to secure payment of the special recreation use fee and/or mitigation of damages.

PERMITS SUBJECT TO THE FOLLOWING CONDITIONS:
*(The conditions and stipulations required by the
authorized officer are checked below.)*

[✓] 1. This permit is issued for the period specified herein. It is revocable for any breach of conditions hereof or at the discretion of the authorized officer of the Bureau of Land Management, at any time upon notice. This permit is subject to valid adverse claims heretofore or hereafter acquired.

[✓] 2. This permit is subject to all applicable provisions of the regulations (43 CFR 18 and 43 CFR Group 8300) which are made a part hereof.

[✓] 3. This permit is subject to the provisions of Executive Order No. 11246 of September 24, 1965, as amended, which sets forth the Equal Opportunity clauses. A copy of this order may be obtained from the signing officer.

[✓] 4. This permit may not be reassigned or transferred by permittee.

[ ] 5. Permittee *must* pay the sum of estimated user fees in advance of permit issuance. Adjustments to user fee charges will be based on actual use reported on the Post Use Report. No refund of less than ten dollars ($10) will be made.

[✓] 6. Permittee *must* observe all Federal, State, and local laws and regulations applicable to the premises; to erection or maintenance of signs or advertising displays including the regulations for the protection of game birds and game animals, and shall keep the premises in a neat, orderly, and sanitary condition.

[✓] 7. Permittee *must* take all reasonable precautions to prevent and suppress forest, brush, and grass fire and to prevent polluting of waters on or in vicinity of the lands.

[ ] 8. Permittee *must* not enclose roads or trails commonly in public use.

[✓] 9. Permittee *must* pay the United States for any damage to its property resulting from this use.

[✓] 10. Permittee *must* notify the authorized officer of address change immediately.

[✓] 11. Permittee *must* not cut any timber on the lands without prior written permission from the authorized officer.

[✓] 12. Permittee *must* indemnify, defend, and hold harmless the United States and/or its agencies and representatives against and from any and all demands, claims, or liabilities of every nature whatsoever, including, but not limited to, damages to property, injuries to or death of persons, arising directly or indirectly from, or in any way connected with the permittee's use and occupancy of the lands described in this permit or with the event authorized under this permit.

[✓] 13. Authorized representatives of the Department of the Interior, other Federal agencies, and game wardens *must* at all times, have the right to enter the premises on official business.

[✓] 14. Permittee *must* abide by all special stipulations attached hereto.

[✓] 15. Permittee *must* not disturb archeological and historical values, including, but not limited to, petroglyphs, ruins, historic buildings, and artifacts.

[✓] 16. Permittee *must* leave in place any hidden cultural values uncovered through authorized operations.

NOTICE

☆U.S. GOVERNMENT PRINTING OFFICE: 1988573-017/81456

<u>APPLICATION</u>

<u>TWO YEAR PERMIT FOR USING THE JAMES RIVER DURING TIME OF HIGH WATER</u>

<u>NAME</u>_____ <u>ADDRESS</u>_____

<u>SEX</u>_____ <u>WEIGHT</u>_____ <u>HEIGHT</u>_____ <u>BORN</u>_____

I certify that I am a paddler with advanced skills, and that I have paddled rivers with difficulty rating equal to or greater than that of the James River at 9 feet and above. I also certify that I will follow the guidelines of the American Whitewater Affiliation Safety Code, and that I have read and agree to abide by the conditions set forth in Section 22-2.20 of the Richmond City Code as stated in Ordinance # 82-24-31 adopted March 22, 1982.

<u>CONDITIONS OF PERMIT</u>

1. United States Coast Guard Approved Personal Flotation Devices must be worn at all times.

2. Helmets must be worn at all times.

3. Minimum group size shall be 3 craft. All persons must have a permit.

4. Each group must carry a rescue line and first aid kit while on the river.

I agree to abide by the conditions stated above.

Date_____   Signature_____

<u>(Applicant under 18 years of age</u>   Signature_____

<u>must have parental or guardian</u>   (Parent or Guardian)

<u>approval)</u>

<u>THE WAIVER ON THE REVERSE SIDE OF THIS APPLICATION MUST</u>

<u>BE COMPLETED AS A CONDITION FOR ISSUANCE OF A PERMIT</u>

<u>PERMIT FEE OF $10 MUST BE SUBMITTED WITH APPLICATION. MAKE CHECK OR MONEY ORDER PAYABLE TO CITY OF RICHMOND</u>

Richmond Public Safety Expert Boater Permit Application, James River, VA

WAIVER

The undersigned,_____, permittee residing at_____
                        FULL NAME

_____
                              STREET ADDRESS

in the_____State of_____
        CITY, TOWN, COUNTY

being of lawful age, having made an application for issuance of a permit to enable
and allow me to enter the waters of the James River in the City of Richmond, between
the West City Limits and the City Locks, pursuant to the provisions of Section
22-2.20 of the Richmond City Code (Ordinance No. 82-24-31 adopted March 22, 1982),
do hereby, in the event a permit is issued to me, for and on behalf of myself,
successors and assigns, including legal representatives, WAIVE, all claims demands,
damages, actions and causes of action, whatsoever, against the City of Richmond or
any City employee or any agent of the City, which may arise by reason of, or, in any
manner growing out of my entering the James River in the City of Richmond between
the West City Limits and the City Locks by virtue of my holding such permit, and do
acknowledge that issuance of such permit is the result of my satisfying all
requirements prescribed for issuance of the permit, the issuance of what I deem,
consider and acknowledge to be valid consideration for the execution of this waiver
and I shall assume all risks attendant to my entering and my use of the James River
at all times when my possession of the permit is requisite.

Pursuant to the terms and conditions of this Permit, I agree to defend, save harmless
and idemnify the City from and against any claims for damages against the City
allegedly caused by issuance of this permit.

_____
                              SIGNATURE

_____
         WITNESS

                              _____
                                  DATE

Mail check to   Director of Public Safety
                501 N. 9th Street   131
                Richmond, VA 23219

KERN RIVER BOATING PERMIT APPLICATION

NAME _____

ADDRESS _____

CITY _____STATE_____ZIP_____

I PLAN TO BOAT THE   LOWER   UPPER   FORKS
SEGMENT OF THE KERN RIVER. (PLEASE CIRCLE)

START DATE _____

FINISH DATE _____

LOCATION OF ENTRY(IES)_____

_____

LOCATION OF EXIT(S) _____

_____

TYPE OF WATERCRAFT   RAFT   KAYAK   CANOE
                      (PLEASE CIRCLE)

NUMBER OF PEOPLE IN GROUP _____(LIMIT 15)

NUMBER OF WATERCRAFT _____

PHONE (OPTIONAL) (   )   -_____

SEQUOIA NATIONAL FOREST REGULATIONS REQUIRE
ALL RAFTERS, CANOEISTS AND KAYAKERS TO
OBTAIN A PERMIT TO BOAT THE KERN RIVER.
GROUP SIZE IS LIMITED TO 15 PEOPLE ON ALL
SEGMENTS OF THE RIVER. PERMITS ARE ONLY
REQUIRED FROM MAY 15 TO SEPTEMBER 15,
BETWEEN 7:00AM AND 4:00PM

PLEASE RETURN APPLICATION TO:

USDA, FOREST SERVICE
CANNELL MEADOW RANGER DISTRICT
P.O. BOX 6
KERNVILLE, CA. 93238

Forest Service Permit Application Form, Kern River, CA

Form I-01-6223-1
November 1983

OWYHEE RIVER BOATER REGISTRATION
(ONLY ONE PERSON PER PARTY NEED REGISTER)

NAME _____

ADDRESS _____
_____

TELEPHONE (in case of emergency) _____

DATES OF TRIP _____

NUMBER OF PEOPLE IN PARTY _____

HOMETOWN OF PARTY MEMBERS _____
_____

NUMBER AND TYPES OF BOATS

____ Raft ____ Kayak ____ Canoe ____ Drift Boat ____ Other

PUT-IN POINT (circle)

Owyhee River	East Fork	South Fork
Three Forks	Indian Reservation	"YP" Ranch
Rome	Pipeline (Garat)	Pipeline
	Crutchers	"45" Ranch

TAKE-OUT POINT (circle)

Three Forks	Crutchers	"45" Ranch
Rome	Owyhee Reservoir (Leslie Gulch)	

WILL YOU FILL OUT A POST-USE QUESTIONNAIRE (circle)

                                        yes   no

Please read the enclosed information and please practice low
impact camping techniques while on the river. FIRE PANS REQUIRED
IN OREGON (MALHEUR COUNTY ORDINANCE).

(Space on back for your comment and/or suggestions)

Bureau of Land Management   Bureau of Land Management
3948 Development Avenue   P.O. Box 700
Boise, Idaho 83705   Vale, Oregon 97918
Phone: (208) 334-1582   Phone: (503) 473-3144

BLM Permit Application Form, Owyhee Rivers, ID/OR

1990
FLOAT TRIP RESERVATION APPLICATION
Main Salmon, Snake, Middle Fork Salmon and Selway Rivers
(see instructions on reverse of form)

__Applicant Identification (Print or Type)__

    1) Photo Identification (ID) Number: _____

    State of Identification (ID): _____

    · Type of ID: _____   Drivers License=D, Bank or State ID=B, Fish & Game ID=F
                     Other=O

Name:2)Last:_____ 3)First:_____ Initial:____

4)Mailing Address: _____

5)City: _____ 6)State: _____

7)Zip: _____ _____   8)Phone: (___) _____ - _____

__Launch Dates and Rivers__

River Code Numbers: Main Salmon=**1**, Snake=**2**, Middle Fork Salmon=**3**, Selway=**4**

  9) 1st choice launch: _____   _____,   River Code No.: _____
                    Month   Day

  10) 2nd choice launch: _____   _____,   River Code No.: _____
                    Month   Day

  11) 3rd choice launch: _____   _____,   River Code No.: _____
                    Month   Day

  12) 4th choice launch: _____   _____,   River Code No.: _____
                    Month   Day

__Fee and Application Validity__

A five dollar ($5.00) nonrefundable application fee must accompany this
form. Send check or money order only; please do not send cash. Checks or money
orders should be made payable to: USDA Forest Service. Applications that are
not legible, incomplete or not accompanied by the required fee will not be
entered into the drawing. Only one application will be accepted from each
person. All applicants must be at least 18 years of age. Applications from
people subject to a no-show penalty for the previous year will be ineligible for
a launch on the river or rivers for which the penalty was imposed.
Applications must be received no earlier than **December 1** and no later than
January 31st. Applications received outside of the time period will be
rejected.

__1990 River Control Dates__

  1 MAIN SALMON: June 20 through September 7
  2 SNAKE: May 25 through September 15
  3 MIDDLE FORK SALMON: June 1 through September 3
  4 SELWAY: May 15 through July 31

__If you make copies of this application form, please make copies of the instructions and__
__information handout also.__

INSTRUCTIONS

General: Print or type all entries; be sure they are legible.

Applicant Identification:

1)   Photo ID Number: The trip leader will be asked to produce the
      identification document with a photograph attached when the permit is
      issued. Do not send a photo or ID with this application. Enter this
      identification number in the space provided. Show the standard two
      letter abbreviation for the state in which the identification was
      issued (for example: CA for California or OR for Oregon). Enter the
      proper code for the type of identification (for example D for drivers
      license).

2)   and 3) Enter last name, complete first name and middle initial.

4)   Mailing address: Show street, house number, P.O. Box, etc.

5)   Self-explanatory.

6)   State: Show the standard two letter abbreviation for your state.

7)   Zip: The first five digits of the zip code are required; the last 4
      digits are optional.

8)   Self-explanatory.

Launch Dates and Rivers:

9)   Show the month and day for your first choice launch. Following the
      date, enter the code number for your first choice river in the space
      provided. For example, if your first choice is to launch on July 9 on
      the Selway, your entry would be
      <u> 7   </u>   <u> 9 </u> , River Code No. <u> 4 </u>.
      Month   Day

10), 11) and 12) Enter your second, third and fourth choices in the same manner
as the first choice. You may use any mix of dates and rivers you wish. For
example, the choices may be all applied to one river or they may be spread among
all four rivers. You may use up to four choices if you wish but do not need to
fill in all four choices for your application to be considered.

Send this application to any one of the following offices to be **received** no earlier than
December 1 or later than January 31:

North Fork Ranger District   Middle Fork Ranger District
P. O. Box 780   P. O. Box 750
North Fork, ID 83466   Challis, ID 83226
(208) 865-2383   (208) 879-5204

Hells Canyon National Recreation Area   West Fork Ranger District
3620-B Snake River Avenue   Darby, MT 59829
Lewiston, ID 83501   (406) 821-3269
(208) 743-2297

<u>1990</u>

<u>INFORMATION</u>

<u>FLOAT LAUNCH RESERVATION APPLICATIONS</u>

Centralized Private Float Reservation System
for the
Main Salmon, Snake, Middle Fork Salmon and Selway Rivers

Private (non-commercial) floaters may now apply for launch reservations for the Main Salmon, Middle Fork Salmon, Selway and Snake Rivers on one application form.

Application forms and information are available at the following offices beginning October 1 each year:

North Fork Ranger District
P. O. Box 780
North Fork, ID 83466
(208)865-2383

Middle Fork Ranger District
P. O. Box 750
Challis, ID 83226
(208)879-5204

Hells Canyon National Recreation Area
3620-B Snake River Avenue
Lewiston, ID 83501
(208)743-2297

West Fork Ranger Station
Darby, MT 59829
(406)821-3269

Applications will be accepted at any one of the above offices from December 1 through January 31. Applications **received** before December 1 or after January 31 will be considered invalid and will not be entered into the drawing. **DON'T WAIT UNTIL THE LAST MINUTE.** The date received determines acceptance, **NOT** the post mark.

Applications may be submitted on the form provided for that purpose to any one of the above offices. They may also be submitted electronically by visiting one of the above offices.

Only one application will be accepted from each person at one of the above offices. Duplicate applications will be rejected. One application covers all four rivers. Applications from all four offices are entered into a single data base. Therefore, there is no advantage to submitting applications to more than one office.

Applicants must be at least 18 years of age.

People subject to a no-show penalty will be ineligible to apply for a launch on the river (or rivers) for which the penalty was imposed for a one year period.

A $5.00 non-refundable reservation application fee must accompany the application: Group checks will be accepted. **Please do not send cash.** Checks or money orders should be sent with mailed applications and made payable to USDA, Forest Service. This fee covers the costs of allocating launches, including processing applications and conducting the drawing. If checks are returned for insufficient funds the application will be rejected or, if a launch has been reserved, the launch date will be cancelled and reissued.

Page 1

People who obtain a reservation after the initial application period and drawing, including walk-ons at the launch site, will also be charged a $5.00 reservation fee. Those who applied during the initial application period and have already paid the fee, will not be charged a second fee for their first reserved launch. For those rivers that allow a second reservation after the first trip is run, a second reservation fee will be charged.

Those people making post-drawing reservations will be asked to submit payment within two weeks of making the reservation to the office at which the reservation was made, unless the launch was reserved less than two weeks prior to the launch date. Those late reservations and walk-ons will make payment by check or money order when the permit is filled out. Cash will not be accepted at the launch site. If the fee is not paid as indicated above, the person's reservation or waiting list position will be cancelled.

No alternate trip leaders will be designated. The person holding the reservation must pick up the permit and participate in the trip.

ALLOCATION OF LAUNCH RESERVATIONS - DRAWING

A computer generated random drawing will be made in February to determine the identity of successful applicants.

Successful applicants only will be notified by mail in February and early March.

Once the initial drawing is complete, each river management team will operate their individual programs with respect to confirmations, cancellations, open dates, waiting lists, etc.

Each successful applicant will receive an information packet describing the process for obtaining the permit and other requirements such as confirmations, special equipment, etc.

INFORMATION SPECIFIC TO EACH RIVER

Because of differences in management plans and the characteristics of the rivers, it is not possible to achieve total uniformity in management systems between the four rivers. As plans are revised, efforts will be made to bring more consistency into the program.

Main Salmon River

The section of river covered by this private float application reservation system extends from Corn Creek to Long Tom Bar.

The control period during which reservations are required extends from June 20 through September 7. Reservations are not required outside of the control period. Voluntary permits can be obtained from either the North Fork District Office or a self-issue station at the launch site for trips outside of the control period.

Four private (non-commercial) launches are reserved for each day in the control period.

Any unassigned, cancelled or unconfirmed launches will be allocated by telephone on a first-come, first-served basis during the call-in period starting at 0800 AM on the second Monday following April 15 (April 23, 1990) and continuing throughout the control period. Calls will be accepted from 8:00 AM to 4:30 PM Mountain time on weekdays, Monday through Friday. No collect calls will be accepted. The office will be closed on Federal Holidays.

There will be no waiting list.

Maximum party size is 30 persons.

Maximum trip duration is 10 days.

Portable toilets and fire pans are required.

Snake River

The section of river covered by the private float application reservation system extends from Hells Canyon Dam to the bottom of Rush Creek Rapid. Parties floating that section of river must have a reservation and trip permit issued by a Forest Officer during the control period.

Float trips launching at points downstream from Rush Creek Rapids to the Scenic River boundary near the Oregon/Washington state line, or those entering the Snake from the Lower Salmon river, must complete a self-issue permit during the control period.

The control period (regulated season) during which reservations are required extends from the Friday preceding Memorial Day weekend through September 15. Reservations and permits are not required outside of the control period.

Three private (non-commercial) launches are reserved each day during the control period.

Any unassigned, cancelled or unconfirmed launches will be allocated by telephone on a first-come, first-served basis starting at 8:00 AM on the third Monday in March, and continuing throughout the control period. Calls will be accepted from 8:00 to 11:30 AM and from 12:30 to 4:00 PM Pacific Time during weekdays, Monday through Friday on the river reservation confirmation telephone line (208) 743-2297. No collect calls will be accepted. The office will be closed on Federal Holidays. Only one launch will be reserved per person. Only one person will be served with each call. After using a reserved launch, an individual may apply for another launch, but only one launch may be reserved at any given time.

During the call-in period, if all launch dates an individual is interested in are reserved, that person's name can be placed on a waiting list for one date. When a launch date becomes available to people on the waiting list, they will be called collect, person to person, in the order in which their names have been placed on the list. If we are unable to contact a person on the waiting list, we will drop to the next name until the date is assigned or the list exhausted. If

the collect call is refused, we will assume that individual is no longer
interested in a launch date and remove that person's name from the waiting list.
No one who has a reserved launch will be eligible for any waiting list until the
reserved launch is used. If three waiting list dates are refused, the applicant
will not be eligible for further waiting list dates during the current season.

All persons requesting reservations after the initial allocation period will be
asked for the information on the application form including name, address,
telephone number and a photo ID number.

Party size limit is 30.

Middle Fork Salmon River

All boaters floating the Middle Fork of the Salmon are required to obtain a trip
permit before launching at any time of the year.

The control period (heavy use season) during which advanced reservations are
required extends from June 1 through September 3. Before and after this period
launches are given out on a first-come, first-served basis. At any time during
the year, users are required to obtain a trip permit. No more than seven
launches are allowed each day, including both private and commercial parties.

During the control period, there are 373 private (non-commercial) launch
opportunities and 288 commercial launches available. Of the seven launches
allowed per day, the number of private vs commercial will vary.

Any unassigned, cancelled or unconfirmed launches will be allocated (**by telephone
only**) on a first-come, first-served basis after the initial lottery in February
and continuing throughout the control period. Calls will be accepted from 8:00
AM to 4:30 PM Mountain time during weekdays, Monday through Friday on the river
reservation telephone line (208)879-5204. No collect calls will be accepted.
The office will be closed on Federal Holidays.

Maximum length of trip is 8 days during the heavy use period.

Maximum party size is 24 people.

People who apply for early June or late August dates may need to fly into
intermediate launch points. Snow often blocks access in the spring and low water
may stop floaters in the upper section of river in late August.

Selway River

The section of river covered by the private float application reservations system
extends from the Paradise launch Site to Selway Falls. Parties floating that
section of river must have a reservation and trip permit during the control
period.

The control period (regulated season) during which reservations are required extends from May 15 through July 31. Reservations and permits are not required outside of the control period for private non-commercial floaters.

One private launch opportunity is reserved each day for 62 days of the control period. The remaining 16 days are reserved for commercial outfitters with one launch per day.

A trip is <u>commercial</u> if any of the participants makes a profit, receives a reimbursement or salary in the form of cash, goods, or service, receives rental for use of rafts or equipment, increases the value of equipment; or supports in any part other programs or activities from amounts received from other party members. A trip is <u>noncommercial</u> if there is a bona fide sharing of costs where no part of the fees are collected in excess of actual costs of the activity, for salary or financial gain in any manner for any of the group, its leaders or sponsors or for captial increase or amortization of the major equipment. Noncommercial trips include the genuine "do-it-yourselfers" who get together to participate in river trips. Group leaders may not be paid in any manner. They must participate equally in sharing costs with other members of the group. Paid advertising is not permitted for noncommercial trips.

Any unassigned, cancelled or unconfirmed launches will be allocated on a first-come first-served basis by telephone starting at 8:00 A.M. on the last Monday in March and continuing throughout the control period. Calls will be accepted from 8:00 AM to 4:30 PM Mountain time during weekdays, Monday through Friday. No collect calls will be accepted. The office will be closed on Federal Holidays.

Party size limit is 16 persons.

No person may take more than one trip per year.

People who apply for May launch dates may find snow blocking their access. Those with late launch dates may encounter low flows.

There will be no waiting list.

Contact the West Fork Ranger District with specific questions.

If you desire any additional information please send self addressed stamped envelope.

Do not apply for the Outfitter/Guide launch dates listed below:

    June 2, 8, 14, 20, 22, 26, 28 and 30
    July 2, 5, 8, 9, 12, 15, 16, and 18

APPLICATION FOR TUOLUMNE RIVER NON-COMMERCIAL PERMIT
(Please supply all information requested)

A separate application must be completed for each trip and accompanied by a check or money order for $10.00, made payable to: U.S.D.A. - Forest Service. The application will be returned if the reservation fee is not included. Include alternative trip dates in case your first choice is filled.

Name_____Organization/Group Name_____

Day Phone_____Address_____

Start Date_____Finish Date_____

Entry Point_____Exit Point_____

No. of Rafts____No. of Kayaks_____Total No. People in group_____

Length of stay limited to 3 days.

CERTIFICATION OF NON-COMMERCIAL TRIP

Please read before signing:

A river trip is non-commercial if there is a bona-fide sharing of expenses. There shall be no fees, charges, or other compensation collected from individual participants in excess of actual costs or expenses incurred. By contrast, a trip is commercial if anyone on the trip makes a profit, receives a reimbursement or salary, receives rental for use of equipment, or supports, in any part, other programs or activities from amounts received from passengers. Accordingly, fund raising trips are commercial and sponsers will have to arrange for an existing commercial launch from a permitted outfitter. Why the concern? Operating under the guise of non-commercial boaters, illegal outfitters are stealing carrying capacity from the private sector for their own profit. They compete unfairly with legitimate outfitters by avoiding use fees, insurance reguirements, and the need to comply with standards of the industry. Their guides may or may not be qualified; their equipment may or may not be safe.

Your signature on this form signifies that, to the best of your knowledge, your trip is not commercial (persons involved in unauthorized commercial operations or falsifying this document are subject to fine and/or imprisonment).

I agree to abide by all laws, and regulations which apply to this area.

Group Leaders Signature_____Date _____

*DRIVER'S LICENSE NUMBER OR SOCIAL SECURITY NUMBER _____

*You may be required to present valid identification to the River Patrolman.

01/01/90

GRAND CANYON NATIONAL PARK
NONCOMMERCIAL RIVER TRIP WAITING LIST
CONTINUING INTEREST / NEW ADDITIONS EXAMPLE FORM

FULL LEGAL NAME _____

                   (First)   (Middle)   (Last)

                   Initials are not acceptable.

CURRENT ADDRESS   PREVIOUS ADDRESS

_____   _____

_____   _____

_____   _____

SOCIAL SECURITY # _____ - ___ - _____   CURRENT PHONE # (___) ____ - _____
Only first 7 digits is required

SIGNATURE _____

*Your waiting list position WILL NOT be continued/added if incomplete information
is given. ONLY 1 REQUEST PER ENVELOPE WILL BE ACCEPTED.*

/ /   CONTINUING INTEREST: I am currently on the waiting list and would like to
remain on the list. In order to be accepted this letter <u>MUST BE POSTMARKED
BETWEEN DECEMBER 15 AND JANUARY 31</u>.

/ /   NEW ADDITIONS: I would like to be placed on the waiting list. This letter
<u>MUST BE POSTMARKED IN FEBRUARY</u> in order to be accepted. *A non-refundable,
non-transferable $25 MONEY ORDER or CASHIER'S CHECK payable to Grand Canyon
National Park is enclosed.*

It is highly recommended that the letters confirming interest in remaining on the
list and letters of new addition to the list be sent by Certified Mail, Return
Receipt Required to ensure that the letter has been received by the River Permits
Office. We cannot take responsibility for letters not received due to Postal
Service error.

MAIL TO:

                River Permits Office
                Grand Canyon National Park
                P.O. Box 129
                Grand Canyon, Arizona 86023-0129

U.S. DEPARTMENT OF AGRICULTURE
FOREST SERVICE

FORM APPROVED
OMB NO. 40R3857

VISITOR'S PERMIT

(14) TRAVEL PLAN

List or code all zones to be traversed, in sequence of travel, and number of nights to be spent in each zone.

In areas where specific campsites are assigned, list and code each site and the number of nights assigned.

TRAVEL ZONES (or campsite)			NIGHTS
32	33	34	35
36	37	38	39
40	41	42	43
44	45	46	47
48	49	50	51
52	53	54	55
56	57	58	59
60	61	62	63
64	65	66	67
68	69	70	71

WHEN SIGNED, THIS SINGLE - VISIT PERMIT AUTHORIZES

(1) NAME (First, Middle Initial, and Last)

(2) MAILING ADDRESS (Optional)

(3) CITY AND STATE

(4) ZIP CODE

| 1 | 2 | 3 | 4 | 5 |

(5) TO VISIT (and to build campfires in accordance with regulations)

| 6 | 7 | 8 | 9 |

(6) DATES (Give best estimate of start and finish dates)

From month/day

| 10 | 11 | 12 | 13 |

Through month/day

| 14 | 15 | 16 | 17 |

(7) LOCATION OF ENTRY POINT

| 18 | 19 | 20 |

(8) LOCATION OF EXIT POINT

| 21 | 22 | 23 |

(9) PRIMARY METHOD OF TRAVEL

| 24 | 25 |

(10) NUMBER OF PEOPLE IN GROUP

| 26 | 27 |

(11) NUMBER OF PACK AND SADDLE STOCK

| 28 | 29 |

(12) NUMBER OF WATERCRAFT OR VEHICLES
(Check Regulations - Vehicles not allowed in many permit areas)

| 30 | 31 |

I agree to abide by all laws, rules and regulations which apply to this area and will do my best to see that everyone in our group does likewise.

(13) VISITOR'S SIGNATURE

DATE

OPTIONAL

(15)(a) NUMBER OF TIMES YOU VISITED THIS AREA IN PAST 10 YEARS (Enter appropriate code)

| 1 | NONE | 3 | TWICE | 5 | FOUR |
| 2 | ONCE | 4 | THREE | 6 | FIVE OR MORE |

| | 72 |

(15)(b) IS VISITING THIS AREA (Enter appropriate code)

1	THE PRIMARY PURPOSE OF YOUR TRIP AWAY FROM HOME?
2	ONE OF SEVERAL IMPORTANT THINGS YOU PLANNED TO DO ON YOUR TRIP?
3	SOMETHING YOU DECIDED TO DO AFTER ARRIVING NEAR THE AREA?

| | 73 |

(16) REMARKS

| 74 | 75 | 76 |

(17) ISSUING OFFICER'S SIGNATURE

| 77 | 78 | 79 | 80 |
| FOREST CODE | | OFFICE CODE | |

VISITORS MUST HAVE THIS PERMIT IN POSSESSION DURING STAY IN REQUIRED PERMIT AREAS

FS-2300-30 (7/79)

LETCHWORTH STATE PARK
CASTILE, NEW YORK
716-493-2611

CANOE PERMIT

This permit is granted to _____ and other petitioners who sign on the reverse, for the purpose of a canoe or kayak trip on the Genesee River within Letchworth State Park for the period of _____, from Lee's Landing to _____.
                    Destination

PERMIT FEE OF $5.00 REQUIRED - Good date of permit ONLY and NON-REFUNDABLE.

This permit is granted subject to the following conditions:

1. All Permittees shall abide by the New York State and Genesee Region Rules and Regulations of the Office of Parks, Recreation and Historic Preservation, except as modified by this permit.

2. Petitioners are subject to the usual Region vehicular use fee and other fee payment schedules. $5.00 fee is required in advance for each permit.

3. Permit is valid only between 8 a.m. and 1/2 hour before sunset.

4. Permittees must enter on the west side of the River at Lee's Landing. They must exit at St. Helena or at Mt. Morris Dam. Mt. Morris Dam must be notified in advance of planned trip (658-4220). Administration Office at Letchworth must be notified when party is out of the river. (493-2611). If no answer, use Geneseo Sheriff (243-1212) and ask that they notify Letchworth Park Police by radio.

5. Cars are not permitted to drive to the River. Trails to the River are barricaded at the top of slopes near developed sections. Permittees are notified and hereby accept that canoes must be portaged from the barricade to the River and return. Cars must be parked in parking area while trip is in progress.

6. Two or more canoes must compose a group in close proximity to one another, with no more than two persons in each canoe. Participants must be 18 years of age or older, must have had some canoeing experience and MUST WEAR Coast Guard approved life jackets at all times. Persons age 12 - 18 may participate ONLY if a release form signed by their parent or legal guardian accompanies the permit application. Each person under 18 must be accompanied by a person age 18 or over on a one to one basis. The release form must designate who will accompany the under age 18 canoeist.

7. Permittees are advised that headgear with chin strap is recommended.

8. Permittees will not leave the river for side trips, hikes or extended lunch breaks.

9. Permittees will avoid canoeing at base of cliffs as much as possible. Falling rock is common.

10. Violation of permit conditions shall cause immediate revocation of the existing permit.

11. This permit must be completed by all parties and returned to the Administration Building, Letchworth State Park for approval at least 2 working days in advance of the canoe trip. The Park Manager, or designee of the Office of Parks, Recreation and Historic Preservation, has the right to cancel any or all trips. CANOEISTS SHOULD CONTACT THE PARK OFFICE PRIOR TO ENTERING THE RIVER TO ASCERTAIN THAT CONDITIONS WARRANT THE TRIP.

12. This permit is issued solely to those members of the group who personally sign on the reverse, or on attached sheet, indicating their acceptance of these conditions. Any other person in the group will be in violation of the Rules and Regulations and subject to arrest.

(See Reverse Side)

W A I V E R

We, the individuals who sign below, in consideration of our being granted a permit to canoe the Genesee River in Letchworth State Park, do hereby voluntarily waive and release on behalf of ourselves, our heirs and assigns, any claims that we or they may have against the State Of New York, the New York State Office of Parks, Recreation and Historic Preservation, its related agencies, employees and servants, on account of any injuries to our persons, including death, that may arise as a result of canoe or kayak use as authorized by this permit.

We certify that we: are able swimmers, are in good health, have had some canoeing experience, and understand the sport of white water canoeing and the potential hazards of the sport; realize we could suffer serious injuries by falling or by being thrown out of the canoe into rough water and rocks, or from rocks falling from the sides of the gorge.

NAME	AGE	DATE	ADDRESS	TELEPHONE

CANOE PERMIT GRANTED:

_____

Signature of Genesee Region Official   Date

Rev:3:28:84
 Rev. 5:25:85

APPENDIX TWO: TABLE OF RECREATIONAL RIVERS MANAGED BY THE BUREAU OF LAND MANAGMENT

RIVER	TRIP LENGTHS (miles)	NATIONAL DESIGNATION			
		Wild	Scenic	Recreation	Wildern
Delta	35, 17	x	x	x	
Gulkana	45	x			
Gulkana, Middle Fork	34	x			
Unalakeet	80	x			
Beaver Creek	127	x			
Birch Creek	126	x			
Forty Mile, Middle Fork	95, 88	x			
Forty Mile, South Fork	72, 88		x		
Deschutes	50, 50, 10, 10				x
John Day	46, 65	x		x	
Klamath, Upper	11				
Rogue	33, others	x			
Grande Ronde	60				
North Umpqua	32				
Owyhee (Oregon)	38, 57				x
Owyhee (Idaho)	50, 35				
Owyhee, South Fork (Idaho)	30				
Owyhee, South Fork (Nevada)	25				
Bruneau and Jarbridge	30, 30, 40				
Payette	10, 7, 9				
Snake (near Boise)	25, 11				
Snake (near Shoshone)	23, 20, 20				
Snake, South Fork	15, 26				
Coeur d'Alene	40				
Salmon, Lower	70, 75				
Salmon, Upper Main	112				
Missouri, Upper	10 to 149	x	x	x	
Madison	16				x
Trinity	40			x	
Sacramento, Lower	53				
American, South Fork	21				
Kern, Lower	21				
Merced	25				
Eel, Middle Fork	30	x	x	x	
Carson, East Fork	31				
Green, Browns Park	16				
Green	84, 8, 68				
San Juan	20, 27, 56				
Dolores (Utah)	30				
Dolores (Colorado)	102, 58, 44				
Arkansas	10, 13 to 44				
Gunnison	13				
Colorado, Upper	14				
Colorado, Catamount	6 to 43				
Colorado, Ruby Canyon	25				
Colorado, Moab	17, 5 to 32				
Colorado, Lower	17, 25				
Bill Williams	6, 26				
Gila (Arizona)	20				
Gila (New Mexico)	49, 28				
Rio Grande	18, 8	x	x	x	
Rio Chama	30				x
North Platte	6 to 127				
Encampment	6				

ds	ATTRACTIONS				BLM ADDRESS FOR FURTHER INFORMATION	PHONE
	Scenery	Wildlife	Fishing	Historic		
	x	x	x		4700 E. 72nd Ave., Anchorage, AK 99507	907-257-1200
		x	x		4700 E. 72nd Ave., Anchorage, AK 99507	907-257-1200
		x	x		4700 E. 72nd Ave., Anchorage, AK 99507	907-257-1200
		x	x		4700 E. 72nd Ave., Anchorage, AK 99507	907-257-1200
	x	x	x		Box 1150, Fairbanks, AK 99707	907-356-2025
	x	x			Box 1150, Fairbanks, AK 99707	907-356-2025
	x	x		x	Box 1150, Fairbanks, AK 99707	907-356-2025
	x	x		x	Box 1150, Fairbanks, AK 99707	907-356-2025
	x	x	x	x	PO Box 550, Prineville, OR 97754	503-447-4115
	x	x	x	x	PO Box 550, Prineville, OR 97754	503-447-4115
	x	x	x	x	3040 Biddle Road, Medford, OR 97504	503-776-4174
	x	x	x	x	3040 Biddle Road, Medford, OR 97504	503-776-4174
	x	x	x	x	PO Box 987, Baker, OR 97814	503-523-6391
	x	x	x		777 NW Garden Valley Blvd., Roseberg, OR 97470	503-672-4491
	x	x	x	x	PO Box 700, Vale, OR 97918	503-473-3144
	x	x		x	3948 Development Ave., Boise, ID 83705	208-334-1582
	x	x		x	3948 Development Ave., Boise, ID 83705	208-334-1582
	x	x		x	PO Box 831, Elko, NV 89801	702-738-4071
	x	x		x	3948 Development Ave., Boise, ID 83705	208-334-1582
	x		x		3948 Development Ave., Boise, ID 83705	208-334-1582
	x	x	x	x	3948 Development Ave., Boise, ID 83705	208-334-1582
	x	x	x	x	PO Box 2B, Shoshone, ID 83352	208-886-2206
	x	x	x	x	940 Lincoln Road, Idaho Falls, ID 83401	208-529-1020
	x	x	x	x	1801 N. Third St., Coeur d'Alene, ID 83814	208-765-7356
	x	x	x	x	Rt. 3, Box 181, Cottonwood, ID 83522	208-962-3245
	x	x	x	x	PO Box 430, Salmon, ID 83467	208-756-2201
	x	x	x	x	Airport Road, Lewiston, MT 59457	406-538-7461
	x	x	x		PO Box 1048, Dillon, MT 59725	406-683-2337
	x	x	x	x	355 Hemsted Drive, Redding, CA 96002	916-246-5325
	x	x	x	x	355 Hemsted Drive, Redding, CA 96002	916-246-5325
	x	x	x	x	63 Natoma St., Folsum, CA 95630	916-985-4474
	x	x	x	x	520 Butte St., Bakersfield, CA 93305	805-861-4236
	x	x	x	x	63 Natoma St., Folsum, CA 95630	916-985-4474
	x	x	x	x	555 Leslie St., Ukiah, CA 95482	707-462-3873
	x	x	x	x	1050 E. Wm. St., Ste. 335, Carson City, NV 84000	702-882-1631
	x		x		170 S. 500 East, Vernal, UT 84078	801-789-1362
	x			x	PO Drawer AB, Price, UT 84501	801-637-4584
	x			x	PO Box 7, Monticello, UT 84535	801-587-2201
	x				PO Box M, Moab, UT 84532	801-259-8193
	x	x		x	701 Camino Del Rio, Durango, CO 81212	303-247-4082
	x	x		x	PO Box 1470, Canon City, CO 81212	303-275-7578
	x	x	x		2465 So. Townsend, Montrose, CO 81401	303-249-7791
	x	x	x		PO Box 68, Kremmling, CO 80459	303-724-3437
	x	x	x		PO Box 1009, Glenwood Spring, CO 81602	303-945-2341
	x	x	x	x	764 Horizon Drive, Grand Junction, CO 81501	303-243-6552
	x				PO Box M, Moab, UT 84532	801-259-8193
	x	x	x	x	PO Box 5680, Yuma, AZ 85364	602-726-6300
	x	x	x		PO Box 685, Lake Havasu City, AZ 86043	602-855-8017
	x	x	x		425 E. 4th Street, Safford, AZ 85546	602-428-4040
	x	x	x		PO Box 1420, Las Cruces, NM 88004	602-855-8018
	x	x		x	PO Box 1045, Taos, NM 87571	505-758-8851
	x	x		x	PO Box 1045, Taos, NM 87571	505-758-8851
	x	x	x	x	Box 670, Rawlins, WY 82301	307-324-7171
	x	x	x	x	Box 670, Rawlins, WY 82301	307-324-7171

APPENDIX THREE: MINNESOTA DEPARTMENT OF NATURAL RESOURCES RIVER LEVEL INVENTORY FORM

RIVER_____   Dates Canoed _/_ /_ to _/_ /_ Number in party ___people; ___canoes

River Level Gauge Location (river mi.)	Date	Gauge Reading	General condition of level (V. High, High, Med., Low, V. Low)

TRIP EXPERIENCE :

Facility	Location, Name, Description	River Mile	
Put-in Access			
Take-out Access			

Total time spent on trip _____ hours

Total time spent canoeing/floating _____ hours

Total time spent playing, fishing, etc. _____ hours

1. Estimate the number of times your canoe: _____ Hit rocks _____ Dragged bottom

2. Estimate the number of times these occurances were due to low water as opposed to an error.

                    low water error   low water error
     Hit rocks   _____/_____   Dragged bottom   _____/_____

3. How do you feel about the frequency of hitting rocks or dragging bottom? (circle one #)

   Didn't bother me at all   1   2   3   4   5   Wouldn't canoe at this level again

4. We need to know how the flow of the river affected your trip. In general, was the current:

        Slow and placid   1   2   3   4   5   Swift and powerful   (circle one #)

WATER CONDITIONS: Which of the following did you encounter on your trip?

_____Riffles _____Rapids, passable _____Fast water with large standing waves

_____Rapids, not passable due to (high / low) water, circle one

Please comment on particular areas, where you feel the water conditions put you at risk:

Condition	Location (river mile)	Description, Comments, Risk if any
	( )	
	( )	
	( )	
	( )	

OBSTRUCTIONS :   Please check those items that may have been a hazard to you on your trip:

___snags ___low bridges ___overhanging tree limbs ___fences ___other:_____

Item	Location (river mile)	Description, Comments, Risk if any
	( )	
	( )	
	( )	
	( )	

8. Other comments: (e.g. overall canoeability; quality of experience; conditions of facility; maintenance problems; suggestions; etc.)

_____

_____

Estimate the number of rivers you have canoed ___ Years of experience___

Thank you for your time and assisstance.

Name_____   Phone ( )_____

Address_____

2-85   _____ Zip_____

APPENDIX FOUR: SAFETY CODE OF THE AMERICAN WHITEWATER AFFILIATION

Adopted 1959

Revised 1989

This code has been prepared using the best available information and has been reviewed by a broad cross section of whitewater experts. The code, however, is only a collection of guidelines. Attempts to minimize risks should be flexible—not constrained by a rigid set of rules. Varying conditions and group goals may combine with unpredictable circumstances to require alternate procedures.

I. Personal preparedness and responsibility

1. Be a competent swimmer, with the ability to handle yourself underwater.
2. Wear a lifejacket. A snugly-fitting vest-type life preserver offers back and shoulder protection as well as the flotation needed to swim safely in whitewater.
3. Wear a solid, correctly-fitted helmet when upsets are likely. This is essential in kayaks or covered canoes and recommended for open canoeists using thigh straps and rafters running steep drops.
4. Do not boat out of control. Your skills should be sufficient to stop or reach shore before reaching danger. Do not enter a rapid unless you are reasonably sure that you can run it safely or swim it without injury.
5. Whitewater rivers contain many hazards that are not always easily recognized. The following are the most frequent killers:

   A. High water. The river's speed and power increase tremendously as the flow increases, raising the difficulty of most rapids. Rescue becomes progressively harder as the water rises, adding to the danger. Floating debris and strainers make even an easy rapid quite hazardous. It is often misleading to judge the river level at the put-in, since a small rise in a wide, shallow place will be multiplied many times where the river narrows. Use reliable gauge information whenever possible, and be aware that sun on snowpack, hard rain, and upstream dam releases may greatly increase the flow.

   B. Cold. Cold drains your strength, and robs you of the ability to make sound decisions on matters affecting your survival. Cold water immersion, because of the initial shock and the rapid heat loss which follows, is especially dangerous. Dress appropriately for bad weather or sudden immersion in the water. When the water temperature is less than 50 degrees F, a wetsuit or drysuit is essential for protection if you swim. Next best is wool or pile clothing under a waterproof shell. In this case, you should also carry water-proof matches and a change of clothing in a waterproof bag. If, after prolonged exposure, a person experiences uncontrollable shaking, loss of coordination or difficulty speaking, he or she is hypothermic and needs your assistance.

   C. Strainers. Brush, fallen trees, bridge pilings, undercut rocks or anything else which allows river current to sweep through can pin boats and boaters against the obstacle. Water pressure on anything trapped this way can be overwhelming. Rescue is often extremely difficult. Pinning may occur in fast current, with little or no whitewater to warn of the danger.

   D. Dams, weirs, ledges, reversals, holes and hydraulics. When water drops over an obstacle, it curls back on itself, forming a strong upstream current which may be capable of holding boat or a swimmer. Some holes make for excellent sport; others are proven killers. Paddlers who cannot recognize the differences should avoid all but the smallest holes. Hydraulics around man-made dams must be treated with utmost respect regardless of their height or the level of the river. Despite their seeming benign appearance, they can create an almost escape-proof trap. The swimmer's only exit from the "drowning machine" is to dive below the surface where the downstream current is flowing beneath the reversal.

   E. Broaching. When a boat is pushed sideways against a rock by strong current, it may collapse and wrap. This is especially dangerous to kayak and decked canoe paddlers; these boats will collapse and the combination of indestructible hulls and tight outfitting may create a deadly trap. Even without entrapment, releasing pinned boats can be extremely time-consuming and dangerous. To avoid pinning, throw your weight downstream toward the rock. This allows the current to slide harmlessly underneath the hull.

6. Boating alone is discouraged. The minimum party is three people or two craft.
7. Have a frank knowledge of your boating ability, and don't attempt rivers or rapids that lie beyond your ability.

   A. Develop the paddling skills and teamwork required to match the river you plan to boat. Most good paddlers develop skills gradually, and attempts to advance too quickly will compromise your safety and enjoyment.

   B. Be in good physical and mental condition, consistent with the difficulties which may be expected. Make adjustments for loss of skills due to age, health, or fitness. Any health limitation must be explained to your fellow paddlers prior to starting the trip.

8. Be practiced in self-rescue, including escape from an overturned craft. The eskimo roll is strongly recommended for decked boaters who run rapids of Class IV or greater, or who paddle in cold environmental conditions.

9. Be trained in rescue skills, CPR, and first aid with special emphasis on the recognizing and treating hypothermia. It may save your friend's life.

10. Carry equipment needed for unexpected emergencies, including footwear which will protect your feet when walking out, a throw rope, knife, whistle, and waterproof matches. If you wear eyeglasses, tie them on and carry a spare pair on long trips. Bring cloth repair tape on short runs, and a full repair kit on isolated rivers. Do not wear bulky jackets, ponchos, heavy boots, or anything else which could reduce your ability to survive a swim.

11. Despite the mutually supportive group structure described in this code, individual paddlers are ultimately responsible for their own safety, and must assume sole responsibility for the following decisions:

A. The decision to participate on any trip. This includes an evaluation of the expected difficulty of the rapids under the conditions existing at the time of the put-in.

B. The selection of appropriate equipment, including a boat design suited to their skills and the appropriate rescue and survival gear.

C. The decision to scout any rapid, and to run or portage according to their best judgement. Other members of the group may offer advice, but paddlers should resist pressure from anyone to paddle beyond their skills. It is also their responsibility to decide whether to pass up any walk-out or take-out opportunity.

D. All trip participants should constantly evaluate their own and their group's safety, voicing their concerns when appropriate and following what they believe to be the best course of action. Paddlers are encouraged to speak with anyone whose action on the water is dangerous, whether they are a part of your group or not.

II. Boat and equipment preparedness

1. Test new and different equipment under familiar conditions before relying on it for difficult runs. This is especially true when adopting a new boat design or outfitting system. Low volume craft may present additional hazards to inexperienced or poorly conditioned paddlers.

2. Be sure your boat and gear are in good repair before starting a trip. The more isolated and difficult a run, the more rigorous this inspection should be.

3. Install flotation bags in non-inflatable craft, securely fixed in each end, designed to displace as much water as possible. Inflatable boats should have multiple air chambers and be test inflated before launching.

4. Have strong, properly sized paddles or oars for controlling craft. Carry sufficient spares for the length and difficulty of the trip.

5. Outfit your boat safely. The ability to exit your boat quickly is an essential component of safety in rapids. It is your responsibility to see that there is absolutely nothing to cause entrapment when coming free of an upset craft. This includes:

A. Spray covers that won't release reliably or that release prematurely.

B. Boat outfitting too tight to allow a fast exit, especially in low-volume kayaks or decked canoes. This includes low hung thwarts in canoes lacking adequate clearance for your feet and kayak footbraces which fail or allow your feet to become wedged under them.

C. Inadequately supported decks which collapse on a paddler's legs when a decked boat is pinned by water pressure. Inadequate clearance with the deck because of your size or build.

D. Loose ropes which cause entanglement. Beware of any length of loose line attached to a whitewater boat. All items must be tied tightly and excess line eliminated; painters, throw lines, and safety rope systems must be completely and effectively stored. Do not knot the end of a rope, as it can get caught in cracks between rocks.

6. Provide ropes that permit you to hold on to your craft so that it may be rescued. The following methods are recommended:

A. Kayaks and covered canoes should have grab loops of 1/4" + rope or equivalent webbing sized to admit a normal sized hand. Stern painters are permissible if properly secured.

B. Open canoes should have securely anchored bow and stern painters consisting of 8-10 feet of 1/4" line. These must be secured in such a way that they are readily accessible, but cannot come loose accidently. Grab loops are acceptable, but are more difficult to reach after an upset.

C. Many rafts and dories have taut perimeter lines threaded through the loops provided. Footholds should be designed so that a paddler's feet cannot be forced through them, causing entrapment. Flip lines should be carefully and reliably stowed.

7. Know your craft's carrying capacity, and how added loads affect boat handling in whitewater. Most rafts have a minimum crew size which can be added to on day trips or in easy rapids. Carrying more than two paddlers in an open canoe when running rapids is not recommended.

8. Car top racks must be strong and attach positively to the vehicle. Lash your boat to each crossbar, then tie the ends of the boat directly to the bumpers for added security. This arrangement should survive all but the most violent vehicle accident.

III. Group Preparedness and Responsibility

1. Organization. A river trip should be regarded as a common adventure by all participants, except on instructional or commercially guided trips as defined below. Participants share the responsibility for the conduct of the trip, and each participant is individually responsible for judging his or her own capabilities and for his or her own safety as the trip progresses. Participants are encouraged (but are not obligated) to offer advice and guidance for the independent consideration and judgement of others.

2. River Conditions. The group should have a reasonable knowledge of the difficulty of the run. Participants should evaluate this information and adjust their plans accordingly. If the run is exploratory or no one is familiar with the river, maps and guidebooks, if available, should be examined. The group should secure accurate flow information; the more difficult the run, the more important this will be. Be aware of possible changes in river level and how this will affect the difficulty of the run. If the trip involves tidal stretches, secure appropriate information on tides.

3. Group equipment should be suited to the difficulty of the river. The group should always have a throw line available, and one line per boat is recommended on difficult runs. The list may include: carabiners, prussick loops, first aid kit, flashlight, folding saw, fire starter, guidebooks, maps, food, extra clothing, and any other rescue or survival items suggested by conditions. Each item is not required on every run, and this list is not meant to be a substitute for good judgement.

4. Keep the group compact, but maintain sufficient spacing to avoid collisions. If the group is large, consider dividing into smaller groups or using the "buddy system" as an additional safeguard. Space yourselves closely enough to permit good communication, but not so close as to interfere with one another in rapids.

A. The lead paddler sets the pace. When in front, do not get in over your head. Never run drops when you cannot see a clear route to the bottom or, for advanced paddlers, a sure route to the next eddy. When in doubt, stop and scout.

B. Keep track of all group members. Each boat keeps the one behind it in sight, stopping if necessary. Know how many people are in your group and take head counts regularly. No one should paddle ahead or walk out without first informing the group. Weak paddlers should stay at the center of a group, and not allow themselves to lag behind. If the group is large and contains a wide range of abilities, a designated "sweep boat" should bring up the rear.

C. Courtesy. On heavily used rivers, do not cut in front of a boater running a drop. Always look upstream before leaving eddies to run or play. Never enter a crowded drop or eddy when no room for you exists. Passing other groups in a rapid may be hazardous: it's often safer to wait upstream until the group has passed.

5. Float plan. If the trip is into a wilderness area or for an extended period, plans should be filed with a responsible person who will contact the authorities if you are overdue. It may be wise to establish checkpoints along the way where civilization could be contacted if necessary. Knowing the location of possible help and preplanning escape routes can speed rescue.

6. Drugs. The use of alcohol or mind-altering drugs before or during river trips is not recommended. It dulls reflexes, reduces decision-making ability, and may interfere with important survival reflexes.

7. Instructional or Commercially Guided Trips. In contrast to the common adventure trip format, in these trip formats, a boating instructor or commercial guide assumes some of the responsibilities normally exercised by the group as a whole, as appropriate under the circumstances. These formats recognize that instructional or commercially guided trips may involve participants who lack significant experience in whitewater. However, as a participant acquires experience in whitewater, he or she takes on increasing responsibility for his or her own safety, in accordance with what he or she knows or should know as a result of that increased experience. Also, as in all trip formats, every participant must realize and assume the risks associated with the serious hazards of whitewater rivers. It is advisable for instructors and commercial guides to acquire trip or personal liability insurance.

A. An "instructional trip" is characterized by a clear teacher/pupil relationship, where the primary purpose of the trip is to teach boating skills, and which is conducted for a fee.

B. A "commercially guided trip" is characterized by a licensed, professional guide conducting trips for a fee.

IV. Guidelines For River Rescue

1. Recover from an upset with an eskimo roll whenever possible. Evacuate your boat immediately if there is imminent danger of being trapped against rocks, brush, or any other kind of strainer.

2. If you swim, hold on to your boat. It has much flotation and is easy for rescuers to spot. Get to the upstream end so that you cannot be crushed between a rock and your boat by the force of the current. Persons with good balance may be able to climb on top of a swamped kayak or flipped raft and paddle to shore.

3. Release your craft if this will improve your chances, especially if the water is cold or dangerous rapids lie ahead. Actively attempt self-rescue whenever possible by swimming for safety. Be prepared to assist others who may come to your aid.

A. When swimming in shallow or obstructed rapids, lie on your back *with feet held high and* pointed downstream. Do not attempt to stand in fast moving water; if your foot wedges on the bottom, fast water will push you under and keep you there. Get to slow or very shallow water before attempting to stand or walk. Look ahead! Avoid possible pinning situations including undercut rocks, strainers, downed trees, holes, and other dangers by swimming away from them.

B. If the rapids are deep and powerful, roll over onto your stomach and swim aggressively for shore. Watch for eddies and slackwater and use them to get out of the current. Strong swimmers can effect a powerful upstream ferry and get to shore fast. If the shores are obstructed with strainers or undercut rocks, however, it is safer to "ride the rapid out" until a less hazardous escape can be found.

4. If others spill and swim, go after the boaters first. Rescue boats and equipment only if this can be done safely. While participants are encouraged (but not obligated) to assist one another to the best of their ability, they should do so only if they can, in their judgement, do so safely. The first duty of a rescuer is not to compound the problem by becoming another victim.

5. The use of rescue lines requires training; uninformed use may cause injury. Never tie yourself into either end of a line without a quick-release system. Have a knife handy to deal with unexpected entanglement. Learn to place set lines effectively, to throw accurately, to belay effectively, and to properly handle a rope thrown to you.

6. When reviving a drowning victim, be aware that cold water may greatly extend survival time underwater. Victims of hypothermia may have depressed vital signs so they look and feel dead. Don't give up; continue CPR for as long as possible without compromising safety.

V. Universal River Signals

HELP/EMERGENCY: Assist the signaller as quickly as possible. Give three long blasts on a police whistle while waving a paddle, helmet or life vest over your head. If a whistle is not available, use the visual signal alone. A whistle is best carried on a lanyard attached to your life vest.

ALL CLEAR: Come ahead (in the absence of other directions proceed down the center) Form a vertical bar with your paddle or one arm held high above your head. Paddle blade should be turned flat for maximum visibility. To signal direction or a preferred course through a rapid around obstruction, lower the previously vertical "all clear" by 45 degrees toward the side of the river with the preferred route. Never point toward the obstacle you wish to avoid.

(STOP: Potential hazard ahead. Wait for "all clear" signal before proceeding, or scout ahead. Form a horizontal bar with your outstretched arms. Those seeing the signal should pass it back to others in the party.

VI. International Scale Of River Difficulty

This is the American version of a rating system used to compare river difficulty throughout the world. This system is not exact; rivers do not always fit easily into one category, and regional or individual interpretations may cause misunderstandings. It is no substitute for a guidebook or accurate first-hand descriptions of a run.

Paddlers attempting difficult runs in an unfamiliar area should act cautiously until they get a feel for the way the scale is interpreted locally. River difficulty may change each year due to fluctuations in water level, downed trees, geological disturbances, or bad weather. Stay alert for unexpected problems!

As river difficulty increases, the danger to swimming paddlers becomes more severe. As rapids become longer and more continuous, the challenge increases. There is a difference between running an occasional Class 1V rapids and dealing with an entire river of this category. Allow an extra margin of safety between skills and river ratings when the water is cold or if the river itself is remote and inaccessible.

The Six Difficulty Classes:

Class I: Easy. Fast-moving water with riffles and small waves. Few obstructions, all obvious and easily missed with little training. Risk to swimmers is slight; self-rescue is easy.

Class II: Novice. Straightforward rapids with wide, clear channels that are evident without scouting. Occasional maneuvering may be required, but rocks and medium-sized waves are easily missed by trained paddlers. Swimmers are seldom injured and group assistance, while helpful, is seldom needed.

Class III: Intermediate. Rapids with moderate, irregular waves which may be difficult to avoid and which can swamp an open canoe. Complex maneuvers in fast current and good boat control in tight passages or around ledges are often required; large waves or strainers may be present but are easily avoided. Strong eddies and powerful current effects can be found, particularly on large-volume rivers. Scouting is advisable for inexperienced parties. Injuries while swimming are rare; self-rescue is usually easy but group assistance may be required to avoid long swims.

Class IV: Advanced. Intense, powerful but predictable rapids requiring precise boat handling in turbulent water. Depending on the character of the river, it may feature large, unavoidable waves and holes or constricted passages demanding fast maneuvers under pressure. A fast, reliable eddy turn may be needed to initiate dangerous hazards. Scouting is necessary the first time down. Risk of injury to swimmers is moderate to high, and water conditions may make self-rescue difficult. Group assistance for rescue is often essential but requires practiced skills. A strong eskimo roll is highly recommended.

Class V: Expert. Extremely long, obstructed, or very violent rapids which expose a paddler to above average endangerment. Drops may contain large, unavoidable waves and holes or steep, congested chutes with complex, demanding routes. Rapids may continue for long distances between pools, demanding a high level of fitness. What eddies exist may be small, turbulent, or difficult to reach. At the high end of the scale, several of these factors may be combined. Scouting is mandatory, but often difficult. Swims are dangerous, and rescue is difficult, even for experts. A very reliable eskimo roll, proper equipment, extensive experience, and practiced rescue skills are essential for survival.

Class VI: Extreme. One grade more difficult than Class V. These runs often exemplify the extremes of difficulty, unpredictability, and danger. The consequences of errors are very severe and rescue may be impossible. For teams of experts only, at favorable water levels, after close personal inspection, and taking all precautions. This class does **not** represent drops thought to be unrunnable, but may include rapids that are only occasionally run.

INDEXES

INDEX OF RIVERS
REQUIRING PERMISSION

The public authorities require permits, reservations, or registration for you to be allowed to boat the rivers listed below. Rivers where permits are required only for camping or fires are not listed.

River	State	River	State
American River, South Fork, 27	CA	Rio Grande River, Big Bend National Park, 198	TX
Chama River, 143	NM	Rio Grande River, Taos Box, 145	NM
Chattooga River, 72	GA/SC	Rogue River, 158	OR
Colorado River, Cataract Canyon, 203	UT	Salmon River, Lower, 83-84	ID
Colorado River, Grand Canyon, 16	AZ	Salmon River, Main Fork, 82	ID
Colorado River, Westwater, 202	UT	Salmon River, Middle Fork, 84	ID
Deschutes River, 169	OR	Salt River, 17	AZ
Dolores River, Gateway to the Colorado River, 53	CO/UT	San Juan River, 189	UT
Flathead River, Main Stem, 130	MT	Selway River, 86	ID
Genesee River, 151	NY	Skagit River, 228	WA
Green River, Desolation and Gray Canyons, 206	UT	Skykomish River, 228	WA
Green River, Dinosaur, 205	UT	Snake River, 254	WY
Illinois River, 172	OR	Snake River, Hells Canyon, 87	ID
James River, 217	VA	Tuolumne River, 41	CA
Jarbridge and Bruneau Rivers, 79	ID	Yampa River, Dinosaur National Monument, 57	CO/UT
Kennebec River, 96	ME	Youghiogheny River, 170	PA
Kern River, 30	CA		
Klickitat River, 226	WA		
Methow River, 226	WA		
Missouri River, 132	MT		
Nantahala River, 161	NC		
Owyhee River, 80	ID		
Owyhee River, 174	OR		